Human–Wildlife Interactions

Human–Wildlife
Interactions
From Conflict to Coexistence
2nd Edition

Michael R. Conover
Denise O. Conover

CRC Press is an imprint of the
Taylor & Francis Group, an **informa** business

Second edition published 2022
by CRC Press
6000 Broken Sound Parkway NW, Suite 300, Boca Raton, FL 33487–2742

and by CRC Press
2 Park Square, Milton Park, Abingdon, Oxon, OX14 4RN

© 2022 Taylor & Francis Group, LLC

First edition published by CRC Press 2001

CRC Press is an imprint of Taylor & Francis Group, LLC

ISBN: 978-1-138-39409-4 (hbk)
ISBN: 978-1-032-13449-9 (pbk)
ISBN: 978-0-429-40140-4 (ebk)

DOI: 10.1201/9780429401404

Typeset in Times LT Std
by Apex CoVantage, LLC

Contents

Author Bios

Michael R. Conover, PhD, is a professor in the Wildland Resources Department of Utah State University and has taught and studied wildlife biology since the 1970s.

Denise O. Conover, PhD, is a retired senior lecturer in the History Department of Utah State University and has taught and studied diplomatic and military history since the 1970s. She has written several papers on wildlife management.

Preface

"The philosophy of human-wildlife coexistence is based on the concept that wildlife populations can only remain abundant if humans and wildlife can live together on the same land with neither having an adverse impact on the other."

– Michael R. Conover

In 2002, I published, with CRC Press, the book, *Resolving Human-Wildlife Conflicts: The Science of Wildlife Damage Management.* The publisher has been asking me to write a second edition for the last decade, but I resisted doing so because it is an exhausting process. Three years ago, I finally decided to write a second edition because our knowledge of human–wildlife conflicts had expanded so much in the last two decades. If you would like proof of that statement, leaf through the Literature Cited sections at the end of any chapter in this book. You will see that most of the references cited in this book were published since 2002, when the first edition was written.

I want to point out some important items to the readers. First, the scientific names for all species mentioned in this book appear in the Appendix, and a subject index appears at the end of the book. Second, monetary inflation has continually decreased the value of a dollar over time. When I first started working in 1967, I earned the minimum wage of $1.00 an hour by picking vegetables and driving a tractor. Today, the minimum wage in the United States is $7.25. But this does not mean that workers today are better off than I was in my youth because $1.00 in 1967 could buy the same amount as $7.81 today, due to an average of annual inflation rate of 4% over the period from 1967 and 2021. Because of inflation, we tend to underestimate the actual cost of losses reported in papers published previously. For example, a report that deer damage was $1,000 in 1967 is actually over $7,000 in today's dollars. To adjust for inflation, I have revised all monetary values appearing in studies published prior to 2010 to their value in current (2021) $U.S. dollars. This means that economic values I report in this book will differ from the amounts reported in the original reports.

Third, current extinction rates of animals across the world are similar to those during the mass extinction events in earth's distant past, but this time, humans, rather than a meteor, are the cause of the extinctions. There are several reasons why humans are having such an adverse impact on life. We convert natural habitat to our own uses: changing forests, swamps, grasslands, or prairies to agricultural fields, pastures, and housing developments. We are responsible for many exotic species invading new areas where the native species are unable to compete or cope with the new invasive species. Exotic diseases have decimated many wildlife populations. The effect of humans on the environment is now so great that many geologists report that a new geological age has started – the Anthropocene (meaning the "Age of Humans"), owing to our impact on the planet. In the Anthropocene, humans have obtained dominion over the surface of our planet and most plants and vertebrate animals living on it, allowing humans the power to mold the world to their liking. Humans can increase or decrease populations as they see fit.

As human dominion increases, there is an intensifying need to ensure continued abundance of wildlife species in the Anthropocene. There are two philosophies about how to achieve this goal. One is to set aside areas for the exclusive use of wild animals. We call these areas nature preserves, national parks, or wilderness areas. But human demand for land and natural resources is so great that only a small proportion of the earth's continents has been set aside for sanctuaries. Even the world's largest reserves and parks are too small to sustain long-term ecosystem processes (Woodroffe and Ginsberg 1998; Hunter et al. 2007).

The second philosophy (human–wildlife coexistence) is based on the realization that society will never set aside enough land to sustain functioning ecosystems or wildlife populations that existed prior to humans. Instead, the philosophy of human–wildlife coexistence is based on the view that wildlife populations can only remain abundant if humans and wildlife live together on the same land with neither having an adverse impact on the other. Proponents of this coexistence philosophy applaud whenever land is set aside from human uses to preserve nature, while realizing that these efforts will never be sufficient.

I am a proponent of, and champion for, the philosophy of human–wildlife coexistence. My teaching and research are focused on furthering this philosophy. I dream of a world where (1) humans will not have an adverse impact on humans and (2) wildlife will not have an adverse impact on humans. The latter is important not only because it will save human lives and property and help produce the food that people depend upon but also because many wildlife species are at the mercy of society. These species can only remain abundant, or return to abundance, if humans allow them to do so. This will not happen if that species or all wildlife species as a whole are viewed unfavorably by people. As we shall discover in this book, the favorable opinions of people toward a wildlife species become more negative when that wildlife species damages crops, destroys property, or poses a risk to human health and safety. Hence, both humans and wild animals are harmed when human–wildlife conflicts occur. In light of this, I have not named this book: *Resolving Human–Wildlife Conflicts, Second Edition*. Instead, the title of this book is *Human–Wildlife Interactions: From Conflict to Coexistence, Second Edition*.

I hope this book will be a small step in helping to create that world of coexistence. In this book, I focus on how to reduce the adverse impact of wildlife on people and society. In the future, I hope to write a companion book that focuses on the other side of the coexistence coin – how to reduce the adverse impact of people and society on wildlife. I hope you will find the book interesting and useful.

LITERATURE CITED

Conover, M. R., and D. O. Conover. 2022. Human-Wildlife Interactions: From Conflict to Coexistence. Second Edition. CRC Press, Boca Raton, Florida, USA.

Hunter, L. T., K. Pretorius, L. C. Carlisle, M. Rickelton, C. Walker, R. Slotow, and J. D. Skinner. 2007. Restoring lions *Panthera leo* to northern KwaZulu-Natal, South Africa: Short-term biological and technical success but equivocal long-term conservation. *Oryx* 41:196–204.

Woodroffe, R., and J. R. Ginsberg. 1998. Edge effects and the extinction of populations inside protected areas. *Science* 280:2126–2128.

1 Philosophy

"The point of philosophy is to start with something so simple as not to seem worth stating, and to end with something so paradoxical that no one will believe it."

– Bertrand Russell

"To paraphrase Socrates, those animals that are the hardest to love, need it the most. Perhaps the field of wildlife-damage management is to make the unlovable a little less so."

– Anonymous

Human–wildlife coexistence is predicated on the assumption that humans and wildlife need to live in the same space without either adversely impacting the other. There are two parts of human–wildlife coexistence: reducing adverse effects of humans on wildlife, which is the domain of conservation biology, and reducing adverse effects of wildlife on humans, which is the field of wildlife damage management. Humans need wildlife to be truly human, and abundant populations of wildlife cannot exist if the benefits of wildlife for humans do not outweigh the problems they create.

Wildlife damage management is a field within the discipline of wildlife management. To understand wildlife damage management, we need to know how it is related to the broader goals of wildlife management, why we manage wildlife, and how wildlife damage management helps achieve societal goals. Wildlife damage management is built upon the fundamental knowledge gained in the fields of ecology, behavior, population dynamics, and wildlife management. The same principles apply whether we are trying to increase or decrease a wildlife population, regardless of our motives.

1.1 WHAT IS MEANT BY THE TERM WILDLIFE RESOURCE?

Wildlife is one of those terms we use every day without worrying about its precise definition. It is a misnomer to say that wildlife means wild animals because the term "wild" has several meanings. Wild sometimes describes an individual or animal that exhibits erratic, unpredictable, or uncontrollable behavior. We do not mean crazy animals when we use the term wildlife. By wild, we really mean animals with behavior and movements not controlled by humans (i.e., undomesticated animals). To avoid confusion over the different interpretations of "wild," many scientific journals prefer the term "free-ranging animals" rather than wild animals. It is unlikely that the term "wildlife" will ever be replaced by "free-ranging wildlife," but the latter is a more correct term. Moreover, not all free-ranging animals are considered wildlife. Excluded are insects and other invertebrates. Historically, the term meant free-ranging vertebrates, but it was unclear whether fish were included in this

DOI: 10.1201/9780429401404-1

term. To reduce ambiguity, people started using the term "fish and wildlife" when referring to both. By doing so, the term "wildlife" became restricted to vertebrates excluding fish. Hence, the commonly accepted definition of wildlife is free-ranging vertebrates other than fish. It includes amphibians, reptiles, birds, and mammals, including marine mammals.

Wildlife is often referred to as a resource. By definition, a resource provides a benefit to people. Without people, wildlife exists, but it is not a resource. Resources are goods and services that have value for humans. A value is the ability to cause an effect, which can benefit people (i.e., have a positive value) or harm people (i.e., have a negative value). If there were no people, wildlife could not affect them and, therefore, could not be assigned a value. The lives of wildlife and humans are so entwined that wildlife affects people in many different ways. Thus, wildlife creates many values, both positive and negative.

Wildlife management can be defined as the act of influencing or modifying the wildlife resource to meet human needs, desires, or goals. Wildlife management is a science. Wildlife scientists use the scientific method of asking a question, devising hypotheses (i.e., potential answers to that question), and then conducting experiments to try to disprove the hypotheses. Because wildlife management is a science, we can try some form of management, observe the effects of our management actions, and learn of its consequences. Through this process, we can determine how best to achieve our goals for managing wildlife.

1.2 WHAT IS THE NORTH AMERICAN MODEL OF WILDLIFE CONSERVATION?

Both the United States and Canada started as British colonies, and the colonies had to follow British common law. One such law gave the British monarchy ownership of all wildlife. Wildlife was not owned by the citizens or landowners. The monarch created royal hunting preserves where only he and his favored subjects had the right to hunt or trap. These royal preserves not only included forested areas but also contained villages and cultivated fields within them – lands individually owned by other people – with the result that the landowners were not allowed to kill wildlife on their own land. At the time of the American Revolution, English law held that the English Sovereign had complete authority to determine what rights, if any, his or her subjects had to take wildlife.

After the American Revolution, the 13 original colonies became the 13 original states, and the citizenry replaced the king as the sovereign (Figure 1.1). The result was that the states owned the wildlife and held it in trust for its citizens, a concept affirmed by the U.S. Supreme Court in 1896 (Blumm and Ritchie 2005). English law, and later American law, stated that ownership of wildlife transferred to private ownership when captured or possessed by an individual. That is, a wild animal ceased to belong to the state when it was killed or captured. The state maintained the right to restrict the methods, areas, and times that an individual could kill or capture a wild animal. This evolved into the American Rule of Capture (Blumm and Ritchie 2005).

FIGURE 1.1   After the conclusion of the American Revolution with the surrender of English forces at Yorktown, wildlife was held in trust by the states, and people were allowed to hunt with few restrictions.

Source: Everett Collection, Shutterstock 238060738.

Over time, American and Canadian wildlife law evolved into a set of principles known as the North American Model of Wildlife Conservation (NAM), which continues in use today (Organ et al. 2012). Its seven principles are:

1. Wildlife is a public trust. It is owned by the public and held in trust for the benefit of the public.
2. Wildlife is managed for the benefit of as many people as possible. Governments have a responsibility to create those conditions and laws that allow as many citizens as possible to enjoy the pursuit of wildlife. This goal has taken precedence over the desire to generate funds for government by pricing hunting licenses or permits high enough to maximize revenue for the government.
3. Allocation of wildlife to citizens is made by law. In the United States and Canada, the rule of law prevails to avoid capriciousness. Laws are used to decide when, where, and by whom wildlife can be taken.
4. Wildlife cannot be sold. The commercial sale of wildlife in past centuries has led to the extinction of the passenger pigeon and the near extinction of bison and several birds that had feathers used in women's hats. During the

last century, the public has realized that the best use of wildlife is for recreation, either to view wildlife or to hunt it.

5. Wildlife can only be killed for a legitimate purpose. The nonhunting public is willing to tolerate recreational hunting of wildlife as long as hunters appreciate and value the animals they kill and use for food. Killing for just the sake of killing or the wanton waste of an animal is discouraged and usually illegal.

6. Management of wildlife that crosses international borders (mainly migratory birds) may be subject to international treaties or cooperative agreements.

7. Wildlife policy should be based on science. The management of wildlife is complex and more likely to be successful if it is based on science rather than opinion, speculation, or guesses.

The NAM provides the philosophical underpinnings of wildlife management in North America. The basis for the model is that wildlife is a public trust and should be managed under the public trust doctrine (PTD). This doctrine states that some resources, including air, water, fish, and wildlife, are held in trust for the benefit of current and future generations of people, who are the beneficiaries of the public trust. Under PTD, the government and the elected leaders of the people are the trustees of the public trust; they have a fiduciary responsibility (a fiduciary is someone who has a legal and moral obligation to act and make decisions for the benefit of the beneficiary and not for his/her own self-interest or anyone else's interest). A trustee has to preserve the trust assets (wildlife resource) for the long-term benefit of the beneficiaries. The trustee has the responsibility to manage the trust, not just to maintain it in its current condition, but to take prudent actions to increase its value. The trustee also has the responsibility to resolve any competing demands between different beneficiaries, such as the current generation of beneficiaries versus future generations. The judiciary also has an important role as the beneficiary's redress if the trustees fail to perform their duties under the PTD or fail in their fiduciary responsibility.

The trustees set the goals for the trust but may lack the knowledge about how best to achieve those goals. Therefore, they often delegate that responsibility to the government wildlife agency and then provide oversight of that agency. The wildlife agency serves in the role of a trust manager and has the responsibility to (1) monitor and manage the assets in the trust, (2) distribute the proceeds of the trust to the beneficiaries in accordance with the instructions of the trustees, and (3) report to the trustees the status of the trust and any distributions from it (Organ et al. 2012; Smith 2011; Decker et al. 2015).

In the United States, responsibility for managing wildlife as a public trust is divided between the federal and state governments. The federal government reserves the right to manage migratory birds because they cross state borders in their migrations. For this reason, a state's actions concerning migratory birds could have an adverse effect on another state. For example, if one state overharvested ducks during the fall, it would adversely affect the hunting opportunities in states farther south in the Flyway. The federal government also has reserved for itself the right to manage endangered species under the Endangered Species Act because all Americans would suffer if a species became extinct. Each state has management authority for mammals and nonmigratory birds (e.g., quail, grouse, and pheasants) within their state's borders because the home ranges of these animals usually do not cross state boundaries.

For some avian species that cause damage, the federal government has signed depredation orders, allowing people to capture or kill specific avian species. These depredation orders are intended to provide short-term relief for bird damage or threats to human health or safety. By 2018, depredation orders had been issued for blackbirds, cowbirds, grackles, crows, magpies, double-crested cormorants, and resident Canada geese (Table 1.1). These orders remove federal prohibitions against the capture or killing of specific migratory bird species that are causing damage. State laws, however, still apply; in essence, the federal government has given each state the right to manage these species within state boundaries (U.S. Fish and Wildlife Service 2013).

TABLE 1.1

List of Federal Depredation Orders as of 2018 That Allow the Use of Lethal Measures against Certain Avian Species

Regulation	Species	Interest Harmed	States
50 CFR 21.43	Blackbirds, cowbirds, grackles, crows, magpies	Ornamental shade trees, agricultural crops, livestock, wildlife, when concentrated in such numbers and manner that they are a health hazard or other nuisance	All
50 CFR 21.44	Horned larks, golden-crowned, white-crowned, and other crowned sparrows, house finches	Agriculture, horticulture	CA
50 CFR 21.45	Purple gallinules	Rice	LA
50 CFR 21.46	Scrub jay, Steller's jay	Nut crops	OR, WA
50 CFR 21.47	Double-crested cormorants	Freshwater aquaculture, federal and state fish hatcheries	AL, AR, FL, GA, KY, LA, MN, MS, NC, OK, SC, TN, TX
50 CFR 21.48	Double-crested cormorants	Public resources	AL, AR, FL, GA, IL, IN, IA, KS, KY, LA, MI, MN, MS, MO, NY, NC, OH, OK, SC, TN, TX, VT, WV, WI
50 CFR 21.49	Resident Canada geese	Public safety at airports and military airfields	Lower 48 States (implemented by States and Tribes)

(Continued)

TABLE 1.1 *(Continued)*

Regulation	Species	Interest Harmed	States
50 CFR 21.50	Resident Canada geese (nests and eggs)	People, property, agricultural crops, or other interests	See registration website (https://epermits.fws.gov/eRCGR/)
50 CFR 21.51	Resident Canada geese	Agriculture	Atlantic, Central, and Mississippi Flyway portions of AL, AR, CO, CT, DE, FL, GA, IL, IN, IA, KS, KY, LA, ME, MN, MS, MO, MT, NE, NH, NM, NJ, NY, NC, ND, OH, OK, PA, RI, SC, SD, TN, TX, VT, VA, WV, WI, WY (implemented by States and Tribes)
50 CFR 21.52	Resident Canada geese	Human health	Lower 48 states (implemented by States and Tribes)
50 CFR 21.53	Purple swamphens	(Invasive)	All states, Puerto Rico, U.S. Virgin Islands
50 CFR 21.54	Muscovy duck	(Invasive)	All states except TX Counties: Hidalgo, Starr, and Sapata

1.3 WHAT ARE THE ALTERNATIVES TO THE NORTH AMERICAN MODEL OF WILDLIFE MANAGEMENT AND THE PUBLIC TRUST DOCTRINE?

Compassionate conservation model (CCM) is an alternate to the NAM for the management of wildlife and is advocated by people who are concerned about animal welfare. CCM seeks to improve the quality of life of all animals, including companion animals (pets), livestock and poultry, animals used in research, and wild animals. Supporters of CCM worry about the suffering of individual animals and seek to reduce harm to wildlife by an expanding human population. They view NAM as an antiquated philosophy of human dominion of wildlife and nature. The philosophy of CCM is one of mutualism with wildlife rather than dominion over wildlife. CCM rejects the idea that there is a hierarchy that places humans above animals. It seeks a humane approach to wildlife management and seeks to prevent animal suffering, improve animal health, and allow wildlife the opportunity to live in a fashion suitable to their behavior (Dubois and Harshaw 2013). The overarching goal of CCM is to do no harm and to recognize the intrinsic worth of every individual wild animal.

CCM rejects the view that wildlife are a resource for humans (Ramp and Bekoff 2015; Wallach et al. 2015).

The Free Market Model opposes the NAM and the PTD; it takes the position that a resource owned by everyone is actually owned by no one, leading to a "tragedy of the commons" where resources are overexploited by people, who are all acting out of their own personal self-interest (Huffman 2007). NAM argues that if private individuals owned wildlife, then the owners would better care for and manage wildlife out of a desire to maximize their own benefits and profits.

1.4 WHAT IS THE TYRANNY OF THE MAJORITY?

Ancient Greece was a true democracy where people met in an open square and made decisions by majority vote by the citizens who were present at the time of the vote. The United States and Canada are not true democracies but rather are republics where citizens vote for individuals to represent them. These representatives then meet together and make decisions based on the majority vote of the elected representatives. This style of government allows for compromises in which the interests of minorities are heard and, in some cases, prevail through the persuasions of their elected representatives. For example, consider the questions of whether livestock should be allowed to graze in the federal lands in Utah. Most people in the United States would say no, but they do not really care. But the ranchers and rural residents in Utah would vote yes, and for these folks, it is an important issue because their livelihoods are involved. Likewise, their elected representatives in Utah realize that they may not be reelected if they cannot convince the federal government to allow grazing on federal land. Thus, Utah's representatives lobby the representative of other states to allow for public grazing. This style of government was favored by our Founding Fathers because they worried about the tyranny of the majority where the rights of minority groups might be trampled underfoot by the majority.

The alternative to this form of government is a public referendum where decisions are made directly by the citizens, who vote for one alternative or another. Whichever alternative receives the most votes becomes law without regard to the desires of the minority. Referendums are favored by people who seek laws ending hunting and trapping because such laws are more likely to pass in a referendum (Treves et al. 2017). Wildlife laws that have been made by public referendum include the decision by California voters to stop hunting and trapping of cougars, and in some states, voters decided to restrict the use of leghold traps. Wildlife laws are primarily made by elected representatives, but the citizens in many states can require a referendum if enough voters sign a petition requesting one.

1.5 SHOULD WILDLIFE BE MANAGED FOR THE BENEFIT OF WILDLIFE OR PEOPLE?

I often hear wildlife biologists complain that we should be managing for the sake of wildlife and not for society. This sounds like a great idea, but the problem is in the details – starting with what the person means by the term "wildlife" when they say we should be managing for wildlife. People who enjoy big-game hunting probably mean we should manage for ungulates in particular, not wildlife in general. When bird watchers think about managing for wildlife, they probably are thinking about trying to increase avian diversity. In truth, there is no management action that we can take that will benefit all wildlife. Instead, some species will benefit from our actions, while others will lose. For instance, Mathisen et al. (2012) found that managing to increase moose populations had different effects on two insectivorous birds: great tits and pied flycatchers. Great tits had lower reproductive success in areas with high moose activity and preferred to nest in areas with few moose. In contrast, pied flycatchers preferred to nest in areas with high moose activity. These contrasting impacts resulted from how moose herbivory impacted the insect prey of each avian species. People who seek more pied flycatchers would be in favor of a management plan that benefits moose, but not folks who prefer great tits.

1.6 WHAT ARE THE GOALS OF WILDLIFE MANAGEMENT?

An important philosophical question is why do we try to manage wildlife? We must have lofty goals because we spend large amounts of time and money to achieve them. We can draw several conclusions from these large expenditures to manage wildlife. First, we, as individuals and as a society, believe our goals are important. Second, we believe that our goal will not be achieved without our active intervention. The question is, what are we, as a society, trying to accomplish when we manage wildlife? Are we managing wildlife for the benefit of mankind or for the benefit of the wildlife resource itself? These two positions are explained in more detail in Sidebars 1.1 and 1.2.

SIDEBAR 1.1   DEVELOPING A LAND ETHIC – VIEWS OF ALDO LEOPOLD (FIGURE 1.2)

"All ethics so far evolved rest upon a single premise: that the individual is a member of a community of interdependent parts. His instincts prompt him to compete for his place in that community, but his ethics prompt him also to cooperate (perhaps in order that there may be a place to compete for). The land ethic simply enlarges the boundaries of this community to include soils, waters, plants, and animals, or collectively: the land.

This sounds simple: do we not already sing our love for and obligation to the land of the free and the home of the brave? Yes, but just what and whom do we love? Certainly not the soil, which we are sending helter-skelter downriver. Certainly not the waters, which we assume have no function except to turn turbines, float barges, and carry off sewage. Certainly not the plants, of which we exterminate whole communities without batting an eye. Certainly not the animals, of which we have already extirpated many of the largest and most beautiful species. A land ethic of course cannot prevent the alteration, management, and use of these 'resources,' but it does affirm their right to continued existence, and at least in spots, their continued existence in a natural state.

In short, a land ethic changes the role of *Homo sapiens* from conqueror of the land-community to plain member and citizen of it. It implies respect for his fellow-members, and also respect for the community as such." (Leopold 1949).

FIGURE 1.2   Aldo Leopold.

Source: Robert Oetking, courtesy of Aldo Leopold Foundation and the University of Wisconsin – Madison.

SIDEBAR 1.2   SAVING NATURE, BUT ONLY FOR MAN – VIEWS OF CHARLES KRAUTHAMMER

"Environmental sensitivity is now as required an attitude in polite society as is, say, belief in democracy or aversion to polyester. But how are we to choose among the dozens of conflicting proposals, restrictions, projects, regulations, and laws advanced in the name of the environment? Clearly not everything with an environmental claim is worth doing. How to choose?

There is a simple way. First, distinguish between environmental luxuries and environmental necessities. Luxuries are those things it would be nice to have if costless. Necessities are those things we must have regardless. Then apply a rule. Call it the fundamental axiom of sane environmentalism: combating ecological change that directly threatens the health and safety of people is an environmental necessity. All else is luxury . . .

A sane environmentalism is entirely anthropocentric: it enjoins man to preserve nature, but on the grounds of self-preservation. It does not ask people to sacrifice in the name of other creatures. After all, it is hard enough to ask people to sacrifice in the name of other humans." (Krauthammer 1991).

My personal philosophy of wildlife management, which I believe is supported by most people, has two main tenets. First, I adhere to the concept that we do not inherit natural resources from our parents, but borrow them from our children. Every generation has a right to "use the interest" of the wildlife resource but not to "spend the capital." This means that our generation does not has a right to take an action that diminishes the value of the wildlife resource. The problem each generation faces is not knowing what component of the natural resources might become important to a future generation. Former generations viewed wildlife very differently than we do today. Their interest was focused almost exclusively on wildlife species of economic value: beaver, deer, elk, and bison. Our ancestors would not have dreamed that our generation would care if a frog or warbler became extinct. If our wildlife goals changed in ways that were unforeseen by former generations, how then can we foresee the interests of future generations to make sure that our actions today do not prevent them from achieving their goals for the wildlife resource? The answer is that we cannot. Hence, we need to manage wildlife resources cautiously; we should not take any action that is irrevocable, nor should we fail to act and allow an irrevocable loss to occur.

An example of an irrevocable loss is erosion of soil from our agricultural fields. This loss causes a permanent reduction in the land's productivity. Another is the loss of a species through extinction. During the 1700s, one of the most abundant birds in North America was the passenger pigeon and was one of the most popular game birds of the time. However, former generations allowed this species to become extinct, so we and future generations will not have the pleasure of seeing or hunting this magnificent bird. Climate change is another irrevocable loss because once it occurs, future generations cannot undo it.

My philosophy combines elements of both Leopold's and Krauthammer's philosophies. Like Leopold, I believe that society needs to develop an environmental ethic that constrains us from causing environmental degradation. Like Krauthammer's, my philosophy is based on Protagoras' maxim that "man is the measure of all things" and that the focus of environmental protection should be prioritized based on what represents the greatest threat to society and our children.

The second major tenet in my philosophy of wildlife management is that we need to increase the value of wildlife. As individuals, we manage wildlife to benefit ourselves and our families. Some landowners manage their property to reduce wildlife damage to their crops or to grow trophy deer or elk so that they can lease the hunting rights to others. As a society, we manage wildlife to increase the value of the wildlife resource for all members of society. In summary, my personal philosophy is that the goal of wildlife management should be to increase the net value of the wildlife resource for society while avoiding those actions which might cause the irrevocable loss of any part of this resource.

1.7 WHAT POSITIVE VALUES ARE PROVIDED BY WILDLIFE?

Considering the positive and negative values of wildlife is necessary if we are going to manage wildlife. The positive values of wildlife are the benefits that wildlife provide to humans. These values can be grouped into the following categories: (1) physical utility, (2) monetary, (3) recreational, (4) ecological, (5) existence, and (6) historic values (Giles 1978). Physical utility is the use of wildlife for food and clothing or to meet other necessities for human survival. Before the advent of agriculture, this was the main use of wildlife (Figure 1.3). Even today, many people in the world meet at least part of their subsistence needs by harvesting wildlife.

Monetary benefits of the wildlife resource are those that can be exchanged for money. The economic value of wildlife is captured by individuals, governments, and communities. By harvesting animals, individuals capture the value of furs, hides, and meat, which can be sold. Landowners receive a monetary benefit from wildlife when they charge hunters a fee for access to their property. Hunting guides earn money by helping hunters. Government agencies capture some of the monetary value of wildlife by requiring people to buy licenses for the right to hunt or trap. Communities

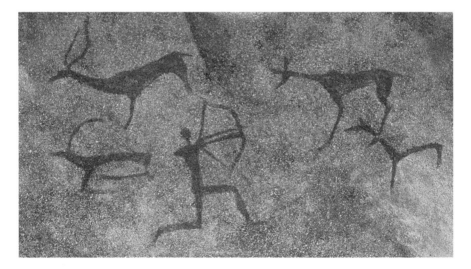

FIGURE 1.3 Before the advent of farming and ranching, wildlife was a major source of protein. This painting using red ocher dye came from a cave wall in Europe.

Source: gerasimov_foto_174, Shutterstock 540399610.

gain an economic benefit when hunters or tourists spend money for meals, lodging, or supplies while recreating in the area.

The recreational value of wildlife can be viewed as the enjoyment people receive from recreational activities involving wildlife. Many hunters derive great pleasure from the sport and often consider it to be one of the most fulfilling activities in their lives. Other people enjoy watching wild birds and mammals and would consider trips to parks or other outdoor activities less enjoyable if they could not see wildlife.

The ecological value of wildlife stems from its importance in maintaining the ecosystem. Wildlife are a vital component of a functioning natural ecosystem. If we want a healthy cougar population, for instance, we need a healthy deer population to sustain it. Therefore, one benefit of deer is sustaining cougar populations. Likewise, without predation from cougars, deer may become too abundant and may overbrowse some plants and cause those plant species to disappear. One ecological value of cougars, consequently, is their ability to keep the deer population from becoming too large.

Wildlife have an existence value, which is its potential to become more valuable in the future. Even the most worthless land in the world can be sold for money because of its potential to become valuable in the future. Likewise, wildlife species may have future values that we fail to recognize today. An example is seen in the value of armadillos, which is the only species other than humans, that is susceptible to leprosy. If we could not use armadillos for medical research, we would know much less about how to treat leprosy in humans. Each species has a unique combination of genes and proteins, which can never be reproduced and may prove useful to humans in the future.

Wildlife have a historic value that stems from mankind's fear of change. We are uneasy about how our actions are changing the world; we are nostalgic for the way things used to be. Thus, we gain a greater sense of well-being from knowing that there still are wild areas and that healthy wildlife populations exist as they have for thousands of years. Many people feel satisfaction from the reintroduction of wolves into Yellowstone National Park. These people have a sense that the world has been made right by their reintroduction – that things have been returned to the way they were (Sidebar 1.3).

SIDEBAR 1.3   WILL RESTOCKING WOLVES IN A WILDERNESS AREA OR NATIONAL PARK MAKE THESE AREAS A ZOO (MIHELL 2018)?

There are two views about how U.S. national parks and wilderness areas should be managed. One view, espoused by A. Sarker Leopold, son of Aldo Leopold, is that national parks should try to recreate "a reasonable illusion of primitive America." In response, Howard Zahniser, author of the Wilderness Act, disagreed stating that Leopold's philosophy was "A serious threat to the wilderness within the national park system and indeed to the wilderness concept itself . . . ." The national park ultimately accepted Sarker Leopold's argument.

Isle Royal in Lake Superior is both a national park and a wilderness area. It is a famous example of the importance of the role wolves play in keeping moose populations from becoming too large (Figure 1.4). Moose arrived on Isle Royal during the early 1900s; their population swelled to 5,000 by 1928, only to crash to 171 by 1943. Around 1950, wolves recolonized the island, and their depredation of moose held the moose population in check since then. However, the Isle Royal wolves are close to being extirpated; only one old pair of wolves is still there, and it is infertile. To prevent the disappearance of wolves from Isle Royal, the National Park Service in 2018 decided to reintroduce 30 wolves to the national park. The Park Superintendent Phyllis Green stated that, "It's about hanging on to an ecological system that's probably been integral to the park since its inception." She believes that it is important to keep all of Isle Royal's biological components as they are now. Environmental historian, Roderick Nash disagrees. "It is not just something to please us. The Wilderness Act tells us to take ourselves out of the picture. It doesn't matter what humans want. What matters is what evolution wants. What wilderness wants. Change is the only constant."

FIGURE 1.4 Without wolves in Isle Royale National Park, moose populations may rise above carrying capacity.

Source: Win Hoek, Shutterstock 591332501.

Some authors have considered historic value synonymous with existence value, but they differ. Consider why we reintroduced wolves into the Yellowstone ecosystem. It was not to preserve wolves because large populations exist elsewhere. If we wanted to maximize the existence value of wildlife, we should have released a predator that is threatened with extinction, perhaps the Siberian tiger. This Asiatic species is much more endangered than wolves and could thrive in the Yellowstone ecosystem. But the idea of having Siberian tigers in Yellowstone is disquieting. Why? The answer is that historically they were not present. If we placed tigers there, the wildlife resource in Yellowstone would increase in existence value, but the loss in historic value would far outweigh the gain.

1.8 WHAT NEGATIVE VALUES ARE PROVIDED BY WILDLIFE?

Wildlife also cause many problems for people, and these can be considered negative values of wildlife. Negative values of wildlife would include loss of food production, wildlife damage to property, human fatalities caused by wildlife or deer-vehicle collision (DVC), and wildlife-related illnesses. To determine the true value of wildlife for society, we need to add up all of the positive values of wildlife and then subtract from them all of the negative values of wildlife to determine the net value of wildlife. The goal of wildlife management is, in essence, to increase this net value of wildlife for society (Sidebar 1.4).

SIDEBAR 1.4 ACTIVITIES TO ALLEVIATE WILDLIFE DAMAGE BY THE USDA WILDLIFE SERVICES

Wildlife Services (WS) is a federal agency with public trust responsibilities to manage wildlife for present and future generations. It is charged with protecting human health and safety, agriculture, natural resources, and property. The agency conducts careful environmental review of its actions through a rigorous NEPA process that includes public involvement to ensure we do not negatively impact ecosystem health or threaten the abundance and longevity of native wildlife populations. Most species that WS actively manages are increasing in population and/or increasing in range, perhaps the best evidence that our focused efforts to resolve wildlife conflicts are in balance with our stewardship responsibilities to manage wildlife for long-term sustainability (U. S. Department of Agriculture 1994).

During 2017, WS protected 185 threatened or endangered wildlife and plants from the impacts of disease, invasive species, and predators. WS conducted 70,000 technical assistance projects which provided information to 1.2 million people. WS employees aided 890 airports in reducing aviation strikes with wildlife and trained more than 5,000 airport personnel. WS collected 59,000 wildlife disease samples to test for 42 different diseases; 30% of the samples were collected to test for rabies and avian influenza. WS approaches wildlife conflicts using an integrated approach that utilizes nonlethal options first and employs lethal options only when others have failed. Two million animals were killed by WS and 99% were targeted animals. Most removals (90%) were European starlings and blackbirds.

Most efforts in wildlife management aim to increase the positive values of wildlife. On the one hand, we try to enhance the value of game species by managing them to produce the maximum sustainable yield, so hunters can obtain the maximum recreational value. On the other hand, the field of wildlife damage management tries to grow the net value of wildlife for society by reducing the negative values of wildlife. Ergo, wildlife damage management can be defined as the science and practice of elevating the value of the wildlife resource by reducing the negative values of wildlife.

By this definition, wildlife damage management is a very large field. Anything that a wildlife species does that causes human injuries or illnesses, loss in economic productivity, physical damage, or a reduction in a person's quality of life or well-being would be considered wildlife damage. Wildlife damage management also seeks to reduce the negative impacts of one wildlife species upon another, such as mammalian predation on nesting ducks. Because people like ducks and want large populations of ducks, wildlife damage occurs when duck populations are reduced by mammalian predation on nesting ducks or their eggs.

1.9 HOW DOES WILDLIFE DAMAGE MANAGEMENT CONTRIBUTE TO THE LARGER FIELD OF WILDLIFE MANAGEMENT?

In recent decades, the field of wildlife damage management has become an integral part of the wildlife profession. As such, it has had a profound impact on the entire field of wildlife management. Historically, wildlife management was concerned with increasing game populations for hunters by protecting the animals from overharvest and by protecting and managing wildlife habitat. This approach has been wildly (pun intended) successful, and many wildlife populations have soared above historic levels. Some people would say that wildlife managers have been too successful and that the current problem is not too few animals, but too many. Several authors have suggested that if wildlife managers are going to maintain their relevance to society and to survive as a profession, they must change their traditional emphasis of increasing wildlife populations to enhancing the net value of the wildlife resource for society (Minnis and Peyton 1995; Decker et al. 1996; Messmer 2000). A major difficulty in achieving this optimization of values is that the benefits and liabilities of wildlife do not fall evenly upon everyone in society. Because of this, some people want more wildlife, and others want less. Trying to reach management decisions when stakeholders cannot agree on what is in the best interest of society is difficult. But in doing so, wildlife agencies will become more relevant to all segments of society. Wildlife damage managers have been doing this for years, and the procedures they have developed can serve as a guide for the rest of the wildlife profession.

1.10   ARE THERE ALTERNATIVE DEFINITIONS FOR WILDLIFE DAMAGE MANAGEMENT?

Some people have defined wildlife damage management as the science and management of overabundant species (Wagner and Seal 1991), but this definition is too narrow. All wildlife species act in ways that harm human interests. Thus, all species cause wildlife damage, not just overabundant ones. One such example involves endangered peregrine falcons in California where they prey upon another endangered species: California least terns. Certainly, we would not consider peregrine falcons as being overabundant, but we wish that they would not feed on another endangered species. In this case, a negative value associated with a peregrine falcon population is that it kills another endangered species. The goal of wildlife damage management in this situation would be to use some nonlethal method to stop the falcons from eating the terns without harming the falcons.

Another problem with defining wildlife damage management as the management of overabundant species is that it implies wildlife damage occurs because there are too many individuals of a particular species. It implies that the way to stop the

FIGURE 1.5   Commensal mice and rats are among the few species which might be called a "pest."

Source: Paulpixs, Shutterstock765224923.

problem is to reduce the wildlife population to an acceptable level. As we will see in Chapter 13, achieving human–wildlife coexistence is rarely resolved by reducing wildlife populations.

Other people have defined wildlife damage management as the science and management of vertebrate pests. A pest population can be defined as one in which negative values outweigh its positive values. But few, if any, wildlife species qualify as pests because the positive values of a wildlife population almost always outweigh its negative values. I can only think of two groups of animals that might be considered pests, and both groups are exotic species. The first group is commensal rodents, such as mice and rats, especially when they occur inside our homes and buildings (Figure 1.5). The second group includes exotic species that have escaped into a new area and are causing great environmental damage, such as the brown tree snake on Guam, which has already caused the extinction of most of the island's endemic bird species. However, brown tree snakes are protected in Australia where they are native and valued by Australians. For this reason, I doubt that any wildlife species can accurately be labeled as a pest species. Is there a wildlife species for which humans would rejoice if it were driven to extinction (Sidebar 1.5)? I think not. Pest species do occur, most frequently as organisms which cause human diseases. Few people would regret the elimination of pathogens responsible for AIDS, rabies, or the common cold.

SIDEBAR 1.5   CONSIDER THE WARTHOG

One of Africa's charismatic herbivores is the common warthog, although its name certainly lacks charisma (Figure 1.6). It has been released in South African game farms and wildlife reserves since the 1970s, owing to the species popularity with tourists and recreational hunters. Game farming relies on the utilization of wildlife through tourism, trophy hunting, the sale of live animals, or game meat. Warthogs are valued in all these respects. Unfortunately, warthogs view game fences as a minor impediment rather than something to curtail their movements. Hence, the introduced warthogs escaped from the farms where they were released, dispersed large distances, and reproduced. Naturalized populations now occur in different parts of South Africa. Warthogs are also agricultural pests because they raid crops, damage water structures, and destroy fences that allow captive animals to escape (Figure 1.7). Farmers also believed that warthogs reduce the carrying capacity of the natural environment through their grazing on native plants. Therefore, warthogs can be viewed as both an income producer and an income destroyer for local farmers. The result being that most local farmers appreciate warthogs for both their financial value and aesthetic beauty, but some farmers believe that warthogs cause more problems than benefits and support the eradication of warthogs from their area (Swanepoel et al. 2016). Such divided opinions about wildlife species are common.

FIGURE 1.6   Warthog.
Source: Shutterstock 14018655265.

FIGURE 1.7   Warthog damage to an animal-proof fence in South Africa.
Source: Louw Swanepoel and used with permission.

1.11   IS THE KILLING OF PROBLEM ANIMALS ETHICAL?

Many people question the ethics of using lethal control to resolve human–wildlife conflicts. They worry that lethal methods are not humane or that the cost of lethal control in terms of animal lives lost may not be worth the benefit. The difficulty is that while it may be possible to assign a value to the benefits, such as dollars saved by farmers or ranchers, it is harder to place a value on a wild animal's life. The use of lethal control is controversial because people view the same lethal control operation differently, based on their own experiences, hopes, and concerns. One group's chief interest is to protect biodiversity, another group wants to protect traditional ways of life for rural residents, and a third group is passionate about preventing animal suffering. Warburton and Norton (2009) argue that the only ethically defensible approach is to apply a knowledge-based ethic that guarantees that today's actions will result in more knowledge that will be applied to future actions. This ethic requires that lethal control be designed to collect information on the action's consequences. Lethal control should be conducted as part of a scientific study, using the experimental method and supervised by a scientist to monitor its consequences and outcomes. A new adaptive management plan should be made as new knowledge is acquired. This new plan should then be open to public debate to determine if it does advance social values, knowledge, and ethical concerns more than prior management plans. The question then becomes, not whether the new plan will be effective and humane, but rather if the proposed management plan is an improvement over the current one?

1.12   WHAT ARE THE NECESSARY INGREDIENTS FOR THE OCCURRENCE OF WILDLIFE DAMAGE?

For wildlife damage to occur, three ingredients are required: a wildlife species that is doing the damage, an object being damaged, and a person who has been adversely affected (Figure 1.8). The object being damaged may be an agricultural crop, livestock, building, human, timber, wildlife, or other natural resources. The affected person often is the owner of the object being damaged, but it may be anyone in society. Examples of people adversely affected by wildlife include a farmer suffering crop damage, a homeowner with a raccoon living in the chimney, a hunter who is unable to shoot a pronghorn because most of the fawns have already been killed by coyotes, and a person who is saddened because a bird population is declining as a result of vegetation loss from deer overbrowsing. It is important to note that if no person is being adversely affected by wildlife, then wildlife damage is not occurring. However, wildlife damage can occur even if no physical object appears to be damaged. For instance, elephants venture out of nature preserves and parks in India to forage in agricultural fields next to rural villages. People in these areas are afraid to walk outside at night because of the danger of encountering an elephant and getting hurt (Gamage and Wijesundara 2014). Even if no one is hurt by an elephant, this situation is a type of wildlife damage because the villagers' fear has reduced their ability to enjoy an evening walk and their sense of well-being.

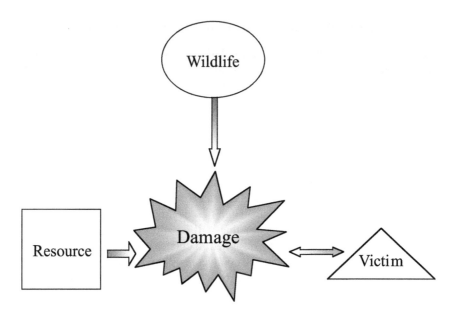

FIGURE 1.8   For wildlife damage to occur, there must be a combination of wildlife, a resource being damaged, and a person who is suffering a loss.

As we will explore throughout this book, several options are available for enhancing human–wildlife coexistence. We can try to remove the animal causing the problem or change its behavior, we can try to modify the object being damaged to reduce its vulnerability, or we can change human behavior and perceptions so that people are willing to tolerate the damage. Any of these approaches can resolve human–wildlife conflicts.

1.13   WHO IS LEGALLY RESPONSIBLE FOR WILDLIFE DAMAGE?

As we have already discussed, wildlife belongs to society in the United States and Canada and is managed for its citizens by their government. But this does not mean that the people or their government are responsible for damage caused by their wildlife. Several U.S. courts have ruled that wildlife are "wild," and therefore by definition, the actions of wildlife are beyond the control of the state, and so, government is not liable for any mischief wildlife may cause. Legally, wildlife damage becomes an "Act of God."

But there are limits to government immunity for wildlife damage. One limitation occurs when the government or its employees know or should have known that wildlife were likely to cause a problem because government has a responsibility to respond to a wildlife problem or at least to warn people of the danger. In such cases, civil suits can be brought against the government and its employees (Dale 2009). The U.S. Forest Service lost a court case and had to pay almost $2 million to compensate the family of an 11-year-old boy who was killed by a black bear in the Uintah National Forest of Utah. Earlier, on the same day and at the same campsite, the bear had attacked another person, but the attack did not result in injuries. The report of this earlier attack was not passed on to other Forest Service employees, who might have warned campers, including the victim's family. The court ruled that the U.S. Forest Service's negligence contributed to the boy's death (Stringham 2013).

Liability may also exist when state or federal employees capture an animal and then decide to release it. If that same animal injures someone thereafter, the attorney for the injured person can argue that the government's actions were reckless and directly contributed to the animal's subsequent destructive behavior. Government liability also exists when its actions create conditions that make wildlife damage inevitable. For example, governments are not liable for damage caused by a DVC, but this may not be true if a state transportation department erects a deer-proof fence on both sides of a highway so that a deer on the highway cannot escape. In this case, the government has created a dangerous situation (i.e., a trapped deer will ultimately cause an accident), and the government may be liable for any damage caused by a trapped deer.

States also have an ethical responsibility when they increase a wildlife population that then causes damage to a person (Sidebar 1.6). Utah, for instance, compensates farmers for damage by pheasants because the state artificially creates large pheasant populations by managing for this goal; the state recognizes an ethical responsibility to help farmers that suffer damage because of pheasants. In contrast, Utah does not compensate for damage by red-winged blackbirds, European starlings, sparrows, or other birds because the state does take actions to increase their numbers.

SIDEBAR 1.6 WHO IS ETHICALLY RESPONSIBLE FOR DAMAGE CAUSED BY WOLVES DESCENDED FROM THOSE RELEASED BY THE U.S. FISH AND WILDLIFE AGENCY IN YELLOWSTONE NATIONAL PARK?

Wolves were extirpated from the Western United States during the 1930s thanks to the efforts of Aldo Leopold and many others who were hired to shoot them. During the 1990s, the U.S. Fish and Wildlife Service introduced 66 wolves into central Idaho and Yellowstone National Park with much fanfare and television coverage. By 2008, these had expanded to more than 1,500 wolves in more than 200 packs. These introductions have been a great success for the U.S. Fish and Wildlife Service, which has received much acclaim (Jimenez et al. 2017). It has benefitted Yellowstone National Park due to an influx of tourists into the park (Figure 1.9) and an increase in its budget ($19 million in 1995 to $35 million in 2015). The introduction, however, has harmed the local ranchers whose livestock are killed by wolves. Should anyone be responsible for reimbursing local ranchers for livestock lost to these wolves?

FIGURE 1.9   Yellowstone National Park has become more popular with tourists who come to view wolves.

Source: Maciej Bledowski, Shutterstock 750992824.

1.14   WHAT LESSONS DID THE INTERNATIONAL UNION FOR CONSERVATION OF NATURE LEARN ABOUT HUMAN–WILDLIFE CONFLICTS?

The International Union for Conservation of Nature (IUCN) is a union of 1,300 national governments and civil society organizations with the mission of simultaneously enabling human progress, economic development, and conservation of nature. It is a global authority on the status of the environment and how to safeguard it. Every ten years, the IUCN's World Parks Congress brings together conservation experts from around the world to share information and ideas and sets a global policy agenda for protected areas. The Fifth World Parks Conference was held in Durban, South Africa during 2004, and brought human–wildlife conflict to the global stage as part of an effort to address current challenges facing protected area management and conservation. The conference had a workshop titled "Creating Coexistence Between Humans and Wildlife: Global Perspectives on Local Efforts to Address Human–Wildlife Conflict." The workshop identified six lessons learned about human–wildlife conflicts. The lessons are important enough that I have included them below by paraphrasing Francine Madden, who was the Chair of the workshop (Madden 2004).

1.14.1   LESSON 1: HUMAN–WILDLIFE CONFLICTS OFTEN INVOLVE HUMAN–HUMAN CONFLICTS

Human–wildlife conflicts frequently involve a struggle between people who have different goals, attitudes, values, feelings, levels of empowerment, or wealth. Human–wildlife conflicts may be rooted in struggles among people over empowerment and access to resources. Many conflicts about wildlife are really clashes between people with historical wounds, cultural misunderstandings, or socioeconomic needs. Conflicts also arise because of gaps in trust and communication over how to conserve wildlife and ensure the well-being of people at the same time.

1.14.2   LESSON 2: BIOLOGY IS A NECESSARY PART OF THE SOLUTION, BUT IT IS NOT SUFFICIENT IN ITSELF

Biological science alone does not provide a complete understanding of, or solutions to, human–wildlife conflicts. In reality, half of the challenge of addressing the conflict is in understanding the human dimension with its social, cultural, political, economic, and legal complexities. A complaint often heard from local communities – that the government cares more for wildlife than the people – is an indication that conservation is not purely a matter of biological science.

1.14.3   LESSON 3: PERCEPTIONS OF CONFLICT ARE IMPORTANT, AND SOLUTIONS MUST ADDRESS THEM

Often, the level of public outcry is not in direct proportion to actual crop, livestock, or property loss. Rather, public outcry often has much more to do with perceptions of potential risk as well as a lack of control over addressing the problem. Neighboring herds of cows or dens of rats may cause more crop damage in a year than a single elephant that wanders through the region once each year. Yet, the elephant's intrusion or threat of intrusion excites more public outrage because people feel that they have less ability to control the threat; given the elephant's size, they pose a greater threat of producing extreme harm. Dealing with their neighbor's intruding cow or a pesky rat is possible; people often have no recourse for dealing with elephants and other wildlife that are protected by law.

1.14.4   LESSON 4: GLOBAL INSIGHTS AND LOCAL VARIABILITY NEED TO BE BALANCED

Two contradictory misconceptions can exist simultaneously. On the one hand, many conservationists believe that "their" species or protected area is unique so that lessons learned from elsewhere or widely held principles of how to assess, address, process, and evaluate conflict do not apply. On the other hand, equally wrong is the belief that a one-size-fits-all solution for mitigation can be applied successfully across the wide spectrum of specific conflict situations. Between these two extremes is a more balanced truism. Widely held global principles and lessons learned, as well as valuable tools and techniques for mitigating conflict, can and should be shared across a wide spectrum. They must, however, be put into perspective with an understanding of the unique, local context of any conflict. This fully integrated view is critical in successfully designing and implementing any conflict mitigation program.

1.14.5 LESSON 5: SUCCESSFUL RESPONSES REQUIRE THE USE OF MULTIPLE AND ADAPTIVE TOOLS

Any given tool, technique, or approach is more likely to succeed if it is incorporated into a full arsenal of conflict mitigation strategies with the flexibility to change strategies as conditions change. Compensation schemes that are not tied to preventive measures and changes in human behavior are more likely to fail than ones that are tied to community participation and good livestock husbandry. Multiple tactics need to be applied together to ensure success. Complex and multifaceted solutions are needed to address the complex and multifaceted reality of human–wildlife conflicts. Rarely, if ever, can a single tactic address the full range of social, economic, and biological aspects of a conflict scenario? By combining a number of tactics, tools, and techniques, we can strengthen and improve the chances of overall success in mitigation efforts.

1.14.6 LESSON 6: DEMONSTRATING GENUINE EFFORT IS A VALUABLE FIRST STEP

Fostering communication and trust, demonstrating effort and a willingness to address the issue, and then following through will often positively impact the attitudes and actions of people in conflict with wildlife. This, in part, reflects the fact that perceptions are major influences on human–wildlife conflicts.

1.15 WHY WORRY ABOUT HUMAN–WILDLIFE CONFLICTS?

A human–wildlife conflict occurs whenever an action by humans or wildlife has an adverse impact upon the other. Human–wildlife conflicts exist when coyotes kill sheep, raccoons destroy someone's garden, a beach is closed because it is littered with goose feces, or mice chew a hole in a cereal box. Human–wildlife conflicts also occur when humans do something that has an adverse impact on wildlife. For instance, a human–wildlife conflict occurs when wildlife habitat is converted into an asphalt parking lot. Humans should be concerned about the impact of their actions on wildlife even from a purely anthropocentric standpoint because wildlife provide many positive benefits to society. In actuality, whenever a human–wildlife conflict occurs, both parties (humans and wildlife) lose. Consider a collision between an automobile and a deer. Both the driver and society lose because of the economic damage to the car and the risk of human injury or death. But the deer also loses because most deer struck by vehicles are killed. Likewise, when coyotes kill sheep, the rancher suffers losses, as does society through higher food costs. But the coyote will also lose if the rancher tries to kill it.

The impact of humans on the earth is now so great that scientists believe that humans have created a new geological era, called the Anthropocene, to distinguish it from the Holocene, which began 11,000 years ago after the end of the last Ice Age.

Humans are changing not only the climate but also the geologic record across the world (Waters et al. 2016). One aspect of the Anthropocene is a defaunation of the earth, which is the sixth mass extinction in the earth's history. Since the year 1500, more than 300 species of terrestrial vertebrates have become extinct (Dirzo et al. 2014). The losses are especially pronounced among the world's largest predators and herbivores (Ripple et al. 2014, 2015).

How can humans mitigate the loss of terrestrial vertebrates? One approach is to create preserves, wildlife refuges, or parks where human impact on wildlife is minimized. Although this approach is well intended, it does little to resolve the problem because only a small fraction of the land is set aside in parks. In reality, most wildlife live outside of parks – the same place people live. Wildlife populations, for example, thrive in densely settled cities. Clearly, if human–wildlife conflicts are going to be resolved, ways must be found for humans and wildlife to coexist harmoniously without either having an adverse impact upon the other. This is the philosophy of human–wildlife coexistence and is the goal of the field of wildlife damage management.

1.16 SUMMARY

Wildlife is considered a public trust in the United States and Canada. It is owned by the citizenry and held in trust for the benefit of both the current and future generations. The wildlife resource provides many benefits for society (i.e., it has many positive values) – physical utility, monetary, recreational, ecological, existence, and historic. Wildlife also causes many problems for people, and these can be considered negative values of wildlife. Anything that wildlife does that causes human injuries or illnesses, loss of economic productivity, physical damage, or a reduction in a person's quality of life or well-being is wildlife damage. The goal of wildlife management is to increase the net value of the wildlife resource for society, which is the sum of wildlife's positive values minus the sum of wildlife's negative values while protecting the resource for the benefit of future generations. Wildlife damage management is an integral part of the field of wildlife management and is devoted to mitigating human–wildlife conflicts and thereby increasing the net value of wildlife by reducing its negative values. Its goal is resolving human–wildlife conflicts so that humans and wildlife can coexist without having an adverse impact upon the other.

Wildlife management in the United States is complicated because society owns wildlife and government manages it, but wildlife habitat is owned and managed by landowners. Legislative bodies have the responsibility to make strategic decisions about how wildlife should be managed to achieve the greatest good for the greatest number of people. Wildlife biologists who work for the government use their scientific knowledge about wildlife to make tactical decisions about how best to achieve the broad wildlife goals set by the government.

1.17 DISCUSSION QUESTIONS

1. Florida's Fish and Conservation Commission implemented a Statewide Nuisance Alligator Program during 1978; this ordered that problem alligators

were to be killed rather than captured and translocated. Nuisance alligators are those that show bold behavior toward humans, show little wariness, or are in situations where they are a perceived threat to people and domestic animals. In 1998, the Commission initiated a policy to remove large alligators proactively from aquatic sites used frequently by humans (Woodward et al. 2019). Poisonous snakes kill similar numbers of Floridians as alligators, yet they are protected by state law. Does this distinction in the management of alligators and poisonous snakes make sense?

2. The Park Superintendent of Isle Royale National Park believes that wolves should be reintroduced into the park because she thinks it is important to maintain all of Isle Royal's wildlife species as they were when the park was created. Others disagree (see Sidebar 1.3 for more information). This leads to a series of questions that need to be considered. Should the national park system be introducing wolves to Isle Royale or should they just let nature take its course? Around 1980, a park visitor violated park rules and brought a dog that was infected with canine parvovirus to Isle Royale; the virus spread to the wolves and killed 36 before the pathogen was eradicated. If this epidemic partially contributed to the collapse of the wolf population, would that change your view about the justification of introducing wolves? Wolves have also been reintroduced into Yellowstone National Park. Why is it more justified to reintroduction of wolves into Yellowstone National Park but not into Isle Royale?

3. The United States supports a worldwide ban on whaling and seeks to embarrass or punish other countries that still allow whale hunting despite our desire that they stop. But the United States supports hunting of large land mammals and the killing of livestock for food. Why does the United States give whales special status? Does this stem from a sense of guilt that U.S. whale hunters almost drove whales to extinction over a century ago?

4. In the preface and in this chapter, I have expressed the view that if wildlife species are to remain abundant in the Anthropocene, then humans and wildlife must be able to coexist on the same land without one having an adverse impact on the other? Do you believe this to be true or do you think I have overstated the need for human–wildlife coexistence?

LITERATURE CITED

Blumm, M. C., and L. Ritchie. 2005. The pioneer spirit and the public trust: the American rule of capture and state ownership of wildlife. *Environmental Law* 35:673–720.

Dale, L. A. 2009. Personal and corporate liability in the aftermath of bird strikes: a costly consideration. *Human-Wildlife Interactions* 3:216–225.

Decker, D. J., A. B. Forstchen, E. F. Pomeranz, C. A. Smith, S. J. Riley, C. A. Jacobson, J. F. Organ, and G. R. Batcheller. 2015. Stakeholder engagement in wildlife management: does the public trust doctrine imply limits? *Journal of Wildlife Management* 79:174–179.

Decker, D. J., C. C. Krueger, R. A. Baer, Jr., B. A. Knuth, and M. E. Richmond. 1996. From clients to stakeholders: a philosophical shift for fish and wildlife management. *Human Dimensions in Wildlife* 1:70–82.

Dirzo, R., H. S. Young, M. Galetti, G. Ceballos, N. J. Isaac, and B. Collen. 2014. Defaunation in the anthropocene. *Science* 345:401–406.

Dubois, S., and H. W. Harshaw. 2013. Exploring "humane" dimension of wildlife. *Human Dimensions of Wildlife* 18:1–19.

Gamage, A., and M. Wijesundara. 2014. *A solution for the elephant-human conflict.* Texas Instruments India Educators' Conference, Bangalore, Karnataka. Pages 169–176.

Giles, R. H., Jr. 1978. *Wildlife management.* W. H. Freeman, San Francisco, CA.

Huffman, J. L. 2007. Speaking of inconvenient truths – a history of the public trust doctrine. *Duke Environment Law and Policy Forum* 18:1–103.

Jimenez, M. D., E. E. Bangs, D. K. Boyd, D. W. Smith, S. A. Becker, D. E. Ausband, S. P. Woodrull, E. H. Bradley, J. Holyan, and K. Laudon. 2017. Wolf dispersal in the Rocky Mountains, Western United States: 1993–2008. *Journal of Wildlife Management* 81:581–592.

Krauthammer, C. 1991. Saving nature, but only for man. *Time* 82, 17 June.

Leopold, A. 1949. *A Sand County almanac and sketches here and there.* Oxford University Press, New York.

Madden, F. 2004. Creating coexistence between humans and wildlife: global perspectives on local efforts to address human-wildlife conflicts. *Human Dimensions of Wildlife* 9:247–257.

Mathisen, K. M., S. Pedersen, E. B. Nilsen, and C. Skarpe. 2012. Contrasting responses of two passerine bird species to moose browsing. *European Journal of Wildlife Research* 58:535–547.

Messmer, T. A. 2000. The emergence of human-wildlife conflict management: turning challenges into opportunities. *International Biodeterioration and Biodegradation* 45:97–102.

Mihell, C. 2018. A reasonable illusion. *Sierra Magazine* 103:30–35.

Minnis, D. L., and R. B. Peyton. 1995. Cultural carrying capacity, modeling a notion. Pages 19–34 *in* J. B. McAninch, editor. *Urban deer: a management resource?* North Central Section of the Wildlife Society, St. Louis, MI.

Organ, J. F., V. Geist, S. P. Mahoney, S. Williams, P. R. Krausman, G. R. Batcheller, T. A. Decker, R. Carmichael, P. Nanjappa, R. Regan, R. A. Medellin, R. Cantu, R. E. McCabe, S. Craven, G. M. Vecellio, and D. J. Decker. 2012. *The North American model of wildlife conservation.* The Wildlife Society Technical Review 12-04, Wildlife Society, Bethesda, MD.

Ramp, D., and M. Bekoff. 2015. Compassion as a practical and evolved ethic for conservation. *BioScience* 65:323–327.

Ripple, W. J., J. A. Estes, R. L. Beschta, C. C. Wilmers, E. G. Ritchie, M. Hebblewhite, J. Berger, B. Elmhagen, M. Letnic, M. P. Nelson, and O. J. Schmitz. 2014. Status and ecological effects of the world's largest carnivores. *Science* 343(6167):1241484.

Ripple, W. J., T. M. Newsome, C. Wolf, R. Dirzo, K. T. Everatt, M. Galetti, M. W. Hayward, G. I. Kerley, T. Levi, P. A. Lindsey, and D. W. Macdonald. 2015. Collapse of the world's largest herbivores. *Science Advances* 1(4):e1400103.

Smith, C. A. 2011. The role of state wildlife professionals under the public trust doctrine. *Journal of Wildlife Management* 75:1539–1543.

Stringham, S. F. 2013. Managing risk from bears and other potentially lethal wildlife: predictability, accountability, and liability. *Human-Wildlife Interactions* 7:5–9.

Swanepoel, M., A. J. Leslie, and L. C. Hoffman. 2016. Farmers' perceptions of the extra-limital common warthog in the Northern Cape and Free State provinces, South Africa. *Wildlife Society Bulletin* 40:112–121.

Treves, A., G. Chapron, J. V. López-Bao, C. Shoemaker, A. R. Goeckner, and J. T. Bruskotter. 2017. Predators and the public trust. *Biological Review* 92:248–270.

U. S. Department of Agriculture. 1994. *Animal damage control program – final environmental impact statement,* volume 2. U.S. Department of Agriculture, Washington, DC.

U. S. Fish and Wildlife Service. 2013. *What you should know about a federal migration bird depredation permit.* U. S. Fish and Wildlife Service, Washington, DC. www.fws.gov/forms/3-200-13.pdf. Accessed 20 June 2018.

Wagner, F. H., and U. S. Seal. 1991. Values, problems, and methodologies in managing overabundant wildlife populations: an overview. Pages 279–293 *in* D. R. McCullough and R. H. Barrett, editors. *Wildlife 2001: populations.* Elsevier Applied Science, New York.

Wallach, A. D., M. Bekoff, M. P. Nelson, and D. Ramp. 2015. Promoting predators and compassionate conservation. *Conservation Biology* 5:1481–1484.

Warburton, B., and B. G. Norton. 2009. Towards a knowledge-based ethic for lethal control of nuisance wildlife. *Journal of Wildlife Management* 73:158–164.

Waters, C. N., J. Zalasiewicz, C. Summerhayes, A. D. Barnosky, C. Poirier, A. Gałuszka, A. Cearreta, M. Edgeworth, E. C. Ellis, M. Ellis, C. Jeandel, R. Leinfelder, J. R. McNeill, D. deB. Richter, W. Steffen, J. Syvitski, D. Vidas, M. Wagreich, M. Williams, A. Zhisheng, J. Grinevald, E. Odada, N. Oreskes, and A. P. Wolfe. 2016. The Anthropocene is functionally and stratigraphically distinct from the Holocene. *Science* 351(6269):aad2622:1–10.

Woodward, A. R., E. H. Leone, H. J. Dutton, J. E. Waller, and L. Hord. 2019. Characteristics of American alligator bites on people in Florida. *Journal of Wildlife Management* 83:1437–1453.

2 Threats to Human Safety

"These [grizzly] bears being so hard to die rather intimidate us all; I must confess that I do not like the gentlemen and had rather be attacked by two Indians than one bear."

– Meriwether Lewis, 11 May 1805, while on the Lewis and Clark Expedition

"Most problems with bears in parks stem not from human malevolence but from too much benevolence. As with most conflicts between powerful adversaries, it is dangerous to appear weak."

– McCullough (1982)

Only a small fraction of human–wildlife interactions results in a human injury or death, but the loss of even one person is a horrible tragedy, and we must do whatever we can to keep people safe. These tragedies also attract a great deal of attention and media coverage and have a great impact on public attitudes about wildlife. There are three ways people become injured or killed from human–wildlife interactions. A person can (1) be bitten, clawed, gored, or attacked by an animal; (2) be involved in a collision between an animal and an automobile or airplane; or (3) become ill from a zoonotic disease or parasite for which a wildlife species served as a vector or reservoir for the pathogen. This chapter will cover the first two topics; zoonotic disease will be the subject of the next chapter.

2.1 WHY DO ANIMALS ATTACK PEOPLE?

There are many reasons why animals attack humans; such attacks can be defensive, predatory, or territorial in nature. Often, the animal is acting defensively when it attacks a human. An animal's best defense against a predator is to hide, flee, or keep its distance. However, when an animal is cornered, trapped, or constrained by a predator, its best chance to survive is to attack in hopes that it can inflict so much pain that the predator will give up and seek easier prey. For this reason, even small animals will bite or attack a predator or a human when they feel trapped. Animals will use any available means to inflict pain. Cats use their claws to scratch, coyotes use their teeth to bite, bison use their horns to gore, moose use their front legs to stomp, porcupines use their quills, and we all know what a skunk will do. Defensive attacks include adult animals trying to protect their offspring from humans. Many bear attacks occur when hikers inadvertently walk between a mother and its cubs. White-tailed deer attacks on people usually involve female deer and occur in the spring. These attacks result when a mother believes that someone is a threat to its fawn, which is hidden nearby (Hubbard and Nielsen 2009).

DOI: 10.1201/9780429401404-2

Predatory attacks occur when the animal views the person as food. Predatory attacks on adult humans are very rare, in part, because human adults are so large that only the largest predators (e.g., cougars, tigers, lions, wolves, bears, and crocodiles) would consider them prey. But sometimes, predatory attacks on adults occur when the predators underestimate the size of the person they are attacking. People are bitten every year by bluefish, which weigh less than a kilogram. In these cases, the fish probably saw an object, perhaps a hand or finger, in turbid water and bit it before realizing that it was part of something much larger. Undoubtedly, some shark and alligator attacks result from this same mistake. If a person is wading in knee-deep water, a submerged alligator might see the legs, but not the rest of the body that is above the water and not realize that it is a person. Young children do not have the benefit of a large size to scare away potential predators. For this reason, a high proportion of predatory attacks on humans are directed at children, who are especially at risk when alone. Even relatively small predators, such as coyotes, occasionally attack young children.

Most wildlife species exhibit territorial behavior or other aggressive behaviors only toward individuals of the same species, but this is not always the case. Some species are aggressive toward individuals of other species and may attack them. Mute swans are an example of the latter, one which I am personally familiar. Some mute swans are aggressive toward other species and drive other birds, especially geese, out of their territories (Conover and Kania 1994). Aggressive mute swans (Figure 2.1)

FIGURE 2.1   An attacking mute swan.

Source: Nounours, Shutterstock 510583507.

often threaten humans during the nesting season by flying at them as if attacking but stop short before making physical contact (i.e., bluff attack). However, I made the acquaintance of one particularly aggressive swan when I was checking swan nests on the Connecticut River. As I was going up one tributary, a boater frantically waved at me and warned me not to proceed further because "there was a mad swan around the bend that attacks people." I thanked him for the warning, but I did not heed it because I knew that swans only make bluff attacks. But, this particular swan was not bluffing; it flew into the boat and attacked me. The attack ended after I pushed it out of the boat, but not before both my legs and ego were bruised.

Many large herbivores, such as bison, travel in herds and have a strict social hierarchy; subordinate animals must keep their distance from dominant individuals. Sometimes, people unknowingly invade the personal space of a dominant animal, provoking an attack. This is especially a problem in parks, where tourists and photographers try to get as close as possible to wildlife. Usually, animals respond to this intrusion by moving away, but sometimes, they attack the person. Tourists in national parks are injured every year by bison, elk, and moose (Figure 2.2).

Animals that are hand reared by humans can imprint on their handlers. When these animals reach maturity, these animals often view humans as members of their species and will attempt to drive people from their territories or attack people in an attempt to establish dominance. An example of this is a deer that lowers its head and uses its antlers to spar with someone during the mating season. For this reason, it is dangerous to release hand-reared animals into the wild.

FIGURE 2.2   Each year, tourists are injured by elk in parks when they get too close to the animal and annoy it. This incident happened in Grand Canyon National Park.

Source: U.S. National Park Photo and in the public domain.

2.2   HOW OFTEN ARE HUMANS INJURED OR KILLED BY WILDLIFE?

We know surprisingly little about the frequency of wildlife attacks on humans across the world; what we do know is too often limited to data collected in a small area. Many countries outside of North America and Europe do not maintain records on human fatalities and injuries. The government records that do exist often underestimate the number of people killed or injured by wildlife because a high proportion of people in these countries do not seek medical attention even for life-threatening injuries. As one example, Khan (2004) documented 41 people killed by tigers in part of Bangladesh during an 18-month period spanning 2001–2003, but official records for the same period listed only 5 fatalities.

My goal for this chapter is to determine the most accurate data on the extent of human fatalities and injuries caused by wildlife in the United States (Table 2.1)

TABLE 2.1

Best estimate of the annual number of people injured or killed in the U.S. after being bitten or attacked by wildlife, involved in a wildlife-vehicle collision, wildlife-aircraft collision, or sickened by a zoonotic disease. These data only include people who sought medical attention or they had a reportable disease (i.e., one that the doctor was required by law to report to state and federal health agencies). The disease statistics include both confirmed and probable cases in humans.

Causes	No. injured or sickened	No. killed	Sources
Sharks	32	1	International Shark Attack Files (2020)
Snakes (non-venomous)	6,135	0	O'Neil et al. (2007)
Snakes (venomous)	7,000	5	CDC (2016)
Alligators	9	1	Florida Fish and Wildlife Conservation Commission (2018), Texas Parks and Wildlife (2004)
Reptiles (excluding snakes)	1,050	?	Langley (2008)
Birds (excluding parrots)	1,594	0	O'Neil et al. (2007)
Bats	1,335	0	O'Neil et al. (2007)
Rodents	27,000	0.2	Conover et al. (1995), Forrester et al. (2012, 2018)
Opossum	375	0	O'Neil et al. (2007)
Skunk	750	0	Conover et al. (1995)
Raccoons	1,310	0	O'Neil et al. (2007)
Foxes	500	0	Conover et al. (1995)
Coyotes	9	0.1	Timm et al. (2004)
Wolves	0.7	0.1	Wikipedia (2018a)
Cougars	3.3	0.3	Wikipedia (2018b), Penteriani et al. (2016)

Causes	No. injured or sickened	No. killed	Sources
Black bears	25	0.3	Herrero (1985)
Grizzly bears	0.8	?	Smith and Herrero (2018)
Polar bears	0.1	0	Smith and Herrero (2018)
Bison	1.7	0	Cherry et al. (2018)
Elk	3.0	0	Conover (unpublished)
All bites and attacks	47,134	8.0	
Deer-vehicle collision	58,622	440	Conover (2019)
Moose-vehicle collisions	640	6	Conover (2019)
Wildlife-civilian aircraft collisions	16	1	Thorpe (2012)
Wildlife-military aircraft collisions	?	3	Richardson and West (2000)
All collisions	59,278	450	
Zoonotic diseases	210,597	–	Chapter 3 of this book. Zoonotic diseases also include AIDS and HIV infections, COVID-19, influenza (avian flu), and salmonellosis, but this number does not include cases of these diseases.
All causes	317,009	458	

and worldwide (Table 2.2). To obtain these data, I searched for unpublished reports and those published in peer-reviewed journals containing information on the extent of human fatalities, injuries, and morbidity in the United States by using Google Scholar, Google, and websites of wildlife agencies. Once an article on the subject was located, I searched its Literature Cited section for additional pertinent literature. Most journal websites also provide information about where their articles have been cited since publication. These articles were likewise searched to locate pertinent articles. I also searched the World Health Organizations (WHO) and Centers for Disease Control and Prevention (CDC) websites and publications for information. Of special importance was the CDC's publication, Morbidity and Mortality Weekly. Some sources citing attacks on humans by large predators did not provide separate data for the United States alone, but instead, reported data for North America, usually meaning the United States and Canada. I included these sources but identified the area of the study as North America rather than the United States. My literature search usually produced several reports about the frequency of attacks by a particular species that differed by the year the data were collected. In these cases, I used the most recent data, and the data that covered the greatest proportion of the United States. Sometimes, I was able to combine data from different studies when they covered nonoverlapping parts of the United States or world.

TABLE 2.2

Studies of Nonfatal and Fatal Injuries to Humans from Wildlife Attacks in Different Parts of the World

Species	Location	Years	Injuries/year		Reference
			Nonfatal	Fatal	
Sharks	Worldwide	2019	100	5	International Shark Files (2020)
Snakes	Worldwide		5 million	95k–125k	WHO (2018)
		2007	400k–1,800k	20k–94k	Kasturiratne et al. (2008)
	Pakistan	?	40k	1k	Alirol et al. (2010)
	India	2005	–	46k	Mohapatra et al. (2011)
	Bangladesh	2009	590k	6k	Rahman et al. (2010)
	Sri Lanka	2002	99k	216	Fox et al. (2006)
	16 West African countries	1975–2015	5.4k*	4.5k	Habib et al. (2015)
	Sub-Saharan Africa	1970–2010	14k	7k	Chippaux (2011)
Crocodilians, all species	Worldwide	2018	162	172	CrocBITES (2019)
Crocodile, saltwater	Worldwide	2018		75	75 CrocBITES (2019)
Crocodile, Mugger	Worldwide	2018	36	18	CrocBITES (2019)
Crocodile, Nile	Worldwide	2018	24	69	CrocBITES (2019)
Crocodile, Morelet's	Worldwide	2018	10	0	CrocBITES (2019)
Crocodile, W. African	Worldwide	2018	1	1	CrocBITES (2019)
Crocodile, America	Worldwide	2018	7	4	CrocBITES (2019)
Alligator, American	Worldwide	2018	5	2	CrocBITES (2019)
Caiman, Yacare	Worldwide	2018	2	0	CrocBITES (2019)
Caiman, black	Worldwide	2018	1	0	CrocBITES (2019)
Caiman, spectacled	Worldwide	2018	1	0	CrocBITES (2019)
Tomistoma	Worldwide	2018	0	4	CrocBITES (2019)
Rat	India	2003	75,000		Sudarshan et al. (2006)
Bear (all species)	India	2003	15,000		Sudarshan et al. (2006)
	Nepal	2010–2014	10	1	Acharya et al. (2016)
Polar bear	Canadian National Parks	1986–2000	0.1	0	Clark (2003)
	Worldwide	1870–2014	0.5	0.2	Wilder et al. (2017)
	Worldwide	2010–2014	3.0	–	Wilder et al. (2017)

Species	Location	Years	Injuries/year		Reference
			Nonfatal	Fatal	
	Worldwide	1900–1999	–	0.1	Löe and Röskaft (2004)
Brown bear	Worldwide	1900–1999	–	3.1	Löe and Röskaft (2004)
	Europe and Asia	2004–2015	3.0	–	Penteriani et al. (2016)
	Asia	1900–1999	–	2.1	Linnell et al. (2002)
	Europe	1900–1999	–	0.4	Linnell et al. (2002)
	Scandinavia	1997–2005	1.4	0.01	Støen et al. (2018)
Sloth bear	Madhya Pradesh, India	1989–1994	128	10	Rajpurohit and Krausman (2000)
	North Bilaspur Forest Division Chhattisgarh, India	1998–2000	46	4.0	Bargali et al. (2005)
Wolf	Worldwide	1900–1999	–	6.0	Löe and Röskaft (2004)
	Worldwide	1950–2000	1.6	5.6	Linnell et al. (2002)
	Madhya Pradesh, India	1989–1994	–	2.6	Rajpurohit and Krausman (2000)
Hyena	Worldwide	1900–1999	–	0.06	Löe and Röskaft (2004)
	Uganda	1923–1994	0.0	0.1	Treves and Naughton-Treves (1999)
	Madhya Pradesh, India	1989–1994	–	0.6	Rajpurohit and Krausman (2000) Jackals
	India	2003		30,000	Sudarshan et al. (2006)
	Mozambique	2006–2008	1	0	Dunham et al. (2010)
Dingo	Australia	1996–2001	37	0.2	Linnell et al. (2002)
Red fox	Kashmir Valley, India	2005–2016	2.3	0.0	Moten et al. (2017)
Lion	Worldwide	1900–1999	–	5.5	Löe and Röskaft (2004)
	Tanzania	1990–2005	21	38	Packer et al. (2005)
	Uganda	1923–1994	1.2	3.6	Treves and Naughton-Treves (1999)
	Mozambique	2006–2008	9	11	Dunham et al. (2010)
	Gir Forest, India	1978–1991	12.6	2.2	Saberwal et al. (1994)
Leopard	Worldwide	1900–1999	–	8.4	Löe and Röskaft (2004)
	Uttar Pradesh, India	1990–1994	4	3	Linnell et al. (2002)
	Pauri Garhwal, India	1987–2000	–	12	Linnell et al. (2002)
	Chamoli Garhwal, India	1900–1994	6	5	Mohan (1997)
	Uganda	1923–1994	1.3	0.6	Treves and Naughton-Treves (1999)

(*Continued*)

TABLE 2.2 *(Continued)*

Species	Location	Years	Nonfatal	Fatal	Reference
			Injuries/year		
	Kashmir Valley, India	2005–2016	6.7	4.9	Moten et al. (2017)
	Maharashtra, India	1999–2005	150.3	33.5	Athreya et al. (2011)
	Madhya Pradesh, India	1989–1994	–	28	Rajpurohit and Krausman (2000)
	Nepal	2010–2014	11	8	Acharya et al. (2016)
Tiger	Worldwide	1900–1999	–	126	Löe and Röskaft (2004)
	Dudhwa, India	1978–1988	–	20	Nowell and Jackson (1996)
	Madhya Pradesh, India	1989–1994	–	24	Rajpurohit and Krausman (2000)
	Sundarbans, India	1991–2000	–	18	Barlow (2009)
	Sundarbans, Bangladesh	1991–2000	–	18	Barlow (2009)
	Sundabans, Bangladesh	2002–2003	–	27	Khan (2004)
	Sundarbans, India and Bangladesh	1881–2006	–	76	Barlow (2009)
	Sumatra	1996–1997	–	4	Linnell et al. (2002)
	Sumatra	1978–1997	1.5	7.3	Nyphus and Tilson (2004)
	Nepal	2010–2014	4	5	Acharya et al. (2016)
	Russia, Far East	2000–2009	1.2	0.2	Goodrich et al. (2011)
	Russia, Far East	1990–1999	1.2	1.2	Miquelle et al. (2005)
Large herbivores	Uganda	1923–1994	–	3.7	Treves and Naughton-Treves (1999)
Elephant	Mozambique	2006–2008	3	14	Dunham et al. (2010)
	Sri Lanka	2005–2012		68	Gamage and Wijesundara (2014)
	Madhya Pradesh, India	1989–1994	–	7	Rajpurohit and Krausman (2000)
	Northern India	1980–2003	–	50	Choudhury (2004)
	Nepal	2010–2014	9	18	Acharya et al. (2016)
Gaur	Madhya Pradesh, India	1989–1994	–	4	Rajpurohit and Krausman (2000)
Hippopotamus	Mozambique	2006–2008	4	5	Dunham et al. (2010)
Rhinoceros	Nepal	2010–2014	14	3	Acharya et al. (2016)
Buffalo, European	Białowieża Forest, Poland	2009–2013	0.3	0	Haidt et al. (2018)
Buffalo, Africa	Mozambique	2006–2008	3	0.4	Dunham et al. (2010)
Feral hogs	Worldwide	2012	9	0	Mayer (2013)
Primates	Uganda	1923–1994	–	0.6	Treves and Naughton-Treves (1999)

Species	Location	Years	Injuries/year		Reference
			Nonfatal	Fatal	
	Mozambique	2006–2008	0	0.4	Dunham et al. (2010)
	Kashmir Valley, India	2005–2016	1.7	0.0	Moten et al. (2017)
	India	2003	330,000	–	(Sudarshan et al. (2006)

*Amputations only.

2.3 SHARKS

The International Shark Attack Files (2020) confirmed 105 worldwide shark attacks on humans during 2019, including five fatal attacks (Tables 2.1 and 2.2). Most years, the United States leads the world in the number of shark attacks. This is not surprising given the long coastline of the United States, large human population, and a warm climate that is conductive to water sports (Figure 2.3). Over half of the U.S. shark attacks occurred in Florida for all of the above reasons. The frequency of shark

Map of World's Confirmed Unprovoked Shark Attacks

1580-Present

1   1301

FIGURE 2.3   Worldwide locations of shark attacks on humans are shown by the size of the circle and by each country's color.

Source: International Shark Attack File, Florida Museum and used with permission.

Unprovoked Shark Attack Trends Worldwide Over the Past Century

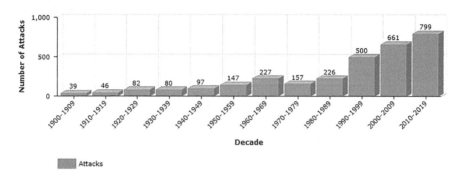

FIGURE 2.4   Change in the frequency of shark attacks across the world since 1900.

Source: International Shark Attack File, Florida Museum and used with permission.

attacks has increased in recent decades as water sports, especially surfing and scuba diving, have become more popular across the globe (Figure 2.4). When attacked, 53% of victims were surfing, 25% were swimming or wading, and 14% were snorkeling, free diving or scuba diving (International Shark Attack Files 2020).

2.4   SNAKES

CDC (2016) estimates that 6,000–8,000 people are bitten by poisonous snakes each year in the United States and about five of those victims die. There are other data sources (Conover 2019), but these CDC data are the most complete and accurate, and I have included 7,000 in Table 2.1 because it is the mean of CDC's range. Information on the snake species responsible for biting people in the United States is available from the American Association of Poison Control Centers (Langley 2008). The proportion of 4,307 callers with bites serious enough to seek medical attention were bitten by rattlesnakes (24%), copperheads (20%), nonpoisonous snakes (11%), pip vipers (5%), exotic snakes (4%), cottonmouths (3%), coral snakes (2%), and unknown snakes (31%).

Contrary to popular opinion, most snakebites in the United States occur where people live: within cities, suburbs, and towns; less common are victims who were bitten while hiking, fishing, or hunting. Children between the ages of 5 and 12 are especially at risk because they are more likely to be barefoot and be less careful about where they step or place their hands. Children also are curious about snakes and may try to catch them.

Worldwide, about five million people are bitten by poisonous snakes annually with most occurring in Africa and Southeast Asia. These snakebites result in 94,000–125,000 deaths and 400,000 amputations or other serious health problems. Many snakebite victims (20%–70%) do not seek medical attention, making accurate

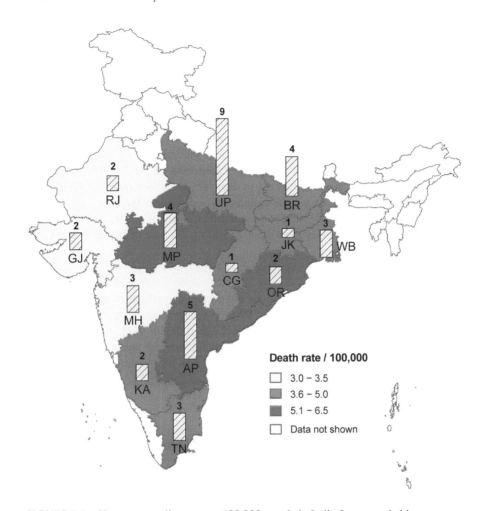

FIGURE 2.5   Human mortality rate per 100,000 people in India from a snakebite.

Source: From Mohapatra et al. 2011 and used with permission.

information on snakebites difficult to obtain (World Health Organization 2018). Mohapatra et al. (2011) believed that worldwide data greatly underestimate the actual number of snakebite victims and deaths; the Indian government reported only 15,000 snakebite deaths, while Mohapatra's own data indicate 46,000 deaths in the country (Figure 2.5). The underestimate resulted because official reports are based on hospital reports, but only 23% of snakebite fatalities in India occurred in a hospital. In much of the world, poor access to health care and antivenoms condemns many snakebite victims to a poor outcome (Kasturiratne et al. 2008). In Bangladesh, 1% of snakebites are fatal; one reason for this is because 86% of snakebite victims first seek treatment from a snake charmer, and only 10% are ever treated by a medical doctor (Rahman et al. 2010).

2.5 ALLIGATORS, CROCODILES, AND CAIMANS

American alligators are found throughout the southeastern United States. Alligators injured 567 people and killed 24 from 1948 to 2009. Most of these attacks occurred in Florida where alligators are most abundant (Table 2.3). During 2018, there were nine alligator attacks in Florida, one of which was fatal; there were a few more victims in other southern states (Langley 2010; Florida Fish and Wildlife Conservation Commission 2018). Most victims in Florida were males (84%) and had an average age of 35 years (range = 2 years old to 83 years). Victims were engaged in a variety of activities when attacked, such as golfing or gardening (Table 2.4). When attacked, 128 victims were in water more than 1 m deep, 96 in shallow water, 81 on land but within a meter of the water, and 68 dangling a body part in the water while out of the water (Florida Fish and Wildlife Conservation Commission 2012). Alligators that attacked people ranged in size from 0.3 m to 3.67 m. The size of alligators that killed someone ranged from 2.0 to 3.8 m.

Florida Fish and Wildlife Conservation Commission (2012) offers these safety tips for avoiding alligator attacks: leave alligators alone; never feed alligators; do not throw fish remains in the water; observe and photograph alligators only from a safe distance; do not swim outside of posted swimming areas; be aware of the possibility of alligators when working or recreating near water; do not swim at dusk, dawn, or night; and do not allow your dog to swim, drink, or exercise near waters that might contain alligators (Figure 2.6). Although Florida also has American crocodiles, no one has been bitten by one in the United States (Langley 2010).

TABLE 2.3
Adverse Alligator–Human Encounters Reported in the United States from 1948 through 2009 (Langley 2010)

State	Number of total attacks documented (fatal)	Number of yearly nuisance complaints	Estimated alligator population
Florida	481 (22 fatalities)*	~16,000	≥1.25 million
Texas	17 (no fatalities)	450	300,000–400,000
Georgia	10 (2 fatalities)	450	200,000–225,000
South Carolina	10 (no fatalities)	700	>100,000
Alabama	5 (no fatalities)	300	20,000–30,000
Louisiana	3 (no fatalities)	2000–2500	1–2 million
North Carolina	2 (no fatalities)	20 permits to relocate	Low thousands
Arkansas	1 (no fatalities)	70	3000–4000
Oklahoma	0 (no fatalities)	4–6	50–100
Mississippi	1 (no fatalities)	250–350	> 40,000
Tennessee	0 (no fatalities)	0	<10

* Thirteen other cases in Florida involved individuals who may have had postmortem alligator-related injuries or body parts found in alligators. These were not included in the table because it was unclear if injuries from an alligator occurred before or after the person's death.

TABLE 2.4

Activities of 305 People When Attacked by an Alligator in Florida (Langley 2005)

Activity	% of attacks
Attempting to capture or handle	17
Swimming	17
Fishing	10
Golfing/retrieving golf balls	10
Wading	5
Snorkeling	4
Pulling weeds/planting along bank	4
Standing/sitting/walking on the water bank	4
Other	30

FIGURE 2.6   Alligator warning sign.

Source: Steve Lowrence, Shutterstock 1674376333.

FIGURE 2.7   An alligator enjoying a sunny day in the pool.

Source: Tim Donovan, Florida Fish and Game Conservation Commission and used with permission.

Alligators have posed a threat to human safety, beginning when the first man first set foot on the North American continent; early explorers of Florida reported that both they and the natives considered alligators dangerous and took precautions to protect themselves from these animals (Le Moyne 1591; Van Doren 1955, as cited by Hines and Keenlyne 1977). Yet, the number of people being attacked by alligators has increased in recent decades. For instance, from 1900 to 1950, only one person was known to have been attacked by an alligator, but ten were injured during 2018. What has caused this increase in the frequency of reported alligator attacks? One reason is a much better reporting system; today, state officials are much more likely to learn about an alligator attack than in the past, especially if there were only minor injuries (Conover and DuBow 1997). Most important for this increase has been the expanding alligator population in recent decades. During the 1800s and 1900s, alligator populations were suppressed due to hunting, and the remaining alligators were confined to remote swamps where few humans ventured. Alligator populations began to recover beginning in 1969 with the passage of an Amendment to the Lacey Act that effectively curtailed interstate shipment of alligator hides. The Endangered Species Act in 1973 provided additional protection for alligators (Conover and DuBow 1997). As alligator populations have recovered, these animals have moved into suburban and urban lakes and canals where they come into contact with humans daily (Figure 2.7). Concomitantly, human population in Florida and residential development of waterfront property have increased.

Another factor for the increasing frequency of attacks is that many alligators have lost their fear of humans. A century ago, alligators would hide or flee at the first sight of man because that person was likely to be an alligator hunter. Today, alligators have less to fear from humans and have learned that most people will not hurt them; some will even feed them. People also have lost their fear of alligators. A century ago, most Floridians rarely saw an alligator, and when they did see one, they stayed at a healthy distance. Today, some alligator attacks occur when people misjudge the danger that alligators pose, and people put themselves in harm's way. Each year, people are injured when they try to pet an alligator or pick it up or when they see an alligator sunning itself on a road and try to push it off the highway.

In the United States, wildlife agencies have responded to the threat of alligator attacks by implementing alligator management plans (Hines and Woodward 1980; Taylor et al. 1991). These plans often call for the removal of nuisance alligators and improved public education about alligators, and the dangers they pose. Some states have started harvesting alligators. These efforts have been successful in reducing attacks in some areas, but further attacks are inevitable as long as humans and alligators share the same space.

Worldwide, there are 23 crocodilian species, which includes alligators, caiman, and crocodiles. Attacks by these species can be defensive, territorial, and predatory in nature (Figure 2.8). During 2018, 334 people were attacked worldwide by crocodilians; over half of these were fatal (Table 2.2). Prior to the attack, 96 victims were fishing, 54 bathing, 45 swimming, 22 collecting water, 20 other shallow water activities, or 14 washing some object. Most attacks occurred in Indonesia (96), India (63), Mexico (14), Zimbabwe (14), and Zambia (14). Most fatal attacks were caused by saltwater crocodiles and Nile crocodiles. More people in Africa are killed by Nile crocodiles than any other wildlife species (IUCN 2019).

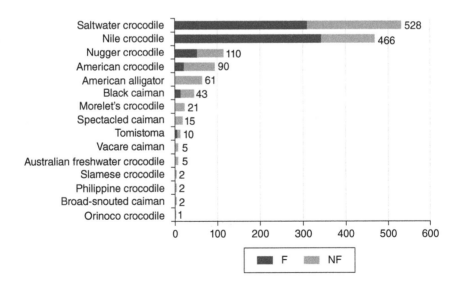

FIGURE 2.8 Number of fatal (*black*) and nonfatal (*gray*) alligator and crocodile attacks from January 2008 through October 2013.

Source: CrocBITE (2019) and used with permission.

2.6   RODENTS AND SMALL MAMMALS

Fourteen states (New Hampshire, Massachusetts, New York, New Jersey, South Carolina, Georgia, Florida, Kentucky, Indiana, Illinois, North Dakota, South Dakota, Texas, and Arizona) require doctors to report to public health officials when someone has been bitten by an animal (Moore et al. 1977). Because these states are widely distributed across the country, we can extrapolate the rates of wildlife attacks to the other 35 states with some degree of confidence. Based on the extrapolation, 27,000 people annually seek medical attention after being bitten by a rodent, 750 after a skunk bite, and 500 after a fox. However, these data are conservative because they only include serious bites for which the victim sought medical attention; they do not include bites for which the person did not see a doctor. These attacks far exceed the number of attacks by any of the large predators but receive less attention because these bites are less severe. Between 2008 and 2015, no one in the United States died from a rat bite, but three died from 1997 through 2007 (Forrester et al. 2012, 2018). In India, rats are responsible for 0.5% of all people bitten by an animal (Sudarshan et al. 2006; Sidebar 2.1).

SIDEBAR 2.1   HOW OFTEN ARE PEOPLE BITTEN BY MAMMALS IN INDIA?

About 15 million people in India are bitten by a mammal annually; this is 1.5% of the total India population of 1.02 billion people (Menezes 2008). Most of these bites are from dogs (91.5%) and cats (4.7%), but 2.2% are from monkeys, 0.5% from rats, 0.2% from golden jackals, and 0.1% from bears (Sudarshan et al. 2006). This means that each year monkeys bite 330,000 people (Figure 2.9), 75,000 by rats, 30,000 by golden jackals, and 15,000 by bears. Most of the dog bites (63%) were from strays, and 37% from pets.

FIGURE 2.9   Monkeys in Jaipur, India.

Source: Luciano Mortula – LGM, Shutterstock 17011771.

2.7 BEARS

Black bears, grizzly bears, and polar bears all pose threats to people in the United States and Canada. About 26 people are attacked in North American annually by bears (Table 2.1). Polar bears have attacked six people in the United States and 38 in Canada from 1870 to 2014. Worldwide, polar bears attack about three people a year and kill someone every third year (Table 2.2). Most (59%) polar bear attacks on humans were predatory in nature; 61% of attacking bears were in poor health (Herrero and Higgins 1999, 2003; Wilder et al. 2017). Polar bear attacks have become more common in recent decades across the world; there were one attack from 1955 to 1974 and nine attacks from 1995 to 2014 perhaps due to a reduction of sea ice from global warming (Penteriani et al. 2016).

Most grizzly bear attacks that cause serious human injuries or fatalities are defensive in nature and involve a female with young (Herrero and Higgins 1999, 2003). Most bear attacks (88%) in Alaska involve grizzlies (Smith and Herrero 2018). Most occurred during the day when people are most active. Attacks were less likely when the habitat provided good visibility and when people were in groups. Most victims were either hunting or hiking when attacked. A person came to the rescue for 18% of attacks and dogs came to the defense for 6% of attacks. When humans intervened, the attack stopped 90% of the time, but 10% of the rescuers were injured. Intervention by dogs ended the attack half of the time (Smith and Herrero 2018). Outside of North America, the grizzly bear is called the brown bear. In Europe and Asia, brown bears attack an average of six people annually, half of the attacks are fatal (Table 2.2).

Across North America, black bears injure more humans than any other bear species. Many of these attacks are defensive in nature. Black bears seeking food want to be left alone while they search for the food and then consume it. If they feel threatened, bears may lash out at the person. Such attacks are normally of short duration and end when the bear perceives that the threat has ended (Herrero and Fleck 1989). Black bears have killed 54 people between 1960 and 2009 with most occurring in Canada and Alaska. Most black bear attacks (88%) resulting in a human fatality were predatory in nature and involved a single bear (usually male); most victims were alone when attacked (Herrero et al. 2011).

India has four bear species: brown bear, Asian black bear, sloth bear, and sun bear; Sudarshan et al. (2006) estimated that 15,000 people in India were attacked by a bear during 2003 (Table 2.2). Many of the bears that attack people in India have lost their fear of humans.

2.8 COYOTES, WOLVES, AND OTHER CANIDS

Coyotes are a 10–20 kg canid that normally prey upon small mammals or the young of large ungulates, which they normally kill by clamping their jaws on the prey's throat and neck, preventing the victim from breathing. Occasionally, a child is attacked and killed by a coyote. Attacks on children are usually predatory but not attacks on adults. Coyotes are proliferating in urban areas where the coyotes find abundant food in the form of rabbits, pets, and garbage, and urbanites do not harm them. Hence,

FIGURE 2.10   Coyotes in many California suburbs have lost their fear of humans.

Source: Troy Boswell and used with permission.

many urban coyotes have habituated to humans (Figure 2.10). From 1999 to 2002, 46 children and adults were attacked by coyotes in California (Table 2.5; Timm et al. 2004). Across North America, there were 159 victims of coyote attacks from 1960 to 2006 (White and Gehrt 2009). There have been two fatalities, a child in California and a grown woman in Canada; both were predatory attacks.

Wolves are much larger than coyotes, weighing 40–70 kg, and are efficient killers of large mammals (e.g., deer, elk, and moose). Wolf populations are expanding in North America, both naturally and with the help of reintroduction efforts. Historically, people have been terrified of wolves, but wolf attacks on humans are uncommon in North America. There have been two fatal wolf attacks in North America, and 17 people were injured by wolves since 2000. Kenton Joel, a 22-year-old engineering student, was killed in 2005 while hiking in northern Saskatchewan. The other victim was Candice Berner, a 32-year-old school teacher; she was killed during 2010 while jogging in Alaska (Streetly 2000; NBC News 2010; Wikipedia 2018a). Wolves also attack people in Europe and Asia. During 1996, a healthy wolf attacked 76 children in Uttar Pradesh, India, over several months, and killed 50 of them [Y. Jhala and B. Jethva, paper given at the Second International Wildlife Management Congress (1999) and abstract published in *The Probe*, Issue 205].

TABLE 2.5
An Accounting of the 46 Coyote Attacks on Humans in California during a Five-Year Period (Timm et al. 2004)

Spr	1999 So. Lake Tahoe. Two adults bitten by coyotes.
Spr	1999 So. Lake Tahoe. Woman bitten by coyote in parking lot of motel.
May	1999 Canyon Country. Coyote attacked dog in yard and would not cease attack; man scratched in melee (night)
Aug	1999 Green Valley Lake. Coyotes attacked woman and her dogs in yard; one dog bitten. Woman and dogs escaped to vehicle; coyotes jumped aggressively on car and scratched it (8:30 AM)
Aug	1999 San Antonio Heights. Three coyotes attacked and killed dog being walked on leash by elderly man
Oct	1999 Ventura County. Six coyotes attacked man on bicycle with his dog; dog bitten
Nov	1999 Hollywood Hills. Coyote attacked and killed pet dog in man's presence; coyote would not leave (morning)
Feb	2000 Calimesa. Adult male attacked in backyard by coyote while attempting to rescue dog; suffered cuts, scrapes, and bruises (9 PM)
May	2000 La Mesa. 3-year-old boy bitten on his side; treated for 4 puncture wounds (7 PM)
May	2000 Dublin area. Coyote killed small dog while woman was taking it for walk
Oct	2000 Oildale. Pair of coyotes treed woman's pet cat, then turned aggressively on her
Apr	2001 Woman received bite on leg; coyote killed the poodle and jumped over fence carrying the carcass (4:30 PM)
Jun	2001 Frazier Park. 22-year-old female camp counselor sleeping outside awakened by coyote sniffing and pawing at her head (2 AM)
Jun	2001 Northridge. 7-year-old girl attacked and seriously injured by a coyote despite mother's attempts to fight off the coyote (7 PM)
Jul	2001 Thousand Oaks. Five coyotes attacked large dog in yard and aggressively threatened residents attempting to rescue dog; coyote would not leave area despite two visits by sheriff
Jul	2001 Irvine. 3-year-old boy bitten in his leg by coyote while he was playing in yard; attack interrupted by father, who was 10–20 ft. away at time of bite (8:15 PM)
Jul	2001 Tustin. Coyote bit woman
Jul	2001 Encinitas. Coyote attacked and took dog, while it was being walked on leash by woman (4 PM)
Aug	2001 Hollywood Hills. Coyotes bit man 8 times as he was defending his dog against their attack (11:50 PM).
Aug	2001 Irvine. Woman walking poodle on leash bitten by coyote while attempting to remove dog from coyote's mouth (4:30 PM)
Aug	2001 Chatsworth. Two coyotes came into yard and took pet cat out of hands of 19-month-old toddler
Sep	2001 Agoura. Woman attacked by coyote when she attempted to stop its attack on her small dog (7:15 AM)
Sep	2001 Lancaster. Man walking encountered 4 coyotes, which crouched, circling him, attempting to attack. Man fought off coyotes with walking stick, hitting one square across the face (morning)
Oct	2001 San Clemente. Coyote attacked children on schoolyard; 8-year-old girl bitten on back of neck and scratched; 7-year-old boy bitten on back and arm. Third student attacked, but coyote bit backpack (12:15 PM)
Nov	2001 San Diego. 8-year-old girl bitten in leg by coyote that family had been feeding at their apartment (1:30 PM)

(Continued)

TABLE 2.5 *(Continued)*

Nov	2001 La Habra Heights. Coyote on golf course ran up to woman, jumped on her back, and bit her on right forearm (daytime)
Dec	2001 San Gabriel. Coyote bit 3-year-old girl in head; grabbed her shoulder in an attempt to drag her off. Father chased coyote away (7:30 PM)
May	2002 Anza Borrego Street Park. Coyote bit boy in sleeping bag on the head
May	2002 Los Angeles. Coyote attacked man walking his dog
July	2002 Woodland Hills. Woman attacked by coyote, bitten on arm (6 AM)
July	2002 Woodland Hills. Man bitten on boot by coyote when he inadvertently came upon it between car and garage
Jul	2002 Canoga Park. Woman walking 2 large dogs accosted by 3 coyotes; she fell backward and fended coyotes off
Jul	2002 Carlsbad. Woman walking Labrador retriever accosted by 8–10 coyotes, which bit at her legs and pants after she tripped and fell; her dog fought off the coyotes until she could escape (10 PM)
Aug	2002 Mission Hills. Coyote approached couple walking dog, attempting to snatch dog out of man's arms; coyotes left only after being kicked (4 AM)
Nov	2002 Carbon Canyon. A coyote came into the trailer park and took a dog in the presence of its owner (3 PM).
Nov	2002 Woodland Hills. Coyote scaled 2-m. wall into yard, attacked and killed small dog in presence of owner; in melee, woman kicked coyote, then fell and fractured her elbow and was attacked and scratched by coyote (1 PM)
Dec	2002 East Highland. Utility worker attacked by coyote, which tore his trousers (evening)
Dec	2002 East Highland. Coyote attacked man (evening)
Feb	2003 Lake View Terrace. Jogger bitten (tooth scrape on ankle) by coyote after jogging past neighborhood coyote feeding station
May	2003 Woodland Hills. Coyote acted aggressively toward man after he intervened during its attack on his dog
May	2003 Highland. Coyote came into neighbor's garage after 2-year-old girl, biting her on arm (10 PM)
May	2003 Woodland Hills. Coyote came into residence to attack small pet dogs (2 PM)
July	2003 Granada Hills. Boy walking family's 2 dogs attacked by 3 coyotes; Boy rescued by father but not before one dog was killed and the other injured
July	2003 Alta Loma. Coyote grabbed small dog while woman was walking it; she was able to rescue it
Aug.	2003 Apple Valley. 4-year-old boy attacked on golf course; bitten on face and neck; saved by father (afternoon)
Nov	2003 Claremont. Man and his dog attacked by 3–4 coyotes; he defended himself, hitting several coyotes with his walking stick (8 AM)

Many of the attacks were initially directed at dogs and cats.

2.9 COUGARS, LIONS, AND TIGERS

During the last century, there have been 53 confirmed cougar attacks on humans, and attacks have become more numerous in recent decades. One reason for the increase is that cougar populations are rebounding from when humans were trying to eradicate them. In California, 12,461 cougars were killed from 1907 to 1963 when the state paid a bounty for them (Torres et al. 1996). Any cougar that managed to stay alive during that period had developed a fear of humans and lived in remote areas where they rarely came in contact with human. Cougars have not been hunted in California since 1973, and they were provided additional protection in 1990 when ballot initiative (Proposition 117) was passed into law by the California voters, designating cougars as a "specially protected mammal" (Torres et al. 1996). From 1990 to 2020, there have been 3 confirmed human fatalities and 13 human injuries by cougars in California. Prior to the ballot initiative, data on confirmed attacks on humans are sparse, but there were three confirmed injuries during 1986 and four fatal incidents involving six victims around the turn of the previous century (California Department of Fish and Wildlife 2020).

Large free-ranging felids pose a danger to people wherever their populations occur in the world. In Tanzania, lions have killed an average of 38 people each year and injured another 21 (Packer et al. 2005). In India, leopards injure over 150 people and kill over 75 (Table 2.1). Tigers kill about 95 people annually in India, Bangladesh, Sumatra, Nepal, and Russia.

African lions have better low-light vision than their herbivore prey and take advantage of this by hunting at night. This same pattern occurs with lion attacks on humans, which is not surprising because most lion attacks are predatory in nature, and human victims are often eaten. Humans are more active during the early evening before they go to bed; it is during these hours when most people are attacked by lions. There also is a lunar cycle to lion hunting and when people are attacked by lions. More people are attacked the week after the full moon than during the full moon or the week before it. Two factors account for this. First, lions are hungrier following the full moon because they are less successful hunting when the moon is full. Second, after the full moon, the moon is below the horizon during early evening when people are awake and outside. Hence, the optimal time for lions to hunt (i.e., total darkness) occurs in the early evening. In contrast, during the week prior to the full moon, the moon is up during the early evening and is below the horizon during the last hours on night when most people are asleep (Packer et al. 2011).

2.10   HERBIVORES

In Yellowstone National Park, bison injure more people than any other large animals; 25 people were injured from 2000 to 2015. Victims were an average distance of only 3.4 m (range 0.3–6.1 m) from the bison when it attacked despite park regulations requiring people not to approach within 23 m of a bison. Of the 25 injured people, ten were thrown into the air, 9 were head-butted, and six were gored; almost half (48%) required hospitalization (Cherry et al. 2018).

Moose also attack people when they feel threatened. During the 1990s, two people were killed by moose in Anchorage, Alaska; one man was stomped to death on the University of Alaska campus, and a woman was trampled to death in her yard. More recently, a woman walking her dog was stomped to death by a moose in Sweden; this was initially considered a homicide by means of a riding lawnmower (Gudmannsson et al. 2018). Herbivores, especially those habituated to humans, attacked when approached too close, especially if the animals had a neonate nearby. White-tailed deer at Southern Illinois University attacked students who came too close to their young, although most victims are unaware that a fawn was near (Hubbard and Nielsen 2009).

Worldwide, large herbivores cause human morbidity and mortality. In South Africa, people are killed or injured by elephants, buffalo, rhino, and zebra (Durrheim and Leggat 1999). Mayer (2013) found 412 reports of feral hogs attacking 665 people worldwide; 24% of which occurred in the United States. These attacks resulted in 391 human injuries and 68 fatalities. During the most recent year for which data are available (2012), there were 12 feral hog attacks worldwide (Mayer 2013). Kangaroos attack people in Australia, and hippopotamuses pose a danger to people in Africa, especially by turning over boats. Elephants kill 100–200 people annually in India (Veeramani et al. 1996). In Nepal, elephants kill an average of 18 people annually, and rhinoceros kill three (Acharya et al. 2016; Sidebar 2.2).

SIDEBAR 2.2 UNFORESEEN CONSEQUENCES OF ELEPHANT ATTACKS ON HUMANS IN SRI LANKA

Sri Lanka has a dense human population of 300 people/km2 and also 6,000 elephants. These human-elephant conflicts result in the death of an average of 68 people and 198 elephants each year (Figure 2.11). Rural farmers usually chase elephants away from their fields and villages upon sight. In response; elephants hide in the deep forests during the day and emerge in night to forage in agricultural fields. Thus, more people are attacked by elephants at night. As a result of these attacks, people who live in rural areas do not walk outdoors during the night; this reduces the rural residents' quality of life (Gamage and Wijesundara 2014).

FIGURE 2.11   At night, elephants leave the forests to raid farmers' fields.

Source: Gideon Ikigai, Shutterstock 1169940217.

2.11 PRIMATES

Gorillas, chimpanzees, bonobos, and orangutans attack people throughout their ranges, resulting in human injuries and occasionally a human fatality. Human primate conflicts are most common when primate species are drawn to urban areas seeking anthropogenic food. Examples of urban primates include rhesus macaques and gray langurs in India, hamadryas baboons in Saudi Arabia, and vervet monkeys and baboons in South Africa (Hoffman and O'Riain 2011; Mormile and Hill 2017). Primates seeking human food often exhibit aggressive behavior toward people in their attempts to obtain food, resulting in human morbidity and an occasional human fatality (Southwick et al. 2005). The number of people bitten by urban primates across the world is unknown (Healy and Nijman 2014; McLennan and Hockings 2016), but primates are responsible for 2.2% of all animal bites in India (330,000 per year), and some of these bites are fatal (Sudarshan et al. 2006). Only dogs bite more people in India than monkeys (World Health Organization 2018).

2.12 WHY HAS THERE BEEN A RECENT INCREASE IN WILDLIFE ATTACKS ON HUMANS IN NORTH AMERICA AND WORLDWIDE?

In North America, attacks by alligators, cougars, grizzly bears, black bears, cougars, and wolves have been increasing in recent decades. Although these predators span the taxonomic spectrum and live in different parts of the continent, the same factors are responsible for the recent increase. Populations of these animals have been rebounding from the early part of the twentieth century when humans killed them. These animals, which currently enjoy either complete or partial legal protection, certainly have less reason to fear humans than previously, and some individual animals have habituated to humans and moved into urban areas. Concomitantly, human populations have increased, and people are spending more time in remote areas frequented by these dangerous animals. The result is much more contact between these animals and humans, occasionally with tragic consequences (Conover 2008).

Considering the large populations of humans and predators coexisting in the same areas, it is not surprising that large predators injure some people. What is really amazing is that so few people are attacked. People are much easier to catch and kill than deer or elk and are more abundant. I hypothesize that many predators are reluctant to attack humans because of a historic memory about how dangerous humans are, which is passed down from mothers to their offspring. But as hunting of cougars and bears becomes uncommon, I fear that this memory will dim and predator attacks on humans will become more common. Another hypothesis was proposed by Seidensticker and Lumpkin (1992); then noted that when humans are standing up, they do not resemble the cat's normal prey (ungulates). Humans heads and necks (where the cat makes its killing bite) are in the wrong place and too high to be attacked efficiently. Perhaps, the upright posture of humans inhibits the normal predator attack of lions. Support for this hypothesis comes from the finding that cougar attacks on humans occur most often when people are leaning over, squatting, or riding a bicycle.

Several steps can be taken to reduce the frequency of such attacks by large predators. In some cases, we can identify the characteristics of individual animals that are most likely to attack people. Some examples of high-threat animals include bears that raid campgrounds for food, alligators that are fed by people, and unusually belligerent bison. These animals could be, and often are, removed proactively to reduce future attacks on humans. Another possible solution is to change animal behavior and to ensure that large predators maintain a fear of man. If hunting becomes less common, new approaches should be used to discourage dangerous animals from becoming habituated to humans, such as shooting them with rubber bullets or spraying them with pepper spray.

We also can reduce predator attacks on people by altering human behavior through education. We should make sure that people have a healthy fear of dangerous animals. Most of these people injured by bison in Yellowstone National Park approached too close to the bison, attempting to pose with it for a photo, pet it, or feed it (Conrad and Balison 1994). We must teach people how to recognize a dangerous situation. For instance, many grizzly bear attacks occur when a bear, often with cubs, is surprised by the sudden appearance of a person near it. Hikers could minimize the risk of such an attack by making loud noises to warn bears of their approach and by avoiding areas with dense vegetation or limited visibility. Campers should locate their cooking areas 100 m downwind of the tent, store food away from the camp in bear-proof containers, and locate their camp near a possible escape tree in grizzly bear country (Herrero 1985). Rajpurohit and Krausman (2000) reported that bear attacks in India could be reduced if people avoided bear habitat during crepuscular periods when bears are more likely to be hunting.

We also should let people know what to do if they are attacked by wildlife to minimize their risk of serious injury. Aggressive responses by people were effective in averting a cougar from making an imminent attack. Yelling, throwing objects, backing away slowly, and increasing one's stature reduced the risk of a close encounter with a cougar turning into an attack. Intervention by other people reduced the odds that an attack will result in a human fatality (Mattson et al. 2011). Running away from a cougar was particularly futile (Brown and Conover 2008).

How a person should respond to a bear attack depends upon whether the attack is defensive or predatory in nature. The victim should fight back during predatory attacks. For black bear attacks in campgrounds, along roads, or other places where bears have become habituated to people, the bear is probably attacking because the person has gotten too close, and the bear wants more space or is trying to get at the food the person might have on them (Herrero 1985). In such situations, the victim should back away and give up the food. When confronted by a grizzly bear, Herrero (1985) recommended climbing at least 5 m up a tree if there is enough time to do so, or to watch the bear, but not stare at it because the bear may interpret staring as a threat. Dropping something while fleeing may distract the bear and provide enough time for escape.

2.13   ARE WILDLIFE ATTACKS CAUSED BY WILDLIFE OR HUMANS?

Whenever someone is injured by a predator, people want to know why the attack occurred and who is responsible for it. Blaming the person for the attack is reassuring; it is comfortable to believe that the attack is due to human folly. Attacks are more terrifying if they occur at random and can claim anyone – even (perish the thought) you or a family member.

Half (48%) of all newspaper articles about wildlife attacks on humans blame wildlife for the attack, 15% blamed humans, 6% blamed both, and 31% did not blame either humans or wildlife (Stafford et al. 2018). Media accounts often state that these attacks occur because the predator is mad at people. In a couple of accounts, humans are reported to have killed the predator's young, and the predator was seeking revenge; but revenge is a human motivation and does not motivate wild animals. Other accounts blame society by arguing that it has destroyed the predators' habitat, perhaps through development, and that the predators had no choice but to attack a person because we had deprived them of their natural food. In actuality, nobody (neither predator nor human) is responsible for a predator attack, and nothing is gained by trying to identify a culprit. Predators are just being predators and that means killing something to eat. Humans are just being humans and going about their lives.

If large predators and humans are going to coexist together, there will be human casualties from predator attacks. This is not to say that predator populations should be reduced. Humans benefit in many ways from having predators to share our environment. But measures can be taken to reduce the number of people injured by predators. Such can be achieved by obtaining a greater understanding of predator behavior (Thiemann et al. 2008), human behavior (Brown and Conover 2008), and the factors that contribute to the successful management of predator–human conflicts (Cotton 2008; Ziegltrum 2008). A major difficulty of predator attacks on humans is that most people can make rational decisions when they have the luxury of viewing them from afar. It is another thing entirely when it is your loved one who is attacked; then humans seek revenge and something to blame. The target may be an individual or agency that did not sufficiently warn them of the danger or the predator. Bereaved families rarely accept the idea that the death of their loved one was an Act of God or that their loved one was just unlucky (Conover 2008; Wolfe 2008).

2.14   WHAT ARE THE CONSEQUENCES OF WILDLIFE ATTACKS ON HUMANS?

There are several consequences whenever someone is attacked by a wild animal. There is an injured person, who will experience pain and suffering. Injured victims will need medical attention and that can be expensive both for the person, insurance companies, and for society. Some victims or their families sue the U.S. Forest Service, Bureau of Land Management, National Park Service, the state, and/or the local government depending upon where the attack occurred. Victims often argue that they were not adequately protected from the animal or were not adequately warned of the danger. Victims may also sue the government, arguing that its actions or the lack of action made the attack inevitable. Juries hearing these lawsuits often empathize with the victim. Such cases are often settled out of court with the government paying large sums of money. The local, state, or federal government often will take steps to avoid similar lawsuits in the future. These actions include curtailing public access to the property by prohibiting camping or hiking, not allowing children to be on the property, restricting the hours when the property is open to the public, or closing it completely. These actions will reduce the risk of a future attack, but they also constrain freedoms or opportunities that the public had previously enjoyed.

When someone is injured or killed by a wild animal, this event often reflects poorly of natural resource agencies, which spend considerable time and money making sure that citizens have a positive opinion of them and the natural resources they manage. Yet, a single wildlife attack on a person can undo all that was gained by a well-funded publicity campaign by a natural resource agency. People are less likely to visit places where they think they are at risk and develop an adverse opinion of predators or wildlife, in general, when they become fearful. Any wildlife attack on a person will attract much attention in the news media, and stories in the media are often designed to elicit empathy for the victim (Stafford et al. 2018). Our natural resources, parks, and wilderness areas are dependent upon public support for their existence. That support wanes when people become fearful of wildlife.

Predators or large herbivores also suffer when someone is injured or killed. After most wildlife attacks, an attempt is made to kill the predator responsible. This is often directed at local individuals of the responsible species. Inskip and Zimmermann (2009) estimated that retaliatory killing by humans for attacking human or killing livestock is responsible for up to 50% of all tiger mortalities and 47% of cheetahs in the world.

2.15 HOW MANY HUMAN INJURIES AND FATALITIES RESULT FROM WILDLIFE–AUTOMOBILE COLLISIONS?

State Farm Insurance Company (2018) reported 1,332,322 claims were filed annually with insurance companies for accidents involving DVCs during a 12-month period stretching from June 2017 to July 2018 (also included are vehicle collisions with elk, moose, and caribou). Given the 223 million drivers in the United States, each U.S. driver had a 0.6% chance each year of filing a claim with an insurance company because of damage from a DVC. This probability varied among states and was highest in states with high deer densities and a high proportion of the state's population living in rural areas. Such states included West Virginia, Montana, Pennsylvania, Iowa, South Dakota, and Wisconsin (Figure 2.12). Only about half of all DVCs were reported to insurance companies or to the police (Decker et al. 1990; Marcoux and Riley 2010); hence, the actual number of DVCs occurring annually in the United States was closer to 2.6 million annually, and the actual risk of a driver being involved in a DVC was approximately 1.2% each year.

CDC (2004) reported that each year 26,726 people visited an emergency medical facility for injuries from a DVC, based on data from 2001 and 2002. Given the 1,332,322 reported DVCs, this means that 2.0% of DVCs result in a person injured serious enough to visit an emergency medical room. Using state highway safety data, Conover (2019) estimated that 58,622 Americans are injured in DVCs annually: double the rate reported by the CDC. I believe that the value provided by Conover (2019) is probably a more realistic record of total injuries because many injured people do not visit emergency medical rooms. Conover (2019) also used the same records to calculate that about 440 people lose their lives annually in the United States due to DVCs, and there are 640 human injuries and 6 fatalities annually from moose-vehicle collisions.

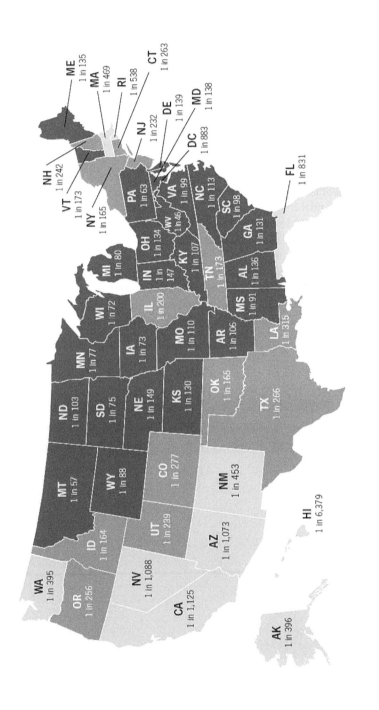

FIGURE 2.12   Probability of a driver colliding with a deer in each state. Data from July 1, 2017 through June 30, 2018 and based on insurance claims.

Source: State Farm Insurance Company 2018 and used with permission.

Being hit by a vehicle is fatal to deer 92% of the time (Allen and McCullough 1976), which means that over 1.3 million deer die each year on U.S. highways. So, many Florida Key deer are killed annually from DVCs that the U.S. Fish and Wildlife Service designated the species as threatened (Sidebar 2.3).

SIDEBAR 2.3 PREVENTING DVCS FROM THREATING THE SURVIVAL OF THE FLORIDA KEY DEER

DVCs are almost always fatal to the deer. This loss is particularly unfortunate when the animal is a threatened or endangered species, such as the Florida Key deer. This white-tailed deer subspecies is famous because it is the size of a dog, standing only 75 cm at the shoulder and being unafraid of humans (Figure 2.13). The deer occurs on a small number of lower Florida Keys, such as Big Pine Key, which have substantial human populations. These keys are crossed by U.S. Highway 1, which provides access between the city of Key West and the Florida mainland. Because of the traffic on this highway, DVCs account for over 25% of all Florida Key deer deaths. To reduce the frequency of DVCs, a continuous 2.6-km fence was erected along U.S. Highway 1 on Big Pine Key; two underpasses also were built, allowing deer to move from one side of the road to the other without having to set foot on the road itself (Figure 2.14). The construction effort was successful. During 2009, over 1,300 deer were

FIGURE 2.13   Key deer are the smallest subspecies of white-tail deer and are about half of the size of other deer. The highway cone provides some perspective of their size.

Source: Agnieszke Bacal, Shutterstock 1365272450.

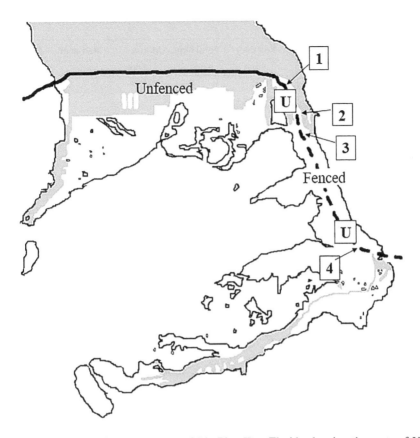

FIGURE 2.14 Map of the lower part of Big Pine Key, Florida showing the route of U.S. Highway 1. The part of the highway that crossed Key deer habitat and was enclosed in a deer fence is show as a dashed line. The location of underpasses is show by a "U." Numbers show where the deer excluders were located.

Source: Adapted from Parker et al. 2011 and drawn by Tara Larkin.

TABLE 2.6
Annual Number of Ungulate–Vehicle Collisions in European Countries

Country	Total	Roe deer	Feral hog	Moose	Red deer	Fallow deer
Germany	233,070	191,590	34,550	2,920	4,010	
UK	74,000					
Sweden	60,857	45,863	6,082	5,941	425	2,546
France	53,418	27,991	20,665		4,762	
Austria	42,279	40,897	602	633		27
Norway	22,396	14,872	4,226	3,298		

(Continued)

TABLE 2.6 (*Continued*)

Country	Total	Roe deer	Feral hog	Moose	Red deer	Fallow deer
Estonia	18,401	1,300	2,000	2,000		
Poland	18,000					
The Czech Republic	12,043	75%	15%			
Spain	9,042	3,441	5,005	581	15	
Hungary	7,650	4,500	2,000	500–800	5,000	2,500
Denmark	6,608	85%	4%	7%		
Latvia	3,190					
Croatia	2,863	2,457	334	72		
Finland	1,842	1,824				
Lithuania	1,000-	2,000				
Italy (South Tyrol)	776	686	90			
Belgium	179	127	44	8		
Italy (Piedmont)	148					
TOTAL	568,159	360,203	73,178	13,831	13,825	7,068

Source: Based on Data from Linnell et al. (2020).

photographed using the underpasses. DVCs decreased 90% along the highway after the fences and underpasses were constructed (Parker et al. 2011).

There are approximately one million DVCs in Europe (Table 2.6), resulting in 30,000 human injuries; human fatalities per year was 12 in the United Kingdom, 3 in Finland, 17 in Spain, and 20 in France (Kämmerle et al. 2017). In Europe, automobiles and trucks hit roe deer, red deer, wild boar, chamois, moose, reindeer, white-tailed deer, and fallow deer with regularity, but roe deer were struck more than any other ungulate in Europe. An additional 10–15 humans are killed annually in Sweden from vehicles colliding with moose (Seiler et al. 2004; Seiler 2005; Neumann and Ericsson 2018).

In Australia, 12 people are killed on average and over 800 injured annually from animal–vehicle collisions, which often involved collisions with wallabies and kangaroos (Rowden et al. 2008). Serious injuries and fatalities often occur when motorists lose control of the vehicle while swerving to avoid the animal, and the vehicle overturns or hits another object. In Saudi Arabia, there were 700 camel–vehicle collisions during 1997, approximately 16 people died and 215 were injured (Al-Ghamdi and AlGadhi 2004; Al Shimemeri and Arabi 2012).

2.16   HOW CAN THE NUMBER OF DEER–VEHICLE COLLISIONS BE REDUCED?

Many deer–automobile collisions occur when deer try to cross from one side of the road to the other; this can be reduced by erecting deer-proof fences along roads, but

FIGURE 2.15   Highway overpasses are constructed so that ungulates and other wildlife do not need to cross the highway. This one is in Russia.

Source: Andrey Vasiliskov, Shutterstock 1452213173.

fencing roads is not a panacea. One problem is that a motivated deer can find ways to get around, over, or through fences. This creates a difficult problem because once deer are inside the fence, it may take them a long time to find a way out, and a deer trapped inside a highway fence faces a high risk of getting hit by a vehicle. For these reasons, one-way gates are built into highway fences so that these trapped deer have a way of getting off the road. Unfortunately, some deer do not recognize these gates as escape routes and ignore them. More recently, earthen ramps have been erected inside highway fences; deer on the road right-of-ways (hereafter ROWs) can climb up the ramp to gain the height needed to jump over the fence. Because the ramp is only built on the highway side of the fence, deer outside the fence cannot use it to jump over the fence. Highway overpasses or underpasses (Figure 2.15) have been built to provide a means for animals to cross safely roads. These passes, however, are expensive to build, costing $400,000 for an underpass and $2,000,000 for an overpass (Sawyer et al. 2016). Some ungulates are reluctant to use the overpasses or underpasses because they want to avoid enclosed areas where they would be vulnerable to predators. For this reason, the best underpasses and overpasses provide an unobstructed view of the far side of the highway.

Deer–automobile collisions can be reduced by modifying the ROWs. For instance, ROWs should be wide and kept clear so that motorists can see deer approaching the road from the side and have time to respond (Meisingset et al. 2014). Also, many deer–automobile collisions occur when deer are attracted to ROWs by some resource, become startled by an approaching car, and try to escape by darting across the road. There are several resources on ROWs that can attract deer. One of the most important is the vegetation growing there. Plants growing along the ROW are especially attractive to deer in forested areas. In many forests, little vegetation is within the reach of deer, and those plants that are may be of poor nutritional quality because they receive only partial sunlight and compete with the trees for water and soil nutrients. ROW plants, on the other hand, grow in full sunlight and are more nutritious because competition with trees is reduced. In arid regions, runoff from the road provides water to vegetation growing adjacent to the pavement, and this vegetation will stay green longer during a drought than other vegetation. Hence, a useful approach to reduce DVCs is to reduce nutritional qualities of ROW vegetation. ROWs could be landscaped with plants that are unpalatable or toxic to deer. Some grass cultivars contain a fungus within their leaves, which produces alkaloids and makes the grass unpalatable to many herbivores (Schmidt and Osborn 1993; Conover and Messmer 1996). Highway departments may be able to reduce DVCs by planting ROWs with fungus-infected cultivars or unpalatable grass species. Grass becomes rank when not mowed; the new leaves are covered by the old ones. This makes it hard for a deer to find new leaves (which are the most palatable) or to bite them without also getting a mouthful of old leaves. Hence, mowing should be reduced along roads where DVCs are common.

In some areas, deer, elk, and moose are attracted to ROWs, especially in the spring, seeking the salt that was spread on the road in the winter to melt snow. This increases the risk of DVCs (Laurian et al. 2008). The Quebec Department of Transportation addressed this problem by covering salt and the salt pools along the ROW with dirt and rock, so they would be inaccessible to moose (Leblond et al. 2007). Another method that could discourage ungulates from entering a ROW is to distribute salt blocks away from the road.

Deer–automobile collisions can also be avoided by changing driver behavior, especially by getting people to drive slower (Meisingset et al. 2014; Neumann and Ericsson 2018); both deer and drivers have less time to react when vehicles are going fast (DeVault et al. 2015). Deer signs were erected at DVC hotspots in Edmonton, Alberta, and were successful in reducing DVCs for the first year but not thereafter (Found and Boyce 2011). To reduce the tendency of drivers to habituate to the deer signs, some states have started placing out deer warning signs only during the rut or when mule deer are migrating across the road (Figure 2.16). Roadside animal detection systems take this a step further. They are designed to detect animals on the ROW and warn drivers by flashing lighted signs warning that animals are standing on the road (Gordon et al. 2004). One such system was placed along a 2-km stretch of highway in Big Cypress Swamp National Park in Florida, USA (Grace et al. 2017). Another approach involved trying to change the behavior of deer when they are crossing or standing on a road. DeVault et al. (2020) found that deer were more likely to move off the road if the front end of the vehicle was clearly lite by a string of LED lights facing the vehicle's grill.

Many deer travel in small groups, and female deer often are accompanied by their fawns (Figure 2.17). When these groups cross a road, the first deer often makes it safely to the other side, but the following deer (usually a fawn) is often the one that

FIGURE 2.16   Deer warning sign in Hertfordshire, England, that lights up when a deer by the highway moves across a laser beam or when a vehicle is traveling too fast.

Source: Jochen Langvein and used with permission.

is killed. Too often, the fawn does not cross the road immediately, but once it realizes that an approaching car is going to come between it and its mother or the rest of the herd, it tries to dart across the road before the car reaches it. DVCs could be reduced by making sure that drivers know that deer often travel in groups and that if they see one deer crossing the road, there may be more crossing shortly. Public service announcements could communicate the message that the deer one sees does not cause the accident; it is the one that is hidden.

DVCs will be more frequent when deer densities increase (Hussain et al. 2007; Grovenburg et al. 2008; Mastro et al. 2008; Rutberg and Naugle 2008). It seems logical that efforts to cull deer should reduce DVCs in the local area. DeNicola and Williams (2008) tested this in three towns where sharpshooting was used to reduce deer abundance. The scientists found that DVCs were reduced 49% in

FIGURE 2.17   Deer often travel in groups, and it is usually the deer that is not seen that the driver collides with when it suddenly darts across the road.

Source: Amy Lutz, Shutterstock 1511428202.

Solon, Ohio; 75% in Princeton, New Jersey; and 78% in Iowa City, Iowa, after a sharpshooting program removed 63 deer in Iowa City, 342 in Princeton, and 171 in Solon, reducing deer populations by 76% in Iowa City, 72% in Princeton, and 54% in Solon.

2.17   HOW MANY HUMAN INJURIES AND FATALITIES RESULT FROM BIRD–AIRCRAFT COLLISIONS?

From 2000 to 2009, wildlife strikes on civilian aircraft across the world have killed more than 51 people and injured 34. Of these, 13 fatalities and 9 injuries occurred in the United States (Thorpe 2012). Collisions with large birds were responsible for most of the human injuries; these included 117 injuries with Canada geese, 42 with vultures, 31 with ducks, and 22 with gulls. Twenty-seven people were injured after their plane collided with a deer on the runway (Dolbeer et al. 2016).

Military aircraft are designed to survive on a modern battlefront, not to survive bird strikes; they are designed more for speed and agility than for safety. For example, many fighters have only one engine, making a crash likely if the engine shuts down after ingesting a bird; in contrast, commercial jets with multiple engines can still fly with the loss of one. Military aircraft also practice flying low to the ground to avoid detection by radar, but this is the same airspace used by birds. For this reason, military aircraft strike birds thousands of times each year (Pfeiffer et al. 2018), often resulting in human injuries and fatalities. During the 1990s, these bird strikes with military aircraft caused 29 and 68 human fatalities in the United States and worldwide, respectively (Richardson and West 2000).

The amount of damage caused by a bird strike depends upon several factors, such as the bird's mass (big birds generally cause more damage than small birds), aircraft speed, and which part of the plane was struck. Most dangerous are birds striking the windshield or being ingested by an engine. Efforts to design aircraft that can withstand a bird strike without sustaining damage have led to safer aircraft. Fernández-Juricic et al. (2011) found that brighter colors on airplanes reduced the number of bird–aircraft strikes, while Dolbeer and Barnes (2017) noted that lights placed along the leading edge of the wings illuminate the wing and help birds see the approaching plane. Washburn et al. (2017) recommended that helicopter manufacturers reinforce and redesign the windshields and rotors so that they can better withstand the impact of a bird.

Few birds fly higher than 500 m above the ground; for this reason, 76% of all bird strikes experienced by civilian aircraft occur on or in the immediate vicinity of an airfield (Dolbeer 2006). Therefore, efforts to reduce the frequency of bird–aircraft collisions are concentrated at airports and are designed to keep birds away from them. The underlying assumption behind these bird control efforts at airports is that a reduction in the localized avian population will result in fewer bird–aircraft collisions; this assumption appears to be accurate (Dolbeer et al. 1993). Bird control efforts at airports can involve removing items that attract birds, such as draining surface water that attracts thirsty birds and removing food sources by closing adjacent landfills. Vegetation on airports can be managed to discourage birds as well (Carragher et al. 2012). For example, fruiting bayberry bushes were drawing tree swallows to John F. Kennedy Airport; removal of the bushes decreased the number of collisions involving tree swallows by 75% (Bernhardt et al. 2009). Other approaches have been to reduce rodent densities on airports because they attract raptors (Witmer 2011) and to reduce earthworm populations because they attract birds after rain events (Seamans et al. 2015). Wedelia is an excellent ground cover at tropical airports because birds find it unpalatable, as do rodents and insects (Linnell et al. 2009). This vegetation helps reduce the numbers of raptors and insectivorous birds at airports that congregate there to feed upon rodents and insects. Bird control efforts on airports appear to have been successful (Dolbeer 2011); airstrike numbers serious enough to produce aircraft damage declined from 764 during 2000 to 601 during 2013 (Dolbeer et al. 2014).

2.18 SUMMARY

Approximately, 47,000 people in the United States are injured annually, owing to attacks or bites by wildlife; 59,000 in collisions with vehicles or aircraft; and another 210,000 contract a zoonotic disease. These problems are much worse outside of the United States. For example, poisonous snakes kill five people in the United States annually, but 100,000 worldwide (Tables 2.1 and 2.2). These numbers do not imply that wildlife populations are too high, only that more needs to be done to reduce human morbidity and mortality that result from human–wildlife interactions. The frequency of wildlife attacks on humans in the United States has been increasing during recent decades. Reasons for the increase include better reporting systems, increasing human and wildlife populations, humans moving into wildlife habitat, wildlife moving into urban and suburban areas, and a change in behavior of both wildlife and humans toward each other. To reduce the frequency of wildlife attacks on humans, we can remove those individual animals which have a high probability of attacking people, teach dangerous animals to fear humans, and educate humans to recognize and avoid dangerous situations involving wildlife. Some people argue that large predators should be limited to national parks and wilderness areas, but few national parks are large enough to maintain a population of large predators given their large home ranges (Enserink and Vogel 2006). The only solution is to accept that predators, and human must coexist on the land and do what we can to reduce the number of wildlife attacks on humans. Mitigation of DVC involves modifying roads to keep deer off them and the roads' ROWs, ideally by erecting deer-proof fences in combination with wildlife overpasses or underpasses. DVCs can also be reduced by modifying the behavior of drivers. The frequency of bird–aircraft collisions has been reduced in recent decades as airports and their surroundings have been modified to make them less attractive to birds.

2.19   DISCUSSION QUESTIONS

1. What are some reasons for why the number of people attacked by wildlife have been increasing in recent decades. Of the reasons you listed, what do you think is the primary reason?
2. How should a country handle the problem of an endangered species, such as a snow leopard, or Siberian tiger, that kills humans? Does your answer change if a single animal is responsible for most of the human deaths?
3. What would you do if you were the director of the South African Department of Wildlife, and the country's prime minister told you to reduce conflicts between humans and elephants?
4. Let's assume you just started your new job as a wildlife extension professor at the University of Florida. Your first job is to educate Floridians about the consequences of feeding alligator, especially in their own backyards. What would you do? The university will judge your success by how many people stop feeding alligators.
5. Do you think the recent passage of state laws to stop all hunting and trapping of cougars will increase the number of people attacked by cougars in the state? Defend your answer.
6. How can you tell if a bear attack is predatory, defensive, or territorial in nature? How should someone respond to a threatening bear based on the reason the bear is attacking?
7. The home ranges of large predators are so large that these animals can across international borders or animals can disperse from one country to another. In such situations, management actions by one country can impact herbivore or predator populations in neighboring countries. This can cause diplomatic tensions between the neighboring countries when their management actions conflict. For example, the number of people killed

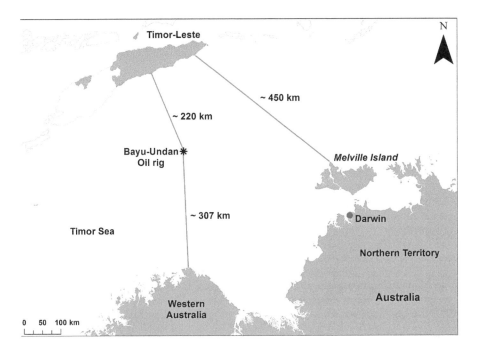

FIGURE 2.18   Some crocodile attacks in East Timor have been caused by crocodiles swimming across the sea from Australia where crocodiles are abundant.

Source: Sebastian Brackhane and used with permission.

in Timor-Leste from saltwater crocodiles has increased dramatically in recent decades despite a lack of suitable nesting habitat for the species. Timor-Leste, however, is close to Australia where crocodile numbers have increased due to conservation measures. The density of large crocodile is now high enough in Australia that some of the large crocodiles are dispersing to Timor-Leste, which requires a swim of at least 450 km across the Timor Sea (Figure 2.18). Although this distance seems great, it is within the swimming ability of crocodiles, and these animals have been found near oil rigs located half way between the two countries (Brackhane et al. 2018). This raises ethical and moral problems when one country's decision to conserve a dangerous predator causes human deaths in another. How should this diplomatic problem be resolved?

LITERATURE CITED

Acharya, K. P., P. K. Paudel, P. R. Neupane, and M. Köhl. 2016. Human-wildlife conflicts in Nepal: patterns of human fatalities and injuries caused by large mammals. *PLoS One* 11(9):e0161717.

Al-Ghamdi, A. S., and S. A. AlGadhi. 2004. Warning signs as countermeasures to camel – vehicle collisions in Saudi Arabia. *Accident Analysis and Prevention* 36:749–760.

Alirol, E., S. K. Sharma, H. S. Bawaskar, U. Kuch, and F. Chappuis. 2010. Snake bite in South Asia: a review. *PLoS Neglected Tropical Diseases* 4(1):e603.

Allen, R. E., and D. R. McCullough. 1976. Deer-car accidents in Southern Michigan. *Journal of Wildlife Management* 40:317–325.

Al Shimemeri, A., and Y. Arabi. 2012. A review of large animal vehicle accidents with special attention to Arabian camels. *Journal of Emergency Trauma and Acute Care* 21. http://doi.org/10.5339/jemtac.2012.21.

Athreya, V., M. Odden, J. D. Linnell, and K. U. Karanth. 2011. Translocation as a tool for mitigating conflict with leopards in human-dominated landscapes of India. *Conservation Biology* 25:133–141.

Bargali, H. S., N. Akhtar, N. P. S. Chauhan. 2005. Characteristics of sloth bear attacks and human casualties in North Bilaspur Forest Division, Chhattisgarh, India. *Ursus* 16:263–267.

Barlow, A. C. D. 2009. *The Sundarbans tiger: adaptation, population status, and conflict management.* Thesis, University of Minnesota Digital Conservancy, Minneapolis, MN.

Bernhardt, G. E., Z. J. Patton, L. A. Kutschbach-Brohl, and R. A. Dolbeer. 2009. Management of bayberry in relation to tree-swallow strikes at John F. Kennedy International Airport, New York. *Human-Wildlife Conflicts* 3:237–241.

Brackhane, S., G. Webb, F. M. Xavier, M. Gusmao, and P. Pechacek, P. 2018. When conservation becomes dangerous: human-crocodile conflict in Timor-Leste. *Journal of Wildlife Management* 82:1332–1344.

Brown, D. E., and M. R. Conover. 2008. How people should respond when encountering a large carnivore: opinions of wildlife professionals. *Human-Wildlife Conflicts* 2:194–199.

California Department of Fish and Wildlife. 2020. *Trends in mountain lion encounters.* https://wildlife.ca.gov/Conservation/Mammals/Mountain-Lion/Attacks. Accessed 1 August 2020.

Carragher, K. A., R. M. Clawges, R. L. Bunn, H. K. Pigage, and J. C. Pigage. 2012. Effects of grassland alterations from mowing and fire on bird activity at a Colorado airfield. *Human-Wildlife Interactions* 6:298–310.

CDC. 2004. Nonfatal motor-vehicle animal crash—related injuries—United States, 2001—2002. *Mortality and Morbidity Weekly Report* 53(30):675–678.

CDC. 2016. *Venomous snakes.* www.cdc.gov/niosh/topics/snakes/. Accessed 6 January 2018.

Cherry, C., K. M. Leong, R. Wallen, and D. Buttke. 2018. Risk-enhancing behaviors associated with human injuries from bison encounters at Yellowstone National Park, 2000–2015. *One Health* 6:1–6.

Chippaux, J. P. 2011. Estimate of the burden of snakebites in sub-Saharan Africa: a meta-analytic approach. *Toxicon* 57:586–599.

Choudhury, A. 2004. Human-elephant conflicts in Northeast India. *Human Dimensions of Wildlife* 9:261–270.

Clark, D. 2003. Polar bear-human interactions in Canadian national parks, 1986–2000. *Ursus* 14:65–71.

Conover, M. R. 2008. Why are so many people attacked by predators? *Human-Wildlife Conflicts* 2:139–140.

Conover, M. R. 2019. Numbers of human fatalities, injuries, and illnesses in the United States due to wildlife. *Human-Wildlife Interactions* 13:264–276.

Conover, M. R., and T. J. DuBow. 1997. Alligator attacks on humans in the United States. *Herpetological Review* 28:120–124.

Conover, M. R., and G. S. Kania. 1994. Impacts of interspecific aggression and herbivory by mute swans on native waterfowl and aquatic vegetation in New England. *Auk* 111:744–748.

Conover, M. R., and T. A. Messmer. 1996. Feeding preference and changes in mass of Canada geese grazing endophyte-infected tall fescue. *Condor* 98:859–862.

Conover, M. R., W. C. Pitt, K. K. Kessler, T. J. DuBow, and W. A. Sanborn. 1995. Review of human injuries, illnesses, and economic losses caused by wildlife in the United States. *Wildlife Society Bulletin* 23:407–414.

Conrad, L., and J. Balison. 1994. Bison goring injuries: penetrating and blunt trauma. *Journal of Wilderness Medicine* 5:371–381.

Cotton, W. 2008. Resolving conflicts between humans and the threatened Louisiana back bear. *Human-Wildlife Conflicts* 2:151–152.

CrocBITE. 2019. *The worldwide crocodilian attack database.* Charles Darwin University. www.crocodile-attack.info/. Accessed 11 December 2019.

Decker, D. J., K. M. Loconti-Lee, and N. A. Connelly. 1990. *Incidence and costs of deer-related vehicular accidents in Tompkins County, New York.* Human Dimensions Research Group 89-7. Cornell University, Ithaca, NY.

DeNicola, A. J., and S. C. Williams. 2008. Sharpshooting suburban white-tailed deer reduces deer-vehicle collisions. *Human-Wildlife Conflicts* 2:28–33.

DeVault, T. L., B. F. Blackwell, T. W. Seamans, S. L. Lima, and E. Fernández-Juricic. 2015. Speed kills: ineffective avian escape responses to oncoming vehicles. *Proceedings of the Royal Society B: Biological Sciences* 282(1801):20142188.

DeVault, T. L., T. W. Seamans, and B. E. Blackwell. 2020. Frontal vehicle illumination via rear-facing lighting reduces potential for collisions with white-tailed deer. *Ecosphere* 11(7):e03187.

Dolbeer, R. A. 2006. Height distribution of birds recorded by collisions with civil aircraft. *Journal of Wildlife Management* 70:1345–1350.

Dolbeer, R. A. 2011. Increasing trend of damaging bird strikes with aircraft outside the airport boundary: implications for mitigation measures. *Human-Wildlife Interactions* 5:235–248.

Dolbeer, R. A., and W. J. Barnes. 2017. Positive bias in bird strikes to engines on left side of aircraft. *Human-Wildlife Interactions* 11:33–40.

Dolbeer, R. A., J. L. Belant, and J. L. Sillings. 1993. Shooting gulls reduces strikes with aircraft at John F. Kennedy international airport. *Wildlife Society Bulletin* 21:442–450.

Dolbeer, R. A., J. R. Weller, A. L. Anderson, and M. J. Begier. 2016. *Wildlife strikes to civil aircraft in the United States 1990–2015.* U. S. Department of Transportation, Federal Aviation Administration, Office of Airport Safety and Standards, Serial Report 22, Washington, DC.

Dolbeer, R. A., S. E. Wright, J. Weller, and M. J. Begier. 2014. *Wildlife strikes to civil aircraft in the United States 1990–2013.* U. S. Department of Transportation, Federal Aviation Administration, Office of Airport Safety and Standards, Serial Report 20, Washington, DC.

Dunham, K. M., A. Ghiurghi, R. Cumbi, and F. Urbano. 2010. Human – wildlife conflict in Mozambique: a national perspective, with emphasis on wildlife attacks on humans. *Oryx* 44:185–193.

Durrheim, D. N., and P. A. Leggat. 1999. Risk to tourists posed by wild mammals in South Africa. *Journal of Travel Medicine* 6:172–179.

Enserink, M., and G. Vogel. 2006. The carnivore comeback. *Science* 314:746–749.

Fernández-Juricic, E., J. Gaffney, B. F. Blackwell, and P. Baumhardt. 2011. Bird strikes and aircraft fuselage color: a correlational study. *Human-Wildlife Interactions* 5:224–234.

Florida Fish and Wildlife Conservation Commission. 2012. *A guide to living with alligators.* Florida Fish and Wildlife Conservation Commission, Tallahassee, FL. https://myfwc.com/media/16070/alligator-brochure.pdf.

Florida Fish and Wildlife Conservation Commission. 2018. *Alligator bites on people in Florida.* Florida Fish and Wildlife Conservation Commission, Tallahassee, FL. https://myfwc.com/media/1716/alligator-gatorbites.pdf. Accessed 1 September 2019.

Forrester, J. A., C. P. Holstege, and J. D. Forrester. 2012. Fatalities from venomous and non-venomous animals in the United States (1999–2007). *Wilderness and Environmental Medicine* 23:146–152.

Forrester, J. A., T. G. Weiser, and J. D. Forrester. 2018. An update on fatalities due to venomous and nonvenomous animals in the United States (2008–2015). *Wilderness and Environmental Medicine* 29:36–44.

Found, R., and M. S. Boyce. 2011. Warning signs mitigate deer – vehicle collisions in an Urban area. *Wildlife Society Bulletin* 35:291–295.

Fox, S., A. C. Rathuwithana, A. Kasturiratne, D. G. Lalloo, and H. J. de Silva. 2006. Underestimation of snakebite mortality by hospital statistics in the Monaragala district of Sri Lanka. *Transactions of the Royal Society of Tropical Medicine and Hygiene* 100:693–695.

Gamage, A., and M. Wijesundara. 2014. *A solution for the elephant-human conflict.* Texas Instruments India Educators' Conference, Bangalore, Karnataka. Pages 169–176.

Goodrich, J. M., I. Seryodkin, D. G. Miquelle, and S. L. Bereznuk. 2011. Conflicts between Amur (Siberian) tigers and humans in the Russian Far East. *Biological Conservation* 144:584–592.

Gordon, K. M., M. C. McKinstry, and S. H. Anderson. 2004. Motorist response to a deer-sensing warning system. *Wildlife Society Bulletin* 32:565–573.

Grace, M. K., D. J. Smith, and R. F. Noss. 2017. Reducing the threat of wildlife-vehicle collisions during peak tourism periods using a roadside animal detection system. *Accident Analysis and Prevention* 109:55–61.

Grovenburg, T. W., J. A. Jenks, R. W. Klaver, K. L. Monteith, D. H. Galster, R. J. Schauer, W. W. Morlock, and J. A. Delger. 2008. Factors affecting road mortality of white-tailed deer in Eastern South Dakota. *Human-Wildlife Conflicts* 2:48–59.

Gudmannsson, P., J. Berge, H. Druid, G. Ericsson, and A. Eriksson. 2018. A unique fatal moose attack mimicking homicide. *Journal of Forensic Science* 63:622–625.

Habib, A. G., A. Kuznik, M. Hamza, M. I. Abdullahi, B. A. Chedi, J. P. Chippaux, and D. A. Warrell. 2015. Snakebite is under appreciated: appraisal of burden from West Africa. *PLoS Neglected Tropical Diseases* 9(9):e0004088.

Haidt, A., T. Kamiński, T. Borowik, and R. Kowalczyk. 2018. Human and the beast-flight and aggressive responses of European bison to human disturbance. *PLoS One* 13(8):e0200635. https://doi.org/10.1371/journal.pone.0200635. Accessed 17 December 2018.

Healy, A., and V. Nijman. 2014. Pets and pests: vervet monkey intake at a specialist South African rehabilitation centre. *Animal Welfare* 23:353–360.

Herrero, S. 1985. *Bear attacks.* Nick Lyons, New York.

Herrero, S., and S. Fleck. 1989. Injury to people inflicted by black, grizzly or polar bears: recent trends and new insights. *International Conference on Bear Research and Management* 8:25–32.

Herrero, S., and A. Higgins. 1999. Human injuries inflicted by bears in British Columbia: 1960–97. *Ursus* 11:209–218.

Herrero, S., and A. Higgins. 2003. Human injuries inflicted by bears in Alberta: 1960–98. *Ursus* 14:44–54.

Herrero, S., A. Higgins, J. E. Cardoza, L. I. Hajduk, and T. S. Smith. 2011. Fatal attacks by American black bear on people: 1900–2009. *Journal of Wildlife Management* 75:596–603.

Hines, T. C., and K. D. Keenlyne. 1977. Two incidents of alligator attacks on humans in Florida. *Copeia* 735–738.

Hines, T. C., and A. R. Woodward. 1980. Nuisance alligator control in Florida. *Wildlife Society Bulletin* 8:234–241.

Hoffman, T., and M. J. O'Riain. 2011. The spatial ecology of chacma baboons (*Papio ursinus*) in a human-modified environment. *International Journal of Primatology* 32:308–328.

Hubbard, R. D., and C. K. Nielsen. 2009. White-tailed deer attacking humans during the fawning season: a unique human-wildlife conflict on a university campus. *Human-Wildlife Conflicts* 3:129–135.

Hussain, A., J. B. Armstrong, D. B. Brown, and J. Hogland. 2007. Land-use pattern, urbaniza-tion, and deer-vehicle collisions in Alabama. *Human-Wildlife Conflicts* 1:89–96.

Inskip, C., and A. Zimmermann. 2009. Human-felid conflict: a review of patterns and priori-ties worldwide. *Oryx* 43:18–34.

International Shark Attack Files. 2020. *Yearly worldwide shark attack summary.* International Shark Attack File, Florida Museum, Gainesville, FL. www.floridamuseum.ufl.edu/shark-attacks/yearly-worldwide-summary/. Accessed 1 August 2020.

IUCN. 2019. *Crocodile attacks.* IUCN Crocodile Specialist Group. www.iucncsg.org/pages/Crocodilian-Attacks.html. Accessed 1 December 2019.

Kämmerle, J. L., F. Brieger, M. Kröschel, R. Hagen, I. Storch, and R. Suchant. 2017. Temporal patterns in road crossing behaviour in roe deer (*Capreolus capreolus*) at sites with wild-life warning reflectors. *PloS One* 12(9):e0184761.

Kasturiratne A, A. R. Wickremasinghe, N. de Silva, N. K. Gunawardena, A. Pathmeswaran, R. Premaratna, L. Savioli, D. G. Lalloo, and H. J. de Silva. 2008. The global burden of snakebite: a literature analysis and modelling based on regional estimates of envenom-ing and deaths. *PLoS Medicine* 5(11):e218.

Khan, M. M. H. 2004. *Ecology and conservation of the Bengal tiger in the Sundarbans man-grove forest of Bangladesh.* PhD Dissertation, University of Cambridge, Cambridge.

Langley, R. L. 2005. Alligator attacks on humans in the United States. *Wilderness and Environmental Medicine* 16:119–124.

Langley, R. L. 2008. Animal bites and stings reported by United States poison control centers. *Wilderness and Environmental Medicine* 19:7–14.

Langley, R. L. 2010. Adverse encounters with alligators in the United States: an update. *Wilderness and Environmental Medicine* 21:156–163.

Laurian, C., C. Dussault, J. P. Ouellet, R. Courtois, M. Poulin, and L. Breton. 2008. Behavioral adaptations of moose to roadside salt pools. *Journal of Wildlife Management* 72:1094–1100.

Leblond, M., C. Dussault, J. P. Ouellet, M. Poulin, R. Courtois, and J. Fortin. 2007. Management of roadside salt pools to reduce moose-vehicle collision. *Journal of Wildlife Management* 71:2304–2310.

Le Moyne, J. 1591. Indorum Floridam provinciam inhabitanitium elcones: Theordore Byr, Liege. *In Voyages en Virginie et en Floride.* Ducharte et Van Buggenhoudt, Paris, France, 1926.

Linnell, J. D., R. Andersen, Z. Andersone, L. Balciauskas, J. C. Blanco, L. Boitani, et al. 2002. The fear of wolves: a review of wolf attacks on humans. *Norsk Institutt for Naturforskning Oppdragsmelding* 731:1–65.

Linnell, J. D., B. Cretois, E. B. Nilsen, C. M. Rolandsen, E. J. Solberg, V. Veiberg, P. Kaczensky, B. Van Moorter, M. Panzacchi, G. R. Rauset, and B. Kaltenborn. 2020. The challenges and opportunities of coexisting with wild ungulates in the human-dom-inated landscapes of Europe's anthropocene. *Biological Conservation* 244:108500.

Linnell, M. A., M. R. Conover, and T. J. Ohashi. 2009. Using wedelia as ground cover on tropical airports can reduce bird activity. *Human-Wildlife Conflicts* 3:223–233.

Löe, J., and E. Röskaft. 2004. Large carnivores and human safety: a review. *AMBIO: A Journal of the Human Environment* 33:283–289.

Marcoux, A., and S. J. Riley. 2010. Driver knowledge, beliefs, and attitudes about deer-vehicle collisions in Southern Michigan. *Human-Wildlife Interactions* 4:47–55.

Mastro, L. L., M. R. Conover, and S. N. Frey. 2008. Deer-vehicle collision prevention tech-niques. *Human-Wildlife Conflicts* 2:80–92.

Mattson, D., K. Logan, and L. Sweanor. 2011. Factors governing risk of cougar attacks on humans. *Human-Wildlife Interactions* 5:135–158.

Mayer, J. J. 2013. Wild pig attacks on humans. *Proceedings of the Wildlife Damage Management Conference* 15:17–35.

McCullough, D. R. 1982. Behavior, bears, and humans. *Wildlife Society Bulletin* 10:27–32.

McLennan, M. R., and K. J. Hockings. 2016. The aggressive apes? Causes and contexts of great ape attacks on local persons. Pages 373–394 *in* F. M. Angelici, editor. *Problematic wildlife.* Springer, Cham, Switzerland.

Meisingset, E. L., L. E. Loe, Ø. Brekkum, and A. Mysterud. 2014. Targeting mitigation efforts: the role of speed limit and road edge clearance for deer – vehicle collisions. *Journal of Wildlife Management* 78:679–688.

Menezes, R. 2008. Rabies in India. *Canadian Medical Association Journal* 175:564–566.

Miquelle, D., I. Nikolaev, J. Goodrich, B. Litvinov, E. Smirnov, and E. Suvorov. 2005. Searching for the coexistence recipe: a case study of conflicts between people and tigers in the Russian far East. Pages 305–322 *in* R. Woodroffe, S. Thirgood, and A. Rabinowitz, editors, *People and wildlife, conflict or co-existence?* Cambridge University Press, Cambridge.

Mohan, D. 1997. Leopard depredation problem in Chamoli Garhwal. *Indian Forester* 123:895–901.

Mohapatra, B., D. A. Warrell, W. Suraweera, P. Bhatia, N. Dhingra, R. M. Jotkar, P. S. Rodriguez, K. Mishra, R. Whitaker, and P. Jha. 2011. Snakebite mortality in India: a nationally representative mortality survey. *PLoS Neglected Tropical Diseases* 5(4):e1018. https://doi.org/10.1371/journal.pntd.0001018.

Moore, R. M., Jr., R. B. Zehmer, J. I. Moulthrop, and R. L. Packer. 1977. Surveillance of animal bite cases in the United States, 1971–1972. *Archives of Environment Health* 32:267–270.

Mormile, J. E., and C. M. Hill. 2017. Living with urban baboons: exploring attitudes and their implications for local baboon conservation and management in Knysna, South Africa. *Human Dimensions of Wildlife* 22:99–109.

Moten, T. L., T. A. Bhat, A. Gulzar, A. Mir, and F. Mir. 2017. Causalities of human wild-life conflict in Kashmir valley, India; a neglected form of trauma: our 10 year study. *International Journal of Research in Medical Sciences* 5:1898–1902.

NBC News. 2010. *Fatal wolf attack unnerves Alaska Village.* www.nbcnews.com/id/35913715/ns/us_news-life/t/fatal-wolf-attack-unnerves-alaska-village/#.XBNGe2fQYTY. Accessed 15 December 2018.

Neumann, W., and G. Ericsson. 2018. Influence of hunting on movements of moose near roads. *Journal of Wildlife Management* 82:918–928.

Nowell, K., and P. Jackson. 1996. *Wild cats: status survey and conservation action plan.* IUCN/SSC, Cat Specialist Group, Gland, Switzerland.

Nyphus, P. J., and R. Tilson. 2004. Characterizing human-tiger conflicts in Sumatra, Indonesia: implications for conservation. *Oryx* 38(1):68–74.

O'Neil, M. E., K. A. Mack, and J. Gilchrist. 2007. Epidemiology of non-canine bite and sting injuries treated in US emergency departments, 2001–2004. *Public Health Reports* 122(6): 764-775.

Packer, C., D. Ikanda, B. Kissui, and H. Kushnir. 2005. Lion attacks on humans in Tanzania. *Nature* 436:927–928.

Packer, C., A. Swanson, D. Ikanda, and H. Kushnir. 2011. Fear of darkness, the full moon and the nocturnal ecology of African lions. *PLoS One* 6(7):e22285. https://doi.org/10.1371/journal.pone.0022285. Accessed 10 August 2018.

Parker, I. D., R. R. Lopez, N. J. Silvy, D. S. Davis, and C. B. Owen. 2011. Long-term effectiveness of US 1 crossing project in reducing Florida key deer mortality. *Wildlife Society Bulletin* 35:296–302.

Pelletier, A. 2006. Injuries from motor-vehicle collisions with moose – Maine, 2000–2004. *Morbidity and Mortality Weekly Report* 55:1272–1274.

Penteriani, V., M. del Mar Delgado, F. Pinchera, J. Naves, A. Fernandez-Gil, I. Kojola, S. Härkönen, H. Norberg, J. Frank, J. M. Fedriani1, V. Sahlén, O. G. Støen, J. E. Swenson, P. Wabakken, M. Pellegrini, S. Herrero, and J. V. López-Bao. 2016. Human behaviour can trigger large carnivore attacks in developed countries. *Scientific Reports* 6: 20552. Accessed 20 December 2018.

Pfeiffer, M. B., B. F. Blackwell, and T. L. DeVault. 2018. Quantification of avian hazards to military aircraft and implications for wildlife management. *PLoS One* 13(11):e0206599. https://doi.org/10.1371/journal.pone.0206599.

Rahman, R., M. A. Faiz, S. Selim, B. Rahman, A. Basher, A. Jones, C. d'Este, M. Hossain, Z. Islam, H. Ahmed, and A. H. Milton. 2010. Annual incidence of snake bite in rural Bangladesh. *PLoS Neglected Tropical Diseases* 4(10):e860.

Rajpurohit, K. S., and P. R. Krausman. 2000. Human-sloth-bear conflicts in Madhya Pradesh, India. *Wildlife Society Bulletin* 28:393–399.

Richardson, W. J., and T. West. 2000. Serious birdstrike accidents to military aircraft: updated list and summary. *Proceedings of International Bird Strike Committee Meeting. Amsterdam, Netherlands* 25:67–98.

Rowden, P., D. Steinhardt, and M. Sheehan. 2008. Road crashes involving animals in Australia. *Accident Analysis and Prevention* 40:1865–1871.

Rutberg, A. T., and R. E. Naugle. 2008. Deer-vehicle collision trends at a suburban immuno-contraception site. *Human-Wildlife Conflicts* 2:60–67.

Saberwal, V. K., J. P. Gibbs, R. Chellam, and A. J. T. Johnsingh. 1994. Lion – human conflict in the Gir Forest, India. *Conservation Biology* 8:501–507.

Sawyer, H., P. A. Rodgers, and T. Hart. 2016. Pronghorn and mule deer use of underpasses and overpasses along U. S. Highway 191. *Wildlife Society Bulletin* 40:211–216.

Schmidt, S. P., and T. G. Osborn. 1993. Effects of endophyte-infected tall fescue on animal performance. *Agriculture, Ecosystems and Environment* 44:233–262.

Seamans, T. W., B. F. Blackwell, G. E. Bernhardt, and D. A. Potter. 2015. Assessing chemical control of earthworms at airports. *Wildlife Society Bulletin* 39:434–442.

Seidensticker, J., and S. Lumpkin. 1992. Mountain lions don't stalk people? True or false. *Smithsonian* 22(11):113–122.

Seiler, A. 2005. Predicting locations of moose – vehicle collisions in Sweden. *Journal of Applied Ecology* 42:371–382.

Seiler, A., J. O. Helldin, and C. Seiler. 2004. Road mortality in Swedish mammals: results of a drivers' questionnaire. *Wildlife Biology* 10:225–233.

Smith, T. S., and S. Herrero. 2018. Human – bear conflict in Alaska: 1880–2015. *Wildlife Society Bulletin* 42:254–263.

Southwick, C. H., I. Malik, and M. F. Siddiqi. 2005. Rhesus commensalism in India: problems and prospects. Pages 241–257 *in* S. Radhakrishna, M. A. Hoffman, and A. Sinha, editors, *The macaque connection: commensalism and conflict between humans and macaques.* Springer, New York.

Stafford, N. T., R. F. Welden, and B. L. Bruyere. 2018. Media reporting of conflict between wildlife and people spending time in nature. *Wildlife Society Bulletin* 42:246–253.

State Farm Insurance Company. 2018. *Deer crashes down: annual report from state farm shows reduction in deer-related crashes.* State Farm Insurance Company, Bloomberg, IN. https://newsroom.statefarm.com/2018-deer-crashes-down/. Accessed 12August 2020.

Støen, O. G., A. Ordiz, V. Sahlén, J. M. Arnemo, S. Sæbø, G. Mattsing, M. Kristofferson, S. Brunberg, J. Kindber, and J. E. Swenson. 2018. Brown bear (*Ursus arctos*) attacks resulting in human casualties in Scandinavia 1977–2016; management implications and recommendations. *PLoS One* 13(5):e0196876. https://doi.org/10.1371/journal.pone.0196876.

Streetly, J. 2000. Wolves between worlds. *BBC Wildlife* 8(12):59–60.

Sudarshan, M. K., B. J. Mahendra, S. N. Madhusudana, D. A. Narayana, A. Rahman, N. S. N. Rao, F. X-Meslin, D. Lobo, and K. Ravikumar. 2006. An epidemiological study of animal bites in India: results of a WHO sponsored national multi-centric rabies survey. *Journal of Communicable Diseases* 38:32–39.

Taylor, D., N. Kinler, and G. Linscombe. 1991. Female alligator reproduction and associated population estimates. *Journal of Wildlife Management* 55:682–688. www.thelocal.se/20180105/wildlife-road-collisions-hi-record-0high-in-sweden.

Texas Parks and Wildlife. 2004. Authorities suggest ways for living with alligators. Texas Parks and Wildlife, Austin, Texas, USA. Accessed January 9, 2019.

Thiemann, G. W., R. S. Stahl, S. Baruch-Modo, and S. W. Breck. 2008. Trans fatty acids provide evidence of anthropogenic feeding by black bears. *Human-Wildlife Conflicts* 2:183–193.

Thorpe, J. 2012.100 years of fatalities and destroyed civil aircraft due to bird strikes. *Proceedings of the International Bird Strike Committee Meeting* 30:1–36.

Timm, R. M., R. O. Baker, J. R. Bennett, and C. C. Coolahan. 2004. Coyote attacks: an increasing suburban problem. *Proceedings of the Vertebrate Conference* 21:47–57.

Torres, S. G., T. M. Mansfield, J. E. Foley, T. Lupo, and A. Brinkhaus. 1996. Mountain lion and human activity in California: testing speculations. *Wildlife Society Bulletin* 24:451–460.

Treves, A., and L. Naughton-Treves. 1999. Risk and opportunity for humans coexisting with large carnivores. *Journal of Human Evolution* 36:275–282.

Van Doren, M. 1955. *Travels of William Bartram.* Dover Publications, New York.

Veeramani, A., E. A. Jayson, and P. S. Easa. 1996. Man – wildlife conflict: cattle lifting and human casualties in Kerala. *Indian Forester* 122:897–902.

Washburn, B. E., P. J. Cisar, and T. L. DeVault. 2017. Impact location and damage to civil and military rotary-wing aircraft from wildlife strikes. *Human-Wildlife Interactions* 11:23–32.

White, L. A., and S. D. Gehrt. 2009. Coyote attacks on humans in the United States and Canada. *Human Dimensions of Wildlife* 14:419–432.

Wikipedia. 2018*a*. *List of wolf attacks in North America.* https://en.wikipedia.org/wiki/List_of_wolf_attacks_in_North_America. Accessed 15 December 2018.

Wikipedia. 2018*b*. *List of fatal cougar attacks in North America.* https://en.wikipedia.org/wiki/List_of_fatal_cougar_attacks_in_North_America#2010s. Accessed 20 December 2018.

Wilder, J. M., D. Vongraven, T. Atwood, B. Hansen, A. Jessen, A. Kochnev, G. York, R. Vallender, D. Hedman, and M. Gibbons. 2017. Polar bear attacks on humans: implications of a changing climate. *Wildlife Society Bulletin* 41:537–547.

Witmer, G. W. 2011. Rodent population management at Kansas City international airport. *Human-Wildlife Interactions* 5:269–275.

Wolfe, M. L. 2008. Avoiding the blame game in managing problem black bears. *Human-Wildlife Conflicts* 2:12–14.

World Health Organization. 2018. *Animal bites.* www.who.int/news-room/fact-sheets/detail/animal-bites. Accessed 6 January 2018.

Ziegltrum, G. J. 2008. Impacts of the black bear supplemental feeding program on ecology in western Washington. *Human-Wildlife Conflicts* 2:153–159.

3 Zoonotic Diseases

Otzi the Iceman, the 5,300-year-old mummy that was found in the Italian Alps when a glacier retreated, was suffering from Lyme disease when he died, making him the earliest person known to have had this disease.

Paraphrased from Hall (2011)

If one plays golf in areas where ehrlichiosis is endemic, one needs to keep oneself and the golf ball on the fairway; ticks are abundant in the rough.

Paraphrased from Standaert et al. (1995)

"Waterbirds, to an influenza researcher, are more than majestic swans and charming mallards. They are instead stealthy vectors of novel influenza viruses, some of nature's bioterrorist agents, chauffeuring dangerous microbes from place to place."

Smith (2013)

Diseases are caused by pathogens, which can be viruses, bacteria, fungi, parasites, or prions. Few pathogens can exist outside a living body for an extended period of time. Yet, a pathogen usually cannot live forever inside any one animal because the animal's immune system will attack the pathogen, eliminating it from the body. For a pathogen to survive, it must spread to another animal before this happens. Pathogens for some human diseases can spread from one human directly to another, meaning the pathogens are "contagious." Pathogens for other human diseases need the help of other species to spread from one person to another. Animals that transmit pathogens from one animal to another are called vectors. Common vectors of human pathogens include biting insects and animals and other animals that humans consume.

For some human diseases, humans are the reservoir host, meaning that the pathogen can maintain itself indefinitely by just infecting humans. These include the pathogens that cause polio and small pox. For other human diseases, the pathogens can infect humans and multiple within them, but the pathogen population cannot maintain itself indefinitely by just infecting humans. These pathogens use another animal species as reservoir host, and humans serve as an amplifying host in which the pathogen population can multiply but not endure. Human diseases that use an animal as a reservoir host, amplifying host, or vector are called "zoonotic diseases" or "zoonoses," which literally means "diseases from animals."

One unfortunate consequence of human–wildlife interactions is the opportunity for the exchange of pathogens between humans and wildlife. Each year, zoonotic diseases sicken hundreds of millions of people worldwide and kill thousands. Most human diseases are zoonotic, and most zoonotic diseases are caused by wildlife pathogens (Conover and Vail 2015). Zoonotic diseases are nearly impossible to eradicate if wildlife species serve as a reservoir host. For example, typhoid, which killed millions of people during the twentieth century, has been eliminated throughout

DOI: 10.1201/9780429401404-3

most of the world. Today, typhoid pathogens only occur in the most impoverished places where medical care is lacking and humans serve as the reservoir host – and in the United States, where flying squirrels are the reservoir host.

One difficulty with determining the number of people killed (mortality) or sickened (morbidity) by zoonotic disease is deciding how close an association between humans and wildlife is required before it is considered a zoonotic disease. Consider an outbreak of salmonellosis, which is one cause of food poisoning (Sidebar 3.1); while the original source of the pathogen for salmonellosis may be the defecation of a mouse or feral hog, the pathogen can then multiple inside food and sicken humans who eat the contaminated food.

Acquired immunodeficiency syndrome (AIDS) is another zoonotic disease; yet few people would consider it to be one because it has become highly contagious. The disease is caused by the human immunodeficiency virus (HIV). This virus originated from the simian immunodeficiency virus (SIV). During the 1920s, SIV developed the ability to infect humans and to become contagious. It was first detected in the U.S. during the 1980s (AVERT 2019). As of 2018, about 700,000 people have died of an AIDS-related illness in the U.S. since the beginning of the HIV epidemic (Wikipedia 2021). During 2019, over a million people in the U.S. and its territories were living with an HIV infection, 15,000 of them died that year, and an additional 37,000 people in the U.S. were diagnosed with an HIV infection (CDC 2021). Worldwide, 38 million prople were living with HIV during 2020, and 680,000 infected people died from an AIDS-related illness (UNAIDS 2021). Fortunately, a group of antiretroviral drugs have been identified, which if taken together, keeps the prevalence of HIV in an infected person low enough that symptoms of AIDS do not develop. Besides AIDS, COVID-19, influenza, and salmonellosis are considered zoonotic diseases because the pathogens originated from some animal. Howver, I had decided not to include the number of people sickened or killed by these zoonotic diseases. If I had, the number of people sickened or killed by zoonotic diseases would be much higher than reported in this book (Sidebar 3.1).

SIDEBAR 3.1 THE 2016 OUTBREAK OF *ESCHERICHIA COLI* IN BAGGED SPINACH

In 2016, more than 200 people located in 26 states became ill after consuming bagged spinach; three people died. Health authorities identified *E. coli* 0157:H7 as the pathogen, and an intense health investigation was initiated to determine its source. Ultimately, the outbreak was traced back to a single field in California, but by that time, the crop had been plowed under and the field was fallow. Interviews with the farmer and harvester failed to identify the source of the pathogen. The investigators could not conclusively identify the source of the infection, but the final report noted the presence of feral hogs in and around the spinach field and near the wells used to irrigate the crop. Both feral hogs and deer are known vectors and reservoirs for *E. coli* and are believed to have been the source of the pathogen. This outbreak encouraged a greater emphasis on enhancing food safety and monitoring along the entire "field-to-fork" food chain (Langholz and Jay-Russell 2013).

The number of different zoonotic diseases are in the hundreds – too many to cover in this chapter. I will only cover 13 zoonotic diseases that occur in the United States. The diseases were selected because they attract interest, usually because they are common among humans or cause serious illnesses or death in humans.

3.1 DATA SOURCES

A case is defined as a patient who has a particular disease, which has been diagnosed by a trained doctor. I will use the terms, case and patients, only for humans, not animals. The "incidence" or "incidence rate" is defined as the number of cases among 100,000 people.

Data on zoonotic diseases often can be obtained from four sources: (1) cases submitted to the U.S. CDC for reportable diseases, (2) doctor reports to state health agencies in those states where such reports are required by law, (3) patient visits to hospital emergency rooms, and (4) queries to poison control centers in the United States. In this book, I report the data that represent the greatest proportion of the patient population and relied on sources in the same order they appear above (i.e., 1, 2, 3, and 4) because that is the order of the completeness of their coverage. Reportable diseases (#1 above) are those diseases and medical problems for which medical providers are required by federal law to report them to federal health agencies. Data on reportable diseases (#1 above), therefore, cover most U.S. patients where a diagnosis was made. These data do not include victims who did not seek medical attention or patients whose disease were not diagnosed. Some states require doctors to report additional diseases or medical problems (such as a bite by a wildlife species), but this varies among states. Hence, these data (#2 above) are not complete for the entire United States but represent a collection of states. It is for this reason that I used CDC data over state data in trying to determine data for the entire United States. Data on patient visits to emergency rooms or calls to poison control centers cover a large proportion of the United States but only include victims who seek their services. The problem with these two data sources is that it is unclear what proportion of victims utilize these services. In this chapter, I report on both confirmed and probable cases. Some cases result from U.S. residents who became infected while traveling outside of the United States. I refer readers to Conover and Vail (2015) *Human Diseases from Wildlife* for more information about zoonotic diseases.

3.2 LEPTOSPIROSIS

Leptospirosis is an ancient disease of humans and has the widest geographic distribution of any zoonotic disease. The disease is caused by aerobic bacteria of the genus *Leptospira* (hereafter these bacteria are called leptospires); these are flexible microorganisms that have the appearance of a tightly wound screw (Figure 3.1). They can move by spinning around their axis; their mobility increases their chances of penetrating a mucous membrane or skin, especially when the skin is scratched or cut. It also allows them to move through tissues once inside a host. Infections also occur

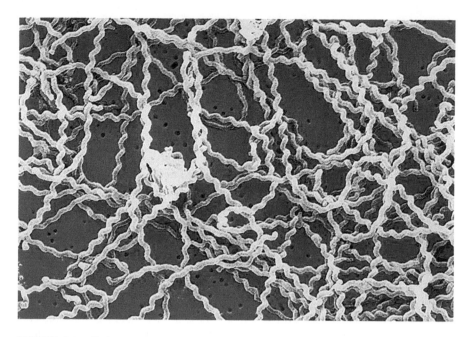

FIGURE 3.1   Corkscrew-shaped leptospires taken with a scanning electron microscope (Janice Haney Carr and CDC).

FIGURE 3.2   People can contract leptospirosis after wading through floodwater that is contaminated with leptospires.

Source: Talukdar David, Shutterstock 1747409963.

through drinking contaminated water. Virulent leptospires have a hook-like structure on one or both ends of their bodies and survive by infecting renal tubules of animals. Over 200 virulent variants of leptospires have been identified that can infect humans (Bharti et al. 2003; CDC 2020d).

Leptospirosis is more prevalent in tropical and subtropical countries than in temperate countries and more common in Hawaii than in the other states of the United States. It is more prevalent during the rainy season or after floods than during droughts. People become infected when they come into contact with urine from an infected animal or water that has been contaminated with infected urine (Figure 3.2). Ninety-one cases of leptospirosis were reported in the United States during 2018 (Table 3.1). Worldwide, the mortality rate is 1 per 100,000 people in temperate climates and 10–100 in the humid tropics (Bovet et al. 1999), but mortality rates vary considerably among adjacent countries. In India, about 12% of all patients admitted to hospitals due to high fevers had leptospirosis (Victoriano et al. 2009). In parts of Peru, 20%–30% of patients seeking medical attention for fever had leptospirosis (Bharti et al. 2003).

TABLE 3.1

Annual Number of Reported Cases in the U.S. of Zoonotic Diseases That Are Notifiable Diseases and Incidence Rates Per 100,000 People in the United States but Excluding U.S. Territories during 2018 (CDC 2019a), Data on AIDS and HIV Infections, COVID-19, Influenza (Avian Flu) and Salmonellosis Are Not Provided Because Most People Currently Contract the Pathogens from Another Person or Infected Food.

Disease	Number of cases	Incidence rate
AIDS and HIV infections	–	–
Anthrax	1	0.0
Arboviral diseases, chikungunya virus disease	117	0.04
Arboviral diseases, eastern equine encephalitis virus disease, neuroinvasive	6	0.00
Arboviral diseases, eastern equine encephalitis virus disease, nonneuroinvasive	–	–
Arboviral diseases, Jamestown Canyon virus disease, neuroinvasive	25	0.01
Arboviral diseases, Jamestown Canyon virus disease, nonneuroinvasive	16	0.00
Arboviral diseases, La Crosse virus disease, neuroinvasive	83	0.03
Arboviral diseases, La Crosse virus disease, nonneuroinvasive	3	0.00
Arboviral diseases, Powassan virus disease, neuroinvasive	21	0.01
Arboviral diseases, Powassan virus disease, nonneuroinvasive	–	–
Arboviral diseases, St. Louis encephalitis virus disease, neuroinvasive	5	0.00

(Continued)

TABLE 3.1 (*Continued*)

Disease	Number of cases	Incidence rate
Arboviral diseases, St. Louis encephalitis virus disease, nonneuroinvasive	3	0.00
Arboviral diseases, West Nile virus disease, neuroinvasive	1,657	0.51
Arboviral diseases, West Nile virus disease, nonneuroinvasive	989	0.30
Arboviral diseases, western equine encephalitis virus disease, neuroinvasive	–	–
Arboviral diseases, western equine encephalitis virus disease, nonneuroinvasive	–	–
Babesiosis, total	2,160	0.79
Babesiosis, confirmed	1,861	0.68
Babesiosis, probable	299	0.11
Botulism, foodborne	17	0.01
Brucellosis	138	0.04
Campylobacteriosis	70,200	21.46
COVID-19	–	–
Cryptosporidiosis, total	12,533	3.83
Cryptosporidiosis, confirmed	8,980	2.74
Cryptosporidiosis, probable	3,553	1.09
Cyclosporiasis	3,519	1.20
Dengue virus infections, dengue	424	0.13
Dengue virus infections, dengue-like illness	41	0.01
Dengue virus infections, severe dengue	9	0.00
Ehrlichiosis and anaplasmosis, *Anaplasma phagocytophilum* infection	4,008	1.27
Ehrlichiosis and anaplasmosis, *Ehrlichia chaffeensis* infection	1,799	0.57
Ehrlichiosis and anaplasmosis, *Ehrlichia ewingii* infection	33	0.01
Ehrlichiosis and anaplasmosis, undetermined ehrlichiosis/anaplasmosis	283	0.09
Giardiasis	15,548	6.06
Hantavirus infection, non-hantavirus pulmonary syndrome	2	0.00
Hantavirus pulmonary syndrome	18	0.01
Influenza (avian flu)	–	–
Leprosy (Hansen's disease)	90	0.03
Leptospirosis	91	0.04
Listeriosis	864	0.26
Lyme disease, total	33,666	10.34
Lyme disease, confirmed	23,558	7.23
Lyme disease, probable	10,108	3.10
Malaria	1,748	0.53
Novel influenza A virus infections	14	0.00
Psittacosis	22	0.01
Q fever, total	215	0.07

(*Continued*)

TABLE 3.1 (*Continued*)

Disease	Number of cases	Incidence rate
Q fever, acute	178	0.05
Q fever, chronic	37	0.01
Rabies, human	3	0.00
Salmonellosis	–	–
Spotted fever rickettsiosis, total	5,544	1.71
Spotted fever rickettsiosis, confirmed	124	0.04
Spotted fever rickettsiosis, probable	5,420	1.67
Trichinellosis	1	0.00
Tularemia	229	0.07
Zika virus, zika virus disease, congenital	2	0.05
Zika virus, zika virus disease, noncongenital	79	0.02
Zika virus, zika virus infection, congenital	8	0.21
Zika virus, zika virus infection, noncongenital	245	0.07
Total number of reported cases in the U.S.*	210,597*	–

*This number excludes U.S. cases of AIDS or HIV infections, COVID-19, influenza, and salmonellosis.

Within minutes of invading a host, leptospires migrate to the lymphatic and circulatory systems. Most infected people are asymptomatic or have only a mild illness with flu-like symptoms (fever, chills, muscle aches, headaches). Other symptoms may include conjunctivitis, vomiting, diarrhea, stomach pain, jaundice, and cough. One indication of leptospirosis is the presence of a red rash that has an irregular border and does not turn white when the skin is pressed. The rash results from the leakage of blood from capillaries into the tissue beneath the skin. Medline Plus (2010) recommends people seek medical attention if they exhibit any of these symptoms and may have been exposed to water contaminated with leptospires. Most patients recover after three to seven days, but in about 10% of patients, the infection enters a second, more severe phase that can include kidney or liver failure, difficulty breathing, and bleeding. Patients can experience mood swings, depression, confusion, and hallucinations. Most patients fully recover from leptospirosis, but this can take months or years. Death from leptospirosis results from renal failure, cardiopulmonary failure, or widespread bleeding. Case fatality rates for patients diagnosed with leptospirosis ranges from less than 5% to 30% in different parts of the world (WHO 2003; Leptospirosis Information Center 2009; Victoriano et al. 2009; Puliyath and Singh 2012; CDC 2019a). Case fatality rate, which is the proportion of cases that resulted in death, is 5%–15% in U.S. cases with severe clinical illness (CDC 2020d).

Species that serve as a reservoir host shed leptospires in their urine. Reservoir hosts species include mice, rats, voles, and shrews; these animals are often asymptomatic when infected. Other vertebrate species are accidental hosts and may become ill if infected but *Leptospira* are unable to survive in them. However, accidental hosts may still excrete leptospires for a few days or weeks (Faine 1994). There are so many serovars (i.e., distinct variations) of *Leptospira* that almost all mammal species can be infected by at least one of them. Infection rates vary widely among wildlife species. In the Florida Panhandle and southwest Georgia, leptospires were found in less than 4% of rabbits, fox squirrels, and gray squirrels but in 38% of raccoons and 41% of opossums (Shotts et al. 1975). Infection rates also vary by area. Antibodies against leptospires were found in 0% of the white-tailed deer from northern Mexico, 8% from Mississippi, 21% from Tennessee, 30% from Virginia, and 60% from Minnesota (Shotts and Hayes 1970; Goyal et al. 1992; New et al. 1993; Cantu et al. 2008).

Early antibiotic intervention is the most significant factor in recovery, but effectiveness of antibiotics decreases rapidly after symptoms develop. For this reason, any patient suspected of having leptospirosis should be placed on antibiotics immediately. Antibiotics can prevent leptospirosis in humans if provided prior to leptospire infections. Hence, they are sometimes taken by military personnel or travelers to areas where leptospirosis is common. The incidence of leptospirosis was reduced 95% among American soldiers training in Panama who were given weekly doses of doxycycline (Takafuji et al. 1984). Antibiotics can also be used to protect residents of endemic areas during disease outbreaks.

3.3 LYME DISEASE

Europeans have suffered from Lyme disease for at least 5,000 years (Hall 2011), but the term, Lyme disease, is of more recent origin. Allen Steere, a physician, observed an unusual concentration of arthritis in children from Lyme, Connecticut, and named the disease after the Connecticut town. This disease is caused by a spirochetal bacterium, *Borrelia burgdorferi* (Figure 3.3).

FIGURE 3.3   A three-dimensional presentation of *Borrelia burgdorferi*, which causes Lyme disease.

Source: Fotoapi, Shutterstock 451652944.

Lyme disease occurs throughout the temperate regions of the Northern Hemisphere, including North America, Europe, Russia, China, and Japan. The reported cases of Lyme disease in the United States has increased fourfold since 1991. CDC reported that there were 33,666 cases of Lyme disease during 2018 and noted that the number of people who contracted the disease was probably ten times higher (Table 3.1; CDC 2020e). There are three endemic areas for Lyme disease in the United States: Northeast, North-central, and Pacific Coast regions which roughly correspond with distribution of its main vectors: blacklegged ticks in the eastern and upper-midwestern United States and western blacklegged tick on the West Coast (Figure 3.4).

Blacklegged ticks seek blood meals from many hosts including birds, reptiles, and mammals. Larval and nymphal blacklegged ticks usually feed on birds and small- or medium-sized mammals, such as mice, voles, chipmunks, squirrels, shrews, skunks, and raccoons. Adult ticks feed primarily on large mammals, especially white-tailed deer. The most important reservoir host for the pathogen is the white-footed mouse; these mice often have an active infection of *B. burgdorferi* throughout their entire lives. In some areas where Lyme disease is endemic, nearly all white-footed mice were infected with *B. burgdorferi* by the end of each summer. A high proportion of *Ixodes* ticks feeding on an infected white-footed mouse became infected themselves. Infected ticks retained the pathogen throughout their lives. White-tailed deer, in contrast, rarely serve as a reservoir for *B. burgdorferi*, but they are important to maintain the blacklegged tick populations in an area and, therefore, also help *B. burgdorferi* maintain itself in the same area (LoGiudice et al. 2003; Bunikis et al. 2004; Eisen et al. 2012).

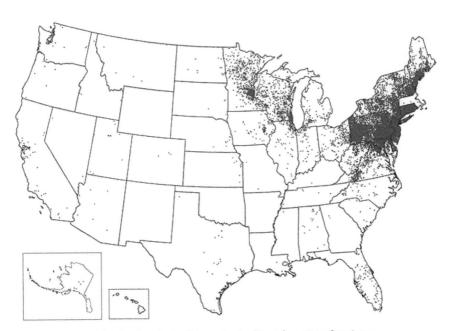

1 dot placed randomly within county of residence for each confirmed case

FIGURE 3.4   Distribution of Lyme disease cases in the United States during 2018. Each dot represents a case (CDC, 2020, www.cdc.gov/lyme/stats/maps.html).

In California, the western fence lizard and alligator lizard are the primary hosts for larval and nymphal western blacklegged tick with up to 90% of these ticks feeding on lizards. Interestingly, neither the west fence lizard nor the alligator lizard serves as reservoir hosts for *B. burgdorferi* because the lizard's immune system kills them. Birds, especially passerines that forage on the ground, also are hosts for western blacklegged tick and transport both ticks and *B. burgdorferi* widely. Mule deer are the primary host for adult western blacklegged tick in California, and the western gray squirrel serves as an important reservoir host for *B. burgdorferi* in California, along with the dusky-footed woodrat, deer mouse, and California kangaroo rat (Castro and Wright 2007; Swei et al. 2011).

Two *Borrelia* species – *B. burgdorferi* and *B. bissettii* – are important in the southeastern United States, where three mammal species serve as their reservoir hosts: cotton mice, hispid cotton rats, and eastern woodrats. All these mammal species occur in high densities, and a high percentage of them are infected with *B. burgdorferi* (Oliver et al. 2003). Three tick species (*Ixodes scapularis*, *I. affinis*, and *I. minor*) transmit *Borrelia* in the South, but the blacklegged tick is the primary tick responsible for spreading these pathogens to humans.

The chief characteristic of Lyme disease is a red bullseye-shaped rash centered at the site of a tick bite; this rash occurs in about 70% of patients (Figure 3.5). Other early signs of Lyme disease include a mild fever, fatigue, pain in the muscles and joints, headache, and swelling of lymph nodes. Within a few days, these symptoms may disappear, but the person is still infected with *B. burgdorferi*. Weeks or months

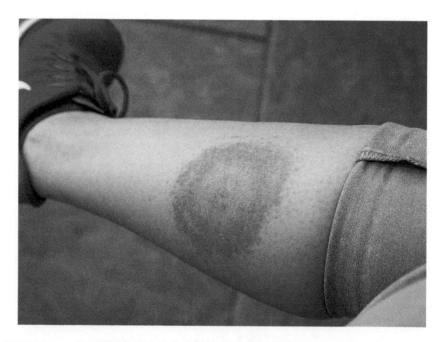

FIGURE 3.5   A red bullseye rash is an early symptom of Lyme disease. The rash is centered where a tick bite occurred.

Source: Anastasia Kopa, Shutterstock 537518422.

later, the disease can reoccur with more serious consequences, such as arthritis in the knee. This condition results when spirochetes invade the joints and is experienced by 30% of patients (Hayes and Piesman 2003; CDC 2020*e*). Finally, neural problems can occur if spirochetes invade nerves and the brain, possibly resulting in a temporary paralysis of facial muscles, meningitis (inflammation of the protective membranes surrounding the brain and spinal cord), and encephalitis (inflammation of the brain). While these conditions are serious and debilitating, Lyme disease is almost never fatal. Chronic Lyme disease can produce a wide variety of neurological problems. These include depression, memory loss, hearing loss, headaches, mood changes, lethargy, and sleep disorders. Late-stage Lyme disease may require intravenous antibiotic therapy, which is usually successful. However, about 30% of patients with late-stage Lyme disease continue to have residual symptoms after antibiotic treatment. These residual symptoms may disappear over time. Up to 10% of patients with Lyme arthritis have persistent joint inflammation that does not respond to antibiotics (Hayes and Piesman 2003; CDC 2020*e*).

Lyme disease is not contagious and is not contracted by direct contact with infected animals. Instead, Lyme disease is transmitted to humans primarily through the bite of nymphal or adult female *Ixodes* ticks. These ticks are tiny: nymphs are the size of a poppy seed, and adults are about the size of a sesame seed (Figure 3.6). More people

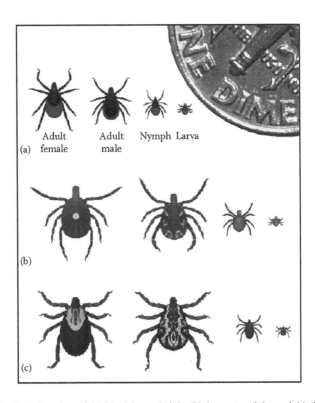

FIGURE 3.6   Relative size of (a) blacklegged tick, (b) lone star tick, and (c) American dog tick relative to a U.S. dime (Chapman and the CDC).

Source: Adapted from Figure 13.8 in Conover and Vail (2015).

are infected from the bite of nymphs than adult ticks because ticks have to remain attached for at least 24 hours before they start to transmit *B. burgdorferri*, and the smaller nymph is easily overlooked. Most people in the United States contract Lyme disease during the summer when nymphal ticks are active and people spend time outdoors. People at risk for Lyme disease are those who spend time outdoors in areas where there are ticks. This includes wildlife biologists, foresters, landscapers, park employees, and people who spend time outdoors (CDC 2018*a*). A Lyme disease vaccine was developed, but the vaccine manufacturer discontinued production during 2002 citing insufficient consumer demand (Sidebar 3.2).

SIDEBAR 3.2 DEATH BY RUMOR: WHAT HAPPENED TO THE VACCINE AGAINST LYME DISEASE? (ABBOTT 2006; NATURE 2006; SOHN 2011)

One of the mysteries in the history of Lyme disease prevention is what happened to the Lyme disease vaccine. During 1998, the pharmaceutical company SmithKline Beecham (now part of GlaxoSmithKline) started to market a vaccine in the United States to protect people from Lyme disease. The vaccine, called LYMErix, was made from a protein on the surface of *B. burgdorferi*; when injected into someone, that person's immune system produced antibodies against that protein. The vaccine was effective, preventing Lyme disease in about 80% of adults.

During the late 1990s, many people were worried about the adverse effects of vaccines, and LYMErix was not above suspicion. Soon, hundreds of people vaccinated with LYMErix claimed they were suffering from the vaccine's side effects. They worried that the vaccine might cause their immune systems not only to attack *B. burgdorferi* but also to attack human proteins, causing serious autoimmune diseases. Soon, SmithKline Beecham was facing a class action lawsuit and numerous individual suits. The U.S. Food and Drug Administration and Centers for Disease Control and Prevention investigated about 900 adverse case reports and found that there was no evidence of a link between the complaints and the vaccine. Still, the adverse publicity caused sales of LYMErix to plummet. By 2002, GlaxoSmithKline stopped making the vaccine.

Many doctors believe this is a public health fiasco. Failing to provide a vaccine when one is available, they say, is failing the many millions of people who live in areas where Lyme disease is endemic. Dr. Markus Simon of the Max Planck Institute for Immunobiology summed up the frustration of many when he said, "This just shows how irrational the world can be. There was no scientific justification for the [Lyme disease] vaccine being pulled."

3.4 ROCKY MOUNTAIN SPOTTED FEVER

Rocky Mountain spotted fever (RMSF) is among the most virulent of human diseases; it is caused by the bacteria *Rickettsia rickettsii* (Figure 3.7). Several species of the hard ticks (Ixodidae) are hosts for this pathogen and can become infected in two ways: an

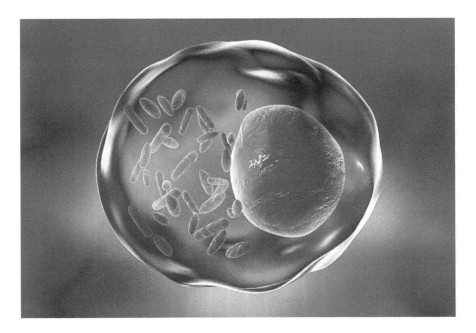

FIGURE 3.7   Three-dimensional illustration of *Rickettsia* (small and red) inside a human cell.

Source: Kateryna Kon, Shutterstock 420181813.

infected female tick can pass the pathogen to its young or a tick can become infected by feeding on an infected host. The tick most responsible for transmitting *R. rickettsii* to people in the eastern United States and Canada is the American dog tick while the Rocky Mountain wood tick is the primary vector in the West. The brown dog tick transmits the pathogen to people in Mexico, and the cayenne tick is a common vector in Central America, South America, and Texas (McDade and Newhouse 1986).

Historically, there were between 250 and 1,200 reported cases of RMSF annually in the United States, but RMSF has become more common in recent years (Figure 3.8). Despite its name, most cases of RMSF do not occur in the Rocky Mountains; instead, the incidence rate is highest in the middle of the United States (Figure 3.9). In humans, *R. rickettsii* live and multiply within the cells that line blood vessels. As these cells die, small holes develop in the blood vessels, causing blood to leak into adjacent tissue. This process causes the characteristic red rash associated with RMSF. If severe enough, this bleeding will damage internal organs and tissue. Early symptoms of RMSF include a rash that normally occurs two to four days following the onset of a fever; the rash consists of flat, red freckles that turn white when pushed in. The rash occurs in most, but not all, patients. Three symptoms of RMSF have historically been used to identify the disease – rash, high fever, and a severe headache (Chapman 2006; Dantas-Torres 2007).

RMSF is a severe illness, and patients commonly require hospitalization. Up to 20% of untreated patients die from the disease, but case fatality rates decrease to between 5% and 10% with proper medical care. Death occurs when RMSF results in

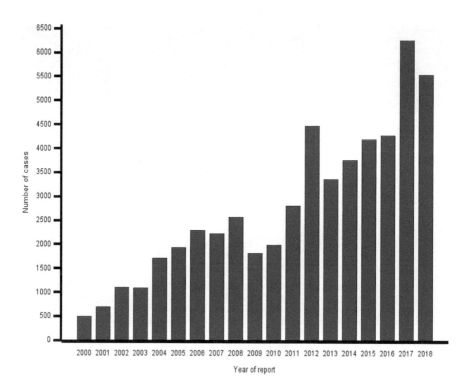

FIGURE 3.8   Number of cases of Rocky Mountain spotted fever and other spotted fevers in the United States from 2000 to 2018 (CDC, www.cdc.gov/rmsf/stats/index.html).

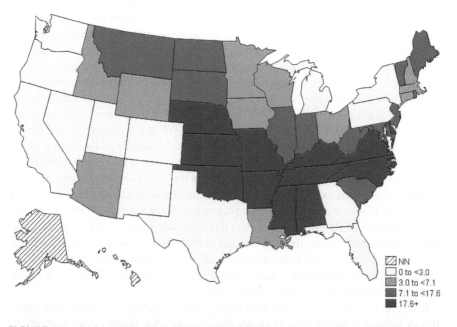

FIGURE 3.9   Incidence (number of cases per 100,000 people) of Rocky Mountain spotted fever and other spotted fevers in the United States (CDC, www.cdc.gov/rmsf/stats/index.html).

kidney failure, a severe infection of the central nervous system, or respiratory failure. RMSF is more likely to be fatal if antibody treatment is delayed for more than five days after the onset of symptoms. For this reason, people who suspect they may have contracted RMSF should seek medical attention and inform their physician if they have been bitten by a tick. Some patients with severe cases of RMSF can experience long-term or permanent problems, including partial paralysis of the legs and feet, movement disorders, loss of bladder control, blindness, hearing loss, and speech disorders (Dumler 1994; Dantas-Torres 2007; CDC 2016).

Several mammal species serve as hosts for *R. rickettsii* including the cotton rat, white-footed mice, meadow vole, pine vole, opossum, cottontail rabbit, and snowshoe hare (McDade and Newhouse 1986). For most of these species, being infected by *R. rickettsii* produces no illness.

Domestic dogs are the main host of adult American dog ticks in eastern Canada and United States, but adult dog ticks also feed on livestock and several wildlife species (e.g., bears, raccoons, opossums, coyotes, and foxes). Many species of mice, voles, and rabbits serve as hosts for larval and nymphal American dog ticks. The Rocky Mountain wood tick will feed on virtually any warm-blooded animal. The primary tick vectors for *R. rickettsii* in Mexico – the brown dog tick and the cayenne tick – feed primarily on domestic dogs (McDade and Newhouse 1986).

RMSF is not contagious; instead, most people in North America contract RMSF from the bite of an infected tick, usually by the Rocky Mountain wood tick or American dog tick. Although cases of RMSF have been reported in large cities, most people contract the disease in rural settings. People who live in wooded areas or own a dog have an elevated risk of contracting the disease. Most RMSF patients (90%) contract the disease between April and September when ticks are active. In the United States and Canada, cases of RMSF are seldom clustered together. In 95% of cases, only one member of a family became infected (CDC 2016). During 2018, there were 5,544 confirmed and probable cases of spotted fevers in the United States (the CDC does not distinguish between RMSF and other spotted fevers; Table 3.1).

There are many species of *Rickettsia* throughout the world, some of which are known to cause human diseases (Conover and Vail 2015). In the United States and Canada, these include 364-D rickettsiosis, which is caused by a pathogen referred to as *Rickettsia* species 364-D. It is vectored by Pacific Coast ticks, which occurs in the coastal ranges of Oregon, California, and Baja Mexico. There were only ten confirmed cases as of 2016. *Rickettsia parkeri* was first confirmed to infect human in 2004. During the next decade, 40 more cases were identified in the United States; fortunately, there are no confirmed fatalities. *R. parkeri* is vectored by Gulf Coast ticks and lone star ticks (CDC 2016). All of these are grouped as other spotted fevers and included with RMSF in Table 3.1. Babesiosis is another tick-borne disease that is common in the United States; there were 2,160 cases reported to the CDC during 2018; this disease can be fatal. It is listed separately in Table 3.1.

3.5   ANAPLASMOSIS AND EHRLICHIOSIS

The human diseases, anaplasmosis and ehrlichiosis, are caused by rickettsial bacteria that infect blood cells or blood platelets and are transmitted by ticks. Anaplasmosis, which also is called human granulocytic anaplasmosis, is caused by *Anaplasma phagocytophilum*. This pathogen infects blood cells. Cases of anaplasmosis have increased in number since 2000 (Figure 3.10) and exceeded 6,000 cases in the United States during 2018; its prevalence among humans, however, is believed to be much higher than that (CDC 2019*a*). Anaplasmosis occurs throughout the United States, but the incidence of the disease is highest in New England and the Upper Midwest (Figure 3.11).

Initial symptoms include fever, chills, headache, muscle aches, and nausea. Some patients develop a cough, have mild liver damage, or exhibit confusion. Few anaplasmosis patients develop a rash; consequently, the presence of a rash may indicate Lyme disease or RMSF rather than anaplasmosis. Half of anaplasmosis patients require hospitalization; 7% require intensive care; the case fatality rate is less than 1%. The risk of death increases when the disease is misdiagnosed or antibiotic treatment is delayed.

The white-footed mouse is the main reservoir host for *A. phagocytophilum* in the United States, but other hosts include raccoons, opossums, tree squirrels, chipmunks, and dusky-footed woodrats. *A. phagocytophilum* is transmitted to humans primarily by the blacklegged tick in the eastern United States and the western blacklegged tick in the West (Thomas et al. 2009; CDC 2016).

Ehrlichiosis is caused by several rickettsial species within the genus *Ehrlichia*. In North America, these species include *E. chaffeensis*, *E. ewingii*, and *E. muris eauclairensis*. Most human infections are caused by *E. chaffeensis*, which infects blood monocytes and is the causative agent for human monocytic ehrlichiosis, cited hereafter as enrlichiosis. The number of reported cases of ehrlichiosis in the United States has increased steadily since 2000 (Figure 3.12). The first symptoms of ehrlichiosis

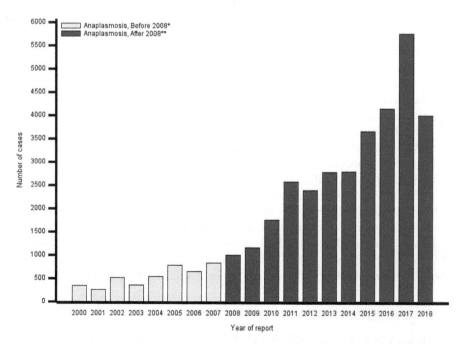

FIGURE 3.10   Number of cases of anaplasmosis in the United States from 2000 through 2018 (CDC, www.cdc.gov/anaplasmosis/stats/index.html).

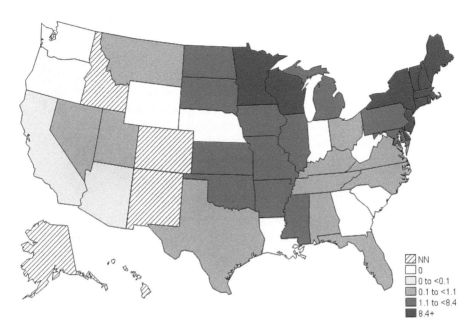

FIGURE 3.11   Incidence of anaplasmosis (number of cases per 100,000 people) in the United States during 2018 (CDC, www.cdc.gov/anaplasmosis/stats/index.html).

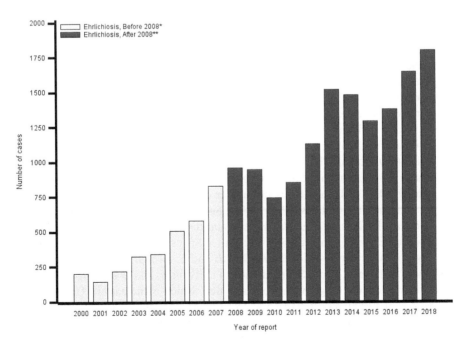

FIGURE 3.12   Number of ehrlichiosis cases caused *E. chaffeensis* in the United States from 2000 through 2018 (CDC, www.cdc.gov/ehrlichiosis/stats/index.html).

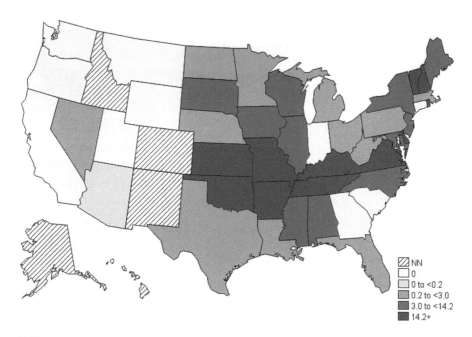

NN
0
0 to <0.2
0.2 to <3.0
3.0 to <14.2
14.2+

FIGURE 3.13 Incidence of ehrlichiosis caused by *E. chaffeensis* (number of cases per 100,000 people) in the United States during 2018 (CDC, www.cdc.gov/ehrlichiosis/stats/index.html).

are similar to other rickettsial diseases and include malaise, muscle aches, headaches, fever, chills, nausea, vomiting, and diarrhea. Patients may exhibit conjunctivitis and confusion. People infected with *E. chaffeensis* can develop a nonitchy rash of small red or purple spots where blood has leaked from capillaries in the skin. Most ehrlichiosis patients have a mild illness that lasts less than 30 days even without antibiotic treatment. But, ehrlichiosis can develop into a serious disease; some patients have difficulty breathing, and others have excessive bleeding. Three percent of patients with an illness severe enough to seek medical attention died from the infection (CDC 2016). The incidence of human cases of *E. chaffeensis* infections is highest in the eastern United States (Figure 3.13).

During 2018, 18 human cases of another disease, *E. ewingii*-ehrlichiosis, were reported in the United States (CDC 2019a). Severe symptoms are less common with *E. ewingii* infections than *E. chaffeensis*, and there have been no reported human deaths from *E. ewingii* infections. In the United States, white-tailed deer and domestic dogs are reservoir hosts for *E. chaffeensis* and *E. ewingii*; the lone star tick vectors these pathogens. The U.S. distribution of ehrlichiosis and *E. ewingii*-ehrlichiosis diseases reflects the range of the lone star tick, which is the eastern United States Thomas et al. (2009) reported that 5%–15% of lone star ticks in the United States are infected with *E. chaffeensis*, and 1%–5% are infected with *E. ewingii*. Most ehrlichiosis cases occur in the eastern United States; most cases of *E. ewingii*-ehrlichiosis occur in Missouri, Tennessee, and Delaware. During 2009, a new *Ehrlichia* species, named *Ehrlichia muris eauclairensis*, was identified in humans living in the upper midwestern United States. It is vectored to humans by the blacklegged tick. There were 115 cases of ehrlichiosis caused by *E. m. eauclairensis* in the United States from 2009 to 2020 and no known fatalities (CDC 2020*b*).

People should seek medical attention if they develop symptoms of anaplasmosis or ehrlichiosis (CDC 2016). Both are difficult to diagnose, so medical physicians usually start patients on antibiotics before a diagnosis can be confirmed. Patients with ehrlichiosis are often clustered together in both time and space (Sidebar 3.3).

SIDEBAR 3.3 OUTBREAK OF EHRLICHIOSIS IN A TENNESSEE RETIREMENT COMMUNITY (STANDAERT ET AL. 1995)

During 1 week in June 1993, four men were hospitalized in the same local hospital; each complained of similar problems: fever, abdominal pain, vomiting, and a severe headache. Blood tests revealed that all had low counts of platelets and white blood cells. One patient developed acute renal and respiratory failure, followed by a coma. All four patients were diagnosed with acute ehrlichiosis and later recovered from their illnesses.

All four patients lived at the same retirement community in Cumberland County, Tennessee, which was adjacent to an 80,000 acre (32,389 ha) wildlife management area (WPA) (Figure 18.8). The community was located on 15,000 acres (6,073 ha) of wooded land and contained four golf courses. White-tailed deer and other wildlife were abundant in the community. All four patients remembered being bitten by ticks while at the retirement community.

An investigation identified seven more people from the county who had confirmed cases of acute ehrlichiosis during the prior six months. Six of the seven new patients also lived in the same retirement community as the initial four victims. Tests revealed that 12% of residents from that endemic community (Figure 18.8) were seropositive for *E. chaffeensis*. In another golf-oriented retirement community from the same area, only 3% of residents were seropositive. One difference between the two communities was that thousands of lone star ticks were recovered from the endemic community but only three ticks from the reference community.

A disease risk assessment was conducted among residents from the endemic community. Golfers were more likely to be seropositive for ehrlichiosis than nongolfers. Among golfers, those who retrieved golf balls that were hit off the fairway and into the tall grass or woods were 3.7 times more likely to be infected than those who just used a new ball. This was likely due to higher tick densities in these areas. Interestingly, poorer golfers had a higher risk of infection than good golfers. Apparently in this golfing community, keeping one's golf ball on the fairway is healthy.

Limiting exposure to ticks is the best means of reducing the risk of contracting anaplasmosis or ehrlichiosis. One example is illustrative. In communities where ehrlichiosis is endemic, golfers have a higher risk of infection than nongolfers, and poor golfers who could not keep their golf ball on the fairway were especially at risk because ticks were more common in the rough (Standaert et al. 1995). Rapid removal of a tick reduces the risk of infection but does not eliminate the risk entirely; a tick can transmit these pathogens within a few hours after attaching to a human. While most patients were infected from a tick bite, some anaplasmosis patients have contracted the disease after butchering an infected white-tailed deer (Bakken et al. 1996). There is no evidence that reducing populations of wild ungulates can decrease the risk of humans, livestock, or companion animals being infected with *A. phagocytophilum* or *Ehrlichia*.

3.6   RABIES

Rabies is a terrifying disease, owing both to its disturbing symptoms and fatal outcome. It is an ancient disease of humans and described in some of the earliest writings. Rabies is caused by a virus that belongs to the genus *Lyssavirus*, which are single-stranded RNA viruses with a distinctive bullet shape (Figure 3.14). All species

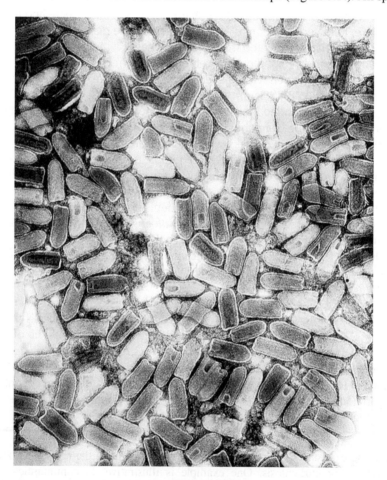

FIGURE 3.14   Image of several bullet-shaped rabies viruses (Fred Murphy and CDC).

of *Lyssavirus* have evolved to infect and replicate in mammalian nerves. There were three human cases in the United States during 2018; worldwide, rabies kills 59,000 people annually with 95% of deaths occurring in Asia and Africa. Half of the victims are children under the age of 15 (CDC 2019*a*, 2019*b*; WHO 2020*a*).

Most humans and other mammals are infected through the bite of a rabid animal, although infection can also occur when the virus is inhaled or crosses mucosal surfaces of the nose, mouth, and eyes; the virus cannot penetrate intact human skin. Once inside a host, the virus enters an incubation phase that may last days or months. During this period, the virus infects muscle cells and nerve cells near the wound and is vulnerable to the host's immune system. The infection then spreads along the neural pathways to the central nervous systems and the brain where the virus replicates rapidly. At the height of the infection, the virus infects the salivary glands, tonsils, and mucous membranes of the mouth, creating an opportunity for the virus to be shed in saliva. This enhances the probability that the virus will spread to a new host when an infected animal bites another (Rupprecht et al. 2001).

The first symptoms of rabies include loss of appetite, vomiting, diarrhea, and restlessness. There may be a tingling, prickly, or itchy sensation around the bite wound; these localized sensations are believed to result from a viral infection of the nerves. These sensations may progressively ascend toward the central nervous system. A weakness and trembling may develop in the affected limb. There are two types of rabies with different symptoms. Patients with furious rabies experience enhanced sensitivity to visual, auditory, and tactile stimuli. Other symptoms include muscle spasms that alternate with periods of agitation, rage, confusion, and lucidity. Hydrophobia (fear of water) and aerophobia (fear of drafts or of fresh air) may develop. Death occurs after a few days due to cardiorespiratory arrest. The other form, paralytic rabies, accounts for about 20% of human cases. Its symptoms are less dramatic and usually occur over a longer period than the furious form. With paralytic rabies, muscles gradually become paralyzed, starting with those near the site of the bite. A coma slowly develops and eventually death occurs. The paralytic form of rabies is often misdiagnosed, contributing to the underreporting of the disease (Beran 1994; Sudarshan et al. 2007; CDC 2019*b*; WHO 2020*a*). Once a rabies infection in humans has progressed to the point where symptoms of rabies appear, it is almost always fatal. Of the 33 rabies cases in the United States from 2002 through 2011, all but three died. The survivors included three girls aged 8-, 15-, and 17-years-old (Blanton et al. 2012). As of 2016, only 15 rabies patients worldwide have survived once symptoms were exhibited, all but one of the survivors had received a rabies vaccine prior to developing symptoms (Jackson 2016; WHO 2018).

All mammal species are susceptible to an infection of the rabies virus. Yet, very few species serve as reservoir hosts for the rabies virus because the virus kills its host so fast that there is not enough time for the virus to infect a new host. Strains of the rabies virus have evolved to be less lethal in specific mammalian hosts so that the virus can maintain itself by infecting other individuals before the virus kills the host.

Canine-strain rabies remains widespread in the developing world and has been documented in more than 90 countries that contain half of the world's human population. Dogs were responsible for vectoring the rabies virus to the person in 99% of human rabies cases worldwide. Public health programs have been successful in reducing cases of rabies by requiring all domestic dogs to be vaccinated against rabies. Vaccination programs have eradicated canine-strain rabies in the United States, Canada, Western Europe, Japan, and many parts of South America. Recommended vaccination programs for dogs and other animals usually involve two vaccinations a year apart, followed by a booster shot every third year. The main challenge in eradicating canine-strain rabies is to ensure adequate coverage of the dog population, which requires that 70% of all dogs be vaccinated (WHO 2018).

Almost 5,000 animals in the United States were found to have rabies during 2018 (CDC 2019a, 2019b); most (90%) of the rabid animals in the United States are wildlife species. The reservoir hosts for the rabies virus in the United States include raccoons, skunks, foxes, and bats. Raccoon-strain rabies is endemic in the eastern states; skunk-strain in the Great Plains and California; and fox-strain in Arizona, New Mexico, and Texas. Additionally, mongoose-strain rabies is found in Puerto Rico where mongooses are the reservoir host. The Arctic fox and domestic dogs are the reservoir hosts for rabies in the Arctic. Rabies in bats is caused by several variants of the rabies virus that have adapted to different bat species. Bats from the southwestern United States were more likely to have antibodies against the rabies virus (19%) than bats in the Northwest (7%), Southeast (7%), and Northeast (4%). In Canada, most animals identified as rabid were (92%) wildlife, 3% were livestock, and 5% were cats or dogs (CDC 2011c; Blanton et al. 2012).

A few people contracted rabies after visiting caves containing roosting bats. Rabid bats shed the virus in their saliva, and tiny droplets can be inhaled by people in the cave. Many U.S. rabies patients acquired the rabies virus from a bat and did not seek medical attention either because the patients dismissed the seriousness of the bite or were unaware that they had been bitten. The CDC (2019b) recommends that treatment for rabies should be initiated whenever someone has been bitten, scratched, or had mucous membrane exposure to a bat unless the bat has been tested for rabies, and the results were negative. Treatment for rabies is advised if a bat was found in a room where someone was sleeping unless the bat is available for testing.

Two rabies vaccines are available for use in humans to prevent rabies prior to a person being bitten or otherwise exposed to the rabies virus: Imovax Rabies[R] uses human diploid cells, and RabAvert[R] uses purified chick embryo cells. Preexposure vaccines against rabies are not recommended for the general public, but they are recommended for people with an elevated risk of infection. These people include wildlife biologists, veterinarians, veterinarian assistants, wildlife rehabilitators, animal control officers, animal handlers, mammalogists, and spelunkers who visit caves containing bat colonies (CDC 2019b).

Postexposure prophylaxis (PEP) is a vaccine protocol for people who have already been exposed to the rabies virus. It consists of a dose of human rabies immune globulin, which provides immediate antibodies against the rabies virus until the body can respond to the vaccine by actively producing antibodies of its own, and rabies vaccine given on the day of the rabies exposure, and then repeated on days 3, 7, and 14. For people who have never been vaccinated against rabies previously, PEP should always include administration of both human rabies immune globulin and rabies vaccines. This PEP is recommended for both bite and nonbite exposures, regardless of the interval between exposure and initiation of treatment (CDC 2019*b*).

One successful approach to controlling rabies in wildlife populations involves the use of oral vaccines. Switzerland tried this by placing virus vaccines in sealed blister packets and inserting the packets inside chicken parts. The chicken baits were distributed in the Rhone Valley and successfully stopped an impending outbreak of rabies (Rupprecht et al. 2001). This success led to an expansion of the oral rabies vaccine (ORV) program throughout Western Europe. During the 1990s, 8–17 million vaccine baits were distributed annually in Europe; this was successful in reducing the number of animals infected with rabies. Excluding bat-strain rabies, seven European countries have become free of rabies as a result of the oral vaccination programs (WHO 2018). Canada started an ORV program aimed at eliminating the Arctic fox variant of rabies from red foxes. For seven years, ORV baits were dropped from airplanes at a rate of 20 baits/km² in Ontario, with the result that this variant has nearly been eliminated from the province (MacInnes et al. 2001; Slate et al. 2009). The United States began an ORV program during the 1990s. It successfully eliminated the coyote variant from the United States during 2004 and the Texas gray fox variant in 2013. During 2019, over eight million ORV baits were distributed by WS across the eastern United States to prevent the westward spread of raccoon rabies (Figure 3.15); another million ORV baits were distributed in Texas to prevent the return of the canine strain from Mexico.

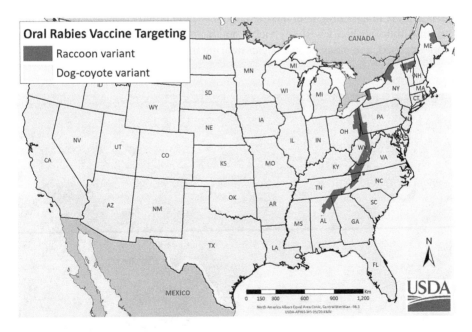

FIGURE 3.15 Map showing cooperative USDA Wildlife Services oral rabies vaccine distribution zones during 2019 targeting raccoons in the eastern United States and coyotes in Texas.

Source: Richard Chipman and used with permission.

3.7 INFLUENZA

Influenza is caused by three species of single-strand RNA viruses (Figure 3.16), influenza virus A, influenza virus B, and influenza virus C (hereafter referred to as type A, B, and C viruses). Humans are reservoir hosts for type B and type C viruses (hereafter referred to as human influenza viruses); these two types rarely infect other species although type B viruses can be found also in marine mammals. Type B viruses cause sporadic outbreaks of respiratory disease in humans, especially in children. Type C viruses are common in humans, causing no symptoms or only a mild illness. Type A viruses mainly infect birds, especially waterbirds, but some strains have developed the ability to infect humans and other mammals including horses, hogs, and marine mammals. It is the type A viruses that produce the flu that sicken and kill people every winter. Sometimes, type A viruses mutate into a more lethal virus that can easily spread from one person to another. When this happens, a worldwide disease epidemic (i.e., pandemic) occurs, which can cause widespread illness and death among people. The most famous pandemic was the Spanish Influenza of 1918 and 1919. This pandemic began during World War I (Figure 3.17); the first wave of this pandemic occurred during spring and summer of 1918, with a second wave occurring that fall, and a third a year later. By the time the pandemic ended during 1920, 25%–30% of the world population or 500 million people had become ill, and 50 million had perished – more casualties than occurred on all of the battles of World War I. In this pandemic, death usually occurred within a couple of days after the onset of illness; the cause of death was suffocation resulting from pneumonia or the lungs filling with fluid. Physicians could do little for their patients, and health authorities had few if any viable options to stem the epidemic. Quarantines were imposed, and many people began wearing masks in public. In some countries,

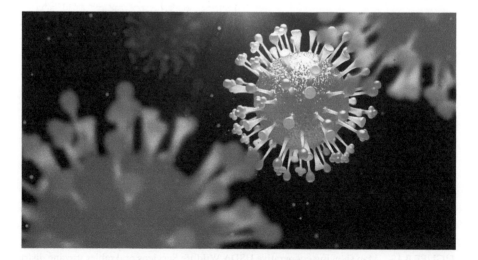

FIGURE 3.16 Three-dimensional illustration of the influenza virus.

Source: Pinkeyes, Shutterstock 1354876142.

laws were passed making it a crime to cough or sneeze in public without covering the mouth. It is this pandemic that haunts medical authorities today because they fear that it will be repeated (Johnson and Mueller 2002; Taubenberger and Morens 2006). Recently, the virus responsible for Spanish Influenza was isolated from frozen tissue obtained from three victims who died during 1918 (two U.S. solders whose lung tissue was archived and an Intuit woman who was buried in permafrost). When the virus was genetically sequenced, it was identified as the type A virus: H1N1 (Taubenberger et al. 2000).

Type A viruses contain two main proteins (antigens) on their outer surfaces: hemagglutinin (H) and neuraminidase (N); each influenza virus is divided into subtypes based on which copy of these two antigens it possesses. For instance, H5N1 and H1N1 are two different subtypes that differ because they possess different H antigens. In total, there are 16 known H antigens and 9 N antigens, and therefore, 144 potential subtypes of the type A virus. Human immune systems recognize influenza viruses by their antigens so that when a person is vaccinated or had a prior infection, the immunity does not extend to subtypes with different antigens. Additionally, type A viruses can mutate and change the proteins on their outer surfaces, using

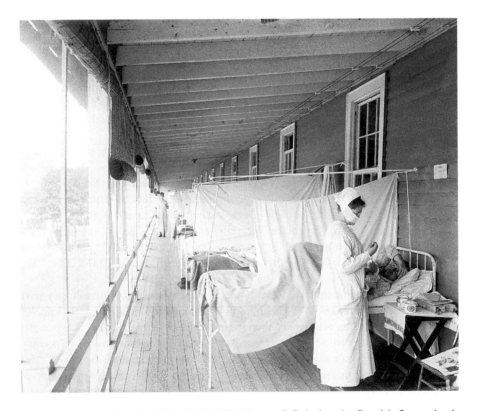

FIGURE 3.17 Walter Reed Hospital in Washington DC during the Spanish flu pandemic (1918–1919). There were so many patients that some had to be kept on the porch.

Source: Everett Collection, Shutterstock 242820250.

two different methods. The first occurs when two influenza viruses change genetic material, a process called antigenic shift. This can create new combinations of the H and N proteins. The second method (antigen drift) occurs when an antigen changes slightly due to a mutation. Antigenic shift and drift continually create new viral strains. In some cases, these changes allow the virus to become more virulent to its host species or be able to infect a new avian or mammalian species (WHO 2005; OSHA 2006; CDC 2011a; Reperant et al. 2012).

Poultry and domestic ducks and geese can become infected with either low or highly pathogenic strains of the type A virus. The low pathogenic strain produces only mild symptoms in birds. Highly pathogenic viruses only occur when a low pathogenic strain mutates into a highly pathogenic strain (CDC 2011b; Reperant et al. 2012). They are so deadly in birds that they cannot maintain themselves (they have no reservoir host). There have been several outbreaks of highly pathogenic strains during the last few decades. Medical authorities are concerned that in the future, one of the type A viruses will cause a pandemic resulting in hundreds of millions of people becoming sick and millions dying. To start a pandemic, an influenza virus needs to have three characteristics. First, the virus needs to be novel so that humans will not have any immunity against it. Second, the virus needs to be able to infect humans and cause illness. Third, the virus needs the ability to be transmitted easily from one person to another (i.e., highly contagious). Three influenza pandemics have occurred during the last century (1918–1919, 1957–1958, and 1968–1969). Influenza pandemics are the disease equivalent of a tsunami or tidal wave. They occur without warning, sweep through an area with devastating speed, and then disappear. While an influenza pandemic is unlikely to happen during any given year, they are recurring events and will occur in the future with potentially devastating health consequences.

Some type A viruses are able to maintain themselves by infecting pigs and cause respiratory diseases in pigs. These are known as swine flu viruses. These viruses are very contagious in pigs and can spread quickly throughout a pig farm. However, these viruses are not usually fatal in pigs. These same influenza viruses also occur in feral hogs, complicating the task of eradicating swine flu at a pig farm because local feral hogs can reinfect them. Normally swine viruses do not infect humans, but sometimes, they evolve the ability to do so. For example, the 2009 pandemic was caused by a H1N1 virus that was circulating in pigs (Reperant et al. 2009, 2012; CDC 2012b, 2013).

People should immediately contact a doctor if they think they suspect they have avian influenza or develop flu-like symptoms within ten days of handling flu-infected birds or who visited an area where there is an influenza outbreak. This is especially true for people who visited a farm or open-air market where there were live poultry. Two antiviral drugs can shorten the duration of influenza and reduce the risk of complications, but the drugs must be started within two days of the onset of symptoms to be effective. CDC (2012b) recommends that the drugs be used to treat patients with confirmed or suspected influenza who are hospitalized or have a severe or progressive illness.

3.8 WEST NILE VIRUS DISEASE

West Nile virus (WNV) is a single-stranded RNA of the *Flavivirus* genus (Figure 3.18). West Nile Virus Disease (WNVD) is defined as a human disease caused by WNV, including neuroinvasive diseases (i.e., infections of the central nervous system that progress into meningitis and encephalitis). WNV was first detected in Africa but spread to Europe and then North America. The first documented cases of WNVD in the United States occurred in New York City during 1999. How the virus crossed the Atlantic Ocean is unknown, but the strain was identical to a strain of WNV isolated from geese in Israel one year earlier. After reaching New York, WNV spread rapidly (Figure 3.19), reaching 44 states by 2002, where it sickened more than 4,000 people; of these, 2,942 developed neuroinvasive diseases and 284 died (Figures 3.20 and 3.21). From the United States, WNV quickly spread to other countries in the Western Hemisphere where it produced high mortality rates in avian species, as well as high rates of neuroinvasive disease among humans (Murray et al. 2010). During 2018, there were 1,657 neuroinvasive cases of WNVD among people living in the United States and 989 non-neuroinvasive cases (Table 3.1, CDC 2018*b*, 2019*a*).

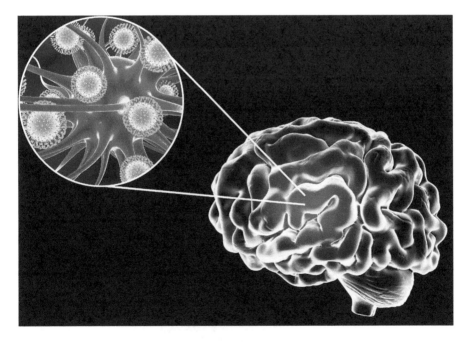

FIGURE 3.18   Three-dimensional picture of the West Nile virus attacking neurons in the brain.

Source: Kateryna Kon, Shutterstock 691709554.

Spread of human cases of WNF in the United States

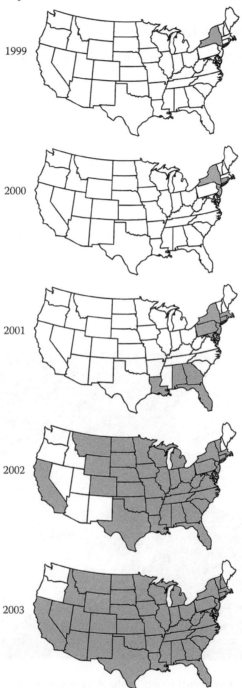

FIGURE 3.19   Map showing the spread of West Nile virus (WNV) disease across the United States during the five years following its introduction into New York City during 1999 (Conover and Vail [2015 and CDC WNV annual maps and data).

Source: Authors.

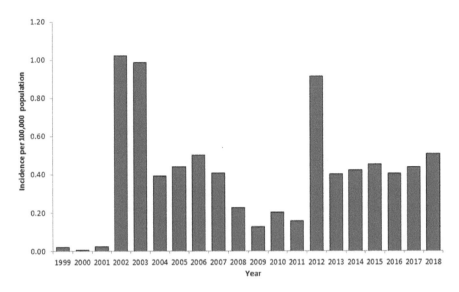

FIGURE 3.20   Annual changes in the incidence of West Nile neuroinvasive disease (number per 100,000 people) in the United States from 1999 to 2018 (CDC, www.cdc.gov/westnile/statsmaps/cumMapsData.html).

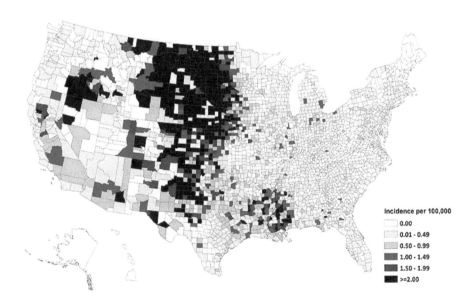

FIGURE 3.21   Map showing the incidence (number of cases per 100,000 people) of West Nile neuroinvasive disease in the United States from 1999 to 2018 (CDC, www.cdc.gov/westnile/statsmaps/cumMapsData.html).

Most people infected with the WNV do not become ill. Those who do may experience fever, headaches, muscle aches, vomiting, swollen lymph nodes, or a skin rash on the chest and back. Symptoms usually last for a few days or a few weeks and typically resolve on their own (Zeller and Shuffenecker 2004; CDC 2018*b*). Symptoms of WNV neuroinvasive disease include a stiff neck, severe headache, stupor, disorientation, confusion, tremors, numbness, convulsions, and coma. Some patients experience paralysis in their arms, legs, or breathing muscles; Some people stricken with the neuroinvasive disease die; survivors may suffer from long-term complications, which include fatigue, weakness, loss of memory, and inability to concentrate (Murray et al. 2010; Rossi et al. 2010).

Avian species, especially passerines, are the reservoir host for WNV; the virus is vectored among birds by mosquitos. American robins are the most important amplifying host for WNV in North America, but the virus has been detected in more than 300 bird species, including domestic chickens, turkeys, geese, and ducks (CDC 2018*b*). In Chicago, Illinois, 66% of mosquitoes infected with WNV acquired the virus from feeding on just a few avian species, including America robins (responsible for 35% of infected mosquitoes), blue jays (17%), and house finches (15%; Hamer et al. 2009). In Guatemala, the great-tailed grackle serves as a reservoir host. In Russia, the marsh frog serves as a reservoir host for WNV (Morales-Betoulle et al. 2012; Wheeler et al. 2012). Most birds are infectious for only four to six days; after which, either the bird's immune system has swept WNV from the blood or the bird has died (Komar et al. 2003; National Wildlife Health Center 2005; CDC 2018*b*). Lethality of WNV varies among avian species; mortality rates were high in American crows (95%) and blue jays (75%), while there were few deaths among mourning doves, European starlings, and feral pigeons. Reports of dead crows are often the first sign of an outbreak of WNV in an area. Since its arrival in North America, WNV has killed millions of wild birds and caused population declines of more than 50% in American crows (Figure 3.22), blue jays, chickadees, titmice, wrens, and thrushes in different regions of North America (Malkinson et al. 2002; Marra et al. 2004; Brown et al. 2012). Even in 2020, two decades after the arrival of WNV in North America, it is still having a consequential impact on some avian populations (Brenner and Jorgensen 2020).

Among mammals, horses are particularly susceptible to WNV. For this reason, horses are a good sentinel species for monitoring the appearance of WNV in an area because they often become ill before humans. Symptoms of WNV neuroinvasive disease in horses include muscle and muzzle twitches, aimless wandering, stiff walking, and balancing problems. One or both sides of the face may be paralyzed so that only one ear is erect. As the illness progresses, horses may lose the ability to stand; some horses collapse on their front legs, so they look as if they are praying. Many infected horses do not become ill from the WNV, but those horses that exhibit symptoms are usually killed by the infection (Marra et al. 2004; National Wildlife Health Center 2005; Farfán-Ale et al. 2006).

Almost everyone with WNVD has been infected from the bite of an infectious mosquito that earlier fed on an infected bird. WNV has been recovered from 62 different mosquito species in North America. However, *Culex* mosquitoes are the primary vectors because they are highly susceptible to infection, feed frequently on

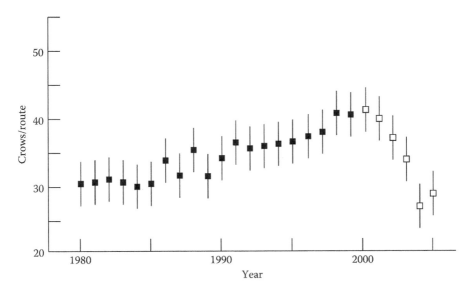

FIGURE 3.22   Change in U.S. population of American crows before (dark squares) and after (open squares) the arrival of WNV to the United States during 1999.

Source: This is Figure 21.6 in Conover and Vail (2015).

passerine birds, and survive long enough to transmit the virus. Many *Culex* also feed frequently on mammals. In some mosquito species, females can pass WNV to their offspring. *Culex restuans* and *Culex pipiens* are responsible for up to 80% of human infections of WNV in the northeastern United States (Anderson and Main 2006).

There is no specific treatment for WNVD, and most people recover on their own. Nonetheless, hospitalization is required for people who develop WNV neuroinvasive disease to provide the supportive care they need. Patients should seek medical attention immediately if they have a severe headache or are confused; these symptoms may indicate encephalitis or meningitis. Such cases are the most serious, and monitoring these patients is critical (Merck 2010; CDC 2020h).

The best way to protect yourself from WNV is to prevent mosquito bites by wearing long sleeve shirts, long pants, and socks and spraying bare skin with DEET insect repellents when outdoors. The risk of contracting WNVD increases with exposure to *Culex* mosquitoes, especially during a WNVD outbreak. The prevalence of WNVD is higher in urbanized and agricultural parts of North America where the mosquito species (e.g., *C. pipens* and *C. tarsalis*) are most abundant. Urban mosquito abundance can be reduced by draining water in buckets, barrels, flower pots, and wading pools. Tire swings should have a hole drilled in the bottom so that water will not accumulate in them. Rain gutters should be checked to ensure that water is draining properly. Water in bird baths should be replaced weekly (Kilpatrick 2011). Water levels in open marshes can be managed to reduce mosquito densities during outbreaks. Mosquito control districts may use insecticides to control either larva or adult mosquitoes.

3.9   CORONAVIRUSES

Coronaviruses are RNA viruses and so named because the spikes on the virus' surface appear "crown-like" and corona mean crown in Ancient Greek and Latin (Figure 3.23). There are many different coronaviruses, which have been divided into four subgroups: alpha, beta, gamma, and delta. These viruses infect both mammals and birds. The alpha group mainly infects birds and mammals, especially bats; the beta group infects bats, while gamma and delta groups primarily infect birds (Lau et al. 2019). Coronaviruses were recognized as a human pathogen during the 1960s. Common coronaviruses known to infect humans are two alpha viruses, 229E and NL63, and two beta coronaviruses, OC43 and HKU1. These may cause flu-like symptoms, but other coronaviruses cause serious illnesses.

The severe acute respiratory syndrome (SARS) is caused by beta coronavirus, SARS-CoV. It originated from the horseshoe bat in China, which is its reservoir host. The virus developed the ability to infect palm civets and then to infect humans during 2002. Humans were first infected in China's markets for live animals, where humans and palm civets are closely associated. It quickly spread to humans in North America, South America, Europe, and Asia (Lau et al. 2019). SARS-CoV is contagious and spreads from one person to another by the inhalation of tiny droplet of saliva from an infected person or indirectly from touching a surface that an infected person touched previously. Symptoms included fever, chills, and muscle aches. In some patients, the infection progresses to pneumonia and causes severe acute respiratory distress (hence the disease's name). Case fatality rate was 10%. Fortunately,

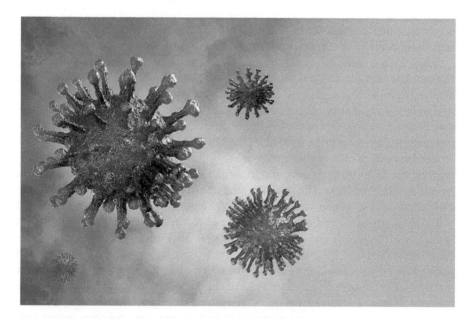

FIGURE 3.23   Three-dimensional picture of the corona virus.

Source: Corona Borealis Studio, Shutterstock 1624415920.

SARS did not last long; there have been no reported human cases of SARS since 2004 (National Foundation for Infectious Diseases 2020; WHO 2020*b*).

The Middle East respiratory syndrome (MERS) is caused by the MERS coronavirus (MERS-CoV). The virus originated in bats, and sometime in the distant past, evolved the ability to infect dromedary camels, which are now a reservoir host for the virus. The virus has been detected in camels in the Middle East, South Asia, and Africa. More recently, it developed the ability to infect humans; the first cases were detected during 2012 in Saudi Arabia. Most MERS cases become infected from contact with dromedary camels. Some human-to-human transmission has been documented, but the virus is not highly contagious and close contact with an infected person is usually necessary, such as providing care to an infected patient without personal protective equipment. From 2012 to 2020, 27 countries have reported cases of MERS, but 80% of cases have been reported in Saudi Arabia (WHO 2019; CDC 2020*a*).

Some people infected with MERS-CoV have been asymptomatic or only experienced mild respiratory symptoms similar to the flu, including fever and a cough. More serious symptoms include difficulty breathing and pneumonia. Among cases, the fatality rate is 35%, usually due to respiratory failure. From 2012 to 2019, there have been 858 human deaths from MERS (WHO 2019).

COVID-19 is by far the most serious threat to worldwide human health since the Spanish flu over a century ago. The "19" in its virus' name signifies that the first human cases were identified during 2019, occurring in Wuhan, China. Bats are the virus' reservoir host, but the virus evolved the ability to infect other mammal species, including humans. From Wuhan, the virus quickly spread around the world, including the United States. The first COVID-19 patient was detected in the United States on January 20, 2020; the patient had recently returned from China. The first U.S. "community spread" (first patient infected who had not left the country) was documented on February 26, 2020. The WHO declared COVID-19 a pandemic on March 11, 2020. The virus spread rapidly. Initially, there was a threat that the U.S. hospital emergency rooms would be overwhelmed and that there were not enough ventilators in some areas. To avoid this, many governors and mayors ordered that all businesses shut down except for essential services and that everyone shelter in place, meaning that everyone was to stay at home and not venture out unless essential. This succeeded in slowing down the virus, but not stopping it. By August 2021 when I am writing this, there were more than 36 million COVID-19 cases and over 600,000 fatalities in the U.S. Worldwide, there were over 200 million reported cases and 4 million fatalities, but worldwide data are conservative because many COVID-19 patients and deaths are not reported in several countries.

COVID-19 is highly contagious and almost every person infected with the virus contracted it from another person. An infected person releases tiny infected droplets into the air by coughing and sneezing. These droplets contain the virus, and another person can be infected by inhaling them. These droplets are heavier than air and land on surfaces. People can also be infected by touching these surfaces with their hands and then later touching their eyes, mouth, or nose. COVID-19 has spread to a few dozen dogs and cats in the United States as well as a couple of captive lions and tigers (CDC 2020*a*).

People infected with COVID-19 experience a wide range of symptoms. Most infected people, especially children and young adults, may be asymptomatic and not even know they are infected. However, these people can infect others, which makes the spread of the virus difficult to control. Other people develop symptoms two days to two weeks after being infected. Symptoms include fever, dry cough, shortness of breath, fatigue, muscle aches, loss of smell or taste, congestion or a runny nose, nausea, and diarrhea. The CDC (2020a) recommends that people seek emergency medical attention if they are having trouble breathing, persistent pain or pressure in the chest, confusion, inability to wake or stay awake, or bluish lips or face. These symptoms may indicate that the person is not getting enough air. Death may follow if the patient's ability to breathe weakens further. Hospitals can help avoid this by constantly monitoring a patient's breathing rate, oxygen levels in the blood, and other symptoms. If necessary, patients can be given oxygen or placed on a ventilator. The goal of medical intervention is to keep the patient alive long enough for the patient's own immune system to overcome the virus. This can take weeks.

To avoid becoming infected, health authorities advised people to stay at home as much as possible and avoid contact with other people. When away from home, people should wear masks over their face and nose and to stay more than 2 m away from others. Urging people to stay home and shutting down all nonessential businesses saved lives and prevented many people from being ill, but it devastated the worldwide economy. About 10% of workers in the United States filed for unemployment insurance after being furloughed or fired. The U.S. economy as measured by the Real Gross Domestic Product or GDP (a measure of the goods and services produced in the United States) shrank 1.5% during the first quarter of 2020 (when the pandemic was just beginning) and 32% during the second quarter of 2020; that was the largest decline since 1947 when record keeping began.

3.10 HANTAVIRUSES

Hantaviruses are a group of viruses in the family Bunyaviridae (Figure 3.24) and cause two diseases in humans: hemorrhagic fever with renal syndrome (HFRS), which is primarily a Eurasia disease, and hantavirus pulmonary syndrome (HPS), which is found in the Americas (Heyman et al. 2012). HFRS is caused by at least five viral species: *Hantavirus hantaan, H. seoul, H. dobrava-belgrade, H. saaremaa,* and *H. puumala* (hantavirus species are usually named after the place where first detected). Worldwide, 150,000–200,000 people annually develop HFRS. In China, there have been over 1.5 million cases with over 46,000 deaths since 1950. In Europe, over 10,000 cases are diagnosed annually with the highest number of patients occurring in Scandinavia, Belgium, and France. However, the actual number of Europeans infected with a hantavirus is five to ten times higher than the number of reported cases. In Europe, 1%–5% of the general population have antibodies for hantavirus, indicating that they have been infected in the past; this rate climbs above 20% in Finland, Bosnia, and Herzegovina (Shakespeare 2009; Zhang et al. 2010; Vaheri et al. 2011, 2013; Heyman et al. 2012). As the disease's name "hemorrhagic fever with renal syndrome" suggests, the main clinical signs of HFRS involve internal bleeding, a high fever, and infection of the renal system. In

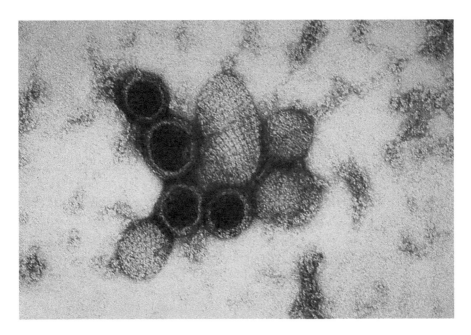

FIGURE 3.24 A photo taken with a transmission electron microscope of a hantavirus (M. L. Marintin, E. L. Palmer, and the CDC).

the most serious cases, the infection of the renal system results in kidney destruction and death. Fatality rates among cases hover around 1% (Zhang et al. 2010; CDC 2020g).

HPS is not a new disease but a newly identified one. It differs from HFRS because the infection occurs mainly in the lungs, not the renal system. HPS has two different stages. During the first stage, symptoms are similar to influenza and include fever, headaches, dizziness, chills, and muscle aches. The second stage occurs four to ten days after the first signs of illness and can begin abruptly. Second-stage symptoms include coughing and difficulty breathing, owing to the lungs filling with fluid. These symptoms result because the hantavirus attacks the capillaries in the lung, causing them to leak and fill the lung with fluid. There also may be a decrease in blood pressure, as the heart becomes less efficient. Lung and heart problems can quickly become life threatening. HPS patients should go immediately to a hospital (Mayo Clinic 2020a). There have been 728 cases on hantavirus in the United States through 2016 with an additional 18 cases of HPS reported to the CDC during 2018 (Table 3.1). Case fatality rate in the United States is 36% (Mertz et al. 2006; CDC 2019a; Mayo Clinic 2020a).

Rats and mice of the Sigmodontinae subfamily are the reservoir hosts for all HPS hantaviruses. There are at least 430 species of these rats and mice, and they are widespread across North and South America. Generally, a single species serves as the reservoir host for each hantavirus. The deer mouse is the reservoir host for Sin Nombre virus, which causes most HPS cases in the United States; annual changes in incidence of HPS among humans are correlated with changes in deer mouse populations (Sidebar 3.4). The deer mouse is common throughout North America and lives in habitat types ranging from desert to alpine tundra. As a result, the Sin Nombre virus occurs in all of these areas. The white-footed mouse is the reservoir host for the New York hantavirus; the cotton rat is the reservoir host for the Black Creek Canal hantavirus, and the rice rat is the reservoir host for the Bayou hantavirus. Nearly the entire continental Unites States falls within the range of one or more of these host species.

SIDEBAR 3.4 WHAT HAPPENED IN 1993 THAT CAUSED THE OUTBREAK OF HPS IN THE FOUR CORNERS OF THE UNITED STATES (HJELLE AND GLASS 2000; YATES ET AL. 2002)

Rodents in the Four Corners region of the United States probably were infected with hantavirus for a long time. Yet, HPS was not known to occur in the region until 1993 when suddenly an HPS outbreak struck 54 people living in the area. In the following years, less than five people were infected annually with HPS. This raised the question of why the outbreak occurred in 1993. One hypothesis was that deer mouse densities may have increased that year; in Europe, the incidence of HFRS in Europe was related to rodent numbers. Perhaps the same was true for HPS. Field research in the Four Corners region supported the hypothesis because the region had been in a multiyear drought. Then, in early 1993, heavy snows and rainfall helped drought-stricken plants and animals to revive and proliferate. The area's deer mice, with ample food, reproduced so rapidly that there were ten times more mice in May 1993 than in May 1992. With so many mice, it was more likely that mice and humans would come into contact and hantavirus would be transmitted from mice to humans.

In most years, precipitation in the Four Corners region is sparse, but rainfall and snow increase when there is an El Niño southern oscillation, which occurred in 1991–1992. This led to the prediction that outbreaks of HPS should occur shortly after an El Niño. To test this hypothesis, researchers examined what happened during the next El Niño southern oscillation, which occurred in 1997–1998. As predicted, there was an outbreak of HPS in the region in 1998–1999 with the number of HPS patients increasing fivefold. Furthermore, HPS patients were clustered in those areas experiencing the greatest increase in precipitation.

Rodents shed hantaviruses in their urine and feces. The virus can survive for up to ten days after being excreted by a rodent. Any activity that brings a person into contact with rodent droppings, urine, or saliva increases their risk of contracting HPS. Most people become infected from inhaling contaminated dust particles stirred up by some event, such as sweeping floors. People can also become infected if bitten by an infected rodent or when rodent urine or fecal material gains entry through broken skin or the mucous membranes of the mouth, nose, or eyes. HPS is not contagious CDC 2020g).

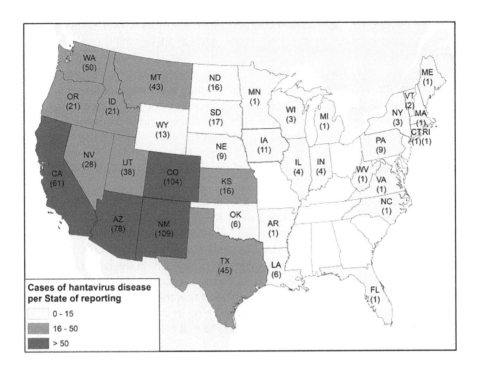

FIGURE 3.25 Location of hantavirus cases since its detection in the United States through 2018 (CDC, www.cdc.gov/hantavirus/surveillance/reporting-state.html).

Most (96%) of HPS patients occur west of the Mississippi River (Figure 3.25). People who live in buildings infested with infected rodents are especially at risk of being infected (Sidebar 3.5). Several methods are effective in reducing rodent numbers inside homes. Rodents can be excluded from building by sealing their access holes and removing brush, lumber, or other items from the yard that rodents can use for shelter. Because mice eat grains and other seeds, items made with grains, such as crackers, cookies, bread, noodles, breakfast cereal, and pet food, should be kept in rodent-proof containers. Mice traps can be baited with peanut butter, nuts, or grain. Nonetheless, trapping mice will be ineffective as long as they have access to food because any trapped mice will quickly be replaced by others.

SIDEBAR 3.5 TIMELINE FOR AN OUTBREAK OF HPS IN YOSEMITE NATIONAL PARK IN (NATIONAL PARK SERVICE 2012; BROWN 2013)

August 27, 2012. The U.S. National Park Service announced that three people visiting Yosemite National Park in 2012 had been diagnosed with HPS; a fourth person probably had the same disease (Figure 23.7). Unfortunately, two of the people died. All four people had stayed at the park's Signature Tent Cabins in Curry Village. The park started contacting other visitors who had stayed there and advised them to seek immediate medical attention if they developed symptoms of HPS.

August 30, 2012. The U.S. National Park Service announced that the number of confirmed cases of HPS among park visitors had increased to six.

November 1, 2012. The U.S. National Park Service announced that there were ten confirmed cases of HPS and three deaths from the disease among people visiting the park that summer. Nine of the patients had stayed at Signature Tent Cabins in Curry Village, and the other person had stayed 24 km away at Tuolumne Meadows and High Sierra campgrounds.

May 25, 2013. Fourteen percent of deer mice collected at Curry Village tested positive for hantavirus, a rate similar to other parts of California. Why so many people staying in the Signature Tent Cabins had contracted hantavirus was due to the cabins' construction. The tents consisted of two walls: an outer wall made of canvas and an inner wall made of drywall. In the space between these two walls, health inspectors found copious amounts of mice feces and shredded insulation. Health officials concluded that the unusually high morbidity rates resulted from mice and humans being in such close proximity. Yosemite National Park spent millions trying to make sure that their facilities were rodent proof.

People should avoid contact with rodent urine, droppings, and saliva, and they should thoroughly wash their hands after touching a contaminated surface. Entering or cleaning buildings that have been closed for an extended period increases the risk of being infected with hantavirus. Therefore, closed rooms and buildings should be thoroughly ventilated before entry, and care should be taken when cleaning rooms or buildings where rodent feces and urine have accumulated. Contaminated surfaces should be wet down with alcohol, disinfectants (e.g., 3% Lysol), or 10% bleach for at least 5 minutes. Surfaces should then be wiped with a wet towel rather than sweeping or vacuuming so that less dust will become airborne. After all dust and organic materials have been removed, clean surfaces should be disinfected a second time to kill any remaining virus (CDC 2020g; Mayo Clinic 2020a).

3.11 HISTOPLASMOSIS

Histoplasmosis is an infectious disease caused by the fungus *Histoplasma capsulatum*. In the United States, histoplasmosis is prevalent in the watersheds of the Ohio, Missouri, and Mississippi rivers (Figure 3.26). An estimated 40 million people in the United States have antibodies against *H. capsulatum*, indicating a prior infection. In Canada, the St. Lawrence River Valley is heavily infested. In Latin America, histoplasmosis is common in Mexico, Guatemala, Venezuela, and Peru (Wilson 1991; Ajello and Padhye 1994).

H. capsulatum is a dimorphic fungus that has two life-forms. The first form is a mycelia (mold) stage that occurs when the fungus is growing in soil enriched with

FIGURE 3.26 Micrograph showing the mycelium form of *H. capsulatum* (the thin branches) and the macrospores they produce, which are the round objects attached to the mycelium (Libero Ajello and the CDC).

bat or bird feces. The mycelia produces two types of spores: microconidia, which are small spores (2–5 μm in diameter), and macroconidia, which are large spores (8–15 μm; Figure 3.26). When growing in soil, many of the mycelia protrude from the ground and produce spores. Because of this, many spores are released into the air, especially when the soil surface is disturbed. If these spores are inhaled by a susceptible host, the warmer temperatures inside the lungs cause *H. capsulatum* to develop into the second form, which has the appearance of oval or round yeast cells with diameters of 1–5 μm; these regenerate by budding. The host's immune cells respond to the yeast cells in the lungs by engulfing them (phagocytosis) and carrying them to the lymph nodes. Once there, the yeasts travel in the blood to many other organs and infect them (Burek 2001; Kauffman 2007). Histoplasmosis is not contagious.

Approximately 500,000 people are infected with *H. capsulatum* annually (Kurowski and Ostapchuk 2002; University of Maryland Medical Center 2011). More than 90% of individuals infected with the *H. capsulatum* do not exhibit symptoms. For those who do, symptoms begin 3–17 days after inhaling spores. Symptoms are often nonspecific and include headache, fever, dry cough, and nausea (CDC 2020c). The Mayo Clinic (2020b) recommends people seek medical attention when they develop flu-like symptoms after exposure to bird or bat droppings. One percent of infected people will develop a serious, sometimes fatal, condition called disseminated histoplasmosis; it results when *H. capsulatum* spreads from the lungs to other organs in the body including liver, spleen, lymph nodes, bone marrow, eyes, skin, and central nervous system. The risk of developing disseminated disease is greatest for people who have weakened immune systems.

Starlings, grackles, red-winged blackbirds, pigeons, and cowbirds form large roosts in the fall and winter that contain thousands of birds. The soil beneath these roosts contains enough bird feces that *H. capsulatum* can thrive (Lenhart et al. 2004). *H. capsulatum* is viable in soil for years so that abandoned roosts and colonies can be a source of infection although no evidence of the roost or colony remains. In areas where *H. capsulatum* is endemic, the spores are released constantly into the air from contaminated soil, and wind can move the spores for kilometers, meaning that people distant from a bird roost can develop histoplasmosis. Hence, human cases of histoplasmosis occur regularly. Still, local outbreaks of histoplasmosis can result when activities, such as plowing, soil excavation, or building construction, disturb the ground surface, releasing large quantities of *H. capsulatum* into the air. Farmers, bulldozer operators, bridge workers, poultry farm workers, pigeon fanciers, demolition crews, construction crews, and landfill employees all have an increased risk of being exposed to *H. capsulatum* spores and developing histoplasmosis (Huhn et al. 2005; Wheat et al. 2007).

H. capsulatum thrives in soil enriched with bat feces. *H. capsulatum* has been isolated from several bat species, and infected bats shed the virus in the feces and carry it on their wings, feet, and body surface. Bats are known to infect the guano-enriched soil under their roost and colonies (Tesh and Schneidau 1966). For this reason, people who visit bat caves have an elevated risk of developing histoplasmosis (Sidebar 3.6).

SIDEBAR 3.6 EXPLORATION OF A CAVE RESULTS IN AN OUTBREAK OF HISTOPLASMOSIS (LOTTENBERG ET AL. 1979)

During February 1973, 29, people on a church outing explored a limestone cave located in central Florida. Two weeks later, one of the participants, an 18-year-old woman, sought medical attention for a respiratory illness that resulted in shortness of breath and cyanosis (i.e., a bluish skin color resulting from a lack of oxygen). The following day, another participant, an 18-year-old male, visited the local hospital with similar symptoms. Both were diagnosed with acute pulmonary histoplasmosis. Further investigation revealed that 23 of the 29 people on the outing had symptoms of cough, afternoon fever and sweats, chest pains, and shortness of breath on exertion. Histoplasmin skin tests were conducted on 24 individuals who were part of the group, and 18 people tested positive for past exposure to the fungus. Pulmonary histoplasmosis is often found in people who spend time in caves where bats roost (Figure 26.4 in Lottenberg et al., 1979). The experiences of this youth group were unique only in the number of people infected simultaneously.

Mild lung infections of histoplasmosis usually last only a few weeks even without treatment. People can develop histoplasmosis several times during their lives, but prior infections provide some immunity; hence, reinfections are less likely to be serious than the first infection (Wheat 2006; Wheat et al. 2007). There is no vaccine to prevent histoplasmosis. The best method to prevent histoplasmosis is to prevent the accumulation of bird or bat feces. Bird roosts can be moved if located at a site frequented by people. When bats are found roosting in a building, action should be taken to exclude them from it. Care needs to be taken not to trap birds or bats inside buildings by making sure that all of the bats or birds have exited the building before the last exit is sealed. A one-way door can also be installed that allows animals to exit a building but prevents their reentry.

3.12 BAYLISASCARIASIS OR RACCOON ROUNDWORMS

Baylisascaris is a genus of roundworms that reside in the intestines of several mammalian species. There are nine *Baylisascaris* species, but only *B. procyonis* causes serious diseases in humans. A raccoon infected with *B. procyonis* can shed millions of roundworm eggs daily in their feces (Figure 3.27). Raccoons often use latrines when defecating and are prone to locate their latrines at the base of trees or on top of raised horizontal structures, such as fallen logs, tree stumps, boulders, woodpiles, or porches. Raccoon feces and these microscopic eggs accumulate in these latrines (Sorvillo et al. 2002). Baylisascariasis is not contagious; instead, people, especially children, become infected when they get their eggs on food or their hands and then touch their mouths. Humans infected with these parasites can develop a disease referred to as baylisascariasis. I will use the term baylisascariasis when referring to the human illness and the term raccoon roundworms when referring to the parasite itself.

FIGURE 3.27   Adult raccoon roundworm removed from the intestine of a raccoon.

Source: Kevin Kazacos, Purdue University and used with permission.

Baylisascariasis is uncommon in humans, but it is a serious disease when it occurs. Ingested eggs hatch in the digestive system; the larvae then burrow through the lining of the intestines and are carried by the bloodstream to different organs (Figure 3.28). The growing larvae start to migrate through organs, muscles, and other tissue, causing inflammation and tissue damage (Sorvillo et al. 2002; Roussere

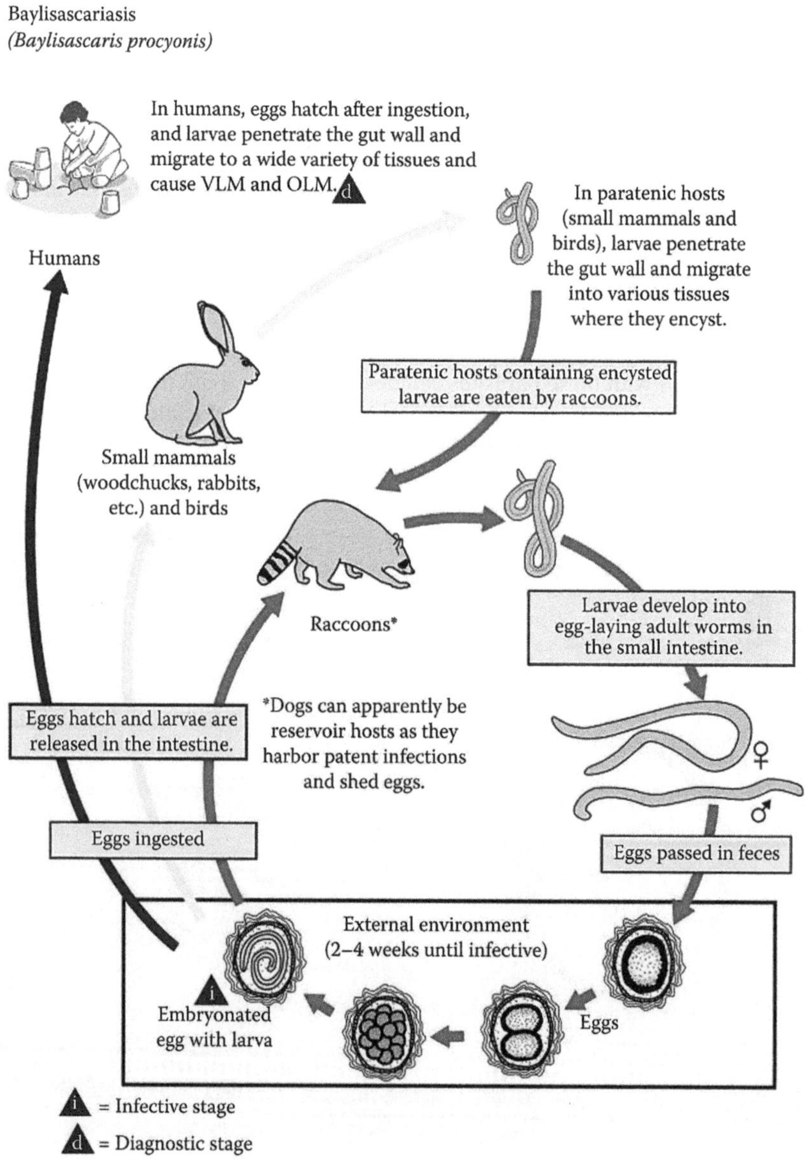

Baylisascariasis
(Baylisascaris procyonis)

In humans, eggs hatch after ingestion, and larvae penetrate the gut wall and migrate to a wide variety of tissues and cause VLM and OLM.

Humans

In paratenic hosts (small mammals and birds), larvae penetrate the gut wall and migrate into various tissues where they encyst.

Paratenic hosts containing encysted larvae are eaten by raccoons.

Small mammals (woodchucks, rabbits, etc.) and birds

Raccoons*

Larvae develop into egg-laying adult worms in the small intestine.

Eggs hatch and larvae are released in the intestine.

*Dogs can apparently be reservoir hosts as they harbor patent infections and shed eggs.

Eggs ingested

Eggs passed in feces

External environment (2–4 weeks until infective)

Embryonated egg with larva

Eggs

= Infective stage

= Diagnostic stage

FIGURE 3.28   Life cycle of raccoon roundworms.

Source: Alexander J. da Silva, Melanie Moser, and the CDC.

et al. 2003). Symptoms vary, based on the number of migrating larvae inside a person and which organs the larvae invade. Neurological problems can result from an invasion of the brain or central nervous system, a condition called neural larva migrans. This can result in lethargy, irritability, slurred speech, minor changes in vision, and a loss of coordination. Symptoms can quickly worsen and progress to seizures, paralysis, tremors, seizures, coma, and death. Neural larva migrans has a fatality rate of 36% in the United States, and many of the survivors are left in a vegetative state or have long-term neurological problems. Dozens of people in North America have been diagnosed with neural larva migrans; most were children under the age of two (CDC 2012a; Center for Food Security and Public Health 2012; Bauer 2013).

The illness, cutaneous larva migrans, results from the larva that invade the skin, causing a skin rash. Visceral larva migrans develops when the larva invades tissue and internal organs, including the lung, heart, or liver, producing abdominal pain. Ocular larva migrans results when roundworm larva invades the eye; dozens of U.S. patients have been diagnosed with ocular larva migrans. Symptoms include sensitivity to light and inflammation of one eye rather than both; blindness can result (Sorvillo et al. 2002; CDC 2012a; Center for Food Security and Public Health 2012).

Humans are an accidental host for raccoon roundworms; the parasite cannot maintain itself by infecting humans; in contrast, raccoons are a definitive host (i.e., the final host in which the parasite reaches sexual maturity). While raccoons are native to North and Central America, they were deliberately imported into Europe for pets or for the fur industry and free-ranging populations now exist in parts of Europe. Some of imported raccoons were infected with raccoon roundworm, and the parasite is now endemic in Europe. In Germany, up to 71% of wild raccoons are infected with raccoon roundworms (Kazacos 2001; Bauer 2013).

Many raccoons in the northeastern and midwestern sections of United States are infected with these parasites, but this is not true in southern states. The roundworms become an adult while in the intestines of raccoons and start to produce eggs that are excreted in the raccoon's feces. Roundworm eggs can survive for years in soil or other moist environments – long after all of the fecal material has decomposed (Kazacos 2001; Sorvillo et al. 2002). Several species of rodents, other small mammals, and ground-foraging birds visit raccoon latrines searching for food. These birds and mammals inadvertently consume the eggs of raccoon roundworms along with any food they find there (Overstreet 1970; Kazacos et al. 2011).

No vaccine is available to prevent infections of raccoon roundworm, and no drug is totally effective against the parasite. Anyone who suspects that they have baylisascariasis should seek immediate medical attention and inform the attending physician about any recent exposure to raccoons or their feces.

Steps should be taken to dissuade raccoons from spending time near homes. Dog or cat food should not be left in areas where raccoons can obtain it; garbage should be kept in raccoon-proof containers. Woodpiles, thick brush, and other dense cover that raccoons can use for den sites should be removed. Sandboxes should be kept covered to prevent raccoons from using them for latrines. Raccoon feces should be removed and latrines sterilized (Sidebar 3.7). Removal of the top 5–10 cm of soil at latrines helps decrease egg numbers, but some viable eggs will remain despite rigorous cleanup measures. The CDCb recommends that feces and soil contaminated with fecal material be removed with a shovel, placed into an inverted plastic bag, and then disposed by putting it in the garbage for disposal at a landfill. Raccoons should not be kept as pets.

SIDEBAR 3.7   CAN THE PREVALENCE OF RACCOON ROUNDWORMS BE REDUCED IN RACCOONS AND THEIR FECES BY A NONLETHAL APPROACH (PAGE ET AL. 2011; SMYSER ET AL. 2013)?

Many people are fond of raccoons and are opposed to killing them to control raccoon roundworms. Kristen Page and others tested the effectiveness of a nonlethal approach. Their study involved comparing eight untreated sites to eight treated sites where all raccoon latrines were removed and sterilized with a propane torch. Anthelmintic baits were then distributed monthly in the treated sites with the number of distributed baits being dependent on the local density of raccoons.

Before treatments began, raccoon roundworm eggs were found in 33% of all latrines. After the anthelmintic baits were distributed, the prevalence of eggs declined more than threefold in treatment plots, but prevalence did not change in untreated plots. One year after the onset of treatments, the proportion of white-footed mice infected with raccoon roundworm larva differed significantly between the treated sites (27% of mice infected) and untreated sites (38%). The results of this study indicate that the prevalence of raccoon roundworms can be reduced by using this nonlethal approach.

3.13   SCHISTOSOMIASIS OR SWIMMER'S ITCH

Swimmer's itch occurs throughout the world and is caused by several species of parasitic flatworms (family Schistosomatidae) including species of the genera *Schistosoma* that use mammals as definitive hosts. The disease can also be caused by species of the genera *Austrobilharzia*, *Gigantobilbarzia*, and *Trichobilharzia*. Swimmer's itch is an allergic reaction to the parasites burrowing through the skin; there often is an immediate tingling or prickling sensation that lasts about an hour (Chamot et al. 1998). The burrowing into the skin also produces reddish skin bumps that appear within minutes or hours of infection. The rash is accompanied by an intense itching sensation; the severity of the itching sensation increases with the number of parasites that burrow into the skin; each bump results from a single parasite burrowed into the skin (Figure 3.28). Symptoms usually end within a few days without medical attention. Most cases of swimmer's itch occur during summer because people are more likely to go swimming when it is hot (Leighton et al. 2000; Coady et al. 2006; Valdovinos and Balboa 2008).

The parasites have a complex lifestyle that requires them to parasitize two different species. Waterbirds and aquatic mammals are a definitive hosts and aquatic snails serve as intermediate hosts for all of these parasites. Hence, the parasite can only survive in water bodies that have snails and are used by waterbirds or mammals. A few studies have examined the prevalence of avian schistosomes among birds from North American lakes where swimmer's itch has been a problem. At Flathead Lake, Montana, schistosome eggs were found in 87% of fecal samples from common mergansers, 5% from gulls, and 3% from Canada geese (Loken et al. 1995). At Cultus Lake, British Columbia, almost all common mergansers shed schistosome eggs in their feces, but this was not true for other avian species including Canada geese, glaucous-winged gulls, and American coots (Leighton et al. 2000). The prevalence rate was 92% among tundra swans collected in the southwestern United States (Brant 2007). Along the coast of Connecticut, prevalence rates were 93% in herring gulls, 93% in ring-billed gulls, 82% in great black-backed gulls, 67% in Canada geese, and 28% in double-crested cormorants (Barber and Caira 1995). Some Schistosomatidae species use aquatic mammals, such as muskrats, beaver, and raccoons for definitive hosts (Bourns et al. 1973; CDC 2020*f*). All of these mammals have a propensity to defecate in water, allowing the shed parasites to infect aquatic snails (Figure 3.25).

Swimmer's itch is not contagious. Instead, humans are a dead-end host for the parasites: the cercariae that burrow into the skin of humans die. Consequently, little need exists for drugs to kill them. Instead, medical attention is designed to relieve the symptoms of the allergic reaction. Scratching the rash can result in a secondary infection if bacteria invade through the abraded skin; thus, patients should avoid the urge to scratch. If the itching sensation becomes overwhelming and lead to insomnia, a medical doctor can prescribe corticosteroids or antihistamines to lessen the itching (Chamot et al. 1998).

Children are more likely to be infected than adults because children spend more time in shallow water where the parasites are concentrated (Leighton et al. 2000; Mayo Clinic 2020*c*). The risk of infection can vary from one day to the next. Cercariae can only survive in water for a couple of days, so daily changes in infection rates probably relate to the number of cercariae released during the prior two days. More are released on warm days and when it is sunny. Cercariae have a propensity to swim upward and toward light so that they accumulate at the surface of the water (Soldánová et al. 2012; Kolářová et al. 2013). Because waterbirds are also on the water surface, these behaviors increase the probability that a parasite will find a waterbird to infect. These behaviors also explain the increased risk of a bather contracting swimmer's itch when there is an onshore wind; such wind blows the surface water and cercariae toward shore (Verbrugge et al. 2004).

One way to mitigate the risk of swimmer's itch is to reduce the populations of aquatic snails that serve as intermediate hosts for the parasites. At popular swimming ponds and lakes, some local governments have killed aquatic snails by applying copper sulfate or other chemicals to the water or using mechanical plows or rototillers that bury or crush the snails (Leighton et al. 2000). The risk of swimmer's itch can also be reduced by excluding mammals and waterbirds from popular swimming ponds or lakes. Biological control methods to reduce swimmer's itch include increasing the density of filter-feeding animals that can remove cercariae from the water or increasing the number of fish that eat aquatic snails. Nonetheless, there is little evidence that these methods can reduce the incidence of swimmer's itch (Soldánová et al. 2012).

3.14   SUMMARY

One unfortunate consequence of human–wildlife interactions is the opportunity for the exchange of pathogens that cause zoonotic diseases between humans and wildlife. Based on the most recent data, there are 210,597 human cases of zoonotic diseases in the U.S. annually. Worldwide, zoonotic diseases sicken hundreds of millions of people and kill thousands each year. These numbers do not include human cases of AIDS and HIV infections, COVID-19, influenza (avian flu), and salmonellosis. Numbers of human fatalites rise into the millions if AIDS, COVID-19, influenza, and salmonellosis are included. The toll on wildlife is unknown. Medical advances have made great progress in preventing and treating zoonotic diseases in humans. While some human-specific diseases have been eradicated, such as small pox, the eradication of zoonotic diseases are difficult because the wildlife population provides a future source for the pathogen if the pathogen was eliminated in humans. Health authorities warn that the question is not if a new disease pandemic will sweep the world, but when that will happen. When it does, the pathogen may well be an animal pathogen that has mutated so that it has the ability to become contagious. Recent examples include the pathogens responsible for AIDS, avian flu, and COVID-19.

Another consequence of zoonotic diseases is that they cause people to view wildlife with apprehension and fear. Although it was not covered in this chapter, millions of livestock and chickens are killed each year from wildlife diseases. This loss is greatest in developing countries where the threat of not having enough to eat is greatest.

3.15   DISCUSSION QUESTIONS

1. Lyme disease has been eliminated on some small offshore islands by eradicating all of the white-tailed deer on an island. Can we assume that a 50% reduction in a deer population will result in a 50% decrease in Lyme disease cases?
2. Should quarantines be used to try to prevent the spread of an epidemic? If so, how should it be enforced, especially considering that many people inside the quarantine area will try to leave to reduce their own risk of being infected?
3. Given the large number of human diseases that are vectored by ticks, should the United States and Canada devote billions of dollars to the mission of trying to eradicate ticks from North America?
4. Viruses are among the simplest forms of life. Do you think they were the first life forms that evolved on earth?
5. The rabies virus is uncommon compared to some other viruses. Why is it not more successful in maintaining large populations?
6. Humans are a dead-end host for the parasite that causes swimmer's itch? Why then do the parasites infect humans?
7. COVID-19 was able to spread rapidly and maintain itself in the United States because a large number of people were unwilling to wear masks? Why was this?

8. What can be done to reduce the risk of avian flu viruses that normally only infect birds from evolving the ability to infect humans and to spread from one human to another?

LITERATURE CITED

Abbott, A. 2006. Lyme disease: uphill struggle. *Nature* 429:509–511.

Ajello, L., and A. A. Padhye. 1994. Systemic mycoses. Pages 483–504 *in* G. W. Beran, editor-in-chief. *Handbook of zoonoses*, second edition. CRC Press, Boca Raton, FL.

Anderson, J. F., and A. J. Main. 2006. Importance of vertical and horizontal transmission of West Nile virus by *Culex pipiens* in the northeastern United States. *Journal of Infectious Diseases* 194:1577–1579.

AVERT. 2019. Origin of HIV and AIDS. http://avert.org/professionals/history-hiv-aids/orgin. Accessed 10 August 2021.

Bakken, J. S., J. K. Krueth, T. Lund, D. Malkovitch, K. Asanovich, and J. S. Dumler. 1996. Exposure to deer blood may be a cause of human granulocytic ehrlichiosis. *Clinical Infectious Diseases* 23:198.

Barber, K. E., and J. N. Caira. 1995. Investigation of the life cycle and adult morphology of the avian blood fluke *Austrobilharzia variglandis* (Trematoda: Schistosomatidae) from Connecticut. *Journal of Parasitology* 81:584–592.

Bauer, C. 2013. Baylisacariasis infections of animals and humans with 'unusual' round-worms. *Veterinary Parasitology* 193:404–412.

Beran, G. W. 1994. Rabies and infections by rabies-related viruses. Pages 307–357 *in* G. W. Beran, editor. *Handbook of zoonoses*. CRC Press, Boca Raton, FL.

Bharti, A. R., J. E. Nally, J. N. Ricaldi, M. A. Matthias, M. M. Diaz, M. A. Lovett, P. N. Levett, R. H. Gilman, M. R. Willing, E. Gotuzzo, and J. M. Vinetz. 2003. Leptospirosis: a zoonotic disease of global importance. *Lancet Infectious Diseases* 3:757–771.

Blanton, J. D., J. Dyer, J. McBrayer, and C. E. Rupprecht. 2012. Rabies surveillance in the United States during 2011. *Journal of the American Veterinary Medical Association* 241:712–722.

Bourns, T. K., J. C. Ellis, and M. E. Rau. 1973. Migration and development of *Trichobilharzia ocellata* (Trematoda: Schistosomidae) in its duck hosts. *Canadian Journal of Zoology* 51:1021–1030.

Bovet, P., C. Yersin, F. Merien, C. E. Davis, and P. Perolat. 1999. Factors associated with clinical leptospirosis: a population-based case-control study in the Seychelles (Indian Ocean). *International Journal of Epidemiology* 28:583–590.

Brant, S. V. 2007. The occurrence of the avian schistosome *Allobilharzia visceralis* Kolářová, Rudolfová, Hampl et Skíirnisson, 2006 (Schistosomatidae) in the tundra swan *Cygnus columbianus* (Anatidae), from North America. *Folia Parasitologica* 54:99–104.

Brenner, S. J., and J. G. Jorgensen. 2020. Declines of black-billed magpie (*Pica hudsonia*) and black-capped chickadee (*Poecile atricapillus*) in the North-Central United States following the invasion of West Nile virus. *Western North American Naturalist* 80:204–214.

Brown, E. 2013. Yosemite makeover seeks to keep hantavirus at bay. *Los Angeles Times* (May 25, 1913).

Brown, E. B. E., A. Adkin, A. R. Fooks, B. Stephenson, J. M. Medlock, and E. L. Snary. 2012. Assessing the risks of West Nile virus-infected mosquitoes from transatlantic aircraft: implication for disease emergence in the United Kingdom. *Vector-Borne and Zoonotic Diseases* 12:310–320.

Bunikis, J., J. Tsao, C. J. Luke, M. G. Luna, D. Fish, and A. G. Barbour. 2004. *Borrelia burgdorferi* infection in a natural population of *Peromyscus leucopus* mice: a longitudinal study in an area where Lyme borreliosis is highly endemic. *Journal of Infectious Diseases* 189:1515–1523.

Burek, K. 2001. Mycotic diseases. Pages 514–531 *in* E. S. Williams and I. K. Barker, editors. *Infectious diseases of wild mammals.* Iowa State University Press, Ames, IA.

Cantu, A., J. A. Ortega-S, J. Mosqueda, Z. Garcia-Vazquez, S. E. Henke, and J. E. George. 2008. Prevalence of infectious agents in free-ranging white-tailed deer in Northeastern Mexico. *Journal of Wildlife Diseases* 44:1002–1007.

Castro, M. B., and S. A. Wright. 2007. Vertebrate hosts of *Ixodes pacificus* (Acari: Ixodidae) in California. *Journal of Vector Ecology* 32:140–149.

CDC. 2011a. *Influenza type A viruses and subtypes.* www.cdc.gov/flu/avianflu/influenza-a-virus-subtypes.htm. Accessed 10 July 2013.

CDC. 2011b. *Key facts about avian influenza (bird flu) and highly pathogenic avian influenza A (H5N1) virus.* www.cdc.gov/flu/avian/gen-info/facts.htm. Accessed 10 September 2020.

CDC. 2011c. *Rabies.* www.cdc.gov/rabies. Accessed 1 May 2013.

CDC. 2012a. *Baylisascaris.* www.cdc.gov/parasites/. Accessed 23 December 2013.

CDC. 2012b. *Seasonal flu (influenza).* www.cdc.gov/flu/avianflu/. Accessed 23 December 2013).

CDC. 2013. *Avian influenza A (H7N9) virus.* www.cdc.gov/flu/avianflu/h7h9-virus.htm. Accessed 10 July 2013.

CDC. 2016. Diagnosis and management of tickborne rickettsial diseases: Rocky Mountain spotted fever and other spotted fever group rickettsioses, ehrlichioses and anaplasmosis – United States. *Morbidity and Mortality Weekly Report* 65(2):1–44.

CDC. 2018a. *Lyme disease vaccine.* www.cdc.gov/lyme/prev/vaccine.html. Accessed 26 July 2020.

CDC. 2018b. *West Nile disease: for health care providers.* www.cdc.gov/westnile/healthcare-providers/healthCareProviders-ClinLabEval.html. Accessed 3 August 2020.

CDC. 2019a. *National Notifiable Diseases Surveillance System, 2018 annual tables of infectious disease data.* www.cdc.gov/nndss/infectioustables.html. Accessed 1 August 2020.

CDC. 2019b. *Rabies.* www.cdc.gov/rabies/index.html. Accessed 29 July 2020.

CDC. 2020a. *Coronavirus 2019 COVID-19.* www.cdc.gov/coronavirus/2019-ncov/symptoms-testing/symptoms.html. Accessed 13 August 2020.

CDC. 2020b. *Ehrlichiosis.* www.cdc.gov/ehrlichiosis/index.html. Accessed 24 July 2020.

CDC. 2020c. *Histoplasmosis.* www.cdc.gov/fungal/diseases/histoplasmosis/. Accessed 23 August 2020.

CDC. 2020d. *Leptospirosis: health care workers.* www.cdc.gov/leptospirosis/health_care_workers/index.html. Accessed 29 July 2020.

CDC. 2020e. *Lyme disease.* www.cdc.gov/lyme/signs_symptoms/index.html. Accessed 16 July 2020.

CDC. 2020f. *Parasites – cercarial dermatitis (also known as swimmer's itch).* www.cdc.gov/parasites/swimmersitch/. Accessed 2 September 2020.

CDC. 2020g. *Tracking a mystery disease: the detailed story of hantavirus pulmonary syndrome (HPS).* www.cdc.gov/hantavirus/outbreaks/history.html. Accessed 10 August 2020.

CDC 2020h. *West Nile virus.* www.cdc.gov/westnile/index.html. Accessed 25 July 2020.

CDC. 2021. *HIV surveillance report* 32: 1–123. http://www.cdc.gov/hiv/library/reports/hiv-surveillance.html. Accessed 10 August 2021.

Center for Food Security and Public Health. 2012. *Baylisascariasis.* Iowa State University, Ames, IA.

Chamot, E., L. Toscani, and A. Rougemont. 1998. Public health importance and risk factors for cercarial dermatitis associated with swimming in Lake Leman at Geneva, Switzerland. *Epidemiology and Infection* 120:305–314.

Chapman, A. S. 2006. Diagnosis and management of tickborne rickettsial diseases: Rocky Mountain spotted fever, ehrlichiosis, and anaplasmosis – United States. *Morbidity and Mortality Weekly Recommendations and Reports* 55(RR04):1–27.

Coady, N. R., P. M. Muzzall, T. M. Burton, R. J. Snider, J. Saxton, M. Sergeant, and A. Sommers. 2006. Ubiquitous variability in the prevalence of *Trichobilharzia stagnicolae* (Schistosomatidae) infecting *Stagnicola emarginata* in three Northern Michigan lakes. *Journal of Parasitology* 92:10–16.

Conover, M. R., and R. M. Vail. 2015. *Human diseases from wildlife*. CRC Press, Boca Raton, FL.

Dantas-Torres, F. 2007. Rocky Mountain spotted fever. *Lancet Infectious Diseases* 7:724–732.

Dumler, J. S. 1994. Rocky mountains spotted fever. Pages 417–427 *in* G. W. Beran, editor. *Handbook of zoonoses*, second edition. CRC Press, Boca Raton, FL.

Eisen, R. J., J. Piesman, E. Zielinski-Gutierrez, and L. Eisen. 2012. What do we need to know about disease ecology to prevent Lyme disease in the northeastern United States? *Journal of Medical Entomology* 49:11–22.

Faine, S. 1994. *Leptospira and leptospirosis*. CRC Press, Boca Raton, FL.

Farfán-Ale, J. A., B. J. Blitvich, N. L. Marlenee, M. A. Loroño-Pino, F. Puerto-Manzano, J. E. García-Rejón, E. P. Rosado-Paredes, L. F. Flores-Flores, A. Ortega-Salazar, J. Chávez-Medina, J. C. Cremieux-Grimaldi, F. Correa-Morales, G. Hernández-Gaona, J. F. Méndez-Galván, and B. J. Beaty. 2006. Antibodies to West Nile virus in asymptomatic mammals, birds, and reptiles in the Yucatan Peninsula of Mexico. *American Journal of Tropical Medicine and Hygiene* 74:908–914.

Goyal, S. M., L. D. Mech, and M. E. Nelson. 1992. Prevalence of antibody titers to *Leptospira* spp. in Minnesota white-tailed deer. *Journal of Wildlife Diseases* 28:445–448.

Hall, S. A. 2011. Iceman autopsy. *National Geographic Magazine*. http://ngm.nationalgeographic.com/2011/11/iceman-autopsy/hall/test. Accessed 7 July 2012.

Hamer, G. L., U. D. Kitron, T. L. Goldberg, J. D. Brawn, S. R. Loss, M. O. Ruiz, D. B. Hayes, and E. D. Walker. 2009. Host selection by *Culex pipiens* mosquitoes and West Nile virus amplification. *American Journal of Tropical Medicine and Hygiene* 80:268–278.

Hayes, E. B., and J. Piesman. 2003. How can we prevent Lyme disease? *New England Journal of Medicine* 348:2424–2430.

Heyman, P., E. P. J. Gibbs, and A. Meredith. 2012. Bunyavirus infections. *In* D. Gavier-Widén, J. P. Duff, and A. Meredith, editors. *Infectious diseases of wild mammals and birds in Europe*. Wiley-Blackwell, West Sussex.

Hjelle, B., and G. E. Glass. 2000. Outbreak of hantavirus infection in the Four Corners region of the United States in the wake of the 1997–1998 El Nino southern oscillation. *Journal of Infectious Diseases* 181:1569–1573.

Huhn, G. D., C. Austin, M. Carr, D. Heyer, P. Boudreau, G. Gilbert, T. Eimen, M. D. Lindsley, S. Cali, C. S. Conover, and M. S. Dworkin. 2005. Two outbreaks of occupationally acquired histoplasmosis: more than workers at risk. *Environmental Health Perspectives* 113:585–589.

Jackson, A. C. 2016. Human rabies: a 2016 update. *Current Infectious Disease Reports* 18(11):38.

Johnson, N. P. A. S., and J. Mueller. 2002. Updating the accounts: global mortality of the 1918–1920 "Spanish" influenza pandemic. *Bulletin of the History of Medicine* 76:105–115.

Kauffman, C. A. 2007. Histoplasmosis: a clinical and laboratory update. *Clinical Microbiology Reviews* 20:115–132.

Kazacos, K. R. 2001. *Baylisascaris procyonis* and related species. Pages 301–341 *in* W. M. Samuel, M. J. Pybus, and A. A. Kocan, editors. *Parasitic disease of wild animals*, second edition. Iowa State University Press, Ames, IA.

Kazacos, K. R., T. P. Kilbane, K. D. Zimmerman, T. Chavez-Lindell, B. Parman, T. Lane, L. R. Carpenter, A. L. Green, P. M. Mann, T. W. Murphy, B. Bertucci, T. L. Goldsmith, M. Cunningham, D. R. Stanek, M. J. Yabsley, S. P. Montgomery, and E. Bosserman. 2011. Racoon roundworms in pet kinkajous – three states, 1999 and 2010. *Morbidity and Mortality Weekly Report* 60:302–305.

Kilpatrick, A. M. 2011. Globalization, land use, and the invasion of West Nile virus. *Science* 334:323–327.

Kolářová, L., P. Horák, K. Skírnisson, H. Marečková, and M. Doenhoff. 2013. Cercarial dermatitis, a neglected allergic disease. *Clinical Reviews in Allergy and Immunology* 45:63–74.

Komar, N., S. Langevin, S. Hinten, N. Nemeth, E. Edwards, D. Hettler, B. Davis, R. Bowen, and M. Bunning. 2003. Experimental infection of North American birds with the New York 1999 strain of West Nile virus. *Emerging Infectious Diseases* 9:311–322.

Kurowski, R., and M. Ostapchuk. 2002. Overview of histoplasmosis. *American Family Physician* 66:2247–2253.

Langholz, J. A., and M. T. Jay-Russell. 2013. Potential role of wildlife in pathogenic contamination of fresh produce. *Human-Wildlife Interactions* 7:140–157.

Lau, S. K., A. C. Wong, L. Zhang, H. K. Luk, J. S. Kwok, S. S. Ahmed, J. P. Cai, P. S. Zhao, J. L. Teng, S. K. Tsui, and K. Y. Yuen. 2019. Novel bat alphacoronaviruses in Southern China support Chinese horseshoe bats as an important reservoir for potential novel coronaviruses. *Viruses* 11(5):423. https://doi.org/10.3390/v11050423. Accessed 1 August 2020.

Leighton, B. J., S. Zervos, and J. M. Webster. 2000. Ecological factors in schistosome transmission, and an environmentally benign method for controlling snails in a recreational lake with a record of schistosome dermatitis. *Parasitology International* 49:9–17.

Lenhart, S. W., M. P. Schafer, M. Singal, and R. A. Hajjeh. 2004. *Histoplasmosis: protecting workers at risk*. National Institute for Occupational Safety and Health, Washington, DC.

Leptospirosis Information Center. 2009. *Leptospirosis*. www.leptospirosis.org. Accessed 15 September 2020.

LoGiudice, K., R. S. Ostfeld, K. A. Schmidt, and F. Keesing. 2003. The ecology of infectious disease: effects of host diversity and community composition on Lyme disease risk. *Proceedings of the National Academy of Sciences of the United States of America* 100:567–571.

Loken, B. R., C. N. Spencer, and W. O. Granath, Jr. 1995. Prevalence and transmission of cercariae causing schistosome dermatitis in Flathead Lake, Montana. *Journal of Parasitology* 81:646–649.

Lottenberg, R., R. H. Waldman, L. Ajello, G. L. Hoff, et al. 1979. Pulmonary histoplasmosis associated with exploration of a bat cave. *Amercian Journal of Epidemology* 110:156–161.

MacInnes, C. D., S. M. Smith, R. R. Tinline, N. R. Ayers, P. Bachmann, D. G. Ball, L. A. Calder, S. J. Crosgrey, C. Fielding, P. Hauschildt, and J. M. Honig. 2001. Elimination of rabies from red foxes in Eastern Ontario. *Journal of Wildlife Diseases* 37:119–132.

Malkinson, M., C. Banet, Y. Weisman, S. Pokamunski, and R. King. 2002. Introduction of West Nile virus in the Middle East by migrating white storks. *Emerging Infectious Diseases* 8:392–397.

Marra, P. P., S. Griffing, C. Caffrey, M. A. Kilpatrick, R. McLean, C. Brand, E. M. I. Saito, A. P. Dupuis, L. Kramer, and R. Novak. 2004. West Nile virus and wildlife. *Bioscience* 54:393–402.

Mayo Clinic. 2020a. *Hantavirus pulmonary syndrome*. www.mayoclinic.org/diseases-conditions/hantavirus-pulmonary-syndrome/diagnosis-treatment/drc-20351844. Accessed 1 August 2020.

Mayo Clinic. 2020b. *Histoplasmosis*. www.mayoclinic.org/diseases-conditions/histoplasmosis/symptoms-causes/syc-20373495. Accessed 1 August 2020.

Mayo Clinic. 2020c. *Swimmers itch*. www.mayoclinic.org/diseases-conditions/swimmersitch/symptoms-causes/syc-20355043. Accessed 1 August 2020.

McDade, J. E., and V. F. Newhouse. 1986. Natural history of *Rickettsia rickettsii. Annual Review of Microbiology* 40:287–309.

Medline Plus. 2010. *Leptospirosis.* www.nlm.nih.gov/medlineplus/ency/article/001376.htm. Accessed 1 June 2012.

Merck. 2010. *Merck veterinary manual*, tenth edition. Merck, Whitehouse Station, NJ.

Mertz, G. J., B. Hjelle, M. Crowley, G. Iwamoto, V. Tomicic, and P. A. Vial. 2006. Diagnosis and treatment of new world hantavirus infections. *Current Opinion in Infectious Diseases* 19:437–442.

Morales-Betoulle, M. E., N. Komar, N. A. Panella, D. Alvarez, M. R. Lopez, J. L. Betoulle, S. M. Sosa, M. L. Müller, A. M. Kilpatrick, R. S. Lanciotti, and B. W. Johnson. 2012. West Nile virus ecology in a tropical ecosystem in Guatemala. *American Journal of Tropical Medicine and Hygiene* 88:116–126.

Murray, K. O., E. Mertens, and P. Despres. 2010. West Nile virus and its emergence in the United States of America. *Veterinary Research* 41:67–80.

National Foundation for Infectious Diseases. 2020. *Coronaviruses.* www.nfid.org/infectious-diseases/coronaviruses/. Accessed 25 August 2020.

National Park Service. 2012. Hantavirus in Yosemite. http://www.nps.gov/ose/planyourvisit/hantafaq.htm. Accessed 26 July 2013.

National Wildlife Health Center. 2005. *West Nile virus.* www.usgs.gov/disease_information/west_nile_virus/. Accessed 23 December 2013.

Nature. 2006. When is a vaccine safe. *Nature* 439:509.

New, J. C., Jr., W. G. Wathen, and S. Dlutkowski. 1993. Prevalence of *Leptospira* antibodies in white-tailed deer, Cades Cove, Great Smoky Mountains National Park, Tennessee, USA. *Journal of Wildlife Diseases* 29:561–567.

Oliver, J. H., Jr., T. Lin, L. Gao, K. L. Clark, C. W. Banks, L. A. Durden, A. M. James, and F. W. Chandler. 2003. An enzootic transmission cycle of *Lyme borreliosis* spirochetes in the southeastern United States. *Proceedings of the National Academy of Sciences of the United States of America* 100:11642–11645.

OSHA. 2006. *OSHA guidance update on protecting employees from avian flu (avian influenza) viruses.* www.osha.gov. Accessed 10 July 2013.

Overstreet, R. M. 1970. *Baylisascaris procyonis* (Sefanski and Zarnowski, 1951) from kinkajou, *Potos flavus*, in Colombia. *Proceedings of the Helminthological Society of Washington* 37:192–193.

Page, K., J. C. Beasley, Z. H. Olsen, T. J. Smyser, et al. 2011. Reducing *Baylisascaris procyonis* roundworm larvae in raccoon latrines. *Emerging Infectious Diseases* 17:90–93.

Puliyath, G., and S. Singh. 2012. Leptospirosis in pregnancy. *European Journal of Clinical Microbiology and Infectious Diseases* 31:2491–2496.

Reperant, L. A., A. D. M. E. Osterhaus, and T. Kuiken. 2012. Influenza virus infections. *In* D. Gavier-Widen, J. P. Duff, and A. Meredith, editors. *Infectious diseases of the wild mammals and birds in Europe.* Wiley-Blackwell, West Sussex.

Reperant, L. A., G. F. Rimmelzwaan, and T. Kuiken. 2009. Avian influenza viruses in mammals. *Revue Scientifique et Technique* 28:137–159.

Rossi, S. L., T. M. Ross, and J. D. Evans. 2010. West Nile virus. *Clinical Laboratory Medicine* 30:47–65.

Roussere, G. P., W. J. Murray, C. B. Raudenbush, M. J. Kutilek, D. J. Levee, and K. R. Kazacos. 2003. Racoon roundworm eggs near homes and risk for larva migrans disease, California communities. *Emerging Infectious Diseases* 9:1516–1522.

Rupprecht, C. E., K. Stöhr, and C. Meredith. 2001. Rabies. *In* E. S. Williams and I. K. Barker, editors. *Infectious diseases of wild mammals*, third edition. Blackwell, Ames, IA.

Shakespeare, M. 2009. *Zoonoses*, second edition. Pharmaceutical Press, London.

Shotts, E. B., Jr., C. L. Andrews, and T. W. Harvey. 1975. Leptospirosis in selected wild mammals of the Florida Panhandle, and Southwestern Georgia. *Journal of the American Veterinary Medical Association* 167:587–589.

Shotts, E. B., Jr., and F. A. Hayes. 1970. Leptospiral antibodies in white-tailed deer of the southeastern United States. *Journal of Wildlife Diseases* 6:295–298.

Slate, D., T. P. Algeo, K. M. Nelson, R. B. Chipman, D. Donovan, J. D. Blanton, M. Niezgoda, and C. E. Rupprecht. 2009. Oral rabies vaccination in North America: opportunities, complexities, and challenges. *PLoS Neglected Tropical Diseases* 3(12):1–8.

Smith, T. C. 2013. *Nature's bioterrorists agents: just how bad is the new bird flu.* www.slate. com/articles/health_and_science/medical_examiner/2013/04/the_h7n9_bird_flu_in_ china_how_dangerous_is_ it.html. Accessed 10 July 2013.

Smyser, T. J., L. K. Page, S. A. Johnson, C. M. Hudson, et al. 2013. Management of raccoon roundworm in free-ranging raccoon populationds via anthelmintic baiting. *Journal of Wildlife Management* 77:1372–1379.

Sohn, E. 2011. *Lyme disease: where is the vaccine?* http://discovery.com/human/lyme-disease-ticks-caccine-110617.html. Accessed 1 July 2012.

Soldánová, M., C. Selbach, M. Kalbe, A. Kostadinova, and B. Sures. 2012. Swimmer's itch: etiology, impact, and risk factors in Europe. *Trends in Parasitology* 29:65–74.

Sorvillo, F., L. R. Ash, O. G. W. Berlin, J. Yatabe, C. Degiorgio, and S. A. Morse. 2002. *Baylisascaris procyonis*: an emerging helminthic zoonosis. *Emerging Infectious Diseases* 8:355–359.

Standaert, S. M., J. E. Dawson, W. Schaffner, J. E. Childs, K. L. Biggie, J. Singleton, Jr., R. R. Gerhardt, M. L. Knight, and R. H. Hutcheson. 1995. Ehrlichiosis in a golf-oriented retirement community. *New England Journal of Medicine* 333:420–425.

Sudarshan, M. K., S. N. Madhusudana, B. J. Mahendra, N. S. N. Rao, D. A. Narayana, S. A. Rahman, F. X. Meslin, D. Lobo, and K. Ravikumar. 2007. Assessing the burden of human rabies in India: results of a national multi-center epidemiological survey. *International Journal of Infectious Disease* 11:29–35.

Swei, A., R. S. Ostfeld, R. S. Lane, and C. J. Briggs. 2011. Impact of the experimental removal of lizards on Lyme disease risk. *Proceedings of the Royal Society B* 278:2970–2978.

Takafuji, E. T., J. W. Kirkpatrick, R. N. Miller, J. J. Karwaki, P. W. Kelley, M. R. Grey, K. M. McNeill, H. L. Timboe, R. E. Kane, and J. L. Sanchez. 1984. An efficacy trial of doxycycline chemoprophylaxis against leptospirosis. *New England Journal of Medicine* 310:497–500.

Taubenberger, J. K., and D. M. Morens. 2006. 1918 influenza: the mother of all pandemics. *Emerging Infectious Diseases* 12:15–22.

Taubenberger, J. K., A. H. Reid, and T. G. Fanning. 2000. The 1918 influenza virus: a killer comes into view. *Virology* 274:241–245.

Tesh, R. B., and J. D. Schneidau, Jr. 1966. Experimental infection of North American insectivorous bats (*Tadarida brasilensis*) with *Histoplasma capsulatum. American Journal of Tropical Medicine and Hygiene* 15:544–550.

Thomas, R. J., J. S. Dumler, and J. A. Carlyon. 2009. Current management of human granulocytic anaplasmosis, human monocytic ehrlichiosis and *Ehrlichia ewingii* ehrlichiosis. *Expert Review of Anti-Infective Therapy* 7:709–722.

University of Maryland Medical Center. 2011. *Histoplasmosis.* www.umm.edu/health/medical/altmed/condition/histoplasmosis.html. Accessed 23 December 2013.

Vaheri, A., H. Henttonen, L. Voutilainen, J. Mustonen, T. Sironen, and O. Vapalahti. 2013. Hantavirus infections in Europe and their impact on public health. *Reviews in Medical Virology* 23:35–49.

Vaheri, A., J. N. Mills, C. F. Spiropoulou, and B. Hjelle. 2011. Hantaviruses. Pages 307–322 *in* S. R. Palmer, L. Soulsby, P. R. Torgerson, and D. W. G. Brown, editors. *Oxford textbook of zoonoses*, second edition. Oxford University Press, New York.

Valdovinos, C., and C. Balboa. 2008. Cercarial dermatitis and lake eutrophication in South-Central Chile. *Epidemiology and Infection* 136:391–394.

Verbrugge, L. M., J. J. Rainey, R. L. Reimink, and H. D. Blankespoor. 2004. Prospective study of swimmer's itch incidence and severity. *Journal of Parasitology* 90:697–704.

Victoriano, A. F. B., L. D. Smythe, N. Gloriani-Barzaga, L. L. Cavinta, T. Kasai, K. Limpakarnjanarat, B. L. Ong, G. Gonal, J. Hall, C. A. Coulombe, and Y. Yanagihara. 2009. Leptospirosis in the Asia Pacific region. *BMC Infectious Diseases* 9:147.

Wheat, L. J. 2006. Histoplasmosis: a review for clinicians from non-endemic areas. *Mycoses* 49:274–282.

Wheat, L. J., A. G. Freifeld, M. B. Kleiman, J. W. Baddley, D. S. McKinsey, J. E. Loyd, and C. A. Kauffman. 2007. Clinical practice guidelines for the management of patients with histoplasmosis: 2007 update by the infectious disease society of America. *Clinical Infectious Diseases* 45:807–825.

Wheeler, S. S., M. P. Vineyard, L. W. Woods, and W. K. Reisen. 2012. Dynamics of West Nile virus persistence in house sparrows (*Passer domesticus*). *PLoS Neglected Tropical Diseases* 6(10):e1860.

WHO. 2003. *Human leptospirosis: guidance for diagnosis, surveillance and control.* World Health Organization. Geneva, Switzerland.

WHO. 2005. *Avian influenza: assessing the pandemic threat, WHO/CDS/2005.29.* World Health Organization, Geneva, Switzerland.

WHO. 2018. *WHO expert consultation on rabies: third report*, volume 1012. World Health Organization, Geneva, Switzerland.

WHO. 2019. *Middle East respiratory syndrome.* World Health Organization, Geneva, Switzerland. www.who.int/health-topics/middle-east-respiratory-syndrome-coronavirus-mers#tab=tab_1. Accessed 22 August 2020.

WHO. 2020a. *Rabies.* www.who.int/health-topics/rabies#tab=tab_1. Accessed 29 July 2020.

WHO. 2020b. *Severe acute respiratory syndrome.* World Health Organization, Geneva, Switzerland. www.who.int/health-topics/severe-acute-respiratory-syndrome#tab=tab_1. Accessed 15 August 2020. HIV/AIDS in the United States.

Wikipedia. 2021. HIV/AIDS in the United States. https://en.wikipedia.org/wiki/HIV/AIDS_in_the_United_States#:~:text=13%20External%20links,Mortality%20and%20morbidity,United%20States%20die%20each%20year. Accessed 8 August 2021.

Wilson, M. E. 1991. *A world guide to infections: diseases, distribution, diagnosis.* Oxford University Press, Oxford.

Yates, T. L., J. N. Mills, C. A. Parmenter, T. G. Ksiazek, et al. 2002. The ecoogy and evolutionary history of an emergent disease: hantavirus pulmonary syndrome. *BioScience* 52:989–998.

Zeller, H. G., and I. Shuffenecker. 2004. West Nile virus: an overview of its spread in Europe and the Mediterranean Basin in contrast to its spread in the Americas. *European Journal of Clinical Microbiology and Infectious Diseases* 23:147–156.

Zhang, Y. Z., Y. Zou, Z. F. Fu, and A. Plyusnin. 2010. Hantavirus infections in humans and animals, China. *Emerging Infectious Diseases* 16:1195–1203.

4 Economics

"We haven't the money, so we've got to think."

– Lord Rutherford

"Ask five economists a question and you'll get five different answers – six if one went to Harvard."

– Edgar Fiedler

"If you put the federal government in charge of the Sahara Desert, in five years they would be a shortage of sand."

– Milton Friedman

4.1 WHY IS IT IMPORTANT TO HAVE ECONOMIC DATA ABOUT HUMAN–WILDLIFE CONFLICTS?

Wildlife causes a myriad of problems (e.g., deer-automobile collisions, diseases, and reduced agricultural productivity). Because of this, making rational decisions about how to manage wildlife is difficult. For instance, if we do not know how much damage deer are causing, how can we determine the optimal deer population in terms of maximizing its value to society? Lack of data makes it difficult to prioritize projects or to allocate resources to solve wildlife problems effectively. Are we better off spending money trying to reduce deer–automobile collisions or bird–airplane collisions? Should the government health service use its funds to control Lyme disease or rabies? Do coyotes kill enough sheep to justify the U.S. government spending $10 million a year to kill coyotes? These questions can only be answered by knowing the monetary losses caused by wildlife. For example, Brewster et al. (2019) compared the cost-effectiveness of several methods to protect calves from coyote predators when used alone and in combination with each other and at varying intensities of use. The scientists found that most cost-efficient was a combination of use of snares and livestock-guarding animals and that management techniques were most cost-effective when the technique is used sparingly. Rust et al. (2013) found that 91% of South African farms that adopted Anatolian guard dogs had no further livestock losses to predators, resulting in a savings of $3,189/farm. The use of these guard dogs sounds like a great success, but the annual cost to maintain a guarding dog was $2,780, so the costs were similar to the benefits: not a strong endorsement for the use of guarding dogs in South Africa.

Amundson et al. (2013) provide another excellent example of what can be achieved through an economic analysis. They trapped mesocarnivores on township-size (93 km^2) areas in North Dakota to increase mallard populations. The trappers increased nest success rates and mallard numbers by 140 annually at a cost of $72 each for each saved duck; an additional cost was the loss of 245 predators each year. Armed with such information, wildlife managers can determine if the costs are justified. In this example, Amundson et al. (2013) did not think that the predator removal effort was cost-effective.

4.2   CAN ECONOMICS BE USED TO ASSESS THE VALUE OF WILDLIFE?

Wildlife provide many types of benefits to people, some of which are intangible and cannot be quantified but, nevertheless, are real. Because so many wildlife benefits are intangible, wildlife biologists are reluctant to discuss the economics of wildlife, less they devalue the animals. But this is counter-productive as it conveys the impression that wildlife has no economic value. A better approach is to try to assess the economic value of wildlife openly while keeping in mind that, in addition to monetary value, wildlife provides many important, intangible benefits.

Monetary benefits of wildlife are those that can be expressed in dollars. Monetary values are obtained in a free-market system, where the price is set through open negotiations between willing sellers, who want to obtain the highest possible price, and willing buyers, who want to pay as little as possible. If the item is easily obtained, then there will be many sellers and the price will decline. Alternatively, if an item is both uncommon and demanded by many people, the many potential buyers will compete against each other to purchase the item, increasing the item's price.

The economic value of wildlife differs for everyone and is based on their personal perspective. Consider, for example, a local deer herd. Its economic value to a hunter is reflected by how much money this person is willing to pay for the right to hunt deer. For a landowner, the economic value of deer could be determined by how much income he or she can obtain by leasing the hunting rights to the land to a deer hunter. For a local community, it can reflect the amount of money spent in local businesses by tourists and hunters, who pay for lodging, meals, hunting equipment, entertainment, and supplies. For a state wildlife agency, it is the amount of money it collects from hunting licenses. Obviously, when speaking of the economic importance of wildlife, we must always specify whose perspective we are considering. Likewise, the costs of wildlife damage do not fall evenly on everyone. As an example, damage by blackbirds will be a much greater problem for sunflower growers than for other people.

Economic analyses also vary depending upon the question being addressed. If we are assessing the value of waterfowl to hunters in the United States, we might randomly sample duck hunters and ask them how much money they would be willing to pay, rather than give up the right to hunt waterfowl for a year. By multiplying the mean value that hunters would be willing to pay by the number of waterfowl hunters in the United States, we could gain an approximation of the value of waterfowl hunting. However, if we are debating whether it is worthwhile to spend a million dollars for habitat improvements to increase duck populations and hunter success, then the appropriate question is: how much money would a duck hunter be willing to spend to harvest one more duck during a day of hunting? Indeed, if the money is not spent, the hunter can still go hunting and have success, but perhaps with slightly less success than if the habitat improvements were not made. The monetary value of shooting one extra duck could be multiplied by the expected increase in duck numbers that would result from the habitat improvements. The resulting value can be considered the rate of return or the "interest" earned annually on the money invested in habitat improvements. We can then decide whether making the habitat improvements would be a wise economic investment. This type of economic approach is referred to as a marginal value analysis.

4.3   HOW CAN THE POSITIVE VALUES OF WILDLIFE BE MEASURED?

There are several ways to assess the economic values of wildlife. Listed below are six methods commonly employed by economists. This list is not complete but rather provides a sample of the range of techniques that can be used to measure economic values. An excellent review of the different economic methods of assessing value is Schwabe and Schuhmann (2002).

4.3.1   MONEY SPENT

People spend money when they take a trip to hunt or view wildlife or to fish. For a fishing trip, the costs might include fishing license fees, fishing equipment and supplies, clothing, meals, lodging, gas, wear on the car, etc. If one adds up all of the money that someone spends while fishing, then the value or enjoyment that this individual derives from fishing must be higher than his or her costs; otherwise, he or she would not do it. The actual value is the enjoyment one obtains from fishing, and it may be several times higher than the amount expended (Figure 4.1). Therefore,

FIGURE 4.1   People derive much pleasure from spending a day fishing.

Source: santypan, Shutterstock 493318369.

this method underestimates the true value of wildlife, but it does provide a solid, conservative estimate of value.

4.3.2 TIME SPENT

Time is a precious commodity for everyone. One way to value wildlife is to determine the total number of hours people spend enjoying the wildlife resource and then multiply this by how much money they could earn if they spent the same amount of time working. A decision to enjoy wildlife rather to work means that the individual values his or her time enjoying wildlife more than the extra income they forego by not working. For example, if someone spends 20 hours hunting deer during the year and values his time at $20 per hour, then that must value deer hunting at more than $400 or he or she would not hunt deer. Like money spent, this method provides a minimal value for wildlife. Time expenditures are often combined with actual monetary expenditures to obtain a more realistic value.

4.3.3 WILLINGNESS TO PAY

This analysis, called the contingent valuation method, is based on asking a person how much he or she is willing to pay for some item or opportunity. We could ask deer hunters in Texas how much money they would be willing to pay for the opportunity to hunt deer during the next season. The average amount can then be multiplied by the number of deer hunters in Texas to estimate the total value of deer hunting to Texas hunters. The maximum amount that someone is willing to pay for an item or service will be more than what the person actually has to pay for it. The difference between these two values (willingness to pay versus actual cost) measures how much the person has gained or how much he/she is better off after making the purchase. Note that if a person's willingness to pay is less than the cost of the item, a rational person will not purchase it.

4.3.4 WILLINGNESS TO DO WITHOUT

This method of evaluation explores how much a person would have to be paid to forego the opportunity to engage in some activity. For instance, to judge the value of beaver ponds to landowners in Toombs County, Georgia, we might go to the county courthouse and obtain a list of all landowners in the county and ask each of them if there is a beaver pond on their land. We could then ask landowners with ponds how much money we would have to pay them to let us fill in the ponds. By adding up all the answers, we could then determine the value of all beaver ponds in the county from the perspective of local landowners. This is another aspect of the contingent valuation method, but it usually results in higher values than the willingness-to-pay method.

4.3.5 INCOME-PRODUCING ABILITY

Landowners can generate income by leasing the hunting rights to their property. The value of a hunting lease is set by the balance of supply and demand. Hence, hunting leases near cities bring much more than those in remote parts of the country. Likewise, scarce hunting opportunities, such as a hunting lease on a prime water-fowl marsh in an arid region, would bring much more than one in the middle of the Prairie Potholes, where marshes are abundant. The wildlife resource can be viewed like a bond or bank account in that the money obtained from the hunting lease can be viewed as the dividend or interest. If a farmer is receiving $1,000 annually for hunting rights while banks are paying 5% interest on savings accounts or bonds, then the wildlife resource of the farm has a value of $20,000 as an income-producing investment because $1,000 is 5% of $20,000.

4.3.6 INCREASE IN PROPERTY VALUES

Throughout much of the United States, advertisements for the sale of land or farms include phrases, such as "good deer hunting," "hunter's paradise," or "abundant wild-life." Realtors add these phrases because they know that land with abundant wildlife will attract more buyers. This price premium for land with wildlife can be used to determine the value of wildlife from the standpoint of the landowner. This method is called hedonic pricing.

4.4 WHO SHOULD BE SURVEYED TO DETERMINE THE ECONOMIC VALUE OF WILDLIFE?

Wildlife biologists must consider who should be surveyed to ensure that the survey group is appropriate for the question they are trying to answer. Consider the question: how much does sports fishing on New York's Oneida Lake increase the economy of the counties adjacent to the lake? The obvious answer is to add up all of the value of items bought by fishermen in the counties including fishing licenses and fees, fishing tackle, gas, meals, and lodging. But the obvious answer is wrong because if county residents were not hunting or fishing, they would still be spending money in the local area for other forms of entertainment. A more accurate method to answer this question would be to determine how much money fishermen who live outside the counties spent when fishing on Oneida Lake; their money would be lost to the counties if outside fishermen either stayed home or went elsewhere to fish. This is the approach that Shwiff et al. (2015) adopted when trying to determine the economic impact of fish eaten by double-crested cormorants in Oneida Lake (and, therefore, not available to fishermen) had on the local economy. They determined that this loss was $5 million to $66 million annually.

4.5 CAN LOSSES TO WILDLIFE BE DETERMINED BY MAKING A DIRECT MEASUREMENT OF LOSES?

There are two methods used to obtain information about the extent of losses from wildlife damage. The first is to visit sites where damage is occurring and directly measure the extent of losses. The second is to identify the people who are suffering from the damage and ask them to estimate their losses. There are advantages and disadvantages to each approach. The direct assessment of damage is more accurate but labor intensive; for that reason, it is most practical for assessing problems involving a single commodity or in a limited area.

Consider the necessary steps to assess directly the losses due to wildlife; first, one must determine exactly what we want to assess. This is a critical question because we will want to be able to extrapolate our findings to a particular group. We can only do so if the group is precisely defined in terms of location (e.g., county, state, country, and world) and class membership (e.g., a cornfield, all cornfields, all grain fields, and all crops). The question of what to survey is harder to answer than it initially seems. For instance, to assess cattle losses to predators, one needs to contact cattle ranchers. But before doing so, we need to answer the question of how to define a cattle rancher. Is a person who has a pet steer a cattle rancher? Do cattle ranchers include dairy farmers or stockyard owners?

Second, we must determine how to collect the data. No lists of agricultural fields or cattle herds are available, so we have to locate these fields or herds through their owners. Cattle herds are too numerous to allow us to sample all of them. Instead, only a sample of them can be surveyed. To produce accurate results, all members in the group must have an equal chance of being sampled. This means that the investigator must have some way to identify all members in the group or at least a random sample of them. To survey all U.S. cattle ranches, we might obtain a membership list from the U.S. Cattlemen's Association or from the American Farm Bureau Federation, a list of cattle ranchers from a company that maintains and sells such lists, or a list of subscribers to the magazine *Beef Today* or *Drover*. Obviously, one question with the use of each of these methods is whether the names on the list are representative of all cattle ranchers or whether the list is biased in some way.

The third step involves selecting the sites. Most farmers own more than one field, so we will need to select which fields on each farm to survey, perhaps by assigning a number to each field and then randomly selecting a number. Once this has been accomplished, we need some way to estimate losses in the selected fields. This will involve one or more site visits and a measurement of damage. If the field is too large to assess in its entirety, we must divide it into units small enough to be measured and use some random method to determine which units should be surveyed.

The fourth step involves determining how best to assess damage, which will vary with each crop and also with the intended use of the crop. Consider the problem of trying to determine the amount of bird damage in a cornfield. If it is a sweet corn field and the ears are intended for the fresh food market, we could count the number of corn ears damaged by birds because buyers will reject any damaged corn ear. The number of damaged ears could then be multiplied by the amount of money the farmer can sell a corn ear. On the other hand, if the grain will be harvested for animal feed, it will be necessary to determine how much of the grain biomass on each damaged ear has been lost due to birds. We might be able to do this by determining what proportion of the kernels on a corn ear have been eaten by birds, the weight of an average corn kernel, and the price for 100 kg of corn grain. However, another problem is that damaged ears are susceptible to the pathogen that produces aflatoxin. Bird-damaged corn may contain higher levels of this toxin than permissible. If that occurs, the entire crop may become worthless.

A useful approach to assess damage is to place a wildlife-proof fence around part of a field and then to compare crop yields within the enclosed area to crop yields in another part of the same field that is accessible to wildlife. Nichols (2014*a*, 2014*b*) used this approach to determine if grazing by Canada geese is responsible for the decline in stands of southern wild rice in New Jersey. To test this, the scientists established goose exclosures in some tidal marshes and compared the growth of wild rice inside the exclosures to other plots where geese could graze. He found that the density of rice plants and rice shoots was four times higher inside the exclosures than outside areas where geese could forage (Figure 4.2). Colligan et al. (2011) used the same approach to determine that deer grazing was reducing the height of soybean

FIGURE 4.2   Photos of a stand of wild rice located in a New Jersey tidal marsh in June and then in August when the grain ripens. Note that the marsh is devoid of vegetation due to grazing by Canada geese except within a small exclosure. You can see the wire fence if you look close.

Source: Ted Nichols and used with permission.

plants (Figure 4.3). Govind and Jayson (2018) used this same approach to determine damage by peacocks to fields adjacent to the Chulannur Peafowl Sanctuary, Kerala, India (Figure 4.4). The scientists determined that peacocks were reducing rice yields by 43%, resulting in a monetary loss of $236/ha. Pérez and Pacheco (2006) used this approach to determine that wildlife damage to small fields of yucca and walusa in Bolivia reduced yields by half.

It is difficult to determine what impact the grazing of growing plants will have on the ability of the plant's production when mature. Deer may browse most leaves of young soybean or corn plants, but grain yields may not be impacted when the plants are harvested (Coulter et al. 2011; Rogerson et al. 2014; Hinton et al. 2017). Winter grazing in British wheat fields by Brent geese reduced the leaf and shoot biomass by 75%, but by the time the fields were harvested, there was only a 6%–10% reduction in grain yields (Summers 1990). This is due to the plant's ability to compensate for damage if the damage occurs early enough in the growing season.

If a plant is destroyed by wildlife, the space that the dead plant had occupied will be filled in by the neighboring plants, providing they are close to the dead plant. Haney and Conover (2013) found that deer and elk killed or damaged over 9% of all safflower plants in fields located in San Juan County, Utah, but seed yields were reduced by only 3% because neighboring plants filled in the open gaps. What becomes important is the size of the open gap left by the dead plants (Figures 4.5 and

FIGURE 4.3   Exclosure in a soybean field to monitor what the weight of soybean plants would have been without browsing by white-tailed deer.

Source: Courtesy of Jacob Bowman.

FIGURE 4.4 An exclosure set up in an Indian rice field to measure what yields would have been if peacocks had not depredated the field.

Source: Photo from Govind and Jayson 2018 and used courtesy of Suresh Govind.

FIGURE 4.5 Sunflowers cannot compensate for seeds removed by blackbirds after the seeds have matured or if more than 15% of the seeds are removed.

Source: Photo by George Linz and used with permission.

FIGURE 4.6   A gap caused by squirrels in a cornfield is so large that the corn plants surrounding it will be unable to compensate for the corn seedlings removed by wildlife.

Source: Courtesy Brian MacGowan and Purdue Extension-Forestry & Natural Resources, FNR-265-W, the-education-store.com.

4.6). If deer eat all of the plants within a 10-m circle, the neighboring plants cannot expand enough to fill in the entire gap, and safflower yields will decline. In contrast, if a deer goes down a row and eats every third growing plant, yields may not suffer at all.

4.6 CAN ENERGETIC MODELS HELP DETERMINE LOSSES TO WILDLIFE?

Energetic models, which use information on how much an animal needs to consume daily to survive, can be used to assess economic losses. For example, Dorr et al. (2012) counted the number of double-crested cormorants roosting in the Yazoo Valley of Mississippi and along the Mississippi River by conducting roost counts throughout the year. The scientists also knew how many grams of fish a cormorant must consume daily to survive and how much of their diet consisted of commercial catfish. Dorr et al. (2012) determined that 14% and 75% of the diets of cormorants roosting near the Mississippi River and Yazoo Valley, respectively, are composed of commercial catfish. With this information, scientists were able to calculate that cormorants foraging during 2001–2002 killed $0.5 million worth of fingerling catfish and $11.6 million worth of mature catfish (Sidebar 4.1).

SIDEBAR 4.1 RISE OF CATFISH AQUACULTURE IMPACTS THE POPULATION OF CORMORANTS AND THE BIRDS' MIGRATORY BEHAVIOR

You have to feel some empathy for aquaculture farmers in the Mississippi Delta. The aquaculture industry, which started during the 1960s, has grown substantially and now produces 200 million kg of catfish annually in 50 million hectares of fish ponds. When the industry started, waterbirds populations, including double-crested cormorants (Figure 4.7), had collapsed due to

FIGURE 4.7 Double-crested cormorant preparing to swallow a catfish.

Source: Brian Lasenby, Shutterstock 728234683.

the pesticide DDT. But after DDT was banned, cormorant numbers made a dramatic comeback. Cormorants winter along the Mississippi River and Gulf of Mexico, and as their numbers increased, some began to appear at catfish farms. Cormorants quickly discovered that catfish were much more abundant in aquaculture ponds than what occurred in nature and were much easier to catch. But what started as a small number quickly increased until cormorants became a major problem. After decades of growth, cormorant populations in North America exceeded one million birds. During this period, cormorant populations declined in Atlantic and western regions of North America but increased in the Mississippi Flyway. King et al. (2010) wanted to determine if the catfish aquaculture industry was responsible for the increasing cormorant population in the Mississippi Flyway where the catfish industry was located. The scientists banded young cormorants in their breeding colonies and then waited to determine where they spent the winter. The scientists found that cormorants had changed their migratory behavior and that an increasing number of cormorants were spending winters in the Mississippi Delta and foraging at catfish ponds rather than continuing on to the Gulf of Mexico. This is an interesting example of a new food industry causing an avian species not only of making a dramatic comeback in numbers but also of altering its migratory behavior. While the aquaculture industry has greatly benefitted North American cormorants, the reverse is not true.

4.7 CAN LOSSES TO WILDLIFE BE DETERMINED BY SURVEYING PEOPLE?

Wildlife damage is best assessed through direct measurement, but this method is labor intensive and expensive. It is simply too costly to survey an adequate number of randomly selected fields across a large geographic area. Hence, this method has been used almost exclusively to measure losses to a single crop or item and in a limited area. There are hundreds of different species of cereal crops, fruits, vegetables, trees, and landscaping plants grown in the world, and almost all suffer damage from some wildlife species. Thus, we will never be able to obtain an accurate accounting of wildlife damage by direct measurement. Most economists, instead, rely upon the estimates of the people who are suffering the damage, such as farmers and ranchers.

Conducting a systematic survey is one approach to sample people. This technique is based on selection who to question (defining the target audience), how to select which members of the target audience to be surveyed, and how to question these people. People might be questioned during a face-to-face meeting, a telephone call, sending them a questionnaire through the mail, or emailing them. As one example, Butler et al. (2011) calculated the economic losses caused by seals to the Atlantic salmon fisheries of Moray Firth, Scotland, by surveying fishermen to determine how many days they could not fish due to interference by seals. The cost of lost workdays to the local economy was obtained from published reports. The results revealed that the fishing industry using rods to catch salmon lost $19,000 annually because of seals while fishermen using nets lost $20,900 annually.

Anderson et al. (2013b) surveyed over 7,000 U.S. fruit growers and found annual production losses due to birds totaled $70 million to wine grapes, $51 million to sweet cherries, $33 million to blueberries, $30 million to honeycrisp apples, and $4 million to tart cherries. American crows caused most of the damage to honeycrisp apples, while the other fruit was damaged primarily by European starlings and American robins.

A problem with surveys is the reluctance of people to respond to the survey or answer the questions. In such cases, researchers must determine if the potential answers from people who did not respond (i.e., nonrespondents) differ from those individuals who did respond (respondents). People who are interested in the subject are more likely to respond than those who are uninterested, and this can affect the results. This is called a nonresponse bias. For example, people who have contracted Lyme disease, or are afraid of it, would be more likely to respond to a survey about this disease than someone who has never heard of it. Hence, the incidence of Lyme disease among respondents might be higher than it is in the general population; a false conclusion might be drawn from the survey unless the scientist conducts a second survey of the nonrespondents and compares their answers to the respondents.

4.8   ARE PEOPLE'S PERCEPTIONS OF LOSSES TO WILDLIFE ACCURATE?

One difficulty with using survey data is that the perceptions of the respondents may not be accurate; they may be either overestimating or underestimating the actual level of damage. There are several reasons for this occurrence. One is variance in the conspicuousness of wildlife. Farmers may see large conspicuous animals, such as sandhill cranes, in newly seeded cornfields and overestimate how much seed they are eating, but the same farmers may underestimate vole damage in their alfalfa fields because voles are small, secretive animals and easy to overlook. Deer and many other wildlife species do not venture far from cover, so their browsing may be concentrated along the edge of the field. Most farmers survey their fields by driving along the field's borders; if damage is concentrated along the field's edge, it will be more conspicuous to the farmer. This will cause him or her to overestimate how much the field is damaged if the farmer assumes the same level of damage is widespread.

Some commodities are difficult to survey for evidence of wildlife damage. In these cases, losses are estimated by counting the number of depredating animals foraging on a crop. This method of estimating losses may result in biased estimates. For instance, a fish farmer cannot count his fish while they are growing and, therefore, must estimate bird predation by noting the number of birds at his ponds (Parkhurst et al. 1992). Many farmers assume that all predators present at their fish farm are meeting their nutritional needs from the fish they are raising. If this is not the case, damage will be less than perceived. In contrast, if there is a turnover in the animals during the day, farmers may underestimate the total number of birds they are feeding and their loss of fish.

Some people believe that agricultural producers are more likely to overestimate their losses than to underestimate them. To test this, scientists need to survey farmers and then determine the accuracy of a farmer's perceptions by directly measuring the damage in the same farmer's fields (Sidebar 4.2). One such study was conducted by Moore et al. (1999*b*) to measure the extent of European badger damage in England and Wales. They sent questionnaires to 3,600 farmers and received 1,962 completed questionnaires. They then visited 150 farms of respondents to measure losses directly. They found that differences were minimal between the farmers' perceptions and the measured losses. In Indiana, 73% of farmers reported wildlife damage to their corn or soybean fields, but scientists found wildlife damage in 93% of the fields when they checked the fields. These same farmers, while overestimated their monetary losses, were more accurate when estimating the proportion of their yield that was loss to wildlife (MacGowan et al. 2006). Elser et al. (2019) compared perceptions of farmers growing sweet cherries, wine grapes, and honeycrisp apples in Oregon, Washington, Michigan, and New York with field surveys of damage. The authors reported that grape and sweet cherry growers accurately assessed bird damage while apple growers overestimated damage. In Montana, alfalfa growers estimated that ground squirrels were reducing their crop yields by 24% but actually losses were 31% (Johnson-Nistler et al. 2005).

SIDEBAR 4.2   COMPARING FARMERS' PERCEPTIONS OF DAMAGE WITH ACTUAL MEASUREMENTS OF DAMAGE

Rarely can we compare farmers' perceptions of crop damage with on-the-ground measurements of crop damage on the same farm, but Tzilkowski et al. (2002) conducted such a study of wildlife damage to cornfields in

FIGURE 4.8   Raccoon damage in a cornfield usually consists of half-eaten corn ears littering the ground and corn stocks that have been pulled down.

Source: Brian MacGowan and Purdue Extension-Forestry & Natural Resources, FNR-265-W, the-education-store.com.

Pennsylvania. They randomly selected 222 corn farmers in the state and asked them about their perceptions of wildlife damage to their cornfields. The scientists also assessed wildlife damage in one of each farmer's cornfields (222 fields). Fields were stratified into four areas based on distance from the field's edge, owing to damage being more severe close to the edge. A 4.4-m long transect was randomly located in each of the four areas in every field. In these transects, the scientists counted the number of corn plants with and without ears, the number of plants with damaged ears, the number and weight of all harvestable ears, and the number and weight of all damaged ears (Figure 4.8).

Average losses in corn yields from all wildlife were 339 kg/ha or 8.4% of the total crop. Deer were responsible for 6.4% of the loss, birds 0.5%, raccoons 0.4%, black bears 0.3%, American crow 0.2%, woodchuck 0.2%, and squirrels 0.1%. Farmers estimated that their corn losses from wildlife were 9.7%. There was no significant difference between the farmers' estimates (perceived losses) and actual losses measured in the fields. That same year, there were 558,000 ha of corn planted in Pennsylvania. When losses reported in this study were extrapolated to the entire state, corn loss to wildlife was $28 million (Tzilkowski et al. 2002).

Surprisingly, recent studies have found that the indirect effect of wildlife damage may be just as great as direct losses of crops and livestock. Steele et al. (2013) found that the financial losses to cow–calf ranches in Wyoming from indirect losses of wolf depredation were similar in magnitude to direct losses. Direct losses were defined as the loss of calves and cows due to injury and deaths of cows. Indirect losses included a reduction in weaning weights of surviving calves, a decreased conception rate, and an increase in cattle illnesses.

One indirect cost of wildlife damage is that agricultural producers have to spend time and supplies to mitigate the problem. In Sweden, farmers who lost sheep to predators spent an average of €71 in labor costs per lost sheep because they had to start bringing the sheep at night, maintaining fences, and searching for lost animals (Widman et al. 2019).

4.9   WHAT IS A LOST-OPPORTUNITY COST?

Lost-opportunity costs reflect an economic loss for individuals who had to forego an opportunity to make money because they know that wildlife damage will be too high. For example, some farmers in South Africa have abandoned sheep farming because their losses to predators would have been unacceptably high (Swanepoel et al. 2016). Thereafter, no dead sheep will be found on these farms, but the opportunity to make money from sheep farming has nonetheless been lost. I own a ranch in Idaho that would be suitable for grazing sheep, but I cannot put sheep there because I know that too many would be killed by coyotes, which are abundant in the area. In my case, I have not lost a single sheep to the coyotes, but I have still suffered a lost – a lost opportunity to make money. While wildlife biologists may acknowledge a lost-opportunity cost associated with wildlife damage, I am unaware of any studies which have tried to measure it.

4.10   WHAT ARE SOME CONSIDERATIONS REGARDING THE ECONOMICS OF WILDLIFE DAMAGE?

Before calculating losses in terms of dollars and cents, one must consider several problems. First, wildlife damage does not affect everyone evenly. Deer will strike many cars, but most cars will not suffer this fate. Most people visiting Yellowstone National Park will not be killed by wildlife but a few will. As citizens, we accept these risks as part of the price society pays for receiving all the positive benefits wildlife brings to society. But if one's vehicle is totaled in a deer collision or if one's child is killed by a predator, it is hard to be stoic in the face of such losses. Instead, there is often a search for a government agency or someone who must be at fault; incriminations and lawsuits often follow.

Likewise, wildlife damage is not evenly distributed across all fields or felt by all agricultural producers. Many farmers will have no damage to their crops while others in the same area will lose a large proportion of their crop. Most (50%) grapefruit orchards in Texas received no damage from grackles but 43% received more than $200/ha in damage yearly, and one suffered more than $1,800/ha (Johnson et al. 1989). In Uganda, Africa, wildlife annually destroy about 10% of the corn crop; most farmers had no losses, but those who did suffer damage lost an average of 27% of their corn; some farmers lost over half their crop (Hill 2004). Brewster (2018) questioned a sample of Texas cattle ranchers and discovered that most (57%) lost less than 1% of their herd to coyotes, but 22% of ranchers reported that coyotes killed more than 3% of their herd each year.

Determining the amount of money that a farmer lost from wildlife damage is an important measure, but we should not lose sight that it is the minimal value of the farmer's loss. It does not account for the hours and dollars spent trying to prevent damage. Another cost to the farmer and his/her family is the stress of not being able to stop the damage from occurring; this stress is greatest when the offending animal is protected by law so that the farmer cannot kill it. Ranchers have empathy for their livestock and feel hurt when one of their animals is killed by a predator.

Consider a rural farmer in Africa that is confronted by elephants that feed in the family's field at night. Losses to a farming family include the loss of income from destroyed crops, but other consequences include (1) a need to guard the fields all night (Figure 4.9); (2) a need to pull the children from school because there is no one else to guard the fields at night; (3) an increased risk of mosquito-borne diseases, such as malaria, for those people who have to guard the fields at night rather than being able to stay inside; and (4) increased risk of injury from trying to drive marauding elephants out of a field. Not surprisingly, children who have to guard fields at night do poorer in school. Wildlife damage can also increase the income disparity between men and women. In parts of Africa, women are restricted or discouraged from leaving the village at night. This means that female-headed farms are left unprotected at night but not male-headed farms. Even if women can hire men to guard the family fields, women cannot oversee their employee's activities at night to make sure that

FIGURE 4.9 A small hut (called an Ikwiriri) that farmers occupy continually to keep animals from their ripening crops.

Source: Courtesy of Hamas Kushnir and Craig Parker.

he is working (Hill 2004; Mackenzie and Ahabyona 2012). Finally, elephants that damage crops are likely to spark retribution killing of elephants by people who have suffered the loss (Kissui 2008).

One difficulty with monetary values is that each year the U.S. dollar or any other currency decreases in value; this is called inflation. For example, 100 years ago, most U.S. employees earned between $500 and $1,000 annually; most workers today would earn that much in a week. This poses a problem in that economic values reported in past studies reflect the value of a dollar at the time the study was conducted, not the value of a dollar today. To correct for inflation, I have adjusted all monetary values reported in studies published prior to 2010 to the value of a dollar in 2020 using the U.S. Consumer Price Index as the measure of inflation because it is the most widely used measure of inflation. Correcting for inflation, however, means that the monetary values that I report in this book will be higher than the values reported in the original study. All monetary values in this book are expressed in U.S. dollars except for those reported in English pounds (£) or Euros (€). When the original study reported values in a foreign currency, I converted their values to U.S. dollars using the exchange rate that existed on August 12, 2020.

4.11   HOW MUCH WILDLIFE DAMAGE IS THERE IN THE UNITED STATES AND WORLDWIDE?

4.11.1   DEER–AUTOMOBILE COLLISIONS

State Farm Insurance Company (2018) reported 1,332,322 claims were filed annually with insurance companies for accidents involving vehicle collisions with deer, elk, or moose during a 12-month period stretching from July 1, 2017 to June 30, 2018. Given the 223 million drivers in the United States, State Farm estimated that each driver in the United States has a 1 in 164 (0.6%) chance each year of filing a claim with an insurance company because of damage from a vehicle collision with an ungulate. Of course, the risk of hitting a deer varies by state and is highest in states that have high deer densities, and a large proportion of driving occurs in rural and suburban areas (Figure 4.10). The average cost to repair a vehicle involved in a DVC was $3,995 in 2016 (State Farm Insurance Company 2016). If this amount is extrapolated to the 1,332,322 claims, then the cost of damaged vehicle from DVCs in the United States is $5.3 billion dollars annually (1,332,322 accidents × $3,995 average repair cost).

Only about half of all DVCs are reported to the police or insurance companies (Decker et al. 1990; Romin 1994; Marcoux 2005). Hence, the actual number of DVCs occurring annually in the United States is closer to 2.6 million, and the actual risk of being involved in a DVC is 1.2% each year. The amount of damage to vehicles involved in unreported deer collisions is less than that of reported collisions because people are less likely to report accidents when damage was minimal. I assume that damage to an automobile from an unreported DVC is $1,000 because most of these vehicles will sustain at least some damage from striking a deer, and even minor collision repairs cost more than $1,000. Thus, the damage to vehicles in the United States

FIGURE 4.10   Cars wait while a deer crosses the road.

Source: jgolby, Shutterstock 422543800.

from unreported DVCs equals $1.3 billion (1.3 million accidents × $1,000 average repair bill). Finally, the annual cost of repairing or replacing vehicles involved in a DVC in the United States (both reported and unreported collisions) is $6.5 billion.

CDC (2004) reported that each year 26,726 people visited an emergency medical facility for injuries from a DVC, based on data from 2001 and 2002. Given the 1,332,322 reported DVCs, this means that 2.0% of DVCs result in a person injured serious enough to visit an emergency medical room. Using state highway safety data, Conover (2019) estimated that approximately 58,000 Americans are injured in DVCs annually, double the rate reported by the CDC, and 440 people were killed. I believe that the Conover (2019) value is probably a more realistic record of total injuries because many injured people do not visit emergency medical facilities. Conover (2019) used the highway safety data to calculate that there are 640 human injuries and 6 fatalities annually in the United States from moose–vehicle collisions. Haskell and Langley (2020) reported that CDC data may underestimate the actual fatality rate by 18%, but I did not correct for this potential under reporting.

The U.S. Department of Transportation (2016) assigned a value of $9.6 million to a human life during 2016, making the total annual loss for all human fatalities resulting from DVCs to be $4.2 billion ($9.6 million × 440 fatalities). Bissonette et al. (2008) estimated the cost of human injuries from DVCs by examining DVCs in Utah data available on the Crash Outcome Data Evaluation System from 1996 to 2001. The data contained information on the types of human injuries resulting from DVCs based on police officers at the scene and charges from a hospital for treating each of these patients. Bissonette et al. (2008) found that 20,873 people (drivers and passengers) in Utah were involved in 13,020 DVCs from 1996 to 2001 (1.6 people inside a vehicle involved in a DVC). Of these people, 2.1% (448 people) involved in a DVC incurred a charge for seeking help at an inpatient medical facility or hospital emergency room. Total medical costs for these patients totaled $1,002,401 or $2,338 per patient. I assume that there were no medical expenses for DVCs that went unreported. If extrapolated these values to the 1,332,322 reported DVCs in the United States during 2016, then 2,131,715 people were involved in a DVC and 44,766 vehicle occupants sought medical attention at a total medical cost of $1.047 billion.

Another cost of a DVC is a dead deer. Being hit by a vehicle is fatal to deer 92% of the time (Allen and McCullough 1976), which means that over 2.4 million deer die after being struck by a vehicle annually on U.S. highways (2.6 million DVCs × 0.92). Bissonette et al. (2008) assigned a value of $300 for each deer; this value seems reasonable to me. If extrapolated to the 2.4 million deer killed annually in DVCs, the total value of these dead deer is $720 million. Finally, I can determine the annual cost of all DVCs in the United States is $12.4 billion (Table 4.1) by adding the damage to vehicle ($6.5 billion), loss of human life ($4.2 billion), medical costs for human injuries ($1.0 billion), and value of dead deer ($0.7 billion).

Estimates by the U.S. Federal Highway Administration (2008) for damage from a vehicle collision with a deer, elk, or moose are much higher than mine (Table 4.2). One reason for this is because they considered costs that I did not, such as towing costs or the disposal of a deer carcass. However, the primarily reason why their estimates are higher result from their estimate of a higher cost per injured person

TABLE 4.1

Summary of Wildlife Damage Occurring Annually in the United States

Human–wildlife conflict	Dollars (in billions)
Damage from DVCs	$12.5
Damage from bird–aircraft collisions	0.2
Damage to metropolitan households	11.6
Damage to rural households	6.0
Damage to timber industry	1.2
Damage to agricultural producers	4.0
Economic losses from zoonotic diseases	Unknown, but in the billions
Total losses	$35.5

The monetary values include both damage to property and money and time spent to prevent the problem.

TABLE 4.2

Summary of Estimated Costs in Dollars ($) for an Average Deer, Elk, and Moose Collision with a Vehicle

Description of cost	Deer	Elk	Moose
Vehicle repair costs	$1,840	$3,000	$4,000
Human injuries	2,702	5,403	10,807
Human fatalities	1,671	6,683	13,366
Towing, police costs	125	375	500
Value of ungulate	2,000	3,000	2,000
Carcass removal and disposal	50	100	100
Total	8,388	18,461	30,773

Source: Based on the U.S. Federal Highway Administration (2008).

($2,700–$10,000 versus my estimate of $2,338) and a higher value for each dead ungulate ($2,000–$3,000 per accident versus my estimate of $300).

Ungulate–vehicle collisions are a worldwide problem. Transportation Canada (2012) estimated that each year an average of 40,000 cars and trucks in Canada sustained damage after colliding with a large animal, usually a deer, elk, or moose; I estimate that another 40,000 DVCs were unreported (same rate as in the United States) Seventeen people died in those collisions, and 2,003 people were injured. If Canada's DVC costs the same as in the United States, then the annual cost of DVCs in Canada is $333 million ($106 million in human fatalities, $4.7 million for medical expenses for human injuries, $160 million for damage to the 40,000 vehicles damaged in reported DVCs, $40 million for damage to vehicles in unreported DVCs, and $22 million for the value of dead ungulate).

In Europe, there are 571,711 reported DVCs annually (Table 2.6), resulting in 30,000 human injuries and 300 deaths (Bruinderink and Hazebroek 1996). The annual repair cost in Europe for vehicles damaged in DVCs is in excess of €1 billion, including €163 million in Finland, €100 million in both Sweden and France, and €447 million in Germany (Kämmerle et al. 2017). The €1 billion amount does not include human injuries and fatalities or the value of dead deer. If Europe's fatality and morbidity cost the same as in the United States, then the annual cost of DVCs in Europe is €4.76 billion; this includes €2.89 billion in human fatalities, €93 million for medical expenses for human injuries, €1 billion for damage to the 40,000 vehicles in reported DVCs, €500 million for damage to vehicles in unreported DVCs, and €276 million for the value of dead deer.

In the United Kingdom, ungulate mortality caused by DVCs as a proportion of the spring ungulate population is 3%–7% for roe deer, 1%–3% for red deer, and 7%–13% for red deer. In Slovenia, 11%–15% of roe deer population are killed in DVCs, 1.6% in Norway, and 6% in Germany (Kämmerle et al. 2017).

Collisions between wildlife and trains probably do not cause much damage to a locomotive considering its mass relative to that of an animal, but such collisions kill millions of wildlife annually across the world. In Norway, moose–train collisions increased from 50 per year during the 1950s to 1,000 during the 1990s (Andreassen et al. 2005). There was an average of 911 train collisions involving these species from 2012 through 2015. These collisions occurred with roe deer (52%), red deer (14%), moose (5%), and wild boar (29%). Given the population size of the wildlife populations, wild boars are particularly vulnerable to being struck by a train, while roe deer were lower than expected (Krauze-Gryz et al. 2017).

4.11.2 Bird–Aircraft Collisions

Over 2,300 reports of civilian aircraft in the United States colliding with wildlife are filed annually with the U.S. Federal Aviation Agency. Yet only 20% of bird–aircraft collisions are ever reported (U.S. Department of Defense-Partners in Flight 2019). The cost of a single bird strike can be catastrophic. One example is the forced landing of U.S. Airways Flight 1549 into the Hudson River after striking a flock of geese (Figure 4.11). Although no one was killed or seriously injured, the airplane was a complete loss (Marra et al. 2009). From 1990 to 2015, there were 616 bird strikes with civilian aircraft in the United States that resulted in damage to the aircraft, 229 strikes that injured 400 people, and 12 strikes that killed 26 people (Dolbeer et al. 2016).

Given the high cost to repair a commercial jet, these collisions are expensive. Annual economic losses from strikes with civil aircraft are conservatively estimated to exceed $1.2 billion worldwide and $142 million within the United States (Dolbeer and Beiger 2019). Birds are stuck in most wildlife–aircraft accidents (96%), but deer or other large mammals can be struck by an airplane during takeoff or landing. According to Federal Aviation Administration, there were almost 900 deer–aircraft collisions from 1990 to 2009, resulting in $75 million in damages, 26 human injuries, and 1 fatality (Biondi et al. 2011). Deer–aircraft collisions occur mainly at small airfields, and their number could be reduced if all airfields were enclosed in deer-proof fences.

FIGURE 4.11   U.S. Airways Flight 1549 after crashing into the Hudson River.

Source: Photograph by Greg Lam Pak Ng, Flikr, CC-BY 2.0, https://creativecommons.org/licenses/by/2.0/.

The U.S. military also incurs substantial losses from bird–aircraft strikes because military planes and birds both fly in the same airspace, which is close to the ground. As a couple of examples, an AWACs military plane crashed during 1995 after colliding with a flock of geese on takeoff, killing all 24 crew members and destroying the $200 million aircraft. During 2011, a U.S. Marine Corp helicopter collided with a red-tailed hawk. Two servicemen (the pilot and copilot) were killed, and $25 million Super Cobra aircraft was destroyed (Washburn et al. 2014).

Over 3,000 U.S. Navy and Air Force aircraft strike wildlife annually (U.S. Department of Defense-Partners in Flight 2019). Each year, an average of $20 million in aircraft damage is caused by wildlife strikes on U.S. Navy aircraft, while the U.S. Air Force averaged $38 million annually (Pfeiffer et al. 2018). U.S. Army has more aircraft than the U.S. Navy, but information of bird strikes to Army airplanes is lacking. I assume that the annual losses to Army planes equals that of the Navy ($20 million). Hence, total losses to U.S. military aircraft are approximately $78 million. When added to the cost of commercial aircraft, the total cost of wildlife–aircraft collision in the United States comes to $220 million (Table 4.1).

4.11.3   WILDLIFE DAMAGE TO HOUSEHOLDS

Conover (1997) surveyed 1,000 households, randomly selected from the 100 largest metropolitan centers in the United States. Over half of the respondents (61%) reported that they or their household had a problem with one or more wildlife species during the prior year and suffered a mean loss of $105 in damage. Mice were the most common culprits (Figure 4.12), followed by squirrels, raccoons, moles, pigeons, starlings, and skunks (Table 4.3). Almost half (42%) of all urban households reported that they tried to solve a wildlife damage problem in the prior year and spent an average of $55 in the attempt. Unfortunately, half reported that their efforts to solve the

FIGURE 4.12   Mice inside homes are a common problem across the world.

Source: Horvath82, Shutterstock 1574343130.

TABLE 4.3

Percentage of U.S. Agricultural Producers and the Number of Agricultural Producers (2 Million Total) and Metropolitan Households (60 Million) Who Reported that the Following Wildlife Species Had Caused Damage on Their Property during the Prior Year (Conover 1997, 1998).

Wildlife	Agricultural producers		Metropolitan households	
	%	Number (in thousands)	%	Number (in thousands)
Deer	51	1,086	4	2,400
Raccoons	25	522	16	9,600
Coyotes	24	501	?	?
Ground hogs	21	438	4	2,400

(Continued)

TABLE 4.3 (*Continued*)

Wildlife	Agricultural producers		Metropolitan households	
	%	Number (in thousands)	%	Number (in thousands)
Beavers	19	396	?	?
Blackbirds	18	376	6	3,600
Mice	18	376	22	13,200
Starlings	16	334	11	6,600
Rabbits	16	334	7	4,200
Foxes	12	50	?	?
Skunks	9	19	11	6,600
Squirrels	?	?	18	10,800
Moles	?	?	14	8,400
Pigeons	?	?	12	7,200

problem were unsuccessful. When these results are extrapolated to the 60 million metropolitan households in the United States (160 million residents), metropolitan households suffered $6.3 billion a year in wildlife damage, despite spending $3.3 billion and 268 million hours trying to prevent these problems (Conover 1997). If we conservatively value people's time at the federal minimum wage ($7.25 in 2020), the total labor cost would be $2.0 billion. Hence, the total cost of wildlife damage (actual damage plus money and time spent to prevent the problem) to metropolitan residents equals approximately $11.6 billion.

An additional 34 million households (92 million residents) live in smaller cities, towns, and rural areas (U.S. Bureau of the Census 1992). Because wildlife populations should be higher in rural areas, I assume that these households suffer at least as much from wildlife problems as do people living in large metropolitan areas. This means the total annual cost of wildlife damage to rural households (damage plus money and time spent to prevent the problem) would conservatively amount to $6.0 billion. The total cost for all households (both metropolitan and rural) in the United States would equal $17.6 billion.

4.11.4 WILDLIFE DAMAGE TO THE TIMBER INDUSTRY

The U.S. timber industry is centered in the Southeast, the Northeast, and the Pacific Northwest. Each area has its own distinctive wildlife problems.

4.11.4.1 Southeast

There are 13 million ha of bottomland forests in the Southeast, and beaver impoundments have flooded 288,000 ha in 6 of the 13 southern states (Arner and DuBose 1980). Trees die when they are flooded by a beaver impoundment or when beavers gnaw or fell nonimpounded timber (Figure 4.13). Both types of beaver damage were estimated by Nolte and Dykzeul (2002) to produce $1 billion annually in losses to

FIGURE 4.13   Trees killed by beaver during winter.

Source: Irina Orlova, Shutterstock 759278614.

timber in the southeastern United States. But more recently, West and Godwin (2011) lowered the annual losses to only $100 million. In this book, I will accept the more recent estimate ($100 million) as the most accurate.

4.11.4.2   Northeast

Although many wildlife species cause damage to forests in the Northeast, white-tailed deer are responsible for most of the economic losses in this region. Experiments using enclosures have demonstrated that deer browsing on tree seedlings and sprouts can reduce tree growth and result in understocked stands and longer periods of time before trees are large enough to harvest. Furthermore, deer browsing can change the species composition of forested stands. Unfortunately, the tree species most desirable for timber production are the same species that deer prefer to browse (Redick et al. 2020; Redick and Jacobs 2020). Marquis (1981) estimated that annual timber losses across Pennsylvania's Allegheny hardwood forest amounted to over $147/ha. This high-quality hardwood forest covers 6.5 million ha in Pennsylvania, but it is unclear if Marquis' data can be extrapolated to the entire Allegheny forest. Hence, I believe that deer-induced losses in this region may be $95 million/year or $15/ha/ year. Pennsylvania's Allegheny hardwood forest represents 14% of the oak–hickory (*Quercus–Carya*) type hardwood that covers 45 million ha in the northeastern United States. Commercial forests cover 72 million ha in the Northeast (Gedney and Van Sickle 1979). Unfortunately, losses to timber production from wildlife damage are unknown for most of this area, but deer populations are high throughout the region. If we assume that deer damage in the oak–hickory forests in the rest of the Northeast (38 million ha) is at least 33% of the damage that occurs in the Alleghenies, or $5/ ha per year, then deer damage to the oak-hickory forest industry in the Northeast is approximately $285 million annually ($95 million in the Alleghenies and $190 million in the rest of the Northeast).

4.11.4.3   Northwest

Washington state has 620 million cubic meters of live trees growing on 9 million ha of forestland, while Oregon has 850 million cubic meters of live trees growing on 12 million km^3 of forestland (U.S. Forest Service 2020). Animal damage to forests and forest regeneration in these two states is caused by numerous wildlife species. The principal damaging species are black bears, beaver, deer, elk, mountain beaver, pocket gopher, porcupine, and rabbits. In a large-scale study using exclosures, Black et al. (1979) found that, after five years, wildlife damage in Washington and Oregon reduced the survival of newly planted Douglas fir trees by 20%, their height by 24%, and the survival and height of ponderosa pine by 31% and 22%, respectively. Based on these data, Brodie et al. (1979) calculated that losses to newly planted tree stands in Oregon and Washington exceeded $460 million annually. Nolte and Dykzeul (2002) considered the studies listed earlier as accurate and concluded that wildlife damage in Oregon resulted in an annual financial loss of $500 million, including $10 million due to mountain beaver and $17 million to black bears. Washington state has the same wildlife species in its forest and the same wildlife damage as Oregon but only 73% of Oregon's forests. Hence, I estimate that wildlife damage to forestland in Washington is $370 million or $870 million for the entire Pacific Northwest although I have not included any losses in Idaho, Montana, or California in these estimates. Across the entire United States, wildlife damage to timber is estimated to be $1.2 billion ($100 million in the Southeast, $285 million in the Northeast, and $870 in the Pacific Northwest; Table 4.1).

4.11.5   WILDLIFE DAMAGE TO AGRICULTURAL PRODUCTION

Conover (1998) surveyed a random sample of 2,000 farmers and ranchers and found that 80% had suffered wildlife damage in the prior year; 53% reported that the damage exceeded their tolerance. Problems were caused most often by deer, raccoons, coyotes, and ground hogs (Table 4.3). When asked to categorize their losses from wildlife damage in the prior year, 22% of farmers reported losses of less than $100, 45% between $100 and $999, 23% between $1,000 and $4,999, and 6% between $5,000 and $9,999. Three percent said that their losses in the prior year exceeded $10,000. In addition, farmers and ranchers reported spending an average of 44 hours and $1,000 in the prior year trying to prevent a wildlife problem. When extrapolated to the nation's 2,029,200 farms, Conover (1998) estimated that despite spending 90 million hours and $2 billion trying to prevent wildlife problems, U.S. agricultural producers still suffered $2 billion in damage annually (Sidebar 4.3). Hence, losses equal $4 billion in direct losses and money spent in damage prevention. Examples of studies that have measured the wildlife damage to specific crops are shown in Table 4.4.

TABLE 4.4

Examples of studies that have measured agricultural losses due to wildlife damage. The examples are not the most serious problems caused by wildlife in each country but were selected to illustrate local problems. Dollar values are adjusted for inflation for papers published prior to 2010 and expressed as the value of a U.S. dollar in the year 2020. All currencies were converted to U.S. dollars ($), except for those reported in British pounds (£) or Euros (€).

Commodity	Wildlife species	Location	Extent of wildlife damage		Reference
			Loss on a country or area-wide basis	Loss on a per-ha basis	
UNITED STATES					
Blueberries	Birds	U.S., nationwide	5% of crop, $8.600,000		De Grazio (1978)
Corn	Birds	U.S., nationwide	1.7 billion kg		De Grazio (1978)
Cherries, Sweet	Birds	U.S. nationwide	13% of crop		Elser et al. (2016)
Rice	Birds	U.S., nationwide	$13 million		Cummings et al. (2005)
Sorghum, grain	Birds	U.S. nationwide	$23 million		De Grazio (1978)
Sunflowers	Blackbirds	U.S., nationwide	2.1%, 19,000 metric tons, $3 million		Linz et al. (2011)
Sunflowers	Blackbirds	U.S., nationwide	Confectionary 1.7%, Oilseed 2.6%	$18.25/ha $18.65ha	Ernst et al. (2019)
Alfalfa	Ground squirrels	U.S., California	25% in fields with ground squirrels	892 kg/ha	Sauer (1984)
Alfalfa	Ground squirrels	U.S., California	35% to 45%	$409	Whisson et al. (1999)
Grapes, wine	Birds	U.S., California, central	2%	$466	DeHaven (1974)
Grapes, wine	Birds	U.S., California, central	2%	$466	DeHaven (1974)
Sunflowers	Birds	U.S., California, Sacramento Valley	1%	$108	Avery and DeHaven (1982)
Soybeans	Deer	U.S., Delaware	0%	$0	Rogerson et al. (2014)
Wheat	White-tailed deer	U.S., Delaware	0%	0%	Springer et al. (2013)

(Continued)

TABLE 4.4 (*Continued*)

Commodity	Wildlife species	Location	Extent of wildlife damage		Reference
			Loss on a country or area-wide basis	Loss on a per-ha basis	
Blueberries	Birds	U.S., Florida	15%–19%		Nelms et al. (1990)
Macadamia nuts	Rodents	Hawaii	16%		Jackson (1977)
Corn	Turkey	U.S., Indiana	0%	$0	Humberg et al. (2007), DeVault et al. (2007)
Peanuts	Birds	U.S., Oklahoma, central		<$3	Mott et al. (1972)
Corn	All wildlife species	U.S., Midwest	0.7%, $92 million	$4.80	Wywialowski (1996)
Catfish	Double-crested cormorants	U.S., Mississippi	4%, $3 million,		Glahn and Bruggers 1995
Catfish	Double-crested cormorants	U.S., Mississippi	2.3%–4.6%		Dorr et al. (2012)
Soybeans	Deer	U.S., Mississippi	0% in 5 fields	$0	Hinton et al. (2017)
Alfalfa	Belding's ground squirrels	U.S., Oregon, SE	44% in fields with ground squirrels		Kalinowski and deCalestra (1981)
Corn	All wildlife species	U.S., Pennsylvania	8.4%	$720	Tzilkowski et al. (2002)
Corn	Deer	U.S., Pennsylvania	4.8%	$53	Tzilknowski et al. (2002)
Corn	Birds (mostly blackbirds)	U.S., Pennsylvania	0.6%	$8	Wakeley and Mitchell (1981)
Corn	Blackbird	U.S., North Dakota	0.3%, $3.4 million		Klosterman et al. (2012)
Sunflowers	Blackbirds	U.S., North Dakota	2.1%, $5.3 million		Klosterman et al. (2012)
All crops	Canada geese	U.S., South Dakota	$250,000		Amount the state paid to compensate farmers Radtke and Dieter (2011)
Safflower	Deer and elk	U.S., Utah	3%	$9.42/ha	Haney and Conover (2013)
Corn	Racoons	U.S., Wyoming	1.1%	$10.75/ha	Anderson et al. (2013a)

TABLE 4.4 (*Continued*)

Commodity	Wildlife species	Location	Extent of wildlife damage		Reference
			Loss on a country or area-wide basis	Loss on a per-ha basis	
SOUTH AMERICA					
Livestock	Cougar	Brazil, Santa Catarina	0.3% cattle, 32% sheep, 38% goats		Mazzolli et al. (2002)
Coconuts	Black rats	Columbia, San Andres Island	34%		Valencia (1980)
Coconuts	Black rats	Columbia, Gorgona Island	60%		Valencia (1980)
Coconuts	Black rats	Columbia	20%		Valencia (1980)
Wheat, sunflowers	Doves, parakeets	Uruguay	$9 million sunflowers, $11 million wheat		De Grazio (1978)
Rice and sorghum	Dickcissels	Venezuela	0.7% rice, 0.4% sorghum, $3 million,		Basili and Temple (1999)
THE UNITED KINGDOM					
Cereal	Wood-pigeon	Britain	$7–14 million		De Grazio (1978)
Rapeseed	Brant geese	Britain	11%		McKay et al. (1993)
Wheat	Brant geese	Britain	65%–10%		Summers (1990)
All crops	European badgers	England and Wales	£73 million	£37 per farm	Moore et al. (1999*b*)
Wheat	Pink-footed geese	Scotland	15%		Pattersen et al. (1989)
EUROPE					
Barley	Pink-footed geese	Denmark	7%–20%		Lorenzen and Madsen (1986)
Grapes, cherries	Birds	Germany	$16 million		De Grazio (1978)
All crops	Big Game	Hungary	€6 million		
All crops	Feral hogs	Luxembourg	0.3%, €527,000		Schley et al. (2008)
Domesticated reindeer	Eurasian lynx	Norway	7% for yearlings, 23% of calves		Nybakk et al. (2002)
Sheep	Grizzly bears	Norway, North Trondelag	11%		Knarrum et al. (2006)
Cereal, hay, rapeseed	European buffalo	Poland, northeast	€17,800		Hofman-Kamińska and Kowalczyk. (2012)

(*Continued*)

TABLE 4.4 (*Continued*)

Commodity	Wildlife species	Location	Extent of wildlife damage		Reference
			Loss on a country or area-wide basis	Loss on a per-ha basis	
Fruit	Monk parakeets	Spain	37% pears, 36% round plums, 17% persimmons, 7% quinces		Senar et al. (2016)
All crops	Feral hogs	Switzerland		€208/farm	Geisser (2000)
AFRICA					
Grains	Birds	Africa	13%, $8 billion		de Mey et al. (2011)
Millet	Elephants	Botswana	2%	?	Songhurst and Coulson (2014)
Livestock	Predators	Botswana, Kweneng	0.3%		Schiess-Meiser et al. (2007)
Millet	Birds	Chad	12%		Manikowski and Da Camara-Smeets (1979)
Livestock	Predators (all) Lions Hyenas Cheetah	Kenya, around Tsavo National Park	2.3% 2.1% 0.1% 0.1%		Patterson et al. (2004)
Grains	Birds	Senegal	907 million kg		De Grazio (1978)
Corn	Birds (mostly weavers)	Somalia	0%–2%		Bruggers (1980)
Rice	Birds (mostly quelea)	Somalia	0%–33%		Bruggers (1980)
Barley and wheat	Egyptian geese	South Africa, Agulhas Plain	3%–7%		Mangnall and Crowe (2002)
Livestock	Predators	South Africa		$5127 cattle $3,222 sheep $2,449 goats	Rust et al. (2013)
Sorghum	Quelea	Sudan	$1.3 million		De Grazio (1978)
Corn	All wildlife	Uganda	10%		Hill (2004)
Olives	Birds	Tunisia	1.4 million kg		De Grazio (1978)
Livestock	Baboons, lions, and leopards	Zimbabwe	5%	$22/ household	Butler (2000)

Commodity	Wildlife species	Location	Extent of wildlife damage		Reference
			Loss on a country or area-wide basis	Loss on a per-ha basis	
ASIA					
Crops	Rodents	All Southeast Asia	15 billion kg		John (2014)
Wheat	Rodents	Bangladesh	12%		Jackson (1997)
Grain	Rodents	Bangladesh	1%–3%, 270 million kg		Sultana et al. (1983)
Peanuts	Rodents	Bangladesh	3%, 2.7 million kg		Sultana and Jaeger (1992)
Banana	Elephant	India, Coimbatore Forest Division	$34,872, 56 ha lost		Ramkumar et al. (2014)
Sweet potato	Macaque, feral hogs	Indonesia, Sulowski	6% 11%		Priston (2009)
Barley	All wildlife	Nepal	1%		Awasthi and Singh (2015)
Buckwheat and sweet potato	All wildlife	Nepal	1%		Awasthi and Singh (2015)
Corn	All wildlife	Nepal	39%		Awasthi and Singh (2015)
Millet	All wildlife	Nepal	19%		Awasthi and Singh (2015)
Potato	All wildlife	Nepal	30%		Awasthi and Singh (2015)
Pulses	All wildlife	Nepal	0.2%		Awasthi and Singh (2015)
Wheat	All wildlife	Nepal	4%		Awasthi and Singh (2015)
Wheat	All wildlife	Nepal	7%		Awasthi and Singh (2015)
Rice	Birds	Pakistan	20%		De Grazio (1978)
Peanuts	All wildlife	Pakistan, Punjab	5%		Brooks et al. (1988)
Stored grain	Rats	Pakistan, Punjab	0.3%		Ahmad et al. (1995)
Australia					
Wine and table grapes	Birds	Australia	7%, $100 million,		Tracey et al. (2007)
Apples and pears	Birds	Australia	13%, $82 million		Tracey et al. (2007)
Stone fruits	Birds	Australia	16%, $53 million		Tracey et al. (2007)
Nuts	Birds	Australia	22%, $44 million,		Tracey et al. (2007)
All crops	Marsupials	Australia	$57 million		McLeod (2004) as cited by Cox et al. (2015)

(Continued)

TABLE 4.4 (*Continued*)

Commodity	Wildlife species	Location	Extent of wildlife damage		Reference
			Loss on a country or area-wide basis	Loss on a per-ha basis	
Pome fruit	Birds	Australia, western	$194,000 to $485,000		Chapman (2007)

SIDEBAR 4.3 DOWNSIDE OF FREE-RANGING POULTRY

Many people believe that raising chickens in cages is cruel to the birds and prefer to buy free-ranging chickens, which have the run of the farm (Figure 4.14). Hawks and eagles also like farms that have free-ranging chickens and consider them an all-you-can-eat restaurant. White Oak Pastures is a family farm in Georgia that provides free range to 60,000 chickens. Sixty-five bald eagles also call the farm home and each eats as many as four chickens daily, costing the farmers more than $1,000 in losses daily. It wasn't always this way. At first,

FIGURE 4.14   Free-ranging chickens in Nebraska.

Source: Weldon Schloneger, Shutterstock 32473363.

there were no eagles; then one winter, 10 eagles showed up; 30 were there the next year. Photographs from the third year showed 78 eagles loafing in trees around the farm. The owner turned to the U.S. Fish and Wildlife Service and Georgia Department of Natural Resources for help. They recommended putting up wires over the pastures and moving the chickens closer to humans, but both were impractical at White Oak Pastures. The farm spent over $5,000 on propane cannons, which are placed beneath the trees used by the eagles for loafing. The cannons have scattered the eagles but have not endeared the farm to the neighbors. The eagles have made his farm popular with bird watchers and photographers. "Buy a chicken from us before you go home." the farmer tells visitors. "You can be sure that it is a healthy chicken, only the quick ones survive around here" (Matthews 2016).

4.12 WHAT IS THE TOTAL ECONOMIC LOSS DUE TO WILDLIFE IN THE UNITED STATES?

Wildlife damage in the United States costs approximately $35.5 billion annually (Table 4.1). I believe this to be a conservative number as I usually rounded down or based the figures on conservative assumptions. These losses include the cost of property damage caused by wildlife and the time and money people spent trying to prevent wildlife damage. Presumably, damage from wildlife would have been much higher if people had not spent their time and money to prevent a problem. That is, I assume that people were rational and spent time and money when they believed that their savings in damage outweighed the costs of the preventive steps. This estimate of $35.5 billion excludes the cost of zoonotic diseases.

4.13 DO HIGH LEVELS OF WILDLIFE DAMAGE MEAN THAT WILDLIFE POPULATIONS ARE TOO HIGH?

Economic losses, injuries, and diseases caused by wildlife are a substantial problem, but this does not imply that wildlife populations are too high or should be controlled. All wildlife species or populations have both positive and negative values. To determine the net value of a wildlife species, all of the positive values must be summed up and all the negative values must be subtracted from them. I used such an approach to determine the positive and negative values of deer (Conover 2011). I calculated that the total positive values of deer in the United States were $16.6 billion dollars, while negative values were $4.4 billion. Hence, the net value of deer was highly positive (approximately $12.2 billion annually).

4.14 WHAT HUMAN–WILDLIFE CONFLICTS OCCUR IN OTHER COUNTRIES?

Thus far, I have concentrated on economic losses in the United States, but human–wildlife conflicts are a global problem. Therefore, it is worthwhile to consider wildlife problems in other parts of the world. The human–wildlife conflicts that are discussed should not be considered an exhaustive list of problems in each country; rather, they are intended to provide a sampling of local problems with wildlife.

4.14.1 CENTRAL AMERICA AND SOUTH AMERICA

The eared dove is probably the most destructive pest of Central and South American grain fields, damaging ripening sorghum, sunflowers, soybeans, wheat, barley, and rice. This species can breed throughout the year and is found throughout South America with the exception of the Amazonia Rain Forest. This nomadic bird concentrates in areas when food is abundant, such as ripening grain fields. Some roosts contain over 10 million doves. Large-scale campaigns have been conducted for decades in Argentina, Brazil, and Uruguay to reduce eared dove populations. Methods included the use of poison bait, aerial spraying of roosting colonies, nest destruction, and incentives for hunting (Bucher and Ranvaud 2006; Bucher and Bocco 2009; Linz et al. 2015). Monk parakeets also damage crops wherever they occur in South America with sunflower, corn, sorghum, and fruit being particularly hard hit. Its large nests create nuisance problems and short out electrical systems (Canavelli et al. 2013; Bucher and Aramburú 2014; Linz et al. 2015).

Many North American birds migrate to Central and South America to winter and produce agricultural damage once on the wintering grounds. One of them is the dickcissel, which is one of the most destructive species to South American grain crops. It breeds in the North American prairies, where they consume mainly insects. During winter, most dickcissels are found in grain-growing regions of Venezuela, Columbia, and Trinidad, where they are particularly destructive of grain sorghum fields (Linz et al. 2015). Winter roosts can number into the millions, and flocks numbering into the thousands forage in ripening grain fields. Damage is acute at grain farms near roosts.

Ranchers in South America have to contend with losses caused by jaguar and cougars. Vulnerable livestock include cattle, horses, sheep, and pigs. The mean value of loss for an animal is $178 in Costa Rica, where more farms have less than eight head of livestock (Amit et al. 2013). After losing livestock, some ranchers retaliate by killing these predators; this practice is believed by many TO explain the decline in jaguar and cougar populations in parts of South America (Crawshaw 2004; Kissling et al. 2009). Ranchers in Venezuela, Colombia, Ecuador, Peru, and Bolivia also have to contend with the loss of livestock to Andean bears (Goldstein et al. 2006; Zukowski and Ormsby 2016). Other examples of wildlife damage to farms and ranches in South America appear in Table 4.4. The examples shown in the table are not the worse problems but illustrate some of the problems that occur in South America.

4.14.2 UNITED KINGDOM

In the U.K., British farmers consider the European rabbit to be their greatest wildlife pest due to its herbivory in grain fields, horticultural crops, and pastures (Wilson and McKillop 1986; Hardy 1990). Often, rabbits are controlled by fumigating their burrows and by trapping, but some British consider these methods to be inhumane. Fencing is often used to exclude rabbits from agricultural fields. Rats and house mice occupy many farm buildings and cause post-harvest losses to stored grain and

FIGURE 4.15   European badger.

Source: Paul A. Carpenter, Shutterstock 1492901462.

feed. In England and Wales, European badgers caused problem for 26% of farmers through their burrowing and 21% through damage to crops (Figure 4.15). Most farmers reported that their losses to badgers were minor, but 5% reported that their losses exceeded £1,800. Nationwide, farm losses from badgers were £73 million (Table 4.4). Coppice woodlands and tree plantations in Great Britain are damaged by red, roe, fallow, and muntjac deer (Putman 1994; Moore et al. 1999*a*).

Several avian species damage agricultural crops in Great Britain. Sparrows and doves are pests in sunflower fields, while wood pigeons damage growing fields of rapeseed and bullfinches ruin fruit in orchards. During winter, large numbers of Brant geese graze in fields of winter grain, as do Canada geese, an exotic species introduced from North America (Patterson et al. 1989; Summers 1990; McKay et al. 1993; Linz and Hanzel 1997).

The urban and suburban parts of the United Kingdom have their own share of wildlife problems; house mice and brown rats invade homes and buildings, damage stored grains, and pose health risks to both animals and people. Starlings, house sparrows, pigeons, and gulls litter urban areas with fecal matter and cause nuisance problems. Gray squirrels damage yards and property and steal food left out for birds. Still, U.K. residents had positive attitudes toward badgers, rabbits, moles, squirrels, and mice. Only pigeons, gulls, and rats produced a negative response (Baker et al. 2020).

Atlantic salmon are raised in large net enclosures in the coastal waters of Great Britain and other North Atlantic countries. Over half of the salmon farms in Scotland reported problems with predators with the main threats being harbor seals and grey seals; only 3% of salmon farmers were unconcerned about predators. Most salmon farms were using top nets to exclude predators and acoustical devices to annoy them (Quick et al. 2004).

4.14.3 Europe

Agriculture is an important land use in the European Union, where there is 137 million ha of farmland and permanent pasture (43% of land use), and 12 million people are employed in the industry. There are also 40 million ha of planted forest plantations (Young et al. 2010). Goose populations have been expanding throughout Europe where the birds are damaging pastures and agricultural fields (Bergjord Olsen et al. 2017; Petkov et al. 2017; Clausen et al. 2019).

Europe has several free-ranging ungulate species, including roe deer, red deer, white-tailed deer, fallow deer, chamois, moose, and reindeer, which provide many benefits to Europeans. For example, over seven million ungulates are harvested by hunters annually (Linnell et al. 2020). Populations of these large herbivores have increased greatly in recent decades (Linnell and Zachos 2010). As discussed in Chapter 2, these species cause numerous collisions with vehicles throughout Europe. Agricultural crops suffer from their grazing and browsing, and the timber industry suffers when they eat newly planted tree seedlings or when they kill mature trees by stripping the bark (Bergquist and Örlander 1998; Verheyden et al. 2006).

Feral hogs are particularly destructive of agricultural crops, and feral hog populations in Europe have increased in recent decades. This increasing population has benefitted European hunters but not farmers. Feral hog damage to agricultural crops and timber across Europe is estimated at €80 million, including €30 million in France and Italy alone (Linnell et al. 2020). Luxembourg receives over 1,300 feral hog complaints from farmers each year; losses to hogs averaging over €500,000 annually (Table 4.4). Losses were greatest in cornfields, wheat fields, and pastures. Feral hog damage per farm averaged €145 in Switzerland and €328 in the German region of Baden-Württemberg (Geisser 2000; Linderoth and Elliger 2002 as cited by Schley et al. 2008).

Europe is also blessed with several large predators: wolves, lynx, and brown bears (European name for grizzly bears). These predators kill sheep, goats, and cattle (Rigg et al. 2011). Each year between 500 and 600 of Sweden's 600,000 sheep are killed by large predators (Elofsson et al. 2015 as cited by Widman et al. 2019). Wolverines, wolves, and bears kill cattle and reindeer throughout Scandinavia. In Spain, griffon vultures attack sheep and cattle (Margalida et al. 2014). Northern Europe has its own problems with seals. Grey seals create many difficulties to the coastal fisheries of Sweden and Finland. These problems include seals stealing catches and damaging nets of fishermen. Seals also vector parasites to the fish, making the fish unsuitable for sale or consumption. The amount of fish consumed by seals is equivalent to the fish harvested by humans in the Baltic Sea, creating a competition for fish between fishermen and seals (Klenke et al. 2013). Sperm whales have also learned to steal the catch of fishermen (Sidebar 4.4).

SIDEBAR 4.4 WORLD'S BIGGEST WILDLIFE PROBLEM

Some of my students ask me what is biggest problem caused by wildlife? I do not know the answer, but I do know what is the largest wildlife to cause problems. That would be sperm whales, which weight up to 50,000 kg as adults (Figure 4.16). Sperm whales forage in the ocean's dark depths where they can use their sonar to locate prey including fish and squid. Fishermen also seek fish, such as black cod and halibut, from same deep depths by deploying long lines of baited hooks. Both killer whales and sperm whales around Alaska have learned that it is much easier to catch a fish that has been already hooked than to try to catch one that can swim away. Videos confirm the whale's thievery. Fishermen complain that whales eat most of their catch and leave only rockfish which the whales do not find palatable. Estimates of losses exceed $100,000 annually. The whales have learned how to grab the fish and get them off the hook. Over the years, the whales have learned the sounds that boats emit when they are pulling up their lines and that sound can attract whales located more than a km away. There are ten individual whales that are the main culprits. Whales are protected by law, so there is little fishermen can do to mitigate the problem, other than admire the whale's intelligence. Scientists hope to place GPS transmitters on these individual whales so that boats can avoid setting their lines near these whales (Gouch 2015; Chen 2017).

FIGURE 4.16   Sperm whale.

Source: Wildeanimal, Shutterstock 1196794360.

4.14.4 AFRICA

Africa is blessed with an abundance of wildlife, which pose problems for the continent's farmers and ranchers. In Uganda, farmers near wildlife reserves must contend with multiple herbivores. Sugarcane is damaged by chimpanzees and baboons; cassava by bush pigs; corn by baboons, monkeys, and bush pigs; and peanuts by African crested porcupines. Baboons, however, are the most destructive. Much of the damage occurs at night, forcing farmers and family members to spend long nights in the fields protecting their crops from wildlife (Tweheyo et al. 2005).

African elephants pose a difficult problem for people who farm close to parks or preserves, owing to the great beasts' propensity to forage in agricultural fields. Their damage not only includes the large amounts of food they consume, but they also trample vegetation and cause considerable damage to fences and structures (Sitati et al. 2003, 2005). About 16,000 people and about the same number of elephants live on the eastern side of the Okavando Delta Panhandle of Botswana. From 2008 through 2010, the government received approximately 200 reports annually of elephants damaging crops (Songhurst 2017). Villagers and small-scale farmers within a few kilometers of a national park or wildlife reserve are in a difficult situation because the wildlife come out from the park to eat their crops; villagers, nonetheless, cannot kill the animals because they are owned by the government and protected by law (Gillingham and Lee 2003).

African ranchers face losses from a variety of predators. In South Africa, ranches lose an average of 6% of their small livestock to black-backed jackals and caracals. This amounts to an annual loss of eight million animals in the Northern Cape and six million in the Free State provinces (De Wet 2010 as cited by Swanepoel et al. 2016). The problem has been made worse by the spread of warthogs because these animals burrow beneath predator-proof fences; then other predators use these same openings to gain access to livestock (Bothma and Du Toit 2010; Swanepoel et al. 2016). Warthogs also consume crops, especially corn, and their rooting damages the veld (Smit 2014). Offsetting these negative impacts, warthogs are considered a game species, and hunting them is popular on game farms.

In Gokwe communal land, Zimbabwe, predators killed 241 livestock of which 75% were goats, 10% sheep, 7% cattle, and 7% donkeys; the losses represented 5% of total livestock holdings. Baboons were responsible for half of the kills; they killed mainly young goats and sheep; lions were responsible for 34% of the kills and leopards for 12%. Yet, lions caused most of the economic losses due to their killing of cattle, which are the most valuable (Table 4.4). Gusset et al. (2009) documented 938 predator attacks on livestock in northern Botswana; black-backed jackals were responsible for 77% of attacks, spotted hyenas for 8%, lions 5%, leopards 5%, African wild dogs 2%, cheetahs 1%, and caracals 1%.

More than 40 species of birds attack grain crops in northern Africa, with most of the damage caused by red-billed quelea, village weavers, yellow-backed weavers, and glossy starlings (Manikowski and Da Camara-Smeets 1979). Quelea and weaver birds live in semi-arid parts of Africa and breed in large colonies during the rainy season. During the rest of the year, they form large flocks that can number into the millions (Crook and Ward 1968). These birds cause extensive damage to ripening grain fields (Table 4.4). These birds may cause more agricultural damage than any other bird species in the world. It is not uncommon for these birds to reduce grain yields in sorghum and wheat fields by more than 50% (Table 4.4). Rock pigeons and red-eyed turtle doves are the main avian threat to sunflower fields in South Africa (Linz and Hanzel 1997).

4.14.5 ASIA

Crops in parts of Asia are damaged by several mammals including rhinoceros, wild buffalo, hog deer, wild pig, rhesus macaque, and elephant. Ten percent of the world's Asian elephant population resides in Sri Lanka, where these animals cause much damage on farms. Affected crops include banana, corn, jackfruit, coconut, manioc, sugarcane, sesame, rice, mango, and papaya. Most of the damage (88%) is caused by male elephants (Ekanayaka et al. 2011). Northeast India contains 10,000 wild elephants, and crop raiding by elephants is common, especially in fields that border forests. Between 1980 and 2003, more than 1,150 humans and 370 elephants died as a result of these conflicts (Choudhury 2004). In Nepal's Terai, 10% of households have someone who was injured or killed by elephants, and half of the households experienced property damaged by elephants (Neupane et al. 2017).

About 94,000 people live in 33 rural villages adjacent to Kumbhalgarh Wildlife Sanctuary in Rajasthan India. The average farm is 4 ha and a single depredation event can destroy a farm's annual production. Most (73%) households reported damage from nilgai; these large herbivores travel in groups and a household's entire crop can be destroyed in a single night. Thirty-six percent of farmers reported damage by wild hogs and 18% by langurs (Chhangani et al. 2008). Macaques cost rural farmers in India $66 per household per year from crop damage, significantly reducing the farmers' annual income (Wang et al. 2006).

In northern Laos, village farmers near wildlife-protected areas face considerable losses from wildlife in their small fields. Corn was the main crop damaged, but rice and pumpkins were also impacted. Most problems are caused by Asiatic black bears and sun bears; perceived losses varied from 11% to 39% among local villagers. Farmers relied on several local remedies for relief: piling trees and branches around the field's edge to create a physical barrier; surrounding the field with human excrement or urine, a colorful string, stripes of cloth soaked in soap or diesel oil; deploying wind chimes or scarecrows within the field; or having someone stay in the field at night. None of these have solved the problem (Scotson et al. 2014).

Feral pigs and macaques cause damage throughout Southeast Asia (Table 4.4). Around Kerinci Seblat Nation Park in Sumatra, Linkie et al. (2007) recorded over 5,000 crop raids by wildlife during a 1-year period; 99% of the raids were carried out by feral hogs and pig-tailed macaques (Priston 2009). Rural farmers in Nepal and Tibet lose much of their annual income to crop damage from primates (Wang et al. 2006). Farmers in Bhutan suffer crop losses by foraging wild hogs, barking deer, macaques, and sambars. Damaged crops included rice, corn, wheat, buckwheat, and chili. Most damage occurs in small fields near forested areas or the national park. In Indonesia, 9% of the rice crop was damaged by ricefield rats (Jacob et al. 2006).

Within the Ramnagar Forest Division of Uttarakhand, India, crops located close to the forest are damaged by sambar, nilgai, and feral pigs. Fields farther away are raided by wild pig and nilgai, but they received less damage. Elephants were less common a problem. To protect their crops, most farmers (86%) used scarecrows, dogs, tin boxes to make noise, and marhans, which are temporary nocturnal shelters where farmers spend the night to guard their crops (Kumar et al. 2017).

Many Asian farmers lack rodent-proof storage facilities for grain. Because of this, additional losses occur after harvest. For instance, Ahmad et al. (1995) found that the average grain shop in Pakistan was home to 40 rats. Given the large number of poor, subsistence farmers in Southeast Asia, a reduction of rice yields due to rodents is a serious problem that results in much human hunger. Multiple crops of grain and rice are produced yearly in some parts of Southeast Asia, and this practice provides ample food all year, allowing rodent populations to reach high levels. Rodent control often involves the use of toxicants and traps to try to reduce their numbers.

Predation on livestock and wildlife damage to crops are becoming serious problems around many of the India's wildlife reserves and national parks. Two-thirds of the villagers near India's Sariska Tiger Reserve spent considerable time and money protecting crops and livestock from wildlife, primarily by personally guarding them or building fences. Despite these efforts, nearly half of the households living near the tiger reserve experienced losses to their livestock or crops due to wildlife depredation. Nilgai and wild boar caused most of the crop losses; tigers and leopards were the main predators of livestock. Despite their losses to wildlife, neighboring villagers had a positive attitude about the tiger reserve because the reserve provided them with fodder and firewood (Sekhar 1998).

In the Himalayan Mountains of northern India, village herders maintain small flocks of goats and sheep. The primary source of loss is to predators, including snow leopards, which kill 18% of all livestock, but tigers, leopards, jackals, dholes, wild-cats, civets, and mongooses also kill livestock or poultry (Jackson and Wangchuk 2004). Many (26%) rural households adjacent to a wildlife sanctuary in Rajasthan, India, reported livestock losses or other problems caused by hyenas, leopards, jackals, and wolves (Chhangani et al. 2008).

4.14.6 AUSTRALIA

Much of the wildlife damage in Australia is caused by exotic species, which were brought to the continent by European settlers. Feral pigs, red foxes, European rabbits, goats, donkeys, horses, water buffalo, and rats are all exotic species in Australia and have become serious environmental threats. Native flora and marsupial fauna did not evolve with these mammalian herbivores and predators and too often cannot compete with them or have no defense against them. These exotic mammals also have become major agricultural pests in Australia; the losses to Australia's wool industry due to European rabbits are over $110 million annually (Williams et al. 1995). Lethal means, including shooting, poisoning, and releasing exotic diseases, are often employed to control populations of exotic species. For instance, myxoma virus was released in 1950 to control European rabbits, producing a dramatic reduction of rabbit populations initially. But the impact waned over time as myxoma virus became less virulent, and the rabbits evolved some resistance to the disease. In 1996, rabbit calicivirus (also known as rabbit hemorrhagic disease virus) was deliberately released in Australia to control rabbits. The virus reduced some rabbit populations by 90%, while having little impact on other rabbit populations. Six years after the outbreak, rabbit numbers recovered to about 15%–17% of what it had been prior to the virus' release (Mutze et al. 2008).

The house mouse is an exotic species in Australia, arriving with European settlers. Mouse numbers are low most years, but about once a decade, their populations erupt to incredible levels. Such an eruption, called a mouse plague, occurred in 1993 in South Australia. Crop losses were estimated at $65 million, mainly from the destruction of newly planted legume and grain fields. Livestock producers also suffered from mice consuming and fouling livestock feed. Problems were not limited to the agricultural community. Mice migrated into towns, where they invading homes, hospitals, and businesses. Interestingly, fires also became more common as mice gnawed through electrical wires, causing short circuits. The 1993–1994 mouse plague cost businesses and community services about $1.3 million and households about $3.2 million (Caughley et al. 1994; Brown and Singleton 2000).

Other problems are caused by the native wildlife. Native marsupials, such as the red-necked wallabies and eastern grey kangaroos, compete with livestock for food, resulting in annual losses of $57 million (McLeod 2004 as cited by Cox et al. 2015). Wallabies and kangaroos create a nuisance in urban and suburban areas and pose a hazard to automobiles and trucks (Ramp and Roger 2008). Livestock are preyed upon by dingoes, a canid brought to Australia by the Aborigines before the arrival of Europeans. Over 60 species of native birds, such as silvereyes, galahs, and sulfur-crested cockatoos, cause losses to sunflower, grain, nut, and fruit growers (Table 4.4). Losses to just the fruit industry by birds during 2005 exceed $210 million, including $72 million to the wine and table grape industry, $59 million to apples and pears, $38 million to stone fruits, and $32 million to the nut industry (Tracey et al. 2007).

4.15 SUMMARY

Wildlife causes a myriad of problems (e.g., deer–automobile collisions, diseases, and reduced agricultural productivity). Because of this, making rational decisions about how to manage wildlife is difficult. Fortunately, economic analysis can express the positive and negative values of wildlife in dollars. Monetary values can be determined using various methods: expenditure of money and time, income-producing ability, increase in property values, willingness to pay, and willingness to do without. With economic data, wildlife biologists can prioritize projects and allocate resources to mitigate wildlife damage (i.e., negative impacts). Wildlife damage can be estimated by directly measuring damage in a random selection of fields where harm has resulted or by surveying people that are impacted by the damage. In the United States, total economic losses in the United States from human–wildlife conflicts are $35.5 billion. This includes losses of $12.5 billion from DVCs, $0.2 billion from bird–aircraft collisions, $17.6 billion to metropolitan and rural households,

$1.2 billion to timber production, and $4.0 billion to agricultural producers. Similar human–wildlife conflicts occur in most countries, but there are not enough data to calculate worldwide losses. Deer are the most destructive wildlife species in the United States due to vehicle collisions, zoonotic diseases, and their damage to timber industry and agriculture. The benefits provided by every wildlife species, including deer, for society greatly exceeds the problems they cause (negative values).

4.16   DISCUSSION QUESTIONS

1. Because of inflation, a dollar was worth more in the past. This causes monetary loss reported in past studies to seem less serious today than they did at the time of the study. For example, a $1,000 loss in 1951 is the same as a $10,000 loss in 2020. In this study, I adjusted monetary values reported over 10 years ago to current values. Do you think this was a wise approach or should I have just reported the values in the original study?
2. What are some methods that can be used to determine the positive values that wildlife provide to society? Which one do you think is most accurate?
3. What is a lost-opportunity cost? Do you think it is worth trying to measure lost-opportunity costs caused by wildlife? If so, how would you assess it?
4. When visiting a cornfield to measure deer damage, why is it necessary to examine several plots rather than just one big one? Why is it necessary to use a random method to determine where to locate your plots in the cornfield? If you just examine one or two cornfields in a state, can you extrapolate your findings to all cornfields in the state?
5. The United States has a much better understanding of the extent of wildlife damage to crops than European countries. Why is this?
6. I estimated that wildlife damage in the United States is over $35 billion annually. Do you consider this a lot of money?
7. African farmers often spend long days and nights in their fields driving away hungry wildlife. But this practice is almost unheard on in the United States, Canada, and Europe. What accounts for the difference?
8. Most village farmers in Africa own only a couple of cattle, and the loss of a single animal can cause the farmer's family to go hunger. Should these farmers be allowed to kill the predator? If not, what else can be done to resolve the situation?
9. Australia releases a myxoma virus, which did not previously exist in the country, to control populations of European rabbits. If we identified an exotic virus that could kill deer, should we release it in the United States to reduce DVCs? Would you be more supportive of releasing an exotic virus in the United States to kill house mice, given that house mice are an exotic species and mainly occur in homes and buildings?

LITERATURE CITED

Ahmad, E., I. Hussain, and J. E. Brooks. 1995. Losses of stored foods due to rats in grain markets in Pakistan. *International Biodeterioration and Biodegradation* 36:125–133.

Allen, R. E., and D. R. McCullough. 1976. Deer-car accidents in Southern Michigan. *Journal of Wildlife Management* 40:317–325.

Amit, R., E. J. Gordillo-Chávez, and R. Bone. 2013. Jaguar and puma attacks on livestock in Costa Rica. *Human – Wildlife Interactions* 7:77–84.

Amundson, C. L., M. R. Pieron, T. W. Arnold, and L. A. Beaudoin. 2013. The effects of predator removal on mallard production and population change in northeastern North Dakota. *Journal of Wildlife Management* 77:143–152.

Anderson, A., K. Gebhardt, W. T. Cross, and S. A. Shwiff. 2013*a*. Spillover benefits of wildlife management to support pheasant populations. *Wildlife Society Bulletin* 37:278–280.

Anderson, A., C. A. Lindell, K. M. Moxcey, W. F. Siemer, G. M. Linz, P. D. Curtis, J. E. Carroll, C. L. Burrows, J. R. Boulanger, K. M. M. Steensma, and S. A. Shwiff. 2013*b*. Bird damage to select fruit crops: the cost of damage and the benefits of control in five states. *Crop Protection* 52:103–109.

Andreassen, H. P., H. Gundersen, and T. Storaas. 2005. The effect of scent-marking, forest clearing, and supplemental feeding on moose-train collisions. *Journal of Wildlife Management* 69:1125–1132.

Arner, D. H., and J. S. DuBose. 1980. The impact of the beaver on the environment and economics in the southern United States. *International Wildlife Conference* 414:241–247.

Avery, M. L., and R. DeHaven. 1982. Bird damage to sunflowers in the Sacramento Valley, California. *Proceedings of the Vertebrate Pest Conference* 10:197–200.

Awasthi, B., and N. B. Singh. 2015. Status of human-wildlife conflict and assessment of crop damage by wild animals in Gaurishankar Conservation Area, Nepal. *Journal of Institute of Science and Technology* 20:107–111.

Baker, S. E., S. A. Maw, P. J. Johnson, and D. W. Macdonald. 2020. Not in my backyard: public perceptions of wildlife and "pest control" in and around UK homes, and local authority "pest control". *Animals* 10(2):222.

Basili, G. D., and S. A. Temple. 1999. Dickcissels and crop damage in Venezuela: defining the problem with ecological models. *Ecological Applications* 9:732–739.

Bergjord Olsen, A. K., J. W. Bjerke, and I. M. Tombre. 2017. Yield reductions in agricultural grasslands in Norway after springtime grazing by pink-footed geese. *Journal of Applied Ecology* 54:1836–1846.

Bergquist, J., and G. Örlander. 1998. Browsing damage by roe deer on Norway spruce seedlings planted on clearcuts of different ages: 1. effect of slash removal, vegetation development, and roe deer density. *Forest Ecology and Management* 105:283–293.

Biondi, K. M., J. L. Belant, J. A. Martin, T. L. DeVault, and G. Wang. 2011. White-tailed deer incidents with U. S. civil aircraft. *Wildlife Society Bulletin* 35:303–309.

Bissonette, J. A., C. A. Kasser, and L. J. Cook. 2008. Assessment of costs associated with deer-vehicle collisions: human death and injury, vehicle damage, and deer loss. *Human-Wildlife Interactions* 2:17–27.

Black, H. C., E. J. Dimock, II, J. Evans, and J. A. Rochelle. 1979. *Animal damage to coniferous plantations in Oregon and Washington: part 1. survey, 1963-1975.* Forest Research Laboratory Research Bulletin 25, Oregon State University, Corvallis, OR.

Bothma, J. du P., and J. G. du Toit. 2010. *Game ranch management.* Van Schaik, Pretoria, South Africa.

Brewster, R. K. 2018. *Cost: benefit analysis of coyote removal as a management option in Texas cattle ranching.* Thesis, Texas A &M University, Kingsville, TX.

Brewster, R. K., S. E. Henke, B. L. Turner, and J. M. Tomeček. 2019. Cost – benefit analysis of coyote removal as a management option in Texas cattle ranching. *Human – Wildlife Interactions* 13:400–422.

Brodie, D., H. C. Black, E. J. Dimock II, J. Evans, C. Kao, and J. A. Rochelle. 1979. *Animal damage to coniferous plantations in Oregon and Washington: part II. an economic evaluation.* Research Bulletin 26, Forest Research Laboratory, Oregon State University, Corvallis, OR.

Brooks, J. E., E. Ahmad, and I. Hussain. 1988. Characteristics of damage by vertebrate pests to groundnuts in Pakistan. *Proceedings of the Vertebrate Pest Conference* 13:129–133.

Brown, P. R., and G. R. Singleton. 2000. Impacts of house mice on crops in Australia – costs and damage. *Human Conflicts with Wildlife: Economic Considerations* 6:48–58.

Bruggers, R. L. 1980. The situation of grain-eating birds in Somalia. *Proceedings of the Vertebrate Pest Conference* 9:5–16.

Bruinderink, G. W. T. A., and E. Hazebroek. 1996. Ungulate traffic collisions in Europe. *Conservation Biology* 10:1059–1067.

Bucher, E. H., and R. M. Aramburú. 2014. Land-use changes and monk parakeet expansion in the Pampas grasslands of Argentina. *Journal of Biogeography* 41:1160–1170.

Bucher, E. H., and P. J. Bocco. 2009. Reassessing the importance of granivorous pigeons as massive, long distance seed dispersers. *Ecology* 90:2321–2327.

Bucher, E. H., and R. D. Ranvaud. 2006. S31-4 eared dove outbreaks in South America: patterns and characteristics. *Acta Zoologica Sinica* 52:564–567.

Butler, J. R. 2000. The economic costs of wildlife predation on livestock in Gokwe communal land, Zimbabwe. *African Journal of Ecology* 38:23–30.

Butler, J. R., S. J. Middlemas, I. M. Graham, and R. N. Harris. 2011. Perceptions and costs of seal impacts on Atlantic salmon fisheries in the Moray Firth, Scotland: implications for the adaptive co-management of seal-fishery conflict. *Marine Policy* 35:317–323.

Canavelli, S. B., M. E. Swisher, and L. C. Branch. 2013. Factors related to farmers' preference to decrease monk parakeet damage to crops. *Human Dimensions of Wildlife* 18:124–137.

Caughley, J., V. Monamy, and K. Heiden. 1994. *Impact of the 1993 mouse plague.* Grains Research and Development Corporation, Occasional Papers Series No. 7, Canberra, Australia.

CDC. 2004. Synopsis for August 6, 2004. Nonfatal motor-vehicle animal crash—related injuries—United States, 2001–2002. *Morbidity and Mortality Weekly Report* 53:675–678.

Chapman, T. F. 2007. An endangered species that is also a pest: a case study of Baudin's cockatoo *Calyptorhynchus baudinii* and the pome fruit industry in South-West Western Australia. *Journal of the Royal Society of Western Australia* 90:33–40.

Chen, A. 2017. Killer whales are stalking boats and stealing their fish. *The Verge.* www.theverge.com/2017/6/20/15840336/killer-whale-depredation-fishing-thievery-halibut. Accessed 29 May 2018.

Chhangani, A. K., P. Robbins, and S. M. Mohnot. 2008. Crop raiding and livestock predation at Kumbhalgarh Wildlife Sanctuary, Rajasthan India. *Human Dimensions of Wildlife* 13:305–316.

Choudhury, A. 2004. Human-elephant conflicts in Northeast India. *Human Dimensions of Wildlife* 9:261–270.

Clausen, K. K., L. K. Marcussen, N. Knudsen, T. J. Balsby, and J. Madsen. 2019. Effectiveness of lasers to reduce goose grazing on agricultural grassland. *Wildlife Biology* wlb00560.

Colligan, G. M., J. L. Bowman, J. E. Rogerson, and B. L. Vasilas. 2011. Factors affecting white-tailed deer-browsing rates on early growth stages of soybean crops. *Human-Wildlife Interactions* 5:321–332.

Conover, M. R. 1997. Wildlife management by metropolitan residents in the United States: practices, perceptions, costs, and values. *Wildlife Society Bulletin* 25:306–311.

Conover, M. R. 1998. Perceptions of American agricultural producers about wildlife on their farms and ranches. *Wildlife Society Bulletin* 26:597–604.

Conover, M. R. 2011. Impacts of deer on society. Pages 399–407 *in* D. Hewitt, editor. *Biology and management of white-tailed deer.* CRC Press, Boca Raton, FL.

Conover, M. R. 2019. Numbers of human fatalities, injuries, and illnesses in the United States due to wildlife. *Human-Wildlife Interactions* 13:264–276.

Coulter, J. A., E. D. Nafziger, L. J. Abendroth, P. R. Thomison, R. W. Elmore, and M. E. Zarnstorff. 2011. Agronomic responses of corn to stand reduction at vegetative growth stages. *Agronomy Journal* 103:577–583.

Cox, T. E., P. J. Murray, A. J. Bengsen, G. P. Hall, and X. Li. 2015. Do fecal odors from native and non-native predators cause a habitat shift among macropods? *Wildlife Society Bulletin* 39:159–164.

Crawshaw, P. G. 2004. Depredation of domestic animals by large cats in Brazil. *Human Dimensions of Wildlife* 9:329–330.

Crook, J. H., and P. Ward. 1968. The quelea problem in Africa. Pages 211–229 *in* R. K. Murton and E. N. Wright, editors. *The problems of birds as pests*. Institute of Biology Symposium 17, Academic Press, London.

Cummings, J. L., S. A. Shwiff, and S. Tupper. 2005. Economic impacts of blackbirds to the rice industry. *Proceedings of the Wildlife Damage Management Conference* 11:317–322.

Decker, D. J., K. M. Loconti-Lee, and N. A. Connelly. 1990. *Incidence and costs of deer-related vehicular accidents in Tompkins County, New York*. Human Dimensions Research Group 89-7. Cornell University, Ithaca, NY.

De Grazio, J. W. 1978. World bird damage problems. *Proceedings of the Vertebrate Pest Conference* 8:9–24.

DeHaven, R. W. 1974. Bird damage to wine grapes in Central California, 1973. *Proceedings of the Vertebrate Pest Conference* 6:248–252.

de Mey, Y., M. Demont, and M. Diagne. 2011. Estimating bird damage to rice in Africa: evidence from the Senegal River Valley. *Journal of Agricultural Economics* 63:175–200.

DeVault, T. L., J. C. Beasley, L. A. Humberg, B. J. MacGowan, M. I. Retamosa, and O. E. Rhodes, Jr. 2007. Intrafield patterns of wildlife damage to corn and soybeans in Northern Indiana. *Human-Wildlife Interactions* 1:205–213.

De Wet, P. 2010. *Predation management forum: norms and standards for the management of damage-causing animals in South Africa*. Meeting of the Parliamentary Monitoring Group, Cape Town, South Africa. www.pmg.org.za/report/20101102-norms-and-standards-management-damage-causing-animals-south-africa.

Dolbeer, R. A., and M. J. Beiger. 2019. *Wildlife strikes to civil aircraft in the United States, 1990–2017*. U. S. Department of Transportation, Federal Aviation Administration, Office of Airport Safety and Standards, Serial Report No. 24, Washington, DC.

Dolbeer, R. A., J. R. Weller, A. L. Anderson, and M. J. Begier. 2016. *Wildlife strikes to civil aircraft in the United States 1990–2015*. U.S. Department of Transportation, Federal Aviation Administration, Office of Airport Safety and Standards, Serial Report 22, Washington, DC, USA.

Dorr, B. S., L. W. Burger, S. C. Barras, and K. C. Godwin. 2012. Economic impact of double-crested cormorant, *Phalacrocorax auratus*, depredation on channel catfish, *Ictalurus punctatus*, aquaculture in Mississippi, USA. *Journal of the World Aquaculture Society* 43:502–513.

Ekanayaka, S. K. K., A. Campos-Arceiz, M. Rupasinghe, J. Pastorini, and P. Fernando. 2011. Patterns of crop raiding by Asian elephants in a human-dominated landscape in Southeastern Sri Lanka. *Gajah* 34:20–25.

Elofsson, K., M. Widman, T. Häggmark Svensson, and M. Steen. 2015. *Påverkan från rovdjursangrepp på landsbygdsföretagens ekonomi* No. 167. Sveriges lantbruksuniversitet, Institutionen för ekonomi, Uppsala.

Elser, J. L., A. Anderson, C. A. Lindell, N. Dalsted, A. Bernasek, and S. A. Shwiff. 2016. Economic impacts of bird damage and management in US sweet cherry production. *Crop Protection* 83:9–14.

Elser, J. L., C. A. Lindell, K. M. M. Steensma, P. D. Curtis, D. K. Leigh, W. F. Siemer, J. R. Boulanger, and S. A. Shwiff. 2019. Measuring bird damage to three fruit crops: a comparison of grower and field estimates. *Crop Protection* 123:1–4.

Ernst, K., J. Elser, G. Linz, H. Kandel, J. Holderieath, S. DeGroot, S. Shwiff, and S. Shwiff. 2019. The economic impacts of blackbird (*Icteridae*) damage to sunflower in the USA. *Pest Management Science* doi:10.1002/ps.5486.

Gedney, D. R., and C. Van Sickle. 1979. Geographic context of forestry. Pages 301-318 *in* W. A. Duerr, D. E. Teeguarden, N. B. Christiansen, and S. Guttenberg, editors. *Forest resource management.* Saunders Publishing, Philadelphia, PA.

Geisser, H. 2000. *Das Wildschein (Sus scrofa) im Kanton Thurgau (Schweiz): analyse der Populationsdynamik, der Habitatansprüche und der Feldschäden in einem anthropogen beeinflussten Lebensraum.* Thesis, University of Zurich, Zurich, Switzerland.

Gillingham, S., and P. C. Lee. 2003. People and protected areas: a study of local perceptions of wildlife crop-damage conflict in an area bordering the Selous Game Reserve, Tanzania. *Oryx* 37:316–325.

Glahn, J. F., and K. E. Brugger. 1995. The impact of double-crested cormorants on the Mississippi Delta catfish industry: a bioenergetics model. *Colonial Waterbirds* 18:168–175.

Goldstein, I., S. Paisley, R. Wallace, J. P. Jorgenson, F. Cuesta, and A. Castellanos. 2006. Andean bear – livestock conflicts: a review. *Ursus* 17:8–15.

Gouch, Z. 2015. Sperm whales target fishing boats for an easy meal. *BBC Earth.* www.bbc.com/earth/story/20150204-sperm-whales-target-fishing-boats-for-an-easy-meal. Accessed 25 May 2018.

Govind, S. K., and E. A. Jayson. 2018. Damage to paddy *Oryza sativa* by Indian peafowl *Paro cristatus* near Chulannur Peafowl Sanctuary, Kerala, India. *Indian Birds* 14:149–150.

Gusset, M., M. J. Swarner, L. Mponwane, K. Keletile, and J. W. McNutt. 2009. Human-wildlife conflict in Northern Botswana: livestock predation by endangered African wild dog *Lycaon pictus* and other carnivores. *Oryx* 43:67–72.

Haney, M. J., and M. R. Conover. 2013. Ungulate damage to safflower in Utah. *Journal of Wildlife Management* 77:282–289.

Hardy, A. R. 1990. Vertebrate pests of U.K. agriculture: present problems and future solutions. *Proceedings of the Vertebrate Pest Conference* 14:181–185.

Haskell, M. G., and R. L. Langley. 2020. Animal-encounter fatalities, United States, 1999–2016: cause of death and misreporting. *Public Health Reports*, 15 September. https://doi.org/10.1177/0033354920953211.

Hill, C. M. 2004. Farmers' perspectives of conflict at the wildlife-agriculture boundary: some lessons learned from African subsistence farmers. *Human Dimensions of Wildlife* 9:279–286.

Hinton, G. C., B. K. Strickland, S. Demarais, T. W. Eubank, and P. D. Jones. 2017. Estimation of deer damage to soybean production in eastern Mississippi: perceptions versus reality. *Wildlife Society Bulletin* 41:80–87.

Hofman-Kamińska, E., and R. Kowalczyk. 2012. Farm crops depredation by European bison (*Bison bonasus*) in the vicinity of forest habitats in northeastern Poland. *Environmental Management* 50:530–541.

Humberg, L. A., T. L. DeVault, B. J. MacGowan, J. C. Beasley, and R. E. Rhodes, Jr. 2007. Crop depredation by wildlife in northcentral Indiana. *Proceedings of the National Wild Turkey Symposium* 9:199–205.

Jackson, R. M., and R. Wangchuk. 2004. A community-based approach to mitigating livestock depredation by snow leopards. *Human Dimensions of Wildlife* 9:307–315.

Jackson, W. B. 1977. Evaluation of rodent depredations to crops and stored products. *EPPO Bulletin* 7:439–458.

Jacob, J., Rahmini, and Sudarmaji. 2006. The impact of imposed female sterility on field populations of ricefield rats (*Rattus argentiventer*). *Agriculture, Ecosystems and Environment* 115:281–284.

John, A. 2014. Rodent outbreaks and rice pre-harvest losses in Southeast Asia. *Food Security* 6:249–260.

Johnson, D. B., F. S. Guthery, and N. E. Koerth. 1989. Grackle damage to grapefruit in the Lower Rio Grande Valley. *Wildlife Society Bulletin* 17:46–50.

Johnson-Nistler, C. M., J. E. Knight, and S. D. Cash. 2005. Considerations related to Richardson's ground squirrel (*Spermophilus richardsonii*) control in Montana. *Agronomy Journal* 97:1460–1464.

Kalinowski, S. A., and D. S. deCalestra. 1981. Baiting regimes for reducing ground squirrel damage to alfalfa. *Wildlife Society Bulletin* 9:268–272.

Kämmerle, J. L., F. Brieger, M. Kröschel, R. Hagen, I. Storch, and R. Suchant. 2017. Temporal patterns in road crossing behaviour in roe deer (*Capreolus capreolus*) at sites with wildlife warning reflectors. *PloS One* 12(9):e0184761.

King, D. T., B. F. Blackwell, B. S. Dorr, and J. L. Belant. 2010. Effects of aquaculture on migration and movement patterns of double-crested cormorants. *Human-Wildlife Interactions* 4:77–86.

Kissling, D. W., N. Fernández, and J. M. Paruelo. 2009. Spatial risk assessment of livestock exposure to pumas in Patagonia, Argentina. *Ecography* 32:807–817.

Kissui, B. M. 2008. Livestock predation by lions, leopards, spotted hyenas, and their vulnerability to retaliatory killing in the Maasai steppe, Tanzania. *Animal Conservation* 11:422–432.

Klenke, R. A., I. Ring, A. Kranz, N. Jepsen, F. Rauschmayer, and K. Henle, editors. 2013. *Human-wildlife conflicts in Europe: fisheries and fish-eating vertebrates as a model case.* Springer Science and Business Media, Heidelberg, Germany.

Klosterman, M. E., G. M. Linz, T. A. Slowik, and W. J. Blier. 2012. *Assessment of bird damage to sunflower and corn in North Dakota.* USDA National Wildlife Research Center Staff Publications, 1325, Fort Collins, CO. www.aphis.usda.gov/wildlife_damage/nwrc/publications/11pubs/linz112.pdf. Accessed 1 November 2018.

Knarrum, V., O. J. Sorensen, T. Eggen, T. Kvam, O. Opseth, K. Overskaug, and A. Eidsmo. 2006. Brown bear predation on domestic sheep in central Norway. *Ursus* 17:67–75.

Krauze-Gryz, D., M. Żmihorski, K. Jasińska, Ł. Kwaśny, and J. Werka. 2017. Temporal pattern of wildlife-train collisions in Poland. *Journal of Wildlife Management* 81:1513–1519.

Kumar, A., H. S. Bargali, A. David, and A. Edgaonkar. 2017. Patterns of crop raiding by wild ungulates and elephants in Ramnagar Forest Division, Uttarakhand. *Human-Wildlife Interactions* 11:41–49.

Linderoth, P., and A. Elliger. 2002. Schwarzwildschäden an landwirtschaftlichen Kulturen in Baden-Württemberg im Jagdjahr 2000/2001. *WFS-Mitteilungen* 1:1–4.

Linkie, M., Y. Dinata, A. Nofrianto, and N. Leader-Williams. 2007. Patterns and perceptions of wildlife crop raiding in and around Kerinci Seblat National Park, Sumatra. *Animal Conservation* 10:127–135.

Linnell, J. D. C., B. Cretois, E. B. Nilsen, C. M. Rolandsen, E. J. Solberg, V. Veiberg, P. Kaczensky, B. Van Moorter, M. Panzacchi, G. R. Rauset, and B. Kaltenborn. 2020. The challenges and opportunities of coexisting with wild ungulates in the human-dominated landscapes of Europe's anthropocene. *Biological Conservation* 244:108500.

Linnell, J. D. C., and F. E. Zachos. 2010. Status and distribution patterns of European ungulates: genetics, population history and conservation. *Ungulate Management in Europe: Problems and Practices* 12–53.

Linz, G. M., E. H. Bucher, S. B. Canavelli, E. Rodriguez, and M. L. Avery. 2015. Limitations of population suppression for protecting crops from bird depredation: a review. *Crop Protection* 76:46–52.

Linz, G. M., and J. J. Hanzel. 1997. Birds and sunflowers. *Sunflower Technology and Production, Agricultural Monograph* 35:381–394.

Linz, G. M., H. J. Homan, S. J. Werner, H. M. Hagy, and W. J. Beier. 2011. Assessment of bird-management strategies to protect sunflowers. *BioScience* 61:960–970.

Lorenzen, B., and J. Madsen. 1986. Feeding by geese on the Filsø farmland, Denmark, and the effect of grazing on yield structure of spring barley. *Ecography* 9:305–311.

MacGowan, B. J., L. A. Humbug, J. C. Beasley, T. L. Devault, M. I. Retamosa, and O. E. Rhodes, Jr. 2006. *Corn and soybean crop depredation by wildlife.* Purdue University, Department of Forestry and Natural Resources Publication, FNR-265-W, Purdue, IN.

Mackenzie, C. A., and P. Ahabyona. 2012. Elephants in the garden: financial and social costs of crop raiding. *Ecological Economics* 75:72–82.

Mangnall, M. J., and T. M. Crowe. 2002. Population dynamics and the physical and financial impacts to cereal crops of the Egyptian goose *Alopochen aegptiacus* on the Agulhas Plain, Western Cape, South Africa. *Agriculture Ecosystems and Environment* 90:231–246.

Manikowski, S., and M. Da Camara-Smeets. 1979. Estimating bird damage to sorghum and millet in Chad. *Journal of Wildlife Management* 43:540–544.

Marcoux, A. 2005. *Deer-vehicle collisions: an understanding of accident characteristics and drivers' attitudes, awareness and involvement.* Thesis, Michigan State University, East Lansing, MI.

Margalida, A., D. Campión, and J. A. Donázar. 2014. Vultures vs livestock: conservations relationships in an emerging conflict between humans and wildlife. *Oryx* 48:172–176.

Marra, P. P., C. J. Dove, R. Dolbeer, N. F. Dahlan, M. Heacker, J. F. Whatton, N. E. Diggs, C. France, and G. A. Henkes. 2009. Migratory Canada geese cause crash of US airways flight 1549. *Frontiers in Ecology and the Environment* 7:297–301.

Marquis, D. A. 1981. *The effect of deer browsing on timber production in Allegheny hardwood forests of Northwestern Pennsylvania.* Northeast Forest Experiment Station, Broomall, PA.

Matthews, S. 2016. An organic chicken farm in Georgia has become an endless buffet for bald eagles. *Audubon* 119:38–43.

Mazzolli, M., M. E. Graipel, and N. Dunstone. 2002. Mountain lion depredation in Southern Brazil. *Biological Conservation* 105:43–51.

McKay, H. V., J. D. Bishop, C. J. Feare, and M. C. Stevens. 1993. Feeding by brent geese can reduce yield of oilseed rape. *Crop Protection* 12:101–105.

McLeod, R. 2004. *Counting the cost: impact of invasive animals in Australia. Cooperative Research Centre for Pest Animal Control.* Australian Capital Territory, Canberra, Australia.

Moore, N. P., J. D. Hart, and S. D. Langton. 1999a. Factors influencing browsing by fallow deer *Dama dama* in young broad-leaved plantations. *Biological Conservation* 87:255–260.

Moore, N. P., A. Whiterow, P. Kelly, D. Garthwaite, J. Bishop, S. Langton, and C. Cheeseman. 1999b. Survey of badger *Meles meles* damage to agriculture in England and Wales. *Journal of Applied Ecology* 36:974–988.

Mott, D. F., J. F. Besser, R. R. West, and J. W. DeGrazio. 1972. Bird damage to peanuts and methods for alleviating the problem. *Proceedings of the Vertebrate Pest Conference* 5:118–120.

Mutze, G., P. Bird, B. Cooke, and R. Henzell. 2008. Geographic and seasonal variation in the impact of rabbit haemorrhagic disease on European rabbits, *Oryctolagus cuniculus*, and rabbit damage in Australia. Pages 279–293 *in* P. C. Alves, N. Ferrand, and K. Hackländer, editors. *Lagomorph biology: evolution, ecology, and conservation.* Springer-Verlag, Berlin, Germany.

Nelms, C. O., M. L. Avery, and D. G. Decker. 1990. Assessment of bird damage to early-ripening blueberries in Florida. *Proceedings of the Vertebrate Pest Conference* 14:302–306.

Neupane, D., S. Kunwar, A. K. Bohara, T. S. Risch, and R. L. Johnson. 2017. Willingness to pay for mitigating human-elephant conflict by residents of Nepal. *Journal for Nature Conservation* 36:65–76.

Nichols, T. C. 2014a. Integrated damage management reduces grazing of wild rice by resident Canada geese in New Jersey. *Wildlife Society Bulletin* 38:229–236.

Nichols, T. C. 2014b. Ten years of resident Canada goose damage management in a New Jersey tidal freshwater wetland. *Wildlife Society Bulletin* 38:221–228.

Nolte, D. L., and M. Dykzeul. 2002. Wildlife impacts on forest resources. Pages 163–168 in L. Clark, editor. *Human conflicts with wildlife: economic considerations.* National Wildlife Research Center, Fort Collins, CO.

Nybakk, K., O. Kjelvik, T. Kvam, K. Overskaug, and P. Sunde. 2002. Mortality of semi-domestic reindeer *Rangifer tarandus* in central Norway. *Wildlife Biology* 8:63–68.

Parkhurst, J. A., R. P. Brooks, and D. E. Arnold. 1992. Assessment of predation at trout hatcheries in central Pennsylvania. *Wildlife Society Bulletin* 20:411–419.

Patterson, B. D., S. M. Kasiki, E. Selempo, and R. W. Kays. 2004. Livestock predation by lions (*Panthera leo*) and other carnivores on ranches neighboring Tsavo National Parks, Kenya. *Biological Conservation* 119:507–516.

Patterson, I. J., S. Abdul Jalil, and M. L. East. 1989. Damage to winter cereals by greylag and pink-footed geese in Northeast Scotland. *Journal of Applied Ecology* 26:879–895.

Pérez, E., and L. F. Pacheco. 2006. Damage by large mammals to subsistence crops within a protected area in a montane forest of Bolivia. *Crop Protection* 25:933–939.

Petkov, N., A. L. Harrison, A. Stamenov, and G. M. Hilton. 2017. The impact of wintering geese on crop yields in Bulgarian Dobrudzha: implications for agri-environment schemes. *European Journal of Wildlife Research* 63(4):66.

Pfeiffer, M. B., B. F. Blackwell, and T. L. DeVault. 2018. Quantification of avian hazards to military aircraft and implications for wildlife management. *PloS One* 13(11):e0206599.

Priston, N. E. C. 2009. Enclosure plots as a mechanism for quantifying damage to crops by primates. *International Journal of Pest Management* 55:243–249.

Putman, R. J. 1994. Deer damage in coppice woodlands: an analysis of factors affecting the severity of damage and options for management. *Quarterly Journal of Forestry* 88:45–54.

Quick, N. J., S. J. Middlemas, and J. D. Armstrong. 2004. A survey of antipredator controls at marine salmon farms in Scotland. *Aquaculture* 230(1–4):169–180.

Radtke, T. M., and C. D. Dieter. 2011. Canada goose crop damage abatement in South Dakota. *Human-Wildlife Interactions* 5:315–320.

Ramkumar, K., B. Ramakrishnan, and R. Saravanamuthu. 2014. Crop damage by Asian elephants *Elephas maximus* and effectiveness of mitigating measures in Coimbatore forest division, South India. *International Research Journal of Biological Sciences* 3:1–11.

Ramp, D., and E. Roger. 2008. Frequency of animal – vehicle collisions in NSW. Pages 118–126 in D. Lunney, A. Munn, and W. Meikle, editors. *Too close for comfort: contentious issues in human – wildlife encounters.* Royal Zoological Society of New South Wales, Mosman, New South Wales, Australia.

Redick, C. H., and D. F. Jacobs. 2020. Mitigation of deer herbivory in temperate hardwood forest regeneration: a meta-analysis of research literature. *Forests* 11(11):1220.

Redick, C. H., J. R. McKenna, D. E. Carlson, M. A. Jenkins, and D. F. Jacobs. 2020. Silviculture at establishment of hardwood plantations is relatively ineffective in the presence of deer browsing. *Forest Ecology and Management* 474:118339.

Rigg, R., S. Find'o, M. Wechselberger, M. L. Gorman, C. Sillero-Zubiri, and D. W. Macdonald. 2011. Mitigating carnivore-livestock conflict in Europe: lessons from Slovakia. *Oryx* 45:272–280.

Rogerson, J. E., J. L. Bowman, E. L. Tymkiw, G. M. Colligan, and B. L. Vasilas. 2014. The impact of white-tailed deer browsing and distance from the forest edge on soybean yield. *Wildlife Society Bulletin* 38:473–479.

Romin, L. 1994. *Factors associated with mule deer highway mortality at Jordanelle Reservoir, Utah.* M.S. Thesis, Utah State University, Logan, UT.

Rust, N. A., K. M. Whitehouse-Tedd, and D. C. MacMillan. 2013. Perceived efficacy of live-stock-guarding dogs in South Africa: implications for cheetah conservation. *Wildlife Society Bulletin* 37:690–697.

Sauer, W. C. 1984. Impact of the Belding's ground squirrel, *Spermophilia beldingi*, on alfalfa production in Northeastern California. *Proceedings of the Vertebrate Pest Conference* 11:20–23.

Schiess-Meier, M., S. Ramsauer, T. Gabanapelo, and B. König. 2007. Livestock preda-tion – insights from problem animal control registers in Botswana. *Journal of Wildlife Management* 71:1267–1274.

Schley, L., M. Dufrêne, A. Krier, and A. C. Frantz. 2008. Patterns of crop damage by wild boar (*Sus scrofa*) in Luxembourg over a 10-year period. *European Journal of Wildlife Research* 54:589–599.

Schwabe, K. A., and P. W. Schuhmann. 2002. Deer-vehicle collisions and deer value: an anal-ysis of competing literatures. *Wildlife Society Bulletin* 30:609–615.

Scotson, L., K. Vannachomchan, and T. Sharp. 2014. More valuable dead than deterred? Crop-raiding bears in Lao PDR. *Wildlife Society Bulletin* 38:783–790.

Sekhar, N. U. 1998. Crop and livestock depredation caused by wild animals in protected areas: the case of Sariska Tiger Reserve, Rajasthan, India. *Environmental Conservation* 25:160–171.

Senar, J. C., J. Domènech, L. Arroyo, I. Torre, and O. Gordo. 2016. An evaluation of monk parakeet damage to crops in the metropolitan area of Barcelona. *Animal Biodiversity and Conservation* 39:141–145.

Shwiff, S. A., K. N. Kirkpatrick, T. L. DeVault, and S. S. Shwiff. 2015. Modeling the eco-nomic impacts of double-crested cormorant damage to a recreational fishery. *Human-Wildlife Interactions* 9:36–47.

Sitati, N. W., M. J. Walpole, and N. Leader-Williams. 2005. Factors affecting susceptibility of farms to crop raiding by African elephants: using a predictive model to mitigate conflict. *Journal of Applied Ecology* 42:1175–1182.

Sitati, N. W., M. J. Walpole, R. J. Smith, and N. Leader-Williams. 2003. Predicting spatial aspects of human-elephant conflict. *Journal of Applied Ecology* 40:667–677.

Smit, Z. M. 2014. *The ecological planning of Doornkloof nature reserve, Northern Cape Province.* Thesis, University of the Free State, Bloemfontein, South Africa.

Songhurst, A. 2017. Measuring human-wildlife conflicts: comparing insights from different monitoring approaches. *Wildlife Society Bulletin* 41:351–361.

Songhurst, A., and T. Coulson. 2014. Exploring the effect of spatial autocorrelation when identifying key drivers of wildlife crop-raiding. *Ecology and Evolution* 4:582–593.

Springer, M. T., J. L. Bowman, and B. L. Vasilas. 2013. The effect of white-tailed deer brows-ing on wheat quality and yields in Delaware. *Wildlife Society Bulletin* 37:155–161.

State Farm Insurance Company. 2016. *Look out! Deer collisions can be costly.* State Farm Insurance Company, Bloomington, IN. https://newsroom.statefarm.com/state-farm-releases-2016-deer-collision-data/. Accessed 15 September 2020.

State Farm Insurance Company. 2018. *Deer crashes down: annual report from state farm shows reduction in deer-related crashes.* State Farm Insurance Company, Bloomberg, IN. https://newsroom.statefarm.com/2018-deer-crashes-down/. Accessed 15 August 2020.

Steele, J. R., B. S. Rashford, T. K. Foulke, J. A. Tanaka, and D. T. Taylor. 2013. Wolf (*Canis lupus*) predation impacts on livestock production: direct effects, indirect effects, and implications for compensation ratios. *Rangeland Ecology and Management* 66:539–544.

Sultana, P., J. E. Brooks, and R. M. Poché. 1983. Methods for assessing rat damage to growing wheat in Bangladesh, with examples of applications. *Vertebrate Pest Control and Management Materials Symposium* 4:231–238.

Sultana, P., and M. M. Jaeger. 1992. Control strategies to reduce preharvest rat damage in Bangladesh. *Proceedings of the Vertebrate Pest Conference* 15:261–267.

Summers, R. W. 1990. The effect on winter wheat of grazing by brent geese *Branta bernicla*. *Journal of Applied Ecology* 27:821–833.

Swanepoel, M., A. J. Leslie, and L. C. Hoffman. 2016. Farmers' perceptions of the extralimital common warthog in the northern cape and free state provinces, South Africa. *Wildlife Society Bulletin* 40:112–121.

Tracey, J., M. Bomford, Q. Hart, G. Saunders, and R. Sinclair. 2007. *Managing bird damage to fruit and other horticultural crops*. Bureau of Rural Sciences, Canberra, Australia.

Transportation Canada. 2012. Update of data sources on collisions involving motor vehicles and large animals in Canada. *Transportation Canada, Road Transportation, Statistical Review*. www.tc.gc.ca/eng/motorvehiclesafety/tp-tp14798-menu-160.htm. Accessed 5 May 2018.

Tweheyo, M., C. M. Hill, and J. Obua. 2005. Patterns of crop raiding by primates around the Budongo Forest Reserve, Uganda. *Wildlife Biology* 11:237–248.

Tzilkowski, W. M., M. C. Brittingham, and M. J. Lovallo. 2002. Wildlife damage to corn in Pennsylvania: farmer and on-the-ground estimates. *Journal of Wildlife Management* 66:678–682.

U. S. Bureau of the Census. 1992. *Statistical abstract of the United States*, 111th edition. U. S. Government Printing Office, Washington, DC.

U. S. Department of Defense-Partners in Flight. 2019. *Bird/wildlife aircraft strike hazard*. U. S. Department of Defense. www.dodpif.org/groups/bash.php. Accessed 1 March 2019.

U. S. Department of Transportation. 2016. *Revised department guidance 2016: treatment of the value of preventing fatalities and injuries in preparing economic analyses*. Department of Transportation, Washington, DC.

U. S. Federal Highway Administration. 2008. *Wildlife-vehicle collision reduction study*. Report to Congress. FHWA-HRT-08-034, U. S. Federal Highway Administration, Washington, DC.

U. S. Forest Service. 2020. *Forest inventory and analysis nation program*. U. S. Forest Service, Washington, DC.

UNAIDS. 2021. Global HIV and AIDS statistics – fact sheet. https://www.unaids.org/sites/default/files/media_asset/UNAIDS_FactSheet_en.pdf. Accessed 10 August 2021.

Valencia, D. G. 1980. Rat control in coconut palms in Columbia. *Proceedings of the Vertebrate Pest Conference* 9:110–113.

Verheyden, H., P. Ballon, V. Bernard, and C. Saint-Andrieux. 2006. Variations in bark-stripping by red deer *Cervus elaphus* across Europe. *Mammal Review* 36:217–234.

Wakeley, J. S., and R. C. Mitchell. 1981. Blackbird damage to ripening field corn in Pennsylvania. *Wildlife Society Bulletin* 9:52–55.

Wang, S. W., P. D. Curtis, and J. P. Lassoie. 2006. Farmer perceptions of crop damage by Wildlife in Jigme Singye Wangchuck National Park, Bhutan. *Wildlife Society Bulletin* 34:359–365.

Washburn, B. E., P. J. Cisar, and T. L. DeVault. 2014. Wildlife strikes with military rotary-wing aircraft during flight operations within the United States. *Wildlife Society Bulletin* 38:311–320.

West, B. C., and K. Godwin. 2011. *Managing beaver problems in Mississippi.* Extension Service of Mississippi State University and U. S. Department of Agriculture, Starkville. Published in Furtherance of Acts of Congress, 8 May and 30 June 1914.

Whisson, D. A., S. B. Orloff, and D. L. Lancaster. 1999. Alfalfa yield loss from Belding's ground squirrels in Northeastern California. *Wildlife Society Bulletin* 27:178–183.

Widman, M., M. Steen, M., and K. Elofsson. 2019. Indirect costs of sheep depredation by large carnivores in Sweden. *Wildlife Society Bulletin* 43:53–61.

Williams, K., I. Parer, B. Coman, J. Burley, and M. Braysher. 1995. *Managing vertebrate pests: rabbits.* Bureau of Resource Sciences/CSIRO Division of Wildlife and Ecology, Australian Government Publishing Service, Canberra, Australia.

Wilson, C. J., and I. G. McKillop. 1986. An acoustic scaring device tested against European rabbits. *Wildlife Society Bulletin* 14:409–411.

Wywialowski, A. P. 1996. Wildlife damage to field corn in 1993. *Wildlife Society Bulletin* 24:264–271.

Young, J. C., M. Marzano, R. M. White, D. I. McCracken, S. M. Redpath, D. N. Carss, C. P. Quine, and A. D. Watt. 2010. The emergence of biodiversity conflicts from biodiversity impacts: characteristics and management strategies. *Biodiversity and Conservation* 19:3973–3990.

Zukowski, B., and A. Ormsby. 2016. Andean bear livestock depredation and community perceptions in Northern Ecuador. *Human Dimensions of Wildlife* 21:111–126.

5 Exotic Species

"Intercontinental invasions of non-indigenous species are leading towards gradual homogenization of the earth's biota and a homogenized global biota would also be a substantially impoverished biota."

– Cox (1999)

"The most common reason for a species to become extinct is biological pollution – the invasion of its habitat by an exotic species."

– Anonymous

Exotic, introduced, invasive, nonindigenous, alien, or nonnative species are terms used interchangeably to describe an animal living outside its normal range. Temple (1992) defined an exotic species as one that exists outside of its natural range as a result of human activity. In contrast, a native or indigenous species is one that occurs within its normal range (i.e., the area that it occupied prior to the arrival of Europeans). Some people believe that this definition should be changed to encompass the time before any humans arrived in the area, not just Europeans. For instance, the popular definition of a native species in Hawaii is one which existed there when the first European explorer (Captain James Cook) visited Hawaii in 1778. However, the Hawaiian flora and fauna that he observed had already been altered by Polynesians, who had earlier introduced several plants and animals into the Hawaiian Islands (Wilcove 1989; Temple 1992). Hence, the debate is whether the species the Polynesians brought with them should be considered exotic or native species of Hawaii.

An interesting case of what constitutes an exotic species occurred in the southwestern United States when one ocelot was killed on a road in Texas and another in Arizona. Ocelots are endangered in the United States where only about 100 exist, and both dead ocelots were found far from any known ocelot population. The question was whether these two ocelots were wild individuals of an endangered species or were they escaped pets? DNA was used to provide the answer by tracing the geographic origin of the animals. The Texas ocelot came from southern Mexico or Guatemala and was likely a pet, given the distance to its place of origin. In contrast, the Arizona ocelot originated from southern Texas or northern Mexico and was considered to be a wild individual and covered by the Endangered Species Act (Holbrook et al. 2011).

Temple's definition of an exotic species includes the phrase: with the help of man. A few species have arrived and occupied a new area following the arrival of Europeans but did so entirely by their own means and without help (either intentional or unintentional) from humans. These animals are considered native species, not exotic species. One example is cattle egrets that are new arrivals in North America, but they are still considered a native species because they were blown to North America by a hurricane. If a species expanded its geographic range in response to

DOI: 10.1201/9780429401404-5

human-caused changes to the habitat, then the species would be considered an exotic species because its dispersion was made possible by unnatural events (Temple 1992). Examples would include mammals that expand their range northward in response to new sources of winter food provided by people. The question becomes even more clouded when trying to define an exotic species in Europe, Asia, and Africa, where humans have existed for thousands of years.

Many people do not consider domesticated livestock or pets as exotic species, but they are exotics and can cause environmental damage. Worldwide, domestic cats have contributed to the extinction of 63 vertebrate species (Loss and Marra 2017). There are 50–157 million cats in North America, and 57 million of them are allowed to roam outside (Winter 2004; Schmidt et al. 2007; Dauphiné and Cooper 2009, 2011). Domestic cats in the United States kill between 1–4 billion birds and 6–22 billion mammals annually (Loss et al. 2013). As one example of the problem, the endangered Lower Keys marsh rabbit is predicted to become extinct within a decade if nothing is done to protect them from free-roaming cats (LaFever et al. 2008). In response to such staggering numbers, the Wildlife Society adopted a policy statement about the management of domestic and feral cats (Sidebar 5.1).

SIDEBAR 5.1 POLICY OF THE WILDLIFE SOCIETY REGARDING FERAL AND FREE-RANGING DOMESTIC CATS

THE WILDLIFE SOCIETY
Leaders in Wildlife Science, Management and Conservation

1. Support and encourage the humane elimination of feral cat populations, including feral cat colonies, through adoption into indoor-only homes of eligible cats and humane euthanasia of unadoptable cats.
2. Support the passage and enforcement of local and state ordinances prohibiting the feeding of feral cats, especially on public lands, and the release of unwanted pet or feral cats into the wild.
3. Oppose the passage of any local or state ordinances that legalize the maintenance of "managed" (trap/neuter/release) free-ranging cat colonies.
4. Support educational programs and materials that provide scientific information on feral cats and the negative effects on cats from living outdoors and call on pet owners to keep cats indoors, in outdoor enclosures, or on a leash.
5. Support programs to educate and encourage pet owners to neuter or spay their cats and encourage all pet adoption programs to require potential owners to spay or neuter their pet.
6. Support the development and dissemination of information on what individual cat owners can do to minimize predation by free-ranging cats and to minimize potential disease transmission to humans, wildlife, cats, and other domestic animals.
7. Pledge to work with the conservation and animal welfare communities to educate the public about the effects of free-ranging and feral cats on native wildlife, including birds, small mammals, reptiles, amphibians, and endangered species.

8. Support educational efforts to encourage the agricultural community to keep farm-cat numbers at low, manageable levels and use alternative, environmentally safe rodent control methods.

9. Support efforts to reduce risks to the health of humans and other animals posed by diseases and parasites of feral cats, including, but not limited to, removal of free-ranging cats and elimination of feral cat colonies. Encourage researchers to develop, obtain, and disseminate information on the impacts of feral and free-ranging cats on native wildlife populations, relative to predation, competition, and diseases.

10. Recognize that cats as pets have a long association with humans and that responsible cat owners are to be encouraged to continue caring for the animals under their control.

The feral cat problem is not limited to North America. Cats were introduced to Australia 200 years ago and now exist on 99% of the continent. Feral cat numbers in Australia range from 1.5 million during continent-wide droughts to 5.5 million during wet periods (Legge et al. 2017). Although these numbers are lower than those in North America, the environmental impact caused by feral cats has been great on Australia's native species. Feral cats have been implicated in most of Australia's marsupial extinctions with many of the remaining species thriving only on cat-free islands (Moseby et al. 2015; Short 2016).

There are 700 million domestic dogs worldwide, and 75% are allowed to roam free at least some of the time. When they do, domestic dogs impact wildlife by killing or harassing wild animals, competing with them for food, hybridizing with wild canines, and serving as a reservoir or vector for the pathogens responsible for rabies and canine distemper (Hughes and Macdonald 2013). Domestic dogs have played a role in causing 188 species to become threatened or endangered (Doherty et al. 2017). For example, there are only 600 Ethiopian wolves left in the world, due, in part, to high mortalities during periodic rabies outbreaks. Domestic dogs are the reservoir host for the rabies virus that spills over into the Ethiopian wolf population (Randall et al. 2006).

People in Canada and the United States do not consider American mink, gray squirrels, and raccoons to be exotic species because their native range is in North America, but these animals are exotic species when they occur in Europe or Asia. The American mink has become established in Britain, and predation by mink is a major reason why the population of a native mammal, the water vole, has been declining. Efforts are now underway to eradicate mink in parts of Britain to provide a sanctuary for water voles (Reynolds et al. 2013).

5.1 WHAT IMPACTS DO EXOTIC SPECIES HAVE ON NATIVE FLORA AND FAUNA?

Exotic species in their new locations often reach higher densities than in their native range because the diseases, parasites, competitors, or predators that limited their population in their native range may be absent in the new location that they have colonized. For instance, European starlings, which are an exotic species in North America, have become the most abundant birds in North America.

Exotic populations, especially when abundant, can cause several problems for native species. Exotic species may outcompete them for food or shelter. Normally, only one species can occupy the same niche at the same time; if the needs of the exotic species and the native species are similar enough, only one will survive. For instance, the establishment of gray squirrels into England caused a decline in the native red squirrel, owing to competition for food (Hale and Lurz 2003). In Australia, feral goats compete for food and water with two endangered native species: the yellow-footed rock wallaby and the brush-tailed rock wallaby and thereby reduce wallaby densities (Bomford 1991).

Exotic predators can greatly impact the native fauna, especially on oceanic islands where native species evolved in the absence of predators. Over 90% of reptiles that have gone extinct across the world since the 1600s were island species (Honnegger 1981); as were 93% of avian extinctions (King 1980) and 81% of mammalian extinctions (Ceballos and Brown 1995). One reason why animals on predator-free islands are so vulnerable to exotic predators is that they lack wariness or the ability to defend themselves or escape from predators (Case and Bolger 1991). Even exotic rats can become major predators of defenseless animals (Figure 5.1) and have been responsible for the decline or extinction of birds from over 30 islands (Atkinson 1985).

Invasions of exotic species can cause habitat changes for which the native species are ill-suited. Introduced carp have been implicated in decline of waterfowl in many wetlands. Not only do carp directly compete with some waterfowl species for food, but their spawning and feeding activities also increase water turbidity, which decreases numbers of aquatic invertebrates upon which many waterbirds forage. Carp also alter wetland habitats by destroying aquatic vegetation used by birds for food, cover, and nesting. In just one year, carp caused an 80% decline in pondweed in an Oregon lake (Ivey et al. 1998).

Establishment of one exotic species can cause a cascade effect by creating conditions allowing other exotic species to compete successfully against the native species. An exotic predator may feed much more heavily on native animals than other exotic herbivores because native herbivores are easier to capture. For this reason, the arrival of an exotic predator may give an exotic herbivore a competitive advantage over a native species than it, otherwise, would not have. Similarly, exotic plants might initially struggle to complete against native plants, but introduction of an exotic herbivore could change this. Rat eradication on Palmyra Atoll (Figure 5.2) increased seedling recruitment for five of the six native trees species on the atoll (Wolf et al. 2018). While pre-eradication monitoring found no seedlings of *Pisonia grandis*, a dominant tree species that is important throughout the Pacific region, post-eradication monitoring documented large increases in the number of seedlings *P. grandis* and two other locally rare native trees. The results demonstrate the effects that a rat eradication program can have on tree recruitment with expected long-term effects on canopy composition.

Introducing exotic animals is problematic if they interbreed with genetically similar native species, causing a loss of genetic integrity in the native population. For example, native Iberian water frogs hybridized with introduced frogs (Arano et al. 1995); mallards introduced in New Zealand, Hawaii, Australia, and Florida interbred

FIGURE 5.1   Trail camera catching a Bulwer's petrel returning to the burrow containing its nest, followed shortly by a black rat.

Source: Kawakami Kazuto, copyright of Institute of Boninology and used with permission.

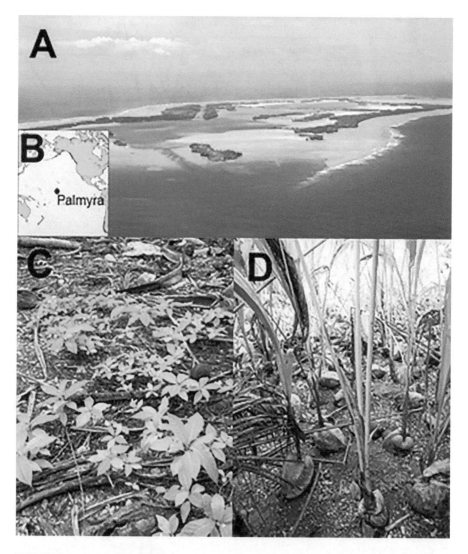

FIGURE 5.2   Palmyra Atoll and two of its native plant species – *Pisonia grandis* and *Cocos nucifera* – that significantly increased after the eradication of invasive rats from the atoll.

Source: Photo from Wolf et al. 2018 and published in PLOS ONE, an open-access journal.

with indigenous duck species, threatening their genetic integrity (Simberloff 1996). Exotic species can also spread exotic diseases (O'Brien 1989). In Queensland, Australia, a rapid decline in native frog populations resulted from a virus introduced by pet fish (McNeely 2000). On a global basis, exotic species have had a profound impact. They have been the major cause of 42% of reptile extinctions, 25% of fish extinctions, 22% of avian extinction, and 20% of mammal extinctions (Cox 1999). To investigate the impact of exotic species in more detail, I want to examine the consequences of exotic species on native biota in different parts of the world. Exotic species having a great impact include diseases, plants, insects, and vertebrates. However, we will limit our discussion to vertebrates.

5.2   WHAT IS THE IMPACT OF EXOTIC SPECIES ON HAWAII?

The flora and fauna of the Hawaiian Islands evolved over a period of 40 million years. Its 100 endemic land birds evolved from as few as 20 colonizing species, and its 1,000–2,000 native plant species evolved from about 300 colonizing species (Stone and Loope 1987). Hawaii's native avifauna evolved in the absence of mammalian predators, humans, and most avian diseases. Hence, Hawaii's flora and fauna were ill-prepared for the arrival of the Polynesians, 1,400 years ago, along with their fellow travelers: rats, dogs, pigs, and junglefowl. The Polynesians also introduced 32 plant species that the they depended on for food or fiber (Stone and Loope 1987). The end result was that at least 38 of Hawaii's native bird species including 18 species of honey creepers, 8 geese, 7 rails, 3 owls, and 2 flightless ibises became extinct soon after the arrival of Polynesians (Wilcove 1989).

When Captain Cook first visited Hawaii in 1778, there were still at least 50 native land bird species remaining (Figure 5.3). However, a second wave of exterminations began after European and American settlers introduced livestock, other mammals, and birds. Some of the introduced birds were infected with the pathogens responsible

FIGURE 5.3   A U.S. postage stamp commemorating the arrival of Captain's Cook's ships the Resolution and Discovery at Hawaii.

Source: Painting by John Webber, photo by brandonht, Shuttlestock 88841944.

for malaria and avian pox. Hawaii's indigenous birds lacked resistance to these diseases, and most of those living below the elevation of 1,000 m were eradicated. Birds above this height were spared because the exotic mosquito that served as the vector for these disease pathogens could not survive above this elevation (van Riper et al. 1982). The result was the loss of 13 more native species. In total, more than two-thirds of Hawaii's native birds have become extinct after the arrival of humans (Wilcove 1989). Populations of Hawaii's remaining native birds have been reduced by exotic species. As just one example, the population of an endemic thrush, the puaiohi is now down to about 500 birds, all located on the island of Kauai (Pitt et al. 2011). Hawaii's avian community has not been silenced, but native birds have been replaced by many exotic bird species from across the world.

5.3   WHAT IS THE IMPACT OF EXOTIC SPECIES ON GUAM?

Brown tree snakes accidentally reached the island of Guam in the Pacific during World War II when vehicles and equipment harboring some of those snakes were brought in from New Guinea (Figure 5.4). Guam's native fauna evolved in the absence of snakes and thus was unable to adapt to brown tree snakes; only two of Guam's 12 native forest bird species currently survive in the wild as does only one of its three native mammals (Engeman et al. 2018). Brown tree snakes are now so abundant on Guam (50–100 snakes/ha in some areas) that there is little hope of eradicating them from the island. Instead, the focus has been on not allowing the snake to escape from

FIGURE 5.4   The brown tree snake.

Source: Trent Townsend, Shutterstock 85847269.

Guam and reaching other Pacific islands, such as Hawaii (Vice and Vice 2004; Kahl et al. 2012). Hence, cargo, ships, and planes are checked closely for any stowaway snakes by using dogs trained to detect them by odor (Savidge et al. 2011).

Acetaminophen, a common painkiller taken by people, is toxic to brown snakes, and one method to reduce snake numbers has been to place 80 mg of acetaminophen in a dead mouse and then putting the dead mouse in a PVC pipe. Clark and Savarie (2012) distributed treated mouse baits that had been frozen (humorously called "mouse-sicles") to reduce snake numbers in small plots. Aerial bait distribution appeared to have reduced snake numbers in a 110-ha forested plot (Siers et al. 2019). Still, only a tiny fraction of Guam's landmass has been reclaimed by removing snakes (Engeman et al. 2018).

5.4   WHAT IS THE IMPACT OF EXOTIC SPECIES ON AUSTRALIA?

Twenty-seven bird species have established exotic populations in Australia, along with two exotic reptiles and one amphibian (Bomford 1991). Exotic mammals, however, have been the most successful in invading Australia and devastating the native biota. This is not surprising because all of Australia's native mammals are marsupials, allowing exotic mammals to find open niches and outcompete native species. The dingo is a subspecies of dog; it was brought to Australia by the Aborigines, making it one of the first exotic species to reach Australia. Since then, 25 species of exotic mammals have established free-ranging populations in Australia. These include 12 species of domestic mammals that went on to establish feral populations, 9 species purposely released for hunting, four commensal species accidently introduced, and 1 species that escaped from a zoo (O'Brien 1993). Some of these exotic mammal populations have exploded in Australia. There are now millions of European rabbits, feral pigs, and foxes, and thousands of feral goats, horses, donkeys, camels, and water buffalo on the continent. The introduction of so many exotic species has devastated Australia's native mammals. Over 29 land mammals have become extinct since Europeans arrived in Australia, and another 56 species are threatened with extinction (Burbidge et al. 2014). Islands off the Australian coast have become the last sanctuary for some of the endemic species that are now endangered.

5.5   WHAT IS THE IMPACT OF EXOTIC
SPECIES ON NORTH AMERICA?

In the United States and its territories, at least 75 free-ranging populations of exotic birds have become established since the arrival of European colonists (Temple 1990). Concomitantly, many native birds have expanded their range or moved to new locations due to environmental changes brought by humans. For instance, the Great Plains once posed an effective barrier to prevent the dispersal of woodland bird species from one coast to the other. However, humans planted trees throughout the region, making it possible for many forest-dependent species to survive on the Great Plains. As an example, 90% of the birds which now nest in eastern Colorado were not there a century ago (Knopf 1986).

Hogs were introduced to North America by early European colonists centuries ago. The feral hogs occupying the continent today are the descendants of these early introduced hogs, domestic swine, and introduced European wild boar. Feral hogs have expanded their range from 18 U.S. states during 1982 to 35 states during 2016 (Figure 5.5); in doing so, feral hogs have tripled their range in the United States (Corn and Jordan 2017). Public opinion of local residents is divided about whether feral hogs are a bane or boon; people suffering losses because of feral hogs are less likely to enjoy their presence than someone who rarely sees one. A great example of this is provided by West (2009) whose experiences came from the Mississippi Delta. For years, wildlife biologists there preached about the evils of feral hogs, but their warnings about increasing feral hog numbers fell on deaf ears. Delta farmers did not mind sharing space with the critters because they enjoyed hunting them, and the main Delta crops were catfish aquaculture and cotton farming. Fortunately for the farmers, "a hog has to be close to starving before it will eat a cotton boll, and so far, no hog has mastered the art of fishing" (to quote Ben West). But farmers' perceptions about feral hogs changed quickly after high corn and soybean prices convinced many Delta farmers to switch to growing corn and soybeans rather than cotton. Suddenly, the state wildlife agency was awash with farmer complaints about feral hogs. What changed? Not hogs, they had always loved to eat soybeans and corn, but there was none around. It was the change in local crops that suddenly made feral hogs an agricultural problem in the Delta.

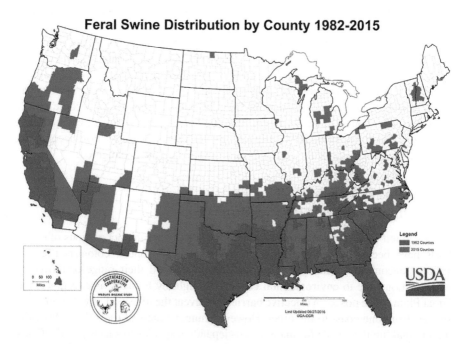

FIGURE 5.5   Distribution of feral hogs in the United States during 1982 (blue) and 2015 (Red).

Source: Stephanie Swiff, USDA National Wildlife Research Center and used with permission.

Anderson et al. (2016) calculated that feral hogs in the United States caused over $190 million in losses to just six crops, which included corn and soybeans. Other problems caused by feral hogs include a decrease in water quality; increased risk of disease transmission to humans, livestock, and other wildlife; and destruction of native vegetation (Chavarria et al. 2007; Clay 2007; Ditchkoff and West 2007; Engeman et al. 2007; Kaller et al. 2007).

Approximately 50 exotic mammals have been imported into Mexico by ranching operations that wanted them to satisfy hunters seeking exotic animals to hunt. Several of these mammals escaped and established free-ranging populations in Mexico, including European wild boar, European red deer, nilgai, and aoudad. Tilapia have escaped from fish farms; dogs and cats have become feral (Weber et al. 2006; Valdez 2019).

In the western United States, feral horses and burros have existed at least since the California Gold Rush in the 1800s (Figure 5.6). In arid regions, these herbivores cause numerous environmental problems by competing with native herbivores; overgrazing the native vegetation; disturbing water sources; compacting soil; reducing ant densities; and increasing abundance of cheatgrass, an exotic plant (Beever and Brussard 2004; Beever et al. 2008; Beever and Aldridge 2011). Yet, efforts to reduce feral horse and burro populations have been controversial because many people consider them to be native to the West and symbols of the region's colorful history.

FIGURE 5.6   Feral horses in the western United States.

Sources: Ventin, Shutterstock 38432761.

In south Florida, over two million people live on a slightly elevated strip of land previously covered with a continuous stand of pine trees. South Florida residents have replaced the native pine forest community with hundreds of colorful exotic plant species gathered from across the tropics. Over 1,000 exotic insect species and 900 exotic plant species have established free-ranging populations in Florida; another 25,000 plant species are cultivated in Florida but have not yet established themselves in the wild (Frank and McCoy 1995a, 1995b). In turn, these new plant and insect communities created a favorable habitat and open niches for tropical insects, reptiles, mammals, and birds, allowing them to become established in south Florida. One exotic species that has invaded the Everglades is the Burmese python (Sidebar 5.2).

SIDEBAR 5.2 WHAT ARE BURMESE PYTHONS DOING IN FLORIDA'S EVERGLADES?

Burmese pythons have long been a favorite of people who enjoy raising pet snakes (Figure 5.7). Hence, it should come as no surprise that some of these snakes were either deliberately or accidently released in south Florida and made their way to the Everglades. There they found a hospitable environment, not unlike their native habitat in Southeast Asia. The snakes are so secretive that it is unknown how many are now living in Florida. Burmese pythons can grow large enough to kill alligators and adult deer by constriction. Snakes have killed so many native mammals that there is a noticeable decline in

FIGURE 5.7   Burmese python in Florida's Everglades.

Source: Patrick K. Campbell, Shutterstock 722064310.

some mammal populations (Snow et al. 2007). Before 2000, native mammals were encountered frequently during nocturnal road surveys within Everglades National Park. After 2003, road surveys documented a decrease of 99% in the abundance of raccoons, 88% of opossums, 84% of white-tailed deer, and 83% of bobcats. The same surveys failed to detect any marsh rabbits, which had been common prior to pythons (Dorcas et al. 2012).

People living in South Florida worry about large pythons killing their children, but that risk is minor. While pet Burmese pythons have killed people in the United States, free-ranging pythons in Florida have not. The few times they bit someone, the attacks seemed to be defensive in nature, and there was no attempt to constrict the person, which would occur during a predatory attack (Reed and Snow 2014). Efforts to remove pythons have included encouraging people to capture or kill them during roundups; but, the number of snake captures have been too small to have any on impact the snake population.

5.6 CAN ENVIRONMENTAL PROBLEMS CAUSED BY EXOTIC ANIMALS BE RESOLVED?

Exotic species pose the greatest threat to the world's biodiversity and natural ecosystem functions (Vitousek et al. 1996; Wilcove et al. 1998). In 1992, the United Nation's Convention on Biological Diversity called on nations to "as far as possible and as appropriate . . . prevent the introduction of, control or eradicate those alien species which threaten ecosystems, habitats or species" (Baskin 1996). Several methods can be used to prevent exotic species from reaching new areas, establishing themselves, and becoming abundant, but none of these tasks are easy to achieve.

5.6.1 PREVENTING EXOTIC ANIMALS FROM REACHING FOREIGN SHORES

The first line of defense against exotic species is to prevent them from reaching new areas. Most countries quarantine all imported animals, including livestock and pets, to make sure that they are free of disease, parasites, or harmful insects. Countries also ban the importation of live plants and animals without governmental approval. But quarantine efforts often fail due to the desire of their citizens to import and raise a wide range of exotic animals as pets or for aquariums. Deciding which exotic species can be safely brought into a country is difficult but should be based on the probability of escapees being able to establish a free-ranging population and the consequences to the native ecosystem if they do (Table 5.1).

5.6.2 PREVENTING EXOTIC ANIMALS FROM ESTABLISHING A FREE-RANGING POPULATION

Once exotic animals have reached a new area, the best chance to eradicate them is before they can become established and spread. Often, exotic animals initially do poorly in their new environment, and their population may die out. But if the

TABLE 5.1

A Risk-Assessment Model to Decide Whether an Application to Import an Exotic Species Should Be Approved (BomFord 1991)

Question	Answer	Decision
(1) What is the probability of the species providing a substantial benefit for society?	Low	Reject
	Unknown	Collect necessary data
	High	Consider next question
(2) What is the probability of an escaped animal causing substantial harm?	High	Reject
	Unknown	Collect necessary data
	Low	Consider next question
(3) What is the probability of escaped animals establishing a free-ranging population?	High	Reject
	Unknown	Collect necessary data
	Low	Consider next question
(4) What is the probability that a free-ranging population can be eradicated?	Low	Reject
	Unknown	Collect necessary data
	High	Consider next question
(5) What is the probability of a free-ranging population having a major adverse impact?	High	Reject
	Unknown	Collect necessary data
	Low	Grant importation request

Source: Adapted from Bomford (1991).

exotic species can survive this period of adjustment, the exotic population can enter a period of explosive population growth. Thus, government should err on the side of caution and not assume that a small exotic population is destined to die out on its own.

Efforts to eradicate exotic species generally are more successful against large and conspicuous animals (e.g., horses) than against small, secretive animals (mice). Populations of feral cattle, dogs, and goats have been exterminated on several Galápagos Islands, while exotic rats have proven harder to eliminate (Brockie et al. 1988). The size of the island is also an important factor in the success of an eradication program. Efforts to eradicate exotic species on small islands in the Galápagos Archipelago have been more successful than on large ones. On large islands, progress has only been achieved by dividing the island into manageable units using wildlife-proof fences. The advantage of this approach is that once a fenced unit has been cleared of an exotic animal, the fence can keep the area from being repopulated by immigrants from other parts of the island.

5.6.3 Eradicating Populations of Exotic Animals

Efforts to eradicate an established population of an exotic species usually fail, owing to the difficulty of removing the last few individuals in the population. When Cruz et al. (2009) removed 79,000 feral goats from Santiago Island in the Galápagos Islands, it cost an average of $51 per goat to remove the first 78,000 but $2,000 per goat to remove the last thousand. Eradicating an exotic population from a large island or a continent is especially difficult (Sidebar 5.3).

SIDEBAR 5.3 ERADICATING FERAL GOATS FROM KANGAROO ISLAND, SOUTH AUSTRALIA

Australia's Kangaroo Island (4400 km²) serves as a refuge for some of Australia's native species, but their future on the island is threatened by the presence of feral goats. The feral goats were introduced to Kangaroo Island over 200 years ago and were located on the rugged, western side of the island. The 2006 management plan to eradicate feral goats from Kangaroo Island called for this side of the island to be divided into seven management units (Figure 5.8). Goats are social animals, and the management plan took advantage of this by using 90 Judas goats, which had been sterilized and fitted with radio collars. The Judas goats quickly joined groups of the feral goats. The Judas goats wore radio collars that were used to locate the Judas goats, and any goats with them were shot

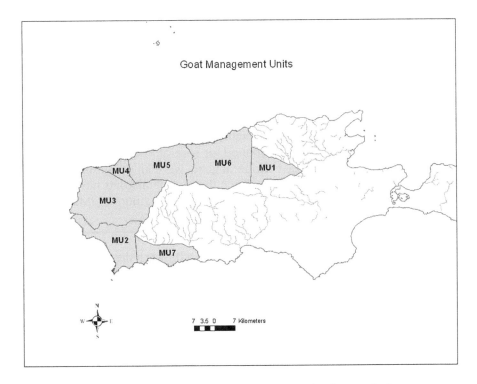

FIGURE 5.8   Map of Kangaroo Island, Australia, showing the six areas in the western part of the island where feral goats were removed.

Source: Courtesy of Pip Masters.

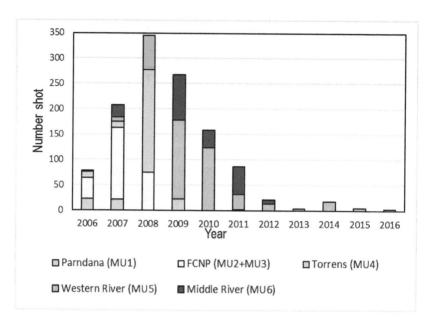

FIGURE 5.9   Number of feral goats shot in the six areas on Kangaroo Island 2006–2016.
Source: Courtesy of Pip Masters. See Figure 5.8 for a map of these areas.

by sharpshooters. The Judas goats had a darker coat than the feral goats, reducing the risk of accidently shooting a Judas goat. By 2013, most of the feral goats had been removed (Figure 5.9), but constant checking of trail cameras and Judas goats continued for several more years. Over 700 feral goats were killed; the last two feral goats were killed during 2016: ten years after the program began. Since then, no feral goats have been located on the island, but the surveillance for them continues (Masters et al. 2018).

Attempts at eradication have been most successful when the exotic population was isolated on a small island. Exotic populations of feral goats have also been eradicated from over 120 islands across the world, feral donkeys from 7 islands, feral cats from 48, black rats from 159, Norway rats from 104, Polynesian rats from 55, house mice from 30, and Arctic fox from 39 (Ebbert 2000; Nogales et al. 2004; Campbell and Donland 2005; Carrion et al. 2007; Howard et al. 2007).

Feral pigs have been eradicated from some sites in North America, but only after the construction of a wildlife-proof fence, preventing the immigration of new animals into the area (Table 5.2). For instance, feral hogs invaded Pinnacles National Monument in California during the 1960s and, since then, have had an adverse impact on wetland habitat critical to native frogs and salamanders that are now rare. The National Park System decided to eradicate feral hogs in the 57-km² Pinnacles

TABLE 5.2
Successful Efforts to Eradicate Feral Hogs

Location	Years	Area (km²)	No. hogs	Cost
Santiago Island, Ecuador	1973–2003	585	18,800	Unknown
Hawaii Volcanoes National Park	1983–1989	30	175	Unknown but fence cost $600,000
Annadel State Park, CA	1985–1987	20	144	$165,000
Santa Catalina Island, CA	1990–2005	194	>12,000	$3,400,000
Santa Rosa Island, CA	1991–1993	215	1,175	$800,000
Pinnacles National Monument, CA	2003–2006	57	200	$2,600,000
Santa Cruz, CA	2004–2006	249	5,036	$1,200,000

Source: Adapted from McCann and Garcelon (2008).

Monument by first building a 42-km, woven-wire fence around the monument at a cost of $2.8 million to prevent the immigration of new hogs into the monument. Hogs were removed through trapping, hunting with dogs, and using Judas hogs. Two hundred hogs were removed at a cost of $800,000 (McCann and Garcelon 2008).

A major impediment to the successful eradication of an exotic population is being unable to determine when the last individual has been removed (Morrison et al. 2007). This problem was exemplified on Grassy Key, Florida, when an attempt was made in 2006 and 2007 to eradicate the Gambian giant pouched rats that had become established after a pet store owner released them on the island. U.S.D.A. Wildlife Services employees distributed more than 1,000 toxic bait stations across the 400-ha island. The effort appeared successful when no pouch rats were seen or trapped for several months. But a female pouch rat was discovered during September 2009 on a 1-ha house lot, where the landowner had prohibited baiting. In response to this discovery, toxic bait stations were once again deployed on Grassy Key; this second effort appears to have eradicated the last pouch rats from Grassy Key (Witmer and Hall 2011).

5.7   CAN POPULATIONS OF EXOTIC SPECIES BE REDUCED WHEN ERADICATION IS NOT AN OPTION?

The advantage of eradicating an exotic population is that it is a permanent solution to the problem and only has to be successful once. In contrast, efforts to reduce the population of an exotic species have to be repeated constantly or the exotic population will rebound as soon as those efforts stop. Although eradication may be the preferred alternative, it is not always an option in situations where it may be possible to reduce the population. For example, invasive rats have become a problem in New Zealand where they threaten native bird species, such as the North Island robin. Rat control was implemented in five areas with native habitat to test whether reducing rat numbers would help these birds reproduce successfully. The control effort was successful with robin numbers increasing from 57 to 134 during the course of a 4-year effort (Armstrong 2017). Another example comes from Henderson Island, which is one of the Pitcairn Islands located in the southern Pacific. It also is home to several endemic bird species that were suffering from the arrival of exotic rodents. A rodent control effort on Henderson Island failed to eradicated rodents, but it reduced their populations. As a consequence, Henderson reed warblers more than doubled in abundance, and Henderson fruit dove increased slightly in numbers. Unfortunately, rodent control has no impact on Henderson lorikeets and Henderson crakes (Brooke et al. 2018).

Nutria were introduced to the Eastern Shore of Maryland during the 1940s, and their numbers had increased to 50,000 by the 1990s. Their herbivory adversely impacted the marshes by converting marshland habitat to open water. From 2003 to 2008, over 12,000 nutria were removed from 61,000 ha of wetlands on the Eastern Shore of Maryland. Damaged marshes recovered rapidly after nutria were removed (Kendrot 2011). Results were less successful in Italy where nutria were widespread and abundant; a nutria control program removed more than 200,000 nutria at a cost €2,614,000, but 200,000 nutria were too few to impact their population on a national scale (Panzacchi et al. 2007).

Efforts to control populations of exotic species often involve identifying the limiting factors in the species' native range and creating the same limiting factors in the species' new range. This is called biocontrol and involves introducing other exotic organisms (such as diseases, parasites, and predators) to control an exotic population. In one innovative approach of biocontrol, red foxes were sterilized and then introduced to some Alaskan islands where exotic arctic foxes were threatening native wildlife populations. Initially, red foxes outcompeted Arctic foxes and excluded them from the islands. The sterilized red foxes could not reproduce and died out within five years, leaving the islands free of all foxes (Bailey 1992).

Biocontrol can backfire: the biocontrol species deliberately released to control one exotic species can itself become an environmental hazard. The mongoose was introduced into many sugarcane-producing islands, including Puerto Rico St. Lucia, and Hawaii to control exotic rats that thrived in the sugarcane fields. Unfortunately, mongoose not only failed to control the rat population but also became a major pest itself due to its predation on native birds and reptiles. Cane toads introduced into Australia to control sugarcane beetles are another example of biocontrol gone awry. Many native predators have died after trying to eat the poisonous toads (Pimentel 1955; Tyler 1994).

5.8   ARE THERE UNINTENDED CONSEQUENCES OF ERADICATING AN EXOTIC POPULATION?

Sometimes, eradicating an exotic population can have unexpected consequences (Sidebar 5.4). Goats were introduced to the Galápagos Islands during the 1800s by sailors, and goat numbers on Santiago Island had increased to 100,000 by 1970. A goat eradication was initiated, and the last goat was eliminated by 2006. After this, several native birds began to recover, such as the Galápagos rail (Donlan et al. 2007), but not all native species benefitted from the eradication. Goat herbivory had changed the island's habitat from a dense shrubby vegetation into more open habitat which was favorable to the hunting style of the endemic Galápagos hawk. The vegetation became less open after goat eradication, and survival rates of these native hawks decreased (Rivera-Parra et al. 2012). As another example, eradication of feral hogs on California's Channel Islands caused golden eagles on the islands to switch from preying on feral hogs to the endemic island fox (Courchamp et al. 2003; Collins et al. 2009).

Another unintended consequence of eradication, or a population reduction, is a public uproar from people who disagree with the eradication policy or the methods used to accomplish it. Mute swans are much loved in Europe but are an exotic species in the United States, after being deliberately introduced. They produce mixed emotions among Americas; some people love them, while others worry that swans are hurting native waterfowl (Figure 5.10).

The question of how to manage feral horses on public lands is another explosive issue. On one side are ranchers and many rural residents who think that the horses are overabundant on public land and threatening the survival of native fauna and flora. Other people believe the BLM is removing excessive numbers of horses to appease ranchers and using inhumane methods to do it. This polarization results in lawsuits, publicity campaigns that depict the BLM engaging in cruel behavior toward horses, and accusations that the BLM is engaging in genocide against horses (Nimmo and Miller 2007; Bies et al. 2011).

SIDEBAR 5.4   UNEXPECTED SETBACK IN SAVING A THREATEN SKINK POPULATION IN NEW ZEALAND

Whitaker's skink is threatened with extinction after a severe restriction of its range and a sharp decline in its numbers. Its last population on the mainland of New Zealand occurs at Pukerua Bay, where the skink is threatened by habitat change and exotic rats. During the 1990s, livestock grazing ceased in the area so that the vegetation could recover and provide protection for the skinks against exotic predators. Unfortunately, the numbers of skinks continued to decline because the habitat changes produced by removing livestock were not as expected. Rather than returning to the plant community that existed before the arrival of Europeans, exotic grass species began to proliferate and dominate the area. This vegetational change led to periodic eruptions of rodents, which preyed upon the skinks. The unexpected mortality pushed the skinks closer to extinction. Scientists are now examining the feasibility of constructing a mammal-proof fence around the core habitat of this skink and trapping all predators located within the exclosure (Hoare et al. 2007).

5.9   CAN WE PREDICT WHEN AN EXOTIC SPECIES WILL CAUSE ENVIRONMENT DAMAGE?

Usually, when an exotic animal escapes into a new area, it does not survive. About 10% of escaped animals will become established, and 10% of those that become established will cause environmental damage. Thus, most invasions can be ignored. However, by the time a population has become established or is causing environmental damage, it usually is too large to eradicate. What is needed is some way to predict (1) where an invasion is likely to occur, (2) which animals are likely to invade, and (3) when an invasive animal is likely to establish a free-ranging population. These topics will be discussed next.

FIGURE 5.10(a)   Mute swans, an exotic species in North America, produce mixed emotions in people: some people love to watch them (David Benton, Shutterstock 8554303).

FIGURE 5.10(b)   Others worry that they threaten Canada geese and other native waterfowl due to their extreme aggressiveness (MrWildLife, Shutterstock 439876945).

5.9.1   WHICH SITES ARE VULNERABLE TO INVASION OF EXOTIC SPECIES?

Habitat characteristics and environmental factors are important in determining whether an invasive species will become established. An invasion is more likely to succeed if it occurs in a habitat similar to the invasive species' native habitat or in a human-altered habitat. In general, an invasive species is more likely to survive when it invades an isolated site, such as an oceanic island, than when it invades a site on a large continent; isolated sites are more likely to contain open niches that an invasive species can occupy. An exotic species trying to invade a large continent will find that native species have already filled most of the niches. Human endeavors can create unique habitats that exotic species are able to occupy because exotic species are preadapted to the open niches. On Pacific islands, exotic lizards are abundant in agricultural habitats and in cities (which are newly created habitats), but few can successfully compete with the native lizards in the undisturbed forests (Case and Bolger 1991). Similarly, pigeons, starlings, house sparrows, house mice, and rats are able to occupy the newly created habitats in urban areas and have spread across the world. In the city of Melbourne, Australia, exotic birds are twice as common as native birds (Green 1984). In Tucson, Arizona, 95% of the birds are exotics (Emlen 1974; Knopf 1992).

5.9.2   WHICH ANIMALS ARE LIKELY TO INVADE?

As humans have expanded across the globe, three groups of species have been able to take advantage of human mobility and have moved across the earth with us (Lockwood 1999). One group consists of plants and animals that are beneficial to humans; people have deliberately taken these species with them when settling a new area. Fruits, vegetables, flowers, ornamental plants, and domestic animals have been transported across the world. Animals are also imported for recreation (e.g., pets), education (e.g., zoo animals), and medical research. Although our intention may have been to keep these animals in captivity, many are able to escape or are deliberately released (e.g., many people release aquarium fish into waterbodies when they get tired of caring for them).

A second group of exotic species includes those that were imported into a country with the intention of releasing them into the wild to establish free-ranging populations in their new surroundings. Plants and animals were often introduced into a new area by settlers who were homesick and longed to see the animals of their homeland. Others were deliberately released to provide food, fiber, or economic gains. For instance, sailors in the 1700s and 1800s released livestock on oceanic islands so that the animals would proliferate and provide a future food supply for themselves or other sailors. One deliberate release that has become infamous is the release of European starlings into New York City's Central Park. Starlings were released in 1890 by the head of the American Acclimation Society because he felt that any bird mentioned in one of Shakespeare's plays deserved a place in Central Park. Of course, the starlings took to their new home, and their descents were so prolific that starlings are now the most abundant avian species in North America.

The extent of these deliberate introductions of "beneficial animals" becomes clear when one realizes that the European rabbit was deliberately released on at least 598 islands (Flux and Fullagar 1983). Over 162 bird species have been deliberately released in Hawaii, 133 in New Zealand, and 56 in Tahiti (Eldredge 1992). Half of the exotic birds in the United States were introduced on purpose (Temple 1992). Many game animals have been deliberately introduced into new areas because people enjoy watching or hunting them (Figure 5.11). For instance, there were 94 different species or subspecies of exotic big-game species on Texas ranches (Payne et al. 1987).

The third group of exotic species comprises those which people inadvertently move from place to place. These include human diseases and parasites or the plants and animals that people took with them. They also include small, secretive animals (mice, rats, snakes, insects, etc.) that humans unknowingly transported with them. As one example of the extent of these inadvertent releases, rats have reached 82% of the world's islands (Atkinson 1985).

5.9.3   WHEN IS AN INVASIVE ANIMAL LIKELY TO ESTABLISH
A FREE-RANGING POPULATION?

Being able to cross an immigration barrier is only one part of becoming a successful exotic species. Upon reaching a foreign shore, the exotic individuals must be able to survive, reproduce, and establish a free-ranging population. Of 162 avian species introduced into Hawaii, 117 failed to establish a free-ranging population (Eldredge 1992).

FIGURE 5.11   Pheasants are only one of many game birds introduced to North America so that they could be hunted.

Source: Piotr Krzesak, Shutterstock 1491221411.

Exotic species that have been able to establish a free-ranging population in a new area have several characteristics in common. The most successful species are those that (1) originate from a similar area and climate as the new site, (2) have a large original range and are abundant within it, (3) successfully colonized elsewhere, (4) reach sexual maturity at an early age and have a high reproductive rate, (5) have a generalist diet, (6) can thrive in human-modified environments, (7) are nonmigratory, and (8) are social and live in flocks or herds (Green 1997).

Other species characteristics will determine how difficult it might be to eradicate an exotic population. Species with high intrinsic growth rates and the propensity to disperse over large distances will be much harder to eradicate than more stationary ones. Small, secretive, or wary animals will be harder to eradicate than those that lack these traits. In addition, animals preferring remote or inaccessible habitats or thick cover will be difficult to eradicate (Bomford 1991).

5.10   CAN AN INTEGRATED PROGRAM BE DEVELOPED TO STOP THE SPREAD OF EXOTICS TO NEW AREAS?

Brockie et al. (1988) recommended an eight-point program to protect endemic species on islands from exotic species. (1) The native flora and fauna need to be inventoried. Surprisingly, species lists have not been compiled for many islands. Efforts to catalog species often concentrate on vertebrates, and less effort is spent surveying plants, insects, and other invertebrates. (2) Because we lack the resources to protect everything, islands with relatively intact native flora and fauna should be given the highest priority for preservation. (3) The conversion of native habitats to agriculture or other uses should be slowed because converted habitats are more vulnerable to invasions of exotic species. (4) Quarantines should be required before any plant or animal is imported into a new area. (5) Hunting and collecting of native species need to be regulated. (6) Predator-free islands need to be identified and used to harbor species that are endangered in their native habitat. This should be done, however, only after ascertaining that the purposeful introduction of endangered animals will not create problems for the island's own native species. (7) Populations of exotic animals and plants need to be eradicated or controlled. (8) Research needs to be conducted to determine the impact exotic species have on the native biota. The success of eradication or control programs should also be monitored.

Wildlife biologists can predict broad trends involving exotic species and their impacts, but they cannot predict with confidence the outcome of any single invasive threat or what environmental consequences might result if an exotic species becomes established. To gain more accuracy, every invasion needs to be studied. Until we can sort out which of the thousands of invasions pose a threat and require our intervention and which can be safely ignored, exotic species will remain a serious environmental threat.

5.11   SUMMARY

A native species is one that currently occupies the same area where it existed before the arrival of humans. Conversely, an exotic species is one that exists outside of its natural range as a result of human activity. Densities of exotic species in new areas are often higher than in their native range because the diseases, parasites, competitors, or predators that limited their population in their native range may be absent in the new area that they have colonized. People have, either deliberately or accidently, brought many species into new areas. Exotic species often cause environmental changes in their new surroundings by threatening the survival of native plants and animals. This is especially true for oceanic islands where many endemic species have become extinct after the arrival of an exotic species.

Almost all countries have laws governing the importation of plants and animals that may become exotic species and may require a long quarantine to make sure imported animals are free of diseases or parasites. Despite these precautions, many exotic populations have become established throughout the world. When the potential threat posed by an exotic species is detected before the population has had time to spread, it may be possible to eradicate the exotic species. But there is little interest in removing an exotic species until it begins to cause damage; by that time, the exotic population is so large and dispersed that eradication is impossible. What is needed is a way to identify which species are likely to invade, which invaders are likely to establish free-ranging populations, and which free-ranging populations are likely to harm the native biota so that an early response can be taken.

5.12 DISCUSSION QUESTIONS

1. Society is confronted with several environmental threats – climate change, loss of habitat, pesticides, threats to endangered species, wildlife diseases, and overexploitation of wildlife – to name a few. Where would you put exotic species in this list of environmental threats? Should it get more funding than the others or do other threats pose more serious problems?
2. The best time to eradicate an exotic species is when it has just arrived in a new area and its population is still small; but then, it is not causing any problems. Should we attempt to eradicate an exotic species at this stage? If so, how can we best determine if a newly arrived species is going to pose a future threat to the environment?
3. The dingo is a dog brought to Australia by the Aborigines about 4,000 years ago: long before European seafarers arrived. Should the dingo be considered an exotic species in Australia?
4. Should feral cats be sprayed, neutered, and released or should they be euthanized?
5. What is the best method to eradicate or control Burmese pythons in Florida?
6. Why are islands more susceptible to invasion by an exotic species than sites on a continent?
7. What are some precautions that should be taken before the use of biocontrol to eradicate or control an exotic species?
8. Should an invading species be treated differently if it invaded a new area by its own means rather by arriving with the help of man?

LITERATURE CITED

Anderson, A., C. Slootmaker, E. Harper, J. Holderieath, and S. A. Shwiff. 2016. Economic estimates of feral swine damage and control in 11 US states. *Crop Protection* 89:89–94.

Arano, B., G. Llorente, M. Garcia-Paris, and P. Herrero. 1995. Species translocation menaces Iberian waterfrogs. *Conservation Biology* 9:196–198.

Armstrong, D. P. 2017. Population responses of a native bird species to rat control. *Journal of Wildlife Management* 81:342–346.

Atkinson, I. A. E. 1985. The spread of commensal species of *Rattus* to oceanic islands and their effects on island avifauna. Pages 35–83 *in* P. J. Moors, editor. *Conservation of island birds: case studies for the management of threatened island species.* International Council for Bird Preservation, Cambridge.

Bailey, G. P. 1992. Red foxes, *Vulpes*, as a biocontrol agent for introduced Arctic fox, *Alopex lagopus*, on Alaskan islands. *Canadian Field-Naturalist* 106:200–205.

Baskin, Y. 1996. Curbing undesirable invaders. *Bioscience* 46:732–736.

Beever, E. A., and C. L. Aldridge. 2011. Influences of free-roaming equids on sagebrush ecosystems, with focus on greater sage-grouse. *Studies in Avian Biology* 38:273–290.

Beever, E. A., and P. F. Brussard. 2004. Community-and landscape-level responses of reptiles and small mammals to feral-horse grazing in the Great Basin. *Journal of Arid Environments* 59:271–297.

Beever, E. A., R. J. Tausch, and W. E. Thogmartin. 2008. Multi-scale responses of vegetation to removal of horse grazing from Great Basin (USA) mountain ranges. *Plant Ecology* 196:163–184.

Bies, L., M. Hutchins, and T. J. Ryder. 2011. The Wildlife Society responds to CNN report on feral horses. *Human-Wildlife Interactions* 5:171–172.

Bomford, M. 1991. *Importing and keeping exotic vertebrates in Australia.* Department of Primary Industries and Energy, Bureau of Rural Resources Bulletin 12, Australian Government Publishing Service, Canberra, Australia.

Brockie, R. E., L. L. Loope, M. B. Usher, and O. Hamann. 1988. Biological invasions of island nature reserves. *Biological Conservation* 44:9–36.

Brooke, M. D. L., E. Bonnaud, B. J. Dilley, E. N. Flint, N. D. Holmes, H. P. Jones, P. Provost, G. Rocamora, P. G. Ryan, C. Surman, and R. T. Buxton. 2018. Seabird population changes following mammal eradications on islands. *Animal Conservation* 21:3–12.

Burbidge, A., P. Harrison, and J. Woinarski. 2014. *The action plan for Australian mammals 2012.* CSIRO Publishing, Canberra, Australia.

Campbell, K., and C. J. Donland. 2005. Feral goat eradications on islands. *Conservation Biology* 19:1362–1374.

Carrion, V., C. J. Donlan, K. Campbell, C. Lavoie, and F. Cruz. 2007. Feral donkey (*Equus asinus*) eradications in the Galàpagos. *Biodiversity and Conservation* 16:437–445.

Case, T. J., and D. T. Bolger. 1991. The role of introduced species in shaping the distribution and abundance of island reptiles. *Evolutionary Ecology* 5:272–290.

Ceballos, G., and J. H. Brown. 1995. Global patterns of mammalian diversity, endemism and endangerment. *Conservation Biology* 9:559–568.

Chavarria, P. M., R. R. Lopez, G. Bowser, and N. J. Silvy. 2007. A landscape-level survey of feral hog impacts to natural resources of the big thicket national preserve. *Human-Wildlife Interactions* 1:199–204.

Clark, L., and P. J. Savarie. 2012. Efficacy of aerial broadcast baiting in reducing brown treesnake numbers. *Human-Wildlife Interactions* 6:212–221.

Clay, W. H. 2007. Hogs gone wild. *Human-Wildlife Interactions* 1:137–138.

Collins, P. W., B. C. Latta, and G. W. Roemer. 2009. Does the order of invasive species removal matter? The case of the eagle and the pig. *PLoS One* 4(9):e7005.

Corn, J. L., and T. R. Jordan. 2017. Development of the national feral swine map, 1982–2016. *Wildlife Society Bulletin* 41:758–763.

Courchamp, F., J. L. Chapuis, and M. Pascal. 2003. Mammal invaders on islands: impact, control, and control impact. *Biological Reviews* 78:34–383.

Cox, G. W. 1999. *Alien species in North America and Hawaii.* Island Press, Washington, DC.

Cruz, F., V. Carrion, K. J. Campbell, C. Lavoie, and C. J. Donlan. 2009. Bio-economics of large-scale eradication of feral goats from Santiago Island, Galàpagos. *Journal of Wildlife Management* 73:191–200.

Dauphiné, N., and R. J. Cooper. 2009. Impacts of free-ranging domestic cats (*Felis catus*) on birds in the United States: a review of recent research with conservation and management recommendations. *Proceedings of the Fourth International Partners in Flight Conference: Tundra to Tropic* 4:205–219.

Dauphiné, N., and R. J. Cooper. 2011. Pick one: outdoor cats or conservation. *Wildlife Professional* 5:50–56.

Ditchkoff, S. S., and B. C. West. 2007. Ecology and management of feral hogs. *Human-Wildlife Interactions* 1:149–151.

Doherty, T. S., C. R. Dickman, A. S. Glen, T. M. Newsome, D. G. Nimmo, E. G. Ritchie, A. T. Vanak, and A. J. Wirsing. 2017. The global impacts of domestic dogs on threatened vertebrates. *Biological Conservation* 210:56–59.

Donlan, C. J., K. Campbell, W. Cabrera, C. Lavoie, V. Carrion, and F. Cruz. 2007. Recovery of the Galápagos rail (*Laterallus spilonotus*) following the removal of invasive mammals. *Biological Conservation* 138:520–524.

Dorcas, M. E., J. D. Willson, R. N. Reed, R. W. Snow, M. R. Rochford, M. A. Miller, W. E. Meshaka, Jr., P. T. Andreadis, F. J. Mazzotti, C. M. Romagosa, and K. M. Hart. 2012. Severe mammal declines coincide with proliferation of invasive Burmese pythons in Everglades National Park. *Proceedings of the National Academy of Sciences* 109:2418–2422.

Ebbert, S. 2000. Successful eradication of introduced arctic foxes from large Aleutian Islands. *Proceedings of the Vertebrate Pest Conference* 19:127–132.

Eldredge, L. G. 1992. Unwanted strangers: an overview of animals introduced to Pacific islands. *Pacific Science* 46:384–386.

Emlen, J. T. 1974. An urban bird community in Tucson, Arizona: derivation, structure, and regulation. *Condor* 76:184–197.

Engeman, R. M., A. B. Shiels, and C. S. Clark. 2018. Objectives and integrated approaches for the control of brown tree snakes: an updated overview. *Journal of Environmental Management* 219:115–124.

Engeman, R. M., J. Woolard, H. T. Smith, J. Bourassa, B. U. Constantin, and D. Griffin. 2007. An extraordinary patch of feral hog damage in Florida before and after initiating hog removal. *Human-Wildlife Interactions* 1:271–275.

Flux, J. E. C., and P. J. Fullagar. 1983. World distribution of the rabbit *Oryctolagus cuniculus*. *Acta Zoologica Fennica* 174:75–77.

Frank, J. H., and E. D. McCoy. 1995a. Invasive adventive insects and other organisms in Florida. *Florida Entomologist* 78:1–15.

Frank, J. H., and E. D. McCoy. 1995b. Precinctive insect species in Florida. *Florida Entomologist* 78:21–35.

Green, R. E. 1997. The influence of numbers released on the outcome of attempts to introduce exotic bird species to New Zealand. *Journal of Animal Ecology* 66:25–35.

Green, R. J. 1984. Native and exotic birds in a suburban habitat. *Australian Wildlife Research* 11:181–190.

Hale, M. L., and P. W. Lurz. 2003. Morphological changes in a British mammal as a result of introductions and changes in landscape management: the red squirrel (*Sciurus vulgaris*). *Journal of the Zoology* 260:159–167.

Hoare, J. M., L. K. Adams, L. S. Bull, and D. R. Towns. 2007. Attempting to manage complex predator-prey interactions fails to avert imminent extinction of a threatened New Zealand skink population. *Journal of Wildlife Management* 71:1576–1584.

Holbrook, J. D., R. W. DeYoung, M. E. Tewes, J. H. Young, J. L. Mays, and E. Meyers. 2011. Natural dispersal or illegal pets? Limitations on assigning origin to road-killed ocelots in the southwestern United States. *Wildlife Society Bulletin* 35:504–507.

Honnegger, R. E. 1981. List of amphibians and reptiles either known or thought to have become extinct since 1600. *Biological Conservation* 19:141–158.

Howard, G., C. J. Donlan, J. P. Galvan, J. C. Russell, J. Parkes, A. Samaniego, Y. Wang, D. Veitch, P. Genovesi, M. Pascal, A. Saunders, and B. Tershy. 2007. Invasive rodent eradication on islands. *Conservation Biology* 21:1258–1268.

Hughes, J., and D. W. Macdonald. 2013. A review of the interactions between free-roaming domestic dogs and wildlife. *Biological Conservation* 157:341–351.

Ivey, G. L., J. E. Cornely, and B. D. Ehlers. 1998. Carp impacts on waterfowl at Malheur national wildlife refuge, Oregon. *Transactions of the North American Wildlife and Natural Resources Conference* 63:66–74.

Kahl, S. S., S. E. Henke, M. A. Hall, A. R. Litt, G. Perry, and D. K. Britton. 2012. Examining a potential brown treesnake transport pathway: shipments from Guam. *Human-Wildlife Interactions* 6:204–211.

Kaller, M. D., J. D. Hudson III, E. C. Achberger, and W. E. Kelso. 2007. Feral hog research in western Louisiana: expanding populations and unforeseen consequences. *Human-Wildlife Interactions* 1:168–177.

Kendrot, S. R. 2011. Restoration through eradication: protecting Chesapeake Bay marsh-lands from invasive nutria (*Myocastor coypus*). Pages 313–319 *in* C. R. Veitch, M. N. Clout, and D. R. Towns, editors. *Island invasives: eradication and management.* Proceedings of the International Conference on Island Invasives, IUCN, Gland, Switzerland.

King, W. B. 1980. Ecological basis of extinctions in birds. *Proceedings of the International Ornithological Congress* 17:905–911.

Knopf, F. L. 1986. Changing landscapes and the cosmopolitism of the eastern Colorado avi-fauna. *Wildlife Society Bulletin* 14:132–142.

Knopf, F. L. 1992. Faunal mixing, faunal integrity, and the biopolitical template for diver-sity conservation. *Transactions of the North American Wildlife and Natural Resources Conference* 57:330–342.

LaFever, D. H., P. M. Schmidt, N. D. Perry, C. A. Faulhaber, R. R. Lopez, N. J. Silvy, and E. A. Forys. 2008. Use of a population viability analysis to evaluate human-induced impacts and mitigation for the endangered lower keys marsh rabbit. *Human-Wildlife Interactions* 2:260–269.

Legge, S., B. P. Murphy, H. McGregor, J. C. Z. Woinarski, J. Augusteyn, G. Ballard, M. Baseler, T. Buckmaster, C. R. Dickman, T. Doherty, G. Edwards, T. Eyre, B. A. Fancourt, D. Ferguson, D. M. Forsyth, W. L. Geary, M. Gentle, G. Gillespie, L. Greenwood, R. Hohnen, S. Hume, C. N. Johnson, M. Maxwell, P. J. McDonald, K. Morris, K. Moseby, T. Newsome, D. Nimmo, R. Paltridge, D. Ramsey, J. Read, A. Rendall, M. Rich, E. Ritchie, J. Rowland, J. Short, D. Stokeld, D. R. Sutherland, A. F. Wayne, L. Woodford, and F. Zewe. 2017. Enumerating a continental-scale threat: how many feral cats are in Australia? *Biological Conservation* 206:293–303.

Lockwood, J. L. 1999. Using taxonomy to predict success among introduced avifauna: rela-tive importance of transport and establishment. *Conservation Biology* 13:560–567.

Loss, S. R., and P. P. Marra. 2017. Population impacts of free-ranging domestic cats on main-land vertebrates. *Frontiers in Ecology and the Environment* 15:502–509.

Loss, S. R., T. Will, and P. P. Marra. 2013. The impact of free-ranging domestic cats on wildlife of the United States. *Nature Communications* 4:1396. https://doi.org/10.1038/ncomms2380p.1396.

Masters, P., N. Markopoulos, B. Florance, and R. Southgate. 2018. The eradication of fall deer (*Dama dama*) and feral goats (*Capra hircus*) from Kangaroo Island, South Australia. *Australasian Journal of Environmental Management* 25:86–98.

McCann, B. E., and D. K. Garcelon. 2008. Eradication of feral pigs from Pinnacles national monument. *Journal of Wildlife Management* 72:1287–1295.

McNeely, J. A. 2000. The future of alien invasive species: changing societal views. Pages 171–189 *in* H. A. Mooney and R. J. Hobbs, editors. *Invasive species in a changing world.* Island Press, Covelo, CA.

Morrison, S. A., N. Macdonald, K. Walker, L. Lozier, and M. R. Shaw. 2007. Facing the dilemma at eradication's end: uncertainty of absence and the Lazarus effect. *Frontiers in Ecology and the Environment* 5:271–276.

Moseby, K. E., D. E. Peacock, and J. L. Read. 2015. Catastrophic cat predation: a call for pred-ator profiling in wildlife protection programs. *Biological Conservation* 191:331–340.

Nimmo, D. G., and K. K. Miller. 2007. Ecological and human dimensions of management of feral horses in Australia: a review. *Wildlife Research* 34:408–417.

Nogales, M., A. Martín, B. R. Tershy, C. J. Donlan, D. Veitch, N. Puerta, B. Wood, and J. Alonso. 2004. A review of feral cat eradication on islands. *Conservation Biology* 18:310–319.

O'Brien, P. H. 1989. Introduced animals and exotic disease: assessing potential risk and appropriate response. *Australian Veterinary Journal* 66:382–385.

O'Brien, P. H. 1993. Managing introduced pests. *Resource Sciences Interface* 1:4–11.

Panzacchi, M., R. Cocchi, P. Genovesi, and S. Bertolino. 2007. Population control of coypu *Myocastor coypus* in Italy compared to eradication in U.K.: a cost-benefit analysis. *Wildlife Biology* 13:159–171.

Payne, J. M., R. D. Brown, and F. S. Guthery. 1987. Wild game in Texas. *Rangelands* 9(5):207–211.

Pimentel, D. 1955. Biology of the Indian mongoose in Puerto Rico. *Journal of Mammalogy* 36:62–68.

Pitt, W. C., L. C. Driscoll, and E. A. VanderWerf. 2011. A rat-resistant artificial nest box for cavity-nesting birds. *Human-Wildlife Interactions* 5:100–105.

Randall, D. A., J. Marino, D. T. Haydon, C. Sillero-Zubiri, D. L. Knobel, L. A. Tallents, D. W. Macdonald, and M. K. Laurenson. 2006. An integrated disease management strategy for the control of rabies in Ethiopian wolves. *Biological Conservation* 131:151–162.

Reed, R. N., and R. W. Snow. 2014. Assessing risks to humans from invasive Burmese pythons in Everglades national park, Florida, USA. *Wildlife Society Bulletin* 38:366–369.

Reynolds, J. C., S. M. Richardson, B. J. Rodgers, and O. R. Rodgers. 2013. Effective control of non-native American mink by strategic trapping in a river catchment in mainland Britain. *Journal of Wildlife Management* 77:545–554.

Rivera-Parra, J. L., K. M. Levenstein, J. C. Bednarz, F. H. Vargas, V. Carrion, and P. G. Parker. 2012. Implications of goat eradication on the survivorship of the Galàpagos hawk. *Journal of Wildlife Management* 76:1197–1204.

Savidge, J. A., J. W. Stanford, R. N. Reed, G. R. Haddock, and A. A. Y. Adams. 2011. Canine detection of free-ranging brown treesnakes on Guam. *New Zealand Journal of Ecology* 35:174–181.

Schmidt, P. M., R. R. Lopez, and B. A. Collier. 2007. Survival, fecundity, and movements of free-roaming cats. *Journal of Wildlife Management* 71:915–919.

Short, J. 2016. Predation by feral cats key to the failure of a long-term reintroduction of the western barred bandicoot (*Perameles bougainville*). *Wildlife Research* 43:38–50.

Siers, S. R., W. C. Pitt, J. D. Eisemann, L. Clark, A. B. Shiels, C. S. Clark, R. J. Gosnell, and M. C. Messaros. 2019. In situ evaluation of an automated aerial bait delivery system for landscape-scale control of invasive brown treesnakes on Guam. *Occasional Paper of the IUCN Species Survival Commission* 62:348–355.

Simberloff, D. S. 1996. Hybridization between native and introduced wildlife species: importance for conservation. *Wildlife Biology* 2:143–150.

Snow, R. W., M. L. Brien, M. S. Cherkiss, L. Wilkins, and F. J. Mazzotti. 2007. Dietary habits of Burmese python, *Python molurus bivittatus*, from Everglades National Park, Florida. *British Herpetological Bulletin* 101:5–7.

Stone, C. P., and L. L. Loope. 1987. Reducing negative effects of introduced animals on native biotas in Hawaii: what is being done, what needs doing, and the role of national parks. *Environmental Conservation* 14:245–258.

Temple, S. A. 1990. The nasty necessity: eradicating exotics. *Conservation Biology* 4:113–115.

Temple, S. A. 1992. Exotic birds: a growing problem with no easy solution. *Auk* 109:395–397.

Tyler, M. 1994. *Australian frogs: a natural history*. Reed Books, New South Wales, Australia.

Valdez, R. 2019. Historical and conservation perspectives. Pages 1–16 *in* R. Valdez and J. Alfonso Ortega-S, editors. *Wildlife conservation management challenges and strategies in Mexico*. Texas A&M University Press, College Station, TX.

van Riper, C., S. G. van Riper, M. L. Goff, and M. Laird. 1982. *The impact of malaria on birds in Hawaii volcanoes national park*. University of Hawaii Cooperative National Park Resources Studies Unit, Technical Report 47, Honolulu, HI.

Vice, D. S., and D. L. Vice. 2004. Characteristics of brown treesnakes *Boiga irregularis* removed from Guam's transportation network. *Pacific Conservation Biology* 10:216–220.

Vitousek, P. M., C. M. D'Antionio, L. L. Loope, and R. Westbrooks. 1996. Biological invasions as global environmental change. *American Scientist* 84:468–478.

Weber, M., G. A. García-Marmolejo, and R. A. Reyna-Hurtado. 2006. The tragedy of the commons: wildlife management units in southeastern Mexico. *Wildlife Society Bulletin* 34:1480–1408.

West, B. C. 2009. The human side of invasive species. *Human-Wildlife Interactions* 3:6–7.

Wilcove, D. S. 1989. Silent Hawaii. *Living Bird Quarterly* 8(3):8–13.

Wilcove, D. S., D. Rothstein, J. Dubow, A. Phillips, and E. Losos. 1998. Quantifying threats to imperiled species in the U. S. *Bioscience* 48:607–615.

Winter, L. 2004. Trap-neuter-release programs: the reality and the impacts. *Journal of the America Veterinary Medical Association* 225:1369–1376.

Witmer, G. W., and P. Hall. 2011. Attempting to eradicate invasive Gambian giant pouched rats (*Cricetomys gambianus*) in the United States: lessons learned. Pages 131–134 *in* C. R. Veitch, M. N. Clout, and D. R. Towns, editors. *Island invasives; eradication and management.* IUCN, Gland, Switzerland.

Wolf, C. A., H. S. Young, K. M. Zilliacus, A. S. Wegmann, M. McKown, N. D. Holmes, B. R. Tershy, R. Dirzo, S. Kropidlowski, and D. A. Croll. 2018. Invasive rat eradication strongly impacts plant recruitment on a tropical atoll. *PloS One* 13(7):e0200743, 17 July. doi:10.1371/journal.pone.0200743.

6 Fear-Provoking Stimuli

As James Thurber said; "You can fool too many of the people too much of the time." But, unfortunately, animals are a lot smarter.

– Adapted from William Fitzwater

Fear-provoking stimuli can be classified scientifically into three categories – those that don't work, those that break, and those that get lost.

– Adapted from Russell Baker

The optimal foraging theory predicts that animals should forage in a way that maximizes their nutritional benefits. Foraging, however, can be dangerous, as hungry animals must venture from the safety of cover into areas that they otherwise would avoid. Hence, foraging decisions are tempered by the need to avoid predators, including the avoidance of some good foraging opportunities that are too risky. Because animals need to find food and to avoid being killed, they often exhibit risk-adverse foraging.

Wildlife managers can reduce wildlife damage to agricultural crops by exploiting an animal's reluctance to forage in risky areas. This can be accomplished through the use of fear-provoking stimuli that increase the animals' fear of areas where crops are grown. Fear-provoking stimuli can be visual (e.g., predator models or scarecrows), auditory (e.g., distress calls or loud noises), or olfactory (e.g., predator's urine).

6.1 WHAT VISUAL STIMULI CAN SERVE AS FEAR-PROVOKING STIMULI?

Several visual stimuli can be used as fear-provoking stimuli. They are designed primarily to repel birds, which rely more on vision than on their other senses to detect danger. Many of these visual stimuli are models of their predators. The use of predator models is based on the fact that foraging is more dangerous when predators are present, and birds respond to this threat by spending more time being alert and less time foraging (Cherry et al. 2015). Thus, predator models can be placed in areas experiencing human–wildlife conflicts to convince animals that foraging elsewhere is safer.

Some predator models are designed to mimic hawks or owls, but the most common predator model is the scarecrow, which is a model of a human. Scarecrows have been used for centuries to reduce bird predation on agricultural crops (Figure 6.1). They are effective because many avian species view humans as dangerous. For instance, Canada geese, which are hunted in North America, stopped visiting agricultural fields once scarecrows were erected in them (Heinrich and Craven 1990). Scarecrows, especially those capable of some movement, have provided at least some protection

DOI: 10.1201/9780429401404-6

FIGURE 6.1   Scarecrows have been used for hundreds of years to scare birds away from agricultural crops. This one is in field in Thailand.

Source: Patpitchaya, Shutterstock 539319679.

from birds at fish farms (Stickley et al. 1995), polluted ponds (Boag and Lewin 1980), grain fields (Knittle and Porter 1988), and sunflower fields (Cummings et al. 1986).

Some birds avoid sites where there are several dead conspecifics. The method works best with flocking species, such as gulls, magpies, and corvids, which can learn about dangerous predators by watching the misfortune of other flock members (Conover 1987). Ring-billed and herring gulls avoided areas on landfills and airports where dead gulls were strewn on the ground, although dead gulls had no effect when placed in nesting colonies (Seamans et al. 2007). Merrell (2012) found that the most effective method to convince ravens to abandon roost sites inside buildings was to hang a dead raven upside down from a rafter (Figure 6.2). Hanging vulture effigies from towers at the U.S. Marine Corps Air Station at Cherry Point, North Carolina, deterred both turkey vultures and black vultures (Ball 2009).

Most animals are neophobic or fearful of novel objects, and many fear-provoking stimuli exploit this phobia. Spot lights, flashing lights, and strobe lights are often used to repel nocturnal animals. Unfortunately, these lights are often ineffective or work for only short periods of time (Koehler et al. 1990; Andelt et al. 1997). Wildlife warning reflectors are angled glass mounted on roadside posts and are designed to make deer wary of highway ROWs and approaching vehicles. When a vehicle approaches at night, the reflectors deflect light from a moving car's headlights into the roadside vegetation to deter deer from crossing the road until the vehicle passes (Figure 6.3). The reflectors can provide either a flashing light or a continuous wall

FIGURE 6.2   Effigy of a vulture hangs from a tower at U.S. Marine Corps Air Station at Cherry Point, North Carolina.

Source: Courtesy of Human–Wildlife Interactions.

FIGURE 6.3   Wildlife warning reflector.

Source: Falko Brieger and used with permission.

of light (depending on reflector type and spacing). Wildlife warning reflectors are popular because they are inexpensive and easy to install but are usually ineffective as countless studies have shown (Langbein et al. 2010, 2011; Brieger et al. 2016; Kämmerle et al. 2017). In an interesting turn of events, Riginos et al. (2018) found that the control he used in these tests, which consisted of covering the reflectors with white canvas bags, was more effective than the reflectors themselves.

Lasers are a visual stimulus that can be effective in scaring birds, especially at night. Lasers were effective in reducing damage by barnacle geese and dark-bellied geese to pastures in Denmark (Clausen et al. 2019). Merrell (2012) used them to disperse common ravens that were roosting inside buildings, but he found that the birds quickly learned that the lasers posed no threat and started moving only a few meters to avoid the laser's annoying light. Lasers were more valuable when used in conjunction with other tools, such as raven effigies. One advantage of lasers was that they can be used by staff members of the facility when professional wildlife management personnel were not available. Lasers allowed facility employees help deal with the situation and offered proof that all available nonlethal means are being employed to alleviate the problem. Merrell (2012) reported that expensive, high-powered lasers were not needed; the small pen-type lasers used as pointers for presentations were just as effective.

Lasers successfully prompted Canada geese to evacuate sites at night, although almost 5 minutes of laser use was needed before the geese left the site. The birds usually moved less than 2 km to another urban site (Sherman and Barras 2004). Lasers have also been tested as a means to repel mammals. VerCauteren et al. (2003, 2006) reported that red, blue, and green lasers were ineffective at dispersing deer at night, perhaps because deer are color blind.

6.2 WHAT AUDITORY STIMULI CAN BE USED AS FEAR-PROVOKING STIMULI?

6.2.1 EXPLODERS AND BANGERS

Several fear-provoking stimuli are based on sound. Most common is the use of a loud bang to scare animals from areas where they are unwanted. There are many ways to produce a loud bang, including the use of firecrackers or firearms. A number of projectiles, including cracker shells, bird bombs, and whistle bombs, scare birds when fired from a starter pistol or shotgun. Cracker shells are fired from a shotgun and explode with a bang after traveling 100–150 m. Hence, cracker shells produce two loud blasts: the shotgun blast, which propels the cracker shell through the air, followed by the exploding cracker shell. The latter is especially alarming to animals because the explosion occurs closer to them. For this reason, cracker shells are particularly useful in scaring birds from aquaculture facilities where people are along the edge of a pond and the birds are in the middle of the pond. Bird bombs are fired from a modified starter pistol and travel up to 100 m before exploding. Whistle bombs, racket bombs, and screamer shells make a whistling or screaming sound as they travel through the air. They are usually less effective than cracker shells but still are useful because they generate a different sound.

FIGURE 6.4   A propane exploder is being used to protect this German vineyard from birds.

Source: Mabeline72, Shutterstock 1501327628.

Propane exploders function by releasing a measured amount of propane into a firing chamber where a spark ignites the gas (Figure 6.4). The explosions are loud; a timer can be set so that the cannon fires at preselected intervals ranging from a minute to an hour. The advantage of propane exploders is their safety and the fact that they can be used when no one is around. Their disadvantage is that they can disturb the neighbors and, therefore, should not be used if homes or people are nearby. Further, animals can habituate to them over the course of a few days. Propane exploders have been used to reduce bird damage in citrus groves (Hobbs and Leon 1987), aquaculture facilities (Parkhurst et al. 1987), and soybean fields (Radtke and Dieter 2011). A single exploder protected 3 ha of sunflowers at a cost of $110 per ha (Linz et al. 2011), but propane exploders were unable to reduce deer damage in corn-fields (Gilsdorf et al. 2004*a*).

6.2.2 Novel Sounds

Animals are wary of unfamiliar sounds, and some auditory devices designed to repel wildlife are based on this principle. The Electron Guard® was developed by the USDA National Wildlife Research Center; it combined a warbling siren with a strobe light. It experienced some short-term success in scaring coyotes away from sheep flocks but was ineffective in protecting cornfields from deer (Gilsdorf et al. 2004*a*).

The underwater broadcast of sharp, brief pulses of sounds deterred earless seals for 19 months from preying upon captive Atlantic salmon at fish farms in Scotland.

Nontarget sea mammals in the area, including Eurasian otters and harbor porpoises, were unaffected by the sound playbacks (Götz and Janik 2016). Similar acoustical devices have been used to keep seals away from marine construction sites and salmon trap nets (Fjälling et al. 2006; Brandt et al. 2013).

Devices capable of emitting ultrasonic frequencies are often advertised by companies to repel nuisance birds. Because humans cannot hear these high frequencies, these devices are supposed to annoy birds and not people; but, we have known for a long time that birds cannot detect ultrasonic frequencies (Brand and Kellogg 1939a, 1939b). So not surprisingly, birds are not repelled or bothered by these devices (Marsh et al. 1991). In contrast, some mammals can hear ultrasonic frequencies. But little evidence suggests that ultrasound is useful in repelling rodents, deer, or other mammals. Langbein et al. (2010, 2011) investigated the response of roe deer, fallow deer, and red deer when exposed to an acoustical device that emitted both ultrasonic and audible signals. After the device began broadcasting every 15–30 seconds, videos revealed that every deer species approached and fed calmly close (0–5 m) to the devices within three days of their activation. Ultrasonic "deer whistles" designed to be mounted on automobiles are ineffective despite the claim that they frighten deer away from moving vehicles.

Deer whistles and other devices produce sound when attached to a moving vehicle. Advertisements for deer whistles claim that they alert deer to an approaching vehicle and keep them from crossing in front of a vehicle. These auditory devices, nonetheless, did not alter the behavior of either fallow deer or white-tailed deer (Ujvári et al. 2004; Valitzski et al. 2009). Such is not surprising because vehicles make considerable noise when traveling at highway speeds; the addition of a new sound to noise already created by the vehicle probably does not make much difference.

6.2.3   Distress Calls and Alarm Calls

When a bird has been captured by a predator, it may emit a loud distress call that sounds more like a scream than a normal bird song. Distress calls function both by startling the predator into accidently dropping the bird and by attracting so much attention that the predator gives up and releases the bird (Conover 1994; Wise et al. 1999). When other birds hear a distress call, they know that a bird has been captured and will often approach the source of a distress call rather than fleeing. Approaching a predator may seem suicidal, but by doing so, birds can learn valuable information about predators in the area and how to avoid them.

Alarm calls are emitted when a bird detects a predator. This is a soft call and sounds like "seee." Birds often respond to alarm calls by gathering in tree branches where they can watch the predator. During the breeding season, birds with nests or young nearby may dive at a predator or mob it to drive it away.

Recordings of distress or alarm calls have been employed to scare starlings from airports and vineyards, gulls from landfills, finches from grain fields, herons from fish farms, and flying-fox bats from orchards (Bomford and O'Brien 1990; Andelt and Hooper 1996). Some airports even have special trucks equipped with mounted speakers that are used to broadcast distress and alarm calls. But, distress or alarm calls are not always effective. To keep wild turkeys from eating grapes in vineyards, Coates et al. (2010) broadcasted three calls that wild turkeys emit when confronted by a predator: the alarm putt call (emitted when there is a predator on the ground), a predator alarm call (produced when the predator is close), and a distress call (given by a captured turkey). Unfortunately, the calls did not lessen damage by wild turkeys.

The main drawback with distress and alarm calls is that birds ultimately learn they are not real and habituate to them; although, birds take longer to habituate to these calls than to loud noises that have no biological meaning to them. For instance, Spanier (1980) compared the effectiveness of distress calls to a loud bang in repelling black-crowned night herons from a fish farm. He reported that the loud bang lost its effectiveness within a week, while the distress calls remained effective for several weeks. Recordings of distress and alarm calls are most effective if made from the same species that is causing the problem.

Because distress calls are given when a bird is being held by a predator and alarm calls are given when there is a predator in the neighborhood, birds probably expect to see a predator whenever they hear one of these calls. If they do not, they may realize that something is not right and habituate more rapidly to the distress and alarm calls. For this reason, it is wise to pair the broadcast of these calls with a predator model. Conover (1985) designed an owl model which held a model of a crow in its talons, and this model was paired with the playback of crow distress calls. In this case, the visual predator model reinforced the distress call playback because crows that flew closer to investigate saw what they expected: a crow captured by a predator. Crows habituated more slowly to this model than to an owl model placed out by itself.

6.2.4 SOUNDS FROM DOMINANT OR AGGRESSIVE INDIVIDUALS

Territorial animals use vocalizations to scare away subordinate animals from their territories. These might have the potential to keep depredating animals away from the area where they are causing problems. For example, male Asian elephants were more likely to flee a food source when vocalizations of an Asian elephant matriarchal group were broadcasted rather than the sounds of a chainsaw (Wijayagunawardane et al. 2016). This was not surprising because matriarchal families avoid solitary males (Sukumar 2003).

6.3 WHICH OLFACTORY STIMULI CAN BE USED AS FEAR-PROVOKING STIMULI?

Odors can be used to repel animals. When herbivores smell a predator, they remain stationary initially and then move to secure areas where predator odors are absent (Apfelbach et al. 2005; Conover 2007). By doing so, herbivores can avoid danger-ous situations. Wildlife biologists have exploited this avoidance behavior by spread-ing predator odors, especially their feces or urine, in crops and orchards to repel herbivores.

Many types of predator odors have been effective in repelling herbivores. Seamans et al. (2016) distributed hair of bobcats, black bears, or coyotes at feeding sites and observed the response of white-tailed deer to the predator odors. Deer were more alert during the first four days but not thereafter. Unfortunately, food consumption by deer was not deterred by the presence of hair. But, Severud et al. (2011) reduced beaver use of trails by spraying trails with wolf urine.

Bobcat urine reduced woodchuck damage to fruit trees (Swihart 1991; Belant et al. 1998). Predator urine or feces discouraged white-tailed deer and elk from browsing (Melchiors and Leslie 1985; Swihart et al. 1991). Feral goats changed their loafing sites after the sites were littered with tiger feces (Cox et al. 2012). Dingo urine repelled western grey kangaroo (Parsons et al. 2007).

Several studies have investigated which components of predator urine are responsible for repelling animals. Identifying the active ingredients would make it possible to produce a synthetic spray and eliminate the need to collect predator urine. Sulfur-containing compounds in predator urines provoke an avoidance response or inhibit browsing by European rabbits (Sullivan et al. 1988a), pocket gopher (Sullivan et al. 1988b), rats (Tobin et al. 1995; Burwash et al. 1998), mice (Epple et al. 1995), and deer (Melchiors and Leslie 1985; Belant et al. 1998). Ferrero et al. (2011) isolated 2-phenylethylamine from the urine of bobcats (Figure 6.5) and found that rodents avoided the area where the chemical was sprayed.

Many animals, including coyotes, mark the boundaries of their territories with urine and odors from scent glands to warn away other members of their species. This suggests that it may be possible to keep animals out of an area where they are unwanted by spraying the perimeter of the area with the specific odor that dominant individuals use to mark their territory. Shivik et al. (2011) examined how other

FIGURE 6.5   Bobcat urine can repel rodents.

Source: Holly Kuchera, Shutterstock 1525714751.

coyotes would react to an area that he sprayed with coyote urine. Local coyotes responded to the urine, but not the way Shivik expected. Coyotes spent twice as much time inside the sprayed area than unsprayed areas. The results did not support the use of coyote urine to repel coyotes from areas where they were causing problems.

6.4   CAN PUNISHMENT ALTER AN ANIMAL'S BEHAVIOR?

Punishment can be defined as an activity or stimulus that reduces the frequency of a behavior. Sequoia National Park used punishment to stop bears from entering campgrounds and picnic areas and from consuming anthropogenic foods. When a bear was located within 50 m of one of these areas, it was punished by a group of people who chased it, fired rubber bullets or pepper spray at it, and threw rocks. Only rubber bullets were effective against bears habituated to humans and anthropogenic food (Mazur 2010). Most bears (75%) stayed away for more than an hour after being punished but did not change their behavior over longer periods.

One way to punish problem animals is by using an electronic collar that shocks the animal wearing it when the collar receives a specific radio frequency. These collars were developed to train dogs in the field. They allow the dog's handler to punish the dog instantly for misbehaving. Andelt et al. (1999) tested whether such a system could be used to teach coyotes to stop killing sheep. The scientists placed shock collars on captive coyotes and shocked them whenever they approached within 2 m of a lamb. Coyotes quickly associated the electric shocks with lambs, stopped trying to kill them, and kept their distance from lambs.

Using shock collars on free-ranging wildlife might not seem practical because capturing predators and placing place shock collars on them are difficult. However, these collars may be useful for resolving some specific human–wildlife conflicts. For instance, bears that raid campgrounds are usually relocated. Too often, these bears simply repeat their camp-raiding behavior in their new surroundings and have to be euthanized. One possible method to stop these bears from repeating their destructive behavior is to place a shock collar on them before they are released. Park employees could signal the collar to shock the bear whenever they see the bear misbehaving. Alternatively, campgrounds could be equipped with a radio transmitter that constantly broadcasted a low-power radio signal that would activate the collar to shock the bear whenever it approached the campground and came in range of the radio signal.

Rossler et al. (2012) and Hawley et al. (2009, 2013) used shock collars to keep wolves from visiting a bait station; the shock collar was triggered by a signal device that was at the bait station so that a collared wolf was shocked if it got too close. Interestingly, other members of the pack took a cue from their collared pack member and also avoided the site. Breck et al. (2006) developed a device that would give bears an electric shock when they tried to pull down a bird feeder. The device consisted of two parallel metal plates, which would rock and touch each other when pressure was applied at the edges. The plates were mounted between the bird feeder and the support pole. When a bear pulled or pushed on the bird feeder, the two plates would touch, complete an electric circuit, and shock the hear. When tested in Minnesota, bears stopped raiding feeders with a shocking device but continued to raid unprotected feeders.

6.5 WHAT LIMITS THE EFFECTIVENESS OF FEAR-PROVOKING STIMULI?

Habituation is the main factor that limits the effectiveness of fear-provoking stimuli as a method to resolve human–wildlife conflicts. Once an animal has learned that a fear-provoking stimulus is harmless, the animal will remember that for a long time, often its entire life. That knowledge can also be conveyed from one generation to the next (Guinn 2013). Offspring learn from their parents what poses a danger to them and what does not. For example, if a bald eagle ignores a scarecrow and kills sheep right beside one, its young will learn to do likewise.

Unless the fear-provoking stimuli are actually capable of harming animals, habituation is inevitable, but it takes time before it occurs. In the meantime, fear-provoking stimuli can be used to reduce wildlife damage. Hence, fear-provoking stimuli are most suitable for problems lasting only a few days. For example, when fields are planted in the spring, birds often go down the rows digging up the newly planted seeds. Fear-provoking stimuli may be useful in this situation because birds lose interest in the seeds when they sprout, and germination occurs a few days after the seeds are planted. Fear-provoking stimuli may be successful in reducing raccoon damage to sweet corn fields because raccoons only eat ripe corn ears. Thus, protection is needed only for a few days before the corn is harvested. Fear-provoking stimuli can also be used to reduce bird damage in a ripening blueberry

FIGURE 6.6   This plastic owl model is supposed to keep birds from loafing on the tower, but it is ineffective based on the number of birds loafing there when this photo was taken.

Source: Photo by Leah Delahoussaye and used with permission.

field because there may only be a few days between when the berries are ripe enough to attract birds and when they are harvested. Unfortunately, the most common usage of fear-provoking stimuli is to place owl models in barns or other buildings, where they are supposed to repel pigeons and starlings (Figure 6.6). They have little chance of being successful because this protection is needed for months or years.

6.6   CAN HABITUATION TO FEAR-PROVOKING STIMULI BE DELAYED?

Several methods can be used to retard an animal's habituation to a fear-provoking stimulus. One method is to use fear-provoking stimuli that mimic real predators. Scarecrows are most effective against species, such as ducks and geese, that are often hunted by humans. They are also more effective during hunting seasons and in areas where hunting is popular. Scarecrows are a poor choice for keeping songbirds out of an orchard because these birds have no reason to fear humans. Distress and alarm calls are effective fear-provoking stimuli because real birds give these calls when attacked. These observations reinforce a bird's fear when it hears the playback of a distress or alarm call and delay the bird's habituation to them.

Lack of movement is an obvious cue to animals that something is not alive. Thus, predator models that are capable of movement are more effective than stationary ones. One visual model that moves is the pop-up scarecrow: the Scary-Man®, which is an inflatable model of a person attached to an air pump. At timed intervals, the air pump inflates the scarecrow, making it appear to be standing up. These scarecrows, often combined with an exploder or siren, have been used in keeping birds out of sunflower fields, aquaculture facilities, and airports (Cummings et al. 1986; Stickley et al. 1995).

The more animals are exposed to a fear-provoking stimulus, the faster they will habituate to it. For this reason, bangers and shell crackers should be used sparingly, and propane cannons should be set so that they fire only a couple of times per hour. Fear-provoking stimuli should be moved often to new locations to delay habituation. Ideally, a propane cannon or other auditory stimuli should fire only when wildlife are close to it. To accomplish this, the fear-provoking stimuli should be activated when a motion or infrared sensor signals that an animal is within a few meters of it. One device designed to stop woodpeckers from drilling holes in wooden utility poles only plays distress calls or predator calls when it detected the vibration in the pole produced by a pecking woodpecker (Blackwell et al. 2012). Beringer et al. (2003) developed an animal-activated fear-provoking stimulus by wiring a fear-provoking stimulus to lasers surrounding a 0.5-ha soybean plot. The fear-provoking stimulus was activated when a horizontal laser beam was interrupted by an object passing through it. The fear-provoking stimulus consisted of a pop-up scarecrow that would inflate and rise from the ground when activated; a strobe light that would flash; and a sound system that broadcasted deer distress calls, the barking of dogs, or a person shouting. Deer spent less time in protected plots than in unprotected ones, and soybean plants were larger in the protected plots.

Not all experiments testing fear-provoking stimuli have been successful. VerCauteren et al. (2005) tested whether a device that made a loud noise and emitted red-flashing lights could prevent elk from foraging on an alfalfa bale placed nearby. The device only fired when motion or infrared sensors detected the presence of a deer. The numbers of alfalfa bales consumed were similar at sites with fear-provoking devices and those without them. Initially, a few elk (21%) were momentarily startled when the device was first activated but quickly resumed feeding. Most elk never reacted to the device, suggesting that the failure may have been in the fear-provoking device, not in the motion detection system. Gilsdorf et al. (2004b) evaluated an auditory device that broadcasted distress and alarm calls of deer. The device was attached to infrared light beams, which activated it when a beam was interrupted by an animal. The device, unfortunately, did not deter deer from entering the plots or reduce corn losses.

Trains pose a danger to large mammals, such as bears or moose, that are on the railroad track but do not detect the oncoming train soon enough to flee. Backs et al. (2017) tested a device that used magnetic or vibration sensors to detect an approaching train and then relay a signal further down the railroad track to where wildlife normally crossed. The signal then activated a siren or loud noise 20 seconds before the train arrived at the scene, enough time for the animals to flee. Because the noise was an accurate predictor of the train's arrival, animals did not habituate to the stimulus.

One method to delay habituation is to fire bullets at a few animals during the period that bangers are being employed. At a U.K. landfill frequented by thousands of gulls and corvids, Baxter and Allan (2008) found that firing blanks at the scavenging birds quickly lost its effectiveness. But after 136 gulls were shot over 7 weeks, the firing of blanks reduced gull number by more than 90%. In contrast, the combination of firing live and blank rounds had little impact on corvids.

I learned the hard way that catching gulls also increases their wariness. As a graduate student, I needed to band all of the adults in a small colony. The first day I baited gulls at a nearby landfill, I caught, banded, and released about 25% of the gulls in the colony. Based on that first day, I was sure that I could easily catch every gull, but I failed to catch another gull despite trying the same technique a dozen times over the next few weeks. The gulls had learned to steer clear of the landfill. Moving elsewhere did not help because the gulls had learned to identify my cannon net and other telltale signs of my baiting operation.

6.7   CAN LIVE PREDATORS SERVE AS FEAR-PROVOKING STIMULI?

The problem of habituation is lessened if live predators are used as fear-provoking stimuli, rather than innocuous models of them. One interesting approach is to attract free-ranging predators to the site. For instance, some farmers with vole and bird problems erect perches in their orchards to attract hawks and owls. Shave et al. (2018) found that supplying artificial perch sites had no impact on raptor abundance but that providing nest boxes in orchards increased the number of nesting American kestrels. Although kestrels rarely prey on birds, the abundance of fruit-eating birds (primarily American robins, common grackles, and European starlings) was reduced in sweet cherry orchards where kestrels were nesting.

FIGURE 6.7   A trained Harris's hawk with a falconer in England.

Source: KeoghanBellew87, Shutterstock 1560734468.

Trained falcons and hawks have been used to frighten corvids and gulls from landfills in England (Baxter and Allan 2006; Baxter and Robinson 2007). Both falcons and hawks reduced bird numbers, but neither could eliminate birds from scavenging at landfills. Peregrine falcons were especially effective against black-headed gulls and corvids; these small gulls are common prey of falcons, but herring gulls were indifferent to the falcons. This was not surprising because herring gulls do not fear falcons; this gull species is so large that falcons rarely chased them (Baxter and Allan 2006). The experiment also showed two limitations of using trained raptors: they could not be released at night or when their handlers were absent.

African golf courses have problems with nuisance geese, except it is not Canada geese but another species, the Egyptian goose. Atkins et al. (2017) tested whether flying trained Harris's hawks at geese could persuade the geese to go elsewhere and not return (Figure 6.7). Golf carts were used to bring the hawks close to the geese before releasing them. Results were promising; goose abundance declined 73% on golf courses where some geese were killed by the hawks. Interestingly, geese also developed a fear of approaching golf carts.

6.8   ARE GUARD DOGS EFFECTIVE AS FEAR-PROVOKING STIMULI?

Live dogs can be used as fear-provoking stimuli to scare wildlife. Dogs have been used to keep Canada geese away from sites where they are unwanted (Castelli and Sleggs 2000) and deer out of apple orchards and plant nurseries (Beringer et al.

1994). One way to use dogs as fear-provoking stimuli is simply to keep the dog under the control of its handler. Dogs, such as border collies, can add an extra frightening dimension to human patrols (Castelli and Sleggs 2000). Use of dogs to harass geese is not only effective but also labor intensive because the dogs must be under human supervision to be successful (Smith et al. 1999).

Another approach is to use dogs by surrounding the property with a fence. Dog-proof fences are much easier to build than wildlife-proof fences. Dogs can also be kept from wandering by having the dog wear a shock collar that shocks the dog whenever it comes within a few meters of a wire that gives off a weak radio wave of the right frequency. The wire can either be buried or left on the ground around the area needing protection. Dogs quickly learn that if they try to cross the wire, they will get a shock and cease doing so. This method can be quite cost-effective when the dogs behave as expected (Beringer et al. 1994). However, when guard dogs are left alone, some quickly tire of chasing animals that they cannot catch and start to ignore them.

Dogs have also been used to protect livestock from predators. In Kenya, livestock herds accompanied by both herders and dogs lost fewer animals to predators, especially to leopards, than those accompanied by just herders. The same was true at night when the livestock were penned inside kraals; predators killed fewer animals when dogs were kept by the kraals (Woodroffe et al. 2006).

Usually, guard dogs undergo a prolonged training period, starting when they are young; puppies are raised with the livestock they are to guard so that they bond with them; this bonding is more likely to occur if human contact with the pups is minimal. A trained guard dog that has imprinted on the herd will stay with the livestock and defend them against predators. Trained guard dogs have prevented coyotes from killing ewes and lambs (Andelt 1992) and kept white-tailed deer from foraging on haystacks (VerCauteren et al. 2008).

Many people view guard dogs as a humane and acceptable method of predator control, but they are not a panacea. Some guard dogs harass, injure, or kill the livestock that they are supposed to protect; some stray from the herd; and others attack wildlife or people that ventured too near to the livestock herd. Considerable time, effort, and money must be invested in guard dogs for them to be effective protectors. One company in New Jersey spent over $18,000 to implement a program using border collies to control nuisance Canada geese and $4,000 annually to maintain the program (Castelli and Sleggs 2000). This investment does not guarantee that a guard dog will be effective. One problem with guard dogs is that they are subject to premature death or injury (Lorenz et al. 1986). In Namibia, the life expectancy of a guard dog was about four years (Marker et al. 2005a, 2005b). For these reasons, donkeys and llamas also are used to guard sheep (Figure 6.8). Whether it is cost-effective to use a guard animal depends on many factors: the ability and longevity of the guard animal, the cost to purchase and maintain it, and the number of livestock lost to predators. Encouragingly, Brewster et al. (2019) found that a combination of guard animals and snares was the most cost-efficient method of mitigating calf losses to coyotes in Texas.

FIGURE 6.8   Llama guarding a herd of sheep.
Source: C. Hamilton, Shutterstock 1794107254.

6.9   WHAT IS HAZING OR HARASSMENT?

When an animal is constantly chased away from a site, it will stop returning to that site, especially if it has to travel some distance to get there. This approach, called hazing or harassment, has been used successfully to keep wood pigeons from agricultural fields (Kenward 1978), grey herons and cormorants from fish farms (Draulans and van Vessem 1985; Moerbeek et al. 1987), baboon troops from venturing into urban areas for food (van Doorn 2009 as cited by Kaplan et al. 2011), and Canada geese from golf courses (Castelli and Sleggs 2000). Chasing wildlife away from their crops was the most common method used by farmers living near India's Sariska Tiger Reserve, to reduce wildlife damage (Sekhar 1998).

The chief drawback of hazing and harassment is that it is labor intensive because many chases may be necessary before the animals stop returning (Sidebar 6.1). Around Nepal's Bardia National Park, villagers use harassment to protect their small fields from elephants, rhinos, blue bulls, wild boars, chitals, and peacocks. Villagers build wooden towers in their fields and occupy the towers throughout the night (Figure 6.9). Villagers bang on tin cans, shout, and throw flaming sticks at any animals entering the fields. Although effective, guarding the fields all night long is also labor intensive (Thapa 2010).

FIGURE 6.9   In Southeast Asia, farmers build small shelters in their fields and occupy them all day and night when their crop is ripening and vulnerable to hungry animals.

Source: Inside_Bhutan, Shutterstock 1602594100.

SIDEBAR 6.1 USING HARASSMENT TO PROTECT VILLAGE CROPS FROM ELEPHANTS IN KENYA

Crop raiding by elephants in Africa is widespread and tragic for both villagers and elephants. Elephants can wipe out a farmer's entire field in a single night, and the ill will this generates within rural villages threaten local elephants. One common method combines an early warning system with human harassment. The Ilmejoli Farmers Association built watchtowers in the tops of trees along the outside edge of the village's fields, and farmers manned them on a rotational basis. The job of the watch guards was to maintain fires around the fields and use spotlights to detect elephants emerging from the forest. The guards blew whistles when elephants were sighted to alert the village. The villagers then emerged in a large group with fires, hand-held torches, whistles, and drums to drive the elephants back to the forest. Sometimes, the Kenyan government provided stun grenades, which made the harassment more frightening for the elephants. Villages that used this combined method reduced incidents of elephant raiding by 90%. Once elephants were already within a field, there was little that could be done to reduce the amount of damage they caused.

Counterintuitively, the use of fear-provoking stimuli to drive elephants out of a field, once they are inside, increased damage because the elephants panicked and trampled much of the field as they tried to escape (Sitati et al. 2003, 2005; Sitati and Walpole 2006).

In the western United States, one use of harassment to reduce wolf depredation of livestock is the Range Rider Program, which increases human presence around livestock herds to deter wolves (Figure 6.10). The program employs horsemen and horsewomen to spend time near livestock herds that are located in wolf country. These programs are usually jointly sponsored by the state wildlife agency, an environmental group, and ranchers (Bradley and Pletscher 2005; Parks and Messmer 2016).

Many U.S. cities are experiencing increased in conflicts with coyotes. In the Denver Metropolitan Area, over 200 citizen volunteers were trained to haze coyotes from sites where they were causing problems. These volunteers hazed coyotes 96 times using loud voices and noisemakers, while approaching the coyotes. The coyotes always fled immediately. It was hoped that the coyotes would be reluctant to return to these hazing sites, but instead it shifted the coyotes' use of these sites to those times when people were absent (Bonnell and Breck 2017; Breck et al. 2017).

FIGURE 6.10   Range rider in Montana monitoring wolf activity near a cattle herd.

Source: Tyler Parks and used with permission.

Nuisance bears are usually relocated, so there is considerable interest in making the capture experience so terrifying that the bears will not become repeat offenders. Beckmann et al. (2004) compared three approaches to scaring captive bears. Bears in the first group were just released without fanfare; bears in the second group were hit with pepper spray and rubber bullets and exposed to cracker shells and yelling when released. Bears in the third group were treated the same as the second group, but they were additionally chased by dogs upon release. Sadly, none of the treatments were successful in keeping bears from returning; 57 of 62 captured bears returned to the urban area where they were captured, regardless of which scare tactics were employed. Similar experimental actions also had little impact on brown bears in Europe (Rauer et al. 2003) or on black bears in Louisiana (Leigh and Chamberlain 2008).

Human-piloted aircraft, including fixed-wing airplanes, ultralight recreational aircraft, and helicopters, are used to haze wildlife. Helicopters have kept bison from wandering outside of Yellowstone National Park (Meagher 1989). Fixed-wing aircraft have been employed to scare blackbirds away from ripening sunflower fields and roosting sites (Linz et al. 2011).

Radio-controlled, model aircraft and drones have proven to be an effective tool to disperse birds. They are both cheaper and safer than an aircraft with a pilot. They have been successful in dispersing dunlins, robins, gulls, pigeons, geese, lapwings, and starlings. Though effective, use of drones or model aircraft is labor intensive and requires a skilled operator (Blokpoel 1976; Bhusal et al. 2018). Furthermore, birds often return to the area soon after the drones land. For these reasons, drones and model airplanes are best employed as one part of an integrated hazing program.

Airboats and outboard motorboats have been used to haze birds on large ponds and lakes where the birds are too far offshore to be repelled by someone standing on the bank. On New York's Oneida Lake, cormorant numbers had expanded to the point where they were impacting the lake's sports fishery. In response, two boats were used from dawn to dusk throughout the spring and fall when cormorant numbers were high. This intensive effort was successful in reducing cormorant numbers on the lake (De Vault et al. 2012).

Canada geese cause numerous nuisance problems in urban and suburban areas in North America and, increasingly, in Europe (Fox 2019). Holevinski et al. (2007) tested whether hazing can produce a local redistribution of geese or can push nuisance geese into rural areas where hunters can reduce their numbers. The authors harassed the geese with border collies, lasers, remote-controlled boats, kayaks, pyrotechnics, and goose distress calls. The most successful approach employed the simultaneous use of border collies and remote-controlled boats. While each hazing event was successful in getting geese to leave the site, the geese moved only an average of 1.2 km and returned within 2 hours. Geese had a strong affinity to sites despite being hazed; an average goose was harassed 17 times. Hazing was unsuccessful in getting the geese to move to areas where hunting was allowed, even though hunting sites were only a few kilometers away.

6.10   IS IT POSSIBLE TO CREATE A LANDSCAPE OF FEAR?

An animal's apprehension varies with habitat. For example, a woodchuck's sense of security is high when it is close to its burrow; but, as it ventures farther away from the burrow in search of food, the woodchuck becomes more alert and more nervous, owing to the growing likelihood that it will be unable of return safely to its burrow if ambushed by a predator. Likewise, animals feel more at ease in habitat where it is safer. A Canada goose prefers to graze in the middle of open fields, rather than close to a forest edge because of its fear that an ambush predator might rush out of the woods and catch it before it can take flight. A bighorn sheep wants to remain in steep, rocky terrain where its climbing ability will allow it to put distant between it and any wolf or cougar trying to catch it. The concept that an animal's sense of fear and security varies by habitat is called the "landscape of fear" and is based on the anticipation of danger (Laundré et al. 2010). But what should an animal do in a world where there are many different predators? Thaker et al. (2011) tested five hypotheses: (1) animals should avoid areas that are utilized by their most dangerous predator, (2) animals should avoid areas that are used by any of their predators, (3) animals should avoid areas used by sit-and-pursue predators, (4) animals should avoid risky habitats, where their predators make many kills, and (5) animals should select for safer habitats where their predators make few kills. The first three hypotheses are techniques designed to reduce the probability of encountering a predator, while the last two are designed to avoid the probability of being killed after being detected by a predator. When tested using seven ungulate species in South Africa, all seven species avoided risky habitat (5). Small herbivores also avoided areas used by any predators (2), while large herbivores (wildebeest, zebra, and giraffe) only avoided areas used by lions and leopards (1).

The landscape-of-fear concept implied that a fear-provoking stimulus may be effective in areas where the problem animal has a heightened sense fear, but not in areas that offer security (Sidebar 6.2). An animal's fear of an area can be increased by making habitat modifications, such as removing hiding cover, which makes the animal more vulnerable to predators. Habitat modification is discussed in Chapter 10 rather than in this chapter.

SIDEBAR 6.2   CREATING A "LANDSCAPE OF FEAR" IN YELLOWSTONE NATIONAL PARK

For much of the last century, elk and bison in Yellowstone National Park lived in an environment free of wolves. Because of this, elk or bison populations were so high that they overbrowsed native plants, including willow, and caused problems when large numbers of elk migrated outside of the park during the winter and onto private ranches. In 1994, the U.S. Fish and Wildlife Agency started releasing wolves into the park to prey upon adult elk and bison. The main impact of wolves on these herbivores, however, was not in the number of ungulates killed, but in changing the behavior of adult elk and bison, especially

females with calves. These herbivores became warier and spent less time forag-
ing in the open meadows where they were vulnerable to wolves and more time
foraging inside forests where the trees offered some protection from wolves.
This decrease in foraging in meadows had a cascading effect on the habitat.
Willows and other plants that had been heavily browsed started to recover
(Figures 6.11 and 6.12), and beaver densities in meadows increased because
there were now more willows for them to consume (Laundré et al. 2001, 2010;
Beyer et al. 2007; Ripple and Beschta 2012).

6.11   SUMMARY

Fear-provoking stimuli, whether visual (e.g., scarecrows and predator models), auditory (e.g., firecrackers, exploders, and distress calls), or olfactory stimuli (e.g., predator
odors), function by increasing the animal's fear of the area where they are deployed.
Most fear-provoking stimuli are effective for a few days, but animals quickly habituate to them. Thus, these stimuli are useful in alleviating wildlife problems which are
of short duration. Habituation occurs because animals learn that the fear-provoking
stimuli are actually innocuous and pose no danger to them. Habituation to fear-
provoking stimuli can be delayed by using lifelike stimuli that are capable of movement, by switching among different stimuli, and by changing their location. Some
fear-provoking stimuli, such as hazing, harassment by humans, trained falcons and
hawks, and guard dogs, pose a real threat to wildlife and, therefore, are effective for
longer periods of time than other fear-provoking stimuli.

6.12   DISCUSSION QUESTIONS

1. At the beginning of this chapter, I wrote that wildlife managers can reduce
   wildlife damage to agricultural crops by exploiting an animal's reluctance
   to foraging in risky areas. This can accomplish through the use of fear-
   provoking stimuli that increase the animals' fear of areas where crops are
   grown. If you were tasked with using fear-provoking stimuli to keep deer
   out of an alfalfa field, how would you do it?
2. What measures can be taken to delay how quickly animals habituate to a
   visual fear-provoking stimulus?
3. What are some human–wildlife conflicts that fear-provoking stimuli have a
   good chance of resolving?
4. Some biologists believe that all possible fear-provoking stimuli should be
   used all at once to create an area that is so terrifying that wildlife will
   never come close enough to habituation to them. Other biologists believe
   that it is best to only use one fear-provoking stimulus at a time and to rotate
   to the second one as soon as the animals habituate to the first one. This process should continue until all of the fear-provoking stimuli have been used.
   Which strategy do you favor?

FIGURE 6.11   Photos taken in the same spot in the Lamar Valley within Yellowstone National Park before wolves were reintroduced (a), four years after their reintroduction and (b), and eight years after their reintroduction. In (a), the only willows are inside a deer-proof exclosure, but in (b) and (c), willows are now growing outside the exclosure.

Source: William Ripple and used with permission.

FIGURE 6.12 Aspen growth after wolves were reintroduced into Yellowstone National Park. Part (A) shows a site where wolves pose a threat to elk due to the lack escape terrain for elk and part (B) shows a location where escape terrain is lacking and elk seldom venture. These differences in aspen heights were likely due to differences in perceived predation risk due to differences in escape terrain.

Source: William Ripple and used with permission.

5. Some biologists tell people that they should use a particular fear-provoking stimulus although there is almost no chance that it will be effective. They argue that they are at least providing hope to people who need it. This practice enrages others who feel that biologists should not be snake oil salesmen who encourage people to waste their money on worthless products. What is your opinion?

6. What methods can be employed to encourage live predators to remain in areas where wildlife are causing problems?

7. Other than the problems already mentioned in the book, can you think of a human–wildlife conflict for which the use of an electronic shock collar may help alleviate the situation?

8. Large flocks of blackbirds can quickly devastate a ripening sunflower field. How could a landscape of fear be created to deter blackbirds from foraging in a sunflower field?

LITERATURE CITED

Andelt, W. F. 1992. Effectiveness of livestock guarding dogs for reducing predation on domestic sheep. *Wildlife Society Bulletin* 20:55–62.

Andelt, W. F., and S. N. Hooper. 1996. Effectiveness of alarm-distress calls for frightening herons from a fish rearing facility. *Progressive Fish-Culturist* 58:258–262.

Andelt, W. F., R. L. Phillips, K. S. Gruver, and J. W. Guthrie. 1999. Coyote predation on domestic sheep deterred with electronic dog-training collar. *Wildlife Society Bulletin* 27:12–18.

Andelt, W. F., T. P. Woolley, and S. N. Hopper. 1997. Effectiveness of barriers, pyrotechnics, flashing lights, and Scarey Man® for deterring heron predation on fish. *Wildlife Society Bulletin* 25:686–694.

Apfelbach, R., C. D. Blanchard, R. J. Blanchard, R. A. Hayes, and I. S. McGregor. 2005. The effects of predator odors in mammalian prey species: a review of field and laboratory studies. *Neuroscience and Biobehavioral Reviews* 29:1123–1144.

Atkins, A., S. M. Redpath, R. M. Little, and A. Amar. 2017. Experimentally manipulating the landscape of fear to manage problem animals. *Journal of Wildlife Management* 8:610–616.

Backs, J. A. J., J. A. Nychgka, and C. C. St. Clair. 2017. Warning systems triggered by trains could reduce collisions with wildlife. *Ecological Engineering* 106:563–569.

Ball, S. A. 2009. Suspending vulture effigies from roosts to reduce bird strikes. *Human-Wildlife Conflicts* 3:257–259.

Baxter, A. T., and J. R. Allan. 2006. Use of raptors to reduce scavenging bird numbers at landfill sites. *Wildlife Society Bulletin* 34:1162–1168.

Baxter, A. T., and J. R. Allan. 2008. Use of lethal control to reduce habituation to blank rounds by scavenging birds. *Journal of Wildlife Management* 72:1653–1657.

Baxter, A. T., and A. P. Robinson. 2007. A comparison of scavenging bird deterrence techniques at UK landfill sites. *International Journal of Pest Management* 53:347–356.

Beckmann, J. P., C. W. Lackey, and J. Berger. 2004. Evaluation of deterrent techniques and dogs to alter behavior of "nuisance" black bears. *Wildlife Society Bulletin* 32:1141–1146.

Belant, J. L., T. W. Seamans, and L. A. Tyson. 1998. Predator urines as chemical barriers to white-tailed deer. *Proceedings of the Vertebrate Pest Conference* 18:359–362.

Beringer, J., L. P. Hansen, R. A. Heinen, and N. F. Giessman. 1994. Use of dogs to reduce damage to a white pine plantation. *Wildlife Society Bulletin* 22:627–632.

Beringer, J., K. C. VerCauteren, and J. J. Milspaugh. 2003. Evaluation of an animal-activated scarecrow and monofilament fence for reducing deer use of soybean fields. *Wildlife Society Bulletin* 31:492–498.

Beyer, H. L., E. H. Merrill, N. Varley, and M. S. Boyce. 2007. Willow on Yellowstone's Northern range: evidence for a trophic cascade? *Ecological Applications* 17:1563–1571.

Bhusal, S., K. Khanal, M. Karkee, K. M. M. Steensma, and M. E. Taylor. 2018. Unmanned aerial systems (UAS) for mitigating bird damage in wine grapes. *International Conference on Precision Agriculture* 14:1–6.

Blackwell, B. F., T. W. Seamans, L. A. Tyson, J. L. Belant, and K. C. VerCauteren. 2012. Exploiting antipredator behavior in white-tailed deer for resource protection. *Wildlife Society Bulletin* 36:546–553.

Blokpoel, H. 1976. *Bird hazards to aircraft.* Clarke, Irwin and Co., Ltd., Ottawa, Canada.

Boag, D. A., and V. Lewin. 1980. Effectiveness of three waterfowl deterrents on natural and polluted ponds. *Journal of Wildlife Management* 44:145–154.

Bomford, M., and P. H. O'Brien. 1990. Sonic deterrents in animal damage control: a review of device tests and effectiveness. *Wildlife Society Bulletin* 18:411–422.

Bonnell, M. A., and S. W. Breck. 2017. Using resident-based hazing programs to reduce human-coyote conflicts in urban environments. *Human-Wildlife Interactions* 11:146–155.

Bradley, E. H., and D. H. Pletscher. 2005. Assessing factors related to wolf depredation of cattle in fenced pastures in Montana and Idaho. *Wildlife Society Bulletin* 33:1256–1265.

Brand, A. R., and P. P. Kellogg. 1939a. Auditory responses of starlings, English sparrows, and domestic pigeons. *Wilson Bulletin* 51:38–41.

Brand, A. R., and P. P. Kellogg. 1939b. The range of hearing of canaries. *Science* 90:354.

Brandt, M. J., C. Höschle, A. Diederichs, K. Betke, R. Matuschek, and G. Nehls. 2013. Seal scarers as a tool to deter harbour porpoises from offshore construction sites. *Marine Ecology Progress Series* 475:291–302.

Breck, S. W., N. Lance, and P. Callahan. 2006. A shocking device for protection of concentrated food sources from black bears. *Wildlife Society Bulletin* 34:23–26.

Breck, S. W., S. A. Poessel, and M. A. Bunnell. 2017. Evaluating lethal and nonlethal management options for urban coyotes. *Human-Wildlife Interactions* 11:133–145.

Brewster, R. K., S. E. Henke, B. L. Turner, and J. M. Tomeček. 2019. Cost – benefit analysis of coyote removal as a management option in Texas cattle ranching. *Human – Wildlife Interactions* 13:400–422.

Brieger, F., R. Hagen, D. Vetter, C. F. Dormann, and I. Storch. 2016. Effectiveness of light-reflecting devices: a systematic reanalysis of animal-vehicle collision data. *Accident Analysis and Prevention* 97:242–260.

Burwash, M. D., M. E. Tobin, A. D. Woodhouse, and T. P. Sullivan. 1998. Field testing synthetic predator odors for roof rats (*Rattus rattus*) in Hawaiian macadamia nut orchards. *Journal of Chemical Ecology* 24:603–630.

Castelli, P. M., and S. E. Sleggs. 2000. The efficacy of border collies for nuisance Canada goose control. *Wildlife Society Bulletin* 28:385–392.

Cherry, M. J., L. M. Conner, and R. J. Warren. 2015. Effects of predation risk and group dynamics on white-tailed deer foraging behavior in a longleaf pine savanna. *Behavioral Ecology* 26:1091–1099.

Clausen, K. K., L. K. Marcussen, N. Knudsen, T. J. Balsby, and J. Madsen. 2019. Effectiveness of lasers to reduce goose grazing on agricultural grassland. *Wildlife Biology* wlb00560.

Coates, R. W., M. J. Delwiche, W. P. Gorenzel, and T. P. Salmon. 2010. Evaluation of damage by vertebrate pests in California vineyards and control of wild turkeys by bioacoustics. *Human-Wildlife Interactions* 4:130–144.

Conover, M. R. 1985. Protecting vegetables from crows using an animated crow-killing owl model. *Journal of Wildlife Management* 49:631–636.

Conover, M. R. 1987. Acquisition of predator information by active and passive mobbers in ring-billed gull colonies. *Behaviour* 102:41–57.

Conover, M. R. 1994. Stimuli eliciting distress calls in adult passerines and response of predators and birds to their broadcast. *Behaviour* 131:19–38.

Conover, M. R. 2007. *Predator-prey dynamics: the role of olfaction*. CRC Press, Boca Raton, FL.

Cox, T. E., P. J. Murray, G. P. Hall, and X. Li. 2012. Manipulating resource use by goats with predator fecal odors. *Wildlife Society Bulletin* 36:802–806.

Cummings, J. L., C. E. Knittle, and J. L. Guarino. 1986. Evaluating a pop-up scarecrow coupled with a propane exploder for reducing blackbird damage to ripening sunflower. *Proceedings of the Vertebrate Pest Conference* 12:286–291.

De Vault, T. L., R. B. Chipman, S. C. Barras, J. D. Taylor, C. P. Cranker III, E. M. Cranker, and J. F. Farquhar. 2012. Reducing impacts of double-crested cormorants to natural resources in central New York: a review of a collaborative research, management, and monitoring program. *Waterbirds* 35:50–55.

Draulans, D., and J. van Vessem. 1985. The effect of disturbance on nocturnal abundance and behaviour of grey herons (*Ardea cinerea*) at a fish-farm in Winter. *Journal of Applied Ecology* 22:19–27.

Epple, G., J. R. Mason, E. Arnov, D. L. Nolte, R. L. Hartz, R. Kaloostian, D. Campbell, and A. B. Smith. 1995. Feeding responses to predator-based repellents in the mountain beaver. *Ecological Applications* 5:1163–1170.

Ferrero, D. M., J. K. Lemon, D. Fluegge, S. L. Pashkovski, W. J. Korzan, S. R. Datta, M. Spehr, M. Fendt, and S. D. Liberles. 2011. Detection and avoidance of a carnivore odor by prey. *Proceedings of the National Academy of Sciences* 108:11235–11240.

Fjälling, A., M. Wahlberg, and H. Westerberg. 2006. Acoustic harassment devices reduce seal interaction in the Baltic salmon-trap, net fishery. *ICES Journal of Marine Science* 63:1751–1758.

Fox, A. D. 2019. Urban geese – looking to North America for experiences to guide management in Europe? *Wildfowl* 69:3–27.

Gilsdorf, J. M., S. E. Hygnstrom, K. C. VerCauteren, E. E. Blackenship, and R. M. Engemann. 2004*a*. Propane exploders and electronic guards were ineffective at reducing deer damage in cornfields. *Wildlife Society Bulletin* 32:524–531.

Gilsdorf, J. M., S. E. Hygnstrom, K. C. VerCauteren, G. M. Clements, E. E. Blankenship, and R. M. Engemann. 2004*b*. Evaluation of a deer-activated bio-acoustics frightening device for reducing deer damage in cornfields. *Wildlife Society Bulletin* 32: 515–523.

Götz, T., and V. M. Janik. 2016. Non-lethal management of carnivore predation: long-term tests with a startle reflex-based deterrence system on a fish farm. *Animal Conservation* 19:212–221.

Guinn, J. E. 2013. Generational habituation and current bald eagle populations. *Human-Wildlife Interactions* 7:69–76.

Hawley, J. E., T. M. Gehring, R. N. Schultz, S. T. Rossler, and A. P. Wydeven. 2009. Assessment of shock collars as nonlethal management for wolves in Wisconsin. *Journal of Wildlife Management* 73:518–525.

Hawley, J. E., S. T. Rossler, T. M. Gehring, R. N. Schultz, P. A. Callahan, R. Clark, J. Cade, and A. P. Wydeven. 2013. Developing a new shock-collar design for safe and efficient use on wild wolves. *Wildlife Society Bulletin* 37:416–422.

Heinrich, J. W., and S. R. Craven. 1990. Evaluation of three damage abatement techniques for Canada geese. *Wildlife Society Bulletin* 18:405–410.

Hobbs, J., and F. G. Leon III. 1987. Great-tailed grackle predation on south Texas citrus. *Proceedings of the Eastern Wildlife Damage Control Conference* 3:143–148.

Holevinski, R. A., P. D. Curtis, and R. A. Malecki. 2007. Hazing of Canada geese is unlikely to reduce nuisance populations in urban and suburban communities. *Human-Wildlife Interactions* 1:257–264.

Kämmerle, J. L., F. Brieger, M. Kröschel, R. Hagen, I. Storch, and R. Suchant. 2017. Temporal patterns in road crossing behaviour in roe deer (*Capreolus capreolus*) at sites with wildlife warning reflectors. *PLoS One* 12(9):e0184761.

Kaplan, B. S., M. J. O'Riain, R. van Eeden, and A. J. King. 2011. A low-cost manipulation of food resources reduces spatial overlap between baboons (*Papio ursinus*) and humans in conflict. *International Journal of Primatology* 32:1397–1412.

Kenward, R. E. 1978. The influence of human and goshawk *Accipiter gentilis* activity on wood-pigeons *Columba palumbus* at brassica feeding sites. *Annals of Applied Biology* 89:277–286.

Knittle, C. E., and R. D. Porter. 1988. *Waterfowl damage and control methods in ripening grain: an overview.* U. S. Fish and Wildlife Service Technical Report 14, Washington, DC.

Koehler, A. E., R. E. Marsh, and T. P. Salmon. 1990. Frightening methods and devices/stimuli to prevent mammal damage – a review. *Proceedings of the Vertebrate Pest Conference* 14:168–173.

Langbein, J., R. Putman, and B. Pokorny. 2010. Traffic collisions involving deer and other ungulates in Europe and available measures for mitigation. Pages 215–259 *in* R. Putnam, M. Apollonio, and R. Andersen, editors. *Ungulate management in Europe: problems and practices.* Cambridge University Press, Cambridge. www.researchgate.net/publication/284890667_Traffic_Collisions_involving_deer_and_other_ungulates_in_Europe. Accessed 7 March 2019.

Langbein, J., R. J. Putman, and B. Pokorny. 2011. Road traffic accidents involving ungulates and available measures for mitigation. Pages 215–259 *in* R. J. Putman, M. Apollonio, and R. Andersen, editors. *Ungulate management in Europe: problems and practices.* Cambridge University Press, Cambridge.

Laundré, J. W., L. Hernández, and K. B. Altendorf. 2001. Wolves, elk, and bison: reestablishing the "landscape of fear" in Yellowstone national park, U.S.A. *Canadian Journal of Zoology* 79:1401–1409.

Laundré, J. W., L. Hernández, and W. J. Ripple. 2010. The landscape of fear: ecological implications of being afraid. *Open Ecology Journal* 3:1–7.

Leigh, J., and M. J. Chamberlain. 2008. Effects of aversive conditioning on behavior of nuisance Louisiana black bears. *Human-Wildlife Conflicts* 2:175–182.

Linz, G. M., H. J. Homan, S. J. Werner, H. M. Hagy, and W. J. Bleier. 2011. Assessment of bird-management strategies to protect sunflowers. *BioScience* 61:960–970.

Lorenz, J. R., R. P. Coppinger, and M. R. Sutherland. 1986. Causes and economic effects of mortality in livestock guarding dogs. *Journal of Range Management* 39:293–295.

Marker, L. L., A. J. Dickman, and D. W. Macdonald. 2005a. Perceived effectiveness of livestock-guarding dogs placed on Namibian farms. *Rangeland Ecology and Management* 58:329–336.

Marker, L. L., A. J. Dickman, and D. W. Macdonald. 2005b. Survivorship and causes of mortality for livestock-guarding dogs on Namibian rangeland. *Rangeland Ecology and Management* 58:337–343.

Marsh, R. E., W. A. Erickson, and T. P. Salmon. 1991. *Bird hazing and frightening techniques.* University of California, Davis, CA.

Mazur, R. L. 2010. Does aversive conditioning reduce human-black bear conflict? *Journal of Wildlife Management* 74:48–54.

Meagher, M. 1989. Evaluation of boundary control for bison of Yellowstone national park. *Wildlife Society Bulletin* 17:15–19.

Melchiors, M. A., and C. A. Leslie. 1985. Effectiveness of predator fecal odors as black-tailed deer repellents. *Journal of Wildlife Management* 49:358–362.

Merrell, R. J. 2012. Some successful methods to mitigate conflicts caused by common ravens in an industrial environment. *Human-Wildlife Conflicts* 6:339–343.

Moerbeek, D. J., W. H. van Dobben, E. R. Osieck, G. C. Boere, and C. M. Bungenberg de Jong. 1987. Cormorant damage prevention at a fish farm in the Netherlands. *Biological Conservation* 39:23–38.

Parkhurst, J. A., R. P. Brooks, and D. E. Arnold. 1987. A survey of wildlife depredation and control techniques at fish-rearing facilities. *Wildlife Society Bulletin* 15:386–394.

Parks, M., and T. Messmer. 2016. Participant perceptions of range rider programs operating to mitigate wolf – livestock conflicts in the western United States. *Wildlife Society Bulletin* 40:514–524.

Parsons, M. H., B. B. Lamont, B. R. Kovacs, and S. J. Davies. 2007. Effects of novel and historic predator urines on semi-wild Western grey kangaroos. *Journal of Wildlife Management* 71:1225–1228.

Radtke, T. M., and C. D. Dieter. 2011. Canada goose crop damage abatement in South Dakota. *Human-Wildlife Interactions* 5:315–320.

Rauer, G., P. Kaczensky, and F. Knauer. 2003. Experiences with aversive conditioning of habituated brown bears in Austria and other European countries. *Ursus* 14:215–224.

Riginos, C., M. W. Graham, M. J. Davis, A. B. Johnson, A. B. May, K. W. Ryer, and L. E. Hall. 2018. Wildlife warning reflectors and white canvas reduce deer – vehicle collisions and risky road-crossing behavior. *Wildlife Society Bulletin* 42:119–130.

Ripple, W. J., and R. L. Beschta. 2012. Trophic cascades in Yellowstone: the first 15 years after wolf reintroduction. *Biological Conservation* 145:205–213.

Rossler, S. T., T. M. Gehring, R. N. Schultz, M. T. Rossler, A. P. Wydeven, and J. E. Hawley. 2012. Shock collars as a site-aversive conditioning tool for wolves. *Wildlife Society Bulletin* 36:176–184.

Seamans, T. W., B. F. Blackwell, and K. E. Linnell. 2016. Use of predator hair to enhance perceived risk to white-tailed deer in a foraging context. *Human-Wildlife Interactions* 10:300–311.

Seamans, T. W., C. R. Hicks, and K. J. Preusser. 2007. *Dead bird effigies: a nightmare for gulls?* Bird Strike Committee USA, Canada, Ninth Annual Meeting, Kingston, ON.

Sekhar, N. U. 1998. Crop and livestock depredation caused by wild animals in protected areas: the case of Sariska Tiger Reserve, Rajasthan, India. *Environmental Conservation* 25:160–171.

Severud, W. J., J. L. Belant, J. G. Bruggink, and S. K. Windels. 2011. Predator cues reduce American beaver use of foraging trails. *Human-Wildlife Interactions* 5:296–305.

Shave, M. E., S. A. Shwiff, J. L. Elser, and C. A. Lindell. 2018. Falcons using orchard nest boxes reduced fruit-eating bird abundances and provide economic benefits for a fruit-growing region. *Journal of Applied Ecology* 55:2451–2460.

Sherman, D. E., and A. E. Barras. 2004. Efficacy of a laser device for hazing Canada geese from urban areas of northeast Ohio. *Ohio Journal of Science* 103:38–42.

Shivik, J. A., R. R. Wilson, and L. Gilbert-Norton. 2011. Will an artificial scent boundary prevent coyote intrusion? *Wildlife Society Bulletin* 35:494–497.

Sitati, N. W., and M. J. Walpole. 2006. Assessing farm-based measures for mitigating human-elephant conflicts in Transmara District, Kenya. *Oryx* 40:279–286.

Sitati, N. W., M. J. Walpole, and N. Leader-Williams. 2005. Factors affecting susceptibility of farms to crop raiding by African elephants: using a predictive model to mitigate conflict. *Journal of Applied Ecology* 42:1175–1182.

Sitati, N. W., M. J. Walpole, R. J. Smith, and N. Leader-Williams. 2003. Predicting spatial aspects of human-elephant conflict. *Journal of Applied Ecology* 40:667–677.

Smith, A. E., S. R. Craven, and P. D. Curtis. 1999. *Managing Canada geese in urban environments.* Jack Berryman Institute Publication 16, Logan, UT.

Spanier, E. 1980. The use of distress calls to repel night herons (*Nycticorax nycticorax*) from fish ponds. *Journal of Applied Ecology* 17:287–294.

Stickley, A. R., D. F. Mott, and J. O. King. 1995. Short-term effects of an inflatable effigy on cormorants at catfish farms. *Wildlife Society Bulletin* 23:73–77.

Sukumar, R. 2003. *The living elephants: evolutionary ecology, behaviour and conservation.* Oxford University Press, New York.

Sullivan, T. P., D. R. Crump, and D. S. Sullivan. 1988*b*. Use of predator odors as repellents to reduce feeding damage by herbivores. IV. Northern pocket gophers (*Thomomys talpoides*). *Journal of Chemical Ecology* 14:379–389.

Sullivan, T. P., D. S. Sullivan, D. R. Crump, H. Weiser, and E. A. Dixon. 1988*a*. Predator odors and their potential role in managing pest rodents and rabbits. *Proceedings of the Vertebrate Pest Conference* 13:145–150.

Swihart, R. K. 1991. Modifying scent-marking behavior to reduce woodchuck damage to fruit trees. *Ecological Applications* 1:98–103.

Swihart, R. K., J. J. Pignatello, and M. J. I. Mattina. 1991. Aversive responses to white-tailed deer, *Odocoileus virginianus*, to predator urines. *Journal of Chemical Ecology* 17:767–775.

Thaker, M., A. T. Vanak, C. R. Owen, M. B. Ogden, S. M. Niemann, and R. Slotow. 2011. Minimizing predation risk in a landscape of multiple predators: effects on the spatial distribution of African ungulates. *Ecology* 92:398–407.

Thapa, S. 2010. Effectiveness of crop protection methods against wildlife damage: a case study of two villages at Bardia National Park, Nepal. *Crop Protection* 29:1297–1304.

Tobin, M. E., R. M. Engeman, and R. T. Sugihara. 1995. Effects of mongoose odors on rat capture success. *Journal of Chemical Ecology* 21:635–639.

Ujvári, M., H. J. Baagøe, and A. B. Madsen. 2004. Effectiveness of acoustic road markings in reducing deer-vehicle collisions: a behavioural study. *Wildlife Biology* 10:155–160.

Valitzski, S. A., G. J. D'Angelo, G. R. Gallagher, D. A. Osborn, K. V. Miller, and R. J. Warren. 2009. Deer responses to sounds from a vehicle-mounted sound-production system. *Journal of Wildlife Management* 73:1072–1076.

Van Doorn, A. C. 2009. *The interface between socioecology and management of chacma baboons (Papio ursinus) in the Cape Peninsula, South Africa.* Ph.D. Thesis, University of Cape Town, Cape Town, South Africa.

VerCauteren, K. C., J. M. Gilsdorf, S. E. Hygnstrom, P. B. Fioranelli, J. A. Wilson, and S. Barras. 2006. Green and blue lasers are ineffective for dispersing deer at night. *Wildlife Society Bulletin* 34:371–374.

VerCauteren, K. C., S. E. Hygnstrom, M. J. Pipas, P. B. Fioranelli, S. J. Werner, and B. F. Blackwell. 2003. Red lasers are ineffective for dispersing deer at night. *Wildlife Society Bulletin* 31:247–252.

VerCauteren, K. C., M. J. Lavelle, and G. E. Phillips. 2008. Livestock protection dogs for deterring deer from cattle and feed. *Journal of Wildlife Management* 72:1443–1448.

VerCauteren, K. C., J. A. Shivik, and M. J. Lavelle. 2005. Efficacy of an animal-activated frightening device on urban elk and mule deer. *Wildlife Society Bulletin* 33:1282–1287.

Wijayagunawardane, M. P., R. V. Short, T. S. Samarakone, K. M. Nishany, H. Harrington, B. V. P. Perera, R. Rassool, and E. P. Bittner. 2016. The use of audio playback to deter crop-raiding Asian elephants. *Wildlife Society Bulletin* 40:375–379.

Wise, K. K., F. K. Knowlton, and M. R. Conover. 1999. Response of captive coyotes to the starling distress call: testing the startle-predator and predator-attraction hypotheses. *Behaviour* 136:935–949.

Woodroffe, R., L. G. Frank, P. A. Lindsey, S. M. K. ole Ranah, and S. Romañach. 2006. Livestock husbandry as a tool for carnivore conservation in Africa's community rangelands: a case-control study. *Biodiversity and Conservation* 16:1245–1260.

7 Chemical Repellents

Organic chemistry is the study of carbon compounds. Wildlife damage management is the study of organic compounds that keep moving into places where they cause mischief.

– Anonymous

Many plant species are protected from herbivores because they contain toxins, which make them poisonous. Unfortunately, most agricultural crops lack chemical defenses against insect or vertebrate herbivores. This is particularly true of plants grown for human consumption, as toxins would also make them unpalatable or poisonous to humans. Therefore, farmers often apply chemicals to crops to give them protection that they would otherwise lack. For insect pests, lethal chemicals are applied to kill them, but because vertebrates are so valuable, pesticides are rarely applied with the intention of killing birds or mammals. Rather, we apply repellents to dissuade wildlife from eating plants, without causing the animals serious harm. Efficacious use of repellents depends on a knowledge of how plants protect themselves from herbivores and why animals have preferences for certain tastes and foods.

7.1 HOW DO PLANTS USE CHEMICALS TO DEFEND THEMSELVES FROM HERBIVORES?

Plants have contended with herbivores for millions of years. Over this period, plants have evolved mechanisms, such as thorns and toxins, to discourage herbivory. Many plants use nutrient dilution by packing their tissues with hard-to-digest fibers, such as lignin and cellulose to discourage herbivores. Likewise, some grasses contain high concentrations of silica, making them more difficult to digest. Humans refer to plants that are well defended with fibers as "tough" or "stringy" and generally avoid eating them, preferring more "tender" plants.

Animals have similar preferences. Many plants contain high levels of tannins, which also cause nutrient dilution, but in a different way. Tannins bind to proteins and make them harder to be absorbed by the intestines. For instance, condensed tannins from blackbrush and bitterbrush inhibit food ingestion by snowshoe hares (Clausen et al. 1990).

Alkaloids and other plant secondary compounds also discourage herbivory. These chemicals are often toxic even in very low concentrations. Yet, some species have developed methods of detoxifying these chemicals. For instance, quaking aspen trees produce coniferyl benzoate; this chemical is repellent to most birds, but ruffed grouse have the ability to detoxify it (Jakubas et al. 1997), and this bird forages heavily on aspen buds during winter and aspen flowers during spring. As another example, snowshoe hares select which green alder plants to eat based on each plant's concentrations of pinosylvin and pinosylvin methyl ether (Bryant et al. 1983) and which birches to browse based on concentrations of papyriferic acid (Reichardt et al. 1984; Bryant et al. 1994).

DOI: 10.1201/9780429401404-7 **239**

7.2.   IS THERE A BIOLOGICAL BASIS FOR FOOD PREFERENCES?

To survive, every animal must extract enough calories from the foods it consumes to meet its energetic needs. And, it also must consume certain chemicals needed for survival that the animal cannot produce itself, such as salts, minerals, amino acids, and vitamins. Herbivores have a wide array of consumable items to meet their daily metabolic needs. Some choices are nutritious and contain a high concentration of energy, some are poisonous, and others contain such low levels of nutrients and energy that an animal cannot afford to eat them. An animal must be able to sift through these food items and select only those that are able to meet its nutritional needs. How an animal makes these decisions involves a complex array of innate preferences for certain tastes and learned preferences from post-ingestion feedback and early experience.

7.2.1   ROLE OF OLFACTION IN SHAPING FOOD PREFERENCES

Olfaction serves many functions. It provides information about the environment and assists in locating and identifying foods. Olfaction plays a role in social behaviors in some species. Consequently, animals have thousands of different olfactory receptors. Olfactory ability and preferences differ among species and help explain why diets differ among animals. For instance, many herbivores are repelled by sulfur compounds, which are common in meat, while carnivores are attracted to the odor (Conover 2007).

7.2.2   ROLE OF TASTE IN SHAPING FOOD PREFERENCES

Mammals have thousands of different olfactory receptors, but only a small number of specific taste receptors exist. The most important ones are sweet, sour, salty, and bitter. Taste receptors probably evolved for the sole purpose of regulating food intake to ensure the rejection of toxins and the acceptance of nutrient-rich foods. Although taste preferences are modified by experience and learning, an animal's initial response to tastes is innately determined. For example, acidic foods produce a "sour" taste, which animals often find distasteful. Many animals have a craving for salt when deprived of it. In particular, herbivores often exhibit a strong preference for salt, due to its low concentration in plants. Herbivores and omnivores also exhibit a preference for "sweet" foods (i.e., plants containing large concentrations of simple carbohydrates). This preference for sweet foods may help animals identify energy-rich foods. Yet, some predators, such as cats, do not prefer sugar and may not even be able to taste it.

Some foods contain poisonous alkaloids and taste "bitter." The ability to detect these chemicals helps protect animals from poisonous foods because there is a correlation between toxicity and bitterness. Carnivores exhibit a strong dislike of alkaloids, which is not surprising, because their normal diet of meat rarely contains these chemicals. In contrast, many herbivores exhibit a graded response to alkaloids; given a choice, herbivores will select a diet low in alkaloids but will consume larger quantities of bitter foods when there is no alternative. Herbivores often seek a varied diet and consume small amounts of plants protected by alkaloids. By doing so, they can keep their intake of alkaloids within tolerable levels. In the Amazonian Basin, macaws and parrots visit clay deposits almost daily to eat the clay. The clay helps

FIGURE 7.1   Macaws in Brazil visit mineral deposits regularly to eat a dose of clay that helps neutralize the alkaloids they consume.

Source: Jiri Hrebicek, Shutterstock 1248600811.

these birds neutralize some of the toxins that they consume as part of their diet of fruit and vegetation (Figure 7.1).

Animals have a fear of novel foods that look, smell, or taste different (neophobia). Herbivores learn which plants can be eaten safely and which need to be avoided by sampling novel plants in small quantities. Likewise, they can identify plant parts, such as flowers, fruits, or young leaves, containing lower levels of alkaloids. These findings suggest that bitter chemicals are more likely to be effective repellents for use against carnivores rather than herbivores.

7.2.3   Role of Tactile Stimuli in Shaping Food Preferences

Some repellents function by changing the texture or tactile features of food. For instance, beaver do not like eating gritty foods, which can grind down their teeth, and can be dissuaded from gnawing on trees by painting the bark with a latex paint mixed with sand. Likewise, birds can be repelled from food contaminated with dolomitic lime, activated charcoal, or sand (Mason and Clark 1994; Belant et al. 1997).

7.2.4   Role of Animal-Derived Substances in Shaping Food Preferences

Some animals, especially herbivores, avoid substances that come from other animals because such materials may contain pathogens or parasites. These substances include blood, meat, feces, egg, bone meal, casein, proteins, and peptides that are associated with microbial activity. Interestingly, the odor of these substances is ineffective as a repellent even when the substances are placed close to food. Instead, foods are only avoided if they are in contact (i.e., contaminated) with these substances (Kimball et al. 2005, 2009).

7.2.5 ROLE OF IRRITANTS IN SHAPING FOOD PREFERENCES

The trigeminal nerve is the fifth cranial nerve and runs from the brain to the facial skin, eyes, mouth, throat, and nasal passages. Some chemicals, such as capsaicin in hot peppers, stimulate the trigeminal nerve. Sometimes, people seek low levels of stimulation of the trigeminal nerve (e.g., people enjoy eating spicy food), but, usually, stimulation of the trigeminal nerve is perceived as painful. Chemicals that irritate the trigeminal nerve may serve as good repellents because they are innately unpleasant. When capsaicin is consumed, it stimulates the trigeminal nerve, causing irritation in mammals, but apparently does not bother birds due to neurological differences between these two groups of animals (Mason and Maruniak 1983). As a result, capsaicin can be used to repel mammals but not birds.

Crop-raiding elephants can be stopped from entering small fields planted by rural villagers in Africa by surrounding the fields with a chili rope placed 1.5 m above the ground (Figure 7.2). The chili rope is made by soaking a rope in a solution made from hot chili sauce, tobacco, and used engine oil. Sitati and Walpole (2006) observed that elephants avoided fields encircled with a chili rope, but that a 1-km chili rope deployed in a straight line was not effective in stopping elephants because the animals learned to go around the end of the rope.

7.2.6 ROLE OF POST-INGESTION FEEDBACK IN SHAPING FOOD PREFERENCES

Some chemicals inhibit food consumption by causing illness, nausea, or gastrointestinal distress. These chemicals function by a post-ingestion feedback mechanism. That is, when humans eat a food item and become nauseated, they associate the sickness with the food just eaten and develop an aversion to that food. People may rationalize that they are allergic to the food or that it was ill-prepared. The end result, however, is that they become wary of that particular food, no longer like its taste, and time will pass before they are willing to eat it again. We make this association between nausea and the consumed food even when an illness or seasickness is the source of the nausea. Human brains have evolved to make this association innately because doing so helps the avoidance of poisonous foods. Other species have evolved the same response.

Often animals eat various foods in one meal. How animals decide what caused the illness is interesting. When nausea follows the consumption of many items, animals develop an aversion to the food that had an unusual taste or odor. When animals become ill after eating a mix of familiar and novel foods, they develop an aversion to the novel food.

Likewise, animals may feel more energetic after consuming an item high in energy or other essential nutrients. As a result, the animal may develop a preference for the item and increase consumption of it in the future. Horses become more active after eating oats, which contain a high concentration of carbohydrates (this is the source

FIGURE 7.2 Elephants can easily remove barbwire fences blocking their way. Perhaps a chili fence will be more effective.

Source: Photo from Mutinda et al. (2014) and published in PLOS ONE, an open-access journal.

of the phrase, "feeling its oats," which means being frisky). Horses develop a preference for oats as a result of their enhanced vigor. Animals can develop a preference for items which alleviate illnesses. For example, healthy lambs prefer plain water to water containing sodium bicarbonate, but lambs suffering from acidosis prefer the latter (Provenza 1997).

Food preferences are shaped by nutritional needs. Humans, for instance, prefer high-carbohydrate foods when hungry, low-carbohydrate foods when satiated, and salty foods when suffering from a sodium deficiency. Rats develop a preference for foods containing threonine when suffering from a deficiency of this amino acid, but not at other times (Gietzen 1993). Preferences for proteins and carbohydrates depend

FIGURE 7.3   Canada goose goslings learn what to eat by following their parents and watching what their parents eat.

Source: RSL Photo, Shutterstock 1760087795.

on an animal's nutritional state. Thus, food preferences constantly change depending on nutritional needs and generally decline when foods are eaten to satiety.

7.2.7   ROLE OF EARLY-LIFE EXPERIENCES IN SHAPING FOOD PREFERENCES

An animal's early-life experiences have a dramatic, long-lasting effect on its food preferences. A young animal learns what foods to eat based on what its parents feed it, by being escorted by its parents to places where certain foods can be obtained and by watching what its parents eat (Figure 7.3). Young mammals can acquire taste preferences associated with their mother's milk (Galef and Henderson 1972; Nolte and Provenza 1991). Even prenatal experiences with chemicals can influence later taste preferences (Nolte and Mason 1995). As they mature, animals become more reluctant to eat novel foods or familiar foods whose flavors have changed. This phenomenon is referred to as neophobia: a fear of the new.

7.3   WHAT TYPES OF REPELLENTS WORK BEST

7.3.1   BEAR SPRAY

Bear spray was developed during the 1980s and is probably the most successful repellent developed in terms of preventing human injuries and fatalities due to bear

FIGURE 7.4   A can of bear spray. It can be sprayed into the face of aggressive bears.

Source: AIVRAD, Shutterstock 1463994587.

attack. It is sold as a can containing compressed air and contains capsaicin and other capsaicinoids (Figure 7.4). The intended use of bear spray is to spray an attacking or menacing bear in the face. The spray can only travel 4 m, so the bear must be close before bear spray can be used. It is effective; bear spray was used 75 times in Alaska to deter bears, and it was 93% successful in deterring the bear's aggressive behavior; the failures resulted in four people being slightly injured. In fact, Smith et al. (2008, 2012) encouraged all persons, with or without a firearm, to keep bear spray with them because its success rate (defined as when the bear was stopped in its aggressive behavior) was greater than 90% for all three North American species of bear; this was a higher success than observed for firearms (76%–84%).

7.3.2   AREA REPELLENTS

Area repellents emit a repulsive odor that are supposed to repel animals from specific areas by imparting a particular odor to the area. Area repellents are used to keep deer out of orchards by hanging rags dipped in bone tar oil, open-mesh bags containing human hair, or soap bars from the trees. In Africa, a chili–dung mixture is burned at night to deter elephants. Although some area repellents provide some protection, most (including the chili–dung) are ineffective (Kimball et al. 2009; Hedges and Gunaryadi 2010).

Some area repellents function by increasing an animal's fear of an area. Predator urine or feces are efficacious against a broad range of herbivores when used as an area repellent, including beaver (Severud 2011). The repellency is associated with the odor of sulfur compounds in the urine, which result from the digestion of meat. Research has shown that urine of coyotes maintained on a meat diet repels herbivores while the urine of coyotes on a vegetarian diet does not (Nolte et al. 1994). In Australia, feces of tigers, lions, and dingoes are effective in protecting feeding sites from kangaroos and wallabies. In fact, both kangaroos and wallabies not only reduce their consumption of food but also shift their home range to avoid sites where lion feces were left, an interesting observation because lions do not occur in Australia (Cox et al. 2015). But predator odors do not always work. Stober and Conner (2007) tried to use fox urine and musk from a rat snake to deter southern flying squirrels from usurping tree cavities used by the endangered red-cockaded woodpecker but found that neither scent deterred flying squirrels.

Many species use chemicals (pheromones) to mark their territories. These chemicals may serve as area repellents for juveniles and subadults of the same species. Presumably, young animals avoid treated areas because they fear they are entering a territory defended by an adult (Lindgren et al. 1997).

Several problems limit the usefulness of area repellents in reducing wildlife damage. One is that animals lose their ability to detect an odor after repeated or continuous exposure. Another limitation is that starving animals will enter a site containing food regardless of how bad it smells. Hence, area repellents may fail when needed most (i.e., when alternate food supplies are lacking and animals are hungry).

7.3.3 CONTACT REPELLENTS

Contact repellents are chemicals designed to be applied directly to food items needing protection, thus the repellents are ingested along with the food, hence, also called food repellents. The idea is that an animal that cannot eat food without consuming the repellent will stop eating the food. Hopefully, application of a repellent will cause the animal to shift its food preference from the treated food to an alternate food. This is more likely to happen when the treated food contains lower energy than alternate foods that are available.

Contact repellents function by imparting a noxious taste or odor to the food (taste repellents), by producing illness when consumed (aversive conditioning chemicals), or by a combination of both (dual-action chemicals). An advantage of taste repellents is that they have an immediate effect. In contrast, aversive conditioning chemicals may not inhibit feeding when an animal first consumes them. Because aversive conditioning chemicals produce a learned aversion, it takes time for an animal to become ill and to learn what made it sick. This time lag could be a problem when low levels of damage are intolerable. For instance, taste repellents would be a more effective method to prevent rodents from gnawing the insulation of electric wires than aversive-conditioning chemicals. Taste repellents would also work better when attempting to reduce crop damage near a roost containing thousands of blackbirds. If each bird must become ill before being conditioned to avoid the food, there may be little left by the time all birds averted to it. The disadvantage of taste repellents is that they change only the taste of the food and not the nutritional value; animals may ignore the repellent if they are hungry enough. Therefore, taste repellents work best when alternate foods are available and may not work at all when most needed (e.g., during winter). This disadvantage can be minimized by using dual-action food repellents, which have both a noxious taste and produce illness when consumed. The advantage of dual-action repellents occurs when animals ignore the noxious taste and consume the food anyway and then become ill. Hence, post-ingestion feedback teaches animals the error of ignoring the taste.

Ziram is a repellent that functions with these dual modes of action. Wild European badgers stopped eating food treated with ziram, and the aversion became stronger over time due to badgers developing a conditioned food aversion to the treated food. Interestingly, badger could detect ziram-treated food from a distance, indicating that they could detect ziram by odor. The addition of clove as an odor clue increased the aversion to ziram-treated food. After experiencing ziram-treated corn that smelled of cove, badgers refused to sample corn ears that had a cove odor although they were actually safe to eat (Baker et al. 2005*a*, 2005*b*, 2007, 2008).

A drawback associated with contact repellents is that they usually wear off or decompose in a matter of days, thus providing protection for only a limited period of time. This is not an issue for short-term problems, but it is for long-term ones. For instance, captive red-winged blackbirds consumed fewer rice seeds when they were coated with anthraquinone than when they were left untreated (Werner et al. 2010; Cummings et al. 2011). This approach was successful in reducing bird damage to treated seeds because seeds are vulnerable to birds only during the short time before the seeds germinate. But anthraquinone was ineffective in protecting a ripening field of sunflowers from red-winged blackbirds (Figure 7.5). One major

FIGURE 7.5   Flock of blackbirds hovering over a sunflower field.

Source: Palatinate Stock, Shutterstock 1185986623.

difference was that the field was sprayed on August 22 and damage was assessed two months later (October 22). During that period, the concentration of anthraquinone gradually decreased until little was left on the sunflower seeds (Niner et al. 2015).

Another problem with applying contact repellents is that plants grow constantly. Any new leaves or shoots produced after the repellent was applied will be unprotected. For instance, consider the issue of trying to reduce goose grazing on a lawn. Because grass grows constantly and is mowed often, a repellent would have to be reapplied every few weeks to be effective.

7.3.4 Systemic Repellents

A way to avoid the problem of contact repellents either washing off or decomposing is to use a chemical contained within the plant (i.e., a systemic repellent). Selenium, which is the chemical that gives onions their pungent smell, eye-watering effect, and "hot" taste, repels many animals. Plants absorb selenium through their roots and transport it throughout their system. Selenium pellets have been used to protect conifer tree seedlings from deer herbivory by placing them near the roots. Although selenium protected some trees from deer browsing, it killed others (Allan et al. 1984; Angradi and Tzilkowski 1987; Engeman et al. 1995). Thus, it was not an effective way to resolve this human–wildlife conflict.

Some plants, such as tall fescue grass, do not have the ability to produce chemicals to protect themselves from herbivory but still contain alkaloids, notably ergovaline, through a unique mutualistic relationship with a fungus (Clay 1988, 1993). The fungus grows within the plant and benefits from the relationship by living off the plant's nutrients. In fact, the fate of the fungus is completely tied to that of its plant host. The fungus cannot produce spores or live outside the plant and must pass from one plant to another through the plant's seeds. The only way to get an infected plant is for it to have an infected parent (Clay 1988, 1993). The plant also benefits from this relationship because the fungus produces alkaloids, which sicken both avian and mammalian herbivores. After consuming fungus-infected grass, herbivores develop an aversion to it and stop eating it (Aldrich et al. 1993; Schmidt and Osborn 1993; Conover and Messmer 1996; Conover 1998). For this reason, fungus-infected plants may make an ideal ground cover in areas where vertebrate herbivores are causing damage; it can be planted along dikes and canals where burrowing animals are a threat, or in parks and golf courses where Canada geese are a nuisance (Washburn et al. 2007). Biotechnology offers another approach to developing systemic repellents. Geneticists have protected cotton and corn plants from insect herbivores by inserting a piece of DNA which produces an insect toxin into the cotton or corn genome. The genetically engineered plants produce the toxin and suffer less herbivory from corn rootworms and cotton bollworms. Such an approach can also be used to produce plants containing a systemic repellent effective against vertebrate pests. But, costs of creating such a plant make it unlikely that one will be bioengineered just to resist vertebrate pests. Also, the chemical must not reduce the quality of the crop for human use.

7.4   WHAT ARE THE BENEFITS OF DECEPTION-BASED AVERSIONS?

There are a plethora of problems caused by foraging wildlife for which we cannot apply a contact repellent to protect the resource from predation. For instance, protecting pecans from squirrels is not an easy task. Simply spraying a repellent on pecans is ineffective because squirrels do not eat the shell, but rather crack it open and eat the seed. As another example, consider the problem of trying to protect a duck nest from predation (Figure 7.6). Spraying eggs with repellent is ineffective because most predators eat only the contents of the egg, not the shell. Injecting a repellent into the egg would solve this problem but would kill the embryo. Even if this problem were overcome, there would still be the logistical task of finding duck nests so that we could inject the eggs.

Aversive conditioning can still be used to protect these resources that cannot be directly treated with a repellent, by resorting to a technique called deception-based aversions (DBAs). With this approach, the resource needing protection is not treated. Rather, the aversive chemical is applied to a bait that mimics the resource. DBAs are effective when a depredating animal consumes the treated bait, becomes ill, develops an aversion to the bait, and, finally, generalizes its aversion to the resource. Ideal aversive chemicals for a DBA should have several properties including (1) cause nausea or digestive pain at a dosage far beneath the lethal dose, (2) cause illness quickly

FIGURE 7.6   Contact repellents are ineffective in protecting the eggs of nesting birds because the nests are difficult to locate and most predators eat only the contents of the egg, not the shell where the repellent is located. This is the nest of a mallard.

Source: Vishnevskiy Vasily, Shutterstock 247886953.

after being consumed so that the animal will associate its illness with what it just consumed, (3) are safe for human consumption in case somebody consumes a bait, and (4) are undetectable at a dose sufficient to cause illness so that the animal will not be able to detect any difference between the bait and the item the wildlife manager is trying to save.

Several chemicals have been tested to produce a DBA in wildlife including oral estrogen (Nicolaus 1989), methiocarb (Catry and Granadeiro 2006), emetine (Conover 1990), cinnamamide (Gill et al. 2000), pulegone (Conover and Lyons 2003), carbachol (Gabriel and Golightly 2014), sodium carbonate (Maguire et al. 2010), thiabendazole (Massei et al. 2002, O'Donnell et al. 2010), and levamisole (Nielsen et al. 2015). Dueser et al. (2018) fed captive raccoons chicken eggs containing 17 α-esthinyl estradiol (a powdered form of estrogen). Eighteen captive raccoons were divided into a treated and an untreated group. Each raccoon in the treatment group received an estrogen-injected egg every other day for 2 weeks and dog food on the alternate days. Each raccoon in the untreated group received an untreated egg every other day and dog food on the alternate days. A challenge period followed the treatment period in which each treatment coyote was given two estrogen-injected eggs, two untreated eggs, and dog food every other day for a total of seven days. They were given just dog food on alternate days. The nine raccoons in the untreated group were eager consumers of eggs during both the treatment and challenge periods, consuming 754 eggs out of the 756 eggs given to them. The nine raccoons in the treatment group consumed all estrogen-injected eggs on day one; thereafter, all raccoons exhibited some aversion to estrogen-injected eggs. They ate only 430 of 685 (63%) estrogen-injected eggs during the treatment period. During the challenge period, they consumed only 53% of eggs and avoided eating both injected eggs and untreated eggs. This test demonstrated that estrogen is an effective aversive agent when consumed in eggs and was undetectable to raccoons.

Field trials of DBA produced mixed results. Ratnaswamy et al. (1997) tried to stop raccoons from eating sea turtle eggs laid on beaches by distributing estrogen-injected eggs, but nest depredation rates were similar on these beaches and those that were left untreated. Gabriel and Golightly (2014) distributed eggs that were dyed to resemble the eggs of marbled murrelet and injected then with carbachol in murrelet nesting habitat. Steller's jays depredated a lower percentage of these injected eggs than they did on untreated eggs that were given a red hue. The authors did not test whether jays would transfer the aversion to actual murrelet eggs. Catry and Granadeiro (2006) found that carrion crows initially opened both untreated eggs and eggs injected with methiocarb, but after consuming eggs with methiocarb, crows stopped eating them but continued eating untreated eggs. These results indicate that crows could detect methiocarb in the egg, developing an aversion to methiocarb, but not to eggs.

Brinkman et al. (2018) tried to stop common ravens from depredating the nests of two endangered species: the western snowy plover and California least tern at Camp Pendleton, California (Figure 7.7). The scientists first created over 700 artificial nests containing quail eggs; 90% were depredated within two days. The scientists then placed out 259 nests containing quail eggs injected with the emetic agent carbachol

FIGURE 7.7   Nesting California least tern (a) and snowy plover with chick (b).

Source: Tern photo by Richard Fitzer, Shutterstock 13792759 and plover photo by MTKhaled mahmud, Shutterstock 1726619095.

and 513 nests containing untreated eggs. Ravens depredated 80% of the untreated nests but only 23% of the nests with injected eggs; this demonstrated that carbachol was an effective repellent against ravens but that the birds learned to avoid injected eggs but not untreated eggs. Of course, actual tern eggs and plover eggs cannot be treated with carbachol without killing the embryo, so these results indicate that this technique cannot be used to protect real nests.

Other applications of DBA, however, have been more successful. Nielsen et al. (2015) used conditioned food aversion to teach South American gray foxes not to consume toxic baits intended for other predators in Patagonia. This method has the potential to reduce mortality of nontarget predators. Woodchucks generalized an aversion from treated to untreated tomatoes (Swihart and Conover 1991), and livestock learned not to graze certain plant species after eating the same plant earlier and getting sick (Burritt and Provenza 1989, 1990; Lane et al. 1990). O'Donnell et al. (2010) demonstrated that an endangered species, the northern quoll, could learn not to attack and consume toxic consume cane toads (Sidebar 7.1).

SIDEBAR 7.1 USING DBAS TO SAVE AN ENDANGERED PREDATOR FROM A POISONOUS INVASIVE SPECIES

The northern quoll is a cat-like marsupial in Australia that is critically endangered (Figure 7.8). Following the invasive, highly toxic cane toad, quoll became extinct across northern Australia. These toads were introduced to Queensland, Australia, in 1935 and have spread subsequently across northern

FIGURE 7.8   The endangered northern quoll.

Source: John Carnemolla, Shutterstock 22484149.

Australia. The toads are expected to soon spread to the Kimberly, which is one of the quoll's last strongholds. The cane toad's toxins differ from those found in frogs native to Australia. For this reason, quoll, Merten's water monitor, freshwater crocodiles, and other native predators are killed when they mistakenly consumed the toads (Smith and Phillips 2006; Griffiths and McKay 2007; Letnic et al. 2008; Doody et al. 2009). A potential way to reduce the number of quolls killed from eating a cane toad is to use a DBA, teaching quoll that cane toads are toxic. To test this idea, O'Donnell et al. (2010) gave 31 captive quoll a single, dead toad that was too small to have enough toxin to be fatal. The scientist treated these dead toads with an emetic compound, thiabendazole. Hereafter, these quolls will be referred to as treated quoll; concomitantly, 31 untreated quolls were allowed to see and smell the cane toad but not allowed to taste or eat it. Each treated and untreated quoll was given a small radio collar and released into an area where cane toads were common. Within hours of their release, four untreated quolls attacked large cane toads and died. Overall, treated female quolls survived twice as long in the field as untreated female quolls while treated males survived 5 times longer than untreated males. These findings indicate that a DBA could offer a viable approach to enhancing the survival of quoll. Wildlife agencies in Australia could distribute thiabendazole-treated "toad baits" ahead of the invasion front of cane toads sweeping across the country (O'Donnell et al. 2010).

7.5 IS BATESIAN MIMICRY SIMILAR TO DECEPTION-BASED FOOD AVERSIONS?

Some animals, such as insects and amphibians, have evolved chemical defenses against predators. But, a poisonous animal does not benefit if a predator eats it before learning this. Consequently, many poisonous animals advertise their toxicity by having bright colors, conspicuous color patterns, and odd, conspicuous behaviors that enhance a predator's ability to recognize them. Other species, lacking chemical defenses, have evolved color patterns and behaviors that mimic those of poisonous species. This phenomenon is known as Batesian mimicry; it functions because these palatable prey obtain some degree of protection from predators through their mimicry. DBA can be viewed as a reverse form of Batesian mimicry because, in DBA, the resource is innocuous and the mimics (the chemically treated baits) are poisonous. Nevertheless, the general ecological and behavioral principles that apply to Batesian mimicry also apply to DBA. Two of these principles involve the precision of the mimicry and the cost-to-benefit ratio.

7.5.1 PRECISION OF MIMICRY

Some Batesian mimics are discovered and preyed upon because predators learn to detect subtle differences between them and poisonous animals. Likewise, some attempts to use DBA fail because depredating animals can distinguish between the

FIGURE 7.9   Deception-based aversion conditioning can be used to teach gray squirrels not to accept food from humans.

Source: Michael de Nysschen, Shutterstock 219786949.

chemically treated mimics and the untreated animal. Attempts to use DBA to teach coyotes not to kill sheep were unsuccessful because the baits designed to mimic sheep were created by injecting chemicals into mutton baits wrapped in sheep fur. Coyotes had little difficulty differentiating between chemically treated baits and live sheep; many coyotes developed an aversion to mutton baits but continued killing sheep.

Fortunately, a closer mimicry between the toxic bait and the resource needing protection is possible for other human–wildlife conflicts. Bears can destroy beehives, and a chemically treated beehive can be created that closely mimics untreated bee-hives. It is also possible to create a bait that closely mimics food handouts from humans (Figure 7.9). Attempts to use DBA to address these problems were more successful. Likewise, precise mimics of vegetable crops (Swihart and Conover 1991) or seeded fields (Avery 1989) can be created by treating part of a field while leaving the rest untreated.

7.5.2   Cost–Benefit Ratio

If treated baits (mimics) can be produced that are identical to the resource, then animals will be unable to distinguish between the two and will face a dilemma. Consider, for instance, an attempt to protect turtle eggs from raccoons by distribut-ing treated mimics. If a raccoon finds a nest and eats the eggs, it runs the risk that the eggs are treated mimics and that sickness will ensue. If it does not eat any, it runs the risk of missing a nutritious meal. Which decision the raccoon makes will depend upon which mistake it can least afford. That, in turn, depends on the severity of the potential illness and the nutritive value of the resource. If the risk of making an error and eating a treated mimic is low, the animal probably will take that risk. However, if the illness caused by eating a mimic is severe and long-lasting, the animal is less likely to take the chance of becoming ill. Monarch butterfly populations, for example, vary in their toxicity, and this impacts their mortality rate from predators (Brower and Fink 1985). Aversive conditioning chemicals also vary in the severity of the illness they produce. Nicolaus and Nellis (1987) reported that 9 of 32 mongooses that were fed carbachol-treated eggs were killed by the drug, while the survivors averted from eggs. In contrast, consumption of lithium chloride is rarely fatal, and its effects last only for a few hours. Not surprisingly, most attempts to avert predators from consuming eggs using this chemical have failed (Hopkins and Murphy 1982; Sheaffer and Drobney 1986; Conover 1989).

7.6   WHAT FACTORS INFLUENCE THE EFFECTIVENESS OF REPELLENTS TO REDUCE WILDLIFE DAMAGE?

Usually, the effectiveness of a repellent is correlated with its concentration. Bullard et al. (1978*a*, 1978*b*) showed that the repellency of synthetic fermented egg could be enhanced considerably by increasing its concentration. In a study evaluating the effectiveness of predator fecal odor on mule deer, Melchiors and Leslie (1985) found that repellency of fecal extracts from five predators was correlated with concentration. Repellent concentration also was a determining factor in decreasing browsing damage by elk (Andelt et al. 1992). Unfortunately, rain can reduce the concentration of contact repellents on the resource. Andelt et al. (1991) reported that several repellents were effective in reducing browsing of apple buds by mule deer, but their repellency decreased when the buds were sprinkled with water to simulate rainfall. Sullivan et al. (1985) found that Big Game Repellent® (BGR) or the feces of coyotes, cougars, and wolves completely suppressed feeding by captive mule deer on salal, Douglas-fir, and western red-cedar for 20 days in dry weather. But after just one day of heavy rain, the repellents became ineffective.

Many authors have noted that repellent effectiveness declines over time. Hence, repellents may have to be reapplied repeatedly to retain their effectiveness. Reapplying repellents, however, is not always successful in lowering browsing rates. Conover and Kania (1988) found that even a mid-winter reapplication of BGR was not sufficient to stop deer browsing on young apple trees. Clearly, repellents are more appropriate for short-term problems than long-term ones.

Repellents normally function by reducing the palatability of the treated plant to a level lower than that of other available plants. Consequently, repellent effectiveness depends upon the availability of alternate forage. Andelt et al. (1991, 1992) reported that repellents reduced deer and elk browsing when alternate foods were available but not when the treated food was presented to hungry animals lacking alternative forage. For the same reason, adding a repellent to a less palatable food is more likely to reduce the food's palatability to below that of alternate foods. Support for this hypothesis comes from several studies that evaluated the same repellent on numerous plant species. Dietz and Tigner (1968) found that repellents were more effective at protecting aspen than the more palatable chokecherry. Sodium selenite was more effective at protecting white ash seedlings than the more palatable seedlings of black cherry (Angradi and Tzilkowski 1987). Swihart et al. (1991) found that bobcat and coyote urine were more effective when used on eastern hemlock than on the more palatable Japanese yews.

7.7 WHAT LAWS GOVERN THE USE OF WILDLIFE REPELLENTS?

All repellents sold in the United States and in most other countries require government approval. In the United States, the Federal Insecticide, Fungicide, and Rodenticide Act (FIFRA) of 1947 gave the federal government the right to ban the sale of any repellent or pesticide when the risks to human health or the environment outweigh the benefits. Since 1970, the U.S. Environmental Protection Agency (EPA) has had the responsibility for making these decisions. EPA does so by requiring that all pesticides and repellents be registered with and approved by them before being sold. The EPA makes its decision based on evaluations of scientific tests of product chemistry, toxicity to target and nontarget species, potential hazards to human health, environmental fate, and chemical longevity in the environment. Chemicals intended for use on food crops face an even more rigorous standard. A company wishing to register a pesticide or repellent must demonstrate that it meets the requirements of registration by conducting several medical and environmental tests to verify its safety and effectiveness. These tests can cost millions of dollars to conduct (Fagerstone et al. 1990).

Additionally, repellents or pesticides must be registered with, and approved by, state governments before they can be used in each state. Usually, the states accept the decisions of the EPA and do not require additional testing. However, some states, such as California, Florida, and New York, require their own review of the data and sometimes require additional testing. Dealing with the different state requirements can be laborious for chemical companies because requirements differ among states, and each state requires a separate application and application fee. These requirements provide disincentives to companies or individuals wishing to register a repellent.

Other countries have their own laws governing the use of repellents within their jurisdiction. In Canada, repellents and pesticides fall under the Pest Control Products Acts and must be approved before they can be used. Canada's registration requirements for repellents are even more laborious than those in the United States; it take approximately two years for a potential repellent to be reviewed in Canada (Hushon 1997). In the European Union, repellents are regulated under the Biocides Directive and require rigorous testing before they can be approved for use (Hushon 1997). One potential way to reduce costs associated with registering a new repellent is to use a chemical already registered for other uses on food as chemical repellent. The advantage of registering these chemicals is that much of the required testing has already been conducted. For instance, the bird repellent methiocarb was first used as an insecticide.

Unfortunately, the cost to register a repellent is so prohibitive that chemical companies are not willing to spend the necessary funds because the market for vertebrate repellents is relatively small compared to the use of insecticides on major crops. Even when a repellent is registered for use by the EPA, the company must recover the money it spent conducting the required tests. For this reason, a repellent costing only a few dollars per kilogram to manufacture may sell for several hundred dollars per kilogram to allow the company to recover the money spent registering the chemical. Due to their high cost, the demand for repellents is limited because few people can afford to use them.

7.8 SUMMARY

Through evolution, many plants have developed chemicals that protect them from herbivores. Chemical repellents are designed to protect plants by exploiting the herbivore's need to avoid poisons and to concentrate its foraging on highly nutritious foods. Repellents can be used as area repellents (which keep wildlife out of an area), contact repellents (which are sprayed on or attached to the resource), or systemic repellents (which are incorporated within the plant). DBAs can also be used to protect food items by tricking animals into believing that a safe food is actually poisonous and should be avoided.

Repellents are most effective when used during periods of good weather, in high concentrations, and for problems with a short duration. Because repellents are designed to persuade animals to eat something else rather than the treated food, they function best when alternate food supplies are readily available and when used on plants of low palatability. The biggest factor limiting the use of repellents in wildlife damage management is the fact that all vertebrate repellents require government approval to ensure that the repellent is effective and safe for human health and the environment. Although no one would disagree with these goals, the necessary testing is so expensive that chemical companies have little interest in developing vertebrate repellents. Thus, few repellents can be used legally in the United States or in many other countries.

7.9 DISCUSSION QUESTIONS

1. What is Batesian Mimicry, and how is a deceptive-based aversion similar to it?
2. What are some short-term human–wildlife conflicts that might be mitigated by using repellents?
3. People do not like to eat in restaurants that smell badly, even if the odor is not from the food. If someone was starving and the only food was in a stinky building, do you think this would prevent the person from eating? Do you think this is similar to how animals might respond to food that is defended by an area repellent?
4. Toxic animals often engage in odd and conspicuous behaviors to let predators know that they are poisonous. Do you think this could explain why killer whales rarely attack humans? After all, killer whales specialize in

preying upon marine mammals, including seals, so why not eat a human? I wonder if killer whales interpret our awkward swimming as warning behavior, advertising the toxicity of humans. What do you think?

5. People become seasick or carsick when signals coming from their inner ear do not match those coming from their eyes. That is, our eyes tell the brain that we are not moving, but the inner ears signal otherwise. Why does the brain, reacting to this disconnect, cause vomiting?

LITERATURE CITED

Aldrich, C. G., J. A. Paterson, J. L. Tate, and M. S. Kelley. 1993. The effects of untufted-infected tall fescue on diet utilization and thermal regulation in cattle. *Journal of Animal Science* 71:164–170.

Allan, G. G., D. I. Gustafson, R. A. Mikels, J. M. Miller, and S. Neogi. 1984. Reduction of deer browsing of Douglas-fir (*Pseudotsuga menziesii*) seedlings by quadrivalent selenium. *Forest Ecology and Management* 7:163–181.

Andelt, W. F., D. L. Baker, and K. P. Burnham. 1992. Relative preference of captive cow elk for repellent-treated diets. *Journal of Wildlife Management* 56:164–173.

Andelt, W. F., K. P. Burnham, and J. A. Manning. 1991. Relative effectiveness of repellents for reducing mule deer damage. *Journal of Wildlife Management* 55:341–347.

Angradi, T. R., and W. M. Tzilkowski. 1987. Preliminary testing of a selenium-based systemic deer browse repellent. *Proceedings of the Eastern Wildlife Damage Control Conference* 3:102–107.

Avery, M. L. 1989. Experimental evaluation of partial repellent treatment for reducing bird damage to crops. *Journal of Applied Ecology* 26:433–439.

Baker, S. E., S. A. Ellwood, D. Slater, R. W. Watkins, and D. W. Macdonald. 2008. Food aversion plus odor cue protects crop from wild mammals. *Journal of Wildlife Management* 72:785–791.

Baker, S. E., S. A. Ellwood, R. W. Watkins, and D. W. Macdonald. 2005a. A dose – response trial with ziram-treated maize and free-ranging European badgers *Meles*. *Applied Animal Behaviour Science* 93:309–321.

Baker, S. E., S. A. Ellwood, R. Watkins, and D. W. MacDonald. 2005b. Non-lethal control of wildlife: using chemical repellents as feeding deterrents for the European badger *Meles meles*. *Journal of Applied Ecology* 42:921–931.

Baker, S. E., P. J. Johnson, D. Slater, R. W. Watkins, and D. W. Macdonald. 2007. Learned food aversion with and without an odour cue for protecting untreated baits from wild mammal foraging. *Applied Animal Behaviour Science* 102:410-428.

Belant, J. L., S. K. Ickes, L. A. Tyson, and T. W. Seamans. 1997. Comparison of four particulate substances as wildlife feeding repellents. *Crop Protection* 16:439–447.

Brinkman, M. P., D. K. Garcelon, and M. A. Colwell. 2018. Evaluating the efficacy of carbachol at reducing corvid predation on artificial nests. *Wildlife Society Bulletin* 42:84–93.

Brower, L. P., and L. S. Fink. 1985. A natural toxic defense system: cardenolides in butterflies versus birds. Pages 171–188 *in* N. S. Braveman and P. Braveman, editors. *Experimental assessment and clinical applications of conditioned food aversions.* New York Academy of Science, New York, NY.

Bryant, J. P., R. K. Swihart, P. B. Reichardt, and L. Newton. 1994. Biogeography of woody plant chemical defense against snowshoe hare browsing: comparison of Alaska and eastern North America. *Oikos* 70:385–395.

Bryant, J. P., G. D. Wieland, P. B. Reichardt, V. E. Lewis, and M. C. McCarthy. 1983. Pinosylvin methyl ether deters snowshoe hare feeding on green alder. *Science* 222:1023–1025.

Bullard, R. W., T. J. Leiker, J. E. Peterson, and S. R. Kilburn. 1978a. Volatile components of fermented egg, an animal attractant and repellent. *Journal of Agricultural Food Chemistry* 26:155–159.

Bullard, R. W., S. A. Shumake, D. L. Campbell, and F. J. Turkowski. 1978b. Preparation and evaluation of a synthetic fermented egg coyote attractant and deer repellent. *Journal of Agricultural Food Chemistry* 26:160–163.

Burritt, E. A., and F. D. Provenza. 1989. Food aversion learning: conditioning lambs to avoid a palatable shrub (*Cercocarpus montanus*). *Journal of Animal Science* 67:650–653.

Burritt, E. A., and F. D. Provenza. 1990. Food aversion learning in sheep: persistence of conditioned taste aversion to palatable shrubs (*Cercocarpus montanus* and *Amelanchier alnifolia*). *Journal of Animal Science* 68:1003–1007.

Catry, T., and J. P. Granadeiro. 2006. Failure of methiocarb to produce conditioned taste aversion in carrion crows consuming little tern eggs. *Waterbirds* 29:211–214.

Clausen, T. P., F. D. Provenza, E. A. Burritt, P. B. Reichardt, and J. P. Bryant. 1990. Ecological implications of condensed tannin structure: a case study. *Journal of Chemical Ecology* 16:2381–2392.

Clay, K. 1988. Fungal endophytes of grasses: a defensive mutualism between plants and fungi. *Ecology* 69:10–16.

Clay, K. 1993. The ecology and evolution of endophytes. *Agriculture, Ecosystems and Environment* 44:39–64.

Conover, M. R. 1989. Potential compounds for establishing conditioned food aversions in raccoons. *Wildlife Society Bulletin* 17:430–435.

Conover, M. R. 1990. Reducing mammalian predation on eggs by using a conditioned taste aversion to deceive predators. *Journal of Wildlife Management* 54:360–365.

Conover, M. R. 1998. Impact of consuming tall fescue leaves with the endophytic fungus, *Acremonium coenophialum* on meadow voles. *Journal of Mammalogy* 79:457–463.

Conover, M. R. 2007. *Predator-prey dynamics: the role of olfaction.* CRC Press, Boca Raton, FL.

Conover, M. R., and G. S. Kania. 1988. Effectiveness of human hair, BGR, and a mixture of blood meal and peppercorns in reducing deer damage to young apple trees. *Eastern Wildlife Damage Control Conference* 3:97–101.

Conover, M. R., and K. S. Lyons. 2003. Reducing or delaying egg depredation by punishing free-ranging predators for opening eggs. *Applied Animal Behaviour Science* 83:177–185.

Conover, M. R., and T. A. Messmer. 1996. Feeding preferences and changes in mass of Canada geese grazing fungus-infected tall fescue. *Condor* 98:859–862.

Cox, T. E., P. J. Murray, A. J. Bengsen, G. P. Hall, and X. Li. 2015. Do fecal odors from native and non-native predators cause a habitat shift among macropods? *Wildlife Society Bulletin* 39:159–164.

Cummings, J. L., R. W. Byrd, W. R. Eddleman, R. M. Engeman, and S. K. Tupper. 2011. Effectiveness of AV-1011® to reduce damage to drill-planted rice from blackbirds. *Journal of Wildlife Management* 75:353–356.

Dietz, D. R., and J. R. Tigner. 1968. Evaluation of two mammal repellents applied to browse species in the Black Hills. *Journal of Wildlife Management* 32:109–114.

Doody, J. S., B. Green, D. Rhind, C. M. Castellano, R. Sims, and T. Robinson. 2009. Population-level declines in Australian predators caused by an invasive species. *Animal Conservation* 12:46–53.

Dueser, R. D., J. D. Martin, and N. D. Moncrief. 2018. Pen trial of estrogen – induced conditioned food aversion to eggs in raccoons (*Procyon lotor*). *Applied Animal Behaviour Science* 201:93–101.

Engeman, R. M., D. L. Campbell, D. Nolte, and G. W. Witmer. 1995. Some recent results on non-lethal means of reducing animal damage to reforestation projects in the Western United States. *Australian Vertebrate Pest Control Conference* 10:150–154.

Fagerstone, K. A., R. W. Bullard, and C. A. Ramey. 1990. Politics and economics of maintaining pesticide registrations. *Proceedings of the Vertebrate Pest Conference* 14:8–11.

Gabriel, P. O., and R. T. Golightly. 2014. Aversive conditioning of Steller's jays to improve marbled murrelet nest survival. *Journal of Wildlife Management* 78:894–903.

Galef, D. G., and P. W. Henderson. 1972. Mother's milk: a determinant of the feeding preference of weaning rat pups. *Journal of Comparative Physiological Psychology* 83:374–378.

Gietzen, D. W. 1993. Neural mechanisms in the responses to amino acid deficiency. *Journal of Nutrition* 123:610–625.

Gill, E. L., A. Whiterow, and D. P. Cowan. 2000. A comparative assessment of potential conditioned taste aversion agents for vertebrate management. *Applied Animal Behavioral Science* 67:229–240.

Griffiths, A. D., and J. L. McKay. 2007. Cane toads reduce the abundance and site occupancy of Merten's water monitor (*Varanus mertensi*). *Wildlife Research* 34:609–615.

Hedges, S., and D. Gunaryadi. 2010. Reducing human – elephant conflict: do chillies help deter elephants from entering crop fields? *Oryx* 44:139–146.

Hopkins, S. R., and T. M. Murphy. 1982. Testing of lithium chloride aversion to mitigate raccoon depredation of loggerhead turtle nests. *Proceedings of the Annual Conference of the Southeastern Association of Fish and Wildlife Agencies* 36:484–491.

Hushon, J. M. 1997. Review of regulatory-imposed marketing constraints to repellent development. Pages 423–428 *in* J. R. Mason, editor. *Repellents in wildlife management: proceedings of a symposium*. National Wildlife Research Center, Fort Collins, CO.

Jakubas, W. J., C. G. Guglielmo, and W. H. Karasov. 1997. Dilution and detoxification costs: Relevance to avian herbivore food selection. Pages 53–70 *in* J. R. Mason, editor. *Repellents in wildlife management: proceedings of a symposium*. National Wildlife Research Center, Fort Collins, CO.

Kimball, B. A., D. L. Nolte, and K. B. Perry. 2005. Hydrolyzed casein reduces browsing of trees and shrubs by white-tailed deer. *HortScience* 40:1810–1814.

Kimball, B. A., J. Taylor, K. R. Perry, and C. Capelli. 2009. Deer responses to repellent stimuli. *Journal of Chemical Ecology* 35:1461–1470.

Lane, M. A., M. H. Ralphs, J. D. Olsen, F. D. Provenza, and J. A. Pfister. 1990. Conditioned taste aversion: potential for reducing cattle loss to larkspur. *Journal of Range Management* 43:127–131.

Letnic, M., J. K. Webb, and R. Shine. 2008. Invasive cane toads (*Bufo marinus*) cause mass mortality of freshwater crocodiles (*Crocodylus johnstoni*) in tropical Australia. *Biological Conservation* 141:1773–1782.

Lindgren, P. M. F., T. P. Sullivan, and D. R. Crump. 1997. Review of synthetic predator odor semiochemicals as repellents for wildlife management in the Pacific Northwest. Pages 217–230 *in* J. R. Mason, editor. *Repellents in wildlife management: proceedings of a symposium*. National Wildlife Research Center, Fort Collins, CO.

Maguire, G. S., D. Stojanovic, and M. A. Weston. 2010. Conditioned taste aversion reduced fox depredation on model eggs on beaches. *Wildlife Research* 36:702–708.

Mason, J. R., and L. Clark. 1994. Use of activated charcoal and other particulate substances as food additives to suppress bird feeding. *Crop Protection* 13:219–224.

Mason, J. R., and J. A. Maruniak. 1983. Behavioral and physiological effects of capsaicin in red-winged blackbirds. *Pharmacology, Biochemistry, and Behavior* 19:857–862.

Massei, G., A. J. Lyon, and D. P. Cowan. 2002. Conditioned taste aversion can reduce egg predation by rats. *Journal of Wildlife Management* 66:1134–1140.

Melchiors, M. A., and C. A. Leslie. 1985. Effectiveness of predator fecal odors as black-tailed deer repellents. *Journal of Wildlife Management* 49:358–362.

Mutinda, M., G. Chenge, F. Gakuya, M. Otiende, P. Omondi, S. Kasiki, R. C. Soriguer, and S. Alasaad. 2014. Detusking fence-breaker elephants as an approach in human-elephant conflict mitigation. *PLoS One* 9(3):e91749.

Nicolaus, L. K., J. Herrera, J. C. Nicolaus, and C. R. Gustavson. 1989. Ethinyl estradiol and generalized aversion to eggs among free-ranging predators. *Applied Animal Behaviour Science* 24:313–324.

Nicolaus, L. K., and D. W. Nellis. 1987. The first evaluation of the use of conditioned taste aversion to control predation by mongooses upon eggs. *Applied Animal Behaviour Sciences* 17:329–346.

Nielsen, S., A. Travaini, A. I Vassallo, D. Procopio, and S. C. Zapata. 2015. Conditioned taste aversion in the grey fox (*Pseudalopex griseus*), in Southern Argentine Patagonia. *Applied Animal Behavior Science* 163:167–174.

Niner, M. D., G. M. Linz, and M. E. Clark. 2015. Evaluation of 9, 10 anthraquinone application to pre-seed set sunflowers for repelling blackbirds. *Human-Wildlife Interactions* 9:4–13.

Nolte, D. L., and J. R. Mason. 1995. Maternal ingestion of ortho-aminoacetophenone during gestation affects intake by offspring. *Physiology and Behavior* 58:925–928.

Nolte, D. L., J. R. Mason, G. Epple, E. Aronov, and D. L. Campbell. 1994. Why are predator urines aversive to prey? *Journal of Chemical Ecology* 20:1505–1516.

Nolte, D. L., and F. D. Provenza. 1991. Food preferences in lambs after exposure to flavors in milk. *Applied Animal Behaviour Science* 32:381–389.

O'Donnell, S., J. K. Webb, and R. Shine. 2010. Conditioned taste aversion enhances the survival of an endangered predator imperiled by a toxic invader. *Journal of Applied Ecology* 47:558–565.

Provenza, F. D. 1997. Origins of food preference in herbivores. Pages 81–90 *in* J. R. Mason, editor. *Repellents in wildlife management: proceedings of a symposium.* National Wildlife Research Center, Fort Collins, CO.

Ratnaswamy, M. J., R. J. Warren, M. T. Kramer, and M. D. Adam. 1997. Comparisons of lethal and nonlethal techniques to reduce raccoon depredation of sea turtle nests. *Journal of Wildlife Management* 61:368–376.

Reichardt, P. B., J. P. Bryant, T. P. Clausen, and G. D. Wieland. 1984. Defense of winter dormant Alaska paper birch against snowshoe hares. *Oecologia (Berlin)* 654:58–69.

Schmidt, S. P., and T. G. Osborn. 1993. Effects of endophyte-infected tall fescue on animal performance. *Agriculture, Ecosystems and Environment* 44:233–262.

Severud, W. J., J. L. Belant, J. G. Bruggink, and S. K. Windels. 2011. Predator cues reduce American beaver use of foraging trails. *Human-Wildlife Interactions* 5:296–305.

Sheaffer, S. E., and R. D. Drobney. 1986. Effectiveness of lithium chloride induced taste aversions in reducing waterfowl nest predation. *Transactions of the Missouri Academy of Sciences* 20:59–63.

Sitati, N. W., and M. J. Walpole. 2006. Assessing farm-based measures for mitigating human-elephant conflicts in Transmara District, Kenya. *Oryx* 40:279–286.

Smith, J. G., and B. L. Phillips. 2006. Toxic tucker: the potential impact of cane toads on Australian reptiles. *Pacific Conservation Biology* 12:40–49.

Smith, T. S., S. Herrero, T. D. Debruyn, and J. M. Wilder. 2008. Efficacy of bear deterrent spray in Alaska. *Journal of Wildlife Management* 72:640–645.

Smith, T. S., S. Herrero, C. S. Layton, R. T. Larsen, and K. R. Johnson. 2012. Efficacy of firearms for bear deterrence in Alaska. *Journal of Wildlife Management* 76:1021–1027.

Stober, J. M., and L. M. Conner. 2007. Scent deterrence to reduce Southern flying squirrel kleptoparasitism of red-cockaded woodpecker cavities. *Human-Wildlife Interactions* 1:45–48.

Sullivan, T. P., D. R. Crump, and D. S. Sullivan. 1985. Use of predator odors as repellents to reduce feeding damage by herbivores, II: black-tailed deer (*Odocoileus hemonius columbianus*). *Journal of Chemical Ecology* 11:921–935.

Swihart, R. K., and M. R. Conover. 1991. Responses of woodchucks to potential garden crop repellents. *Journal of Wildlife Management* 55:177–181.

Swihart, R. K., J. J. Pignatello, and M. J. I. Mattina. 1991. Aversive responses of white-tailed deer, *Odocoileus virginianus*, to predator urine. *Journal of Chemical Ecology* 17:767–777.

Washburn, B. E., S. C. Barras, and T. W. Seamans. 2007. Foraging preferences of captive Canada geese related to turfgrass mixtures. *Human-Wildlife Interactions* 1:214–223.

Werner, S. J., G. M. Linz, S. K. Tupper, and J. C. Carlson. 2010. Laboratory efficacy of chemical repellents for reducing blackbird damage in rice and sunflowers. *Journal of Wildlife Management* 74:1400–1404.

8 Exclusion

"Love your neighbor, but don't take down the fence."

– Carl Sandberg

"Sometimes you put walls up not to keep people out but to see who cares enough to tear them down."

– Socrates

Perhaps the best methods of resolving human–wildlife conflicts is the use of physical barriers. The obvious assumption is that if animals cannot obtain access, they cannot cause damage. Fences have been used since the dawn of agriculture to protect crops from wildlife damage and to separate captive animals from free-ranging animals, which might either compete with livestock for forage or prey upon them.

8.1 WHAT INFLUENCES THE COST-EFFECTIVENESS OF FENCING TO REDUCE HUMAN–WILDLIFE CONFLICTS?

Fences are often the most effective techniques to reduce damage by mammals and can be completely effective if properly constructed and maintained; in contrast, other techniques used in wildlife damage management may reduce wildlife damage but will not end it entirely. Cost is the major factor preventing the widespread use of fences. Fences can be so expensive that they cannot be justified based on economics for many human–wildlife conflicts. The cost-effectiveness of fencing is influenced by several factors.

Fences vary tremendously in cost. A 2-m high deer-proof fence costs $5 per linear meter if made of chain-link mesh, $3 if made of woven wire, and $1 if made using electrified wires. As one might expect, cheaper fences are often less effective; therefore, the challenge is to select the least expensive fence that will work. For example, Lavelle et al. (2011) built five types of fences that were designed to exclude feral hogs, which differed greatly on price (Table 8.1). A fence built with woven-wire panels was the most effective in excluding feral hogs and was intermediate in price.

Fences differ in their durability and life expectancies. When a fence lasts for several years, its cost can be amortized over that time. For instance, a fence made of woven wire (also called hog wire) is less expensive than a chain-link fence, but a woven-wire fence may have a life expectancy of 10 years while a chain-link fence may last 30 years. Expensive fences with a long life expectancy should only be employed for problems that are likely to occur at the same place for several years.

DOI: 10.1201/9780429401404-8

TABLE 8.1

Cost to Build Different Fences Intended to Exclude Feral Hogs

Fence type	$/m	$/corner	$ to fence an 0.01-ha area	Hours to fence an area
Electrified polywire	2.62	2.39	315	3
Hog panels	5.73	3.89	688	20
Polypropylene mesh	5.74	11.67	689	15
Electrified netting	6.20	0.00	744	5
Woven wires	7.75	151.25	930	60

The cost per fence and hours per fence are based on the cost the time required to enclose an area of 0.01 ha (Lavelle et al. 2011).

Hence, they should only be used for predictable problems. Elephants, for example, revisit specific fields regularly, selecting those fields that are close to elephant pathways or near nature reserves. Elephants also remember fields they have visited in past years and return to the same fields each year (Sitati et al. 2003, 2005; Songhurst and Coulson 2014). But African farmers cannot afford the high cost to erect and maintain a fence sturdy enough to exclude elephants (Osborn and Parker 2003).

Local topography affects the cost of fence construction. A corner post is needed each time a fence changes direction or elevation. Corner posts bear much of the weight of a fence and, therefore, must be much sturdier and more securely set in the ground than other posts. This makes corner posts expensive. Consequently, fences cost less when built in flat areas where they can run in straight lines and require few corner posts.

While construction costs for a fence are based on its length, its cost-effectiveness is related to the area of land enclosed within it. The important variable is the perimeter-to-area ratio; the length of a field's perimeter influences how much it costs to erect it, but its area determines the magnitude of the benefit. A fence of a set length encloses more area if built around a square field than an oblong one (Figure 8.1). Fences also become more cost-effective if the area they enclose increases in size (Figure 8.2).

Crops, such as corn or soybeans, have such low value on a per hectare basis that enclosing them in a deer-proof fence may not be economical, regardless of the severity of damage. Other crops are so valuable (e.g., nursery plants, vineyards, or orchards) that fencing is economically justified even when damage is minimal. A hectare of Japanese yews, which are used for landscaping, can be worth up to $30,000. If deer damage reduced the value of these plants by 10%, then fencing would be worthwhile, providing it costs less than $3,000/ha annually and completely stops damage. In contrast, a farmer could not afford to build a fence at that price around a cornfield, even if deer were going to destroy the entire crop. A cornfield yielding 250 bushels/ha at $6/bushel has a value of only $1,500/ha. As another

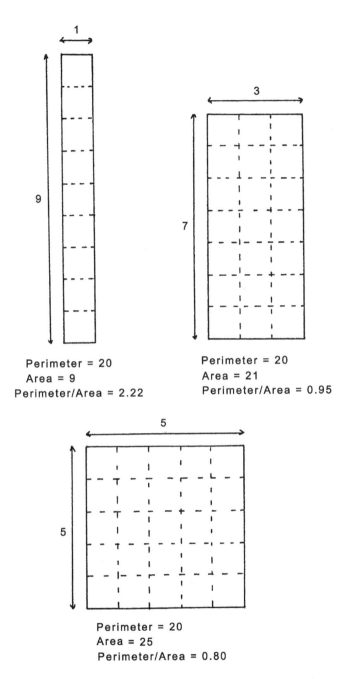

FIGURE 8.1 How the relationship between the length of a fence (perimeter) and the area enclosed within it change as the shape becomes squarer.

Source: This is Figure 13.1 in the first edition of this book.

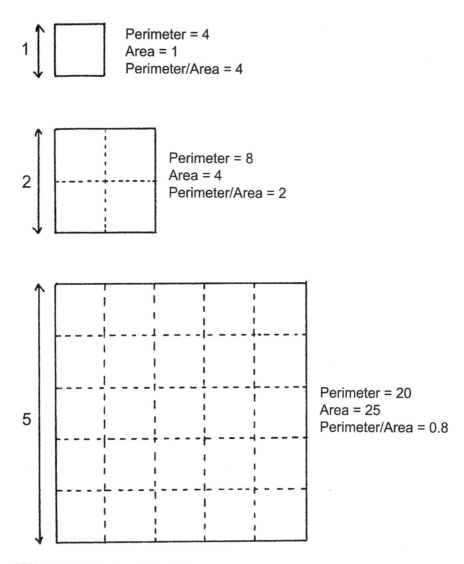

FIGURE 8.2 How the relationship between the length of a fence (perimeter) and the area enclosed within it change as the area increases in size.

Source: This is Figure 13.2 in the first edition of this book.

example, putting a bird-proof net that costs $2,000/ha over a wheat field with a value of $500/ha is not cost-efficient. A wheat farmer, therefore, would be better off losing the entire crop rather than putting up a bird-proof net to save the wheat from birds. On the other hand, wine grapes are so valuable, and birds may eat so many grapes that there is a seven-to-one benefit-to-cost ratio for the use of netting at some vineyards (Fuller-Perrine and Tobin 1993).

8.2 WHAT TYPES OF FENCES ARE USED TO EXCLUDE DEER AND OTHER MAMMALS?

In areas where deer are abundant, fencing may be the only effective method of reducing crop damage. Fences to exclude deer are usually made of chain-link, woven wire or electric wires.

8.2.1 CHAIN-LINK AND WOVEN-WIRE FENCING

The fencing material of chain-link and woven-wire fences consists of metal wires which are woven and welded into a mesh grid (Figure 8.3). These fences function by physically preventing animals from passing through the mesh. Woven-wire and chain-link fences last 10–30 years, require little maintenance, and are effective during all weather conditions. They are the most effective fences at excluding deer (Redick and Jacobs 2020) but are expensive to build, costing $2–$4/m of fence. These fences are used mainly for high-value crops or where effectiveness in excluding deer is more important than cost (e.g., along highways or at airports where deer pose a threat to human safety). Woven-wire and chain-link fences are cost-effective when their cost is amortized over their long life expectancy. To prevent deer from jumping over them, the recommended height for deer-proof fences is at least 2.5 m (Stull et al. 2011). Sometimes, a single strand of barbwire or an electric wire is strung along the top of these fences to increase their height (Sidebar 8.1).

FIGURE 8.3 This horse is looking through a woven-wire or hog-wire fence.

Source: JNix, Shutterstock 379108876.

SIDEBAR 8.1 USING FENCES TO EXCLUDE SOME WILDLIFE SPECIES BUT NOT OTHERS

For decades, Texas had conducted a program to eradicate cattle-fever ticks to prevent the spread of cattle fever to livestock. While it is relatively easy to treat livestock for ticks, white-tailed deer are also a host for the same ticks, and they are difficult to treat with a toxicant that kills ticks (an acaricide). To overcome this difficulty, acaricides are placed on corn seed and then the treated corn is distributing at a bait station where deer can access it. One problem with these bait stations is that the corn is also consumed by several nontarget species, including feral hogs, raccoons, and javelinas. To alleviate this problem, Pound et al. (2012) invented a fence that excluded these nontarget species but not white-tailed deer. The fence surrounding the bait station and was made of woven wire with an electric wire placed on the outside of the fence. The fence was only 0.6-m high, low enough that deer could easily jump over the fence, but tall enough to exclude smaller mammals, such as feral hogs, that are not known for their jumping ability.

8.2.2 ELECTRIC FENCING

Electric fences are built using metal wires spaced close enough together that a deer cannot crawl through them without contacting a wire and being shocked. These fences are designed to make the task of crossing them painful enough that deer will avoid doing so. Poole et al. (2002) tested an electric fence in England to keep European badgers from entering cornfields. Four strands were placed 10, 15, 20, and 30 cm above the ground. With this spacing, badgers could not cross through the fence without getting a shock; damage to cornfields surrounded by this electric fence was only 5% that of unfenced fields.

To receive a shock from an electric fence, an animal must complete an electric circuit. Some fences are built with alternating positive and negative wires so that an animal will receive a shock when it simultaneously touches a positive and negative wire. More commonly, all of the wires are connected to the same pole on the charger, and the other pole is connected to a metal post driven into the ground. With this design, an animal that is standing on the ground completes the circuit and becomes shocked when it touches an electrified wire (Figure 8.4). The advantage of this design is that the animal only has to touch one wire to receive a shock. The disadvantage is that the fence wires must be insulated from the ground or the fence will short circuit. For this reason, plants must be kept from growing beneath an electric fence and contacting a wire. Hence, electric fences require constant weed control and must be checked every few days to ensure the fence is working properly and has not become grounded. This type of electric fences is less effective when the ground is dry (Smith et al. 2018).

Electric fences are usually powered by a fence charger designed to send out a short pulse of power approximately once every second. The fence charger is usually powered by a 12-volt battery, which can be charged with a solar panel. Electric fences should only be powered by a fence charger specifically designed for that purpose.

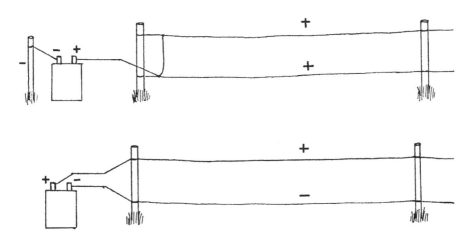

FIGURE 8.4   Two different designs for electric fences. In the top figure, all of the wires are positively charged, the negative lead is grounded, and the deer receives a shock whenever it touches any wire while standing on the ground. With the second design, the wires are either positively or negatively charged (bottom figure); a deer receives a shock when it simultaneously touches a negative and positive wire.

Source: This is Figure 13.5 in the first edition of this book.

They should never be connected to an AC electric outlet (the type found in homes) because a person or animal could be electrocuted by contacting the fence.

Electric fences are not as effective at stopping deer as woven-wire fences because a deer can pass through an electric fence if it is willing to get shocked. Electric fences are most effective at protecting agricultural fields from deer browsing when food supplies outside the fenced area are abundant. During winter, when deer are hungrier and alternative food supplies are fewer, deer are more determined to get through a fence to access the food inside it. Thus, an electric fence working well in the summer may not be effective during the winter.

There are several types of electric fences. High-tensile electric fences are made from a steel wire that can be pulled extremely tight without snapping (i.e., the wire has great tensile strength). This allows fence posts to be spaced farther apart (up to 50 m) because there is less sag in the wires. Powerful springs connect the wires to fence posts, allowing the wires to stretch without breaking if something runs into them. High-tensile fences are most cost-effective when built in a straight line and on flat ground. With this design, only the corner posts need to be sturdy enough to withstand the tremendous pull of the wires. The cost of a high-tensile deer fence with five wires is about $2/m. High-tensile fences have been used to reduce deer damage to a variety of agricultural crops and are cost-effective in many situations.

Temporary electric fences can be assembled and disassembled quickly and cost only $0.50/m. These fences are often made of polywire or polytape, which is a highly visible polyethylene ribbon interwoven with strands of stainless-steel wire. Polytape has the benefit of being durable and easy to roll and unroll from a spool (Hygnstrom and Craven 1988). These temporary fences, nonetheless, are not very sturdy and need to be checked daily.

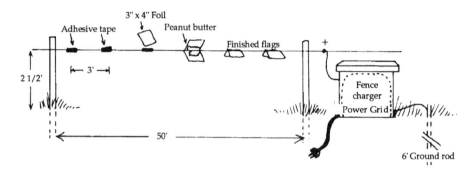

FIGURE 8.5   The peanut butter fence.

Source: Figure from Hygnstrom et al. 1994 and used with permission.

A drawback to temporary electric fences is that gaps will occur along their length, allowing deer to crawl through or under the wires without getting shocked. Once deer learn these locations, these fences become ineffective. Because it takes time for deer to locate these gaps, these fences can be used for short-term problems (i.e., those lasting a week or two). Temporary fences work best when the shock is so painful or frightening that considerable time is required before a deer is willing to attempt another fence crossing. Electric fences have been used successfully to keep bears from beehives and food caches, deer and elk out of sunflower fields, and moose out of road ROW (LeBlond et al. 2007; Johnson et al. 2014; Otto and Roloff 2015; Smith et al. 2018).

A variation of a temporary electric fence is called a peanut butter or baited fence (Figure 8.5). Peanut butter is smeared on the electric wire or on strips of aluminum foil attached to the wire (Hygnstrom and Craven 1988). When a deer investigates the fence and touches the baited foil with its nose or tongue, the deer will get a more painful shock than if it brushes against the electrified fence with its fur. Such fences have been used successfully during the summer to reduce deer damage in apple orchards (Porter 1983) and cornfields (Hygnstrom and Craven 1988).

8.3   CAN FENCES REDUCE DEER–VEHICLE COLLISIONS?

DVCs in North America result in over a billion dollars in damage to vehicles, thousands of injured people, and hundreds of human deaths each year (Chapters 2 and 4). To prevent these losses, federal and state transportation departments are willing to spend considerable money to erect a deer-proof fence along roads. These fences are usually 2–3 m high and made of chain-link fencing material. Unfortunately, many government transportation agencies do a better job building a fence than maintaining it. Over time, gaps enlarge between the fence and the ground, allowing deer to crawl through. Falling trees and branches can smash the top of the fence, lowering it enough for deer to jump over it. For this reason, highway fences must be checked and repaired several times a year.

A deer guard is designed to prevent deer from gaining access to a road at sites where other roads or driveways enter the highway. Deer guards are usually built by placing two cattle guards side by side because deer can easily jump across a single cattle guard. These guards reduced the number of deer trying to cross the road by 83%, compared to access roads without deer guards (Allen et al. 2013). Sometimes, fake wildlife guards are painted onto the road; while these do little harm, they also do little good.

The greatest problem with deer-proof fences along highways is that if a deer is trapped inside a highway fence and wanders down the ROW, it may collide with a vehicle. When this happens, the highway department can be liable for the damage because the victim can argue that the fence made the accident inevitable. Highway departments place one-way exits in their fences so that a deer on the highway side of the fence can exit without deer on the outside being able to get inside. The first one-way gates looked like a subway ticket gate with metal bars that open one way but not the other (Figure 8.6). The idea was that deer trying to exit could squeeze through

FIGURE 8.6   An escape gate on a highway fence that should allow deer on the highway side of the fence to exit while preventing deer on the outside from being able to get inside.

Source: Israel Hervas Bengochea, Shutterstock 90705739.

the bars, but the bars would block any deer trying to enter. Unfortunately, ungulates did not perceive these to exit and rarely used them. Deer exits have been constructed by pushing a mound of dirt along the fence on the highway side to create an earthen ramp that deer can climb up, enabling it to jump over the fence. On the fence side, dirt is held back by a retaining wall so that deer on the outside have no ramp to climb.

Roads, and especially those with deer fences, fragment wildlife habitat because animals cannot cross them. This is a particular problem in the western United States and Canada because mule deer, elk, and pronghorn are migratory and have to cross roads at least twice a year as they move between winter and summer ranges (Seidler et al. 2015). For these reasons, highway departments provide wildlife overpasses and underpasses that allow ungulates to cross the road without ever having to step on the ROW (Dodd and Gagnon 2011). As one example, Wyoming Highway 30 separated winter and summer habitat for mule deer, resulting in hundreds of DVCs each year. To address the problem, Wyoming Department Transportation installed box culvert underpasses along a 21-km stretch of this highway and forced deer to use them by erecting continuous deer-proof fences between the culverts. Almost 50,000 mule deer used the underpasses over a 3-year period. Deer acceptability of the underpasses increased over time; ultimately, 92% of deer used the underpasses to cross the highway (Sawyer et al. 2012).

Ungulates are vulnerable to a predator when in a confined space. For this reason, ungulates prefer to use overpasses rather than underpasses, especially when the overpasses are wide and short and provide a clear view of the area on the other side of the road (Gagnon et al. 2011; Simpson et al. 2016). Yet, underpasses are more common than overpasses because they are easier to build and are cheaper; an average underpass costs $400,000 versus more than $2,000,000 for an average overpass (Sawyer et al. 2016). Placing fences along highways encourages ungulates to use overpasses and underpasses, providing the fences are long enough to prevent ungulates from going around the fence (Gulsby et al. 2011; Gagnon et al. 2015; Huijser et al. 2016).

8.4   CAN INVISIBLE FENCES REDUCE WILDLIFE DAMAGE?

A physical fence is a barrier that uses physical objects, such as rails, woven wire, or electric wires, to prevent animals from crossing it. An invisible fence does not rely on anything physical to prevent animals from crossing. The main use of invisible fences is to keep dogs and cats in yards. The pet wears a collar that produces an electric shock or annoying noise when the pet comes near a buried wire or one along the ground that emits a radio frequency. These fences have the advantage that they can be taken down and put up quickly. Rather than using a wire, the collar can also be activated by radio signals emitted by a ground station; by transmitting the radio signals in a beam, a ground station can serve as a linear fence. Collars can even be equipped so that they are activated by GPS coordinates. Collars can also communicate with each other so that one or more collars fire when collared animals get too close to each other. For example, a collared coyote could receive an electrical shock if it came too close to a collared lamb.

Use of invisible fences to manage wildlife is promising, but largely unfulfilled, because the animal must first be captured and fitted with a collar. For this reason, invisible fences are employed mostly with wild animals that have already been captured for some other reason, such as a bear that has been captured after becoming a nuisance. For social species, such as elk or bison, only a few individuals in a herd need to be fitted with a collar (Correll et al. 2008). Social animals learn to avoid dangerous situations or predators by watching the behavior of other animals. If a collared animal is startled or flees after receiving a shock, other animals in the herd often follow suit.

8.5 CAN FENCES KEEP ELEPHANTS OUT OF AGRICULTURAL FIELDS?

Fencing elephants out of fields is a particularly daunting challenge, but that does not stop African farmers from trying. In Kenya, fences were made from growing plants, dried vegetation, wooden poles, and barbed wire, but these were largely ineffective because elephants easily broke through them. Electric fences proved more effective

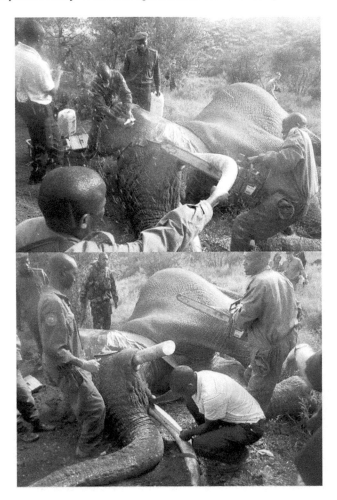

FIGURE 8.7   Kenya wildlife biologists partially detusking problem elephants, so they will stop destroying fences. The tusk is carefully measured to not cut into the nerve.

Source: Photo from Mutinda et al. 2014 and used with permission.

(Sitati et al. 2003, 2005). Despite their general ineffectiveness, fences are popular with elephant conservation organizations because a fence represented a tangible product that could be photographed for funding brochures and annual reports. They were also popular with some villagers because they were effective against zebras, if not elephants.

In Kenya, some individual elephants use their tusks to break fences; these fence-breakers were destroying fences in Kenya an average of once a month: a higher rate than most elephants in the area. Kenya wildlife biologists reduced the ability of these problem elephants to destroy fences by cutting off part of their tusks (Figure 8.7). The procedure removed the elephant's main tool for breaking fences and reduced sixfold the frequency of fences destroyed by problem elephants (Mutinda et al. 2014).

In Sumatra and Africa, villagers dig trenches between forests and their agricultural fields to prevent elephants from raiding crops. The trenches are 2 m deep and wide enough that an elephant cannot step over it and have vertical sides so elephants cannot climb into it. Around Kibale National Park in Uganda, elephant trenches were an effective barrier against elephants and bush pigs, but not baboons (Figure 8.8). The liability of trenches is that they must be maintained, and they sometimes trap elephants in them (Nyhus et al. 2003; Mackenzie and Ahabyona 2012).

Around Nepal's Bardia National Park, local farmers grow crops, which are damaged by elephants, rhinos, buffalo, blue bull, wild boar, and chital. In response, trenches (1.5 m deep and 2.5 m wide) were dug and barbed-wire fences

FIGURE 8.8   An elephant-proof trench.

Source: Catrina Mackenzie and used with permission.

were erected, and living fences of *Euphobia* and *Ipomoea* plants were built. Barb-wired fences and trenches proved effective for one year but usually failed after that because they were too hard to maintain. Living fences were a wall-like structure or thorny plants and were the most effective against elephants and rhino; the plants, nonetheless, take time to grow large and thick enough to be effective (Thapa 2010). One type of living fence built in Africa uses Mauritius thorn bushes planted close together in a row, but MacKenzie and Ahabyona (2012) found that it was not effective in Uganda.

In a novel approach, King et al. (2017) tried to deter elephants from raiding small fields (0.4 ha) by surrounding the fields by a strong wire to which was attached African beehives at 30-m intervals. The wire was designed so that any elephant hitting the wire would disturb several beehives. Most elephants (80%) that raided the village did not break through the fence and enter the protected farm fields. An added benefit was that the farmers were able to harvest the honey.

8.6   CAN FENCES PROTECT LIVESTOCK FROM PREDATORS?

Fences have been used to reduce livestock losses to mammalian predators, including coyotes (Nass and Theade 1988), arctic foxes (Estelle et al. 1996), black bears (Maehr 1982), Asiatic black bears (Huygens and Hayashi 1999), polar bears (Davies and Rockwell 1986), African lions (Weise et al. 2018), badgers (Wilson 1993), skunks (LaGrange et al. 1995), and raccoons (LaGrange et al. 1995). Acorn and Dorrance (1994) interviewed 21 sheep ranchers who used electric fences to reduce coyote predation and found that 17 of them were pleased with their fences and would build another (Sidebar 8.2).

SIDEBAR 8.2 AUSTRALIA'S MONUMENTAL WILDLIFE FENCES

The greatest attempt to reduce wildlife damage by building fences occurred in Australia during the second half of the nineteenth century, when European rabbits were spreading throughout the continent. Fences to stop them were built along the borders of South Australia, New South Wales, and Queensland (Figure 8.9). Subsequently, the governments of Queensland and Western Australia built several parallel fences to stop the range expansion of rabbits. Later, many of the rabbit fences were modified to exclude dingoes. By 1908, there were over 10,000 km of dingo fencing in South Australia. The largest single effort was a dingo-proof fence which stretched for 5,000 km through Queensland, New South Wales, and South Australia.

An interesting question is why such long wildlife fences were built in Australia but not in other countries? The answer lies in the unique landscape of Australia and the nature of its wildlife problems. The topography of Australia is generally flat and the vegetation sparse, making it relatively easy to build long, straight fences. Furthermore, the vast interior of the continent is thinly settled so that fence builders did not have to contend with a multitude of private landowners, who would not want their property bisected by a fence. Moreover,

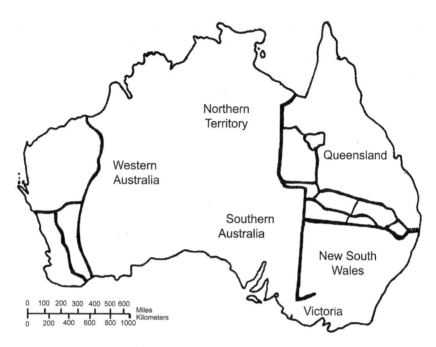

FIGURE 8.9   The wildlife fences (solid lines on map) of Australia in the early 1900s.

Source: This is Figure 13.4 in the first edition of this book.

animals causing problems in Australia, (e.g., rabbits, dingoes, and kangaroos) could be excluded by fencing. Finally, Australians felt a sense of urgency, knowing that once rabbits reached an area, it would be impossible to remove them.

Unfortunately, the long fences in Australia were largely unsuccessful. It was too difficult to maintain such long fences and too easy for rabbits and dingoes to find holes somewhere along them. Furthermore, rabbits were dispersing faster than some fences could be built, and rabbits got around the ends of many fences before they were completed. However, Queensland has had success using fences to exclude dingoes from some livestock areas (McKnight 1969; Allen and Sparkes 2001).

African farmers have used bomas or kraals for centuries to protect their livestock from predators. A boma is a small corral built with poles and acacia plants or other thorny bushes (Figure 8.10). Today, barbwire or electric fences may also surround bomas to add an additional deterrence. Lichtenfeld et al. (2015) fortified 62 traditional bomas with a chain-link fence and fast-growing thorn trees to eliminate any access points for predators. Only two lions penetrated the fortified bomas over a

FIGURE 8.10   Bomas or kraals are used in Africa to confine livestock at night so that predators will be less able to attack them.

Source: Lucian Coman, Shutterstock 1725026707.

period of several months. Ogada et al. (2003) found that the livestock numbers lost
to lions, leopard, cheetahs, and spotted hyenas were reduced when the livestock were
kept in bomas at night. The presence of dogs or people around bomas increased their
effectiveness. Additionally, villagers who used bomas killed fewer predators because
their livestock losses were reduced, creating a win-win situation for both people and
predators. Villagers can build a bomas for $580 (2018 dollars), and bomas prevent a
mean annual loss in livestock of $187. Thus, it takes only three years to recover the
construction costs, which is the functional life of a boma because they deteriorate
with age (Weise et al. 2018).

Hemis National Park is located in India's Himalayan Range of Ladakh. About
1,600 people reside in 16 small settlements that are scattered inside the park. Most
are herders of sheep and goats. These livestock are taken by snow leopards at night.
To reduce the losses, the herders penned their livestock at night inside predator-proof
exclosures (6 × 12 m in size). The exclosures had stonewalls 2.5-m high, and the
roof was made of woven wire. A small door that could be locked provided the only
entrance to the exclosure. During their first year of use, no livestock were killed by
predators (Jackson and Wangchuk 2004).

Game farmers in South Africa employed a combination of electrical fences and
woven-wire fences to keep livestock and game animals inside the farm and predators (e.g., brown hyenas, caracals, and black-backed jackals) outside it. Warthogs
have made this task more difficult by crawling underneath the fences, pushing up the
fences in the process (Swanepoel et al. 2016; Sidebar 8.3).

SIDEBAR 8.3 AUSTRALIA'S NATIVE BULLDOZER, THE BARE-NOSED WOMBAT, IS BAD NEWS FOR FENCES

Bare-nosed wombat have a low center of gravity and great strength. They use both to get under a fence that is blocking their way by using a combination of burrowing beneath a wire fence and using their strength to lift the fence up. This behavior has earned wombats the name "bulldozer of the brush." Unfortunately, their access points are then used by other animals, such as red foxes and swamp wallabies, that cause problems for the farmers who erected the fence to keep out red foxes and wallabies. New South Wales farmers can apply for a permit to kill bare-nosed wombats to maintain the integrity of these fences. As an alternative, Borchard and Wright (2010) developed a heavy, swinging gate that could be placed at wombat access points under fences (Figure 8.11). Wombats had no problem using their low center of gravity to get their heads in the space below the gate and their strength to lift the heavy gate (Figure 8.12). While wombats could push their way through these gates, red foxes and wallabies were unable to lift the heavy door.

FIGURE 8.11   The swinging wombat gate: (1) bushings, (2) steel posts driven in ground, (3) steel tube for added strength, (4, 5) camera and battery pack, (6) woven-wire mesh, (7) log for weight, (8) hemispherical excavation caused by wombats using the gate.

Source: Courtesy of Ian Wright and Human–Wildlife Interactions.

FIGURE 8.12   Photos of wombats using the wombat gate.

Source: Courtesy of Ian Wright and Human–Wildlife Interactions.

8.7   CAN EXCLUSION KEEP NESTS SAFE FROM PREDATORS?

High predation rates on ground-nesting birds and their eggs are a serious problem in many parts of North America. In extreme cases, predation on breeding birds has resulted in extirpation of local populations; more commonly, bird losses contributes to subtle long-term population declines. For example, the puaiohi is an endangered bird restricted to the Hawaiian island of Kauai. Only about 500 birds remain because an exotic species, black rats, consume so many eggs and nestlings (Pitt et al. 2011). Of course, one method of protecting nesting birds is to keep mammalian predators away from them. Puaiohi is a native bird of Hawaii, which nests in cavities that can black rats can easily enter and eat the nestlings. Pitt et al. (2011) developed an artificial nest box that puaiohi can use for nesting but which black rats are unable to enter. There are numerous methods like this that can be used to exclude predators from nest sites.

Elevated nesting structures (e.g., elevated baskets, hay bales, floating platforms) can reduce mammalian predation on duck nests. In the Great Plains, over 80% of mallard nests that were built on structures successfully produced ducklings because raccoons were the only mammalian predator which could reach elevated nests (Bishop and Barratt 1970; Doty et al. 1975). But, raccoons could also be excluded if the support pole was protected with sheet metal or a truncated metal cones that prevent raccoons from being able to reach the nest by climbing up the support pole (Doty et al. 1975). Bailey and Bonter (2017) used data from 24,000 nest records to determine that daily survival rates for eggs in nest boxes increased 7% when predator guards were placed below the nest, keeping predators from climbing up to the nest. These predator guards included stovepipe baffles, cone-type baffles, and entrance-hole extenders. There was an additive effect; nests protected by two or more predator guards had a higher nest success rate than those with one guard.

Fredriksson (2005) used a similar method to stop sun bears from damaging coconut trees; he wrap the tree trucks with sheet metal, preventing bears from climbing them.

Wire-mesh fences built around individual nests have successfully protected nests from predators. Estelle et al. (1996) used wire-mesh fences to exclude Arctic foxes from nests, improving the survival rate of pectoral sandpiper nests in Alaska. Nol and Brooks (1982) used mesh exclosures to exclude gulls from killdeer nests. Raccoons, however, were able to reach the eggs by inserting their paws through the holes in the fences, thus rendering the fences ineffective. In Florida, wire mesh and sheet metal exclosures were used to protect seaside sparrow nests from snakes, rats, and fish crows (Post and Greenlaw 1989). Deblinger et al. (1992) summarized the results of different studies to protect individual piping plover nests and concluded that fences were effective in reducing depredation rates to below 10%. The most successful fences had walls higher than 120 cm, were built of 5 × 5-cm wire mesh, and had the bottom of the fence buried deeper than 10 cm.

Most sea turtles bury their eggs on sandy beaches and then retreat to the ocean. The eggs are then left to hatch on their own, and the baby turtles find their own way back to the sea. Raccoons and ghost crabs are major predators of sea turtle eggs and on some beaches depredate most of them. A method to protect nests is to cover turtle nests with 2 m^2 wire mesh with the edges buried deep in the sand. These meshes hamper raccoons or crabs in digging dig deep enough to reach the eggs. Further, these meshes had 5- × 10-cm holes cut into them so that the baby turtles can escape. Antworth et al. (2006) tested these exclosures on a Florida beach from 1985 through 2003 and found that screened nests had a higher survival rate than unprotected nests. In another study, Ratnaswamy et al. (1997) found that four times as many unscreened sea turtle nests were depredated than screened nests.

In Georgia, 40-ha exclosures designed to exclude mesopredators were tested to determine if they could increase nest success and hatchling survival of gopher tortoises. The fences were built of woven wire and were 1.2-m tall, allowing deer to jump over them. Electric wires were attached to the top, middle, and bottom to prevent predators from climbing over or digging under them. Any predators that made it inside an exclosure were trapped and relocated. Inside the fenced areas, nest success of tortoises was 66% higher and hatchling survival was twice as high as that which occurred outside the fenced areas (Smith et al. 2013). Additionally, deer fawn survival was higher inside the exclosures than outside them (Conner et al. 2016).

8.8 CAN BARRIERS PROTECT INDIVIDUAL TREES FROM HERBIVORES?

During winter, deer often browse the apical meristem (the growing shoot) of trees. Because the meristem contains the bud for the plant's growth in the spring, its loss may have a major impact on the tree's growth. The browsed branch cannot grow until the bud has been replaced. Buds can be protected from browsing by covering them with paper or plastic sleeves, which are called tree guards. These sleeves are open at both ends so that one end can be placed over the shoot, allowing the bud to grow out the other end. These sleeves are often made of biodegradable material and will decompose in a few years.

Deer often browse on tree seedlings, and this can be so severe and persistent that the trees are unable to grow high enough to escape the reach of foraging animals. In such cases, a 30-year-old tree may be less than a meter in height. Long tree guards (1–2 m in length) are used to alleviate this problem by preventing browsing until the tree is tall enough to grow out of the top of the sleeve.

Voles and other small mammals sometimes eat the bark of palatable trees, especially during winter when alternate food supplies are low. Removing all of the bark from around the trunk (i.e., girdling the tree) prevents nutrients from moving between roots and leaves, causing the tree to die. This is a serious problem in fruit orchards, where the loss of a single mature tree has a major effect on an orchard's productivity and may take ten years to replace. A method to protect trees from being girdled is to wrap their trunks with weatherproof cardboard, plastic, or hardware cloth so that small mammals cannot reach the bark. Cylinders designed to encircle tree trunks also can be used for this purpose (Figure 8.13).

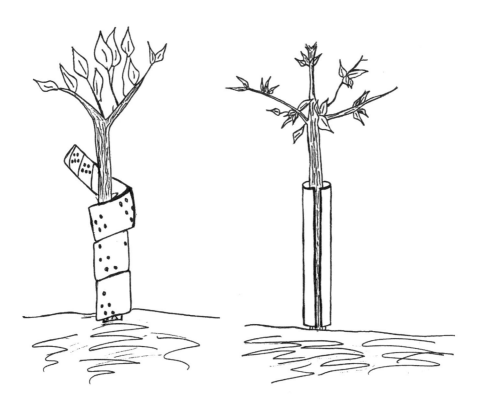

FIGURE 8.13   Wraps and shields to protect tree trunks from girdling by small mammals.

Source: This is Figure 13.14 in the first edition of this book.

8.9   CAN BEAVERS BE STOPPED FROM REBUILDING THEIR DAMS?

Flooding caused by beaver dams can damage roads, homes, agricultural fields, and valuable timber. The short-term solution to these human–wildlife conflicts is to break open the dam and allow the impounded water to escape. But beavers quickly repair breaks, thus requiring dams to be breeched repeatedly. Several exclusionary devices exist that can discourage beavers from rebuilding dams or at least prevent beavers from rebuilding them so quickly.

To prevent beavers from damming culverts, a fence can be constructed around the culvert or by placing a heavy metal grate at both ends of the culvert to exclude beavers. A metal chain is attached to the top of the grate, which allows heavy equipment to lift the grate for cleaning (Taylor and Singleton 2014). A common limitation is that debris will collect along the fence or that beavers may use the fence to build a new dam. Removing these dams is easier than removing those located inside culverts. Debris removal is facilitated if the fence or metal grate is constructed in a way to be easily disassembled for cleaning, such as attaching the fence to posts with metal clips that are easily unfastened. Fencing material should not be placed on the upstream side of the posts or the weight of the water and debris will push the fence panels against the posts with such force that they could not be removed (Figure 8.14).

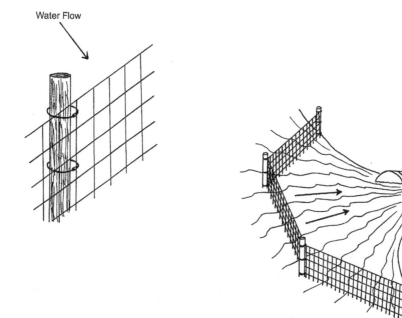

FIGURE 8.14 Keeping beaver from damming up a culvert by building a fence upstream of the culvert, fence panels are attached to the downstream side of the posts with metal clips so the fence panel can be easily removed for cleaning.

Source: This is Figure 13.15 in the first edition of this book.

Another exclusionary method involves the use of water flow devices that allowed beavers to build small dams but not large ones. Beaver locate breaches in their dams by listening for the sound of rushing water and feeling the flow of water around them. Thus, one way to discourage beaver from rebuilding a dam is to place a perforated pipe through the dam leading into the pond. This pipe should have a T-shaped end, with one end of the "T" sticking straight up out of the water and the other facing down. The T-shaped end will force water to flow up through the bottom of the pipe, making it harder for the beaver to dam it, especially if the bottom of the "T" is suspended several feet above the pond's bottom (Figure 8.15). A cleaning rod can be pushed down from the top end of the "T" to clean out any debris lodged inside the bottom end. When the desire is to maintain the beaver pond at a certain level, the outlet pipe should be set at the desired height. This way, water will not flow through the pipe until the water in the pond is above the outlet pipe (Simon 2006).

Another design, the Clemson Beaver Pond Leveler, also uses a perforated pipe, but it is encased in heavy-gauge woven-wire fencing which keeps the beaver from getting close to the perforated pipe (Wood and Woodward 1992). This device works best when the intake pipe is submerged, preventing the beaver from locating and damming underwater breaches. These Levelers have proven successful when used at intermittent and low-flow sites but were less successful in larger streams. Flexible drainage pipes are another option. These pipes are placed upstream from the dam to regulate water flow. The pipes are available in 6-m sections and can be joined together to create a longer section. The end of the pipe needs some sort of filter or fence so that beaver will not block the pipe (Taylor and Singleton 2014).

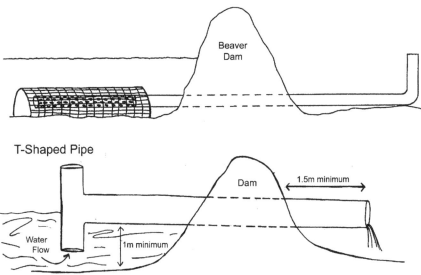

FIGURE 8.15   Using a Clemson Beaver Pond Leveler and a T-shaped pipe to prevent beaver from repairing a dam.

Source: This is Figure 13.16 in the first edition of this book.

8.10   CAN A TRAP-BARRIER SYSTEM REDUCE
RAT DAMAGE IN RICE FIELDS?

Rodent damage in rice fields causes severe economic losses in many parts of the world. A promising method to protect these crops is to use a barrier fence system in which a field is surrounded by a plastic fence. Holes are cut in the fence, through which rodents pass into the field. Every few days, a multiple-capture cage trap is placed on the crop side of the fence so that any rats trying to reach the field by using the hole will now enter the trap instead. This trap-barrier system is easy to build and inexpensive, although labor is required to maintain the fence and check the traps. It is also effective: as many as 6,000 rats have been caught in a single night, and 44,000 were caught in one growing season using a trap barrier around a single field (Singleton et al. 1999). One major advantage of such a system is that the benefits also extend to adjacent fields located outside the fence. For this reason, the trap-barrier system works best as part of a large-scale rodent control program. Another interesting advantage is that ricefield rats are eaten by people of some Asian cultures.

8.11   CAN BIRD DAMAGE BE REDUCED USING
NETTING OR OVERHEAD WIRES?

An effective way to prevent bird damage is to use netting to exclude birds. Unfortunately, netting is one of the most expensive methods of bird control. It costs about $3,000 to erect a bird net over 0.4 ha. The nesting itself can last for five years, but the netting must be erected and taken down each year to avoid damage to the netting from snow or the sun; this takes 30 hours/ha each year. The result is that the yearly cost to cover 0.4 ha is $800 (Dellamono 2006). These costs are for a net placed within 2 m of the ground and supported by poles; this type of netting is suitable for a vineyard or blueberry orchards. But netting would need to be 4 m high for sweet cherries, and this would add considerably to the cost. Due to its expense, netting is used only to protect valuable crops, such as vineyards, blueberry orchards, or aquaculture facilities.

In a simple backyard system, netting can be laid over the fruit trees. This system provides some protection, but birds can still land on the net and reach many berries through the netting. Another drawback is that people and equipment cannot easily work under the draped nets. For this reason, most bird nets are held aloft through the use of support poles that keep the netting above the plants.

A less expensive way to exclude birds is to erect a set of closely spaced wires overhead so that birds have to fly through the wires when landing or taking off. If the wires are close enough together, birds have difficulty flying through them without striking them with their wings. Overhead wires have been used to keep birds from reservoirs (Amling 1980), fish hatcheries (Barlow and Bock 1984), nesting colonies (Morris et al. 1992), public places (Blokpoel and Tessier 1984), and garbage dumps (Laidlaw et al. 1984). Overhead wires are most effective against birds, such as gulls and geese, which have long wings and are not agile fliers. The optimal spacing for parallel wires should be equal to the culprit bird's wingspan. For instance, Andelt and Burnham (1993) found that wires spaced 10 cm apart repelled pigeons, while

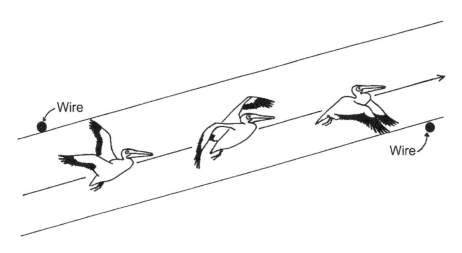

FIGURE 8.16   A bird risks hitting overhead wires with its wings when flying up through a grid or at an angle to parallel lines. That risk is increased if it cannot gain altitude quickly, has a large wing-beat, or if the wires are close together.

Source: This is Figure 13.18 in the first edition of this book.

widely spaced wires did not (Figure 8.16). Parallel lines often work as well as wire grids because birds take off into the wind and cannot always orient themselves to fly parallel to the wire. If parallel lines are used, they should be placed perpendicular to the prevailing winds.

Whether the wires' height above the ground influences their effectiveness is unclear. At present, the height of the wires is usually determined by the most convenient height for the landowners. When birds first take flight, many use their feet to help them gain altitude by jumping. Because of this, their initial ascent (for the first 0.5–1 m) is steeper than their later flight when they can only use their wings to gain altitude. This suggests that overhead wires would be more effective if placed higher than 1 m from the ground, so birds cannot literally jump through them. They also should not be so high that birds taking off can change their flight direction before flying through the wires.

Response to overhead wires varies by species. American robins and European starlings are not deterred by overhead wires, while house sparrows seem particularly bothered by them. Because house sparrows can become nuisances when monopolizing bird feeders, one unique solution is to place wires above feeders where house sparrows are unwanted (Auguero et al. 1991; Kessler et al. 1994).

8.12   CAN RAPTORS AND CORVIDS BE KEPT AWAY FROM POWER LINES?

The placement of power line poles in treeless habitat can adversely affect native wildlife; the poles provide an elevated hunting perch for crows or raptors, which, in turn, allow avian predators to hunt in areas that formerly were unavailable to them.

Unfortunately, commercially available perch deterrents did not stop these birds from perching on distribution line poles or on high-voltage towers (Lammers and Collopy 2007; Prather and Messmer 2010). More success was achieved in preventing birds from building nests on the horizontal beams of high-voltage towers. Dwyer et al. (2015) attached sheet metal at an angle to these beams. When crows started to build their nests, the nesting material would slide off the slick, angled surface, preventing the building of a nest. This innovative approach reduced nesting from 40% on untreated towers to only 2% on treated ones.

Power lines themselves cause problems when birds fly into them and are killed. This is particularly a problem when power lines cross waterbodies. One popular approach to mitigate this problem is to attach devices to the power lines, making them more visible. To determine their effectiveness, Sporer et al. (2013) compared the number of bird carcasses under power lines where these devices were attached to other power lines that were unprotected. The scientists determined that these devices decreased bird fatalities by 29%. Likewise, Barrientos et al. (2012) reported a 10% decrease in avian fatalities after wire markers were deployed.

8.13   CAN NUISANCE ANIMALS BE KEPT OUT OF TRASH?

Black bears often move into towns or parks in search of trash cans containing discarded food. Once in these areas, these bears become a nuisance and a potential threat to human safety and property. As a result, nuisance bears often have to be relocated or killed (Lackey et al. 2018). Johnson et al. (2018) distributed 1,100 bear-proof trash containers free of charge to people in Durango, Colorado, and increased education about bears and enforcement of the city's ordinances concerning bears. The bear-proof container had two latches on the lid, and bears were unable to open it when both latches were locked shut. Bear conflicts were reduced 60% in areas where the containers were distributed versus other parts of Durango. The distribution of bear-proof containers also had an additional benefit of improving residents' perceptions of the city's bear management program and state wildlife agencies.

In suburban areas, Canada geese can become a nuisance in parks, especially during the summer molt. In Cokeville, Tennessee, molting geese in one park were herded to a closed section of the park that was surrounded by a fence, so the flightless birds could not escape. The captive geese were fed corn and allowed to eat the grass in the closed section. Once the geese finished their molt, they simply flew away. This approach turned out to be a cost-effective method of resolving problems caused by molting geese (Mills and Combs 2018).

8.14   CAN BUILDINGS BE MADE WILDLIFE PROOF?

Animals often become a nuisance and health hazard when they get inside buildings. Usually, the best way to correct this problem is to determine how the animals are entering the building and then seal up the opening. This often involves nothing more than capping a chimney, caulking a window, or boarding up a hole in the wall. This is best achieved when the animals are outside the house, rather than trapping them inside. Moreover, adults should not be excluded during the period when they may have young in the building, less the young die there. When it is impossible to observe the comings and goings of animals and to know when they are all outside, a device can be installed, such as a one-way door or a check valve, which will allow animals to leave the building but not to return (Sidebar 8.4).

SIDEBAR 8.4 WHEN THE SOLUTION TO BATS ROOSTING IN BUILDINGS IS TO EXCLUDE PEOPLE

National parks are managed for multiple objectives, such as maintaining its historic resources and keeping visitors safe. The Great Smoky National Park has a number of historical structures, including many on the U.S. National Registry of Historical Places (Figure 8.17). Many of these old buildings are popular with

FIGURE 8.17   Many historical buildings in Great Smoky Mountain National Park are used by bats for roosting.

Source: U.S. National Park Service Digital Image Archives.

tourists and also with eight bat species that roost inside them. Seven of the bat species are known to be infected by WNV, which also infects humans. Park administration took a unique approach to reducing the danger of people being infected by the bats, restricting public access to historic structures during the summer when bats were using them (Fagan et al. 2018).

Birds can cause nuisance problems and health hazards due to their fecal material when roosting or nesting on ledges outside buildings, in aircraft hangers, under bridges, or in barns. To keep birds off ledges, the top of the ledge can be changed from a flat surface to a surface pitched at an angle greater than 45° (Figure 8.18). Another approach is to install porcupine wire on top of the ledges. Porcupine wire is well named: it is a tape consisting of hundreds of metal wires that stick up 10–20 cm at all angles. When these wires are longer than the birds' legs, the birds cannot alight, sit, or walk on ledges with porcupine wire. Bird coils look like giant springs and function much like porcupine wire when installed on ledges. However, some birds will build their nests on porcupine wire and bird coils.

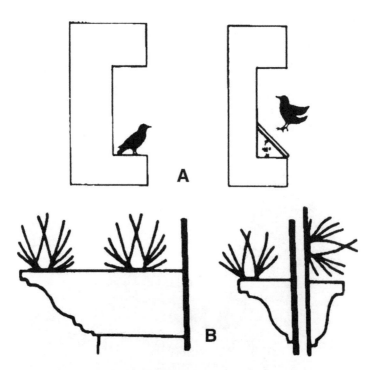

FIGURE 8.18 Birds can be kept off ledges and electrical poles by (a) changing the upper surface to a 45° angle or (b) by installing porcupine wire.

Source: Scott Hygnstrom and used with permission.

8.15   WHAT ARE THE LIMITATIONS OF USING EXCLUSION?

Exclusion, obviously, can be expensive. Matchett et al. (2013) erected 8 km of electric fencing to exclude coyotes from 108 ha of prairie dog colonies, where 2 female black-footed ferrets and 12 young were living. The fencing consisted of nine horizontal wires that alternately charged positive and negative so that a predator would be shocked when it pushed its face or body through the net. The wires were spaced 10-cm apart; this allowed prairie dogs and ferrets to past through the netting without being shocked but not coyotes or badgers. The fencing was effective in reducing coyote activity inside the exclosure and increased ferret survival. But the fence was expensive, costing \$4,464/km to build and \$641/km to maintain for 68 days. The estimated cost to save one ferret young was \$4,500. Such a cost is justifiable to save an endangered species, such as black-footed ferrets, but for few other uses (Sidebar 8.5).

SIDEBAR 8.5 A LESS EXPENSE WOVEN-WIRE FENCE

It is less expensive to make a woven-wire fence out of plastic than metal (Figure 8.19). When a cornfield had a woodlot on only one side, Hildreth et al. (2012) found that placing a plastic fence on just the side of the cornfield with

FIGURE 8.19   A fence made of polypropylene and used to exclude white-tailed deer from a cornfield by placing it between the cornfield and the one side of the field adjacent to a woodlot. The fence extended 50 m past the end of the woodlot to make it harder for deer to just walk around the end of the fence.

Source: Aaron Hildreth and used with permission.

wings of the fence extending an additional 50 m on each side reduced the proportion of corn ears damaged by deer from 20% to 4%. The wings were designed to make it harder for deer to walk around the fence, and they were effective in doing this. Averaged over an estimated life expectancy of ten years, it costs $1.62/m/year to buy the fence, including the labor cost to erect it and remove it each year. The fence was cost-effective and resulted in a savings of $205/ha/year in damaged corn compared with the cost incurred in damaged fields without fences.

Another issue with exclusion is that excluded animals have to go somewhere and that may be to a neighbor's property. I saw this problem on Cutler Reservoir in Utah. The reservoir in the summer has a population of several hundred Canada geese, composed of broods and their parents which stay together as a large flock for protection. There is not much to eat except alfalfa along the reservoir banks, and the goose flock would select the one that was easiest to walk from the water. The farmer whose alfalfa was being browsed by the geese could easily solve the problem by putting up a chicken wire fence, which worked because the chicks could not fly and their parents would not leave them. Once their favorite field was fenced off, the geese would pick the adjacent alfalfa field for lunch, resulting in the farmer of that field also fencing off his field. This continued until most of the fields were fenced. This reduced damage in the fenced fields, but the goose flock always found some other alfalfa field to forage. Thus, total losses to alfalfa farms bordering Cutler Reservoir did not decrease. Yet in the end, farmers had to erect and maintain fences for little overall gain.

A benefit of fences is that they can save wildlife from retaliatory killings by people upset by the wildlife damage. This is an especially difficult problem in Africa when large herbivores and predators leave wildlife reserves to forage. Packer et al. (2013) examined lion densities in 42 protected areas scattered across 11 countries. Lion densities inside unfenced reserves were at half of their estimated carrying capacities while lion densities in fenced reserves were at 85%.

8.16 SUMMARY

Excluding wildlife through the use of fences or netting is one of the most effective methods to eliminate problems with wildlife. Unfortunately, building a fence to enclose a field or using a bird-proof net is very expensive and not economically justified unless the crop is of high value or the problem is particularly serious (deer–automobile collisions). Animals can be excluded by many techniques, which differ in cost, life expectancy, and effectiveness. For instance, birds can be excluded by a complete netting system or with overhead wires. Deer can be excluded with a single-wire peanut butter fence, an electric fence, a wire-mesh fence, or a chain-link fence. Exclusionary devices can also be used for many different problems, such as protecting nesting birds from predators, stopping mammals from gnawing trees, preventing beaver from rebuilding their dams, or keeping wildlife out of buildings. Fences, nets, and other exclusionary devices are most appropriate when effectiveness is more important than cost and when the wildlife problem is expected to persist at the same place for several years.

8.17   DISCUSSION QUESTIONS

1. Exclusion is one of the most effective methods to mitigate human–wildlife conflicts. Why then is it not employed more frequently?
2. What are some methods that can be used to make fences species specific so that they can exclude problem species while allowing other wildlife species to pass through them?
3. A problem with erecting predator-proof fencing to protect turtles or shorebirds that nest along beaches is that they attract the attention of beach goers, who then scare away the nesting birds. If you were the manager of a state park, how would you try to solve this human–wildlife conflict so that both humans and wildlife can coexist on the same beach?
4. The peanut butter electric fence consists of hanging stripes of aluminum foil smeared with peanut butter on an electrified wire. The fence is designed to give deer a powerful shock when they contact the stripes with their tongue or nose. Would you argue that this should be made illegal because it provides a cruel and unusual punishment?
5. Can you design an original bird feeder that can exclude squirrels or a beehive that is bear proof?

LITERATURE CITED

Acorn, R. J., and M. J. Dorrance. 1994. An evaluation of anti-coyote electric fences. *Proceedings of the Vertebrate Pest Conference* 16:45–50.

Allen, L. R., and E. C. Sparkes. 2001. The effect of dingo control on sheep and beef cattle in Queensland. *Journal of Applied Ecology* 38:76–87.

Allen, T. D., M. P. Huijser, and D. W. Willey. 2013. Effectiveness of wildlife guards at access roads. *Wildlife Society Bulletin* 37:402–408.

Amling, W. 1980. Exclusion of gulls from reservoirs in Orange County, California. *Proceedings of the Vertebrate Pest Conference* 9:29–30.

Andelt, W. F., and K. P. Burnham. 1993. Effectiveness of nylon lines for deterring rock doves from landing on ledges. *Wildlife Society Bulletin* 21:451–456.

Antworth, R. L., D. A. Pike, and J. C. Stiner. 2006. Nesting ecology, current status, and conservation of sea turtles on an uninhabited beach in Florida, USA. *Biological Conservation* 130:10–15.

Auguero, D. A., R. J. Johnson, and K. M. Eskridge. 1991. Monofilament lines repel house sparrows from feeding sites. *Wildlife Society Bulletin* 19:416–422.

Bailey, R. L., and D. N. Bonter. 2017. Predator guards on nest boxes improve nesting success of birds. *Wildlife Society Bulletin* 41:434–441.

Barlow, C. G., and K. Bock. 1984. Predation of fish in farm dams by cormorants, *Phalacrocorax* spp. *Australian Wildlife Research* 11:559–566.

Barrientos, R., C. Ponce, C. Palacín, C. A. Martín, B. Martín, and J. C. Alonso. 2012. Wire marking results in a small but significant reduction in avian mortality at power lines: a BACI designed study. *PLoS One* 7(3):e32569.

Bishop, R. A., and R. Barratt. 1970. Use of artificial nest baskets by mallards. *Journal of Wildlife Management* 34:734–738.

Blokpoel, H., and G. D. Tessier. 1984. Overhead wires and monofilament lines exclude ring-billed gulls from public places. *Wildlife Society Bulletin* 12:55–58.

Borchard, P., and I. A. Wright. 2010. Bulldozers and blueberries: managing fence damage by bare-nosed wombats at the agricultural – riparian interface. *Human-Wildlife Interactions* 4:247–256.

Conner, L. M., M. J. Cherry, B. T. Rutledge, C. H. Killmaster, G. Morris, and L. L. Smith. 2016. Predator exclusion as a management option for increasing white-tailed deer recruitment. *Journal of Wildlife Management* 80:162–170.

Correll, N., M. Schwager, and D. Rus. 2008. Social control of herd animals by integration of artificially controlled congeners. Pages 437–446 *in International conference on simulation of adaptive behavior*. Springer, Berlin, Heidelberg, Germany.

Davies, J. C., and R. F. Rockwell. 1986. An electric fence to deter polar bears. *Wildlife Society Bulletin* 14:406–409.

Deblinger, R. D., J. J. Vaske, and D. W. Rimmer. 1992. An evaluation of different predator exclosures used to protect Atlantic coast piping plover nests. *Wildlife Society Bulletin* 20:274–279.

Dellamono, F. 2006. Controlling birds with netting: blueberries, cherries and grapes. *New York Fruit Quarterly* 14:3–5.

Dodd, N. L., and J. W. Gagnon. 2011. Influence of underpasses and traffic on white-tailed deer highway permeability. *Wildlife Society Bulletin* 35:270–281.

Doty, H. A., F. B. Lee, and A. D. Kruse. 1975. Use of elevated nest baskets by ducks. *Wildlife Society Bulletin* 3:68–73.

Dwyer, J. F., D. L. Leiker, and S. N. King. 2015. Testing nest deterrents for Chihuahuan ravens on H-frame transmission structures. *Wildlife Society Bulletin* 39:603–609.

Estelle, V. B., T. J. Mabee, and A. H. Farmer. 1996. Effectiveness of predator exclosures for pectoral sandpiper nests in Alaska. *Journal of Field Ornithology* 67:447–452.

Fagan, K. E., E. V. Willcox, L. T. Tran, R. F. Bernard, and W. H. Stiver. 2018. Roost selection by bats in buildings, great smoky mountains national parks. *Journal of Wildlife Management* 82:424–434.

Fredriksson, G. 2005. Human – sun bear conflicts in East Kalimantan, Indonesian Borneo. *Ursus* 16:130–138.

Fuller-Perrine, L. D., and M. E. Tobin. 1993. A method for applying and removing bird-exclusion netting in commercial vineyards. *Wildlife Society Bulletin* 21:47–51.

Gagnon, J. W., N. L. Dodd, K. S. Ogren, and R. E. Schweinsbury. 2011. Factors associated with the use of wildlife underpasses and importance of long-term monitoring. *Journal of Wildlife Management* 75:1477–1487.

Gagnon, J. W., C. D. Loberger, S. C. Sprague, K. S. Ogren, S. L. Boe, and R. E. Schweinsburg. 2015. Cost-effective approach to reducing collisions with elk by fencing between existing highway structures. *Human-Wildlife Interactions* 9:248–264.

Gulsby, W. D., D. W. Stull, G. R. Gallagher, D. A. Osborn, R. J. Warren, K. V. Miller, and L. V. Tannenbaum. 2011. Movements and home ranges of white-tailed deer in response to roadside fences. *Wildlife Society Bulletin* 35:282–290.

Hildreth, A. M., S. E. Hygnstrom, E. E. Blankenship, and K. C. VerCauteren. 2012. Use of partially fenced fields to reduce deer damage to corn. *Wildlife Society Bulletin* 36:199–203.

Huijser, M. P., E. R. Fairbank, W. Camel-Means, J. Graham, V. Watson, P. Basting, and D. Becker. 2016. Effectiveness of short sections of wildlife fencing and crossing structures along highways in reducing wildlife – vehicle collisions and providing safe crossing opportunities for large mammals. *Biological Conservation* 197:61–68.

Huygens, O. C., and H. Hayashi. 1999. Using electric fences to reduce Asiatic black bear depredation in Nagano prefecture, Central Japan. *Wildlife Society Bulletin* 27:959–964.

Hygnstrom, S. E., and S. R. Craven. 1988. Electric fences and commercial repellents for reducing deer damage in cornfields. *Wildlife Society Bulletin* 16:291–296.

Hygnstrom, S. E., R. M. Timm, and G. E. Larson. 1994. *Prevention and control of wildlife damage*. University of Nebraska Cooperative Extension, Lincoln, NE.

Jackson, R. M., and R. Wangchuk. 2004. A community-based approach to mitigating livestock depredation by snow leopards. *Human Dimensions of Wildlife* 9:307–315.

Johnson, H. E., J. W. Fischer, M. Hammond, P. D. Dorsey, W. D. Walter, C. Anderson, and K. C. VerCauteren. 2014. Evaluation of techniques to reduce deer and elk damage to agricultural crops. *Wildlife Society Bulletin* 38:358–365.

Johnson, H. E., D. L. Lewis, S. A. Lischka, and S. W. Breck. 2018. Assessing ecological and social outcomes of a bear-proofing experiment. *Journal of Wildlife Management* 82:1102–1114.

Kessler, K. K., R. J. Johnson, and K. M. Eskridge. 1994. Monofilament lines and a hoop device for bird management at backyard feeders. *Wildlife Society Bulletin* 22:461–470.

King, L. E., F. Lala, H. Nzumu, E. Mwambingu, and I. Douglas-Hamilton. 2017. Beehive fences as a multidimensional conflict-mitigation tool for farmers coexisting with elephants. *Conservation Biology* 31:743–752.

Lackey, C. R., S. W. Breck, B. F. Wakeling, and B. White. 2018. Human-bear conflicts: a review of common management practices. *Human-Wildlife Interactions Monograph* 2:1–69.

LaGrange, T. G., J. L. Hansen, R. D. Andrews, A. W. Hancock, and J. M. Kienzler. 1995. Electric fence predator exclosure to enhance duck nesting: a long-term case study in Iowa. *Wildlife Society Bulletin* 23:256–260.

Laidlaw, G. W., H. Blokpoel, V. E. F. Soloman, and M. McLaren. 1984. Gull exclusion. *Proceedings of the Vertebrate Pest Conference* 11:180–182.

Lammers, W. M., and M. W. Collopy. 2007. Effectiveness of avian predator perch deterrents on electric transmission lines. *Journal of Wildlife Management* 71:2752–2758.

Lavelle, M. J., K. C. Vercauteren, T. J. Hefley, G. E. Phillips, S. E. Hygnstrom, D. B. Long, J. W. Fischer, S. R. Swafford, and T. A. Campbell. 2011. Evaluation of fences for containing feral swine under simulated depopulation conditions. *Journal of Wildlife Management* 75:1200–1208.

LeBlond, M., C. Dussault, J. P. Ouellet, M. Poulin, R. Courtois, and J. Fortin. 2007. Electric fencing as a measure to reduce moose – vehicle collisions. *Journal of Wildlife Management* 71:1695–1703.

Lichtenfeld, L. L., C. Trout, and E. L. Kisimir. 2015. Evidence-based conservation: predator proof bomas protect livestock and lions. *Biological Conservation* 24:483–491.

Mackenzie, C. A., and P. Ahabyona. 2012. Elephants in the garden: financial and social costs of crop raiding. *Ecological Economics* 75:72–82.

Maehr, D. S. 1982. Beekeeping enters the solar age. *American Bee Journal* 122:280–281.

Matchett, M. R., S. W. Breck, and J. Callon. 2013. Efficacy of electronet fencing for excluding coyotes: a case study for enhancing production of black-footed ferrets. *Wildlife Society Bulletin* 37:893–900.

McKnight, T. L. 1969. Barrier fencing for vermin control in Australia. *Geographic Review* 59:330–347.

Mills, J. T., and D. L. Combs. 2018. Fencing alleviates nuisance molting goose problems in an urban park in Tennessee. *Human-Wildlife Interactions* 12:212–219.

Morris, R. D., H. Blokpoel, and G. D. Tessier. 1992. Management efforts for the conservation of common tern (*Sterna hirundo*) colonies in the Great Lakes: two case histories. *Biological Conservation* 60:7–14.

Mutinda, M., G. Chenge, F. Gakuya, M. Otiende, P. Omondi, S. Kasiki, R. C. Soriguer, and S. Alasaad. 2014. Detusking fence-breaker elephants as an approach in human-elephant conflict mitigation. *PLoS One* 9(3):e91749. https://doi.org/10.1371/journal.pone.0091749.

Nass, R. D., and J. Theade. 1988. Electric fences for reducing sheep losses to predators. *Journal of Range Management* 41:251–252.

Nol, E., and R. J. Brooks. 1982. Effects of predator exclosures on nesting success of killdeer. *Journal of Field Ornithology* 53:263–268.

Nyhus, P., H. Fischer, F. Madden, and S. Osofsky. 2003. Taking the bite out of wildlife damage: the challenges of wildlife compensation schemes. *Conservation in Practice* 4:37–43.

Ogada, M. O., R. Woodroffe, N. O. Oguge, and L. G. Frank. 2003. Limiting depredation by African carnivores: the role of livestock husbandry. *Conservation Biology* 17:1521–1530.

Osborn, F. V., and G. E. Parker. 2003. Towards an integrated approach for reducing the conflict between elephants and people: a review of current research. *Oryx* 37:80–84.

Otto, T. E., and G. J. Roloff. 2015. Black bear exclusion fences to protect mobile apiaries. *Human-Wildlife Interactions* 9:78–86.

Packer, C., A., Loveridge, S. Canney, T. Caro, S. T. Garnett, et al. 2013. Conserving large carnivores: dollars and fence. *Ecological Letters* 16:635–641. https://doi.org/10.1111/ele.12091.

Pitt, W. C., L. C. Driscoll, and E. A. VanderWerf. 2011. A rat-resistant artificial nest box for cavity-nesting birds. *Human-Wildlife Interactions* 5:100–105.

Poole, D. W., I. G. McKillop, G. Western, P. J. Hancocks, and J. J. Packer. 2002. Effectiveness of an electric fence to reduce badger (*Meles meles*) damage to field crops. *Crop Protection* 21:409–417.

Porter, W. F. 1983. A baited electric fence for controlling deer damage to orchard seedlings. *Wildlife Society Bulletin* 11:325–327.

Post, W., and J. S. Greenlaw. 1989. Metal barriers protect near-ground nests from predators. *Journal of Field Ornithology* 60:102–103.

Pound, J. M., K. H. Lohmeyer, R. B. Davey, L. A. Soliz, and P. U. Olafson. 2012. Excluding feral swine, javelinas, and raccoons from deer bait stations. *Human-Wildlife Interactions* 6:169–177.

Prather, P. R., and T. A. Messmer. 2010. Raptor and corvid response to power distribution line perch deterrents in Utah. *Journal of Wildlife Management* 74:796–800.

Ratnaswamy, M. J., R. J. Warren, M. T. Kramer, and M. D. Adam. 1997. Comparisons of lethal and nonlethal techniques to reduce raccoon depredation of sea turtle nests. *Journal of Wildlife Management* 61:368–376.

Redick, C. H., and D. F. Jacobs. 2020. Mitigation of deer herbivory in temperate hardwood forest regeneration: a meta-analysis of research literature. *Forests* 11(11):1220.

Sawyer, H., C. Lebeau, and T. Hart. 2012. Mitigating roadway impacts to migratory mule deer – a case study with underpasses and continuous fencing. *Wildlife Society Bulletin* 36:492–498.

Sawyer, H., P. A. Rogers, and T. Hart. 2016. Pronghorn and mule deer use of underpasses and overpasses along U. S. Highway 191. *Wildlife Society Bulletin* 40:211–216.

Seidler, R. G., R. A. Long, J. Berger, S. Bergen, and J. P. Beckman. 2015. Identifying impediments to long-distance mammal migrations. *Conservation Biology* 29:99–109.

Simon, L. J. 2006. Solving beaver flooding problems through the use of water flow control devices. *Proceedings of the Vertebrate Pest Conference* 22:174–180.

Simpson, N. O., K. M. Stewart, C. Schroeder, M. Cox, K. Huebner, and T. Wasley. 2016. Overpasses and underpasses: effectiveness of crossing structures for migratory ungulates. *Journal of Wildlife Management* 80:1370–1378.

Singleton, G. R., Sudarmaji, Jumanta, T. Q. Tan, and N. Q. Hung. 1999. Physical control of rats in developing countries. Pages 178–198 *in* G. R. Singleton, L. Hinds, H. Leirs, and Z. Zhang, editors. *Ecologically-based rodent management.* Australian Centre for International Agriculture Research Monograph 59, Canberra, Australia.

Sitati, N. W., M. J. Walpole, and N. Leader-Williams. 2005. Factors affecting susceptibility of farms to crop raiding by African elephants: using a predictive model to mitigate conflict. *Journal of Applied Ecology* 42:1175–1182.

Sitati, N. W., M. J. Walpole, R. J. Smith, and N. Leader-Williams. 2003. Predicting spatial aspects of human-elephant conflict. *Journal of Applied Ecology* 40:667–677.

Smith, L. L., D. A. Steen, L. M. Conner, and J. C. Rutledge. 2013. Effects of predator exclusion on nest and hatchling survival in the gopher tortoise. *Journal of Wildlife Management* 77:352–358.

Smith, T. S., B. G. Hopkins, J. Gookin, and S. M. Thompson. 2018. Portable electric fencing for bear deterrence and conservation. *Human-Wildlife Interactions* 12:309–321.

Songhurst, A., and T. Coulson. 2014. Exploring the effect of spatial autocorrelation when identifying key drivers of wildlife crop-raiding. *Ecology and Evolution* 4:582–593.

Sporer, M. K., J. F. Dwyer, B. D. Gerber, R. E. Harness, and A. K. Pandey. 2013. Marking power lines to reduce avian collisions near the Audubon National Wildlife Refuge, North Dakota. *Wildlife Society Bulletin* 37:796–804.

Stull, D. W., W. D. Gulsby, J. A. Martin, G. J. Angelo, G. R. Gallagher, D. A. Osborn, R. J. Warren, and K. V. Miller. 2011. Comparison of fencing designs for excluding deer from roadways. *Human – Wildlife Interactions* 5:47–57.

Swanepoel, M., A. J. Leslie, and L. C. Hoffman. 2016. Farmers' perceptions of the extra-limital common warthog in the Northern Cape and free State Provinces, South Africa. *Wildlife Society Bulletin* 40:112–121.

Taylor, J. D., and R. D. Singleton. 2014. The evolution of flow devices used to reduce flooding by beavers: a review. *Wildlife Society Bulletin* 38:127–133.

Thapa, S. 2010. Effectiveness of crop protection methods against wildlife damage: a case study of two villages at Bardia National Park, Nepal. *Crop Protection* 29:1297–1304.

Weise, F. J., M. W. Hayward, R. C. Aguirre, M. Tomeletso, P. Gadimang, M. J. Somers, and A. B. Stein. 2018. Size, shape and maintenance matter: a critical appraisal of a global carnivore conflict mitigation strategy-livestock protection kraals in northern Botswana. *Biological Conservation* 225:88–97.

Wilson, C. G. 1993. Badger damage to growing oats and an assessment of electric fencing as a means of its reduction. *Journal of Zoology* 231:668–675.

Wood, G. W., and L. A. Woodward. 1992. The Clemson beaver pond leveler. *Proceedings of the Annual Conference of Southeastern Association of Fish and Wildlife Agencies* 46:179–182.

9 Diversion

"For most wildlife, food is an important part of a balanced diet."

Adapted from Fran Lebowitz

You should cut the chicken into four pieces because a fox isn't hungry enough to eat six.

Adapted from Yogi Bera

Providing an alternate source of food for the problem animal is one approach to reducing wildlife damage to agriculture by convincing the animal to consume an alternate food in lieu of the agricultural crop. This is a philosophically appealing approach to resolving a human–wildlife conflict because the animal voluntarily changes its behavior when offered a more attractive alternative.

Usually, diversionary feeding programs involve planting an alternate crop in a separate field and encouraging wildlife to use it, or placing food at feeder stations. Many different names have been used for this approach. Unharvested fields used to feed wildlife have been called lure fields, sacrificial fields, diversionary fields, supplemental fields, alternative fields, or decoy fields. In this chapter, I will refer to them as diversionary fields and will refer to the general approach of providing alternate food to wildlife as the use of diversion because this label seems clearest.

In the context of human–wildlife conflicts, diversion is defined as a method to solve a conflict by creating an alternative which diverts the culprit from its damaging behavior or lures it away from the problem site. Government agencies often distribute supplemental food for the benefit of wildlife, especially in the winter, but this differs from diversion due to human motivation. The purpose of supplemental feeding is to increase the health and survival of wildlife species, while the intention of diversion is to reduce wildlife damage. However, the consequences of diversion and supplemental feeding on wildlife are the same.

Humans have been familiar with the concept of diversion for centuries, although not in the context of wildlife damage. In human history, diversion was used to deal with other people. For example, a vanquished tribe could pay a tribute (often money, gold, or other valuable goods) to their stronger opponents to appease them and to avoid being attacked.

One of the earliest examples of diversion to reduce wildlife damage comes from the 1600s: it is summed in a doggerel that goes like this, "One for the mouse, one for the crow, one to rot, and two to grow," which advised American colonial farmers to plant five corn seeds in every hole so that some will sprout even after birds and mammals eat their fill (Figure 9.1; Conover and Conover 1987). As early as 1943, the U.S. government used diversionary fields to divert ducks from commercial rice fields in California (Horn 1949). Before investigating the uses of diversion in wildlife damage management, we need to consider the optimal foraging theory upon which it is based.

DOI: 10.1201/9780429401404-9

FIGURE 9.1   Drawing of a Puritan family by George Henry Boughton, 1885.

Source: Everett Collection, Shutterstock 238058758.

9.1   WHAT IS THE OPTIMAL FORAGING THEORY?

Optimal foraging theory declares that animals that make optimal foraging decisions have a higher probability of surviving and reproducing. Hence, the genes of wise decision-makers will predominate in future generations. The diet a forager selects should depend upon those factors most important to its survival and reproductive success (i.e., to its genetic fitness). In many species, individuals enhance their fitness by increasing their energy intake; these animals seek a high-caloric diet and are called "energy maximizers."

The foraging decisions of other species that are vulnerable to predation while foraging are shaped by the need to forage as quickly as possible and return to a safe place. These animals are "time minimizers." Many birds are time minimizers; they can quickly stuff themselves with food and then retire to a safe place to digest the food. They are able to do this because many birds have an enlarged esophagus (a sack-like organ called the crop) that allows them to store food in it for later digestion.

Herbivores face their own foraging problems. For them, potential food (i.e., vegetation) is abundant, but most of it is of low nutritional value and difficult to digest because it contains cellulose and lignin. Hence, herbivores may search for plants that are more nutritious and easier to digest. Acquiring sufficient protein is another difficult problem for herbivores, especially for pregnant or lactating females. Thus, the foraging decisions of herbivores during certain times of the year is based more on a need for protein than a need for energy.

Large herbivores, such as elk, elephants, and feral horses, have adapted to the problem of low nutritional forage by developing efficient digestive systems capable of handling large volumes of food. Such digestive systems allow the animals to survive on poor-quality food. The optimal foraging strategy for these animals is one of quantity over quality to ensure their digestive systems are full by the end of the foraging effort. Elephants and elk are so large because their size is needed to support the large digestive system required to extract energy from poor-quality food. Other herbivores select a varied diet and will eat small amounts of many different plants, including toxic ones. This practice allows them to acquire needed nutrients without consuming enough of a poisonous plant to become ill.

Some herbivores, such as Canada geese, are selective foragers; their digestive systems are too small to handle large quantities of food. Their foraging strategy is to seek out those plants, or parts of plants (such as shoots and new leaves) which are both nutritious and easily digested, because their food consumption is limited by how fast they can digest what they have already eaten (Conover 1991). Diversion programs intended to resolve human–wildlife conflicts should consider the foraging strategy of the species involved.

9.2 IS LARGE GROUP FORMATION A NATURAL FORM OF DIVERSION?

Many animals avoid predation by congregating in large groups. This defensive strategy reduces the probability of any one individual falling victim to a predator. For example, thousands of seabirds may nest in a single colony, often located on an island, that mammalian predators have difficulty reaching (Figure 9.2). For those few predators able to reach the nesting colony, the large number of gulls and eggs on the island provides a line of defense: satiate the predator with an abundance of food. This is the same strategy (satiate a predator with food) that forms the basis of diversion, except that in the case of nesting gulls, their neighbors' eggs provide the diversionary food.

Why do not all prey use the defensive strategy of congregating in large groups to avoid predation? The answer is that there are three drawbacks with congregating in large groups: (1) being in a large group can interfere with foraging, due to competition for food with other group members; (2) large groups are detrimental to those animals that rely on hiding and/or being cryptic as their primary antipredator strategy; and (3)

FIGURE 9.2   Colony of nesting guillemots at Farne Island, in Northumberland, UK. So many seabirds nest in a single colony that it is unlikely that any particular nest will be depredated when a predator invades the colony.

Source: Simon Guettier, Shutterstock 1444008557.

predators may respond to the aggregation of prey by congregating around the prey; if predators do this, the preys' strategy of concentration loses its effectiveness (e.g., the main threat to schools of small fish are schools of predatory fish). This suggests that a major limitation to diversion in resolving human–wildlife conflicts is that the problem animals may congregate in large numbers in response and overwhelm the diversionary food supply. For this reason, diversion will be more successful for those species that are territorial or solitary and less unsuccessful for those species which normally travel in groups. Thus, diversion may be an option to protect a blueberry field from territorial mockingbirds, but not from juvenile starlings, which flock in the hundreds or thousands.

9.3   CAN DIVERSION MITIGATE WILDLIFE DAMAGE TO AGRICULTURE?

Diversion has been used mostly by government agencies in response to complaints of agricultural crops being eaten by wildlife populations that have increased as a result of government action. Many U.S. wildlife refuges were established in the twentieth century to provide secure loafing and roosting areas for waterfowl and consist mainly of wetlands and open water. These refuges were successful in increasing local waterfowl populations, which, in turn, caused other problems because ducks and geese foraged outside the refuges. Local farmers became angry when their crops were destroyed, causing conflict between farmers and refuge managers. In the Prairie Potholes region where many North American ducks nest, an anti-duck sentiment developed in the 1950s, and farmers threatened to take matters into their own hands. The Souris Duck Control Association advocated the reduction of waterfowl populations, duck sterilization, the drainage of wetlands, and compensating farmers for crop damage (Fairaizl and Pfeifer 1987). Because the mandate of the U.S. Fish and Wildlife Service was to increase wildlife populations, these complaints created an awkward situation for the agency. The U.S. Fish and Wildlife Service responded to farmers' complaints by trying to scare ducks from the farmers' unharvested grain fields, but the effort failed because alternative food sources for the ducks were lacking. Instead, ducks scared from one field just flew to another one. Realizing the problem, the government set up a series of bait stations in the refuges and planted grain fields to serve as a diversion for ducks scared from agricultural fields. The initial results of this program were encouraging, and the program ultimately was expanded to all of North Dakota. It consisted of planting 12-ha fields of barley or wheat and produced an overall benefit-to-cost ratio of 2-to-1 (Fairaizl and Pfeifer 1987; Knittle and Porter 1988).

In addition to diverting ducks, some refuges in North Dakota planted sunflower fields on idle ground to reduce blackbird depredation in commercial sunflower fields. Blackbird use of these diversionary fields was heavy, and the diversion was successful in reducing damage in nearby sunflower fields (Cummings et al. 1987). In California, waterfowl damage in commercial rice fields near refuges was reduced by renting a rice field that was left to the birds as a diversion.

Diversion has been used to reduce crop damage by ungulates. In one imaginative program, the Utah Division of Wildlife Resources purchased Hardware Ranch. This ranch had historically been a source of friction for the Division, and local farmers did not like elk eating all their hay. The Division began to manage Hardware Ranch for the benefit of elk, and this ranch became a winter home for local elk. This reduced elk damage in the rest of the county and created a popular tourist attraction where people now come to view the large elk herd (Figure 9.3).

The North Dakota Game and Fish Department planted diversionary crops in their WPAs to reduce white-tailed deer damage on farms around them. Lone Tree WPA, planted 40 food plots (each 6–31 ha) annually with sunflowers and corn. In response, deer damage to local farms was reduced, but deer densities within the WPA increased, creating a new concern (Smith et al. 2007).

Diversionary feeding efforts are not always successful. When diversionary sunflower fields were established close to blackbird roosts to divert the birds from commercial sunflower fields, the cost of the program was twice as high as the benefits (Linz et al. 2015). The scientists believed that the program might have been less expensive if the diversionary sunflower fields had been planted inside the refuge to avoid having to pay rent for the land.

In Spain, rabbit herbivory can reduce yields of vineyards by 20%. Barrio et al. (2010) tested if placing fresh alfalfa inside the vineyard would reduce damage to the grape vines. The alfalfa reduced the evidence of rabbit damage but had no impact of grape yields. Rabbit damage also decreased when the ground cover inside a vineyard had a diversity of herbaceous plant species, suggesting that efforts to manipulate the ground cover may be beneficial.

FIGURE 9.3   Utah's Hardware Range is now managed for the benefit of elk and has become a popular tourist attraction.

Source: Shiningkey, Shutterstock 1720188295.

Japanese macaques around Ôito, Japan, were raiding farmers' crops (Figure 9.4). In response, the city started a diversionary feeding program in a park with the dual aims of helping local farmers and creating an opportunity for people to view the free-ranging macaques at an open-range visitor attraction. The city's plan was a remarkable success for promoting tourism. Macaques traveled from the forest to the park daily, and the park became popular as the place to view free-ranging macaques. But the diversion was unsuccessful in protecting farmers' crops. Instead, $80,000 was paid out in compensation for crop damage (Knight 2017).

Elephants, brush pigs, and baboons raid the crops of villagers living near Kibale National Park, Uganda, and damage is consistently higher in fields adjacent to the park than those further away. There is an odd use of diversionary crops around Kibale National Park, Uganda. Most villagers are members of the Batoro tribe, and they have the power to assign fields to different farmers. Their custom is to allocate immigrant farmers (usually members of the Bakiga tribe) the land closer to the park. In doing so, Bakiga farms serve as a buffer from crop-raiding wildlife coming from the national park for their Batoro neighbors. Bakiga farmers may like this idea, but I suspect that Bakiga farmers do not view this diversionary practice favorably (MacKenzie and Ahabyona 2012).

Several efforts have been made to reduce livestock losses to predators by placing out carcasses as an alternative source of food, but most have been unsuccessful in

FIGURE 9.4   A family of Japanese macaques, which also are called snow monkeys.

Source: Tetyana Dotsenko, Shutterstock 766929109.

stopping the killing of livestock. In Slovenia, distributing carcasses and corn did not reduce the number of sheep killed by brown bears (Kavčič et al. 2013). A diversionary feeding program was tested in Canada to protect caribou calves from predators (Sidebar 9.1).

SIDEBAR 9.1 CAN DIVERSION SAVE CARIBOU CALVES FROM PREDATORS?

Woodland caribou populations in Newfoundland, Canada, declined from 94,000 in 1996 to 32,000 in 2013, primarily because black bears and coyotes killed many caribou calves. To save the caribou, the province conducted a massive experiment to determine if diversionary feeding could reduce the problem. Lewis et al. (2017) followed 536 radio-tagged calves located in four areas scattered across the province (Figure 9.5). For the first two years, none of the areas were treated, but in the third and fourth years, diversionary food was distributed by placing 500-kg bags of bakery waste at 25 bait stations scattered in one area. The scientists replenished food as needed so that predators would have an unlimited amount of food. Additionally, six beaver carcasses, each weighing 5–20 kg, were placed in the treated area and also replenished as needed. Bait sites were so remote that helicopters had to be used to fly the food to them. Baits were distributed a week before the start of

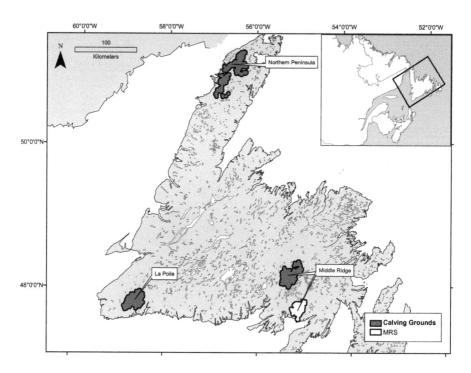

FIGURE 9.5 Map of Newfoundland, Canada showing the study sites in white and calving grounds in dark gray.

Source: Keith Lewis and used with permission.

the calving season and continued until mid-July when most of the surviving calves had left the calving areas. Despite this effort, total calf mortality and depredation rates were similar before and after the use of diversionary food and exceeded 75%.

9.4   CAN DIVERSION REDUCE WILDLIFE DAMAGE TO TIMBER?

Diversion has been used successfully to mitigate wildlife damage to the timber industry. One problem occurred when forest clear-cuts were restocked with trees. Initially, restocking was accomplished by spreading seeds of desirable tree species over the clear-cut, but this approach often failed because too many seeds were consumed by birds and small mammals. Sullivan and Sullivan (1982*a*) were able to increase lodgepole pine seed survival fourfold by spreading sunflower seeds with the pine seeds at a ratio of two sunflower seeds to each pine seed.

In the spring, black bears fed on sugar-rich sapwood of 15- to 30-year-old Douglas fir trees. The injured trees often were killed outright or died as a result of fungi or disease entering through the wounds. This problem was alleviated by providing the bears with alternative food pellets in the spring. The pellets, made from meat meal, bone meal, molasses, sugar beet pulp, and sugar, were more palatable to bears than sapwood but less palatable than berries. By 1996, the Washington Forest Protection Association was trying to save 400,000 ha of trees from 3,000 bears by placing out 225,000 kg of feed annually (Ziegltrum 2008).

Moose herbivory damage stands of young trees in Scandinavia, especially when availability of alternate forage in lacking (Månsson 2009). This suggests that moose herbivory on young tress can be reduced by increasing sources of alternate forage. To test this, Månsson et al. (2010) felled old Scots pines to increase forage close to the ground where moose could reach it. The study revealed that moose browsed heavily on these trees, but it is unknown if this practice reduced damage on young trees.

9.5 CAN WILDLIFE BE PROTECTED THROUGH DIVERSION?

Several attempts have been made to use diversion to protect valuable wildlife. Crabtree and Wolfe (1988) reduced skunk depredation on duck nests in Utah by distributing dead fish during the duck breeding season. Other attempts to use diversion to protect nests have been less successful. In North Dakota, red foxes, skunks, and raccoons depredate most upland-nesting duck nests. To test if diversion might reduce this problem, chicken eggs were distributed weekly at a density of 120/km^2 in five fields with nesting cover while five other nesting cover fields were left untreated. The hypothesis was that predators would stop hunting for duck nests when chicken eggs were abundant and easily found. Despite all of the chicken eggs, the proportion of duck nests that were depredated was similar in the diversionary fields and the untreated fields (Conover et al. 2005).

Difficulties arise when one protected species is depredating another protected species, such as happened when kestrels were eating the chicks of little terns in England. Smart and Amar (2018) examined whether providing nesting Eurasian kestrels with supplemental food (dead mice and poultry chicks) would reduce their depredations of tern chicks. As a control, they provided supplemental food every other year. Depredation rates of tern chicks was cut in half, and tern productivity doubled during those years when supplemental food was provided. Ward and Kennedy (1996) found that providing supplemental food to goshawks during the breeding season increased survival rates of their young, not by reducing starvation, but unexpectedly by reducing depredation rates on the chicks. Apparently, when the parents did not have to spend as much time searching for food, they were able to devote more time to nest defense (Sidebar 9.2).

SIDEBAR 9.2 CAN DIVERSION PREVENT HEN HARRIERS FROM KILLING TOO MANY RED GROUSE?

Hunting red grouse on U.K. heather moorlands is a tradition that goes back centuries (Figure 9.6). Grouse hunting involves a line of men beating the heather to get the grouse to flush and fly over a line of hunters stationed ahead

FIGURE 9.6   A red grouse in its natural habitat of heather and grasses on a moor.

Source: Courtesy, Shutterstock 1195252153).

of them. Hen harriers kill red grouse and can reduce grouse populations during those year when harrier densities are high. A decrease in grouse numbers decreases hunter success, enthusiasm, and ultimately cause an estate to become economically unsustainable as a grouse-hunting moor (Redpath and Thirgood 1997; Thirgood et al. 2000; Thirgood and Redpath 2005). As a result, people have historically killed hen harriers. Hen harriers were protected in the United Kingdom during 1952, and their populations have increased substantially since then. Therein lies the problem. Hunters and landowners believe that the current densities of hen harriers are too high, while harrier enthusiasts disagree.

Diversion has been proposed as a method to alleviate this conflict. Redpath et al. (2001) provided carrion (poultry and white rats) to nesting hen harriers that were feeding their own chicks. These hen harriers delivered an average of one grouse chick every week to their nests. In contrast, unfed hen harriers brought seven grouse chicks to their nests weekly. Surprisingly, the diversionary feeding program did not increase red-grouse density or increase the number of grouse available in the fall to hunters. Instead, other forms of mortality reduced grouse numbers and controlled grouse populations (Thompson et al. 2009).

9.6 CAN DIVERSION BE USED TO REDUCE UNGULATE–VEHICLE COLLISIONS?

To prevent moose–train collisions in Norway, a decision was made to keep moose away from a railroad in the center of the valley by stocking food plots in side canyons. Each food plot was baited with approximately 3,000 kg of hay bales each winter. Sections of railroads with the food plots had half the number of moose–railroad collisions that occurred previously (Andreassen et al. 2005).

Wood and Wolfe (1988) reduced the number of deer located beside Utah's highways and the number of DVCs by providing the deer with food located away from the highways. In contrast, Peterson and Messmer (2011) provided supplement feed to mule deer during the winter, but fed deer and unfed deer were involved in similar rates of DVCs (Peterson and Messmer 2011).

9.7 CAN HABITAT MODIFICATION BE USED TO CREATE A FOOD DIVERSION?

An indirect approach to diversion is to increase the quantity or quality of native foods. One indication that such an approach may have merit comes from observations that wildlife damage often is more severe when natural food supplies are low. For instance, wolf predation on sheep in Poland was highest during those years when red deer numbers were low, and European lynx depredation on sheep in Norway increased when its main prey, roe deer, was scarce (Gula 2008; Odden et al. 2013). In Uganda, crop raiding by baboons decreased when food in their forests became abundant (Tweheyo et al. 2005). But using native browse as a diversion for agricultural crops or nurseries may not be successful; cultivated plants are more nutritious owing to all of the sunlight, water, and fertilizer they receive. Consequently, cultivated plants are more likely to be browsed by wildlife. One approach is to use herbicide or a mechanical treatment, such as disking, to thin out the native plants in the habitat surrounding the agricultural field or area being reforested to increase the growth rates of native plants. Applying fertilizer to native vegetation may also be effective because ungulates prefer to browse fertilized plants over unfertilized plants. However, when these approaches are used in sagebrush habitat, the environmental benefits are less than the environmental costs, including an increase in nitrogen runoff and exotic plants (Wambolt 2004; Beck et al. 2012; Korfanta et al. 2015).

9.8 HOW DO WILDLIFE RESPOND TO SUPPLEMENTAL FOOD?

Animals respond to supplemental food in several ways, which have the effect of increasing the animal density in the area where the food is provided. The most immediate response to supplemental food is a change in the animal's behavior. Harem size in red deer increased, and females moved into areas where supplemental food was provided (Pérez-González et al. 2010). Providing supplemental food also impacted the migratory behavior of mule deer; deer fed during the winter remained on the wintering grounds longer in the spring than unfed deer; fed deer also returned to the wintering grounds the following year earlier than unfed deer perhaps because fed deer had expectations of high-quality food on the wintering grounds and wanted to reach it (Peterson and Messmer 2007).

Animals utilizing supplemental food will have higher survival and fecundity rates when food is provided for several weeks or months. Over time, this may cause the local population to increase (Newey et al. 2010; Newsome et al. 2015). During a 5-year period when supplemental food was provided to white-tailed deer within a 250-ha enclosure, deer density increased sevenfold to 63 deer/km^2 (Ozoga and Verme 1982). Concomitantly, the deer's dependence on supplemental food increased as native forage became overbrowsed. Compared to years prior to the diversionary feeding program, body growth and physical maturation of deer increased producing a higher reproduction rate (Ozoga and Verme 1982). In Utah, mule deer were in better body condition in areas where supplemental food was provided during severe winters; this, in turn, resulted in higher survival rates, and the production of more fawns during the following spring (Peterson and Messmer 2007). Likewise, feral hogs that had access to supplemental food increased their body condition and reproduction (Cellina 2008).

In a meta-analysis, Newsome et al. (2015) found that when large predators were provided foods (usually cattle carcasses), the predators' survival rate, fecundity, home ranges, and diet changed. Black bears that had access to anthropogenic foods had body masses 40% greater than other bears and home ranges half the size of unfed bears (Massé et al. 2014). A single feeder station has the potential to attract and feed several bears; the increased bear density may exceed the cultural carrying capacity of the local area. Therefore, the scientist recommended that feeder station be at least 11 km away from sites where human–bear conflicts might occur (e.g., campgrounds).

9.9   WHAT PROBLEMS ARISE WITH DIVERSIONARY FEEDING OF WILDLIFE?

As noted previously, animals tend to congregate near food supplies by making behavioral changes in home ranges and time budgets. These behavioral changes are welcomed because they must occur if the diversion is going to resolve a human–wildlife conflict elsewhere; nonetheless, concentrating animals near supplement feeding sites can cause problems there. When food was distributed for white-tailed deer in Texas, deer browsing on seedlings intensified near feeders (Cooper et al. 2006). Landowners in Norway fed moose to lure them away from highways and newly planted forest plots, but the feeders concentrated moose and their damage around the feeders (Gundersen et al. 2004). In some areas, food plots were baited with corn, fodder, grain, and beets all year long. The plots were placed in glades located in the middle of forest and attracted several omnivores, including ravens, Eurasian jays, feral hogs, and brown bear. Because of these omnivores, depredation rates on bird nests were higher near these food plots than elsewhere (Selva et al. 2014). Likewise, when a concentrated source of supplemental food, such as a large carcass, was available to predators and scavengers, the success rate of ground nests near the carcass decreased (Cortés-Avizanda et al. 2009).

In the long run, increasing populations constitute a major drawback to the use of diversion to mitigate a human–wildlife conflict. Because of this, effectiveness of a diversion will wane over the years. For this reason, the use of diversion is best suited for short-term problems or those that do not occur on a yearly or regular basis. Diversion may be an excellent way to prevent birds from eating tree seeds that have been distributed to restock a forest clear-cut. In this situation, the seeds only need to be protected for the short period of time before germinating. Moreover, many years will pass before the new trees are harvested and the site has to be reseeded, rendering any temporary increases in seed-eating animals of little consequence.

Another problem with diversion is that animals may become dependent on the food. Once a diversion program ends, the animals may take a long time to disperse or may return in subsequent years expecting food to be provided. Therefore, a considerable period may be required before wildlife numbers return to their original levels. For instance, Douglas squirrel populations that received supplemental food took three months to return to normal levels once the feeding ceased (Sullivan and Sullivan 1982b). Red squirrel populations were still twice as high in plots where food had been provided than in untreated plots one year after a food diversion program ended (Sullivan 1990). After the diversionary food is removed, wildlife damage will be worse than before the diversion because more animals will be present and hungrier.

Diversionary feeding may increase the risk of disease spreading among the animals concentrated at the feeding site (Castillo et al. 2011; Milner et al. 2014). For example, Cross et al. (2013) found that the contact rates among adult female elk were more than twice as high at feeding sites as elsewhere, and this enhanced the direct and indirect transmission of infectious diseases (Creech et al. 2012; Campbell et al. 2013). At feeding sites, contact rates with infectious material in the environment, including feces, aborted fetuses, and prions, are high, causing an increase in bovine tuberculosis and chronic wasting disease (Miller et al. 2003; Creech et al. 2012).

Schley et al. (2008) reported that diverting feral hogs from agricultural crops was only effective when four conditions existed: (1) wild boar densities are lower than $1.5/km^2$, (2) food is supplied only during a limited period, (3) supplemental food is distributed over a large area, and (4) food is supplied in the forest at least 1 km from the forest edge. The scientists also reported that these four conditions are rarely met; therefore, most attempts at using supplemental feeding to protect crops were rarely successful in Europe, a finding that Geisser and Reyer (2004) found to be true in Switzerland.

9.10   IS DIVERSION COST-EFFECTIVE?

Diversion is usually expensive and labor intensive, raising the question of whether the approach is cost-effective. Unfortunately, few studies on diversion provide information on the cost and monetary benefits resulting from the program. Among those studies that did look at economics, the results are mixed (Massei 2010; Kubasiewicz et al. 2016). When protecting agricultural crops, the cost of a diversionary program can be justified only when high-valued crops or commodities need protection. For instance, a 30-year-old Douglas fir tree has considerable value to a timber company, as does a mature apple tree to an orchardist. The use of diversion to keep bears or voles from killing these trees would be cost-effective. The key variable is that the item needing protection should be several times more valuable than the diversionary item being fed to wildlife. One successful example of diversion was spreading corn to reduce wild hog damage in vineyards because corn is much cheaper than wine grapes. After corn was distributed, the proportion of vineyards experiencing wild hog damage dropped from 63% to 36%, and the amount of damage to grapes in the vineyards declined from 193 kg/ha to 151 kg/ha (Calenge et al. 2004). The cost of the diversionary program (cost of corn and its distribution) was €4,600 in 2003, and the price of grapes saved was €21,400, or better than a 4-to-1 benefit-to-cost ratio.

Under most circumstances, planting a sunflower field to lure birds from other sunflower fields is misguided because little is saved in this process, especially given the risk that the targeted wildlife might not use the diversion field. In these cases, a more effective response is to allow wildlife forage where they will and then compensate the farmers for the grain consumed by the wildlife. In one such program, the federal government offered to purchase the grain in fields where ducks were foraging heavily; these fields then became diversionary fields. Under this program, grain yields in diversionary fields were appraised by an independent crop adjustor, and the value determined by the price paid at the local grain elevator. Adjacent landowners were encouraged to scare birds from their fields toward the diversionary fields. After the adjacent fields were harvested, farmers were allowed to harvest diversionary fields and were paid the difference between the earlier appraised yield and the actual yield. Farmers also were compensated for any reduction in grain quality in diversionary fields (Fairaizl and Pfeifer 1987).

Also reducing the cost-effectiveness of diversion is the consumption of food by nontarget species (e.g., grain placed out to divert waterfowl from farmers' fields may be consumed by blackbirds). Further, if diversion fields are planted, there is the danger that target species may consume the resulting crops either too early or too late to do any good as a diversion. For instance, if an alfalfa field is planted to divert deer from a plant nursery, all of the alfalfa may be eaten early in the fall, long before the deer start browsing in the nurseries during the winter.

A most promising use of diversion, even for low-valued crops, is to protect the seeds from being eaten in a newly planted field. A bushel of genetically improved corn seeds (what farmers plant) may cost $50 while a regular bushel of corn sells for $6. Corn seeds acquire more value once planted because each seed may develop into an ear of corn containing hundreds of corn seeds. Sandhill cranes and American crows feed in newly planted corn fields, where they walk down the rows pulling up the seeds and eating them, leaving large gaps where no corn plants will grow. In this case, diversion is a viable option because a farmer can spread a few bushels of inexpensive corn grain on the ground in newly planted fields. Birds will consume the diversionary corn over the planted seeds because they can find grain lying on the ground much faster than buried seeds. To be successful, this diversion has to work only for the few weeks when the seeds are vulnerable to bird depredation; after the corn seeds sprout, birds will not bother them.

9.11   WHERE SHOULD A FEEDER STATION OR DIVERSIONARY CROP BE LOCATED?

As we discussed earlier, diversionary food will attract wildlife, and it may be unwise to attract them to the area where the vulnerable resource. The problem is that most animals seek a varied diet, and while they may eat mainly the diversionary food, they will still eat other things around them. For this reason, the vegetation around feeding stations usually is heavily browsed, sometimes to the point that there is no vegetation left. Deer primarily forage in apple orchards to eat fallen apples and the ground cover but, while in the orchard, they also may reach up and nip the buds of apple trees. The total biomass of apple buds they consume is low, but the damage to the trees is substantial; loss of these buds can alter the shape and growth rate of apple trees. If feeder stations were placed in an apple orchard to deter deer from eating apple buds, the feeder stations would have the opposite effect as more deer would be lured into the orchard. Sullivan and Sullivan (1988) recognized this problem and recommended not placing diversionary food for voles by the trunks of apple trees because this might attract voles and increase the likelihood that trees would be girdled; instead, they thought diversionary food should be placed away from apple trees.

Another example of this dilemma involves the task of protecting the eggs of nesting ducks from mammalian predators. If diversionary food is distributed in the field where ducks are nesting, the effort may actually cause an increase in nest depredation: the food may attract predators to the field, and while looking for the diversionary food, the predators may find duck nests. One way to visualize this is to consider the effect of a feeder containing an unlimited amount of food for skunks. This feeder causes skunks in its vicinity to shift their home ranges and foraging activities toward it. As a consequence, the skunks' activity in the distant parts of their home ranges is reduced. In doing so, the feeder creates a "halo zone," where skunk densities are reduced because that zone's former skunk residents have vacated it and moved closer to the feeder (Figure 9.7). Diversionary feeders or crops should be located at a distance so that the crop needing protection is within the halo zone created by the diversion.

If diversionary crops and feeder stations should be placed away from the crop that needs protection, then the question is how far? The problem is that if the diversion is placed too far away, then some of the culprit animals will not find or use it because it is outside their home ranges. This happened when a feeder station was created to offer bears an opportunity to find food without having to invade a campground. The only marked bears that continued to enter campgrounds after the diversion were two bears that never found the food plot (Rogers 2011). As the distance between the diversionary food and a campground increases, a higher proportion of the bears feeding on the diversionary food would not normally feed at the campground because the latter is outside their home ranges. In that case, the consumed food provides no benefit. Obviously, diversionary feeders should be located as close as possible to the campground needing protection, but at a distance where the feeders will not concentrate animals near the campground. Identifying this ideal distance is difficult, and it will vary depending upon the size of the

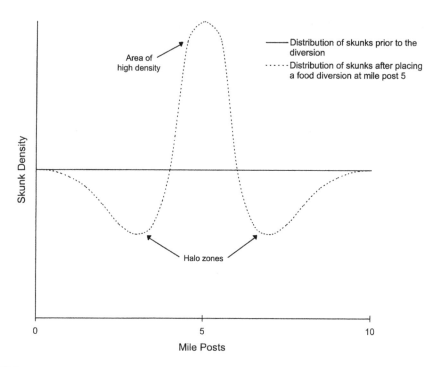

FIGURE 9.7   If a diversionary bait station causes skunks to shift their home ranges toward it and concentrate their foraging there, three zones of skunk density will be created: a zone of high skunk density close to the bait station, a halo zone farther out where the skunk density is reduced, and a zone so far away that the diversion has no effect on skunk behavior.

Source: This is Figure 12.6 in the first edition of this book.

species' home range and its mobility. A good rule of thumb is that a diversionary food should be separated from the item needing protection by a distance equal to one-half of the diameter of that species' home range.

If diversionary feeders or crops are going to be placed away from the crop needing protection, then more than one feeder will be required. Consider Figure 9.8 which depicts a landscape showing the circular and overlapping home ranges of four deer with a field being damaged in the center. If feeder stations are going to be placed away from the field, two would be required so at least one falls within the home range of each deer. Determining where to place the feeder station is easy to solve for those animals which are central-place foragers and radiate out from a single location (often a roost site, den, or colony) to forage. We know from research on the optimal foraging theory that animals attempt to minimize the time and energy required to forage (Sidebar 9.3). For central-place foragers, the diversion should be placed between the resource needing protection and the central place so that the animals can reach the diversion sooner than they can reach the resource (Figure 9.9).

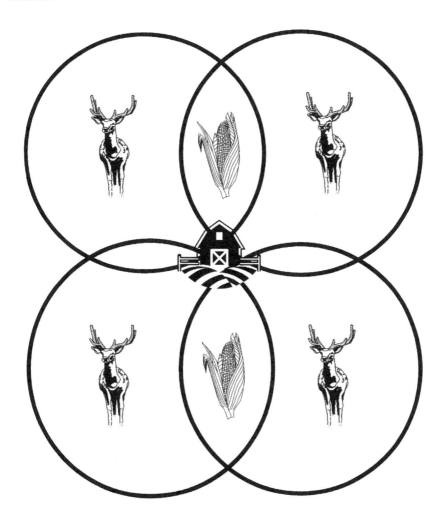

FIGURE 9.8 A hypothetical landscape showing a farm located within the overlapping home ranges of four deer. If bait stations need to be placed away from the farm so as not to attract more deer, a minimum of two bait stations (represented by corn cobs) is required so that all four deer have one within their home range.

Source: This is Figure 12.7 in the first edition of this book.

SIDEBAR 9.3 CAN DIVERSION CONVINCE CORMORANTS TO MOVE THEIR COLONY TO A NEW LOCATION?

Thousands of double-crested cormorants nest on East Sand Island in the Columbia River estuary. From there, they forage on juvenile salmon trying to reach the ocean. Federal, state, and tribal authorities believed that saving the fish was essential, but cormorants are protected by the Migratory Bird Treaty Act.

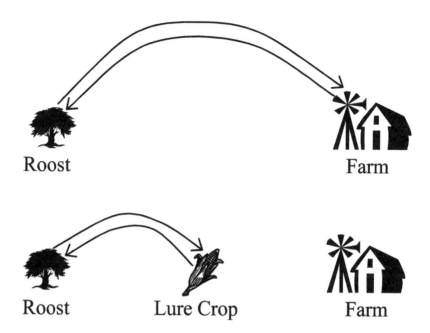

Roost   Farm

Roost   Lure Crop   Farm

FIGURE 9.9   The ideal placement of a diversionary bait station, to protect a crop from a species that is a central-place forager, is between the roost or colony and the crop.

Source: This is Figure 12.8 in the first edition of this book.

Perhaps if the cormorants abandoned their colony and relocated to more remote colony sites where hopefully, the birds would eat something other than salmon smolt. Suzuki et al. (2015) tested this by making habitat improvements at alternate sites that might convince the birds to nest at these alternate sites. The authors enhanced alternate sites by (1) deploying cormorant decoys, (2) broadcasting cormorant vocalizations, (3) moving driftwood to the site similar to those used by nesting cormorants elsewhere, (4) bringing old cormorant nests, and (5) supplying abundant nest material (Figure 9.10). The scientists convinced cormorants to nest in alternate sites on three islands, but not on a fourth island.

9.12   CAN WILDLIFE DAMAGE BE PREDICTED?

To use diversion successfully, wildlife damage must be predictable because diversionary fields have to be planted and diversionary stations established before damage begins. Unfortunately, wildlife damage often varies substantially across years and fields and often cannot be predicted. Because of this, diversion will sometimes be employed in years and places where it is not needed. The opposite problem also occurs. Wildlife may ignore the diversionary fields or bait stations and continue to cause damage. This problem is rather common. In one attempt to use diversion to protect grain fields from ducks, some diversion fields failed to attract any ducks.

As Fairaizl and Pfeifer (1987) stated, "Ducks appear to have their own criteria for feeding site selection and attempts to preselect alternative sites and attract ducks into those fields failed." In my own case, I once tried to divert white-tailed deer from plant nurseries by placing out feeders containing hay and corn as soon as snow was on the ground. However, the experiment failed because no deer ever foraged at my feeders.

9.13 WHICH IS BETTER: DIVERSIONARY CROPS OR FEEDER STATIONS?

Several disadvantages are associated with diversionary crops. Growing them is labor intensive and requires specialized farming equipment. These problems can be overcome by having a local farmer grow the crop in exchange for the right to harvest a proportion of it (usually 50%–66%). Moreover, there may be a great waste of food when diversionary crops are grown, such as food being trampled into the mud by wildlife. There also is the risk that the crop may not be used by any of the intended wildlife. Diversionary crops cannot be created quickly in response to unanticipated wildlife problems, and they cannot be shifted to a new location when needed. For all of these reasons, growing diversionary crops is a risky and inefficient way to feed wildlife.

FIGURE 9.10   A colony enhancement constructed to entice cormorants to move to a new colony. The enhancement included tires filled with nesting material, speakers used to broadcast cormorant calls, and cormorant decoys.

Source: Yasuko Suzuki and used with permission.

Feeder stations, where food will be placed out periodically, are much more efficient (a higher proportion of the food will be consumed by the intended wildlife) and provide more flexibility: they can be easily moved, and the amount of food distributed can be changed daily. Under most circumstances, feeders are more cost-effective than diversionary crops. Several practical problems, however, limit their effectiveness, including the need to distribute food at the feeders regularly. Also, dominate animals may exclude others from the feeders; this was responsible for the failure of one attempt to provide diversionary food to deer (Schmitz 1990).

The consequence of terminating food at a feeder station will be more severe than at a diversionary field. In the latter, animals can observe the depletion of the food and decide when it is time to find an alternative foraging site. In contrast, when food is periodically distributed at a feeder station, animals cannot predict the arrival of food and thus cannot predict when there will be no more food. Hence, animals take longer to abandon a feeder station once it is closed. If this occurs during the harsh conditions of winter, animals may wait too long and starve before abandoning the feeder station. For this reason, the amount of food distributed at a feeder should be slowly decreased over a period of time.

9.14   WHAT IS PREDATOR SWAMPING?

Predator swamping occurs when prey are so abundant that local predators can consume their fill, but most of the prey animals will survive. Ring-billed and California gulls nest together in the thousands on a single island. Sometimes, I have observed a raccoon on a colonial island, and while a single raccoon may destroy dozens of nests, most nests will be successful. Likewise, schools of sardines may contain millions of individuals, and such large schools are only threatened by predators which also occur in large schools or by whales that have such large mouths that they can consume thousands in one swallow.

Predator swamping has been used by wildlife biologists to protect prey from predators, but these efforts are not always successful. Bannister et al. (2016) tried to improve the success of an effort to reintroduce burrowing bettong in South Australia by releasing a large number (1,266) at one time and place. Unfortunately, the large release was no more successful than smaller releases of 50 individuals; in both cases, no introduced bettong survived more than four months.

9.15   CAN DIVERSION BE USED WITH OTHER TECHNIQUES?

Nonlethal techniques to reduce wildlife damage to crops work best when other food sources are available for the wildlife. Diversion can provide this alternate source of food, making other techniques more effective. Hazing or the use of fear-provoking stimuli in fields needing protection can be used to move the wildlife culprits to the diversionary field. Kaplan et al. (2011) tried to keep baboons from foraging in urban areas by creating a feeding station outside of the city but within the baboon troop's home range. The food station consisted of distributing dried corn daily before dawn. Baboons not only quickly started foraging at the feeding station but also continued to forage in local landfills where a plethora of food was available. Success was

FIGURE 9.11   A red-cockaded woodpecker.

Source: Feathercollector, Shuttlestock 128378930.

achieved only when the diversion program was combined with an exclusion program that involved building walls around local landfills to exclude baboons.

Diversion can also be combined with lethal measures. Doing so can potentially overcome the major shortcoming of diversion: the increase in wildlife populations in response to the diversionary food. Philosophically, however, diversion and lethal control are not compatible because of the perception that wildlife managers are luring animals to their deaths or killing animals that otherwise would not have caused problems.

Stopping a diversion program can cause substantially higher levels of damage than when the program was initiated. Using lethal means to reduce quickly the number of culprits may help alleviate this problem. As one example, red-cockaded woodpeckers (an endangered species) will only nest in cavities that it excavates in old pine trees (Figure 9.11). Sometimes, these cavities are usurped by flying squirrels. To keep this from happening, Borgo et al. (2006) used a combination of lethal control of flying squirrels roosting in woodpecker colonies and erecting nest boxes near woodpecker colonies that flying squirrels, but not woodpeckers, were willing to use. The results were successful in decreasing the use of woodpecker cavities by flying squirrels.

9.16 SUMMARY

Diversion is an appealing way to alleviate wildlife damage, but it is not commonly used, owing to its high cost and labor requirements. It works best when high-valued crops need protection and when those crops are not very palatable. A major draw-back with diversion is that wildlife numbers will rise over time, due to an increase in immigration, reproduction, and survival. This problem of increasing wildlife popula-tions will become particularly acute if diversionary food is made available during the winter or whenever natural foods are scarce. Animals also may become dependent upon the food. For these reasons, the amount of food that has to be distributed will increase over time. Stopping a diversion program may cause animals to starve and result in a higher level of damage than what occurred originally. For all of these rea-sons, diversion is most appropriate for problems of a short-term nature.

9.17   DISCUSSION QUESTIONS

1. What are the advantages and disadvantages of using feeder stations or growing a diversionary crop to convince birds to stop foraging at a cherry orchard?
2. Do you think it is ethical to use a diversionary crop to lure wildlife away from a site where they are causing problems and then kill the animals as they eat the diversionary crop?
3. Does a federal wildlife refuge have a responsibility to farmers if geese from the refuge destroy wheat fields planted near the refuge (Figure 9.12)? Does it matter if the wheat fields or the refuge were there first?

FIGURE 9.12   Snow geese feeding in a field.

Source: Ray Hennessy, Shutterstock 1644118027.

4. Elk have been fed for many winters at the National Elk Refuge near Jackson Hole, Wyoming. What effect would this have on elk behavior and their population dynamics?
5. Rather than just providing hay to elk near Jackson Hole, how could a state wildlife agency improve the habitat in the area so that it could support more elk during the winter?

LITERATURE CITED

Andreassen, H. P., H. Gundersen, and T. Storaas. 2005. The effect of scent-marking, forest clearing, and supplemental feeding on moose-train collisions. *Journal of Wildlife Management* 69:1125–1132.

Bannister, H. L., C. E. Lynch, and K. E. Moseby. 2016. Predator swamping and supplementary feeding do not improve reintroduction success for a threatened Australian mammal, *Bettongia lesueur*. *Australian Mammalogy* 38:177–187.

Barrio, I. C., C. G. Bueno, and F. S. Tortosa. 2010. Alternative food and rabbit damage in vineyards of Southern Spain. *Agriculture, Ecosystems and Environment* 138:51–54.

Beck, J. L., J. W. Connelly, and C. L. Wambolt. 2012. Consequences of treating Wyoming big sagebrush to enhance wildlife habitats. *Rangeland Ecology and Management* 65:444–455.

Borgo, J. S., M. R. Conover, and L. M. Conners. 2006. Nest boxes reduce flying squirrel use of red-cockaded woodpecker cavities. *Wildlife Society Bulletin* 34:171–176.

Calenge, C., D. Maillard, P. Fournier, and C. Fouque. 2004. Efficiency of spreading maize in the garrigues to reduce wild boar (*Sus scrofa*) damage to Mediterranean vineyards. *European Journal of Wildlife Research* 50:112–120.

Campbell, T. A., D. B. Long, and S. A. Shriner. 2013. Wildlife contact rates at artificial feeding sites in Texas. *Environmental Management* 51:1187–1193.

Castillo, L., P. Fernández-Llario, C. Mateos, J. Carranza, J. M. Benítez-Medina, W. García-Jiménez, F. Bermejo-Martín, and J. H. de Mendoza. 2011. Management practices and their association with Mycobacterium tuberculosis complex prevalence in red deer populations in Southwestern Spain. *Preventive Veterinary Medicine* 98:58–63.

Cellina, S. 2008. *Effects of supplemental feeding on the body condition and reproductive state of wild boar 'Sus scrofa' in Luxembourg.* Doctoral Dissertation, University of Sussex, Brighton.

Conover, D. O., and M. R. Conover. 1987. Wildlife management in colonial Connecticut and New Haven during their first century: 1636–1736. *Transactions of the Northeast Section of the Wildlife Society* 44:1–7.

Conover, M. R. 1991. Herbivory by Canada geese: diet selection and effect on lawns. *Ecological Applications* 1:231–236.

Conover, M. R., R. L. King, Jr., J. E. Jimenez, and T. A. Messmer. 2005. Evaluation of supplemental feeding to reduce predation of duck nests in North Dakota. *Wildlife Society Bulletin* 33:1330–1334.

Cooper, S. M., M. K. Owns, R. M. Cooper, and T. F. Ginnett. 2006. Effect of supplemental feeding on spatial distribution and browse utilization by white-tailed deer in semi-arid rangeland. *Journal of Arid Environments* 66:716–726.

Cortés-Avizanda, A., M. Carrete, D. Serrano, and J. A. Donázar. 2009. Carcasses increase the probability of predation of ground-nesting birds: a caveat regarding the conservation value of vulture restaurants. *Animal Conservation* 12:85–88.

Crabtree, R. L., and M. L. Wolfe. 1988. Effects of alternate prey on skunk predation of water-fowl nests. *Wildlife Society Bulletin* 16:163–169.

Creech, T. G., P. C. Cross, B. M. Scurlock, E. J. Maichak, J. D. Rogerson, J. C. Henningsen, and S. Creel. 2012. Effects of low-density feeding on elk – fetus contact rates on Wyoming feedgrounds. *Journal of Wildlife Management* 76:877–886.

Cross, P. C., T. G. Creech, M. R. Ebinger, K. Manlove, K. Irvine, J. Henningsen, J. Rogerson, B. M. Scurlock, and S. Creel. 2013. Female elk contacts are neither frequency nor density dependent. *Ecology* 94:2076–2086.

Cummings, J. L., J. L. Guarino, C. E. Knittle, and W. C. Royall, Jr. 1987. Decoy plantings for reducing blackbird damage to nearby commercial sunflower fields. *Crop Protection* 6:56-60.

Fairaizl, S. D., and W. K. Pfeifer. 1987. The lure crop alternative. *Proceedings of the Wildlife Damage Control Workshop* 8:163-168.

Geisser, H., and H. U. Reyer. 2004. Efficacy of hunting, feeding, and fencing to reduce crop damage by wild boars. *Journal of Wildlife Management* 68:939–946.

Gula, R. 2008. Wolf depredation on domestic animals in the Polish Carpathian mountains. *Journal of Wildlife Management* 72:283–289.

Gundersen, H., H. P. Andreassen, and T. Stein Storaas. 2004. Supplemental feeding of migratory moose *Alces*: forest damage at two spatial scales. *Wildlife Biology* 10:213–224.

Horn, E. E. 1949. Waterfowl damage to agricultural crops and its control. *Transactions of the North American Wildlife Conference* 14:577–585.

Kaplan, B. S., M. J. O'Riain, R. van Eeden, and A. J. King. 2011. A low-cost manipulation of food resources reduces spatial overlap between baboons (*Papio ursinus*) and humans in conflict. *International Journal of Primatology* 32:1397–1412.

Kavčič, I., M. Adamič, P. Kaczensk, M. Krofel, and K. Jerina. 2013. Supplemental feeding with carrion is not reducing brown bear depredations on sheep in Slovenia. *Ursus* 24:111–120.

Knight, J. 2017. Commentary: wildlife tourism as crop protection? Double-goal provisioning and the transvaluation of the macaque in postwar Japan. *Human-Wildlife Interactions* 11:217–230.

Knittle, C. E., and R. D. Porter. 1988. Waterfowl damage and control methods in ripening grain: an overview. *U. S. Fish and Wildlife Service Technical Report* 14:6-8.

Korfanta, N. M., M. L. Mobley, and I. C. Burke. 2015. Fertilizing Western rangelands for ungulate conservation: an assessment of benefits and risks. *Wildlife Society Bulletin* 39:1–8.

Kubasiewicz, L. M., N. Bunnefeld, A. I. Tulloch, C. P. Quine, and K. J. Park. 2016. Diversionary feeding: an effective management strategy for conservation conflict? *Biodiversity and Conservation* 25:1–22.

Lewis, K. P., S. E. Gullage, D. A. Fifield, D. H. Jennings, and S. P. Mahoney. 2017. Manipulations of black bear and coyote affect caribou calf survival. *Journal of Wildlife Management* 81:122–132.

Linz, G. M., E. H. Bucher, S. B. Canavelli, E. Rodriguez, and M. L. Avery. 2015. Limitations of population suppression for protecting crops from bird depredation: a review. *Crop Protection* 76:46–52.

Mackenzie, C. A., and P. Ahabyona. 2012. Elephants in the garden: financial and social costs of crop raiding. *Ecological Economics* 75:72–82.

Månsson, J. 2009. Environmental variation and moose *Alces* density as determinants of spatio-temporal heterogeneity in browsing. *Ecography* 32:1–12.

Månsson, J., R. Bergström, A. Pehrson, M. Skoglund, and C. Skarpe. 2010. Felled Scots pine (*Pinus sylvestris*) as supplemental forage for moose (*Alces alces*): browse availability and utilization. *Scandinavian Journal of Forest Research* 25:21–31.

Massé, S., C. Dussault, C. Dussault, and J. Ibarzabal. 2014. How artificial feeding for tourism-watching modifies black bear space use and habitat selection. *Journal of Wildlife Management* 78:1228–1238.

Massei, G., R. J. Quy, J. Gurney, and D. P. Cowan. 2010. Can translocations be used to mitigate human – wildlife conflicts? *Wildlife Research* 37:428–439.

Miller, R., J. B. Kaneene, S. D. Fitzgeral, and S. M. Schmitt. 2003. Evaluation of the influence of supplemental feeding of white-tailed deer (*Odocoileus virginianus*) on the prevalence of bovine tuberculosis in the Michigan wild deer population. *Journal of Wildlife Diseases* 39:84–95.

Milner, J. M., F. M. Van Beest, K. T. Schmidt, R. K. Brook, and T. Storaas. 2014. To feed or not to feed? Evidence of the intended and unintended effects of feeding wild ungulates. *Journal of Wildlife Management* 78:1322–1334.

Newey, S., P. Allison, S. Thirgood, A. A. Smith, and I. M. Graham. 2010. Population and individual level effects of over-Winter supplementary feeding mountain hares. *Journal of Zoology* 282:214–220.

Newsome, T. M., J. A. Dellinger, C. R. Pavey, W. J. Ripple, C. R. Shores, A. J. Wirsing, and C. R. Dickman. 2015. The ecological effects of providing resource subsidies and predators. *Global Ecology and Biogeography* 24:1–11.

Odden, J., E. B. Nilsen, and J. D. C. Linnell. 2013. Density of wild prey modulates lynx kill rates on free-ranging domestic sheep. *PLoS One* 8(11):e79261.

Ozoga, J. J., and L. J. Verme. 1982. Physical and reproductive characteristics of a supplementally-fed white-tailed deer herd. *Journal of Wildlife Management* 46:281–301.

Pérez-González, J., A. M. Barbosa, J. Carranza, and J. Torres-Porras. 2010. Relative effect of food supplementation and natural resources on female red deer distribution in a mediterranean ecosystem. *Journal of Wildlife Management* 74:1701–1708.

Peterson, C., and T. A. Messmer. 2007. Effects of Winter-feeding on mule deer in Northern Utah. *Journal of Wildlife Management* 71:1440–1445.

Peterson, C., and T. A. Messmer. 2011. Biological consequences of Winter-feeding of mule deer in developed landscapes in Northern Utah. *Wildlife Society Bulletin* 35:252–260.

Redpath, S. M., and S. J. Thirgood. 1997. *Birds of prey and red grouse*. Centre for Ecology and Hydrology, Stationary Office, London.

Redpath, S. M., S. J. Thirgood, and F. M. Leckie. 2001. Does supplementary feeding reduce predation of red grouse by hen harriers? *Journal of Applied Ecology* 38:1157–1168.

Rogers, L. L. 2011. Does diversionary feeding create nuisance bears and jeopardize public safety? *Human-Wildlife Interactions* 5:287–295.

Schley, L., M. Dufrêne, A. Krier, and A. C. Frantz. 2008. Patterns of crop damage by wild boar (*Sus scrofa*) in Luxembourg over a 10-year period. *European Journal of Wildlife Research* 54(4):589.

Schmitz, O. J. 1990. Management implications of foraging theory: evaluating deer supplemental feeding. *Journal of Wildlife Management* 54:522–532.

Selva, N., T. Berezowska-Cnota, and I. Elguero-Claramunt. 2014. Unforeseen effects of supplementary feeding: ungulate baiting sites as hotspots for ground-nest predation. *PLoS One* 9(3):e90740.

Smart, J., and A. Amar. 2018. Diversionary feeding as a means of reducing raptor predation at seabird breeding colonies. *Journal for Nature Conservation* 46:48–55.

Smith, J. R., R. A. Sweitzer, and W. F. Jensen. 2007. Diets, movements, and consequences of providing wildlife food plots for white-tailed deer in Central North Dakota. *Journal of Wildlife Management* 71:2719–2726.

Sullivan, T. P. 1990. Response of red squirrel (*Tamiasciurus hudsonicus*) populations to supplemental food. *Journal of Mammalogy* 71:579–590.

Sullivan, T. P., and D. S. Sullivan. 1982a. The use of alternative foods to reduce lodgepole pine seed predation by small mammals. *Journal of Applied Ecology* 19:33–45.

Sullivan, T. P., and D. S. Sullivan. 1982*b*. Population dynamics and regulation of the Douglas squirrel (*Tamiasciurus douglasii*) with supplemental food. *Oecologia* 53:264–270.

Sullivan, T. P., and D. S. Sullivan. 1988. Influence of alternative foods on vole populations and damage in apple orchards. *Wildlife Society Bulletin* 16:170–175.

Suzuki, Y., D. D. Roby, D. E. Lyons, K. N. Courtot, and K. Collis. 2015. Developing nondestructive techniques for managing conflicts between fisheries and double-crested cormorant colonies. *Wildlife Society Bulletin* 39:764–771.

Thirgood, S. J., and S. Redpath. 2005. Hen harriers and red grouse: the ecology of a conflict. Pages 192–208 *in* R. Woodroffe, S. J. Thirgood, and A. Rabinowitz, editors. *People and wildlife: conflict or co-existence?* Cambridge University Press, New York.

Thirgood, S. J., S. Redpath, I. Newton, and P. Hudson. 2000. Raptors and red grouse: conservation conflicts and management solutions. *Conservation Biology* 14:95–104.

Thompson, P. S., A. Amar, D. G. Hoccom, J. Knott, and J. D. Wilson. 2009. Resolving the conflict between driven-grouse shooting and conservation of hen harrier. *Journal of Applied Ecology* 46:950–954.

Tweheyo, M., C. M. Hill, and J. Obua. 2005. Patterns of crop raiding by primates around the Budongo forest reserve, Uganda. *Wildlife Biology* 11:237–248.

Wambolt, C. L. 2004. Browsing and plant age relationships to winter protein and fiber of big sagebrush subspecies. *Journal of Range Management* 57:620–623.

Ward, J. M., and P. L. Kennedy. 1996. Effects of supplemental food on size and survival of juvenile Northern goshawks. *Auk* 113:200–208.

Wood, P., and M. L. Wolfe. 1988. Intercept feeding as a means of reducing deer-vehicle collisions. *Wildlife Society Bulletin* 16:376–380.

Ziegltrum, G. J. 2008. Impacts of the black bear supplemental feeding program on ecology in western Washington. *Human-Wildlife Interactions* 2:153–159.

10 Habitat Manipulation

A public meeting was called to decide the optimal deer population for a Pennsylvania county. The meeting became heated with farmers arguing for fewer deer; but, no matter what farmers suggested, the hunters always wanted more deer. Finally, one old farmer complained, "If there was a deer hiding behind every tree in the county, the hunters would still not be satisfied. They would simply argue that the county needs more trees."

Anonymous

Habitat changes can mitigate many human–wildlife conflicts by (1) altering the resource itself, (2) modifying the habitat in and around the site where the resource is located, or (3) making changes to the surrounding landscape (Figure 10.1). Potential changes to the resource (throughout this chapter, I will refer to the object we are trying to protect as the resource) include planting crop species or varieties that are less susceptible to wildlife damage, altering the time a crop is planted or harvested, changing animal husbandry practices to reduce depredation, and designing buildings to be wildlife-proof. Habitat modification includes modifying the area surrounding the resource so that it is less attractive to wildlife. A landscape ecology approach can be used to increase human–wildlife coexistence, by deciding which crop to plant at a specific location or by managing distant wildlife refugia, such as not allowing birds to roost in the vicinity of the resource.

10.1 CAN HUMAN–WILDLIFE CONFLICTS BE MITIGATED BY MODIFYING THE RESOURCE?

As we discussed in Chapter 7, some plant species suffer greatly from herbivory while others are rarely browsed. Deer prefer to browse apple trees rather than peach or pear trees (Craven and Hygnstrom 1994); an apple orchard with severe deer damage can instead be planted with pears to alleviate the problem. Homeowners experiencing deer damage to plants around their homes could reduce the problem by landscaping with unpalatable plants. Many homeowners are exasperated when they discover in the spring that deer have eaten all of their tulips; yet deer avoid other spring flowers, such as daffodils and irises. Homeowners' angst could be avoided by selecting plants from a list of unpalatable spring flowers (Conover et al. 2018).

In Saskatchewan, Canada, goose are more likely to damage grain fields that are located close to the lakes where they are roosting. Callaghan et al. (2015) recommended that farmers plant canola or other unpalatable crops, rather than grain, in fields close to these lakes. In suburban areas, Canada geese prefer to graze on Kentucky bluegrass and fine fescue while avoiding St. Augustine grass and zoysia grass (Washburn and Seamans 2012). Areas experiencing problems with nuisance Canada geese might experience fewer goose–human conflicts if they are replanted with an unpalatable grass (Conover 1991).

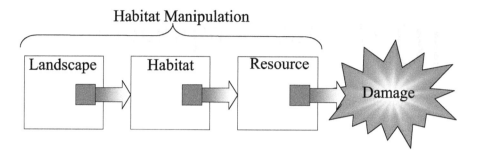

FIGURE 10.1 Human–wildlife conflicts can be reduced by changing the resource, modifying the resource's habitat, or making changes to the surrounding landscape.

Source: This is Figure 14.1 in the first edition of this book.

Linnell et al. (2009) were able to reduce bird numbers on a Hawaiian airport, which suffered multiple bird–aircraft collisions, by replacing grass growing along the runways with an unpalatable ground cover. Planting an unpalatable agricultural crop on airport grounds can also reduce bird hazards (DeVault et al. 2013). American crows are attracted to airports when grassy fields have been mowed, not because the crows consume grass, but the crows are seeking grasshoppers, which are conspicuous in mowed grass. Kennedy and Otter (2015) found that crow numbers could be reduced at a Canadian airport by allowing the grass to grow more than 15 cm in height.

Taylor et al. (2013) discovered a novel approach to an old problem. Many landowners provide supplemental food to white-tailed deer with the goals of increasing fawn survival, adult body condition, and antler size. Unfortunately, the food commonly provided (protein pellets and whole corn) also are consumed by raccoons and feral pigs. This feeding by nontarget species annoys landowners, but more seriously, it increases the survival and reproductive rates of both species, which, in turn, increases nest depredation rates on wild turkeys and bobwhites. What Taylor et al. (2013) found was that deer love to eat whole cottonseed, but raccoons and wild pigs do not, making it a promising food supplement for free-ranging deer.

Some farmers or timber growers are unable to plant unpalatable species because these species do not grow well on their farms or are not as valuable as other plants. When farmers cannot shift to an unpalatable crop, they still may be able to reduce wildlife damage by selecting a subspecies, variety, or cultivar of a palatable species which has chemical or morphological traits, making it less attractive to wildlife. Chemical traits include the presence of substances that give the crop an unpleasant taste, reduce its nutritional value, or are poisonous (see Chapter 7). For instance, deer find some cultivars of Japanese yews highly palatable, but not others.

Morphological traits can reduce the feeding efficiency of wildlife by making a food resource difficult to access or digest. Apple trees provide a great example of this because apple trees come in three sizes. There are dwarf apple trees, which are less than 3 m in height; standard-sized trees, which can reach up to 10 m; and semi-dwarfs, which are intermediate in height. In recent years, dwarf apple trees have become popular with growers because these trees yield well, reach maturity in just a few years, and are easy to harvest (no ladders required). The drawback with dwarf apple trees is that they never outgrow the reach of a hungry deer, whereas deer cannot reach most apples on a standard-sized tree. Hence, taller trees may be a better option for orchards with a history of deer damage.

There are three types of grain sorghum, which differ by the presence or absence of tannins at different stages of maturity. Type I sorghums have seeds that do not contain tannins, Type II sorghums have seeds that only contain tannins in the immature stages, and Type III sorghums contain tannins in both the immature and mature seeds. The presence of tannins in grain not only makes sorghum unattractive to birds but also reduces the palatability and nutritional quality of the grain for humans and livestock. Hence, Type III sorghums not only suffer less from bird damage but also sell for less because it does not make good feed for chickens. Therefore, Type II sorghum may be the best candidate for bird-resistant varieties because it provides protection from bird damage during the immature stages and has similar nutritional qualities as Type I when ripened (Bullard 1988).

Morphological characteristics of plants can increase their bird-resistance by making it difficult for birds to reach the seeds or to open them. In sunflowers, these characteristics include flat or concave seed heads, downward-facing heads, head-to-stem distances greater than 15 cm, long bracts surrounding the head, long chaffs, and tough hulls (Figure 10.2; Seiler and Rogers 1987; Mah et al. 1990). Confectionary

FIGURE 10.2 Great tit feeding on a sunflower seed head. Downward facing ones are difficult for birds to reach and exposes them to predators because it takes longer to flee when a bird is upside down.

Source: Lucie K, Shutterstock 1879955227.

types of sunflowers, with heavy hulls and lower oil content, suffer less damage than oilseed types, which have thinner hulls and more lipids. Sunflower seeds with purple hulls suffer less bird damage than others because they contain greater concentrations of anthocyanin, which is a taste repellent (Mason et al. 1989). Two bird-resistant varieties of sunflowers have been developed. In field tests, they suffered less bird damage than commercial varieties, especially when damage was caused by goldfinches rather than blackbirds (Dolbeer et al. 1986). However, these bird-resistant varieties produced lower yields than commercial varieties and, therefore, were not popular with growers.

10.2   CAN WILDLIFE DAMAGE TO CROPS BE MITIGATED BY MODIFYING THE HABITAT IN OR AROUND THE RESOURCE?

White-fronted geese avoided foraging in growing wheat fields that were close to roads or windbreaks, suggesting that damage could be prevented by planting wheat in fields near them and windbreaks. Amano et al. (2008) also observed that the geese start foraging in wheat fields only after they had consumed waste rice left in other fields that had already been harvested. Thus, anything that can increase the amount of waste rice left in other fields will benefit wheat farmers (Kross et al. 2008).

DeVault et al. (2007) found that deer and raccoon damage in cornfields and soybean fields was more severe along field edges and that the type of adjacent habitat was an important variable. Damage was worse along field edges that bordered woodlots than edges adjacent to pastures, other agricultural fields, or homes.

Another way to reduce herbivory in an agricultural field or orchard is to enhance the palatability and vigor of native vegetation in surrounding habitat; this can be achieved by applying herbicides or mechanical thinning to reduce completion among wild plants or by applying fertilizer, which makes them more nutritious to the wildlife (Beck et al. 2012; Korfanta et al. 2015).

Voles girdle vines and fruit trees, creating losses in vineyards and orchards, but voles forage on the orchard's groundcover during most of the year. By creating an unpalatable groundcover, vole densities can be reduced and their damage in vineyards and apple orchards minimized. Mowing can reduce vole populations by half (Edge et al. 1995), and planting an unpalatable groundcover also helps (Prieur and Swihart 2020).

Whisson and Giusti (1998) noted that newly planted vineyards were susceptible to pocket gopher damage and suggested no groundcover be planted until the vines are a couple of years old and large enough to tolerate some vole herbivory. On grain farms in Victoria, Australia, controlling weeds along fence rows and the borders of fields by mowing them or spraying them with a herbicide during the spring reduced mouse densities in late summer (Brown et al. 1998). Mouse densities can also be reduced by using livestock to graze fields immediately after harvest (Brown et al. 1998). Wood rats cause damage in Malaysian oil palm and cocoa plantations. These rodents spend most of their time hiding in the piles of palm fronds left between the tree rows (Buckle et al. 1997). Removing frond piles by burning or shredding should reduce rat populations in plantations.

10.3   CAN WILDLIFE DAMAGE TO CROPS BE REDUCED BY CHANGING AGRONOMICAL TECHNIQUES?

Several farming practices can change the vulnerability of crops to damage by birds and small mammals. For example, no-till farming allows more voles and mice to survive in fields, resulting in more damage to newly planted crops (Hygnstrom et al. 1996, 2000). In contrast, deep plowing kills voles and pocket gophers and destroys their underground burrows (Whisson and Giusti 1998). Mowing vineyards and orchards or using flood irrigation can reduce vole and pocket gopher densities.

Keeping crops weed free helps reduce wildlife damage. Red-billed quelea damage to ripening wheat in Tanzania is more extensive in weedy portions of fields than in non-weedy areas (Figure 10.3). These birds have difficulty standing on wheat plants and find it easier to forage on the seed heads where weeds are entangled with the wheat, providing stable perches (Luder 1985). In sunflower fields, severity of blackbird damage is related to how weedy the field is (Otis and Kilburn 1988).

Sometimes, bird damage can be reduced by delaying planting in the spring. In Louisiana rice fields, 98% of the rice sprouts were eaten by birds in fields planted in March, but less than 15% were lost in fields planted in mid-April (Wilson et al. 1989). Several factors are responsible for this seasonal pattern. Many blackbirds leave Louisiana between late February and April to migrate north, so fewer birds

FIGURE 10.3   Red-billed quelea.

Source: Alta Oosthuizen, Shutterstock 1708354471.

are around when late-season fields are planted in rice. Furthermore, there is an increase in the availability of alternate food sources as spring progresses, and blackbirds undergo a dietary change that reduces their desire for sprouting rice (Sidebar 10.1).

SIDEBAR 10.1 CAN BIRD DAMAGE TO FRUIT BE MINIMIZED BY ADJUSTING WHEN FRUIT RIPEN?

Many birds are migratory causing large numbers to be present in an area during some seasons but absent during others. A method to reduce crop damage by migratory species is to adjust planting schedules so that crops ripen when birds are absent. In Florida, bird damage to early-season cultivars of highbush blueberries can exceed 50% in some years (Figure 10.4). Yet, late-season cultivars rarely suffer from bird damage in Florida. The reason is that large numbers of cedar waxwings winter in Florida but have left the state before late-season blueberries ripen. However, early-ripening cultivars are still popular with Florida growers despite the bird damage because these cultivars command a premium price, owing to their being some of the first blueberries to ripen in the United States (Nelms et al. 1990).

FIGURE 10.4   Many avian species cannot resist eating ripe blueberries and cherries.

Source: Naturaegeek, Shutterstock 1425950072.

Wildlife damage can sometimes be reduced by moving up the harvest date. In Canada, waterfowl damage to grain fields mainly occurs during those years when wet weather keeps farmers from harvesting their crops in a timely manner (Callaghan et al. 2015). Some wheat farmers spray a desiccant or herbicide on maturing sunflower fields to dry the sunflower heads faster, so they can be harvested a couple of weeks earlier. This earlier harvest reduces blackbird damage by limiting the number of days the sunflowers are in the field (Linz et al. 2011).

The size of a field has a great impact on the severity of wildlife damage. Usually, the total amount of damage caused by wildlife increases slightly as the size of a field increases, while the proportion of the crop that is damaged decreases as field size increases, because the perimeter of the field increases more slowly than its area. Consider a square blueberry field of 1 ha and each side being 100 m in length. The perimeter of this field would be 400 m. Let us assume that the ripe blueberries attract all of the mockingbirds, American robins, and northern orioles nesting within 100 m of its perimeter. Let us assume that 100 birds foraging in the field remove 100 kg of berries during the growing season. If the blueberry field yields 400 kg per ha, then the birds would remove 25% of the blueberries from a 1-ha field. In contrast, each side of a 100-ha square field is 1000 m in length. This field's 4,000-m perimeter would attract 1,000 birds, which would remove 1,000 kg of berries. But, this field contains 100 ha and produces 10,000 kg of blueberries. In this field, birds consume 10% of the blueberry crop because its area increases faster than its perimeter, and there is a one-to-one relationship between a field's size and its yield (Figure 10.5).

The same principle applies to depredation of livestock and poultry. Consider a raccoon breaking into a chicken house one night and eating its fill. The number of chickens it eats will be the same regardless of whether the chicken coop contains 100, 1,000, or 1,000,000 chickens; but, the proportion of the chicken flock that was killed declines as the chicken flock becomes larger. Several authors have noted this "economics of scale" principle. Another factor influencing the level of wildlife damage is the shape of the agricultural field. Most foraging animals, such as deer, seldom venture far from secure cover. Consequently, most deer damage occurs along the edges of a field, rather than in its center. Fields with a straight edge will be less vulnerable to de damage than those that have a convoluted edge (Figure 10.6).

Bird Habitat = 24 ha
Blueberry Field = 1 ha

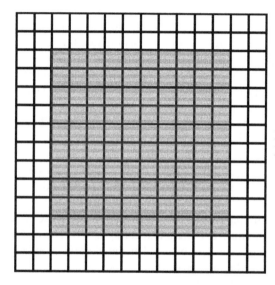

Bird Habitat = 96 ha
Blueberry Field = 100 ha

☐ = 1 ha

☐ = Bird Habitat

▨ = Blueberry Field

FIGURE 10.5 If all songbirds within 200 m of a blueberry field forage in it, then the total amount of blueberries consumed by birds increases as the field increases in size; but, the proportion of the total crop they consume declines.

Source: This is Figure 14.19 in the first edition of this book.

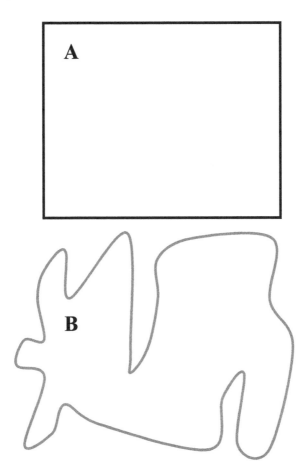

FIGURE 10.6   Fields with straight edges (A) are less vulnerable to deer damage than fields with a convoluted edge (B) because a higher proportion of the convoluted field is located close to the field's edge.

Source: This is Figure 14.11 in the first edition of this book.

10.4   CAN LIVESTOCK LOSSES TO PREDATORS BE REDUCED THROUGH HUSBANDRY PRACTICES?

Sheep farmers can change their operations to reduce the vulnerability of their livestock to predators. Livestock on the open range suffer more depredation than those confined to pastures (Schiess-Meier et al. 2007). Keeping livestock away from areas where predators are likely to congregate will reduce losses. Interestingly, cattle losses increased when elk were nearby, suggesting prey switching when wolves are unable to capture an elk.

Intensive husbandry reduced depredation rates by wolves (Bradley and Pletscher 2005; Miller et al. 2016). In the French Alps, keeping sheep confined at night and having a pack of five guard dogs watch the flock were the best methods of reducing wolf depredation (Espuno et al. 2004). In Poland, sheep losses to wolves were related to how close the sheep were to a wolf rendezvous site or den (Gula 2008). Sheep breeds also differ in their aggressiveness, alertness, group cohesiveness, and intensity of maternal protection. All of these characteristics influence the vulnerability of a particular breed of coyotes (Gluesing et al. 1980; Knowlton et al. 1999).

Grizzly bears prefer to ambush large prey; this hunting style requires trees or brush to provide cover to bears. Wilson et al. (2005) noted that livestock killed by grizzly bears were concentrated in riparian areas, suggesting that one method to protect lambs and calves from attacks is to locate bedding grounds for sheep away from riparian habitat.

Losses to large cats increase when the livestock venture farther from occupied buildings or closer to landscape features that attract large felids, such as rocky and steep slopes, cliffs, or riparian areas (Inskip and Zimmermann 2009). Losses to felids can be reduced by keeping a herder with the sheep when they are on the range and bedding the sheep for the night close to the herder's camp (Inskip and Zimmermann 2009). In rural parts of Pakistan, leopards are the main predator of domestic sheep and goats. Dar et al. (2009) discovered that most losses occurred at night near villages that lacked electricity. The scientists concluded that the most effectiveness method to reduce depredation on livestock was to bring electricity to villages.

10.5 HOW CAN BUILDINGS BE MADE BIRD AND RODENT PROOF?

Birds cause nuisance problems or health hazards when they roost, loaf, or nest on the outside or inside of buildings because of their droppings, noise, and pathogens. Many of these problems could be avoided if buildings were designed without exposed ledges, rafters, I-beams, or architectural decorations that offer birds' places to roost or nest. Other building features that provide access into the building or good nesting sites for birds include the following: eaves, vents, spaces between the gutter and roof, and flat or slightly pitched roofs (Figure 10.7).

Woodpeckers drill holes in buildings when searching either for nest sites or insect prey. Such damage is more likely to occur when the outside walls are made of wood, have a wooden veneer, or when the roof is composed of wooden shingles. Thus, many woodpecker problems could be avoided if other building materials were used. Interestingly, houses painted brown or tan experienced more woodpecker problems than houses painted in other colors (Harding et al. 2007, 2009).

Avoiding rodent infestations are best accomplished by designing buildings to be rodent-proof; this includes foundations deep enough that rodents will not burrowing beneath them. A 30-cm-long horizontal footing extension placed about 60 cm below ground level, or a buried wire-mesh fence (Figure 10.8) can be used to deflect burrowing rodents away from the walls (Timm 1987; Baker et al. 1994). Weeds, woodpiles, and construction debris around buildings attract rodents by providing them with shelter and should be removed. Maintaining a 1-m-wide weed-free area around buildings by close mowing or installing heavy gravel can discourage rodent burrowing. Rats can climb along the outside of vertical pipes that are less than 7 cm

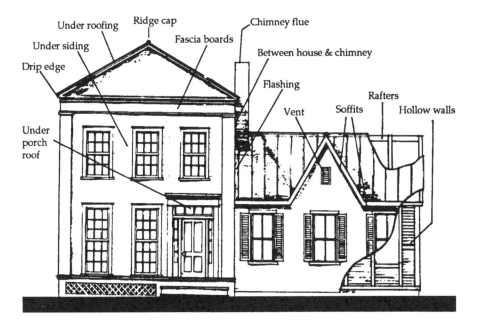

FIGURE 10.7   Common entry points into a home and nesting sites for birds.

Source: From Hygnstrom et al. (1994) and used with permission.

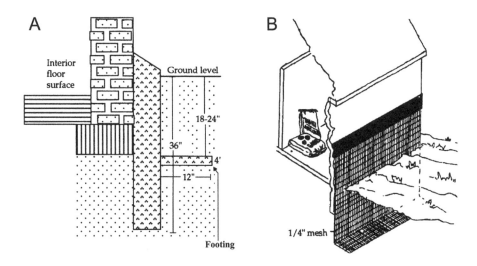

FIGURE 10.8   A concrete footing extending out from the wall (a) or a buried wire screen (b) can be used to keep rodents from burrowing into the basement.

Source: From Hygnstrom et al. (1994) and used with permission.

in diameter. Such pipes can be equipped with metal disks or cones to serve as rodent guards. To prevent rodents from climbing walls, the lower portions of walls should be covered with materials that have a hard, smooth surface. This surface needs to extend above surrounding hedges or plants that rodents can climb.

Common entry points of rodents into buildings include vents; drains; pipes; spaces at the base of doors; and wall opening for electrical, water, and gas lines. By gnawing on the edges to enlarge the openings, rats and mice can enter buildings through holes as small as 1.3 cm and 0.6 cm, respectively. Thus, all holes larger than 0.6 cm should be sealed.

Rodents are particularly attracted to areas where food is stored or handled. Such areas should be kept as clean as possible and should be designed to allow cleaning beneath and behind equipment, such as refrigerators, counters, and dishwashers. Food should be stored in rodent-proof containers. Warehouses should have self-closing doors; loading docks should be equipped with barriers preventing rodent access. Areas around garbage dumpsters should be kept clean, and the dumpster lids should fit tightly and be kept close. Dumpster drains should be equipped with rodent screening.

10.6 CAN HABITAT BE MODIFIED TO INCREASE AN ANIMAL'S FEAR OF A SITE?

Wildlife avoid areas where they are vulnerable to predators. One way to reduce the density of a particular wildlife species is to change the habitat, making wildlife culprits more vulnerable. For example, Andreassen et al. (2005) removed all vegetation higher than 30 cm from the ROW of a Norway railroad track and returned repeatedly to keep the vegetation low. The vegetation removal reduced moose–vehicle collisions by 40% either because the moose no longer had a reason to forage close to the track or because moose moved quicker across the open area where they were more visible to predators. White-tailed deer prefer habitat where they can watch for the approach of predator. Blackwell et al. (2012) exploited this preference to keep deer away from areas, such as haystacks, where they were causing problems. The scientists erected a visual barrier that was high enough that deer could not see over it on three sides of some haystacks. As the scientists predicted, few deer used haystacks that were visually obstructed.

Voles are vulnerable to raptors when vegetation is sparse or absent. Thus, an approach to reducing vole densities in orchards is to remove cover by mowing or applying an herbicide. In contrast, ground squirrels and prairie dogs rely on their vision to detect predators, and ground squirrels avoid areas where thick or tall vegetation blocks their view. Several scientists have tested whether visual barriers can be used to keep prairie dogs from expanding their colonies, but results were inconclusive (Hygnstrom 1996).

Canada geese prefer to forage in the center of large, open fields or lawns where they have a clear view of their surroundings (Figure 10.9; Callaghan et al. 2015). In such areas, they are safe from mammalian predators that seek to ambush them. Therefore, one way to discourage urban Canada geese from using a site where they are unwanted is to landscape the site with trees, bushes, hedges, boulders: anything that could hide a predator (Figure 10.10). Geese also prefer to forage on lawns that are close to a pond or lake where they can flee if they see a mammalian predator.

FIGURE 10.9   A typical site where Canada geese like to forage because nothing impedes their view of any approaching danger.

Source: Iordanis, Shutterstock 1485921071.

FIGURE 10.10   A pond landscaped to be unattractive to Canada geese by using vegetation, boulders, and wooden buckets to obstruct a goose's view of its surroundings.

Source: Josefkubes, Shutterstock 1678172197.

Such sites can also be made less inviting to geese by denying them access to a pond by erecting a fence or placing wires above the pond (see Chapter 8). Interestingly, Mackay et al. (2014) made the same suggestions to discourage Egyptian geese from using golf courses in South Africa. Both Egyptian and Canada goose species prefer foraging sites that are open with excellent visibility, clear beaches, and near waterbodies.

10.7   CAN HUMAN–WILDLIFE CONFLICTS BE REDUCED AT THE LANDSCAPE LEVEL?

The amount of wildlife damage that occurs at any site depends, in part, on what the landscape and land-use patterns are in the broad area surrounding the site. In some cases, we can manipulate the landscape to resolve human–wildlife conflicts. In Scotland, harriers kill red grouse, and Amar et al. (2004) discovered that depredation rates on grouse were correlated with the amount of heather in the landscape, suggesting that steps to increase heather densities will also help save red grouse from harriers.

Several wildlife species cause problems when they burrow into dams or dikes (Bayoumi and Meguid 2011). These ground squirrels often feed on vegetation in areas bordering dikes. McGrann et al. (2014) found that ground squirrel densities along a dike varied based on the type of crop grown adjacent to the dike. Ground squirrels were abundant on dikes adjacent to nut and fruit orchards and scarce on dikes adjacent to rice and grassland. This information is useful to managers who are surveying dikes for damage, allowing them to concentrate their searches where nut and fruit crops are located. Furthermore, as fruit trees grow old and orchards need to be replaced, water companies can encourage adjacent farmers to establish crops less likely to attract ground squirrels.

White-tailed deer thrive in suburban areas where predators and hunters are uncommon, and there is a close proximity of woodlots that give cover for deer and homes that provide food (e.g., ornamental plants and lawns). Gorham and Porter (2011) proposed that towns and suburbs could be designed in the future to minimize deer–human conflicts by building homes with their lawns and landscaping plants away from woodlots. Neighborhoods become less suitable for deer as the distance increases between them and woodlots because deer have to expend more energy journeying between food and shelter. Some urban planners encourage the creation of compact neighborhoods where homes are clustered together.

One approach to mitigating conflicts between large herbivores and predators is through public zoning. That is, local zoning could prohibit certain human activities, such as livestock grazing, in areas where large predators occur. One way to reduce the number of people killed by large predators is to move people away from areas where large predators are abundant. In fact, India moved human settlements out of lion and tiger habitat (Treves and Karanth 2003), but the resettlement of people is an extreme form of zoning and unpopular with villagers who had to leave their home.

An old saying, the enemy of my enemy is my friend, can be true when livestock losses are caused by a specific predator species (Sidebar 10.2). For village farmers in Africa, having a tiger in the vicinity reduces crop damage by herbivores, such as sambar, muntjac, and wild boars. When tigers are present, smaller predators, such as leopards and dholes, moved closer to village fields and killed more of the herbivores that damaged crops (Thinley et al. 2017, 2018).

SIDEBAR 10.2 REDUCING LOSSES TO PREDATORS BY MODIFYING THE PREDATOR GUILD

Red foxes are efficient predators of incubating ducks and their eggs (Figure 10.11). Coyotes also prey on duck eggs, but they are less of a threat to nesting ducks than red foxes. Coyotes will kill red foxes; this causes foxes to avoid them with the result that fox densities are suppressed where coyotes are abundant. Sovada et al. (1995) tested whether the presence of coyotes leads to an increase in duck nesting success. The scientists compared 17 duck-nesting areas in North and South Dakota where coyotes predominated to 13 areas where red foxes were the principal canid. Duck nest success was 32% where coyotes predominated and 17% where red foxes predominated, supporting the hypothesis that managing for more coyotes may be an effective method for increasing the nesting success of ducks.

FIGURE 10.11   A red fox with a recent kill.

Source: Menmo Schaefer, Shutterstock 101928223.

10.7.1 AVOIDING DAMAGE BY CLUSTERING VULNERABLE RESOURCES TOGETHER

Sometimes, human–wildlife conflicts can be mitigated by taking advantage of the "economics of scale;" that is, the proportion of a crop damaged by wildlife decreases as the amount of land devoted to agriculture increases in the area. For example, bird damage to grapefruit in Texas was lower on a per hectare basis when orchards were clumped together rather than widely spaced (Johnson et al. 1989). In New England where cornfields are few and far between, blackbirds often reduce corn yields by 25% (Figure 10.12). Whereas bird damage rarely exceeds 2% in the Midwest Corn Belt, there can be thousands of hectares of cornfields within a small area (Figure 10.13). Therefore, blackbird damage is spread over hundreds of fields in the Midwest, but this is not be true in New England. The "economics of scale" principle is based on the fact that, as production increases, the proportion of it that is damaged by wildlife will decline. Thus, one way to reduce wildlife damage is to concentrate vulnerable crops in a single area.

In addition to clustering vulnerable fields in one area, wildlife damage often can be reduced by clustering them in time (i.e., synchronization). Most crops are vulnerable to wildlife damage only during a particular growth stage. For instance, newly planted cornfields are vulnerable to birds when first planted. One way to minimize damage during this period is to plant all of the fields simultaneously, so they benefit

FIGURE 10.12 In New England, forests dominate the landscape while agricultural fields, such as this ripening wheat field, tend to be small and isolated, making them more vulnerable to wildlife damage.

Source: Miroslav Posavec, Shutterstock 1747904936.

FIGURE 10.13 In some parts of the world, agricultural fields dominate the landscape, and forests are scarce.

Source: LazarenkoD, Shutterstock 210416770.

from the economics of scale. This approach is problematic, however, owing to the difficult of planting or harvest at fields at once. Synchronizing the fields exacerbates the risk that a single event will destroy all fields. For example, corn yields are reduced if hot, dry weather occurs during the 2-week period when pollination occurs.

10.7.2 Reducing Damage by Managing Distant Bird Colonies and Roosts

Sometimes, human–wildlife conflicts are best addressed at distant sites that serve as the source for the wildlife culprits. For avian species that are central-place foragers, a close relationship exists between the severity of bird damage and proximity to a roost or nesting colony. Linz et al. (2011) and Linz and Homan (2011) reported that blackbirds prefer to roost in wetlands with dense stands of cattails; damage by these birds can be minimized if birds are forced to abandon a nearby roost by spraying parts of the cattail stand with an herbicide to create open water. The scientists found they were able to reduce bird damage to sunflowers by forcing birds to abandon a nearby roost for one farther away (Figure 10.14).

Around San Francisco Bay, California, gull populations have increased in recent decades, and their depredation of tern chicks was responsible for more than half of all tern chick deaths. Ackerman et al. (2014) examined whether tern losses could be mitigated by forcing gulls to abandon their colony that was located near tern colonies. The gull colony was located in a dried salt pond; when this pond was deliberately flooded, the gulls left the area to nest elsewhere. This increased fledgling success of Forster's tern chicks. The results were most dramatic at the tern colony closest to the gull colony. When the gull colony was there, only 5% of chicks survived to fledgling compared to a tenfold increase to 50% when the gull colony was abandoned.

For birds that roost together at night, preventing them from roosting close to the resource being damaged mitigates the problem (Linz et al. 2011; Linz and Homan 2011). Blackbird damage in 68 cornfields in New York decreased exponentially with distance from a large blackbird roost located in Montezuma National Wildlife Refuge (Bollinger and Caslick 1985). None of the fields located more than 6 kms from the roost received more than 1% damage, whereas fields located 2–4 kms from the roost

FIGURE 10.14   Cattails can completely take over a pond, leaving no open water. Cattail-choked ponds make excellent roosts for blackbirds. It they were thinned out to create open water, the pond would be more inviting for ducks but not enticing to blackbirds seeking a place to roost.

Source: M. V. Photography, Shutterstock 1773461282.

received up to 29% damage. Grackle damage in Texas was related to the distance between the orchard and sugarcane fields where grackles roost (Johnson et al. 1989).

A drawback of forcing birds to abandon a roost is that we have little ability to move them to the site of our choosing. Hence, we may chase birds from one roost, only to have them move to at a site even less to our liking. This happened in Connecticut where crows using a large roost were forced to relocate because the local residents complained that their fecal material was creating a health hazard. In response, the crows were scared away from that roost, but unfortunately, their new roost was in trees located in the playground of an elementary school.

10.7.3   Reducing Damage by Managing Distant Refugia

Some wildlife populations fluctuate widely, depending upon weather or habitat conditions. When poor conditions occur, these species may be able to survive only in a refugium that provides food or security during hard times. When conditions improve, wildlife venture out of these refugia and repopulate the landscape. An effective approach to suppress the population of culprits is to use lethal control when the number of animals is concentrated in refugia. For example, when sugarcane is planted, the land is first prepared by burning the residual vegetation followed by repeated cultivation. During this period, canefield rats must leave the field and take refuge in noncrop areas. By removing these refugia, densities of canefield rats can be suppressed in the surrounding sugarcane fields (Whisson 1996). This approach was used to manage rabbit populations in semi-arid regions of Australia, where habitat conditions fluctuate with rainfall (Parker et al. 1976). In wet years, rabbits spread over large areas, but during droughts, only a few warrens are active, and they are located where there is water, such as near drainage channels and swamps. Destruction of these warrens can make it impossible for rabbits to survive during droughts and can lower populations over wide areas.

10.8   SUMMARY

Sometimes, human–wildlife conflicts can be avoided by making structural changes to the resource being damaged or the surrounding area. This can be achieved by (1) changing the resource itself or the way it is managed, (2) modifying the habitat at the site where the resource is located, or (3) making changes to the surrounding landscape. Structural changes to the resource include the use of species or varieties that are less susceptible to wildlife damage, rescheduling the timing of planting or harvesting date for a crop and modifying animal husbandry practices to reduce losses to predators. Human–wildlife conflicts can be reduced by making habitat changes near the resource, such as altering the groundcover to reduce wildlife densities or modifying the surrounding habitat so that wildlife will be more vulnerable to predators and fearful when in the area. A landscape approach to mitigating human–wildlife conflicts might involve clustering vulnerable resources together in time and space, growing crops in large fields with straight edges, not allowing birds to roost nearby, or removing wildlife refugia so that the wildlife sub-population will collapse during droughts or periods when habitat conditions have deteriorated.

10.9   DISCUSSION QUESTIONS

1. Universities, biotech industries, and seed companies spend considerable time and money, developing new plant varieties and cultivars that are resistant to insects and diseases, but do not have research programs to develop plants resistant to wildlife damage. Why is this?
2. On one occasion, I investigated a cluster of DVCs in U along a stretch of road that was adjacent to a horse pasture with a tall wooden fence. The landowner had piled bales of hay on the road ROW between the road and his fence. This was convenient for the pasture owner, but the hay attracted several deer to the ROW. Unfortunately, when the deer were startled by a vehicle, the fence prevented them from escaping on their side; so, deer had to reach the far side of the road to escape. If the deer waited too long to escape, they had to dart in front of a moving vehicle, not giving the driver time to swerve or brake. If you were a state wildlife biologist, how would you handle this situation? If you were working for the insurance company

that insured the wrecked vehicle, would you advise the insurance company to sue the owner of the horse pasture?

3. Many nature shows on TV state that wild animals, such as deer, geese, bears, and coyotes, have moved into suburban areas because humans have destroyed their native habitat, leaving them nowhere else to go. Is this the main reason that we find high densities of wildlife in urban and suburban areas? If we repaired their native habitat outside of a city, do you think wildlife would leave the city?

4. The "economics of scale" principle is based on the fact that, as production increases, the proportion of it damaged by wildlife will decline. Can you provide some examples of your own to illustrate the principle?

5. The Mexican wolf is an endangered species that lives in New Mexico and Arizona. The few remaining animals kill a considerable number of livestock. Some biologists excuse the wolves' behavior by arguing that there is nothing else for them to eat where they live. Do you think this problem could be resolved by managing the landscape so that it can support larger numbers of deer and other wild ungulates? If so, how could this be accomplished?

LITERATURE CITED

Ackerman, J. T., M. P. Herzog, C. A. Hartman, and G. Herring. 2014. Forster's tern chick survival in response to a managed relocation of predatory California gulls. *Journal of Wildlife Management* 78:818–829.

Amano, T., K. Ushiyama, and H. Higuchi. 2008. Methods of predicting risks of wheat damage by white-fronted geese. *Journal of Wildlife Management* 72:1845–1852.

Amar, A., B. Arroyo, S. Redpath, and S. Thirgood. 2004. Habitat predicts losses of red grouse to individual hen harriers. *Journal of Applied Ecology* 41:305–314.

Andreassen, H. P., H. Gundersen, and T. Storaas. 2005. The effect of scent-marking, forest clearing, and supplemental feeding on moose-train collisions. *Journal of Wildlife Management* 69:1125–1132.

Baker, R. O., G. R. Bodman, and R. M. Timm. 1994. Rodent-proof construction and exclusion methods. Pages B137–B150 *in* S. E. Hygnstrom, R. M. Timm, and G. E. Larson, editors. *Prevention and control of wildlife damage.* University of Nebraska Cooperative Extension, Lincoln, NE.

Bayoumi, A., and M. A. Meguid. 2011. Wildlife and safety of earthen structures: a review. *Journal of Failure Analysis and Prevention* 11:295–319.

Beck, J. L., J. W. Connelly, and C. L. Wambolt. 2012. Consequences of treating Wyoming big sagebrush to enhance wildlife habitats. *Rangeland Ecology and Management* 65:444–455.

Blackwell, B. F., T. W. Seamans, L. A. Tyson, J. L. Belant, and K. C. VerCauteren. 2012. Exploiting antipredator behavior in white-tailed deer for resource protection. *Wildlife Society Bulletin* 36:546–553.

Bollinger, E. K., and J. W. Caslick. 1985. Factors influencing blackbird damage to field corn. *Journal of Wildlife Management* 49:1109–1115.

Bradley, E. H., and D. H. Pletscher. 2005. Assessing factors related to wolf depredation of cattle in fenced pastures in Montana and Idaho. *Wildlife Society Bulletin* 33:1256–1265.

Brown, P. R., G. R. Singleton, D. A. Jones, and S. C. Dunn. 1998. The management of house mice in agricultural landscapes using farm management practices: an Australian perspective. *Proceedings of the Vertebrate Pest Conference* 18:156–159.

Buckle, A. P., T. H. Chia, M. G. P. Fenn, and M. Visvalingam. 1997. Ranging behaviour and habitat utilisation of the Malayan wood rat (*Rattus tiomanicus*) in an oil palm plantation in Johore, Malaysia. *Crop Protection* 16:467–473.

Bullard, R. W. 1988. Characteristics of bird-resistance in agricultural crops. *Proceedings of the Vertebrate Pest Conference* 13:305–309.

Callaghan, C. J., B. Daneshfar, and D. J. Thompson. 2015. Modeling waterfowl damage to crops surrounding the Quill lakes in Saskatchewan. *Human-Wildlife Conflicts* 9:87–100.

Conover, M. R. 1991. Herbivory by Canada geese: diet selection and effect on lawns. *Ecological Applications* 1: 231–236.

Conover, M. R., K. B. Hulvey, M. L. Monroe, and C. B. Fitzgerald. 2018. Susceptibility of spring-flowering garden plants to herbivory by mule deer. *Wildlife Society Bulletin* 42:131–135.

Craven, S. R., and S. E. Hygnstrom. 1994. Deer. Pages D25–D40 *in* S. E. Hygnstrom, R. M. Timm, and G. E. Larson, editors. *Prevention and control of wildlife damage.* University of Nebraska Cooperative Extension, Lincoln, NE.

Dar, N. I., R. A. Minhas, Q. Zaman, and M. Linkie. 2009. Predicting the patterns, perceptions and causes of human-carnivore conflict in and around Machiara National Park, Pakistan. *Biological Conservation* 142:2076–2082.

DeVault, T. L., J. C. Beasley, L. A. Humberg, B. J. MacGowan, M. I. Retamosa, and O. E. Rhodes, Jr. 2007. Intrafield patterns of wildlife damage to corn and soybeans in Northern Indiana. *Human-Wildlife Conflicts* 1:205–213.

DeVault, T. L., M. J. Begier, J. L. Belant, B. F. Blackwell, R. A. Dolbeer, J. A. Martin, T. W. Seamans, and B. E. Washburn. 2013. Rethinking airport land-cover paradigms: agriculture, grass, and wildlife hazards. *Human-Wildlife Interactions* 13:10–15.

Dolbeer, R. A., P. P. Woronecki, R. A. Stehn, G. J. Fox, J. J. Hansel, and G. M. Linz. 1986. Field trials of sunflower resistant to bird depredation. *North Dakota Farm Research* 43(6):21–24, 28.

Edge, W. D., J. O. Wolff, and R. L. Carey. 1995. Density-dependent responses of gray-tailed voles to mowing. *Journal of Wildlife Management* 59:245–251.

Espuno, N., B. Lequette, M. L. Poulle, P. Migot, and J. D. Lebreton. 2004. Heterogeneous response to preventive sheep husbandry during wolf recolonization of the French Alps. *Wildlife Society Bulletin* 32:1195–1208.

Gluesing, E. A., D. F. Balph, and F. F. Knowlton. 1980. Behavioral patterns of domestic sheep and their relationship to coyote predation. *Applied Animal Ethology* 6:315–330.

Gorham, D. A., and W. F. Porter. 2011. Examining the potential of community design to limit human conflict with white-tailed deer. *Wildlife Society Bulletin* 35:201–208.

Gula, R. 2008. Wolf depredation on domestic animals in the Polish Carpathian mountains. *Journal of Wildlife Management* 72:283–289.

Harding, E. G., P. D. Curtis, and S. L. Vehrenamp. 2007. Assessment of management techniques to reduce woodpecker damage to homes. *Journal of Wildlife Management* 71:2061–2066.

Harding, E. G., S. L. Vehrencamp, and P. D. Curtis. 2009. External characteristics of houses prone to woodpecker damage. *Human-Wildlife Conflicts* 3:136–144.

Hygnstrom, S. E. 1996. Plastic visual barriers were ineffective at reducing recolonization rates of prairie dogs. *Proceedings of the Great Plains Wildlife Damage Control Workshop* 12:74–76.

Hygnstrom, S. E., R. M. Timm, and G. E. Larson. 1994. *Prevention and control of wildlife damage.* University of Nebraska Cooperative Extension, Lincoln, NE.

Hygnstrom, S. E., K. C. VerCauteren, and J. D. Ekstein. 1996. Impacts of field-dwelling rodents on emerging field corn. *Proceedings of the Vertebrate Pest Conference* 17:148–150.

Hygnstrom, S. E., K. C. VerCauteren, R. A. Hines, and C. W. Mansfield. 2000. Efficacy of in-furrow zinc phosphide pellets for controlling rodent damage in no-till corn. *International Biodeterioration and Biodegradation* 45:215–222.

Inskip, C., and A. Zimmermann. 2009. Human-felid conflict: a review of patterns and priorities worldwide. *Oryx* 43:18–34.

Johnson, D. B., F. S. Guthery, and N. E. Koerth. 1989. Grackle damage to grapefruit in the Lower Rio Grande Valley. *Wildlife Society Bulletin* 17:46–50.

Kennedy, L. A., and K. A. Otter. 2015. Grass management regimes affect grasshopper availability and subsequently American crow active at airports. *Human-Wildlife Interactions* 9:58–66.

Knowlton, F. F., E. M. Gese, and M. M. Jaeger. 1999. Coyote depredation control: an interface between biology and management. *Journal of Range Management* 52:398–412.

Korfanta, N. M., M. L. Mobley, and I. C. Burke. 2015. Fertilizing Western rangelands for ungulate conservation: an assessment of benefits and risks. *Wildlife Society Bulletin* 39:1–8.

Kross, J. P., R. M. Kaminski, K. J. Reinecke, and A. T. Pearse. 2008. Conserving waste rice for wintering waterfowl in the Mississippi Alluvial Valley. *Journal of Wildlife Management* 72:1383–1387.

Linnell, M. A., M. R. Conover, and T. J. Ohashi. 2009. Using wedelia as ground cover on tropical airports can reduce bird activity. *Human-Wildlife Conflicts* 3:226–236.

Linz, G. M., and H. J. Homan. 2011. Use of glyphosate for managing invasive cattail (*Typha* spp.) to disperse blackbird (Icteridae) roosts. *Crop Protection* 30:98–104.

Linz, G. M., H. J. Homan, S. J. Werner, H. M. Hagy, and W. J. Beier. 2011. Assessment of bird-management strategies to protect sunflowers. *BioScience* 61:960–970.

Luder, R. 1985. Weeds influence red-billed quelea damage to ripening wheat in Tanzania. *Journal of Wildlife Management* 49:646–647.

Mackay, B., R. M. Little, A. Amar, and P. A. Hockey. 2014. Incorporating environmental considerations in managing Egyptian geese on golf courses in South Africa. *Journal of Wildlife Management* 78:671–678.

Mah, J., G. M. Linz, and J. J. Hanzel. 1990. Relative effectiveness of individual sunflower traits for reducing red-winged blackbird depredation. *Crop Protection* 9:359–362.

Mason, J. R., R. W. Bullard, R. A. Dolbeer, and P. P. Woronecki. 1989. Red-winged blackbird (*Agelaius phoeniceus* L.) feeding response to oil and anthocyanin levels in sunflower meal. *Crop Protection* 8:455–460.

McGrann, M. C., D. H. Van Vuren, and M. A. Ordeñana. 2014. Influence of adjacent crop type on occurrence of California ground squirrels on levees in the Sacramento Valley, California. *Wildlife Society Bulletin* 38:111–115.

Miller, J. R. B., K. J. Stoner, M. R. Cejtin, T. K. Meyer, A. D. Middleton, and O. J. Schmitz. 2016. Effectiveness of contemporary techniques for reducing livestock depredations by large carnivores. *Wildlife Society Bulletin* 40:806–815.

Nelms, C. O., M. L. Avery, and D. G. Decker. 1990. Assessment of bird damage to early-ripening blueberries in Florida. *Proceedings of the Vertebrate Pest Conference* 14:302–306.

Otis, D. L., and C. M. Kilburn. 1988. *Influence of environmental factors on blackbird damage to sunflowers.* U. S. Fish and Wildlife Service Technical Report 16, Washington, DC.

Parker, B. S., K. Myers, and R. L. Caskey. 1976. An attempt at rabbit control by warren ripping in semi-arid western New South Wales. *Journal of Applied Ecology* 13:353–367.

Prieur, A. G. A., and R. K. Swihart. 2020. Palatability of common cover crops to voles (Microtus). *Crop Protection.* https://doi.org/10.1016/jcropro 2020.105141.

Schiess-Meier, M., S. Ramsauer, T. Gabanapelo, and B. Koenig. 2007. Livestock predation – insights from problem animal control registers in Botswana. *Journal of Wildlife Management* 71:1267–1274.

Seiler, G. J., and C. E. Rogers. 1987. Influence of sunflower morphological characteristics on achene depredation by birds. *Agriculture, Ecosystems and Environment* 20:59–70.

Sovada, M. A., A. B. Sargeant, and J. W. Grier. 1995. Differential effects of coyotes and red foxes on duck nest success. *Journal of Wildlife Management* 59:1–9.

Taylor, B. D., E. K. Lyons, D. Rollins, C. B. Scott, J. E. Huston, and C. A. Taylor. 2013. Consumption of whole cottonseed by white-tailed deer and nontarget species. *Human-Wildlife Interactions* 7:99–106.

Thinley, P., J. P. Lassoie, S. J. Morreale, P. D. Curtis, R. Rajaratnam, K. Vernes, L. Leki, S. Phuntsho, T. Dorji and P. Dorji. 2017. High relative abundance of wild ungulates near agricultural croplands in a livestock-dominated landscape in Western Bhutan: implications for crop damage and protection. *Agriculture, Ecosystem and Environment* 248:88–95.

Thinley, P., R. Rajaratnam, J. P. Lassoie, S. J. Morreale, P. D. Curtis, K. Vernes, L. Leki, S. Phuntsho, T. Dorji, and P. Dorji. 2018. The ecological benefit of tigers (*Panthera tigris*) to farmers in reducing crop and livestock losses in the eastern Himalayas: implications for conservation of large apex predators. *Biological Conservation* 219:119–125.

Timm, R. M. 1987. Commensal rodents in insulated livestock buildings. *In* C. G. Richards and T. Y. Ku, editors. *Control of mammal pests.* Taylor and Francis, New York.

Treves, A., and K. U. Karanth. 2003. Human-carnivore conflicts and perspectives on carnivore management worldwide. *Conservation Biology* 17:1491–1499.

Whisson, D. E. 1996. The effect of two agricultural techniques on populations of the cane-field rat (*Rattus sordidus*) in sugarcane crops of North Queensland. *Wildlife Research* 23:589–604.

Whisson, D. E., and G. A. Giusti. 1998. Vertebrate pests. Pages 126–131 *in* C. A. Ingels, R. L. Bugg, G. T. McGourty, and L. P. Christensen, editors. *Cover cropping in vineyards: a grower's handbook.* University of California, Division of Agriculture and Natural Resources Publication 3338, Oakland, CA.

Wilson, E. A., E. A. LeBoeuf, K. M. Weaver, and D. J. LeBlanc. 1989. Delayed seeding for reducing blackbird damage to sprouting rice in southwestern Louisiana. *Wildlife Society Bulletin* 17:165–171.

Wilson, S. M., M. J. Madel, D. J. Mattson, J. M. Graham, J. A. Burchfield, and J. M. Belsky. 2005. Natural landscape features, human-related attractants, and conflict hotspots: a spatial analysis of human-grizzly bear conflicts. *Ursus* 16:117–129.

11 Wildlife Translocation

"Toto, I don't think we're in Kansas anymore."

– Dorothy, after a tornado translocated her to Oz

Wildlife translocation, or relocation, consists of transporting live-captured animals to a location different from their capture site and releasing them. Translocation has been used for various purposes, including the reintroduction of threatened or endangered species into portions of their former range and the stocking of popular game species. In wildlife damage management, translocation has been used either to remove individual animals responsible for depredations (culprits) or to reduce populations in specific areas (subpopulations) by removing larger numbers of animals. Although this chapter discusses translocation in the context of human–wildlife conflicts, data pertaining to other types of translocations will also be presented when relevant.

Many people regard lethal control methods as cruel. Translocation, on the other hand, appears to be the perfect solution: the offending animal is captured and moved to a new area in its natural habitat where it is given another chance to live happily ever after. Unfortunately, the biological realities of translocation are quite different, and this technique is rather controversial, as we will see.

Nuisance wildlife control operators (NWCOs) in urban/suburban area report that live-trapping animals and releasing them off-site is their primary method of controlling raccoons, squirrels, skunks, and woodchucks owing to their customers not wanting to hurt these animals (Barnes 1993, 1995; Curtis et al. 1993). However, the effectiveness of this method is rarely monitored, and the fate of translocated animals is not fully understood.

One might not realize that an endangered species can be numerous enough to cause conflicts with humans until one has met Utah prairie dogs (Figure 11.1). The Utah prairie dog is an endangered species that occurs in southern Utah. In this arid environment, prairie dogs prefer to occupy golf courses, city parks, and alfalfa fields. The presence of any endangered species restricts the development and use of areas that they occupy. Hence, landowners, real developers, and the business community in southern Utah dislike them (Elmore and Messmer 2006). In response, governmental employees catch prairie dogs in urban areas and translocate them to federal land in the hope of establishing new prairie dog colonies. Translocations seem to create a win-win situation. The landowners get help with the nuisance animals, and the prairie dogs are a step closer to having enough colonies on federal land to quality for removal from the endangered species list (Curtis et al. 2014).

Translocation has often been used to manage problem bears at garbage dumps or campgrounds and deer in parks. Managing deer in suburban areas has proved especially challenging because hunting may not be an option if local laws prohibit

FIGURE 11.1   Utah prairie dogs.

Source: Courtesy of National Park Service.

the discharge of firearms or if local residents are opposed to hunting. Surveys of suburban residents in New York and Virginia indicated that the management technique preferred by the highest proportion of respondents was live-trapping and translocating deer (Green et al. 1997; Stout et al. 1997). This action was also perceived as the most effective short-term deer management technique by respondents in New York (Stout et al. 1997).

Before we can evaluate wildlife translocation as a tool to alleviate wildlife damage, we need to address the following questions: (1) Do translocated animals return to their capture site? (2) Do translocated animals cause similar problems in their new homes? (3) Does translocating animals solve the original problem or do new animals just replace them? (4) What is the survival rate of translocated animals, and what effect do they have on the animals that are already living at the release site? (5) What factors influence the probability that translocation will satisfactorily resolve a wildlife problem? (6) Is translocation a cost-effective method to alleviate wildlife damage? These questions are explored next.

11.1 DO TRANSLOCATED ANIMALS RETURN TO THEIR CAPTURE SITE?

Many wildlife species have a well-developed homing instinct. Upon release, they tend to travel in the direction of their capture site and can cover extensive distances in an attempt to reach it. Bears are a classic example; Rogers (1986) summarized data from various studies reporting movements of black bears after translocation. In total, 81% of bears returned to their capture area when translocated less than 64 km, 48% returned from 64 to 120 km, 33% from 120 to 220 km, and 20% from over 220 km. Grizzly bears also demonstrate strong homing tendencies. Of 85 grizzly bears translocated less than 125 km in Yellowstone National Park, 59% returned to their capture site (Brannon 1987). In Alaska, Miller and Ballard (1982) translocated 20 radio-collared grizzly bears over distances of 150–300 km. At least 12 (60%) traveled back to their capture area from an average distance of 198 km.

Less is known about the homing tendencies of canids and felids. In the northwest United States, 20% of 81 individual wolves or groups of wolves returned to their capture site despite being moved 74–316 km. Wolves that failed to return to their capture site still tended to move in its direction after their release (Bradley et al. 2005). Eight of 14 wolves returned to their capture site in Minnesota when released with 50–64 km of it, whereas none of 20 wolves translocated more than 64 km returned (Fritts et al. 1984). Nine female red foxes and 171 pups were translocated 3–171 km in Iowa. One female returned from 14 km, and a litter of four pups, translocated with their mother, returned from 3 km. The remaining foxes showed no homing tendencies (Andrews et al. 1973). In New Mexico, 14 cougars were experimentally translocated an average of 477 km from their capture sites, yet two males were able to return to them (Ruth et al. 1998).

Large herbivores that had been translocated generally remain close to their release sites, although a few individuals travel long distances. Rogers (1988) reviewed a series of papers reporting white-tailed deer movements after translocation and found that most animals remained within 30 km of their release sites. In other studies, translocated white-tailed deer moved between 2 and 5 km in Illinois (Jones and Witham 1990) and 23 km in New York (Jones et al. 1997). Translocated black-tailed deer moved an average of 9 km in California (O'Bryan and McCullough 1985). However, individual deer occasionally find their way home over much longer distances. In Texas, three white-tailed deer successfully returned to their capture site from distances of 530–560 km, which represent the longest homing distances ever recorded for North American mammals. One hundred and nine elephants were translocated from Shimba Hills National Reserve and Mwaluganje Elephant Sanctuary in Kenya to Tsavo East National Park, a distance of 160 km; yet, six elephants still managed to return to their capture site (Pinter-Wollman 2009).

Birds typically have a better homing instinct than mammals. Because of this, translocation is not commonly used to resolve human–bird conflicts. Twelve of 14 resident adult golden eagles captured in Wyoming and released 416–470 km away returned to their former home ranges (Phillips et al. 1991). Some eagles came back within a few weeks, whereas others took over five months to return (Figure 11.2).

FIGURE 11.2   When golden eagles are translocated, many return to their capture site.

Source: Paolo-manzi, Shutterstock 709358215.

Red-tailed hawks (n = 610) were translocated from Chicago's O'Hare International Airport where they posed a hazard to airplanes, but 18% returned to the airport. The hawks were released at four sites that were 81, 121, 181, and 204 km from the airport; homing rates decreased when hawks were released at the more distant sites. Mature hawks were more likely than subadults to return to the airport (Pullins et al. 2018).

When nuisance Canada geese were translocated from urban areas where they were causing problems, most adults (83%) return to the capture site, even though the release site was 400 km from the capture site. In contrast, only 11% of juveniles returned to the capture site (Flockhart and Clarke 2017). Thus, attempts to resolve urban Canada goose problems by translocating adults to rural areas have largely been abandoned because of the propensity of adults to return home or to cause nuisance problems in other areas. In contrast, goslings that are captured just before they are able to fly and translocated to rural areas show little inclination to return home and are likely to remain in rural areas (Cooper and Keefe 1997). One interesting approach to translocating juveniles is to relocate juvenile geese in an area that is open to hunting. At these sites, 23% of relocated juveniles were shot by hunters compared to only 7% of juveniles that were not translocated (Holevinski et al. 2006). Juvenile starlings that were translocated also did not return to their capture, allowing their damage to an orchard to be mitigated (Sidebar 11.1).

SIDEBAR 11.1 TRANSLOCATING JUVENILE STARLINGS CAN PROTECT BLUEBERRY ORCHARDS FROM BIRD DAMAGE

After juvenile starlings fledge, they form large flocks, which contain only juvenile birds. Sometimes, these flocks discover a blueberry orchard when the blueberries are ripening. When that happens, the same flock returns day after day, eating a great number of the fruit, much to the dismay of the farmer. Conover and Dolbeer (2007) wanted to determine if this problem could be

FIGURE 11.3   Modified Australian crow trap taken from the side and from the top, showing the narrow slit through which birds can jump into the trap but cannot fly out.

Source: Author.

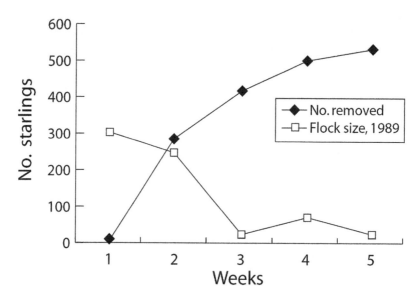

FIGURE 11.4   Relationship between the number of juvenile starlings translocated from a blueberry farm in Connecticut and the size of the remaining flock that fed daily at the blueberry farm.

Source: Author.

mitigated by translocating the starlings. To test this, the scientists positioned Australian crow traps at a farm in Connecticut where a flock of 400 juveniles foraged daily. The traps worked because they have a long, narrow slit on the slanting roof of the trap. Starlings on the outside of the trap can drop through the narrow slit, but birds inside the trap cannot fly out of it (Figure 11.3). A few juvenile starlings were placed inside each trap with plenty of food and water for their survival to lure other starlings into the trap. Starlings on the outside were motivated to get into the trap because they wanted to join the captive starlings. Over a 5-week period, 620 juvenile starlings were captured but not a single adult starling. During this same period, the number of starlings feeding in the blueberries dropped from 300 to less than 50 (Figure 11.4). The trapped starlings were not killed but released 50–100 km away. This program was successful because juvenile starlings are naïve and easy to catch. Few of the released starlings returned, probably because juvenile starlings wandered around looking for food and did not have a territory, mate, or young back at the blueberry orchard.

Several variables influence the propensity of translocated animals to return home. As indicated in previous examples, homing tendencies decrease as distances between the capture and release sites increase (Bradley et al. 2005; Fontúrbel and Simonetti 2011). Because translocating animals great distances is costly and time-consuming, most people want to release the animals at the shortest distance possible while still achieving the purpose of the translocation. For most mammals, this distance is typically 5–10 times the width of the animal's home range so that the animal is released into unfamiliar territory. If a skunk has a home range of 2 km in diameter, it would probably not return to its capture site if released 12–20 km away. The presence of physical barriers, such as rivers or mountain ranges, further impedes the ability of a translocated animal to return to its capture site.

The age of the translocated animal is also a factor in its propensity to return to its capture area. In general, adults are more likely to return than juveniles or subadults, in part, because an adult may have been taken away from an established territory, mate, or young. These provide strong incentives for translocated adults to return. In contrast, many subadults lack territories and may have been in the process of dispersing when captured. Thus, these animals have fewer reasons to return to the capture site.

One way to reduce the tendency for translocated animals to return home is to keep the animals in large pens at the release site for several weeks. This method is called a "gentle," "soft," or "slow" release, whereas the immediate release of animals is called a "hard" or "quick" release. With a soft release, the prerelease captivity period allows animals to acclimatize to their new surroundings and, among social species, promotes long-term bonding of unfamiliar individuals into a cohesive group (Hunter et al. 2007). Translocated wolves shorter distances and were less likely to return to the capture site when they were soft released by keeping them for a month in a 0.5-ha exclosure than those that were hard released (Bradley et al. 2005).

For short-term problems, it matters little if the animals return home if the problem is over by the time they get there. In Great Smoky Mountains National Park, reestablishment of elk to the park was hampered due to high depredation rates on elk calves by black bears. In response, 49 black bears at the elk-calving site were captured and relocated. Bear capturing began a couple of weeks prior to when the elk started to have calves and ended when the last known elk had given birth. Half of the bears returned within a couple of weeks, but by then, most elk calves were fast enough to escape from a bear. Elk calf recruitment increased from 0.31 prior to the removal to 0.54 after it (Yarkovich et al. 2011). As another example, U.S.D.A. Wildlife Services prevented bears from depredating sheep in Oregon by translocating bears. In this case, several migratory bands of sheep traveled together during the summer on a one-way circuit of different grazing areas. Wildlife Services trapped bears in each grazing area shortly before the sheep were scheduled to arrive. The bears were moved less than 33 km to an area where no sheep were present. Most bears returned to their capture sites, but by the time they returned, the sheep had moved on to another area (Armistead et al. 1994).

During the Winter Olympics in Utah, the state Department of Transportation was worried about moose colliding with buses shuttling athletes between Salt Lake City and the Olympic venues in the mountains. To reduce this risk, helicopters relocated moose wintering near the highway to other areas. The Olympics only last a few weeks and if the moose returned after that, it did not matter because they could no longer disrupt the Olympics. The program was successful; there were no moose–vehicle collisions during the Olympics.

11.2   DO NEW ANIMALS REPLACE THE TRANSLOCATED ONES SO THAT THE PROBLEM PERSISTS?

The answer to this question will depend on the species and circumstances, but little information is available on the subject in scientific literature. A study of white-tailed deer movements in a New York forest revealed that the removal of small social groups of deer created a low-density area that persisted for several years (McNulty et al. 1997). Deer from adjacent areas tended not to move into the low-density area, nor did they shift their ranges closer to it. The authors concluded that localized management of white-tailed deer was possible owing to the deer's philopatry (tendency to return or remain near a particular site) to their home ranges. However, deer living in agricultural environments exhibit less philopatry than deer living in forested areas.

Conversely, after an experimental removal of resident golden eagles in Wyoming, all open territories were quickly reoccupied by new eagles (Phillips et al. 1991). Seven of the 14 translocated eagles came back and were able to reclaim their territories, either during the same breeding season or during the next one. Three others were displaced from their territories, and two more were found dead near their original nest tree after fighting with the eagles that had replaced them. The fate of the remaining two eagles was unknown. Replacement of translocated eages would be desirable from a damage management perspective because most eagles do not prey upon lambs or calves and, therefore, are unlikely to kill livestock. Phillips et al.

FIGURE 11.5   Translocation is rarely used to alleviate problems with urban Canada geese because the translocated geese are quickly replaced by others.

Source: Ron Rowan Photography, Shutterstock 263574869.

(1996) reported two cases of eagle predation on calves; the removal of a single eagle in one case, and of a pair in the other case, put an end to all depredations.

When nuisance behavior is exhibited by most individuals in a population, the problem is likely to reoccur as soon as the translocated animal is replaced by another. For example, translocating urban raccoons without removing the attractant will probably result in further depredations by other raccoons. Similarly, when urban Canada geese are captured at a nuisance site and removed, new geese reoccupy the site within a few weeks or months, creating the same nuisance problem (Figure 11.5). For this reason, geese will have to be translocated every year from the same site. In these situations, translocation provides only a temporary solution to a wildlife damage problem.

11.3   DO TRANSLOCATED ANIMALS CREATE THE SAME PROBLEMS ELSEWHERE?

Some individuals causing problems in one area will probably cause the same type of nuisance elsewhere if given the opportunity. In Sir Lanka, almost all elephants continued to cause human–elephant conflicts after being translocated, and most continued to raid crops (Fernando et al. 2012). Because wolves and bears can travel long distances when translocated, a certain proportion of these animals are bound to find their way to human settlements or livestock operations and cause further problems. In Glacier National Park, 11% of translocated black bears caused similar problems elsewhere (McArthur 1981). In Yellowstone National Park, 43% of translocated grizzly bears were involved in further depredation incidents (Brannon 1987).

FIGURE 11.6   Siberian tiger on the Russian taiga.

Source: Ondrej Prosicky, Shutterstock 1727952805.

In the northwestern United States, 27% of 63 wolves that were translocated owing to their history of preying on livestock continued to do so after they were translocated (Bradley et al. 2005). In Minnesota, 107 wolves were translocated after they attacked livestock, and 13% had to be recaptured after causing similar problems elsewhere (Fritts et al. 1985). Four Siberian tigers (Figure 11.6) in Russia that were captured after killing domestic animals or attacking people were relocated 150–350 km to a site considered good tiger habitat. Two of the translocated tigers moved to areas of human activity and were killed by people; the other two caused no further conflicts with people and survived their first winter after being translocated (Goodrich and Miquelle 2005; Sidebar 11.2).

SIDEBAR 11.2 SOMETIMES TRANSLOCATING DANGEROUS PREDATORS GOES HORRIBLY WRONG

One fear of relocating large predators is that the action will backfire. The government of India translocated 20 leopards from a human-dominated rural area in Junnar and moved 40 km to a nearby forest; 11 additional leopards were translocated to other districts in India. An average of four leopard attacks on humans occurred prior to the translocation, but this increased to 17 attacks after it. When leopards were moved 40 km, attacks on humans increased in Junnar; when leopards were moved to other districts, attacks decreased

FIGURE 11.7   Leopard at a recent kill. This was photographed on a morning drive in a forest reserve in Jaipur, India.

Source: Sourabh Bharti, Shutterstock 1235950798.

in Junnar but increased in the districts where the leopards were released. Additionally, leopard attacks became more lethal after the translocation, 18% of attacks resulted in a human fatality before the attack but increased to 36% afterward. Why the translocation had such devastating consequences is unclear. Perhaps, the translocation increased the leopards' stress and aggressiveness or caused the leopards to lose their fear of humans. Alternatively, the translocated leopards may be less able to capture prey (Figure 11.7) at the release sites and sought humans as alternate prey (Athreya et al. 2011).

In the worst-case scenario, animals translocated because of inappropriate behavior may teach that behavior to other individuals through social facilitation. The inappropriate behavior may then quickly spread through the population. For instance, when a few black bears in Yosemite National Park learned how to break into cars to obtain food, the problem bears were relocated to other parts of the park rather than being euthanized. Translocating these bears expanded the problem by spreading the learned behavior throughout the park's bear population.

11.4   WHAT HAPPENS TO TRANSLOCATED ANIMALS?

The general public views translocation as more humane than the use of lethal means, but this is not always the case. To translocate an animal, it first needs to be captured. A varying percentage of individuals are injured or killed during capture, depending on the species, capture technique, experience of the capture crew, season, meteorological conditions, and condition of the animal prior to capture. Some of these deaths result from the physical trauma involved with being captured and constrained. Mortality rates of white-tailed deer differed based on the method used to capture them (Table 11.1). Mortality rates from capture were 1.3% net guns, 1.4% for drive nets, 2.4% from drop nets, 3.3% for box traps, 5.9% dart guns, 7.7% for clover traps, and 11.1% for rocket-cannon nets (Peterson et al. 2003).

TABLE 11.1
Capture-Related Mortality of White-Tailed Deer Reported for Various Capture Techniques (Unless Indicated, These Figures Do Not Include Deaths from Capture Myopathy Following Release)

Method	Number translocated	Mortality rate (%)	References
Box trap	47	0.0	Hawkins et al. (1967)
	2,035	2.1	Palmer et al. (1980)
	85	7.6	Peery (1969)
Clover trap	2	0.0	Ishmael and Rongstad (1984)
	260	4.6	Fuller (1990)
	115	5.1[1]	Beringer et al. (1996)
Corral trap	302	13.9	Hawkins et al. (1967)

(Continued)

TABLE 11.1 (*Continued*)

Method	Number translocated	Mortality rate (%)	References
Crossbow	83	15.7	Hawkins et al. (1967)
Dart gun	47	0.0	Diehl (1988)
	44	13.6	Palmer et al. (1980)
	75	20.0	Hawkins et al. (1967)
	6	33.3	Ishmael and Rongstad (1984)
Drive net	5	0.0	Ishmael and Rongstad (1984)
	430	<1.4[2]	Sullivan et al. (1991)
	668	0.9	David Pac, Mont. Dept Fish and Wildl., personal communication to Sullivan et al. (1991)
Rocket net	300/187	2.6 + 11.2[3]	Beringer et al. (1996)
	33	6.1	Hawkins et al. (1968)
	17	23.5	Palmer et al. (1980)
Tranimul (tranquilizer sprinkled on bait)	36	22.2	Hawkins et al. (1967)

[1] Deaths from capture myopathy = 0.0.

[2] 0.9% from capture myopathy and possibly 0.5% from injuries sustained during capture (the fate of these injured animals is unknown).

[3] 2.6% of 300 deer died from capture accidents, and 11.2% of 187 radio-tagged deer died from capture myopathy.

Capturing animals by running them down or tiring them out is particularly stressful and can result in high mortality. With African big-game species, this method has occasionally resulted in a 100% mortality rate (Harthoorn 1975). Many of these deaths are a consequence of "capture myopathy," a condition associated with the intense muscle activity, fear, and stress experienced during pursuit and capture. When an animal starts running or working hard, its respiration and heart rates increase in response to the body's increased demands for oxygen. But, the needs of rapidly contracting muscles can outstrip the body's ability to deliver oxygen to them. This causes an oxygen deficit in the muscles, but rather than stop contracting, the muscles switch from aerobic metabolism that requires oxygen to anaerobic metabolism that does not, but produces lactic acid. High concentrations of lactic acid can result in muscle lesions, damage to internal organs, paralysis, and death (Paterson 2007). Deaths from capture myopathy can occur immediately or a few days after capture.

Animals can suffer from chronic stress when the frightening stimuli persist, become repetitious, or when multiple frightening stimuli occur repeatedly. This can lead to anxiety, hypertension, heart problems, and a decrease in immune function. All of the components of translocation (e.g., being captured, handed, transported, and released in a novel area) are stressful and can result in chronic shock. Animal mortality may occur when these are combined with a lack of maintenance behavior, although the death may not occur until weeks after the animal is translocated. Chronic stress predisposes an animal to many forms of mortality and is a major reason why the mortality rates are higher during the first few weeks following a relocation (Teixeira et al. 2007). Species differ in their vulnerability to capture myopathy and chronic stress. Mortality within 30 days of capture can be as high as 47% in fragile species, such as pronghorn, and less than 1% in robust species like moose and elk (O'Gara et al. 2004; Arnemo et al. 2006; Bender 2015).

Animals that survive the first few weeks after capture still face more challenges from being released in an unfamiliar area (Matson et al. 2004). Often, they have difficulty finding food and shelter or avoiding predators and other dangers because they are unfamiliar with the release area. When elk were translocated to areas in Ontario, Canada, where both wolves and hunters were present, naïve elk that were unfamiliar with hunters or wolves were twice as likely to die during their first year after being released as resident elk. Predators, especially wolves, killed a higher percentage of translocated elk (38%) than resident elk (14%). Translocated elk were also prone to accidents (vehicle collisions, falls in steep terrain, mired in mud) while no resident elk had an accidental death. Fortunately, translocated elk were able to learn the skills they needed, and those that survived their first year were as likely as resident elk to survive the second year (Frair et al. 2007). The scientists recommended that elk be released in the middle of summer when forage is abundant, elk are in better body condition, and elk are less vulnerable to wolves.

The difficulties of releasing animals into unfamiliar environments are compounded when urban or suburban animals are released in rural environments. A classic example of such problems is the translocation of black-tailed deer from Angel Island, in San Francisco Bay, to the Cow Mountain Recreation Area, in the Mayacmas Mountains of California. Of 13 radio-collared deer whose fate is known, only two (15%) were still alive a year after translocation (O'Bryan and McCullough 1985). In comparison, the annual survival rate for indigenous black-tailed deer was 72% (Taber and Dasmann 1958, cited by O'Bryan and McCullough 1985). Many of the translocated deer were in poor condition when captured, and several of them died of malnutrition within 2 weeks of release. After release, the main cause of death was collisions with vehicles. Predators and hunters also took their toll. The deer failed to recognize dangers that they had not been exposed to prior to translocation, such as fast-moving vehicles, predators, and hunters; all of which were absent from Angel Island. In another translocation of black-tailed deer in California, 27 deer were moved from Ardenwood Regional Park in the city of Fremont to a more remote area; three months later, 23 of these deer were known to be dead (McCullough et al. 1997).

Urban white-tailed deer translocated to a rural area in Illinois had higher mortality than resident deer, particularly during the first hunting season and winter after translocation. Estimated annual mortality rate was 66% for translocated female deer versus 27% for resident females (Jones and Witham 1990). Of 25 translocated bucks, half were known to have died within a year after translocation, mostly due to hunting. In the northern Great Plains, only 3 of 208 white-tailed deer died from injuries sustained from helicopter-based net gunning; none died as a result of capture myopathy. Mortality (9%) was higher when capturing pronghorn; half of the mortalities resulted from injuries sustained during capture, and half occurred after the animals were released (Jacques et al. 2009).

Forty-four koalas were translocated in Australia. All survived the first month after release, so there was no sign of capture myopathy. They had a 62% annual survival rate for the first year after their release versus a 100% survival rate among koalas that were left alone (Whisson et al. 2012). In Africa, the success or failure of translocating black-faced impala depended, in part, on whether cheetah were present at release sites (Matson et al. 2004).

The 1-year survival rate for predators that were translocated ranged from 0.31 for coyotes to 1.00 for African wild dogs (Table 11.2). Problem black bears (66) were relocated in Colorado; the annual survival rate was 50% for translocated adults and 28% for subadults; of all bears, 29% were killed after getting into trouble again, 15% were legally harvested by hunters, and 14% were illegally killed (Alldredge et al. 2015). In Alberta, Canada, 110 grizzly bears were translocated, but only 30% were successful, which was defined as the bear living a year and not causing problems at its new site.

Annual survival rate of 88 translocated wolves in the northwest United States was 0.60; this was significantly lower than 0.72 survival rate of 399 wolves that were not translocated (Bradley et al. 2005). The two leading causes of mortality among

---

TABLE 11.2
The Proportion of Translocated Individuals That Survived for More Than One Year (Annual Survival Rate), the Number of Cattle That Could Be Compensated for by Using the Same Amount of Money Spent Translocating One Carnivore, and Number of Livestock Killed Annually by a Single Carnivore

Fields	Species	Survival Rate	Cost of translocation Expressed as cattle number	No. cattle Killed annually
Felid	Cougar	0.46	4	1–2
	Tiger	0.17	–	–
	Lion	0.39	–	–
	Leopard	–	8	1–3
	Jaguar	0.50	15	1–6
	Lynx	0.61	–	–
	Cheetah	0.36	8	1–4
	Ocelot	–	4	1–1
Canid	Coyote	0.31	2	1–2
	African wild dog	1.00	6	1–2
Bear	Black bear	0.90	1	1–2
	Polar bear	0.75	2	1–2

Source: Data from Fontúrbel and Simonetti (2011).

translocated wolves were illegal killings and governmental removal after the wolves got into trouble. Best release sites contained abundant wildlife, no cattle, and no wolves. In Minnesota, the annual mortality rate (0.40) for translocated wolves was similar to that for nontranslocated wolves (Fritts et al. 1985).

For social species, survival of translocated animals may increase if animals of the same social group are released together (Letty et al. 2007). Black-tailed prairie dogs that were translocated with their entire family were five times more likely to survive than those released alone or with unfamiliar conspecifics. Predators are a major problem for translocated prairie dogs, and when released as a family unit, the prairie dogs were more likely to give warning calls when predators were sighted and more likely to attack small predators as a family and to drive the predators away (Shier 2006).

Several variables interact to increase the mortality rate of translocated animals, including the individual's health and fitness, age, social status, and sex. Characteristics of the release site also are important. Translocated animals are less likely to survive if released in areas with endemic diseases, abundant predators, and high density of the translocated species already present at the release site. Weather at the time of the release also plays a factor (Calvete and Estrada 2004; Letty et al. 2007; Kock et al. 2010; Whisson et al. 2012). An acceptable level of mortality should be defined prior to any translocation of wildlife. The translocated animals should then be monitored using radio-collars for a year, and the project canceled if mortality rates of translocated animals exceed the accepted mortality rate.

11.5 WHAT ARE THE CONSEQUENCES OF TRANSLOCATION ON RESIDENT WILDLIFE AT THE RELEASE SITE?

11.5.1 COMPETITIVE INTERACTIONS

Any given area can only support a limited number of animals; this is the concept of biological carrying capacity. If translocated animals are released in an area where the population is already at carrying capacity, some animals must die or leave. Usually, the translocated animals will be the ones to perish because they do not know as well as the resident animals how to find food or avoid predators.

In territorial species, translocating animals may cause an increase in territorial fights. Territory owners usually win these fights because a territory has much more value to an individual possessing all the information about the resources available on that territory. Hence, the territory owners will be more determined and more likely to win territorial disputes. Although resident animals usually win these disputes, they also suffer from them because they must spend both time and energy to intimidate, chase, and/or fight off these intruders. Doing so reduces their own chances of survival.

11.5.2 DISEASE PATHOGENS AND PARASITE TRANSMISSION

Transmission of pathogens and parasites to resident animals by translocating wildlife is a serious concern; infected individuals translocated to an area where a certain disease is absent could potentially start an epidemic. For example, a major rabies outbreak in the Mid-Atlantic States in 1982 resulted from the translocation of raccoons from Florida to Virginia (Nettles et al. 1979; Jenkins and Winkler 1987). Similarly, during the late 1970s, a rabies outbreak in skunks in Ontario was traced to the translocation of nuisance animals (Rosatte and MacInnes 1989). Likewise, the parasite *Plasmodium kempi* probably spread into new areas through the translocation of infected turkeys (Castle and Christensen 1990). This blood parasite does not pose much of a threat to turkeys but can sicken other species, such as quail, pheasant, and lesser prairie chicken.

Some wildlife diseases also can be transmitted to pets, livestock, or humans. Raccoons, for instance, can carry rabies, pseudorabies, canine parvovirus, canine distemper, canine adenovirus, feline panleukopenia, and the parasite *Baylisascaris procyonis*. Additionally, epidemics can have indirect effects on species that are not infected by the disease; a plague epidemic in prairie dogs was partly responsible for the population decline of the black-footed ferret (Conover and Vail 2015).

The opposite problem can also occur, when translocated individuals, not exposed to a certain disease, are released into an area where that disease is endemic. This is especially a concern in the translocations of threatened or endangered species when every individual is valuable. Exacerbating this problem is the stress caused by being captured and released into a new area; this stress can weaken the immune system and make the translocated animal susceptible to parasites and diseases (Hing et al. 2017).

11.5.3 REPRODUCTION AND POPULATION GENETICS

Occasionally, individuals have been translocated out of the range of their subspecies and into the range of a different subspecies. An influx of genes from a different subspecies can result in individuals that are not as well adapted to local conditions, a term called outbreeding depression. The alpine ibex provides an example of this problem. Following extinction of this species in Czechoslovakia, some individuals were successfully reintroduced from Austria, and a small population became established. The problem began when animals from a different subspecies were introduced from Turkey and Sinai a few years later. These animals bred with the established individuals; the resulting hybrids were fertile but bred in the fall instead of winter. Consequently, their offspring were born in the cold of winter and did not survive, resulting in the second elimination of alpine ibex from Czechoslovakia.

Another example of problems resulting from the translocation of a subspecies out of its range can be found in Mexico, which, in 1952, adopted a law prohibiting the harvest of antlerless deer. Consequently, white-tailed deer populations increased on many ranches in northern Mexico, which eventually led to problems of overabundance. Because the 1952 law precluded doe hunting, landowners and government agencies translocated does to reduce populations. Between 1992 and 1997, over

2,000 deer were captured and moved to ranches that wanted more deer (Martinez et al. 1997). Although expensive, this technique was successful as long as there were local ranches willing to accept the deer. However, their willingness to do so declined over time. By 1997, 65% of the captured deer had to be translocated outside the range of the subspecies. This practice may have had detrimental consequences on the reproduction and genetics of local deer populations at the release sites (Galindo-Leal and Weber 1994). The translocated deer subspecies (*Odocoileus virginianus texanus*) is larger than other subspecies of white-tailed deer found in Mexico, such as the Coues deer (*O. v. couesi*). During mating season, the male offspring of the large translocated deer apparently had a competitive advantage over the smaller resident bucks and obtained a disproportionate number of matings (Galindo-Leal and Weber 1994). In addition to the alteration of population genetics of the local deer, more immediate problems can occur. Small females carrying offspring sired by large males experience difficulties during parturition, sometimes to the point that both mother and fawn die (Galindo-Leal and Weber 1994).

In many wildlife species, females are synchronized so that they all produce young at the same time of year to reduce the risk of their offspring being killed by a predator (Figure 11.8). For example, white-tailed deer breed in November across the northern United States and Canada (Diefenbach and Shea 2011). But this is not true for

FIGURE 11.8   White-tailed deer are synchronized breeders so that most fawns in a population are born within a few weeks of each other.

Source: Tony Campbell, Shutterstock 1129631135.

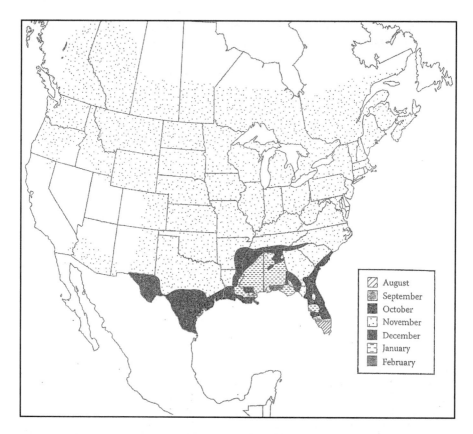

FIGURE 11.9 In the South, white-tailed deer populations vary in when they breed; some breed in August, some in February, and every month in between.

Source: From Diefenbach and Shea (2011) and used with the permission of the publisher.

white-tailed deer in the South where breeding may occur from August to February (Figure 11.9). Using DNA analyses, Sumners et al. (2015) discovered that today's deer population in the South originated from remnant deer that survived the period of overhunting, as well as from numerous reintroductions of deer brought in from other areas. The deer's current lengthy breeding season in the South is a genetic legacy of the diverse areas where the founders originated and may not be beneficial to the deer in their new location. Sumners et al. (2015) caution that potential genetic differences between the local population and the translocated animals must be considered before animals are relocated.

11.6   IS TRANSLOCATION COST-EFFECTIVE?

Translocating an animal is more expensive and requires more hours than to kill it. Huijser et al. (2009) reported that reducing ungulate–vehicle collisions using

FIGURE 11.10   A captured deer being processed for relocation.

Source: Paul Curtis and used with permission.

translocation cost over four times as much as euthanizing them. Fontúrbel and Simonetti (2011) calculated that it cost an average of $4,000 to translocate a bear or felid and $2,875 to translocate a canid. The scientists noted that this was the equivalent of 30 cattle and that the potential costs of translocating a predator exceeded the benefits because most translocated predators would not kill 30 cattle if they had been left alone.

Translocation costs vary based on how the animals are captured. Ishmael and Rongstad (1984) compared the costs of various deer removal techniques at the University of Wisconsin Arboretum during 1982–1983. Shooting over bait was the least expensive technique at $74/deer (for $n = 34$ deer removed), followed by dart gunning at $179/deer ($n = 6$), drive netting at $523/deer ($n = 5$), and using a clover trap at $570/deer ($n = 2$). Palmer et al. (1980) reported that in Ohio it took 1.8, 2.8, 3.3, 4.1, and 6.9 man-hours per deer to remove a deer using public hunting, box trapping, shooting by biologists, dart-gunning, and rocket netting, respectively. Most of the cost of translocating animals is in capturing them alive (Figure 11.10). In general, the cost to capture a single animal will be lowest when (1) densities are high, (2) the animals have not been trapped previously, and (3) wildlife biologists are not trying to capture a particular animal. In any trapping operation, it is always much easier and less expensive to capture the first 10% of a population than the last 10%.

Another cost with translocation is the expense of transporting the captured animals to their release site. The cost of relocating a single red-tailed hawk 81, 121, 181, and 204 km from Chicago's O'Hare Airport was $213, $284, $362, and $426, respectively (Pullins et al. 2018). Likewise, the cost of releasing an animal will be lower if the animal is released immediately (hard or quick release) rather than a gentle release. However, the chances of the translocated animal surviving and remaining near the release site increase if the animal is maintained in a large pen for several weeks prior to release. Because the gentle release is much more expensive than a hard release, it is used mainly for valuable animals.

11.7 WHEN IS TRANSLOCATION WARRANTED?

Translocation is not a panacea. Its effectiveness varies widely with the circumstances, as does its cost. The main benefit of translocation is that it is socially acceptable; people always prefer to "give the animal a second chance," even when knowing that the odds are against that animal surviving. Most people do not want to be responsible for causing an animal's death. When homeowners hire someone to catch a nuisance animal for them, they prefer to think that the animal will be translocated rather than killed. Most NWCOs will comply with their clients' wishes, although the reality of translocation differs from the myth of animals living "happily ever after" in their new homes. Capturing and translocating wildlife can be extremely stressful to the animals and can result in high mortality rates, particularly for urban wildlife released in a rural habitat where they do not know how to survive. In such cases, it may be more humane to euthanize animals rather than to translocate them (Craven et al. 1998). Translocation of problem animals is warranted (1) when the animal is so valuable that euthanasia is not an option, (2) when the population is below carrying capacity at the release site, and (3) when public relations are more important than other factors. These conditions would not apply for most urban wildlife captured by NWCOs. Yet, those people are responsible for translocating hundreds of thousands of animals annually (Craven et al. 1998). State wildlife agencies should consider requiring nuisance animals to be euthanized upon capture, rather than allowing them to be translocated. Wildlife agencies should then also require all NWCOs to inform their clients if captured animals are to be euthanized. This way, clients will realize that one of the costs of removing the nuisance animal will be its death. Then they can make their own decision whether ending the problem caused by the animal is worth that cost.

Translocating nuisance animals creates two other problems that need to be considered before a decision is made to use this technique. The first problem is a moral one. If an animal is likely to cause the same problem elsewhere, then translocating animals merely shifts the problem to someone else. The second problem concerns liability. The person(s), organization, or agency translocating an animal may be held liable for any damage or injuries caused by that animal after translocation and, in some cases, by that animal's offspring. Hence, animals should be translocated only if there is a willingness to assume this liability, which may be in the millions of dollars (Sidebar 11.3). For this reason, species that may cause human injuries or excessive damage should not be translocated. For example, 12 elephants that were causing problems in Sir Lanka were translocated to national parks. Four of translocated elephants entered major towns, resulting in five human deaths and damage to property including vehicles. Twelve other elephants were not translocated, and none of them entered major towns or killed people (Fernando et al. 2012).

SIDEBAR 11.3 COURT CASE: KNOCHEL VERSUS STATE OF ARIZONA

The Arizona Department of Fish and Game had a policy of capturing nuisance black bears and translocating them elsewhere (Figure 11.11). At a release site in a mountain range near Phoenix, one of these translocated bears severely mauled a young girl, who was camping at the time. The attack left her with permanent injuries. The girl and her family sued the state for damages, arguing that the state knew, or should have known, that it was creating a dangerous situation by translocating nuisance bears and that, therefore, the state should be held liable for the girl's injuries. On advice of its counsel, the state of Arizona settled out of court for $4.5 million.

FIGURE 11.11   A black bear.

Source: Jim Cumming, Shutterstock 1179185860.

11.8 SUMMARY

The translocation of nuisance animals is an appealing method of resolving wildlife damage problems because the public perceives it as giving the problem animal a second chance in a new home. Unfortunately, reality is usually different. Translocated animals often return to their original homes or cause similar problems at their release sites. Most translocated animals have a short life expectancy and may adversely affect resident animals at the release sites. Organizations, agencies, or people who translocate animals should be willing to assume liability for any damage or injuries caused by these animals. For this reason, animals posing a threat to human safety should not be translocated. In many cases, translocating animals will not resolve the original problem because new animals will replace them and cause the same problems. Hence, it is often more effective to make the site less attractive to wildlife (e.g., it is better to cap a chimney than constantly translocate raccoons that attempt to nest in it). Capturing animals alive and translocating them is usually expensive. However, while translocating animals is not a panacea, it is a viable option in some situations. Translocation will be most appropriate when (1) the animals have high value (e.g., an endangered species), (2) the population of the species at the release site is below carrying capacity, or (3) public relation concerns outweigh other considerations. Translocated animals are less likely to return to the site where they were captured as the distance between the capture site and release site increases or if separated by physical barriers, such as a river. Translocated animals are more likely to survive if relocated using a gentle release, during summer, and in suitable habitat where the resident population in below carrying capacity.

11.9 DISCUSSION QUESTIONS

1. We discussed in this chapter the management of the Utah prairie dog, which is an endangered species. The presence of an endangered species creates hardships for landowners when an endangered species lives on their property. This raises the question of whether management of endangered species should be considered part of the field of wildlife damage management. Some argue that it should be, but others believe that if management of endangered species is considered part of wildlife damage management, then there is no difference between wildlife management and wildlife damage management. What is your opinion on this matter?
2. Sometimes, juvenile Canada geese that were raised in urban parks are translocated to public lands where hunting is allowed. Some believe that this is a useful practice because it increases opportunities for hunters to harvest a goose during the hunting season. Others argue that juvenile geese raised in parks have learn to trust people, and it is unfair to move these trusting animals to an area where they can be hunted, even if the hunting season is several months away. What is your opinion?
3. What are some methods that can be employed to reduce the risk of a translocated animal returning to its original home?

4. What can be done to reduce the risk that a translocated animal will cause the same problem where it is released?

5. What would you do if you worked for Yellowstone National Park and had to decide how to handle a nuisance black bear captured in campground. Would you euthanize it, let it go, or translocate it?

6. Several years ago, Massachusetts had a law that a person could only release a nuisance animal, such as a raccoon, on their own property, while Connecticut had a policy that a nuisance animal could be released anywhere. Which state had the better policy?

LITERATURE CITED

Alldredge, M. W., D. P. Walsh, L. L. Sweanor, R. B. Davies, and A. Trujillo. 2015. Evaluation of translocation of black bears involved in human – bear conflicts in south-central Colorado. *Wildlife Society Bulletin* 39:334–340.

Andrews, R. D., G. L. Storm, R. L. Phillips, and R. A. Bishop. 1973. Survival and movements of transplanted and adopted red fox pups. *Journal of Wildlife Management* 37:69–72.

Armistead, R. A., K. Mitchell, and G. E. Connolly. 1994. Bear relocations to avoid bear/sheep conflicts. *Proceedings of the Vertebrate Pest Conference* 16:31–35.

Arnemo, J. M., P. Ahlqvist, R. Andersen, F. Bernsten, G. Ericsson, J. Odden, S. Brunberg, P. Segerström, and J. E. Swenson. 2006. Risk of capture-related mortality in large free-ranging mammals: experiences from Scandinavia. *Wildlife Biology* 12:109–113.

Athreya, V., M. Odden, J. D. Linnell, and K. U. Karanth. 2011. Translocation as a tool for mitigating conflict with leopards in human-dominated landscapes of India. *Conservation Biology* 25:133–141.

Barnes, T. G. 1993. A survey comparison of pest control and nuisance wildlife control operators in Kentucky. *Proceedings of the Eastern Wildlife Damage Control Conference* 6:39–48.

Barnes, T. G. 1995. Survey of the nuisance wildlife control industry with notes on their attitudes and opinions. *Proceedings of the Great Plains Wildlife Damage Control Workshop* 12:104–108.

Bender, L. C. 2015. Does body condition affect immediate post-capture survival of ungulates? *Human-Wildlife Interactions* 9:191–197.

Beringer, J., L. P. Hansen, W. Wilding, J. Fischer, and S. L. Sheriff. 1996. Factors affecting capture myopathy in white-tailed deer. *Journal of Wildlife Management* 60:373–380.

Bradley, E. H., D. H. Pletscher, E. E. Bangs, K. E. Kunkel, D. W. Smith, C. M. Mack, T. J. Meier, J. A. Fontaine, C. C. Niemeyer, and M. D. Jimenez. 2005. Evaluating wolf translocation as a nonlethal method to reduce livestock conflicts in the Northwestern United States. *Conservation Biology* 19:1498–1508.

Brannon, R. D. 1987. Nuisance grizzly bear, *Ursus arctos*, translocations in the Greater Yellowstone area. *Canadian Field-Naturalist* 101:569–575.

Calvete, C., and R. Estrada. 2004. Short-term survival and dispersal of translocated European wild rabbits: improving the release protocol. *Biological Conservation* 120:507–516.

Castle, M. D., and B. M. Christensen. 1990. Hematozoa of wild turkeys from the midwestern United States: translocation of wild turkeys and its potential role in the introduction of *Plasmodium kempi*. *Journal of Wildlife Diseases* 26:180–185.

Conover, M. R., and R. A. Dolbeer. 2007. Use of decoy traps to protect blueberries from juvenile European starlings. *Human-Wildlife Interactions* 1:265–270.

Conover, M. S., and R. M. Vail. 2015. *Human-diseases from wildlife.* CRC Press, Boca Raton, FL.

Cooper, J. A., and T. Keefe. 1997. Urban Canada goose management: policies and procedures. *Transactions of the North American Wildlife and Natural Resources Conference* 62:412–430.

Craven, S., T. Barnes, and G. Kania. 1998. Toward a professional position on the translocation of problem wildlife. *Wildlife Society Bulletin* 26:171–177.

Curtis, P. D., M. L. Richmond, P. A. Wellner, and B. Tullar. 1993. Characteristics of the private nuisance wildlife control industry in New York. *Eastern Wildlife Damage Control Conference* 6:49–57.

Curtis, R., S. N. Frey, and N. L. Brown. 2014. The effect of coterie relocation on release-site retention and behavior of Utah prairie dogs. *Journal of Wildlife Management* 78:1069–1077.

Diefenbach, D. R., and S. M. Shea. 2011. Managing white-tailed deer: Eastern North America. Pages 481–500 *in* D. G. Hewitt, editor. *Biology and management of white-tailed deer.* CRC Press, Boca Raton, FL.

Diehl, S. R. 1988. The translocation of urban white-tailed deer. Pages 239–249 *in* L. Nielsen and R. D. Brown, editors. *Translocation of wild animals.* Wisconsin Humane Society, Milwaukee, Wisconsin and Caesar Kleberg Wildlife Research Institute, Kingsville, TX.

Elmore, R. D., and T. A. Messmer. 2006. *Public perceptions regarding the Utah prairie dog and its management: implications for species recovery.* Jack H. Berryman Institute for Wildlife Damage, Publication No. 23. Utah State University Extension, Logan, UT.

Fernando, P., P. Leimgruber, T. Prasad, and J. Pastorini. 2012. Problem-elephant translocation: translocating the problem and the elephant? *PLoS One* 7(12):e50917.

Flockhart, D. T., and J. B. Clarke. 2017. Demographic consequences of translocation of overabundant Canada geese breeding in urban areas. *Wildlife Society Bulletin* 41:231–239.

Fontúrbel, F. E., and J. A. Simonetti. 2011. Translocations and human-carnivore conflicts: problem solving or problem creating? *Wildlife Biology* 17:217–225.

Frair, J. L., E. H. Merrill, J. R. Allen, and M. S. Boyce. 2007. Know thy enemy: experience affects elk translocation success in risky landscapes. *Journal of Wildlife Management* 71:541–554.

Fritts, S. H., W. J. Paul, and L. D. Mech. 1984. Movements of translocated wolves in Minnesota. *Journal of Wildlife Management* 48:709–721.

Fritts, S. H., W. J. Paul, and L. D. Mech. 1985. Can relocated wolves survive? *Wildlife Society Bulletin* 13:459–463.

Fuller, T. K. 1990. Dynamics of a declining white-tailed deer population in north-central Minnesota. *Wildlife Monographs* 110:1–37.

Galindo-Leal, C., and M. Weber. 1994. Translocation of deer subspecies: reproductive implications. *Wildlife Society Bulletin* 22:117–120.

Goodrich, J. M., and D. G. Miquelle. 2005. Translocation of problem Amur tigers *Panthera tigris altaica* to alleviate tiger-human conflicts. *Oryx* 39:454–457.

Green, D., G. R. Askins, and P. D. West. 1997. Public opinion: obstacle or aid to sound deer management? *Wildlife Society Bulletin* 25:367–370.

Harthoorn, A. M. 1975. *The chemical capture of animals: a guide to the chemical restraint of wild and captive animals.* Ralph Curtis Books, Hollywood, FL.

Hawkins, R. E., D. C. Autry, and W. D. Klimstra. 1967. Comparison of methods used to capture white-tailed deer. *Journal of Wildlife Management* 31:460–464.

Hawkins, R. E., L. D. Montoglio, and G. G. Montgomery. 1968. Cannon-netting deer. *Journal of Wildlife Management* 32:191–195.

Hing, S., A. S. Northover, E. J. Narayan, A. F. Wayne, K. L. Jones, S. Keatley, R. C. A. Thompson, and S. S. Godfrey. 2017. Evaluating stress physiology and parasite infection parameters in the translocation of critically endangered woylies (*Bettongia penicillata*). *EcoHealth* 14:128–138.

Holevinski, R. A., R. A. Malecki, and P. D. Curtis. 2006. Can hunting of translocated nuisance Canada geese reduce local conflicts? *Wildlife Society Bulletin* 34:845–849.

Huijser, M. P., J. W. Dufield, A. P. Cleverger, R. J. Ament, and P. T. McGowen. 2009. Cons-benefit analyses of mitigation measures aimed at reducing collisions with large ungulates in the United States and Canada: decision support tool. *Ecology and Society* 14(2). www.ecologyandsociety.org/vol14/iss2/art15/.

Hunter, L. T. B., K. Pretorius, L. C. Carlisle, M. Rickelton, C. Walker, R. Slotow, and J. D. Skinner. 2007. Restoring lions *Panthera leo* to Northern KwaZulu-Natal, South Africa: short-term biological and technical success but equivocal long-term conservation. *Oryx* 41:196–204.

Ishmael, W. E., and O. J. Rongstad. 1984. Economics of an urban deer-removal program. *Wildlife Society Bulletin* 12:394–398.

Jacques, C. N., J. A. Jenks, C. S. Deperno, J. D. Sievers, T. W. Grovenburg, T. J. Brinkman, C. C. Swanson, and B. A. Stillings. 2009. Evaluating ungulate mortality associated with helicopter net-gun captures in the Northern Great Plains. *Journal of Wildlife Management* 73:1282–1291.

Jenkins, S. R., and W. G. Winkler. 1987. Descriptive epidemiology from an epizootic of raccoon rabies in the middle Atlantic states, 1982–1983. *American Journal of Epidemiology* 126:429–437.

Jones, J. M., and J. H. Witham. 1990. Post-translocation survival and movements of metropolitan white-tailed deer. *Wildlife Society Bulletin* 18:434–441.

Jones, M. L., N. E. Mathews, and W. F. Porter. 1997. Influence of social organization on dispersal and survival of translocated female white-tailed deer. *Wildlife Society Bulletin* 25:272–278.

Kock, R. A., M. H. Woodford, and P. B. Rossiter. 2010. Disease risks associated with the translocation of wildlife. *Revue Scientifique et Technique* 29:329–350.

Letty, J., S. Marchandeau, and J. Aubineau. 2007. Problems encountered by individuals in animal translocations: lessons from field studies. *Ecoscience* 14:420–431.

Martinez, A., D. G. Hewitt, and M. Cotera Correa. 1997. Managing overabundant white-tailed deer in Northern Mexico. *Wildlife Society Bulletin* 25:430–432.

Matson, T. K., A. W. Goldizen, and P. Jarman. 2004. Factors affecting the success of translocation of the black-faced impala in Namibia. *Biological Conservation* 116:359–365.

McArthur, K. L. 1981. Factors contributing to effectiveness of black bear transplants. *Journal of Wildlife Management* 45:102–110.

McCullough, D. R., K. W. Jennings, N. B. Gates, B. G. Elliott, and J. E. DiDonato. 1997. Overabundant deer populations in California. *Wildlife Society Bulletin* 25:478–483.

McNulty, S. A., W. F. Porter, N. E. Mathews, and J. A. Hill. 1997. Localized management for reducing white-tailed deer populations. *Wildlife Society Bulletin* 25:265–271.

Miller, S. D., and W. B. Ballard. 1982. Homing of transplanted Alaskan brown bears. *Journal of Wildlife Management* 46:869–876.

Nettles, V. F., J. H. Shaddock, and R. K. Sikes. 1979. Rabies in translocated raccoons. *American Journal of Public Health* 69:601–602.

O'Bryan, M. K., and D. R. McCullough. 1985. Survival of black-tailed deer following relocation in California. *Journal of Wildlife Management* 49:115–119.

O'Gara, B. W., C. J. Knowles, P. R. Knowles, and J. D. Yoakum. 2004. Capture, translocation and handlings. Pages 705–761 *in* B. W. O'Gara and J. D. Yoakum, editors. *Pronghorn: ecology and management.* University of Colorado Press, Boulder, CO.

Palmer, D. T., D. A. Andrews, R. O. Winters, and J. W. Francis. 1980. Removal techniques to control an enclosed deer herd. *Wildlife Society Bulletin* 8:29–33.

Paterson, J. 2007. Capture myopathy. Pages 115–121 *in* G. West, D. J. Heard, and N. Caulkett, editors. *Zoo animal and wildlife immobilization and anesthesia.* Blackwell Publishing, Ames, IA.

Peery, C. H., III. 1969. The economics of Virginia's deer transplantation program. *Proceedings of the Southeastern Association of Game and Fish Commissioners* 22:142–144.

Peterson, M. N., R. R. Lopez, P. A. Frank, M. J. Peterson, and N. J. Silvy. 2003. Evaluating capture methods for urban white-tailed deer. *Wildlife Society Bulletin* 31:1176–1187.

Phillips, R. L., J. L. Cummings, and J. D. Berry. 1991. Responses of breeding golden eagles to relocation. *Wildlife Society Bulletin* 19:430–434.

Phillips, R. L., J. L. Cummings, G. Notah, and C. Mullis. 1996. Golden eagle predation on domestic calves. *Wildlife Society Bulletin* 24:468–470.

Pinter-Wollman, N. 2009. Spatial behaviour of translocated African elephants (*Loxodonta africana*) in a novel environment: using behaviour to inform conservation actions. *Behaviour* 146:1171–1192.

Pullins, C. K., T. L. Guerrant, S. F. Beckerman, and B. E. Washburn. 2018. Mitigation translocation of red-tailed hawks to reduce raptor-aircraft collisions. *Journal of Wildlife Management* 82:123–129.

Rogers, L. L. 1986. Effect of translocation distance on frequency of return by adult black bears. *Wildlife Society Bulletin* 14:76–80.

Rogers, L. L. 1988. Homing tendencies of large mammals: a review. Pages 76–92 *in* L. Nielsen and R. D. Brown, editors. *Translocation of wild animals.* Wisconsin Humane Society, Milwaukee, Wisconsin and Caesar Kleberg Wildlife Research Institute, Kingsville, TX.

Rosatte, R. C., and C. D. MacInnes. 1989. Relocation of city raccoons. *Great Plains Wildlife Damage Control Conference* 9:87–92.

Ruth, T. K., K. A. Logan, L. L. Sweanor, M. G. Hornocker, and L. J. Temple. 1998. Evaluating cougar translocation in New Mexico. *Journal of Wildlife Management* 62:1264–1275.

Shier, D. M. 2006. Effect of family support on the success of translocated black-tailed prairie dogs. *Conservation Biology* 20:1780–1790.

Stout, R. J., B. A. Knuth, and P. D. Curtis. 1997. Preferences of suburban landowners for deer management techniques: a step towards better communication. *Wildlife Society Bulletin* 25:348–359.

Sullivan, J. B., C. A. DeYoung, S. L. Beasom, J. R. Heffelfinger, S. P. Coughlin, and M. W. Hellickson. 1991. Drive-netting deer: incidence of mortality. *Wildlife Society Bulletin* 19:393–396.

Sumners, J. A., S. Demarais, R. W. Deyoung, R. L. Honeycutt, A. P. Rooney, R. A. Gonzales, and K. L. Gee. 2015. Variable breeding dates among populations of white-tailed deer in the Southern United States: the legacy of restocking? *Journal of Wildlife Management* 79:1213–1225.

Taber, R. D., and R. F. Dasmann. 1958. *The black-tailed deer of the chaparral: its life history and management in the North Coast range of California.* California Department of Fish and Game, Game Bulletin 8, Sacramento, CA.

Teixeira, C. P., C. S. De Azevedo, M. Mendl, C. F. Cipreste, and R. J. Young. 2007. Revisiting translocation programmes: the importance of considering stress. *Animal Behaviour* 73:1–13.

Whisson, D. A., G. J. Holland, and K. Carlyon. 2012. Translocation of overabundant species: implications for translocated individuals. *Journal of Wildlife Management* 76:1161–1669.

Yarkovich, J., J. D. Clark, and J. L. Murrow. 2011. Effects of black bear relocation on elk calf recruitment at great smoky mountains national park. *Journal of Wildlife Management* 75:1145–1154.

12 Fertility Control

Contraception in wildlife management is a promising technology for use in the not too distant future; and it always will be.

– Anonymous

You want to sterilize coyotes? Perhaps you don't understand the problem: coyotes are killing my sheep, not mating with them.

– Response of a rancher upon
learning about research on
fertility control of coyotes

As for rabbits, God must have loved them because He made so many of them.

– Anonymous

Reproductive hormones are proteins made in the body that are critical for the production of eggs and sperm. One of them is gonadotropin-releasing hormone (GnRH); it is produced by both sexes in the hypothalamus section of the brain and travels in the bloodstream to the anterior pituitary gland at the base of the brain, where it stimulates the release of gonadotropins (hence its name – GnRH). The two gonadotropins that it stimulates are luteinizing hormone (LH) and follicle-stimulating hormone (FSH). In females, these hormones influence the release of progesterone and estradiol from the ovaries. FSH also stimulates the growth and maturation of eggs while LH induces ovulation. In males, LH and FSH stimulate the release of testosterone and estradiol from the testes. Progesterone, estradiol, and testosterone travel in the bloodstream back to the hypothalamus and pituitary gland, where they regulate the production of GnRH and gonadotropins through a feedback mechanism (Hobbs and Hinds 2018, Figure 12.1).

Infertility or fertility control can be achieved by disrupting this system, thereby preventing the production of eggs or sperm, fertilization of eggs in the oviduct, or implantation of the embryo in the uterus. A contraceptive (meaning "against conception") is an entity that prevents reproduction by preventing egg fertilization. Fertility control uses some form of contraceptive to reduce the fertility of a wildlife population to keep that population in check with the goal of resolving a human–wildlife conflict. Fertility control methods in wildlife can be categorized into three general groups: (1) mechanical and surgical techniques, (2) endocrine disruption, and (3) immunocontraception. Each of these methods has advantages and disadvantages that affect its practicality in managing wildlife populations. Ideally, contraceptive agents should (1) be suitable for field delivery, (2) be effective with a single dose, (3) pose no hazard to nontarget species, (4) not enter the food chain, (5) cause no harmful side effects, and (6) have no impact on the social and reproductive behavior of the treated animal.

DOI: 10.1201/9780429401404-12

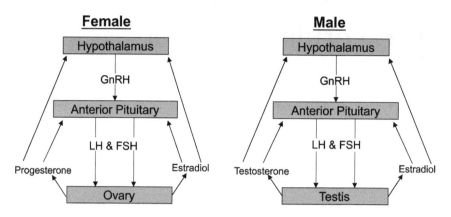

FIGURE 12.1   Diagram of how different hormones regulate reproduction in mammals.
Source: This is Figure 8.1 in the first edition of this book.

12.1   CAN SURGERY OR MECHANICAL METHODS REDUCE FERTILITY IN WILDLIFE?

Surgery and mechanical devices can be used to suppress reproduction in wildlife. Males can be vasectomized to block sperm from exiting the testes; intrauterine devices can be implanted in the uterus to prevent egg implantation. Surgery has been used for years to sterilize domestic pets, zoo animals, and some free-ranging wildlife (Hobbs and Hinds 2018). The primary advantages of mechanical or surgical sterilization are that the animals are permanently incapable of reproducing after a single treatment, and there is no danger to nontarget species. However, these methods are rarely used in wildlife management because each animal must be live-trapped and transported to a veterinarian, making these methods time-consuming and expensive. At present, surgical sterilization of wildlife is used mainly as a research tool to determine if induced sterility will be effective in controlling a population (National Research Council 2013).

12.2   CAN SYNTHETIC HORMONES DISRUPT ENDOCRINE REGULATION?

Normal hormonal function can be disrupted through the use of synthetic hormones that act similar to the normal hormone and bind to hormone receptions. In doing so, the synthetic hormone disrupts sperm production in males and egg development or implantation in females. Initially, synthetic hormones may increase sexual activity, but eventually, infertility occurs because the targeted organ stops releasing hormones.

Synthetic hormones are often used in zoos and livestock to prevent fertility. Four synthetic hormones have been tested with wildlife: melengestrol acetate, norgestomet, levonorgestrel, and quinestrol. Implants of melengestrol acetate and norgestomet have been used for decades to control reproduction in female zoo animals.

Studies with captive white-tailed deer indicated that either can reduce the fertility of females, but melengestrol acetate causes uterine problems, stillbirths, and infant mortality in some species. A single injection of levonorgestrel has reduced fertility in female marsupials, including kangaroos, wallabies, and koalas. Despite the effectiveness of synthetic hormones, their use in the field is contentious due to long-term health effects, environmental concerns, and lack of species specificity (Massei and Cowan 2014). Additionally, high cost and the administration requirements of synthetic hormones make them impractical for use in managing wildlife populations (Asa and Porton 2005).

Large, continuous doses of GnRH or similar chemicals can inhibit the release of gonadotropin by overloading the hormonal receptors of the pituitary gland. Doses of GnRH initially increase pituitary stimulation and stimulate estrus in females and semen production in males. After all of the GnRH receptors become occupied, the pituitary gland cannot be further stimulated and reproduction and sexual behavior cease. A benefit of GnRH is that they should not cause secondary poisoning of nontarget predators or scavengers, owing to their rapid metabolization when consumed. Treatment with GnRH is also reversible and suitable for remote delivery. However, a major problem is GnRH's suppression of sexual and social behavior in the treated animal, which will prevent it from fighting other animals that seek to replace it. If this happens, the population's reproduction may not decline. Another problem is that this treatment may also prolong the breeding season or simply delay it for the treated animal, resulting in off-season births, such as during winter.

12.3   CAN NORMAL REPRODUCTION BE DISRUPTED USING ANTIGENS?

An antigen is a chemical that an animal's immune system recognizes as foreign and develops antibodies to fight it. Scientists have developed antigens that mimic hormones or other proteins essential to reproduction. When these antigens are injected into an animal, the immune system develops antibodies to that antigen and to its own proteins that the antigen mimics. Hence, these vaccines are called immunocontraceptive vaccines. To make sure the body recognizes the antigen as a foreign object, antigens are often injected with adjuvants that stimulate the immune response.

GonaCon is an immunocontraceptive that has prevented reproduction in either sexes for multiple years (Miller et al. 2004) and has safely induced temporary infertility in many wildlife species, including white-tailed deer (Miller et al. 2008; Gionfriddo et al. 2011a, 2011b), mule deer (Perry et al. 2006), coyotes (Young et al. 2018), ground squirrels (Nash et al. 2004), Norway rats (Miller 1997), feral pigs (Killian et al. 2006), eastern gray squirrels, fox squirrels, and black-tailed prairie dogs (Yoder and Miller 2010; Krause et al. 2014, 2015). A single injection of GonaCon can disrupt fertility of female horses for multiple years, although it becomes less effective over time: 94% effectiveness during the first year versus 50%–70% in the second and third year. A booster shot can further increase its duration in some species (Hobbs and Hinds 2018). The USDA National Wildlife Research Center has registered GonaCon with the U.S. EPA during 2003 for use in free-ranging horses and burros, and during 2009 for use with white-tailed deer (Miller et al. 2013). The need for frequent boosters reduces animal welfare concerns because the infertility is reversible; but, this also makes the contraceptive impractical for most free-ranging populations. Vaccinated animals also need to be individually recognized because overdosing is possible if the same animal receives multiple booster shots during a short period of time.

Other promising immunocontraceptive vaccines target the egg's zona pellucida (ZP), which is a glycoprotein membrane that surrounds a mature mammalian egg; sperm must penetrate the ZP before they can fertilize the egg. Injections of ZP proteins into the bloodstream cause the immune system to identify these proteins as foreign bodies and to develop antibodies that specifically recognize the ZP and bind to it. This prevents the ability of sperm to bind with the ZP and, thus, prevents egg fertilization. A common source of ZP is from pig ovaries; thus, this type of ZP is referred to as porcine zona pellucida (PZP). Injections of PZP have been used to decrease fertility in over 80 ungulate species, but PZP injections have not worked so well with felines and rodents (Kirkpatrick et al. 2009; Fagerstone et al. 2010). Three formulations of PZP vaccines are ZonaStat, PZP-22, and SpayVac which vary in their ZP antigens or adjuvants. ZonaStat-H was registered by the Humane Society of the United States and approved by the EPA during 2012 as a contraceptive for feral horses and donkeys.

A single injection of PZP reduced pregnancy rates in white-tailed deer by over 95% in the first year and by 65%–70% during the second year (Rutberg et al. 2013). One problem with PZP is that vaccinated female deer go through multiple estrous cycles in the fall which causes both treated females and local males to increase activity rates and enter the winter in poor body condition. Treated does may also give birth to fawns too late in the year for them to survive the winter. Immunocontraceptive vaccines pose a lower risk to nontarget species than the use of synthetic hormones because the former are less likely to enter the food chain.

12.4   HOW CAN INFERTILITY DRUGS BE ADMINISTERED TO WILDLIFE?

The difficulty of administering a drug to a free-ranging animal limits fertility control in wildlife; the ideal way to do so is through a treated bait (oral delivery). For this, the drug must be constructed so that it is not destroyed in the digestive tract. Placing a contraceptive in a treated bait can be problematic; reproductive hormones are similar in different species, which can cause a nontarget hazard if a treated bait is consumed by the wrong species. The hazard can be reduced by placing the treated bait in a location where it is only available to the target species. An example would include placing treated bait intended for pocket gophers within their burrows. Snow et al. (2017) and Lavelle et al. (2018) created a bait station designed to deliver drugs to feral hogs; it was equipped with a heavy lid that feral hogs could open but not raccoons or deer. Reynolds et al. (2004) developed a floating raft for delivery of a contraceptive to mink, thereby making the drug unavailable to terrestrial mammals.

Another approach of delivering a contraceptive to free-ranging animals is remote delivery systems (RDS), which are mechanical devices designed to administer a contraceptive to a free-ranging animal from a short distance. This is usually accomplished by having a person use a longbow, crossbow, blowgun, pistol, or rifle to fire a hollow dart tipped with a syringe needle and filled with a liquid contraceptive. The effective range of darts is less than 40 m (Massei and Cowan 2014). A limitation of RDS is that animals learn to avoid humans after being darted once or seeing another animal being darted. For this reason, it is particularly difficult to dart an animal more than once (Naugle and Grams 2013). Nevertheless, RDS have the potential to be effective in reducing the fertility of small, isolated populations, and there is little danger of a nontarget species receiving the drug because the animal has to be within sight before it can be darted. A contraceptive could also be delivered using a bioengineered bacteria or virus. Most of the research on this topic has been conducted by Australia. Their interest arises because European rabbits have invaded the country and now number in the hundreds of millions. Australian researchers investigated whether the *Myxoma* virus could be genetically modify to contain a protein found on the surface of rabbit's eggs or sperm. The hope was that rabbits infected with the modified virus would produce antibodies against the virus, and be rendered sterile (Tyndale-Biscoe 1997). Efforts to use a modified virus to sterilize rabbits was successful in the lab. Despite this, this research program was cancelled over concern that the modified virus, once released in Australia, might invade other countries or mutate so that it could infect and sterilize other species.

12.5 DOES THE TYPE OF MATING SYSTEM INFLUENCE CONTRACEPTION?

Male sterilization may be a useful strategy to control polygynous species because the number of breeding males is small relative to the number of breeding females. If the dominant male can be sterilized without affecting his sexual, aggressive, and social behavior, all females in his harem may experience a reduction in fertility. However, male sterility would be ineffective in species with promiscuous mating behavior. Likewise, female sterility may be particularly advantageous in species where the dominant female suppresses reproduction in subordinate females.

Fertility control methods can also be successful in monogamous species that have life-long pair bonds. This would be especially true for species with low immigration rates or that breed only once per year or every few years. Territorial species are also good targets for reproductive control if treated individuals continue to hold their territory and exclude others from it. This seems to be the case with vasectomized wolves and red foxes (Mech et al. 1996; Saunders et al. 2002).

A species' reproductive rate, age at which animals reproduce, and survival rate all influence the outcome of any sterilization strategy. Reproductive rates have a greater impact on population size than mortality rates for short-lived species, such as mice, voles, and lemmings. For these species, a successful infertility program will quickly produce a decrease in population due to the high mortality rates these species experience. Many of these species exhibit cyclic populations with great variance in population size between periods that are favorable and unfavorable for the species. People usually want to reduce these populations when they have peaked because that is when the animals damage crops and people notice them. But this is the wrong time to initiate a sterilization program. Instead, these programs should be delayed until the population has declined. Even then, only remotely delivered contraceptives have any chance of success when many animals needing to be sterilized.

Many wildlife populations are regulated by density-dependent factors. If the target population is at or near carrying capacity, reducing the birth rate through contraception may simply prevent the birth of offspring that would otherwise die. In such cases, reducing the birth rate will have little effect on the size of the population (Bomford 1990). A management program that uses both lethal control and fertility control may be the best option for such populations. An abundant population could first be culled to the extent possible and then followed up with a fertility management program to maintain the population at that low level.

Occasionally, it is possible to increase human–wildlife coexistence by reducing the fertility of specific animals without having any impact on the size of the population. Beaver damage is usually caused by dispersing young rather than by adults. Fertility control could be used to reduce the number of dispersing young each year without having to reduce the population level (Kennelly and Lyons 1983). Fertility control of coyotes also may reduce their predation on livestock without having any impact on coyote populations. Till and Knowlton (1983) demonstrated that most sheep and lambs are killed by adult coyotes feeding pups and only territorial adults produce pups. Hence, a program to sterilize only territorial coyotes near a sheep ranch may end sheep losses without requiring a reduction of the local subpopulation of coyotes.

12.6   WHAT ARE SOME USES OF CONTRACEPTION IN WILDLIFE?

12.6.1   ELEPHANTS

Elephant populations are rapidly increasing in parts of Africa following international legislation that banned the sale of ivory. Unfortunately, elephants cause agricultural damage due to their destructive feeding habits. In the past, elephant overpopulation problems have been alleviated by culling and translocation programs. However, many people oppose the use of lethal methods to manage elephant populations, and sites willing to accept relocated elephants are dwindling. One hope to address the problem of too many elephants is the use of an immunocontraception vaccine, which can be used to delay calving among young females so that reproduction can be shifted to older individuals (Druce et al. 2011). Twenty-one elephants received PZP vaccinations and booster shots in Kruger National Park. These elephants had lower pregnancy rates than untreated elephants (Fayrer-Hosken et al. 1997; Butler 1998; Delsink et al. 2007).

12.6.2   DEER

Human–deer coexistence is difficult inside parks, nature preserves, and suburban areas where hunting is prohibited (Figure 12.2). In such situations, fertility control using surgical sterilization and immunocontraceptives may be a viable method

FIGURE 12.2   Large numbers of white-tailed deer now exist in urban and suburban areas where hunting is not allowed.

Source: Jessica Eldora Robertson, Shuttlestock 1411895036.

because female deer have small home ranges and high rates of site fidelity. Surgical sterilization takes considerable time owing to difficulty of capture deer alive. But this effort is 100% effective and permanent.

Treating a high proportion of deer in the local population is a challenge; Boulanger et al. (2012) reported that more than 80% of the female deer in a population have to be sterilized to achieve a decrease in population. The actual proportion of deer that have to be captured and treated needs to be higher still, given that some procedures will fail. This task becomes near impossible for vaccines that have to be administered more than once. Boulanger and Curtis (2016) tested whether surgical sterilization could reduce the white-tailed deer population on a 445-ha suburban campus in New York state. Despite sterilizing 93 deer from 2007 to 2013, female deer abundance did not change. The authors could not recommend surgical sterilization as a stand-alone method for communities dealing with deer problems. Computer modeling by Pepin et al. (2017) showed that fertility control is much more likely to be successful in managing deer populations in areas, such as offshore islands, where there is no immigration.

Immunocontracptive vaccines via dart guns may be more successful because they do not require the live capture of an animal. PZP and GonaCon immunocontraceptive vaccine are commonly used on deer (Evans et al. 2016). A single injection PZP reduced pregnancy rates in white-tailed deer by over 95% in the first year and by

65%–70% in the second year (Rutberg et al. 2013). At NASA's space center in Texas, Locke et al. (2007) gave 34 white-tailed deer a single injection of SpayVac, a slow-release form of PZP. Deer injected more than a month before the breeding season had no fawns during the next two years versus a 78% fawning rate for uninjected deer. SpayVac has also reduce fertility in fallow deer, elk, and bison (Fraker et al. 2002; Miller et al. 2004; Massei and Cowan 2014). Unfortunately, PZP vaccines cause multiple estrous cycles in female deer and recurrent sexual activity (USDA Animal Plant Health Inspection Service 2018c).

12.6.3 EQUIDS

Horses were introduced to the New World during Columbus' second voyage to the New World; more horses arrived later when Spanish Conquistadors invaded Mexico and South America. Some of these horses escaped, became feral, and their descendants spread across North America. Many people view feral horses as an exotic species because they arrived in North America through the help of man and have no rightful place in the United States or Canada. Others love feral horses and view them as an icon of the American West. Heated debates have arisen over this topic question; what is not debated is that grazing by feral horses has a substantial impact on the semi-arid ecosystem of the Great Basin (Davies et al. 2014; Hall et al. 2016; Gooch et al. 2017) and on barrier islands along the Atlantic Seaboard (Lowney et al. 2005). There are 118,000 wild horses and burros on public lands in the Western United States, an area that should only support 27,000 (Hendrickson 2018). Management of feral horse populations has been difficult since passage of the federal Wild and Free-Roaming Horse and Burro Act in 1971, which bars the use of lethal means to manage horse populations. Instead, public land managers must rely on capturing horses alive and holding them until they are adopted by the public. But not enough horses have been adopted; only 2,700 wild horses and burros are adopted annually, representing only 6% of 46,000 horses that are kept in captivity. This capture-and-hold program has not reduced feral horse numbers, owing to horses' high reproductive potential. The program is also expensive; U.S. Bureau of Land Management (BLM) must pay for the upkeep for 46,000 captured horses and burros that now reside on private pastures at a cost of $50 million during 2018. Captive horses cannot be euthanized; instead, the BLM has to maintain them until they die of natural causes (Jenkins and Ashley 2003; Garrott and Oli 2013; Hendrickson 2018).

Another potential method to manage feral horse populations is fertility control. Surgical sterilization of feral stallions is promising because horses are polygynous, and dominant ones keep other males away from females in their harems (Figure 12.3). Unfortunately, dominant horses are not always success in this effort; some mares in harems controlled by a sterilized stallion still get pregnant by mating with subdominant males.

Collins and Kasbohm (2017) permanently sterilized 1,800 horses (males and females) at Sheldon National Wildlife Refuge in Nevada from 2008 through 2014. The remote population is closed, meaning that there is little immigration of outside horses into it. A helicopter was used to herd horses into a trap corral and was

FIGURE 12.3   Sterilized stallions must be able to maintain their harem and fight off intruding males or fertility control will not succeed in reducing feral horse populations.

Source: Clayton Andersen, Shutterstock 1119541433.

sterilized by a veterinarian (i.e., vasectomy of males and ovariectomy of females).
The feral horse population in the refuge was estimated at 1,400 when the sterilization
program began. Sterilization did not impact horse breeding behavior, and sterilized
horses maintained their former group associations. The sterilization program was
effective in reducing population-level fertility rates; foaling rates, which were more
than 20% prior to treatment, dropped to less than 4% after it.

One PZP vaccine that has promise for use on feral horses is SpayVac. Bechert
et al. (2013; Bechert and Fraker 2018) examined the effects of this vaccine on feral
horses and found that a single vaccine stopped mares from cycling and had no other
effect on the horses' health. The most widely used PZP vaccine is Zonastat-H. This
liquid contraceptive can be hand injected or darted into a mare. It is effective in
preventing conception for a year when the initial vaccine is followed by a booster
shot a month later (Kane et al. 2018). Gonacon-Equine was given to mares in a single
injection at Theodore Roosevelt National Park with mixed results. Half of the treated
mares gave birth during the first or second year after treatment, and by the fourth
year, treated mares were similar to untreated mares. At that point, a booster shot was
provided, and no mares receiving it foaled during the next two years (Baker et al.
2017).

12.6.4 RODENTS

Reducing fertility of small rodents in the field is difficult, owing to the need for wide-scale delivery of an antifertility treatment to rodents. For this reason, most efforts have focused on delivery of contraceptive-treated baits. Ideally, these baits would be species-specific, but such baits are not available. Instead species specificity is achieved by placing them in grain fields or inside rodent burrows where other species are less likely.

A combination of two synthetic hormones – lovonorgestrel and quinestrol (EP-1) – have successfully reduced fertility in several hamsters and gerbils. In field tests conducted in China, EP-1 successfully reduced fertility in plateau pikas and Mongolian gerbils (Liu et al. 2012; Fu et al. 2013). Reproduction in a field population of ricefield rats was reduced after 50%–75% of the population were sterilized (Figure 12.4). Fieldrats are seasonal breeders, making a single treatment effective for the entire breeding season (Sidebar 12.1). In contrast, house mice breed year-round, requiring multiple applications of treated bait. Still, a decrease in reproduction was achieved as long as 67% of female mice were sterile (Jacob et al. 2008).

Alpha-chlorohydrin, also known as Epibloc®, is the only contraceptive approved by the U.S. EPA for rodents. It is specifically registered for fertility control of Norway rats, and the EPA updated its label during 2007 (U. S. Environmental Protection Agency 2007). Its use is restricted to the inside of industrial and commercial buildings and in sanitary sewers. It is an acute toxicant and will kill many rats, but male rates that receive a sublethal dose will be rendered sterilize. But it is no longer being marketed due to a lack of sales.

FIGURE 12.4   Ricefield rats in front of a ripening rice crop.

Source: Sailom, Shutterstock 442289704.

SIDEBAR 12.1 CAN A RAT POPULATION BE REDUCED THROUGH FEMALE STERILITY?

Ricefield rats cause considerable losses of grain yields in flood-irrigated rice fields in Indonesia (Figure 12.4). Fertility control might be an option to reduce this damage because ricefield rats only breed during an 8-week season each year, are territorial, and have a home range of about a hectare. Hence, a 50% reduction of fertility might be achieved if half of the females were sterilized. To test this, Jacob et al. (2006) used multiple methods to capture rats in six 10-ha rice fields. Twenty-one females in two fields were sterilized using tubal ligation, 51 females in two other fields were sterilized using progesterone injections, and 2 fields were left untreated as a control. After the rice was harvested, the scientists captured 1,586 rats from these six fields (26/ha). Fields where the females had been sterilized had as many rats as the untreated fields. All fields also had similar number of active rat burrows, young rats per burrow, and young produced per female. Fertility did not reduce crop damage; there was approximately a 10% loss due to rats in all fields.

Why did treatments not led to a decrease in population growth, breeding performance, or crop damage? One possibility is that only a small proportion of the rats at the start of the nesting season were actually caught, although the scientists believed they had caught most, if not all, of the rats in the treated fields. In confined populations, only 30%–50% of the females had to be sterilized to decrease reproduction in confined populations. But, the fields were not confined in this field experiment. The problem plaguing this experiment probably was the immigration by fertile female rats.

12.6.4.1 Marsupials

Most research on achieving fertility control using GnRH agonists, such as deslorelin, has been conducted on marsupials in Australia. Sustained-release deslorelin has inhibited reproduction in tammar wallabies, grey kangaroos, and brushtail possums (Herbert et al. 2005). The Perth Zoo in Australia had a problem with free-ranging tammar wallabies devouring tree seedlings and food intended for the zoo's captive animals (Figure 12.5). In response, the zoo implanted deslorelin in female wallabies. Eighty percent of the treated wallabies stopped breeding for over a year without any loss in body condition (Lohr et al. 2009).

Implants of levonorgestrel, a progesterone analog, prevented 82% of eastern kangaroos from reproducing (Poiani et al. 2002). In wallabies, implants did not prevent birth in pregnant wallabies but inhibited subsequent estrus so that no other births occurred in treated females. The treatment did not affect lactation for nursing females, and the effects of the treatment were reversible. In addition, a single levonorgestrel implant is effective for three years (Nave et al. 2000).

Kangaroo Island off the coast of South Australia (Figure 12.6) has served for decades as a refuge for marsupial species that are doing poorly on the mainland. One introduced species, the koala, has adapted too well to their new home, and koala densities are now so high (10/ha) in the Island's Flinders Chase National Park, that

FIGURE 12.5   Tammar wallaby are voracious feeders.

Source: Ken Griffiths, Shutterstock 1719785518.

FIGURE 12.6   Map of Kangaroo Island, Australia.

Source: Rainer Lesniewski, Shutterstock 1662970162.12.6.5 Birds

they are denuding their habitat, posing a threat to the survival of the manna gum tree on the island. Koalas are popular with both Australia's citizens and tourists, so killing koalas was not an option. Instead, a combination of translocation and fertility control was implemented. Over 3,000 koalas were surgically sterilized over a four-year period, and another 1,000 were translocated at an annual cost of $240,000. The program was successful in reducing koala reproduction, but the management goal of reducing koala density to 1/ha was not achieved, and the program was discontinued. One problem was that there were 27,000 koalas on the island, far more than the 5,000 that were initially predicted. Furthermore, many koalas were located in inaccessible areas. While the program reduced koala densities in localized parts of Kangaroo Island, in the end, the koala problem on the island was too big for the program to succeed (Duka and Masters 2005).

Fertility in Canada geese, mute swans, cormorants, and gulls has been reduced by addling, puncturing, or oiling their eggs (Figure 12.7). Addling eggs involve forcefully shaking the eggs, which destroy embryos. Puncturing eggs is accomplished by piercing the eggshell with a needle, allowing entry by bacteria. Covering an egg with mineral or corn oil prevents respiratory gases from diffusing through the shell, causing the embryo to asphyxiate. The EPA allows the use of corn oil to reduce

FIGURE 12.7   Numbers of mute swans have increased greatly in North America, and egg oiling has been used to reduce the number of young produced each year.

Source: Elle 1, Shutterstock 1730023390.

reproduction in Canada geese and gulls (Fagerstone et al. 2010). After addling, puncturing, or oiling, the eggs are placed back in the nest so that the parents will continue to incubate them. Just removing eggs from the nest is ineffective because the parents will renest and lay another clutch of eggs (Beaumont et al. 2018). Impairing reproduction in birds through any of these mechanical approaches requires a long-term commitment. In Canada geese, 62% of all eggs have to be treated annually for many years to reduce the growth rate of a goose population (Coluccy et al. 2004; Beston et al. 2016). This is a labor-intensive practice because all nests have to be individually treated. Logistically, this is difficult because geese are synchronized nesters, and they all start egg laying within a few weeks of each other.

Many drugs have been used to reduce fertility in birds. DiazaCon[R] (20, 25 diazacholesterol) prevents cholesterol production. Without cholesterol, the body cannot make reproductive hormones, resulting in infertility in both males and females. DiazaCon reduced reproduction in Japanese quail, rose-ringed parakeets and monk parakeets for a few months (Sidebar 12.2). A major drawback of DiazaCon is that it is not species specific, has a long half-life in birds, and accumulates in animals causing a risk to both predators and scavengers of sterilized birds. Hence, it is best used for those situations where nontarget species are unlikely to consume treated baits or birds (USDA Animal Plant Health Inspection Service 2018a).

SIDEBAR 12.2 REDUCING REPRODUCTION IN INVASIVE POPULATIONS OF MONK PARAKEETS WITH DIAZACON

Feral populations of monk parakeets (Figure 12.8) became established in the United States during the 1960s when pets escaped or were intentionally

FIGURE 12.8   Monk parakeets are beautiful birds but also are a source of human–wildlife conflicts.

Source: CoinUp, Shuttlestock 1388173616.

FIGURE 12.9   The large nests of monk parakeets cause problems when built on electrical equipment and structural sites.

Source: Drew Horne, Shutterstock 142203991.

released. The parakeets build large stick nests in trees and sometimes on electrical poles and substations (Figure 12.9). These nests cause electrical outages when they short out transmission lines. The problems are likely to increase in the future due to the rapid growth of parakeet populations in the United States. Avery et al. (2008) fed DiazaCon-treated seed to parakeets at six electrical substations in south Florida. Four electrical substations served as untreated sites where the parakeet were fed untreated seed. The seed was first distributed in March or April before the nesting season. Monk parakeets readily accepted the DiazaCon-treated bait. Nests were checked for eggs or young in late April or early May. At treated substations, 32% of the nests contained no eggs versus only 6% at untreated substations. There also was a mean of 1.3 eggs or nestlings per nest at treated substations and 4.2 per nest at untreated substations. These findings indicated that ingesting DiazaCon can reduce the reproduction of monk parakeets.

Nacarbazin is an oral contraceptive that reduces fertility of birds but not mammals; it breaks the egg membrane separating the yolk and the albumen causing the two to mix, which prevents embryo development. The company Innolytics registered it with the EPA as a reproduction inhibitor under the name OvoControl[R]. It was approved for use with Canada geese in 2005 and feral pigeons in 2007. It is mixed with bait and fed to Canada geese in areas where the geese are causing problems. Treated geese produce infertile eggs and incubate them for the duration of the nesting season. Bynum et al. (2007) compared reproduction of resident Canada geese at five sites in Oregon where the geese were fed OvoControl and four untreated sites. At OvoControl sites, 56% of the eggs hatched compared to 88% at untreated sites.

OvoControl is more efficient than egg oiling at sites where geese are fed by people because the geese more willing to accept treated bait from people. Moreover, OvoControl is more efficient when nests are spaced widely apart and a boat is required to reach them. OvoControl also become more cost-effective when more than 35 nests have to be treated (Caudell et al. 2010).

A risk using an oral contraceptive against Canada geese is that these geese are a game species, and many are shot and consumed by humans. Nacarbazin poses little risk to humans; in fact, it has already approved for use in broiler chickens. Nacarbazin is rapidly metabolized by birds, so it has to be fed constantly to maintain infertility in birds, but this can be an advantage because infertility can be easily reversed in treated birds. It also does not pose a hazard to predatory birds that might consume a treated bird (Fagerstone et al. 2008; USDA Animal Plant Health Inspection Service 2018*b*).

12.7   WHAT ARE THE DRAWBACKS WITH WILDLIFE CONTRACEPTION?

The main drawback of contraception is that it takes an extended period of time, usually years, to have any effect on population size of most wildlife species. Also, a high proportion of animals in the population must be sterilized if the population is to be reduced or maintained at a level below carrying capacity. With Canada geese, 71% of the females must be sterilized to reduce a population. In actuality, this means that more than 71% of the population must be treated because not all treated animals will be rendered sterile. Bynum et al. (2007) showed that when Canada geese were treated with OvoControl (a contraceptive approved for use on this species), egg infertility decreased by only 36%, not enough to stabilize the population.

While it is relatively easy to treat a proportion of a population, it becomes difficult to sterile the remaining individuals, especially if the animals find the treatment to be unpleasant or frightening (such as being captured). If a contraception program is successful in reducing a population's birth rate, compensatory mortality changes can be expected with a decrease in the natural mortality rate and an increase in the reproductive rate of any untreated individuals because more food and other resources will be available to them and their offspring. A fertility control program that sterilized 80% of female European hares did not reduce adult abundance, owing to improved survival rates, which compensated for the reduced birth rate (Twigg et al. 2000; Williams et al. 2007).

A major problem with fertility control will always be the immigration of fertile individuals into the treated area. Immigration rates will accelerate as the control program successfully reduces the population. Thus, the few wildlife contraception programs that have successfully reduced a wildlife population or maintained it below carrying capacity have been conducted with small, isolated populations where there is no immigration. An example of this is the successful program to reduce feral horse populations on a barrier island in Maryland (Sidebar 12.3). I am unaware of any wildlife population that is open to immigration where fertility control has reduced and maintained the population below carrying capacity.

SIDEBAR 12.3 USE OF PZP INJECTIONS TO MANAGE A FERAL HORSE POPULATION

Assateague Island is a 60-km barrier island that crosses the Maryland and Virginia border. It was designated as a National Seashore in 1965 and is visited by over two million tourists annually. Its stated mission is to preserve

FIGURE 12.10   A pair of wild ponies grazing on the Maryland side of Assateague Island.

Source: Mary Swift, Shutterstock 1245364081.

and protect the unique coastal resources and the natural ecosystem conditions and processes upon which they depend. These objectives are threatened by two populations of wild horses, separated by a horse-proof fence on the state border. On the Virginia side, the horses (known locally as Chincoteague ponies) are rounded up annually and surplus ponies are sold at auction. On the Maryland side, the horses were left alone and their numbers increased to 175 where they were causing ecological damage to the 167 km² national seashore by the mid-1990s (Figure 12.10). At that time, the National Seashore adopted the management goal for Maryland horses of reducing horse numbers using contraception rather than lethal control or adoption. The strategy was to allow each mare to produce a single foal and then permanently sterilize the mare by giving it three PZP injections a year apart. The program began in 1995, and within two years, the horse population had stabilized, but it was not until the eighth year that the population began to decline. By 2007, the population had declined 23%. This is one of the few successful examples of using conceptive to stabilize a population of a long-lived species. There are several reasons for the success of the contraception program: (1) The population is isolated, so there is no immigration into the population; (2) the initial population of 175 was manageable; (3) Assateague Island is small with an open habitat; (4) the horses were habituated to humans and could be approached on foot; and (5) horses could be individually recognized (Kilpatrick and Turner 2008; Hobbs and Hinds 2018).

Another drawback is that contraceptives may lengthen the annual breeding season due to females recycling when they fail to become pregnant the first time. If this happens, treated females and the males that seek them could deplete their energy reserves by participating in prolonged breeding activities and fighting among males (Heilmann et al. 1998). This, in turn, could increase winter mortality if these individuals enter winter with low fat levels. Additionally, offspring may be born at the wrong time of year.

Body condition and longevity can improve from infertility because females are free from the energetic costs of pregnancy, lactation, and rearing a foal (Kilpatrick and Turner 2008). While longevity is normally considered good from an animal welfare perspective, some people argue the opposite – a longer lifespan leads to old-age infirmaries, and they consider it to be inhumane.

Using an immunocontraceptive vaccine to sterilize an animal will be more expensive than the cost to kill it. It costs over $1,000 to vaccinate a white-tailed deer with most of the cost being for drugs and veterinary time (Boulanger et al. 2012; Evans et al. 2016).

12.8   WHAT IS THE PUBLIC'S PERCEPTION OF USING FERTILITY CONTROL IN WILDLIFE?

Public perceptions of wildlife fertility control vary. Some people note that pets are commonly sterilized and see no reason why the same methods would be inappropriate for wildlife. Others counter that many methods of fertility control require that wild animals be captured and handled and worry that these procedures will cause stress. Some people oppose it because they do not believe that humans should be managing wildlife. Others support fertility control as an alternative to lethal control, but they are opposed to using fertility control for species that would otherwise be unharmed. Some hunters and fur trappers are wary of fertility control because one justification for hunting and fur trapping is that it reduces wildlife damage. They worry that fertility control of wildlife populations would reduce opportunities to hunt or trap (Gray and Cameron 2010; Hampton et al. 2015). The Wildlife Society has adopted a policy about the role of fertility control in managing wildlife populations (Sidebar 12.4).

Some wildlife biologists are wary of fertility control because sometimes it is proposed as a replacement for lethal control when there is little or no chance of fertility control solving the problem. For example, feral cats kill millions of native birds, mammals, and reptiles annually in the United States. In response, many towns and cities have adopted programs to trap–neuter–release feral cats as a way to manage feral cat colonies; such action does not reduce the feral cat population; new cats are constantly being release by owners who no longer want to care for them.

SIDEBAR 12.4 THE POLICY OF THE WILDLIFE SOCIETY REGARDING WILDLIFE FERTILITY CONTROL

"The policy of The Wildlife Society in regard to wildlife fertility control is to:

1. Recognize that species overabundance in localized or isolated areas is often largely influenced by landscape features and human manipulation of the environment, and these factors may not be easily modified.

2. Encourage educational efforts to disseminate information on scientifically sound solutions for reducing problems with overabundant wildlife and discuss the benefits and limitations of various wildlife fertility control methods.
3. Recognize that overabundant wildlife populations can be managed via lethal methods, regulated hunting seasons, or other means where they are legal, practical, and cost-effective and that some of these methods can provide a net economic benefit, recreational opportunity, and source of high-quality meat.
4. Recognize that application of wildlife fertility control should be based on appropriate science and species population biology and that in some instances it may be necessary to reduce the population with lethal methods before fertility control can be used effectively to limit population growth.
5. Recommend research into development of cost-effective fertility control techniques, including improved delivery systems.
6. Recognize that fertility-control products must have minimal health effects on target and nontarget animals, and must be safe for human consumption if used in food animals.
7. Encourage local communities to consult with appropriate state and provincial wildlife agencies and certified private wildlife control consultants early in the decision-making process when considering application of fertility control.
8. Recognize that the authority to permit field applications of fertility control measures lie with the state or provincial wildlife agency.
9. Pledge to work toward finding safe, humane, and effective methods for resolving human–wildlife conflicts associated with overabundant species."

12.9 WHAT LAWS GOVERN THE USE OF FERTILITY CONTROL TO MANAGE WILDLIFE?

Two sets of rules govern fertility control of wildlife. First, the contraceptive has to be approved by both state and federal authorities, and it usually takes millions of dollars to conduct the required tests to demonstrate that a vaccine or product is effective, environmentally safe, and poses no threat to humans. The EPA has been responsible for regulating contraceptives since 2006 under the Federal Insecticide, Fungicide, and Rodenticide Act. Any company or agency that wants to use a contraceptive must prepare a registration application that includes the contraceptive's chemistry, toxicity, efficacy, risk to nontarget species, and environmental fate. The EPA then decides whether to register (accept) a contraception for a specific use against a species based on its potential benefits and risks. Each state also has an agency responsible for protecting the environment within the state, and their approval must be obtained before the contraceptive can be used within the state. Most contraceptives are classified as "restricted-use" which means that they may only be used by certified pesticide applicators. Some are further restricted so that they can only be used federal employees (usually employees of USDA Wildlife Services).

Wildlife is managed by state and federal governments so that use of a method to reduce the fertility of a wildlife requires a permit from the state wildlife agency. A permit from the U.S. Fish and Wildlife Service is also required if migratory birds or endangered species are impacted. At present, only a handful of contraceptives have been approved by EPA for use in the United States; none are in widespread use in the United States or elsewhere in the world.

12.10   SUMMARY

Fertility control of wildlife species is a tool that can be used to manage some human–wildlife conflicts. It usually functions by reducing population size but sometimes can be effective by merely changing an animal's behavior. Methods to reduce the fertility of wildlife include mechanical and surgical techniques, chemical sterilization, endocrine disruption, and immunocontraception. Ideally, contraceptive agents should be reversible (depending on the species), suitable for field delivery, and effective with a single dose. Furthermore, treated animals need to maintain their territories, their status in the dominance hierarchy, and their willingness to engage in sexual behavior. Otherwise, the sterile animal will be replaced by a reproductively active individual. Contraceptives should pose no risk to humans or nontarget species.

Contraception in wildlife management is a promising technology, but it is still in the experimental stage. Several problems have to be overcome before these techniques come into widespread use. Current delivery methods are not feasible for treating large populations of wildlife, and there is a need to develop drugs that can be placed in baits and orally deliverable to animals. Questions about cost-effectiveness and public acceptance of fertility control methods remain to be addressed.

Given the problems associated with fertility control in wildlife, why then are we still trying to develop effective contraceptive techniques? For some species, such as coyotes, reducing fertility can reduce wildlife damage without actually reducing the population size. Using contraception for population control may be a useful technique when other forms of population control are ineffective or unavailable. It also is perceived as more humane than using lethal methods of resolving human–wildlife conflicts. It is best suited for situations where patience prevails and public perception and ethical consideration involving humane treatment of animals outweigh efficacy and costs.

12.11   DISCUSSION QUESTIONS

1. Sheep ranchers have long complained about coyotes killing sheep. When they heard that the federal government was going to determine if sterilization of coyotes would help, ranchers joked that the problem was not coyotes mating with sheep. Do the ranchers have a point?

2. If you were a wildlife biologist working with the U.S. Bureau of Land Management (BLM), what steps would you advise your employer to take to resolve the problem of too many feral horses on BLM land in the West.
3. Fertility control of wildlife usually fails in areas where there are high rates of immigration into the area where the sterilized animals are located. Can you think of some human–wildlife conflicts where this would not pose a problem because the local animals are isolated?
4. Before a fertility control agent could be used widely in deer, it would have to be safe for humans who consume venison. Do you think that people opposed to hunting would spread the rumor that anyone eating venison would become sterile? If you were director of the state wildlife program, would you try to counteract their message and if so, how?
5. Many animal welfare groups only support fertility control when it is used in lieu of lethal control or hunting to manage a human–wildlife conflict. They oppose the use of fertility control to manage other populations of free-ranging wildlife. Do you think this view will prevent fertility control from living up to its potential to become a major tool in the resolution of human–wildlife conflicts?
6. Some environmentalists believe that the main barrier to human–wildlife coexistence is not that there are too many animals, but too many people? Do you agree?

LITERATURE CITED

Asa, C. S., and I. J. Porton. 2005. *Wildlife contraception: issues, methods and applications.* John Hopkins University Press, Baltimore, MD.
Avery, M. L., C. A. Yoder, and E. A. Tillman. 2008. Diazacon inhibits reproduction in invasive monk parakeet populations. *Journal of Wildlife Management* 72:1449–1452.
Baker, D., J. Powers, J. Ransom, B. McCann, M. Oehler, J. Bruemmer, N. Galloway, D. Eckery, and T. Nett. 2017. Gonadotropin-releasing hormone vaccine (GonaCon-Equine) suppresses fertility in free-ranging horses (*Equus caballus*): limitations and side effects of treatment. *Proceeding of the International Conference on Wildlife Fertility Control* 8:12.
Beaumont, M., J. Rodrigue, C. Pilotte, É. Chalifour, and J. F. Giroux. 2018. Behavioral response of Canada geese to egg-oiling and nest removal. *Journal of Wildlife Management* 82:1359–1366.
Bechert, U., J. Bartell, M. Kutzler, A. Menino, Jr., R. Bildfell, M. Anderson, and M. Fraker. 2013. Effects of two porcine zona pellucida immunocontraceptive vaccines on ovarian activity in horses. *Journal of Wildlife Management* 77:1386–1400.
Bechert, U. S., and M. A. Fraker. 2018. Twenty years of SpayVac® research: potential implications for regulating feral horse and burrow population in the United States. *Human Wildlife Interactions* 11:117–130.
Beston, J. A., C. K. Williams, T. C. Nichols, and P. M. Castelli. 2016. A population model for management of Atlantic flyway resident population Canada geese. *Wildlife Society Bulletin* 40:106–111.
Bomford, M. 1990. *A role for fertility control in wildlife management?* Australian Government Publishing Service Bulletin No. 7, Canberra, Australia.

Boulanger, J. R., and P. D. Curtis. 2016. Efficacy of surgical sterilization for managing over-abundant suburban white-tailed deer. *Wildlife Society Bulletin* 40:727–735.

Boulanger, J. R., P. D. Curtis, E. G. Cooch, and A. J. DeNicola. 2012. Sterilization as an alternative deer control technique: a review. *Human-Wildlife Interactions* 6:273–282.

Butler, V. 1998. Elephants: trimming the herd. *Bioscience* 48:76–81.

Bynum, K. S., J. D. Eisemann, G. C. Weaver, C. A. Yoder, K. A. Fagerstone, and L. A. Miller. 2007. Nicarbazin OvoControl G bait reduces hatchability of eggs laid by resident Canada geese in Oregon. *Journal of Wildlife Management* 71:135–143.

Caudell, J. N., S. A. Shwiff, and M. T. Slater. 2010. Using a cost-effectiveness model to determine the applicability of OvoControl G to manage nuisance Canada geese. *Journal of Wildlife Management* 74:843–848.

Collins, G. H., and J. W. Kasbohm. 2017. Population dynamics and fertility control of feral horses. *Journal of Wildlife Management* 81:289–296.

Coluccy, J. M., D. A. Graber, and R. D. Drobney. 2004. Population modeling for giant Canada geese and implications for management. Pages 181–186 *in* T. J. Moser, R. D. Lien, K. C. VerCauteren, K. F. Abraham, D. E. Andersen, J. G. Bruggink, J. M. Coluccy, D. A. Graber, J. O. Leafloor, D. R. Luukkonen, and R. E. Trost, editors. *Proceedings of the 2003 international Canada goose symposium*, Dembar Educational Research Services, Madison, WI.

Davies, K. W., G. Collins, and C. S. Boyd. 2014. Effects of feral free-ranging horses on semi-arid rangeland ecosystems: an example from the sagebrush-steppe. *Ecosphere* 5:1–14.

Delsink, A. K., J. J. van Altena, D. Grobler, H. Bertschinger, J. Kirkpatrick, J., and R. Slotow. 2007. Implementing immunocontraception in free-ranging African elephants at Makalali conservancy. *Journal of the South African Veterinary Association* 78:25–30.

Druce, H. C., R. L. Mackey, and R. Slotow. 2011. How immunocontraception can contribute to elephant management in small enclosed reserves: Munyawana population as a case study. *PloS One* 6(12):e27952.

Duka, T., and P. Masters. 2005. Confronting a tough issue: fertility control and translocation for over-abundant koalas on Kangaroo Island, South Australia. *Ecological Management and Restoration* 6:172–181.

Evans, C. S., A. J. DeNicola, and R. J. Warren. 2016. Comparison of treatment effort for immunocontraceptive vaccines and surgical sterilization in deer. *Wildlife Society Bulletin* 40:593–598.

Fagerstone, K. A., L. A. Miller, J. D. Eisemann, J. R. O'Hare, and J. P. Gionfriddo. 2008. Registration of wildlife contraceptives in the United States of America, with OvoControl and GonaCon immunocontraceptive vaccines as examples. *Wildlife Research* 35:586–592.

Fagerstone, K. A., L. A. Miller, G. Killian, and C. A. Yoder. 2010. Review of issues concerning the use of reproductive inhibitors, with particular emphasis on resolving human – wildlife conflicts in North America. *Integrative Zoology* 5:15–30.

Fayrer-Hosken, R. A., P. Brooks, H. J. Bertschinger, J. F. Kirkpatrick, J. W. Turner, and I. K. M. Liu. 1997. Management of African elephant populations by immunocontraception. *Wildlife Society Bulletin* 25:18–21.

Fraker, M. A., R. G. Brown, G. E. Gaunt, J. A. Kerr, and B. Pohajdak. 2002. Long-lasting, single-dose immunocontraception of feral fallow deer in British Columbia. *Journal of Wildlife Management* 66:1141–1147.

Fu, H., J. Zhang, D. Shi, and X. Wu. 2013. Effects of levonorgestrel-quinestrol (EP-1) treatment on Mongolian gerbil wild populations: a case study. *Integrative Zoology* 8:277–284.

Garrott, R. A., and M. K. Oli. 2013. A critical crossroad for BLM's wild horse program. *Science* 341:847–848.

Gionfriddo, J. P., A. J. DeNicola, L. A. Miller, and K. A. Fagerstone. 2011*a*. Efficacy of GnRH immunocontraception of wild white-tailed deer in New Jersey. *Wildlife Society Bulletin* 35:142–148.

Gionfriddo, J. P., A. J. DeNicola, L. A. Miller, and K. A. Fagerstone. 2011*b*. Health effects of GnRH immunocontraception of wild white-tailed deer in New Jersey. *Wildlife Society Bulletin* 35:149–160.

Gooch, A. M. J., S. L. Petersen, G. H. Collins, T. S. Smith, B. R. McMillan, and D. L. Eggett. 2017. The impact of feral horses on pronghorn behavior at water sources. *Journal of Arid Environments* 138:38–43.

Gray, M. E., and E. Z. Cameron. 2010. Does contraceptive treatment in wildlife result in side effects? A review of quantitative and anecdotal evidence. *Reproduction* 139:45–55.

Hall, L. K., R. T. Larsen, M. D. Westover, C. C. Day, R. N. Knight, and B. R. McMillan. 2016. Influence of exotic horses on the use of water by communities of native wildlife in a semi-arid environment. *Journal of Arid Environments* 127:100–105.

Hampton, J. O., T. H. Hyndman, A. Barnes, and T. Collins. 2015. Is wildlife fertility control always humane? *Animals* 5:1047–1071.

Heilmann, T. J., R. A. Garrott, L. L. Cadwell, and B. L. Tiller. 1998. Behavioral response of free-ranging elk treated with an immunocontraceptive vaccine. *Journal of Wildlife Management* 62:243–250.

Hendrickson, C. 2018. Managing healthy wild horses and burros on healthy rangeland: tools and the toolbox. *Human-Wildlife Interactions* 12:143–147.

Herbert, C. A., T. E. Trigg, M. B. Renfree, G. Shaw, D. C. Eckery, and D. W. Cooper. 2005. Long-term effects of deslorelin implants on reproduction in the female tammar wallaby (*Macropus eugenii*). *Reproduction* 129:361–369.

Hobbs, R. J., and L. A. Hinds. 2018. Could current fertility control methods be effective for landscape-scale management of populations of wild horses (*Equus caballus*) in Australia? *Wildlife Research* 45:195–207.

Jacob, J., and S. Rahmini. 2006. The impact of imposed female sterility on field populations of ricefield rats (*Rattus argentiventer*). *Agriculture, Ecosystems and Environment* 115:281–284.

Jacob, J., G. R. Singleton, and L. A. Hinds. 2008. Fertility control of rodent pests. *Wildlife Research* 35:487–493.

Jenkins, S. H., and M. C. Ashley. 2003. Wild horse. Pages 1148–1163 *in* G. A. Feldhamer, B. C. Thompson, and J. A. Chapman, editors. *Wild mammals of North America*, second edition. Johns Hopkins University Press, Baltimore, MD.

Kane, A. J. 2018. A review of contemporary contraceptive and sterilization techniques of feral horses. *Human-Wildlife Interactions* 12:111–118.

Kennelly, J. J., and P. J. Lyons. 1983. Evaluation of induced sterility for beaver (*Castor canadensis*) management problems. *Eastern Wildlife Damage Control Conference* 1:169–175.

Killian, G., L. Miller, J. Rhyan, and H. Doten. 2006. Immunocontraception of Florida feral swine with a single-dose GnRH vaccine. *American Journal of Reproductive Immunology* 55:378–384.

Kilpatrick, J. F., and A. Turner. 2008. Achieving population goals in a long-lived wildlife species (*Equus caballus*) with contraception. *Wildlife Research* 35:513–519.

Kirkpatrick, J. F., A. Rowan, N. Lamberski, R. Wallace, K. Frank, and R. Lyda. 2009. The practical side of immunocontraception: zona proteins and wildlife. *Journal of Reproductive Immunology* 83:151–157.

Krause, S. K., D. A. Kelt, J. P. Gionfriddo, and D. H. Van Vuren. 2014. Efficacy and health effects of a wildlife immunocontraceptive vaccine on fox squirrels. *Journal of Wildlife Management* 78:12–23.

Krause, S. K., D. H. Van Vuren, C. Laursen, and D. A. Kelt. 2015. Behavioral effects of an immunocontraceptive vaccine on Eastern fox squirrels. *Journal of Wildlife Management* 79:1255–1263.

Lavelle, M. J., N. P. Snow, J. M. Halseth, J. C. Kinsey, J. A. Foster, and K. C. verCauteren. 2018. Development and evaluation of a bait station for selectively dispensing bait to invasive wild pigs. *Wildlife Society Bulletin* 42:102–110.

Liu, M., J. Qu, M. Yang, Z. Wang, Y. Wang, Y. Zhang, and Z. Zhang. 2012. Effects of quinestrol and levonorgestrel on populations of plateau pikas, *Ochotona curzoniae*, in the Qinghai – Tibetan Plateau. *Pest Management Science* 68:592–601.

Locke, S. L., M. W. Cook, L. A. Harveson, D. S. Davis, R. R. Lopez, N. J. Silvy, and M. A. Fraker. 2007. Effectiveness of Spayvac® on reducing white-tailed deer fertility. *Journal of Wildlife Diseases* 43:726–730.

Lohr, C. A., H. Mills, H. Robertson, and R. Bencini. 2009. Deslorelin implants control fertility in urban brushtail possums (*Trichosurus vulpecula*) without negatively influencing their body-condition index. *Wildlife Research* 36:324–332.

Lowney, M., P. Schoenfeld, W. Haglan, and G. Witmer. 2005. Overview of impacts of feral and introduced ungulates on the environment in the eastern United States and Caribbean. *Proceedings of the Wildlife Damage Management Conference* 11:64–81.

Massei, G., and D. Cowan. 2014. Fertility control to mitigate human-wildlife conflicts: a review. *Wildlife Research* 41:1–21.

Mech, L. D., S. H. Fritts, and M. E. Nelson. 1996. Wolf management in the 21st century, from public input to sterilization. *Journal of Wildlife Research* 1:195–198.

Miller, L. A. 1997. Delivery of immunocontraceptive vaccines for wildlife management. Pages 49–58 *in* T. J. Kreeger, editor. *Contraception in wildlife manage.* U. S. Government Printing Office, Washington, DC.

Miller, L. A., K. A. Fagerstone, and D. C. Eckery. 2013. Twenty years of immunocontraceptive research: lessons learned. *Journal of Zoo and Wildlife Medicine* 44:S84–S96.

Miller, L. A., J. P. Gionfriddo, J. C, Rhyan, K. A. Fagerstone, D. C. Wagner, and G. J. Killian. 2008. GnRH immunocontraception of male and female white-tailed deer fawns. *Human-Wildlife Interactions* 2:93–101.

Miller, L. A., J. C. Rhyan, and M. Drew. 2004. Contraception of bison by GnRH vaccine: a possible means of decreasing transmission of brucellosis in bison. *Journal of Wildlife Diseases* 40:725–730.

Nash, P. B., D. K. James, L. T. Hui, and L. A. Miller. 2004. Fertility control of California ground squirrels using GnRH immunocontraception. *Proceedings of the Vertebrate Pest Conference* 21:274–278.

National Research Council. 2013. *Using science to improve the BLM wild horse and burro program: a way forward.* National Academies Press, Washington, DC.

Naugle, R., and K. Grams. 2013. Long-term methods and effects of remotely treating wildlife with immunocontraception. *Journal of Zoo and Wildlife Medicine* 44:S138–S140.

Nave, C. D., G. Shaw, R. V. Short, and M. B. Renfree. 2000. Contraceptive effects of levonorgestrel implants in a marsupial. *Reproduction, Fertility and Development* 12:81–86.

Pepin, K. M., A. J. Davis, F. L. Cunningham, K. C. VerCauteren, and D. C. Eckery. 2017. Potential effects of incorporating fertility control into typical culling regimes in wild pig populations. *PLoS One* 12(8):e0183441.

Perry, K. R., W. M. Arjo, K. S. Bynum, and L. A. Miller. 2006. GnRH single-injection immunocontraception of black-tailed deer. *Proceedings of the Vertebrate Pest Conference* 22:72–77.

Poiani, A., G. Coulson, D. Salamon, S. Holland, and C. D. Nave. 2002. Fertility control of eastern grey kangaroos: do levonorgestrel implants affect behavior? *Journal of Wildlife Management* 66:59–66.

Reynolds, J. C., M. J. Short, and R. J. Leigh. 2004. Development of population control strategies for mink *Mustela vison*, using floating rafts as monitors and trap sites. *Biological Conservation* 120:533–543.

Rutberg, A. T., R. E. Naugle, J. W. Turner, M. A. Fraker, and D. R. Flanagan. 2013. Field testing of single-administration porcine zona pellucida contraceptive vaccines in white-tailed deer (*Odocoileus virginianus*). *Wildlife Research* 40:281–288.

Saunders, G., J. Mcilroy, M. Berghout, B. Kay, E. Gifford, R. Perry, and R. Van De Ven. 2002. The effects of induced sterility on the territorial behaviour and survival of foxes. *Journal of Applied Ecology* 39:56–66.

Snow, N. P., M. J. Lavelle, J. M. Halseth, C. R. Blass, J. A. Foster, and K. C. verVauteren. 2017. Strength testing of raccoons and invasive wild pigs for a species-specific bait station. *Wildlife Society Bulletin* 41:264–270.

Till, J. A., and F. F. Knowlton. 1983. Efficacy of denning in alleviating coyote depredations upon domestic sheep. *Journal of Wildlife Management* 47:1018–1025.

Twigg, L. E., T. J. Lowe, G. R. Martin, A. G. Wheeler, G. S. Gray, S. L. Griffin, C. M. O'Reilly, D. J. Robinson, and P. H. Hubach. 2000. Effects of surgically imposed sterility on free-ranging rabbit populations. *Journal of Applied Ecology* 37:16–39.

Tyndale-Biscoe, C. H. 1997. Immunosterilization for wild rabbits: the options. Pages 223–234 *in* T. J. Kreeger, editor. *Contraception in wildlife management.* U. S. Government Printing Office, Washington, DC.

USDA Animal Plant Health Inspection Service. 2018*a*. *Diazacon as an induced infertility agent.* U. S. D. A. Animal Plant Health Inspection Service, Washington, DC. www.aphis.usda.gov/aphis/ourfocus/wildlifedamage/programs/nwrc/research-areas/sa_reproductive_control/ct_diazacon. Accessed 20 July 2018.

USDA Animal Plant Health Inspection Service. 2018*b*. *Nicarbazin research.* U. S. D. A. Animal Plant Health Inspection Service, Washington, DC. www.aphis.usda.gov/aphis/ourfocus/wildlifedamage/programs/nwrc/research-areas/SA_Reproductive_Control. Accessed 20 July 2019.

USDA Animal Plant Health Inspection Service. 2018*c*. *Porcine zona pellucida immunocontraception in mammals.* U. S. D. A. Animal Plant Health Inspection Service, Washington, DC. www.aphis.usda.gov/aphis/ourfocus/wildlifedamage/programs/nwrc/research-areas/sa_reproductive_control/ct_pzp. Accessed 20 July 2018.

U. S. Environmental Protection Agency. 2007. *Epibloc.* U. S. Environment Protection Agency, Washington, DC. https://www3.epa.gov/pesticides/chem_search/ppls/042882-00002-20070316.pdf. Accessed 1 August 2018.

Williams, C. K., C. C. Davey, R. J. Moore, L. A. Hinds, L. E. Silvers, P. J. Kerr, N. French, G. M. Hood, R. P. Pech, and C. J. Krebs. 2007. Population responses to sterility imposed on female European rabbits. *Journal of Applied Ecology* 44:291–301.

Yoder, C. A., and L. A. Miller. 2010. Effect of GonaCon™ vaccine on black-tailed prairie dogs: immune response and health effects. *Vaccine* 29:233–239.

Young, J. K., M. J. MacGregor, E. M. Gese, and D. C. Eckery. 2018. Experimental tests of non-surgical reproductive inhibitors to prevent coyote reproduction. *Human-Wildlife Interactions* 12:171–185.

13 Lethal Control

One way to change an animal's behavior is to kill it, but that is a rather crude way to accomplish the task.

Anonymous

The only thing you need to do to manage elk is to manage the air-to-bullet ratio.

– Anonymous

I drank what?

– Socrates

Humans have used lethal means to reduce wildlife damage for thousands of years. Although it seems obvious that killing animals should reduce the amount of damage they cause, the relationship is rarely straightforward. This chapter examines questions and issues involving the use of lethal methods to reduce human–wildlife conflicts.

13.1 WHAT IS THE INTRINSIC GROWTH RATE OF A WILDLIFE POPULATION?

Most wildlife populations have the potential to grow by an ever-increasing number. Consider a population where there is no mortality, each animal can breed when one-year old, and each pair of animals can produce two young annually. If we start with 2 individuals in the first year, the population will grow to 4 in the second year, 8 in the third, 16 in the fourth, and 32 in the fifth (Figure 13.1). If this rate is maintained, the population passes 1,000 in the tenth year and exceeds 1,000,000 in 20th year. The potential for a population to increase over time is not linear but exponential.

Exponential growth may be observed in populations recovering from a severe population crash or when an exotic species invades a new habitat where food is abundant, and there are no predators or diseases to check its growth. This rate of population growth under ideal conditions is called the intrinsic growth rate. It varies among species depending upon the age at which individuals reach sexual maturity and how many offspring each female can produce annually. In our hypothetical population described in Figure 13.1, offspring were able to breed after one year. If two years were required to reach sexual maturity, the growth rate of the population would be slower (Figure 13.2). Obviously, the longer it takes for an individual to reach sexual maturity, the slower the population will increase. Growth rates will increase with the number of young each female can produce in a year. If instead of producing two offspring per year, a pair of adults can produce four, then only 13 years would be

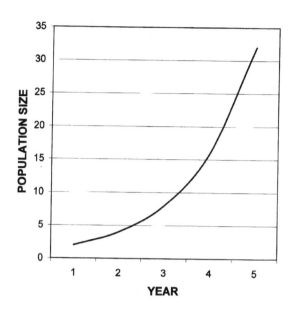

FIGURE 13.1   Exponential curve that shows how a wildlife population would increase over time if every female reaches sexual maturity in one year, each sexually mature female produces two young every year, and there is no mortality.

Source: This is Figure 7.1 in the first edition of this book.

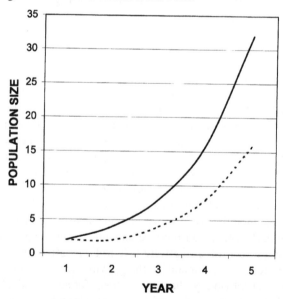

FIGURE 13.2   Comparison of the growth rates of two wildlife populations – in one population, the females reach sexual maturity in one year (solid line), and in the other (dotted line), the females need two years to reach sexual maturity (assumes that each female produces two young/year and no mortality).

Source: This is Figure 7.2 in the first edition of this book.

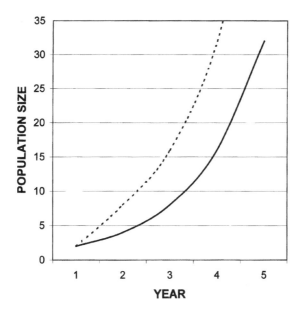

FIGURE 13.3   Comparison of the growth rates of two wildlife populations – in one population, each female produces two young/year (solid line), while females in the other population (dotted line) produce four young/year (assumes that females reach sexually maturity in one year and no mortality).

Source: This is Figure 7.3 in the first edition of this book.

required for the population to increase to a million (Figure 13.3), providing females reach sexual maturity in one year. The population would increase to over three million in nine years if each female produced ten offspring annually and all survived.

13.2   WHAT EFFECT DOES LETHAL CONTROL HAVE ON A WILDLIFE POPULATION'S BIRTH AND MORTALITY RATES?

When wildlife densities in a suitable habitat are low and food is plentiful, birth rates are high because females are in good health and can produce large and raise litters of young or clutches of eggs. For the same reason, parents also have little difficulty feeding several young. As populations increase and competition for food intensifies, the health of females deteriorates, and they produce smaller litters. Hence, birth rates decrease as populations increase. For example, twins are less common among deer when food is scarce. If lethal control reduces a wildlife population, competition for food will decrease and birth rates will increase. For this reason, most wildlife populations can recover quickly from any population reduction due to lethal control. This is especially true for species, such as rodents, that normally have high birth rates.

When populations increase, mortality rates rise because food becomes scarce and animals starve. At the same time, diseases spread more easily among higher densities of animals. Losses to predators also become more common because predator

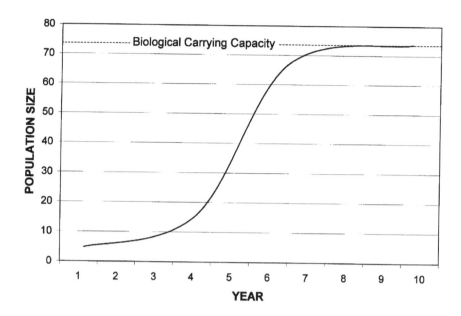

FIGURE 13.4 Logistic growth curve that shows a wildlife population growing exponentially when it is small; but as the population increases, its rate of increase slows because of increasing mortality from predators, disease, and/or starvation.

Source: This is Figure 7.4 in the first edition of this book.

populations expand in response to the availability of prey and because individual predators concentrate their feeding activities on the abundant species. Ultimately, the mortality rate from starvation, disease, and predators expands until it equals the birth rate and the population stabilizes. The point at which the population stabilizes is called the biological carrying capacity. It is a characteristic of the habitat and can be viewed as the number of animals that can be sustained by annual food production or the number of animals that can find safe hiding places from predators. The resource (e.g., food or shelter) in the shortest supply acts to limit the size of the wildlife population. This type of equation, where the population initially grows exponentially and then slows as it approaches the carrying capacity, is called a logistical equation (Figure 13.4).

A wildlife population is usually large by the time it causes enough damage that people begin to apply lethal methods. Therefore, the population is probably already experiencing a high rate of natural mortality. If, by using lethal methods, we are only killing animals that would have died anyway before the next breeding season, then lethal control will have no impact on the population. In this case, the mortality caused by lethal control is considered to be "compensatory" and simply replaces a natural form of mortality (Blomberg 2015). Hence, the population during the next breeding season will be the same whether or not lethal means are employed

(Sidebar 13.1). Murton et al. (1974) tested whether shooting wood pigeons in England was an effective method to reduce their damage to agricultural crops. For a decade, up to 60% of the wood pigeon population was removed each winter. By late spring, wood pigeon populations and the amount of damage they caused had returned to pre-removal levels. Compensating for the loss of birds from shooting was a decrease in natural mortality rates and immigration by birds from nearby areas. Murton et al. (1974) found that the food supply, not shooting, determined the amount of winter mortality from year to year.

SIDEBAR 13.1 EFFECT OF LETHAL CONTROL ON COYOTE POPULATIONS

In areas such as Yellowstone National Park, where coyotes are not subjected to hunting or lethal control, their population dynamics are very different than in areas where they are heavily culled. In protected areas, females normally do not breed before two years of age, and litter sizes are 3–4. Coyotes often live in packs containing a dominant breeding pair and several subordinate individuals that do not breed but help feed and raise the pups produced by the dominant pair. These helpers are often offspring of the dominant pair from previous years. The dominant pair and their pack keep other coyotes out of their territory. At high densities, all suitable habitat is filled up with territories. Coyotes unable to secure a territory of their own become transient individuals and confine their movements to the spaces between occupied territories or areas of poor habitat. Like helpers, transient coyotes do not breed. Hence, at high densities, only a small proportion of coyotes breed. In protected areas, such as in national parks, over half of the coyotes die annually from natural causes.

In areas where coyotes are subjected to high rates of lethal control and coyote densities are low, coyotes leave their parents' territory during their first year of life, establish a territory of their own, and breed. They do not become helpers or transient coyotes. In these areas, litters may average 7–8 pups. When most female coyotes produce large litters every year, the coyote population is capable of tripling or quadrupling its numbers each year. Furthermore, in a heavily controlled population, few coyotes starve to death or die from diseases. Instead, natural forms of mortality have been replaced by human-caused mortality. For this reason, more than 60% of the coyote population must be killed by humans annually before there is any reduction in coyote densities (Wagner 1988).

Sometimes, animals removed by lethal methods do not simply replace animals that were destined to die anyway; instead, these deaths may be "additive" to those from natural causes. In these cases, wildlife populations during the next breeding season would be smaller than what would have occurred in the absence of culling. Thus, lethal control is compensatory to a point and additive thereafter, meaning that when only a small number of animals are killed, lethal control has little effect on populations, but as more and more animals are killed, it will begin to reduce the population. Although it may be possible to kill many animals using lethal methods, suppressing wildlife populations to a low enough level where the population cannot recover within a year is difficult. Lethal control almost always must be repeated each year to be effective.

Most wildlife populations go through a critical period during the year when much of the mortality occurs. These critical periods (hereafter called population bottlenecks) often occur in winter when food resources are lowest. Any mortality that occurs before the bottleneck is compensatory because only enough resources exist for a limited number of animals to survive the winter. For this reason, hunting normally occurs in the fall because wildlife agencies want hunters to have a minimal impact on game populations. However, if we want to use lethal control to suppress a population, the control is much more likely to have an effect if it is delayed until after the population's bottleneck has occurred. Lethal control is, therefore, more effective if conducted in late winter or early spring (Lieury et al. 2015). For instance, Anthony et al. (1991) improved the nesting success of black brant by shooting and trapping Arctic foxes immediately before the brant started to nest.

13.3   WHAT EFFECT DOES LETHAL CONTROL HAVE ON THE IMMIGRATION RATE OF WILDLIFE?

If lethal control reduces the density of a wildlife population in an area, individuals from outside this area typically move in and occupy the void. This immigration of individuals into an area helps nullify any population reduction produced by the lethal technique (Baker and Harris 2006; Kilgo et al. 2017). This is especially true for populations that are close to carrying capacity and contain transient individuals that have been unable to secure a territory of their own. Lieury et al. (2015) tried to cull red fox populations on 246-km^2 plots but was largely unsuccessful because immigration negated the impact of the removal effort. The scientists determined that about 45% of the pre-breeding population had to be removed annually to drop the fox density from the carrying capacity of 1.5 foxes/km^2 to an optimal population of 1.0 foxes/km^2.

Immigration rates will be fastest for those species that disperse long distances. Norway's efforts to reduce lynx-caused livestock losses by reducing lynx numbers were thwarted because lynx, which have large home ranges, immigrated from neighboring Sweden (Herfindal et al. 2005). Efforts to reduce populations over large areas are more effective than those in small areas because the sources of immigrants are more distant, and more immigrants are required to fill the larger void. To reduce goose–aircraft collisions, Rutledge et al. (2015) recommended that culling resident Canada geese at an airport should not be restricted to the airport; instead, any goose within 8 km of the airport should be removed because, otherwise, new geese will start to recolonize the airport within the first month. Garrettson et al. (1996) doubled the nesting success of ducks when predators were trapped from large areas (over 40 km^2), whereas predator trapping on small areas (1.4 km^2) had little effect (Sargeant et al. 1995). Likewise, Frey et al. (2003) found that culling predators to enhance pheasant populations was effective in large areas (40 km^2), but not in smaller ones.

13.4 IS THERE A CORRELATION BETWEEN WILDLIFE POPULATION LEVELS AND WILDLIFE DAMAGE?

The amount of wildlife damage is often correlated with the size of local wildlife populations. Raccoon damage in cornfields, for example, is related to raccoon abundance in adjacent woodlots (Beasley and Rhodes 2008). A reduction in white-tailed deer densities in suburban areas produced a similar decline in DVCs (DeNicola and Williams 2008). But the assumption that there is a direct one-to-one relationship between a change in a wildlife population and the amount of damage it produces (e.g., a 50% reduction in a deer population will decrease the damage deer cause by 50%) is often wrong. Instead, a 50% reduction in a deer population can have little impact on deer damage in some situations and completely prevent it in others. The actual relationship between a reduction in a wildlife population and a reduction in wildlife damage depends, in large part, on why the animals are causing the damage. To illustrate this, consider the problem of deer–automobile collisions. If most collisions result from deer just roaming throughout their home range as part of their daily activities, then reducing the deer population by half will probably reduce deer–automobile collisions by a similar amount at least over the short term. However, if most of the collisions are caused by hungry deer which have eaten all the food within their home ranges and are searching for new food sources, then most collisions will occur when deer populations exceed the biological carrying capacity. In this case, reducing the deer population by half may prevent most deer–automobile collisions because deer will not need to travel far in search of food.

Consider a population of 100 elk that are consuming crops of local farmers. Let us assume the elk have 20 different plant species in their home ranges that they can consume and will concentrate their forage on the plant species that is most palatable. Under this scenario, elk concentrate foraging exclusively on the most palatable plant until that plant becomes scarce. At which time, elk will start eating the second most palatable plant. The elk will continue this pattern: grazing each plant species, in turn, based on the plant's palatability relative to the other species that are still available. Let us also assume that foraging by the 100 elk is intense enough that they have over-grazed nine plant species. Hence, they are now concentrating their foraging on the tenth most palatable plant species and grazing the more palatable plants as they grow back. Now, assume that the farmers complain about elk damage, and the state has sent hunters to reduce the elk population from 100 to 50. What impact will this have on reducing elk damage to a farmer's crops? That will depend upon how palatability the farmer's crops are compared to the other 20 plant species within the elk's home range. If the farmer is growing apples, which typically is very palatable, any elk in the area will preferentially forage on it. For apples, reducing the elk herd from 100 to 50 animals will have little impact on its damage if 50 elk are sufficient to consume all of the fruit. To reduce herbivory on apples, almost all elk in the area would have to be removed. However, if farmers are growing wheat, which elk find only moderately palatable, and elk are just starting to forage on it when their population contains 100 individuals, then reducing the elk population by half may completely stop foraging on wheat, owing to the availability of more palatable plant species in the area. Hence,

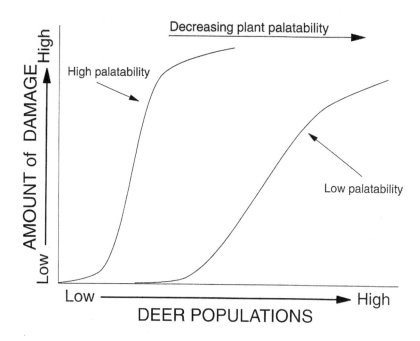

FIGURE 13.5   A small reduction in an elk population may significantly reduce damage to less palatable plants, but a large reduction may be required to reduce damage to a very palatable plant species.

Source: This is Figure 7.5 in the first edition of this book.

reducing an elk population may not significantly reduce damage to highly palatable crops but may stop damage to less palatable ones (Figure 13.5).

13.5   DO THE BENEFITS AND LIABILITIES OF WILDLIFE CHANGE AS WILDLIFE POPULATIONS INCREASE?

Although there may not be a direct one-to-one relationship between an increasing wildlife population and the severity of a specific wildlife problem, human–wildlife conflicts become more intense and more frequent as wildlife populations increase. Thus, the negative values of a wildlife species increase exponentially as its populations expands (Figure 13.6). This occurs because there are more animals to cause damage, and humans become less tolerant as their losses mount. As wildlife populations expand, the positive values of wildlife will also increase but at an ever-slowing rate. With more deer, there are more opportunities for people to see them, and more hunters will have the opportunity to shoot one; thus, positive values rise. But the amount of pleasure people receives from seeing their one-thousandth deer is less than when they saw a deer for the first time.

At low populations, positive values provided by a wildlife species greatly exceed the negative values, but as a wildlife population rises, negative values accelerate

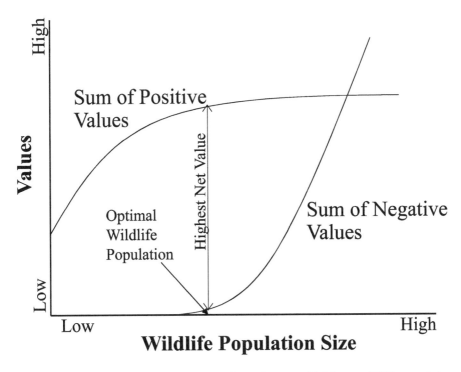

FIGURE 13.6 How the positive and negative values provided by a wildlife population change as the wildlife population increases.

Source: This is Figure 7.6 in the first edition of this book.

faster than positive values. Ultimately, a wildlife population can grow to the point where the sum of its negative values exceeds its positive values. At this point, it could be considered a pest, and both nonlethal and lethal methods might be employed to reduce the population. The optimal wildlife population is the one with the greatest net value (positive benefits minus negative benefits).

13.6 SHOULD LETHAL TECHNIQUES BE DIRECTED AT SPECIFIC INDIVIDUALS, SPECIFIC SUBPOPULATIONS, OR THE ENTIRE POPULATION?

A wildlife population is a group of animals of the same species that is isolated from other groups of that same species by physical barriers. For instance, gray squirrels in England can breed with each other, but they cannot breed with those in North America. Therefore, the squirrels in England constitute a separate population from the North American population. Each population is composed of many subpopulations (Figure 13.7). When wildlife damage is occurring on a farm, the wildlife subpopulation can be defined as the group of animals that have a home range that includes the farm. These are the animals that have the potential to cause damage

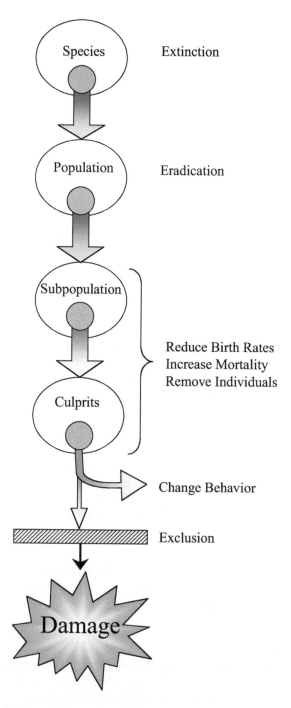

FIGURE 13.7   Relationship between culprits, subpopulations, and populations and how lethal control might be directed at any of these levels.

Source: This is Figure 7.8 in the first edition of this book.

because they can travel to the farm. Not all members of the local subpopulation may actually be causing damage. Instead, only a small number of individuals may be responsible for the damage; these individuals are called the "culprits" (Figure 13.7).

When lethal means are used in wildlife damage management, selectivity is best because the goal should be to stop the damage by killing as few animals as possible due to their high positive values (Chapter 1). Ideally, we should remove only the culprits from the local subpopulation and leave all other individuals alone. The difficulty involves identifying the culprits. Sometimes, the culprits have distinctive markings and can be identified visually or by using cameras at problem sites. A few seals in the Baltic Sea, for instance, learned how to capture salmon inside traps set by fishermen. Seals can be individually identified by the spotting pattern on their fur. By placing cameras inside the traps, Königson et al. (2013) identified which individual seals were entering traps to feed. Wildlife managers then live captured and translocated some of these culprit seals. This approach was successful in reducing salmon losses.

Every animal's DNA is unique, providing another method to identify culprits. Even DNA extracted from feces can be used to identify the culprit. Chiyo et al. (2011) identified crop-raiding elephants by collecting feces from farms after an elephant raid. The scientists found that 12% of the elephants in the area were responsible for the crop raiding. Sanz-Aguilar et al. (2009) were able to identify which yellow-legged gulls had developed an appetite for European storm-petrels by using DNA analysis. Scientists and wardens were able to identify 16 pairs of gulls out of 500 pairs on a Spanish island that were depredating storm-petrels by inspecting fecal pellets in each gull territory for the remains of petrels. The selective removal of these individual gulls reduced the number of petrels killed by gulls by over half, resulting in an increase in the breeding success of petrels by 23%.

When animals are shot while in the process of causing damage, we can be assured that only culprits are being removed. Some states only allow farmers to kill deer when they are observed foraging on their agricultural crops. Other deer are left alone. Sometimes, animals leave the depredation scene before wildlife biologists arrive, but they can still be individually identified, by using hound dogs to follow the scent of individuals. When people have been attacked by bears, hound dogs can be utilized to track down the culprit by releasing the dogs at the attack site and allowing them to find the bear by following its odor trail. Confirmation that the correct individual bear was located can be made by locating human DNA under its claws or human remains in its digestive system.

Sometimes, culprits can be identified by their location. Wolf packs are territorial and keep other wolves at bay. Hence, most livestock killing will be the result of the resident pack. Bradley et al. (2015) found that removing the entire pack was more effective than removing only part of it. The time between recurrent livestock attacks was 19 days when no wolves were removed, 64 days following partial pack removal, and 730 days following removal of an entire pack.

One lethal technique that removes only culprits is the Livestock Protection Collar®, which is placed around the neck of sheep or lambs. This collar has pouches filled with a toxicant, sodium monofluoroacetate (also called 1080). Coyotes normally kill sheep by biting hard enough on the throat to close the sheep's windpipe and suffocate it. When a coyote bites the throat of sheep wearing a Livestock Protection Collar, its teeth puncture one or more of the pouches, and the coyote gets some of the toxicant in its mouth and dies. Hence, these collars only remove culprits. After all, if a coyote has its teeth around the throat of a sheep, it is pretty good evidence that it was trying to kill that sheep. Unfortunately, Livestock Protection Collars have not lived up to their potential to solve the problem of predation on livestock. They are too expensive ($15–20 each) to put one on every sheep in a flock, and it is impossible to predict which sheep a coyote is going to attack next (Knowlton et al. 1999). This technique is more effective if most of the flock can be temporarily moved from the pasture where sheep have been killed so that the pasture now contains only sheep with collars. Of course, such action requires additional work and a safe area where the rest of the sheep can be moved. Another limitation is that the U.S. EPA requires states to have registration, training, and record-keeping programs before these collars can be used. Anytime, a coyote is killed by a Livestock Protection Collar; its carcass has to be treated as a hazardous waste site.

Sometimes, we cannot identify, locate, or target only the culprits. In such situations, the best we can do is to identify members of the subpopulation most likely to be culprits and to target that group, a process called profiling. Adult wolves, not juveniles, are responsible for most livestock depredations; therefore, juveniles can be ignored in any culling programs designed to address livestock depredations (Harper et al. 2008). In Europe, male lynx kill more livestock than females, allowing people to avoid killing females if the desire is to protect livestock (Herfindal et al. 2005). Blejwas et al. (2002) found that most coyotes that kill sheep and lambs were adults that had pups to feed. Apparently, the additional stress caused by hungry pups drove their parents to shift their hunting efforts to large food items, such as lambs and sheep, which they might have otherwise avoided. Coyotes with pups can be targeted by killing adults at the den sites or by selectively removing territorial coyotes (only territorial adults produce pups). Territorial coyotes can also be targeted because they will chase small dogs that are inside their territories, and shooters can use this knowledge to bring territorial coyotes within gun range (when the dog returns to the shooter, the coyote often comes with it).

Sometimes, removing only culprits is impossible because we cannot identify them, or because all members of the local subpopulation are culprits. For example, thousands of red-winged blackbirds or eared doves may occupy a single roost in an area with ripening grain fields and fly out every morning in large flocks to search for fields of ripening grain. In such situations, all blackbirds are seeking grain to consume and are culprits; thus, any lethal program should be targeted at the subpopulation (Linz et al. 2015). In the moorlands of England, abundance of red foxes was reduced 43% and carrion crows by 78% by culling them for eight consecutive years. This resulted in a threefold increase in breeding success of ground-nesting birds and a 14% annual increase in the abundance of lapwings, curlews, golden plovers, and red grouse (Fletcher et al. 2010). The scientists concluded that controlling predators was a better use of money than spending it on habitat improvement.

Lethal control is used more frequently when an exotic species is causing the problem. In such situations, lethal control may be employed not just to reduce a population of an exotic species but to eradicate it from an invaded area (Siers et al. 2019).

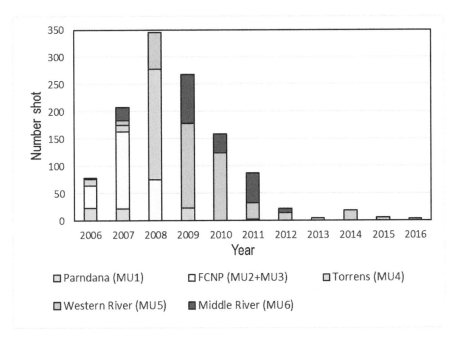

FIGURE 13.8   Number of kangaroos removed by sharpshooters per night declined as the removal program continued, and the cumulative number of kangaroos removed by the program increased. The program was conducted in a nature reserve in Australia that was surrounded by a wildlife-proof fence. At the end of the sharpshooting program, 12% of the original population was still alive.

Source: P. Mawson and used with permission.

Most efforts to eradicate a wildlife population fail; while it may be relatively easy to kill most individuals in a population, it becomes difficult to kill the last ones, which are warier and live in the most inaccessible areas. This was discovered in a small Australian nature preserve, which was overrun with western grey kangaroos; sharpshooters initially killed 70 kangaroos a night when they started and the kangaroo population numbered over a thousand; a year later, they were not killing any kangaroos during most nights, and the program was halted (Figure 13.8). Yet, 12% of the original kangaroo population remained at the time the sharpshooting program ended (Mawson et al. 2016).

Eradication efforts are more successful if the wildlife population is confined to a small area, such a small island. Anacapa Island (280 ha) is one of the Channel Islands located off the coast of California. It used to be a great place for seabirds to nest, but few did so after black rats were accidently released on the island. After much effort, the rats were eradicated from Anacapa in 2002. Since then, nests of Scripps's murrelets have increased from 11 to 60, Cassin's auklets nests increased from 0 to 42, and hatching success of Xanthus's murrelets doubled (Whitworth et al. 2005, 2015; Whitworth and Carter 2018).

13.7 CAN LETHAL METHODS CREATE A LANDSCAPE OF FEAR AMONG PROBLEM ANIMALS?

Animals are wary of areas where they are vulnerable to predators and learn from their experiences to avoid such areas (Ferrari et al. 2009). For example, cougars need to stalk or ambush their prey; this requires a terrain with boulders or brush that provide cover. This explains why 73% of cougar kills occurred along forest edges versus only 6% in open areas (Laundré and Hernández 2003). Deer and elk recognize these risky areas and avoid them (Ripple and Beschta 2003, 2004a, 2004b, 2006; Sullivan et al. 2018).

Can wildlife biologists reduce human–wildlife conflicts by creating a landscape of fear in the problem animals? Hunters or sharpshooters can create a landscape of fear if shooting is concentrated in open, agricultural fields so that animals learn that agricultural fields are dangerous (Conover 2001). The goal of creating a landscape of fear is not to keep animals in a continual state of fear but only to make them fearful of entering agricultural fields (Cromsigt et al. 2013). Of course, creating an atmosphere of fear will only be successful if wildlife are able recognize and respond to risks posed by hunters. Anecdotal evidence supports this. During the culling program, the scientists found that during the day, deer avoided areas around hunting stands immediately after the stand had been occupied by a hunter. During the hunting season, deer also avoid previously preferred habitats, such as young pine plantations, forest clear cuts, and open areas where they are more exposed to hunters (Kilgo et al. 1998).

13.8 ARE LETHAL METHODS LEGAL?

Societies usually allow their citizens a free hand in using most nonlethal techniques to resolve the wildlife problems confronting them. Governmental approval is not required if citizens want to place a fence around their alfalfa fields to protect them from deer, to put a scarecrow in the garden, or to manipulate the habitat on their property to reduce animal numbers. Likewise, no permits are required if a person wants to kill insects. But wildlife are different; laws protect wildlife species because of their high value, and governmental approval is required before they are killed. The only exceptions are a few species classified by the government as "vermin." Starlings, pigeons, house sparrows, rats, house mice, and coyotes are the species most often excluded from protection. Additionally, it is illegal to discharge a firearm in most municipalities.

Many lethal techniques are dangerous if used by inexperienced people and could result in human deaths or harm nontarget species. For this reason, state and federal governments require people employing most lethal techniques to have a state and/or federal permit to use them. For instance, a pesticide applicator's license is required to use toxicants, and a hunter safety certificate is required to use a firearm to shoot wildlife. To protect wildlife and the environment, the federal government uses its own employees to mitigate human–wildlife conflicts, especially when lethal measures are required. These U.S.D.A. Wildlife Services employees work in all 50 states to mitigate human–wildlife conflicts in ways that are safe, effective, and environmentally benign (Table 13.1).

TABLE 13.1

During 2019, U.S.D.A. Wildlife Services (WS) Killed 2.1 Million Animals of Which Almost One Million Were Exotic Species

Number of birds killed		Number of mammals killed	
Species	Number	Species	Number
European starlings	687,000	Feral hogs	84,000
Brown-headed cowbirds	407,000	Coyotes	62,000
Red-winged blackbirds	365,000	Beaver	25,000
Common grackles	120,000		
Feral pigeons	60,000		
Chestnut munias	41,000		
Scaly-breasted munias	26,000		
Canada geese	26,000		
Mourning doves	23,000		
House sparrows	15,000		
Java sparrows	13,000		
Common ravens	11,000		
Double-crested cormorants	11,000		
Black vultures	11,000		
Zebra dove	10,000		

Listed here are all avian and mammalian species where WS killed more than 10,000 individuals. Other species where more than 10,000 were killed included 53,000 pike minnows and 18,000 brown tree snakes. www.aphis.usda.gov/aphis/ourfocus/wildlifedamage/pdr/?file=PDR-G_Report&p=2019:INDEX

13.9 ARE LETHAL METHODS EFFECTIVE AT REDUCING WILDLIFE DAMAGE?

A pressing question is whether the use of lethal methods is successful in alleviating wildlife damage. If not, there is no reason to use them. Intuitively, we know that if all individuals of a damaging wildlife species are killed, then damage by that species will stop. However, the issue is what has been accomplished when some, but not all, of the animals are killed (Figure 13.9). Many studies have reported that lethal control was effective in alleviating wildlife problems. For instance, Stahl et al. (2001) found that sheep losses in France declined after the removal of European lynx. Several studies compared livestock losses at ranches with and without predator control and found that loss rates on ranches with predator control were lower than those observed on ranches without predator control (Nass 1980; Wagner 1988). In one interesting experiment, all efforts to kill predators were stopped at a Washington ranch to assess what effect this would have on livestock losses to predators (Sidebar 13.2).

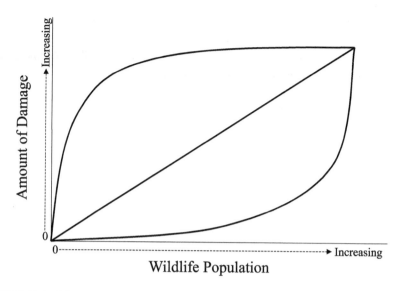

FIGURE 13.9 Three potential relationships between an increasing wildlife population and the amount of damage it causes.

Source: This is Figure 7.9 in the first edition of this book.

SIDEBAR 13.2 PREDATION AT A WASHINGTON SHEEP RANCH WHEN LETHAL CONTROL OF PREDATORS WAS TERMINATED

Some people believe that high rates of sheep losses to coyotes result from poor husbandry. Their assumption is that overgrazing leads to sick and weak sheep, and this leads to easy pickings for predators. To test this hypothesis and determine what would happen if there was no predator control, scientists convinced the owner of the Eight Mile Ranch in Washington state not to use lethal control to protect his sheep from predators, with the understanding that the scientists would compensate him for the value of any sheep killed by predators. This ranch was selected because it was well managed, the pastures lightly grazed, shed lambing was practiced, and coyotes had been a problem in prior years. After the first year of the study, the scientists had to change the study design and reinitiate predator control because sheep and lamb losses were so high that the scientists were in danger of running out of money to compensate the owner. The study was discontinued after 30 months because the researchers had already paid the owner over $50,000 in compensation. During the entire study, predators (mostly coyotes) killed 1,223 sheep. Before predator control was renewed, approximately 25% of the lambs and 6% of the ewes were killed by predators (O'Gara et al. 1983).

Overall, the effectiveness of lethal control is mixed: with success has also come setbacks. For instance, during the 1950s and 1960s, a major effort was made in the western United States to reduce livestock losses by reducing coyote populations over large areas by distributing large carcasses that had been poisoned with thallium or compound 1080 (sodium monofluoroacetate). To reduce the nontarget hazard to birds, these baits were distributed in the winter after most birds had migrated to warmer climates. Only one poisoned carcass was placed in each township (93 km^2). It was assumed that most coyotes would find a poisoned carcass while roaming within their large home ranges, as would some smaller predators, such as foxes and skunks. Because small predators have smaller home ranges than coyotes, most small predators would not have a poisoned carcass within their home range and would be spared (Wagner 1988). These poisoned carcasses were distributed in most of the townships of Utah, Idaho, and Wyoming. During years when these poisoned carcasses were used, coyote densities in these states were lower than they had been previously (Linhardt and Robinson 1972; Wagner 1988). In other western states (Colorado, Nevada, New Mexico, and Texas), poisoned carcasses were distributed more sporadically, and the results were more ambiguous. Although coyote populations were reduced in some states, Wagner (1988) concluded that the program had little effect on reducing depredation on sheep and lambs. The widespread distribution of poisoned carcasses ended in 1972 when President Nixon issued an executive order banning the use of toxicants by federal employees or on federal land. Since then, lethal control to protect livestock from predators has become site specific. Current efforts target culprits or sub-populations around individual ranches rather than trying to reduce coyote populations over large areas. Still, the work of U.S.D.A. Wildlife Services to use lethal control on predators is controversial. Critics argue that culling predators is ineffective, causes environmental damage, and is immoral (Bergstrom et al. 2014).

The Australian government distributed over a million baits laced with 1080 annually to control dingoes. The baits caused an immediate decrease in dingo populations and sheep losses. Distribution of 1080 baits remains a major component in the country's efforts to reduce problems caused by dingoes. The people in Australia are less concerned about the use of this toxicant than people in the United States because many plant species in Australia produce the same chemical to protect themselves from herbivores (Allen and Sparkes 2001).

Stands of southern wild rice in New Jersey have been declining due to over-grazing by resident Canada geese (Figure 13.10). To address the problem, an integrated program was initiated that involved the lethal control of adult Canada geese, egg destruction, and harassment. The integrated program was successful in reducing the number of goose nests by 70%. After implementation of the program, the number of wild rice plants exhibiting goose damage was four times lower than before the program began. A major concern was that all this human activity in tidal marshes would deter ospreys from nesting, but their numbers were higher at the end of the ten-year study than at the beginning (Nichols 2014a, 2014b).

FIGURE 13.10   In New Jersey's tidal marshes, grazing by resident Canada geese threatens stands of wild rice. The rice stands appear as light green in this photo.

Source: Theodore Nichols and used with permission.

13.10   ARE LETHAL TECHNIQUES COST-EFFECTIVE?

The benefits provided by any method to reduce wildlife damage should always exceed the cost of the method. In other words, the benefit-to-cost ratio should be greater than 1.0. Usually, lethal techniques are cost-efficient and less expensive than other alternatives for reducing wildlife damage. For instance, in Minneapolis/St. Paul, Minnesota, the cost of removing one Canada goose was $0 using sport hunters, $10 using relocation, $24 to kill and process it for food, $45 using egg destruction, $100 using sterilization, and even more using habitat modification (Cooper and Keefe 1997). Campa et al. (1997) estimated that it annually costs less than $3/ha to protect an agricultural field from deer by using hunters, $54/ha using a multiwire electric deer fence, and $77/ha using a woven-wire fence. Another study examined how much it cost to save a duckling from predators (Sidebar 13.3).

SIDEBAR 13.3   WHAT DOES IT COST TO INCREASE DUCK NUMBERS BY REMOVING PREDATORS?

It has long been debated whether predator removal can increase reproduction in upland-nesting ducks; more biologists favor habitat improvement over predator removal. In 1994, Delta's Waterfowl Foundation addressed the question by hiring trappers to remove mesopredators (mainly skunks, raccoons, and ground squirrels) within five town sections (each 93 km²) and compared nesting success in these areas to four town sections that were left alone. An average of 245 predators were removed from each section. Trapped sections had higher duck nest success levels than untreated sites, but brood size and prefledgling survival were similar. An estimated 150 more mallards were added to the fall population by the trapping program at a cost of $74 per additional bird. While the results were positive in producing more ducks, it was not cost-effective (Amundson and Arnold 2011; Amundson et al. 2013). Additionally, an increase in duck numbers during the fall may not translate into more duck breeding pairs during the following spring (Pieron et al. 2013).

The money spent to employ a lethal technique is only one of its costs. Other costs occur because wildlife are killed, and they have value (Chapter 1). Lethal control creates political and ethical problems because wildlife are owned by society, but the damage they inflict is usually to private property. It is in the self-interest of property owners who are suffering from wildlife damage to stop the damage by any means possible, including lethal methods. After all, property owners receive the economic benefit if the damage stops. The perspective of other people can be different. What they see is that their wildlife, which they own as members of society, are being destroyed for someone else's private gain. These people are only remotely impacted by the wildlife damage. After all, it is not their livestock that are being preyed upon or their crops that are being eaten. The various stakeholders pursue their own self-interest but differ in where their self-interest lies, making lethal control of wildlife controversial.

When nonlethal techniques are used to stop wildlife damage, there is little controversy. In this case, the rancher has to pay the cost of the nonlethal technique and also reaps its benefits if successful (all of the costs and benefits fall upon the same individual, so he/she can make rational decisions). With nonlethal techniques, wildlife are usually unharmed, and society allows ranchers to make their own decisions about whether the cost of using a nonlethal technique is economically justified. When one wildlife species is killed to protect another wildlife species, society can decide whether a lethal control program is worthwhile because society owns both species. An example can be found in a predator control program to kill arctic foxes to help nesting brant. By killing an average of 13 arctic foxes annually, the program saved approximately 3,000 brant eggs each year from depredation. Anthony et al. (1991) believed that this trade-off of foxes for brants was justified because brants were uncommon and declining in the area while arctic foxes were abundant.

13.11 SHOULD PREDATOR CONTROL BE DIRECTED AT A SINGLE SPECIES OR MULTIPLE SPECIES?

Wildlife managers are often tasked with increasing populations of wild birds or mammals by controlling predators. Often, these programs target the specific predator species that is causing most of the depredation. A benefit of this approach is that all of the resources can be directed at a single predator. Doing so enhances the probability that enough individuals of that predator species will be removed to have an effect. But programs to eliminate a single predator often fail to increase prey numbers because depredation by other predator species may accelerate when one predator species is eliminated (Holt et al. 2008). Greenwood (1986) demonstrated this in a classical study in which he tried to increase nesting success of ducks in North Dakota by selectively removing skunks. Despite removing 69 skunks, nest success barely budged because other predator species continued to depredate nests. More success was obtained when removal efforts targeted all predator species (Garrettson et al. 1996).

13.12   SHOULD LETHAL METHODS BE USED PREEMPTIVELY TO PREVENT A CONFLICT OR ONLY AFTER DAMAGE HAS BEGUN?

Lethal control is normally used in a "corrective" mode, meaning that it is employed only after damage has already begun. Furthermore, lethal control is normally used only after potential nonlethal methods were unsuccessful. Thus, lethal methods are often employed only for intractable problems of a long-standing nature. The liability of this approach is that some people endure considerable damage before lethal methods are employed.

Sometimes, lethal control is employed in a "preventive" mode, meaning that lethal methods will be used to prevent a potential problem from starting. Farmers are often encouraged to start using nonlethal techniques before wildlife damage begins; once animals start feeding in a field, changing their behavior is more difficult than not allowing the behavior in the first place. However, lethal methods are rarely employed in a preventive mode, due to the reluctance of society to allow wildlife to be killed unless absolutely necessary.

The main use of lethal methods in a preventive mode occurs when there is a threat to human health or safety or when economic losses occur so quickly that losses reach unacceptable levels before lethal control can be employed in a corrective sense. In the Rocky Mountains, coyote predation on livestock often occurs at the same places every year, usually during the spring or summer when the sheep are in remote pastures. Ranchers employ several methods (traps, snares, and shooting) to kill the coyotes responsible for killing their livestock. These methods, nonetheless, are often labor intensive, and it may take weeks or months to kill the culprits. An easier, faster, and cheaper method of killing coyotes is to shoot them from an airplane or helicopter during the winter, when snow makes coyotes easier to spot and track. The shooting of coyotes during the winter was successful in reducing lamb and sheep losses during the following spring and summer when sheep were moved to the areas where coyotes had been removed earlier (Wagner and Conover 1999). In Texas, a combination of snares and livestock guard animals was the most cost-effective in preventing calf losses to coyotes when employed one month before the calving period (Brewster et al. 2019).

13.13   WHAT RISK DO TRAPS POSE TO NONTARGET SPECIES?

A problem with any lethal technique is the danger that the wrong species will be killed; this is called a "nontarget hazard." The species that we are trying to kill is referred to as the "target species," while all other animals are "nontarget species." When animals are shot, the nontarget hazard is low because the shooter must see the animal before it can be killed. Thus, the shooter has an opportunity to avoid killing the wrong species by simply not pulling the trigger.

Traps, of course, are less selective because no one is present when an animal is captured; hence, traps pose a danger to nontarget species. This happened in Nevada where some cougars were injured as a result of recreational use of leg-hold traps and snares set for bobcats. Although most cougars were alive when released from the device, their survival rate over the next couple of years was lower than that of untrapped cougars. Apparently, leg or paw injuries sustained from the trapping adversely impacted cougars in the future (Andreasen et al. 2018). The risk to nontarget species can be reduced if the trap is equipped with a radio capable of signaling the trapper whenever the trap is sprung so that the trapper can check it immediately and release any nontarget animal (Benevides et al. 2008).

Species selectivity can be obtained by using traps of the proper size so that larger or smaller animals are excluded. Most leg-hold traps use a pan tension device for the trigger; the pan can be adjusted so that the trap will not be sprung unless an animal over a specific weight steps on the pan. Snares also can be equipped with a breakaway device that allows a deer or large animal to break free if trapped.

Some traps are designed to catch only specific species (Muñoz-Igualada et al. 2008; Massei et al. 2010; Short et al. 2012). There are egg traps, which is an egg-shaped plastic container and is designed to catch only raccoons. This trap contains a small hole so that an animal can only be caught by the trap if the animal can reach inside the trap's opening to reach the trigger; raccoons are one of the few species in North America that has the dexterity to do this (Figure 13.11). Another

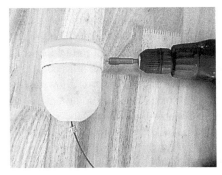 

FIGURE 13.11   Egg trap is designed to catch only raccoons because an animal has to reach inside the egg trap to reach the trigger, and raccoons are one of the few animals in North America with the dexterity to do this. When the white bar is pushed, the spring powers the black bar across the trap's opening and pins the animal's paw inside the trap. The photos show the outside and inside of the trap.

Source: Egg Trap Company and used with permission.

FIGURE 13.12 Testing of a hog-specific bait box that raccoons cannot open because the lid is too heavy for them; deer cannot open it with their nose as the hog in the photo is doing.

Source: N. P. Snow and used with permission.

species-specific trap is designed to catch hogs. Unlike most mammals, hogs use their noses to turn things over and lift them up. Snow et al. (2017) and Lavelle et al. (2018) used this knowledge to create a bait station that feral hogs could access but not raccoons or deer, meaning these bait stations would deliver toxic bait to kill feral hogs but not other animals. The scientists realized that both raccoons and hogs could open the lid of a box if they left a gap between the hinged lid and the box, allowing hogs to insert their noses and then their heads into the boxes, but deer could not do this. Through testing, the scientists realized that raccoons did not have the strength to open the lid if it weighed more than 14 kg, but feral hogs could do so (Figure 13.12). This knowledge allowed the scientists to create a bait station that could help make a toxic bait intended for feral hogs inaccessible to both deer and raccoons.

Traps also can be set in locations where only the target species can access them. Squirrel traps should be set on tree branches where only arboreal mammals can reach them; mole traps should be set in mole burrows, and beaver traps set in water (Sovada et al. 1995).

Traps can also be made more species specific by using bait that is attractive only to the target species. Many species use chemicals (called pheromones) to mark their territories or attract a member of the opposite sex. These pheromones are of great interest to members of a particular species, but seldom attract others, allowing them to target selectively that species. Beaver traps are baited with secretions from a beaver's castor gland. Additionally, species specificity can be obtained by using a scent that the target species finds attractive, but nontarget species do not. For instance, feral hogs are attractive to an artificial strawberry scent, but peccaries and raccoons are not (Campbell and Long 2008).

Traps can be made quite selective through careful selection of the proper trap, location, and bait, but this requires considerable training and experience (Muñoz-Igualada et al. 2008; Baldwin 2014). This is one of the major benefits of having professional employees, such as those employed by the U.S.D.A. Wildlife Services or professional game keepers in Europe be responsible for using lethal means to control predators, rather than expecting landowners to do it themselves (Holt et al. 2008).

13.14   CAN TOXICANTS BE EMPLOYED WITHOUT POSING A RISK TO NONTARGET SPECIES?

Toxicants pose a considerable risk to nontarget species that find and consume a toxic bait. Nontarget predators and scavengers may also be killed by consuming the carcass of a poisoned animal (this is called secondary poisoning) or if a poisoned animal vomits and another animal consumes it. To reduce these risks, EPA only approves toxicants that decompose rapidly and do not accumulate in the food chain.

There are many ways to make toxicants more species specific, such as using a poison that can kill the target species but not other species. Species specificity also can be achieved by placing toxic baits in locations where they are accessible only to the target species. Pocket gophers and ground squirrels can be targeted by placing toxic baits in their burrows, rather than scattering them on the ground (Whisson 1999; Hygnstrom et al. 2000). Baits can be used that do not attract the attention of nontarget species. For instance, baits intended for small mammals can be dyed green so as not to attract the attention of birds (Brunner and Coman 1983; Bryant et al. 1984).

An assessment of the nontarget hazard is especially difficult when using toxicants because dead animals might be dispersed over an extended area, the size of which depends on the home range of the species, and how quickly the animal is killed by the toxicant. For instance, strychnine kills quickly, and most dead animals are found within a few meters of the poisoned bait. In contrast, DRC-1339 kills over several days. Animals killed by slow-acting toxicants might be located over a wide region, and only a small proportion of them will be found during a search for carcasses. Hence, determining the actual number of animals killed by the toxicant is challenging. Estimating the true number of nontarget kills is made even more difficult because carcasses of small mammals and birds are easy to overlook during a search and can be quickly consumed by scavengers.

To determine a toxicant's risk to nontarget species, the first steps involve determining how much of the toxicant the nontarget species might obtain, how long the toxicant persists in the animal before it is excreted or detoxified, and what the average lethal dose is for that species (referred to as the LD_{50} or the lethal dose that kills 50% of the individuals receiving it). Receiving a sub-lethal dose of a pesticide may not kill an animal immediately, but the dose may be sufficient to cause illness or increase the animal's risk of dying. This danger is difficult to assess. A small dose might cause such a slight impairment of motor function that its effects might not be detected in a captive animal study, but this slight impairment could prevent a free-ranging animal from evading a predator (Sidebar 13.4).

SIDEBAR 13.4 ASSESSING THE RISK OF A BAITING PROGRAM IN A COLONY USED BY DIFFERENT AVIAN SPECIES

Sometimes, nontarget animals are killed not by traps or toxicants but by the disturbance caused by people conducting the operation. Populations of double-crested cormorant on the Great Lakes are reduced by going into nesting colonies to hand spray cormorant eggs to prevent them from hatching. Black-crowned night herons, great blue herons, ring-billed gulls, and herring gulls often nest in the same colony sites as cormorants. Although no night heron eggs were sprayed, Wyman et al. (2018) reported that the number of night herons nesting inside the cormorant colony declined the year following the oiling of cormorant eggs, presumably because of the disturbance. In contrast, the gull populations increased in the same colonies. Spraying cormorant eggs benefitted the gulls by providing an extra source of food. The results indicate how difficult it can be to predict or prevent an impact on nontarget species.

13.15   DOES CULLING APEX PREDATORS OR KEYSTONE HERBIVORES PRODUCE A TROPHIC CASCADE?

Reducing populations of a wildlife species can have unintended consequences unless all the roles played by that species in the ecosystem are known. This is especially true for apex predators (those at the top of the food chain) and keystone animals (those that impact other species). Consider the potential consequences of killing prairie dogs: a keystone species. Their intensive grazing around their burrows create islands of short grasses where other animals forage. Many predators hunt prairie dogs. Their burrows are used for shelter by many species, including rattlesnakes and burrowing owls. The black-footed ferret, which is an endangered species, is dependent on prairie dogs for food and their burrows for cover.

The danger of unintended consequences become more likely when apex predators are targeted for removal. Large carnivores interact with other species, and the absence of apex carnivores may cause faunal and flora changes, a process called trophic cascade. Apex predators are believed to suppress populations of medium-sized predators (called mesopredators) and the herbivores that they consume (Ballard et al. 2003). The presence of apex predators also can change the behavior of both mesopredators and herbivores by making them move their home ranges, avoid unsafe habitat, increase their vigilance, and remain close to dens and other safe cover. For example, wolf reintroduction has induced tropic cascades in the Yellowstone Ecosystem of North America (Hebblewhite and Smith 2010; Eisenberg 2013). Wolves prey upon elk and reduce elk populations (Eberhardt et al. 2007); wolves also change elk behavior. Due to these effects, wolf reintroductions have allowed aspen and willow to recover from decades of overbrowsing, and the regrowth of these plants has allowed beaver to reoccupy their former ranges. Beaver dams create more riparian habitat and increase avian abundance in arid areas. Additionally, wolves kill coyotes, and this has allowed the prey of coyotes to increase in abundance (Ballard et al. 2003). Carcasses left by wolves benefit scavengers from insects to golden eagles and bears (Wilmers et al. 2003), but see Mech (2012) for alternate interpretations.

Occasionally, the unintended consequences of predator removal can be beneficial. Lethal control of coyotes in Colorado and Wyoming for the protection of livestock also produced an increase in pronghorn populations (Harrington and Conover 2007). Other times, the consequences can be deleterious. In areas without wolves, coyotes serve as the apex predator and culling them may cause an explosion in populations of deer mice, ground squirrels, and chipmunks, which, in turn, can increase depredation rates on the nests of small songbirds (Sanders and Chalfoun 2019).

13.16   ARE LETHAL TECHNIQUES ETHICAL, HUMANE, AND SOCIALLY ACCEPTABLE?

Many people who object to lethal methods for reducing wildlife damage do so on moral grounds, viewing them as unethical and inhumane. This is especially true when lethal methods target charismatic animals. California voters approved a ballot initiative (Proposition 117) over 30 years ago that banned the killing of cougars in the state. Most people empathize with the animal that will be killed and are concerned about an animal's pain and suffering. These concerns led to the creation of best management practices (BMPs) for the trapping of mammals in the United States and Canada (International Association of Fish and Wildlife Agencies 1997). The main purpose of these BMPs was to develop standards about how to trap animals as humanely as possible.

If animals must be killed, everyone wants them killed as humanely as possible to prevent needless suffering. For example, Massachusetts voters approved a ballot initiative, the Wildlife Protection Act, which banned body-gripping traps and prohibited the use of dogs or bait in hunting black bears and bobcats (Jackman and Way 2018). A framework for assessing humane outcomes was presented by Hampton et al. (2015, 2016). There are four key parameters to assess the humaneness of shooting wildlife: the wounding rate (i.e., the proportion of animals that are wounded but not killed), time to death, instantaneous death rate (proportion of animals that die instantaneously), and the anatomical location of bullet wounds. Bullet type makes a difference in Hampton's four parameters; high-velocity bullets are more humane than bullets with low energy because the former produces a more rapid death and a lower wounding rate. The wounding rate also increased as the distance between the shooter and the animal increased (Caudell 2013; Hampton et al. 2016). This suggests that animals should only be shot when they are close to the shooter.

If target animals are live trapped, they should be euthanized as humanely as possible. Fortunately, the American Veterinary Medical Association (2013) published guidelines about how to euthanize animals humanely; these guidelines should be consulted and followed before killing any animal. Further, it is important to euthanize captured animals as soon as possible to reduce their stress, and this means that it is best to euthanize animals in a field setting (Julien et al. 2010). In this regard, research is leading to new methods to accomplish this quickly, such as employing portable gas chambers that can be moved to where wild animals are being captured, rather than moving the captured animal to a distant gas chamber (Kinsey et al. 2016).

Many people believe that lethal control is acceptable but only under specific circumstances. For instance, many people would support killing wildlife if there is a risk to human life or health (such as preventing bird–aircraft collisions to save passengers), but not if lethal control was used to alleviate a nuisance problem. All leaders of animal rights and animal welfare groups interviewed by Hooper (1992) felt that it was acceptable to kill animals if a human life was at stake. Baker et al. (2020) pointed out that people's perceptions about animals are complex and can be paradoxical in how different groups of animals are treated. U.K. residents protested the government's plans to cull invasive hedgehogs on the island of Uist and badgers in other parts of the kingdom. Yet, there was no protest against the use household products to kill rats and mice. Hence, society is divided over the question of using lethal techniques in wildlife damage management. This is a personal question and depends on a person's experiences, perspectives, and values. Nonetheless, the following principles are generally agreed upon: (1) nonlethal techniques that are efficacious and efficient should be used in lieu of lethal techniques and (2) if lethal techniques are used, we should select those that are as humane, selective, and socially acceptable as possible.

13.17 WHAT METHODS ARE USED IN LETHAL CONTROL?

13.17.1 RECREATIONAL HUNTING

Hunting is intended to provide a recreational opportunity to those who enjoy the sport, but it also can be a tool to reduce human–wildlife conflicts when designed to do so. For instance, bear populations increased 6% in 17 U.S. states or Canadian provinces that allowed bear hunting in the spring, 51% in 21 states or provinces that allowed only fall hunting of bears, and 87% where hunting was not allowed. Jurisdictions with liberal hunting seasons did not see an increase in bear complaints while those that did not allow bear hunting or only had a restricted hunting season experienced a plethora of complaints (Hristienko and McDonald 2007). Of course, recreational hunting does not always solve wildlife conflicts. In Washington state, both livestock losses and complaints about cougars were higher in those counties where many cougars were killed the previous year than in counties where few cougars were killed. Peebles et al. (2013) hypothesized that this resulted because young male cougars immigrated into counties when resident cougars were killed; these young males were responsible for much of the complaints and the depredation of livestock.

Recreational hunting in suburban and urban areas is problematic due to safety concerns. For this reason, many towns and cities restrict deer hunting to archery only. Hidden Valley Lake, Indiana, is 7.1 km², and there were 424 deer living within it when the city decided to reduce deer populations through a managed archery hunt. During the first two years of the program, 302 deer were removed (Stewart et al. 2013).

Some urban and suburban areas only allow controlled hunts where hunter numbers and locations are strictly regulated. These controlled hunts have been conducted in local towns, parks, government facilities, and land controlled by a single landowner. Most controlled hunts require potential hunters to take a training course, practice shooting on a range to improve their marksmanship, and check in upon entering and leaving the property. Most controlled hunts are designed to be intensive and of short duration so that the management objective, usually defined as a reduction in animal density, can be achieved quickly (Bowman 2011; Hubbard and Nielsen 2011). Longer hunting seasons become less effective due to animals locating refuges where they are safe (Rhoads et al. 2013).

White-tailed deer were so abundant in a 30,000-ha forest in northwest Pennsylvania that the local landowners created a quality-deer cooperative during 2000, and a decision was made to decrease deer densities through hunting. Hunters who brought a harvested buck to a check station received a free lottery ticket and an invitation to an annual deer hunter appreciation banquet; hunters that brought in antlerless deer received a second lottery ticket. Roads were plowed after snows to keep them open for hunters. The program decreased deer densities from 10/km² when the program first started to 4/km² a decade later (Figure 13.13). During this same period, body mass of deer and antler diameter increased. The habitat started

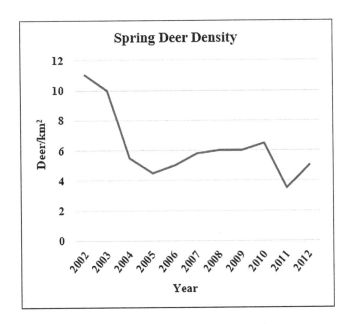

FIGURE 13.13   Spring deer densities in the quality deer cooperative during the decade after it was created.

Source: Adapted from DeCalesta (2017).

to recover from overgrazing, and seedling densities of red maple, American beech, and black cherry increased substantially after deer densities declined (DeCalesta 2017).

White-tailed deer were so abundant on Anticosti Island (Quebec, Canada) that they were in poor body condition and had reduced fecundity. Simard et al. (2013) created five areas (each 20 km²) on the island where deer hunting regulations were liberalized with the objective of removing 50% of antherless deer during the first year and an additional 30% over the next four years. Overall, harvest objectives were met 93% of the time. Yet deer densities and vegetation abundance and growth were not met, perhaps because of emigration of deer from other parts of the island. Better results were obtained by using hunting at the Quabbin Reservoir in Massachusetts. The management objective was to reduce the current deer population of 11–28 deer/km² to 4 deer/km². This objective was met after two years of a controlled hunt (McDonald et al. 2007). Williams et al. (2013) examined the impact of a combination of recreational hunting with liberalized regulations and organized hunts on white-tailed deer densities at sites in Pennsylvania and New Jersey. The program was able to reduce deer densities from 30–80/km² prior to the program to 17–18/km² after 3–10 years of the program, but hunters were unable to reduce densities below this level. Likewise, liberalization of deer hunting along the interface of rural and urban areas failed to increase harvest rates because few hunters were able to gain access to private property. Landowners were unwilling to allow hunters on their property because they were wary of how the hunters would behave and if allowing them access would decrease hunting opportunities for themselves and family members (Siemer et al. 2016).

Recreational hunting to control sika deer populations was tested in Japan by escalating its intensity over a series of years; the hunting season expanded from two to four months, and the number of female deer that could be harvested went from zero to two per day. Thirty percent of the entire deer population were removed, including 25% of all females (Ueno et al. 2010). In Norway, sheep are free ranging (i.e., there are no shepherds or livestock guard dogs watching them), and lynx depredate many lambs. Annual lamb losses to all causes range from 5% to 12%, and lynx were responsible for a high proportion of the lost lambs. Herfindal et al. (2005) examined if recreational hunting of lynx was effective in reducing lamb losses. Hunters killed 294 lynxes from 2001 to 2005. The scientists found that total lambs loses declined when hunting was intense enough to reduce lynx densities. But the magnitude of the benefit was so small (13 lambs saved for every male lynx killed and two lambs saved for every female lynx killed) that it did not justify the use of recreation hunting for this benefit (Herfindal et al. 2005).

Resident Canada geese have become so numerous that they cause nuisance problems throughout the cities and suburbs of North America. In an attempt to reduce populations through recreational hunters, special early and late hunting seasons were created when migratory geese were not in the area, and special hunting zones were created in urban areas. Unfortunately, the liberal hunting regulations were unsuccessful in reducing populations because the resident goose populations had grown too large and had a reproductive rate that was too high (Sheaffer et al. 2005; Groepper et al. 2012).

13.17.2 LEG-HOLD TRAPS

Leg-hold traps are designed to hold the animal until the trapper returns (Figure 13.14). This allows the trapper to release nontarget animals that might have been captured. Some people consider such traps to be inhumane because the animal is held (sometimes for an extended period) rather than being killed immediately. They note that animals are often injured during this holding period (Van Ballenberghe 1984; Olsen et al. 1988). Currently, there is much research aimed at reducing this injury rate. For instance, a padded-jaw leg-hold trap has been developed that causes fewer leg injuries than nonpadded traps (Frame and Meier 2007). Wolves captured in cable restraints recovered more quickly than wolves captured with foothold traps (Gese et al. 2019). Another approach is to attach a tranquilizer tablet on the trap. Trapped animals normally bite at the trap and, in doing so, consume some of the sedative (Sahr and Knowlton 2000).

13.17.3 KILLING TRAPS AND SNARES

Some traps are designed to kill the animal rather than hold it. Snap traps are the most widely used traps in the world and are used in many households to kill mice and

FIGURE 13.14   Leg-hold trap.

Source: Courtesy of Bill Duke.

rats in buildings (Figure 13.15A). They have a baited trigger that releases a spring-powered bar that snaps over and breaks the animal's spine. Spring-powered harpoon traps are used to control moles in yards and gardens by placing them in a mole's tunnel (Figure 13.15B). Conibear traps are rectangular in shape (Figure 13.16). When an animal walks through the trap, two spring-powered bars snap shut, crushing the animal. These traps are commonly placed in shallow water to kill beaver, muskrats, and nutria or along an animal trail.

Snares are a wire noose with a locking device that allow movement in only one direction, resulting in a tightened noose, which cannot be loosened by the trapped

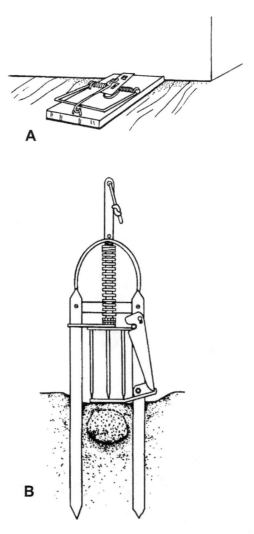

FIGURE 13.15   Snap trap commonly used to kill mice inside buildings (A), and a harpoon-type trap (B) used to kill moles.

Source: Courtesy of Scott Hygnstrom.

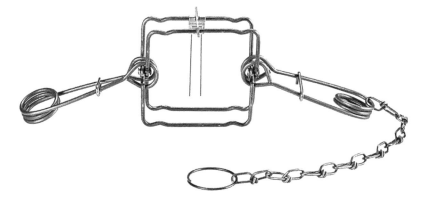

FIGURE 13.16   Conibear traps.

Source: Bill Duke and used with permission.

animal. Snares are set at sites where the target animal must pass through a restricted path or crawl under a fence. When an animal does so, the snare closes on its neck; the animal's attempts to free itself only serve to tighten the noose. Death results from suffocation, but snares can also be set to hold an animal without killing it. Trapping wolves in Minnesota after livestock have been killed was effective in reducing sheep losses, but not cattle losses (Sidebar 13.5).

SIDEBAR 13.5 EFFECTIVENESS OF TRAPPING WOLVES IN MINNESOTA AFTER LIVESTOCK ARE DEPREDATED

During a 20-year period, 923 livestock were verified as wolf kills at 434 different farms in the northern part of Minnesota. In response, 1,440 wolves were trapped by the U.S. Fish and Wildlife Service or by the U.S.D.A. Wildlife Services. Harper et al. (2008) examined these data to determine whether trapping and killing wolves was an effective means to protect livestock. The authors determined that trapping wolves reduced losses of sheep but not cattle. Sheep are more vulnerable to wolves than cattle, and wolves often return repeatedly to sheep flocks, whereas cattle depredations are more of a one-time event. The benefits, however, lasted only for a short time; there was no impact on depredation rates the following year. Interestingly, Harper et al. (2008) also found that sometimes livestock depredations decreased even when the traps caught nothing. Apparently, an increase in human activity was enough to deter wolves.

13.17.4   USE OF JUDAS ANIMALS TO REDUCE OR ERADICATE POPULATIONS OF INVASIVE SPECIES

With exotic or invasive species, the management goal is often to eradicate a population. This is difficult to achieve, especially when the animals are widely dispersed or in inaccessible habitat. An approach that is effective for social species is the use of Judas animals, so-called because a few individuals of the same species that can be tracked are released in the area inhabited by the exotic animals. These Judas animals seek out and join conspecifics in the area and thereby betray the location of feral members of their species. Managers can then shoot the exotic animals while sparing the Judas animals, allowing them to "betray" the location of other individuals. This technique has been used successfully to eradicate feral goats and donkeys from some of the Galapagos Islands (Carrion et al. 2007; Cruz et al. 2009), and feral pigs from Pinnacles National Monument, California (McCann et al. 2008). Judas animals have also been used to reduce populations of red deer, fallow deer, water buffalo, dromedary camels, and feral cattle (Spencer et al. 2015). Judas starlings were employed to locate the roost sites of starlings along the edge of the expanding range of European starlings in Australia (Woolnough et al. 2006).

13.17.5 TOXICANTS

Numerous chemicals have been used to poison depredating animals (Table 13.2), most of which have to be consumed to be fatal. These chemicals are placed in baits, so target species will ingest them. The advantage of toxicants is that they do not require much labor and can be used to kill large numbers of animals, even in remote areas. Their disadvantage is that toxins may not be as species specific as we would prefer.

Any chemical that is used in the United States to mitigate a human–wildlife conflict or to kill animals must be approved and registered with the EPA. Before being approved, the company or agency that seeks to have a chemical registered must show that the chemical does not pose a hazard to the environment or to people. This requires many tests that are costly to conduct; usually several million dollars are required to conduct the tests needed to register a chemical with the EPA. In fact, it is so expensive that few chemicals are registered with the EPA for use in resolving wildlife problems (Table 13.2).

Burgeoning populations of common ravens in the western United States prey upon many species of conservation concern including the desert tortoise and sage-grouse. Ravens are more susceptible to the toxicant DRC-1339 than other avian species, and the toxin can be sprayed on dried dog food that few birds, other than crows and ravens, will consume. By distributing the treated dogfood at landfills in the winter, the risk to nontarget species can be minimized and large number of ravens can be killed quickly (Peebles and Conover 2016). Doing so improves the nesting success of sage-grouse hens during the following spring (Dinkins et al. 2016) and increases the number of adult sage-grouse a year later (Peebles et al. 2017).

One widespread program to poison predators was conducted in Queensland, Australia, starting in 1968 when the toxicant 1080 became available to control dingoes. The toxicant was sprayed on meat baits, and the government distributed one million baits annually; ranchers also distributed the baits on their land. The program decreased dingo abundance and the number of sheep killed by predators (Allen and Sparkes 2001; Allen 2015).

TABLE 13.2

Toxicants Registered as of November 2020 with the U.S. EPA for Use in Resolving Human–Wildlife Conflicts Involving Terrestrial Vertebrates (Burrow Fumigants Are Not Included)

Pesticide active ingredient	Trademarks and brand names or registered product names[*]	Target species[**]
4-Aminopyridine CAS No. 504–24–5	Avitrol®	American crow, boat-tailed grackle, Brewer's blackbird, brown-headed cowbird, bronzed cowbird, common grackle, European starling, house sparrow, fish crow, great-tailed grackle, northern crow, red-winged blackbird, rock pigeon, rusty blackbird, yellow-headed blackbird
3-Chloro-p-toluidine hydrochloride (DRC-1339; CPTH) CAS No. 7745–89–3	Compound DRC-1339 Concentrate, Starlicide®	American crow, black-billed magpie, boat-tailed grackle, Brewer's blackbird, brown-headed cowbird, common grackle, California gull, Chihuahuan raven, common raven, Eurasian collared dove, European starling, fish crow, great black-backed gull, great-tailed grackle, herring gull, laughing gull, red-winged blackbird, ring-billed gull, rock pigeon, western gull, yellow-headed blackbird
Acetaminophen CAS No. 103–90–2	Acetaminophen for Brown Treesnake Control	Brown tree snake
Alphachloralose CAS No. 15879–93–3	Alpha, Black Belt, Black Pearl, Flash	House mouse
Alpha-chlorohydrin CAS No. 96–24–2	Epibloc®	Norway rat
Brodifacoum CAS No. 56073–10–0	BDF, De-Mize, Final®, Formus®, Havoc®, Jaguar®, Talon®, WeatherBlok®	Cotton rat, eastern harvest mouse, golden mouse, house mouse, meadow vole, Mexican woodrat, Norway rat, Polynesian rat, roof rat, southern plains woodrat, white-throated woodrat

(Continued)

TABLE 13.2 (*Continued*)

Pesticide active ingredient	Trademarks and brand names or registered product names[*]	Target species[**]
Bromadiolone CAS No. 28772–56–7	Boot Hill®, Brigand®, Contrac®, Hawk®, JT Eaton™, Just One Bite®, Kaput®, Maki®, Ratrac®, Resolv®, Revolver®	Cotton rat, deer mice, eastern harvest mouse, golden mouse, house mouse, meadow vole, Mexican woodrat, Norway rat, Polynesian rat, roof rat, southern plains woodrat, white-footed mouse, white-throated woodrat
Bromethalin CAS No. 63333–35–7	Assault®, Black Flag®, Cannon®, CyKill®, F-Trac®, Fast-Kill®, Fastrac®, Gladiator®, Gunslinger®, JT Eaton™, Prowler™, Rampage®, Sweeney's®, TakeDown®, Talpirid®, Tomcat®, Victor®	Broad-footed mole, coast mole, cotton mouse, cotton rat, deer mice, eastern harvest mouse, eastern mole, golden mouse, house mouse, meadow vole, Mexican woodrat, Norway rat, Polynesian rat, roof rat, southern plains woodrat, star-nosed mole, Townsend's mole, white-footed mouse, white-throated woodrat
Chlorophacinone CAS No. 3691–35–8	BorderLine®, Flatline®, JT Eaton™ AC Formula 90™, Rozol®	Black-tailed prairie dog, California ground squirrel, Columbian ground squirrel, cotton rat, deer mice, eastern harvest mouse, golden mouse, house mouse, Mexican woodrat, Norway rat, pocket gophers (*Geomys* spp. and *Thomomys* spp.), Polynesian rat, Richardson's ground squirrel, roof rat, southern plains woodrat, voles (*Microtus* spp.), white-footed mouse, white-throated woodrat
Cholecalciferol CAS No. 67–97–0	Agrid3®, Selontra®, Terad3®	Cotton rat, eastern harvest mouse, golden mouse, house mouse, meadow vole, Mexican woodrat, Norway rat, Polynesian rat, roof rat, southern plains woodrat, white-throated woodrat
Difenacoum CAS No. 56073–07–5	Monark®	Cotton rat, eastern harvest mouse, golden mouse, house mouse, meadow vole, Mexican woodrat, Norway rat, Polynesian rat, roof rat, southern plains woodrat, white-throated woodrat

Pesticide active ingredient	Trademarks and brand names or registered product names*	Target species**
Difethialone CAS No. 104653–34–1	BlueMax™, Fastdraw®, FirstStrike®, Generation®, Hombre®, Renegade™	Bushy-tailed woodrat, cotton mouse, cotton rat, deer mice, eastern harvest mouse, golden mouse, house mouse, meadow vole, Mexican woodrat, Norway rat, Polynesian rat, roof rat, southern plains woodrat, white-footed mouse, white-throated woodrat
Diphacinone CAS No. 82–66–6	Adios™, Answer®, D-Con®, Ditrac®, Gopher Getter, J.T. Eaton™, Kaput®, P.C.Q.®, Ramik®, RCO, Sure Stop™, SureKill®, Tomcat®, Zero™	Black-tailed prairie dog, broad-footed mole, California ground squirrel, coast mole, cotton rat, eastern harvest mouse, eastern mole, golden mouse, hairy-tailed mole, house mouse, meadow vole, Mexican woodrat, Norway rat, pine vole, pocket gophers (*Geomys* spp. and *Thomomys* spp.), Polynesian rat, roof rat, southern plains woodrat, star-nosed mole, Townsend's ground squirrel, Townsend's mole, white-throated woodrat, Wyoming ground squirrel
Diphacinone, sodium salt CAS No. 42721–99–3	Liqua-Tox®	House mouse, Norway rat, roof rat
Sodium cyanide CAS No. 143–33–9	M-44 Cyanide Capsules	Coyote, gray fox, red fox, wild (feral) dog
Sodium fluoroacetate (Compound 1080) CAS No. 62–74–8	Sodium Flouroacetate (Compound 1080) Livestock Protection Collar	Coyote
Strychnine CAS No. 57–24–9	Cooke, Martin's, Petersen's, RCO, Wilco	Pocket gophers (*Cratogeomys* spp., *Geomys* spp., and *Thomomys* spp.)
Warfarin CAS No. 81–81–2	Kaput®, Rodex™	Broad-footed mole, California vole, coast mole, cotton rat, deer mice, eastern harvest mouse, eastern mole, feral swine, golden mouse, hairy-tailed mole, house mouse, meadow vole, montane vole, Norway rat, pine vole, Polynesian rat, roof rat, star-nosed mole, Townsend's mole, white-footed mouse

(Continued)

TABLE 13.2 (*Continued*)

Pesticide active ingredient	Trademarks and brand names or registered product names*	Target species**
Zinc phosphide CAS No. 1314–84–7	Bonide®, Eraze™, Force's, Gopha-Rid®, MoleTox®, Prozap®, RodentRid®, Sweeney's®, Tomcat®, Victor®, Wilco, ZP®	Banner-tailed kangaroo rat, Belding's ground squirrel, black-tailed jackrabbit, black-tailed prairie dog, broad-footed mole, bushy-tailed woodrat, California ground squirrel, California vole, Columbian ground squirrel, common muskrat, cotton rat, deer mice, desert woodrat, dusky-footed woodrat, eastern mole, eastern woodrat, Franklin's ground squirrel, golden-mantled ground squirrel, Gunnison's prairie dog, hairy-tailed mole, house mouse, long-tailed vole, meadow jumping mouse, meadow vole, Merriam's ground squirrel, Merriam's kangaroo rat, Mexican woodrat, montane vole, Norway rat, nutria, oldfield mouse, Ord's kangaroo rat, Oregon vole, pine vole, Piute ground squirrel, pocket gophers (*Cratogeomys* spp., *Geomys* spp., and *Thomomys* spp.), Polynesian rat, prairie vole, rice rat, Richardson's ground squirrel, rock squirrel, roof rat, round-tailed ground squirrel, round-tailed muskrat, southern plains woodrat, star-nosed mole, thirteen-lined ground squirrel, Townsend's ground squirrel, Townsend's mole, Uinta ground squirrel, white-footed mouse, white-tailed antelope squirrel, white-tailed prairie dog, white-throated woodrat, woodchuck, Wyoming ground squirrel, yellow-bellied marmot

Information was compiled by Emily Ruell, USDA-Wildlife Services National Wildlife Research Center using EPA's Pesticide Product and Label System (PPLS) database (https://iaspub.epa.gov/apex/pesticides/f?p=PPLS:1).

*Trademarks and commercial brand names are often just part of the full pesticide product names registered with EPA. Registered products may be sold under additional brands and product names not listed here. In addition, not all registered product names contain trademarks or brand names. For active ingredients with no registered products containing trademarks or brand names, examples of registered full product names are listed instead.

**Target species lists do not include target species registered under state-specific or emergency use registrations. Pesticide labels may contain additional geographic use restrictions for some target species.

13.17.6   BOUNTIES

Queensland, Australia, has paid a bounty on dingoes since 1885 with over 1.5 million bounties being paid since then. Yet the bounties have had little impact on dingo abundance in the state (Allen and Sparkes 2001). Queensland still has faith in the bounty system and in 2017 paid $22 for a dead dingo and $7 for a fox or a feral cat (Guardian Newspaper 2017).

Feral hog numbers have been expanding at Fort Benning army base (737 km²) in Georgia since the early 1900s. During 2008, the base offered a $40 bounty on feral hogs, hoping to reduce their negative impact on the base's flora, fauna, and army training exercises. From June 2007 through 2008, 1,138 hogs were harvested by 2,600 licensed hunters. But the hog population did not decline despite the bounties, owing, in part, to an increase in hog fertility (Ditchkoff et al. 2017). Bounty programs also have been created to control nutria in Britain (Baker 2006) and seals in Maine and Massachusetts (Lelli et al. 2009).

13.17.7   DISEASES AND PARASITES

Diseases and parasites, such as sarcoptic mange, can spread rapidly through wildlife populations when animal densities are high and can limit wildlife populations. When exotic wildlife species escape into a new area, their populations can increase to levels much higher than in their native range, due to the absence of the diseases or other natural constraints (competitors or predators) that limit their numbers in their native area (see Chapter 6 for more details). For this reason, diseases or parasites are sometimes released where an exotic species is causing destruction in an effort to control the exotic population (Singleton et al. 1995; Williams et al. 1995). In Australia, the virus responsible for myxomatosis was released to control European rabbits. This virus caused a substantial reduction in rabbit populations, but resistance to the virus subsequently developed in rabbit populations. A feral population of domestic cats became established on Marion Island in the Pacific Ocean and adversely impacted nesting seabirds. The pathogen for feline leucopenia disease was introduced to the island and caused a substantial decrease in the cat population. The few remaining cats were shot or trapped, eradicating cats from the island (Bester et al. 2002).

13.18   SUMMARY

Lethal control offers a potential means to solve human–wildlife problems in a more effective and economical manner than nonlethal techniques. Lethal methods are usually employed after a wildlife problem has already begun, but lethal control can be used as a preventive strategy when problems are predictable. Lethal methods are often reserved for problems involving threats to human safety or when unacceptable economic losses can occur quickly. When lethal control is employed, it is best to focus on those individuals actually causing the problem (the culprits) or, if this is not possible, to target the group of animals that have home ranges, overlapping the site where the problem is occurring (the subpopulation). Only rarely are attempts made to reduce entire wildlife populations, and these usually target an exotic species that is causing environmental destruction in the area it invaded. Lethal techniques often produce ephemeral results because a population reduction usually results in an increase in the birth rate, a decrease in natural forms of mortality, and an increase in immigration of animals into the area. Consequently, wildlife populations can quickly recover once a lethal control program ends. Therefore, most lethal control programs have to be continued annually and can become quite costly over the long term. Lethal control often is controversial because it is in the self-interest of people suffering damage to solve their problem even if they have to kill wildlife to accomplish this. In contrast, the self-interest of other members of society lie in prohibiting the killing of wildlife because these people are not harmed by the damage and may feel a sense of loss if wildlife are killed. The use of any lethal control technique raises questions about whether such action is humane and poses no threat to nontarget species. When used by trained personnel, however, the risk of such techniques to nontarget species is usually minimal.

13.19   DISCUSSION QUESTIONS

1. An experimental predator control program in Texas costs $7,000 but resulted in additional deer and turkeys valued at $21,000; thus, so on a strictly economic basis, the program was cost-effective (Beasom 1974). But while the program produced an extra 87 male turkeys, 170 deer, and unknown numbers of nongame birds, it also costs the lives of 188 coyotes, 120 bobcats, and over 140 other predators (skunks, badgers, and opossums). Was the increase in deer and turkeys worth the number of predators killed?

2. Some people believe that lethal control should be an option whenever there is a human–wildlife conflict and sympathize with those people who are suffering damage. Others feel that wildlife species are too precious to permit their killing and that animals have a right to exist despite any damage they may cause. Still others think the suffering caused by overpopulation (e.g., starvation) is worse than death from lethal control because the latter is much quicker. What is your opinion on this matter?

3. Some U.S. states have created a bounty system to reduce predator numbers in the hope that this will increase the abundance of deer (Lelli et al. 2009). The state of Utah pays a bounty of $50 for killing a coyote. For payment, the hunter must turn in the lower jaw and ears of the dead coyote, which the government keeps to prevent double counting. Hunters who want to collect the bounty have to register with the state ahead of time, allowing the state to contact the coyote hunters with updates. Are you supportive of this program, and do you think it is successful in increasing deer numbers?

4. Utah determined that most coyotes turned in for bounties were killed during the fall, meaning that many of the coyotes turned in for bounties would have died during the winter from starvation or diseases. Does this change your opinion on the effectiveness of Utah's bounty system?

5. Some people in Utah argue that the state's bounty of coyotes has been a success simply because it has made coyotes a more sought-after target for hunters. Their argument is that the enjoyment of hunters is sufficient to justify the bounty. Do you agree with this argument?

LITERATURE CITED

Allen, L. R. 2015. Demographic and functional responses of wild dogs to poison baiting. *Ecological Management and Restoration* 16:58–66.

Allen, L. R., and E. Sparkes. 2001. The effect of dingo control on sheep and beef cattle in Queensland. *Journal of Applied Ecology* 38:76–87.

American Veterinary Medical Association. 2013. *Guidelines for the euthanasia of animals*, 2013 edition. American Veterinary Medical Association, Schaumber, IL.

Amundson, C. L., and T. W. Arnold. 2011. The role of predator removal, density-dependence, and environmental factors on mallard duckling survival in North Dakota. *Journal of Wildlife Management* 75:1330–1339.

Amundson, C. L., M. R. Pieron, T. W. Arnold, and L. A. Beaudoin. 2013. The effects of predator removal on mallard production and population change in northeastern North Dakota. *Journal of Wildlife Management* 77:143–152.

Andreasen, A. M., K. M. Stewart, J. S. Sedinger, C. W. Lackey, and J. P. Beckmann. 2018. Survival of cougars caught in non-target foothold traps and snares. *Journal of Wildlife Management* 82:906–917.

Anthony, R. M., P. L. Flint, and J. S. Sedinger. 1991. Arctic fox removal improves nest success of black brant. *Wildlife Society Bulletin* 19:76–184.

Baker, P. J., and S. Harris. 2006. Does culling reduce fox (*Vulpes vulpes*) density in commercial forests in Wales, UK? *European Journal of Wildlife Research* 52:99–108.

Baker, S. E. 2006. The eradication of coypus (*Myocaster coypus*) from Britain: the element required for a successful campaign. Pages 142–147 *in* F. Koike, M. N. Clout, M. Kawamichi, M. De Poorter, and K. Iwatsuki, editors. *Assessment and control of biological invasions risks*. International Union for the Conservation of Nature, Gland, Switzerland.

Baker, S. E., S. A. Maw, P. J. Johnson, and D. W. Macdonald. 2020. Not in my backyard: public perceptions of wildlife and "pest control" in and around UK homes, and local authority "pest control". *Animals* 10(2):222.

Baldwin, R. A. 2014. Determining and demonstrating the importance of training and experience for managing pocket gophers. *Wildlife Society Bulletin* 38:628–633.

Ballard, W. B., L. N. Carbyn, and D. W. Smith. 2003. Wolf interactions with non-prey. Pages 259–271 *in* L. D. Mech and L. Boitani, editors. *Wolves: behavior, ecology and conservation*. University of Chicago Press, Chicago, IL.

Beasley, J. C., and O. E. Rhodes, Jr. 2008. Relationship between raccoon abundance and crop damage. *Human-Wildlife Interactions* 2:248–259.

Beasom, S. L. 1974. Intensive short-term predator removal as a game management tool. *Transactions of the North American Wildlife and Natural Resource Conference* 39:230–240.

Benevides, F. L., Jr., H. Hansen, and S. C. Hess. 2008. Design and evaluation of a simple signaling device for live traps. *Journal of Wildlife Management* 72:1434–1436.

Bergstrom, B. J., L. C. Arias, A. D. Davidson, A. W. Ferguson, L. A. Randa, and S. R. Sheffield. 2014. License to kill: reforming federal wildlife control to restore biodiversity and ecosystem function. *Conservation Letters* 7:131–142.

Bester, M. N., J. P. Bloomer, R. J. Van Aarde, B. H. Erasmus, P. J. J. Van Rensburg, J. D. Skinner, P. G. Howell, and T. W. Naude. 2002. A review of the successful eradication of feral cats from sub-Antarctic Marion Island, Southern Indian Ocean. South African *Journal of Wildlife Research* 32:65–73.

Blejwas, K. M., B. N. Sacks, M. M. Jaeger, and D. R. McCullough. 2002. The effectiveness of selective removal of breeding coyotes in reducing sheep predation. *Journal of Wildlife Management* 66:451–462.

Blomberg, E. J. 2015. The influence of harvest timing on greater sage-grouse survival: a cautionary perspective. *Journal of Wildlife Management* 79:695–703.

Bowman, J. L. 2011. Managing white-tailed deer: exurban, suburban, and urban environments. Pages 599–620 *in* D. G. Hewitt, editor. *Biology and management of white-tailed deer.* CRC Press, Boca Raton, FL.

Bradley, E. H., H. S. Robinson, E. E. Bangs, K. Kunkel, M. D. Jimenez, J. A. Gude, and T. Grimm. 2015. Effects of wolf removal on livestock depredation recurrence and wolf recovery in Montana, Idaho, and Wyoming. *Journal of Wildlife Management* 79:1337–1346.

Brewster, R. K., S. E. Henke, B. L. Turner, and J. M. Tomeček. 2019. Cost – benefit analysis of coyote removal as a management option in Texas cattle ranching. *Human – Wildlife Interactions* 13:400–422.

Brunner, H., and B. J. Coman. 1983. The ingestion of artificially coloured grain by birds, and its relevance to vertebrate pest control. *Australian Wildlife Research* 10:303–310.

Bryant, H., J. Hone, and P. Nicholls. 1984. The acceptance of dyed grain by feral pigs and birds. I. Birds. *Australian Wildlife Research* 11:509–516.

Campa, H., III, S. R. Winterstein, R. B. Peyton, and G. R. Dudderar. 1997. An evaluation of a multidisciplinary problem: ecological and sociological factors influencing white-tailed deer damage to agricultural crops in Michigan. *Transactions of the North American Wildlife and Natural Resources Conference* 62:431–440.

Campbell, T. A., and D. B. Long. 2008. Mammalian visitation to candidate feral swine attractants. *Journal of Wildlife Management* 72:305–309.

Carrion, V., C. J. Donlan, K. Campbell, C. Lavoie, and F. Cruz. 2007. Feral donkey (*Equus asinus*) eradications in the Galapagos. *Biodiversity and Conservation* 16:437–445.

Caudell, J. N. 2013. Review of wound ballistic research and its applicability to wildlife management. *Wildlife Society Bulletin* 37:824–831.

Chiyo, P. I., C. J. Moss, E. A. Archie, J. A. Hollister-Smith, and S. C. Alberts. 2011. Using molecular and observational techniques to estimate the number and raiding patterns of crop-raiding elephants. *Journal of Applied Ecology* 48:788–796.

Conover, M. R. 2001. Effect of hunting and trapping on wildlife damage. *Wildlife Society Bulletin* 29:521–532.

Cooper, J. A., and T. Keefe. 1997. Urban Canada goose management: policies and procedures. *Transactions of the North American Wildlife and Natural Resource Conference* 62:412–430.

Cromsigt, J. P., D. P. Kuijper, M. Adam, R. L. Beschta, M. Churski, A. Eycott, G. I. Kerley, A. Mysterud, K. Schmidt, and K. West. 2013. Hunting for fear: innovating management of human – wildlife conflicts. *Journal of Applied Ecology* 50:544–549.

Cruz, F., V. Carrion, K. J. Campbell, C. Lavoie, and C. J. Donlan. 2009. Bio-economics of large-scale eradication of feral goats from Santiago Island, Galápagos. *Journal of Wildlife Management* 73:191–200.

DeCalesta, D. S. 2017. Achieving and maintaining sustainable white-tailed deer density with adaptive management. *Human-Wildlife Interactions* 11:99–111.

DeNicola, A. J., and S. C. Williams. 2008. Sharpshooting suburban white-tailed deer reduces deer – vehicle collisions. *Human-Wildlife Interactions* 2:28–33.

Dinkins, J. B., M. R. Conover, C. P. Kirol, J. L. Beck, and S. N. Frey. 2016. Effects of common raven and coyote removal and temporal variation in climate on greater sage-grouse nesting success. *Biological Conservation* 202:50–58.

Ditchkoff, S. S., R. W. Holtfreter, and B. L. Williams. 2017. Effectiveness of a bounty program for reducing wild pig densities. *Wildlife Society Bulletin* 41:548–555.

Eberhardt, L. L., P. J. White, R. A. Garrott, and D. B. Houston. 2007. A seventy-year history of trends in Yellowstone's Northern elk herd. *Journal of Wildlife Management* 71:594–602.

Eisenberg, C. 2013. *The wolf's tooth: keystone predators, trophic cascades, and biodiversity.* Island Press, Washington, DC.

Ferrari, M. C., A. Sih, and D. P. Chivers. 2009. The paradox of risk allocation: a review and prospectus. *Animal Behaviour* 78:579–585.

Fletcher, K., N. J. Aebischer, D. Baines, R. Foster, and A. N. Hoodless. 2010. Changes in breeding success and abundance of ground-nesting moorland birds in relation to the experimental deployment of legal predator control. *Journal of Applied Ecology* 47:263–272.

Frame, P. F., and T. J. Meier. 2007. Field-assessed injury to wolves captured in rubber-padded traps. *Journal of Wildlife Management* 71:2074–2076.

Frey, S. N., S. Majors, M. R. Conover, T. A. Messmer, and D. L. Mitchell. 2003. Effect of predator control on ring-necked pheasant populations. *Wildlife Society Bulletin* 31:727–735.

Garrettson, P. R., F. C. Rohwer, J. M. Zimmer, B. J. Mense, and N. Dion. 1996. Effects of mammalian predator removal on waterfowl and non-game birds in North Dakota. *Transactions of the North American Wildlife and Natural Resource Conference* 61:94–101.

Gese, E. M., P. A. Terletzky, J. D. Erb, K. C. Fuller, J. P. Grabarkewitz, J. P. Hart, C. Humpal, B. A. Sampson, and J. K. Young. 2019. Injury scores and spatial responses of wolves following capture: cable restraints versus foothold traps. *Wildlife Society Bulletin* 43:42–52.

Greenwood, R. J. 1986. Influence of striped skunk removal on upland duck nest success in North Dakota. *Wildlife Society Bulletin* 14:6–11.

Groepper, S. R., M. P. Vrtiska, L. A. Powell, and S. E. Hygnstrom. 2012. Evaluation of the effects of September hunting seasons on Canada geese in Nebraska. *Wildlife Society Bulletin* 36:524–530.

Guardian Newspaper. 2017. Queensland council stands by $10 bounty for adult feral cat scalps. *Guardian Newspaper, London.* www.theguardian.com/australia-news/2017/nov/13/queensland-council-stands-by-10-bounty-for-adult-feral-cat-scalps. Accessed 6 January 2018.

Hampton, J. O., P, J. Adams, D. M. Forsyth, B. D. Cowled, I. G. Stuart, T. H. Hyndman, and T. Collins. 2016. Improving animal welfare in wildlife shooting: the importance of projectile energy. *Wildlife Society Bulletin* 40:678–686.

Hampton, J. O., D. M. Forsyth, D. I. MacKenzie, and I. G. Stuart. 2015. A simple quantitative method for assessing the animal welfare outcomes of wildlife shooting: the European rabbit as a case study. *Animal Welfare* 24:307–317.

Harper, E. K., W. J. Paul, L. D. Mech, and S. Weisberg. 2008. Effectiveness of lethal, directed wolf-depredation control in Minnesota. *Journal of Wildlife Management* 72:778–784.

Harrington, J. L., and M. R. Conover. 2007. Does removing coyotes for livestock protection benefit free-ranging ungulates? *Journal of Wildlife Management* 71:1555–1560.

Hebblewhite, M., and D. W. Smith. 2010. Wolf community ecology: ecosystem effects of recovering wolves in Banff and Yellowstone national park. Pages 69–120 *in* M. L. Musiani, L. Boitani, and P. C. Paquet, editors. *The wolves of the world: new perspectives on ecology, behaviour and management.* University of Calgary Press, Calgary, Alberta, Canada.

Herfindal, I., J. D. Linnell, P. F. Moa, J. Odden, L. B. Austmo, and R. Andersen. 2005. Does recreational hunting of lynx reduce depredation losses of domestic sheep? *Journal of Wildlife Management* 69:1034–1042.

Holt, A. R., Z. G. Davies, C. Tyler, and S. Staddon. 2008. Meta-analysis of the effects of predation on animal prey abundance: evidence from UK vertebrates. *PLoS One* 3(6):e2400.

Hooper, J. K. 1992. Animal welfarists and rightists: insights into an expanding constituency for wildlife interpreters. *Legacy* 20–25, November–December.

Hristienko, H., and J. E. McDonald. 2007. Going into the 21st century: a perspective on trends and controversies in the management of the American black bear. *Ursus* 18:72–89.

Hubbard, R. D., and C. K. Nielsen. 2011. Cost-benefit analysis of managed shotgun hunts for suburban white-tailed deer. *Human-Wildlife Interactions* 5:13–22.

Hygnstrom, S. E., and K. C. VerCauteren. 2000. Efficacy of five fumigants for managing black-tailed prairie dogs. *International Biodeterioration and Biodegradation* 45:159–168.

International Association of Fish and Wildlife Agencies. 1997. *Improving animal welfare in U.S. trapping programs: process recommendations and summaries of existing data.* International Association of Fish and Wildlife Agencies, Washington, DC.

Jackman, J. L., and J. G. Way. 2018. Once I found out: awareness of and attitudes toward coyote hunting policies in Massachusetts. *Human Dimensions of Wildlife* 23:187–195.

Julien, T. J., S. M. Vantassel, S. R. Groepper, and S. E. Hygnstrom. 2010. Euthanasia methods in field settings for wildlife damage management. *Human-Wildlife Interactions* 4:158–164.

Kilgo, J. C., R. F. Labisky, and D. E. Fritzen. 1998. Influences of hunting on the behavior of white-tailed deer: implications for conservation of the Florida panther. *Conservation Biology* 12:1359–1364.

Kilgo, J. C., C. E. Shaw, M. Vukovich, M. J. Conroy, and C. Ruth. 2017. Reproductive characteristics of a coyote population before and during exploitation. *Journal of Wildlife Management* 81:1386–1393.

Kinsey, J. C., J. A. Foster, and R. L. Reitz. 2016. Development of a self-contained carbon dioxide euthanasia trailer for large-scale euthanasia of feral swine. *Wildlife Society Bulletin* 40:316–320.

Königson, S., A. Fjälling, M. Berglind, and S. G. Lunneryd. 2013. Male gray seals specialize in raiding salmon traps. *Fisheries Research* 148:117–123.

Knowlton, F. F., E. M. Gese, and M. M. Jaeger. 1999. Coyote depredation control: an interface between biology and management. *Journal of Range Management* 52:398–412.

Laundré, J. W., and L. Hernández. 2003. Winter hunting habitat of pumas *Puma concolor* in Northwestern Utah and Southern Idaho, USA. *Wildlife Biology* 9:123–130.

Lavelle, M. J., N. P. Snow, J. M. Halseth, J. C. Kinsey, J. A. Foster, and K. C. verCauteren. 2018. Development and evaluation of a bait station for selectively dispensing bait to invasive wild pigs. *Wildlife Society Bulletin* 42:102–110.

Lelli, B., D. E. Harris, and A. M. Aboueissa. 2009. Seal bounties in Maine and Massachusetts, 1888 to 1962. *Northeastern Naturalist* 16:239–255.

Lieury, N., S. Ruette, S. Devillard, M. Albaret, F. Drouyer, B. Baudoux, and A. Millon. 2015. Compensatory immigration challenges predator control: an experimental evidence-based approach improves management. *Journal of Wildlife Management* 79:425–434.

Linhardt, S. D., and W. B. Robinson. 1972. Some relative carnivore densities in areas under sustained coyote control. *Journal of Mammalogy* 53:880–884.

Linz, G. M., E. H. Bucher, S. B. Canavelli, E. Rodriguez, and M. L. Avery. 2015. Limitations of population suppression for protecting crops from bird depredation: a review. *Crop Protection* 76:46–52.

Massei, G., J. Coats, R. Quy, K. Storer, and D. P. Cowan. 2010. The boar-operated-system: a novel method to deliver baits to wild pigs. *Journal of Wildlife Management* 74:333–336.

Mawson, P. R., J. O. Hampton, and B. Dooley. 2016. Subsidized commercial harvesting for cost-effective wildlife management in urban areas: a case study with kangaroo sharpshooting. *Wildlife Society Bulletin* 40:251–260.

McCann, B. E., and D. K. Garcelon. 2008. Eradication of feral pigs from Pinnacles national monument. *Journal of Wildlife Management* 72:1287–1295.

McDonald, J. E., Jr., D. E. Clark, and W. A. Woytek. 2007. Reduction and maintenance of a white-tailed deer herd in central Massachusetts. *Journal of Wildlife Management* 71:1585–1593.

Mech, L. D. 2012. Is science in danger of sanctifying the wolf? *Biological Conservation* 150:143–149.

Muñoz-Igualada, J., J. A. Shivik, F. G. Domínguez, J. Lara, and L. M. González. 2008. Evaluation of cage-traps and cable restraint devices to capture red foxes in Spain. *Journal of Wildlife Management* 72:830–836.

Murton, R. K., N. J. Westwood, and A. J. Isaacson. 1974. A study of wood-pigeon shooting: the exploitation of a natural animal population. *Journal of Applied Ecology* 11:61–81.

Nass, R. D. 1980. Efficacy of predator damage control programs. *Proceedings of the Vertebrate Pest Conference* 9:205–208.

Nichols, T. C. 2014*a*. Integrated damage management reduces grazing of wild rice by resident Canada geese in New Jersey. *Wildlife Society Bulletin* 38:229–236.

Nichols, T. C. 2014*b*. Ten years of resident Canada goose damage management in a New Jersey tidal freshwater wetland. *Wildlife Society Bulletin* 38:221–228.

O'Gara, B. W., K. C. Brawley, J. R. Menoz, and D. R. Henne. 1983. Predation on domestic sheep on a Western Montana ranch. *Wildlife Society Bulletin* 11:253–264.

Olsen, G. H., R. G. Linscombe, V. L. Wright, and R. A. Holmes. 1988. Reducing injuries to terrestrial furbearers by using padded foothold traps. *Wildlife Society Bulletin* 16:303–307.

Peebles, K. A., R. B. Wielgus, B. T. Maletzke, and M. E. Swanson. 2013. Effects of remedial sport hunting on cougar complaints and livestock depredations. *PLoS One* 8(11):e79713. https://doi.org/10.1371/journal.pone.0079713.

Peebles, L. W., and M. R. Conover. 2016. Effectiveness of the toxicant DRC-1339 in reducing populations of common ravens in Wyoming. *Wildlife Society Bulletin* 40:281–287.

Peebles, L. W., M. R. Conover, and J. B. Dinkins. 2017. Adult sage-grouse numbers rise following raven removal or an increase in precipitation. *Wildlife Society Bulletin* 41:471–478.

Pieron, M. R., F. C. Rohwer, M. J. Chamberlain, M. D. Kaller, and J. Lancaster. 2013. Response of breeding duck pairs to predator reduction in North Dakota. *Journal of Wildlife Management* 77:663–671.

Rhoads, C. L., J. L. Bowman, and B. Eyler. 2013. Movements of female exurban white-tailed deer in response to controlled hunts. *Wildlife Society Bulletin* 37:631–638.

Ripple, W. J., and R. L. Beschta. 2003. Wolf reintroduction, predation risk, and cottonwood recovery in Yellowstone national park. *Forest Ecology and Management* 184:299–313.

Ripple, W. J., and R. L. Beschta. 2004*a*. Wolves and the ecology of fear: can predation risk structure ecosystems? *BioScience* 54:755–766.

Ripple, W. J., and R. L. Beschta. 2004*b*. Wolves, elk, willows, and trophic cascades in the upper Gallatin range of southwestern Montana, USA. *Forest Ecology and Management* 200:161–181.

Ripple, W. J., and R. L. Beschta. 2006. Linking wolves to willows via risk sensitive foraging by ungulates in the northern Yellowstone ecosystem. *Forest Ecology and Management* 230:96–106.

Rutledge, M. E., C. E. Moorman, B. E. Washburn, and C. S. Deperno. 2015. Evaluation of resident Canada goose movements to reduce the risk of goose-aircraft collisions at suburban airports. *Journal of Wildlife Management* 79:1185–1191.

Sahr, D. P., and F. F. Knowlton. 2000. Evaluation of tranquilizer trap devices (TTDs) for foothold traps used to capture gray wolves. *Wildlife Society Bulletin* 28:597–605.

Sanders, L. E., and A. D. Chalfoun. 2019. Mechanisms underlying increased nest predation in natural gas fields: a test of the mesopredator release hypothesis. *Ecosphere* 10(5):e02738.

Sanz-Aguilar, A., A. Martínez-Abraín, G. Tavecchia, E. Mínguez, and D. Oro. 2009. Evidence-based culling of a facultative predator: efficacy and efficiency components. *Biological Conservation* 142:424–431.

Sargeant, A. B., M. A. Sovada, and T. L. Shaffer. 1995. Seasonal predator removal relative to hatch rate of duck nests in waterfowl production areas. *Wildlife Society Bulletin* 23:507–513.

Sheaffer, S. E., W. L. Kendall, and E. F. Bowers. 2005. Impact of special early harvest seasons on subarctic-nesting and temperate-nesting Canada geese. *Journal of Wildlife Management* 69:1494–1507.

Short, M. J., A. W. Weldon, S. M. Richardson, and J. C. Reynolds. 2012. Selectivity and injury risk in an improved neck snare for live-capture of foxes. *Wildlife Society Bulletin* 36:208–219.

Siemer, W. F., D. J. Decker, and R. C. Stedman. 2016. Hunter and landowner views on a periurban deer-hunting program. *Wildlife Society Bulletin* 40:736–746.

Siers, S. R., A. B. Shiels, and W. C. Pitt. 2019. Brodifacoum residues in fish three years after an island-wide rat eradication attempt in the tropical Pacific. *Management of Biological Invasions* 11:105–121.

Simard, M. A., C. Dussault, J. Huot, and S. D. Côté. 2013. Is hunting an effective tool to control overabundant deer? A test using an experimental approach. *Journal of Wildlife Management* 77:254–269.

Singleton, G. R., L. K. Chambers, and D. M. Spratt. 1995. An experimental field study to examine whether *Capillaria hepatica* (Nematoda) can limit house mouse populations in eastern Australia. *Wildlife Research* 22:31–53.

Snow, N. P., M. J. Lavelle, J. M. Halseth, C. R. Blass, J. A. Foster, and K. C. VerCauteren. 2017. Strength testing of raccoons and invasive wild pigs for a species-specific bait station. *Wildlife Society Bulletin* 41:264–270.

Sovada, M. A., A. B. Sargeant, and J. W. Grier.1995. Differential effects of coyotes and red foxes on duck nest success. *Journal of Wildlife Management* 59:1–9.

Spencer, P. B., J. O. Hampton, C. Pacioni, M. S. Kennedy, K. Saalfeld, K. Rose, and A. P. Woolnough. 2015. Genetic relationships within social groups influence the application of the Judas technique: a case study with wild dromedary camels. *Journal of Wildlife Management* 79:102–111.

Stahl, P., J. M. Vandel, V. Herrenschmidt, and P. Migot. 2001. The effect of removing lynx in reducing attacks on sheep in the French Jura mountains. *Biological Conservation* 1011:15–22.

Stewart, C. M., B. Keller, and C. R. Williamson. 2013. Keys to managing a successful archery deer hunt in an urban community: a case study. *Human-Wildlife Interactions* 7:132–139.

Sullivan, J. D., S. S. Ditchkoff, B. A. Collier, C. R. Ruth, and J. B. Raglin. 2018. Recognizing the danger zone: response of female white-tailed to discrete hunting events. *Wildlife Biology* 1. http://doi.org/10.2981/wlb.00455.

Ueno, M., K. Kaji, and T. Saitoh. 2010. Culling versus density effects in management of a deer population. *Journal of Wildlife Management* 74:1472–1483.

Van Ballenberghe, V. 1984. Injuries to wolves sustained during live-capture. *Journal of Wildlife Management* 48:1425–1429.

Wagner, F. H. 1988. *Predator control and the sheep industry*. Regina Books, Claremont, CA.

Wagner, K. K., and M. R. Conover. 1999. Effect of preventive coyote hunting on sheep losses to coyote predation. *Journal of Wildlife Management* 63:606–612.

Whisson, D. A. 1999. Modified bait stations for California ground squirrel control in endangered kangaroo rat habitat. *Wildlife Society Bulletin* 27:172–177.

Whitworth, D. L., and H. R. Carter. 2018. Population trends for Scripps's murrelet following eradication of black rats. *Journal of Wildlife Management* 82:232–237.

Whitworth, D. L., H. R. Carter, R. J. Young, J. S. Koepke, F. Gress, and S. Fangman. 2005. Initial recovery of Xantus's murrelets following rat eradication on Anacapa Island, California. *Marine Ornithology* 33:131–137.

Whitworth, D. L., A. L. Harvey, H. R. Carter, R. J. Young, J. S. Koepke, and D. M. Mazurkiewicz. 2015. Breeding of Cassin's auklets *Ptychoramphus aleuticus* at Anacapa Island, California, after eradication of black rats *Rattus*. *Marine Ornithology* 43:19–24.

Williams, K., I. Parer, B. Coman, J. Burley, and M. Braysher. 1995. *Managing vertebrate pests: rabbits*. Bureau of Resource Sciences/CSIRO Division of Wildlife and Ecology, Australian Government Publishing Service, Canberra, Australia.

Williams, S. C., A. J. Denicola, T. Almendinger, and J. Maddock. 2013. Evaluation of organized hunting as a management technique for overabundant white-tailed deer in suburban landscapes. *Wildlife Society Bulletin* 37:137–145.

Wilmers, C. C., R. L. Crabtree, D. W. Smith, K. M. Murphy, and W. M. Getz. 2003. Trophic facilitation by introduced top predators: grey wolf subsidies to scavengers in Yellowstone National Park. *Journal of Animal Ecology* 72:909–916.

Woolnough, A. P., T. J. Lowe, and K. Rose. 2006. Can the Judas technique be applied to pest birds? *Wildlife Research* 33:449–455.

Wyman, K. E., L. R. Wires, and F. J. Cuthbert. 2018. Great Lakes double-crested cormorant management affects co-nester colony growth. *Journal of Wildlife Management* 82:93–102.

14 Human Dimensions

"Wildlife management is, at its core, the management of people."

– Anonymous

"Knowledge speaks but wisdom listens."

– Jimi Hendrix

For wildlife damage to occur, three elements must come together. There must be a resource being damaged, an animal causing the damage, and an injured person. If no one has been injured or has suffered a loss, then there has been no damage. Usually, the injured person is the owner of the damaged resource, but other people can also suffer a loss. When urban Canada geese roost on a public beach, the injured people include swimmers, who have to step around goose manure, and local citizens, who through their taxes, have to pay more to keep the beach clean. If the state decides to address the problem by killing the geese, the injured people would also include those individuals who like to feed the geese at the beach, neighbors who like to see them, hunters who have been looking forward to the fall's goose season, and those individuals who have empathy for the geese and worry about their pain and suffering. Hence, individuals who are affected by wildlife damage issues can form a complicated web of people. The area of wildlife management that is concerned with people and society is called human dimensions and is the focus of this chapter.

14.1 HOW DOES SOCIETY RESPOND TO WILDLIFE DAMAGE?

There are many ways that society can respond to complaints about wildlife damage (Figure 14.1). Some wildlife species, such as coyotes, striped skunks, or European starlings, are classified as "vermin" and are not protected by law in some states. For conflicts involving these animals, society may provide injured persons a free hand to solve the wildlife problem any way they wish. Society restricts the use of some techniques for solving wildlife damage because they are considered too cruel or inhumane or because the techniques pose too great a threat to human safety, non-target animals, or the environment. Further, society may prevent the person suffering damage from killing the offending animal, especially when the animal is rare or valuable. Sometimes, government use its own employees to help reduce wildlife damage; for instance, U.S.D.A. Wildlife Services fulfills this function for the federal government. Other times, government may compensate landowners for their losses caused by wildlife. How society responds to wildlife damage depends, in part, on people's attitudes about wildlife.

DOI: 10.1201/9780429401404-14

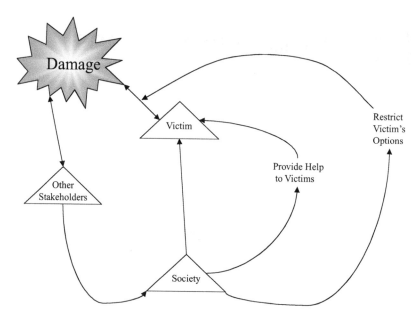

FIGURE 14.1   Conceptual model of how human dimensions fit into the science of resolving human–wildlife conflicts.

Source: This is Figure 15.1 in the first edition of this book.

14.2   WHAT ARE STAKEHOLDER PERCEPTIONS OF HUMAN–WILDLIFE CONFLICTS?

People who suffer from or are concerned about wildlife damage are called "stake-holders." Other segments of society are also stakeholders because they are concerned about the person being injured, wildlife, or the methods used to alleviate the damage. The views of the various stakeholders influence how the government responds to wildlife problems. The major stakeholders involved with the management of wildlife damage are discussed in the following sections.

14.2.1   FARMERS, RANCHERS, AND PRIVATE LANDOWNERS

There are approximately 3.2 million farmers in the United States operating 2.1 mil-lion farms (U.S. Census of Agriculture 2012). Although they comprise less than 2% of the U.S. population, agricultural producers are an important group owing to their control of 45% of the land in the United States (Berg 1986). Their support is essential if wildlife conservation is going to occur on private land (Leopold 1933). Unfortunately, relationships between wildlife agencies and private landowners are often strained. The difficulty stems from the paradox that wildlife is publicly owned but is dependent upon a habitat base that is largely owned by individuals, who may have dreams for this land other than producing wildlife (Hegel et al. 2009).

Agricultural producers are a unique occupational group; their attitudes about wildlife differ from people employed in other professions. They view wildlife in utilitarian terms and focus on how wildlife affects them economically. Farmers are more supportive of hunting to eliminate depredating animals than the general public and are more likely to seek lower numbers of predators and deer (Sidebar 14.1). They are also more supportive of programs to compensate for wildlife damage (Naughton-Treves et al. 2003; Smith et al. 2016). Agricultural producers who are economically dependent on their land or who derive most of their income from farming are less tolerant of wildlife damage than part-time or hobby farmers.

SIDEBAR 14.1 WHY CYPRESS HILLS, CANADA, HAS BECOME THE LAND OF WILDLIFE CONFLICT

Canada's Cypress Hills is a hilly area on the border between Saskatchewan and Alberta. It was made a park in 1931 and expanded in 1951. Conflicts between the park and the local community began decades ago when elk numbers increased; the elk often ranged outside the park where haystacks and agricultural fields of cereal and alfalfa offered the elk better food than what was inside the park. The park expected the local community to accept the burden of supporting elk as a public duty. The local community resented this attitude and questioned why they should feed the park's elk. Belatedly, the government started compensating farmers for verifiable wildlife damage if the agricultural producer had first taken steps to mitigate the problem. But by the time these concessions were made, the attitudes of local farmers and ranchers toward elk had hardened.

A second approach taken by government was to decrease the elk herd to minimize the number of local complaints from the local community. But this angered other stakeholders who believed that the rights of hunters were being ignored. Hegel et al. (2009) noted that this system of compensating landowners for damage to high risk crops, reducing elk numbers to satisfy the low cultural carrying capacity of the local community, and not providing an opportunity for others to enjoy more abundant elk constitutes a perverse measure that rewards poor land-use practices of farmers and ranchers and fails to serve the public interest. Hegel et al. (2009) believed that a better policy was to increase landowners' willingness to accept elk and hunters on their property by creating opportunities for landowners to benefit from elk.

Yet, agricultural producers appreciate wildlife despite suffering wildlife damage (Willcox and Giuliano 2011). Half of the agricultural producers in the United States spend their time and money to enhance wildlife habitat on their property (Conover 1998). The American Farm Bureau Federation and National Farmers' Union are two groups that represent U.S. agricultural producers. There are several active farmer groups organized around specific commodities (e.g., American Soybean Association, National Cattlemen's Association, and National Woolgrowers' Association).

In many third-world countries, wildlife can completely destroy the crops and live-stock of a small rural farmer, leaving the farmer and his family destitute and without food. The costs of these human–wildlife conflicts to village farmers are varied; these include an increasing workload for farmers, a decrease in the family's well-being, loss of control over their own future, economic hardship, and at times, an increase in illegal activities. Women often bear a disproportionate burden of these effects (Ogra and Badola 2008).

14.2.2 Hunters and Fur Trappers

Only a small proportion of the U.S. population hunts or traps: there were about 11.5 million hunters and 175,000 licensed trappers in the United States during 2016 (U.S. Department of the Interior 2016; Association of Fish and Wildlife Agencies 2018). Many hunters and trappers, however, are passionate about their sports, derive great enjoyment from it, and spend considerable time and money engaging in hunting and trapping activities (Figure 14.2). During 2016, Americans spent $26 billion annually in hunting-related activities (U.S. Department of Interior 2016). Funds obtained from hunters through hunting licenses, federal duck stamps, and special taxes on hunting supplies provide most of the funding for state and federal wildlife agencies. Nongovernmental agencies that represent the interest of hunters and trappers in the United States include the Boone and Crockett Club, Ducks Unlimited, Mule Deer Foundation, National Rocky

FIGURE 14.2   Many hunters receive great enjoyment from this recreational activity.

Source: Roman Kosolapov, Shutterstock 1728685786.

Mountain Elk Foundation, National Wild Turkey Foundation, Pheasants Forever, Quail Unlimited, and National Trappers Association.

Hunters and trappers want large and healthy populations of game and fur-bearing species. Hence, their ideas of what constitutes the optimal size of a wildlife population are often higher than those of agricultural producers. This difference was put humorously at a meeting in Iowa to discuss the ideal deer population for the local area. One hunter continually interrupted any proposal by arguing that more deer were needed. Finally, one farmer spoke up, "Ralph: if there was a deer behind every tree, you would just argue that we need more trees in the county!"

Actually, the views of hunters and trappers are similar to those of farmers and ranchers with regard to many environmental issues and in seeking to preserve the right to hunt and trap (D'Angelo and Grund 2015). Both hunters and trappers seek fewer large predators capable of killing elk and deer because they believe that large predators suppress big-game populations (Andersone and Ozolinš 2004; Jonzén et al. 2013; Smith et al. 2016).

14.2.3 WILDLIFE ENTHUSIASTS

Wildlife enthusiasts are people who place a high value on wildlife or derive great pleasure from it. Bird watchers and outdoor recreationists are members of this group, as are many hunters and fur trappers (Figure 14.3). Also included are people who sit at home and enjoy watching nature programs on television. When hearing about wildlife damage, wildlife enthusiasts often sympathize with the wildlife rather than the person suffering the damage. Wildlife enthusiasts want healthy wildlife populations and the preservation of wildlife habitat; they are concerned about the impact of increasing human populations on nature. During 2016, 86 million people in the United States participated in watching wildlife and spent $76 billion doing so (U.S. Department of the Interior 2016). Defenders of Wildlife, National Audubon Society, National Wildlife Federation, and World Wildlife Fund are some of the organizations in the United States that represent these stakeholders.

FIGURE 14.3 Millions of people enjoy watching wild birds and mammals.

Source: Kim Kuperkova, Shutterstock 1745739560.

14.2.4 ANIMAL WELFARE SUPPORTERS

Animal welfare concerns arose during the 1700s over human cruelty and neglect of domestic and captive animals and later expanded to a more general concern over the adverse effects of humans on all animals. Early successes in the 1800s included laws to prohibit cruelty to cattle and horses.

Animal welfare supporters are sensitive to human activities that result in animal suffering. For instance, many oppose the use of leg-hold traps, preferring either that trapping be banned or that only live traps be used. Many seek the end of hunting and the use of lethal control to resolve wildlife problems. Instead, they support the use of nonlethal techniques, especially if those techniques do not cause pain to animals. As one example, the Animal Welfare Institute has the aims of protecting companion animals from cruelty and violence, abolishing factory farms, ending the use of steel-jaw leghold traps, improving conditions for research animals, and protecting wild animals from harmful exploitation or loss of critical habitat (Animal Welfare Institute 2019).

During interviews, 77% of the national leaders of animal welfare groups reported that it was unacceptable for people to hunt, fish, or trap for sport (Hooper 1992). In contrast, 82% believed that it was acceptable for native people to do so for subsistence, and 100% thought it was acceptable if a matter of human survival (e.g., someone lost in the wilderness). The American Society for the Prevention of Cruelty to Animals has more

FIGURE 14.4 People around the world have strong emotional ties to individual animals. The man feeding the squirrel is in a park in Moscow, Russia.

Source: YuryKara, Shutterstock 1820465003.

than two million members; Humane Society of the United States has ten million members (American Society for the Prevention of Cruelty to Animals 2019; Nolen 2019).

Animal welfare science is concerned with the health of individual animals or groups of animals, their suffering, and their quality of life (Figure 14.4). This focus differs from wildlife management and conservation biology, which focus on populations, species, ecosystem function, and the environment. To quote Michael Soulé (1985), one of the founders of the discipline of conservation biology, about the differences between the science of conservation biology and animal welfare: "Although disease and suffering in animals are unpleasant and, perhaps regrettable, biologists recognize that conservation is engaged in the integrity and continuity of natural processes, not the welfare of individuals."

14.2.5 Animal Rights Supporters

In the second half of the twentieth century, a movement arose among people who believed that animals should have the same rights as humans. They believe that "specism" – the attitude that humans were placed above other species and have a right to exploit other animals – is just as immoral as racism or sexism (Schmidt 1991*a*, 1991*b*). They feel that causing animals to suffer is morally the same as causing human suffering (Figure 14.5). Animal rights supporters are opposed to hunting, trapping, or the lethal control of animals because they believe that it is morally and ethically improper to subject animals to such treatment. Many supports of animal rights argue that animals should have legal status, which means that animals possess legal rights

FIGURE 14.5   Animal rights proponents believe that animals and humans should be treated the same.

Source: Yurina Photo, Shuttlestock 734121238.

that should be protected in the courts. They are opposed to what they perceive as an alliance between hunters and wildlife management agencies. They believe that wildlife agencies try to create a surplus of animals for the benefit of hunters, who provide political and economic support for the wildlife agency (Decker and Brown 1987).

14.2.6 METROPOLITAN RESIDENTS

In the United States, most people live and work in metropolitan areas. Most metropolitan residents enjoy watching wildlife in their neighborhood or while visiting parks or engaging in outdoor recreation. Most metropolitan residents (57% of them) spend time and money each year on efforts to encourage wildlife around their homes, such as erecting bird feeders (Conover 1997).

While metropolitan residents enjoy having wildlife in their neighborhoods, they are also concerned with the problems these animals cause (Thornton and Quinn 2010; Mcgovern and Kretser 2015); most experience some type of wildlife problem each year. Common wildlife problems for U.S. metropolitan residents include raccoons eating food placed out for pets, birds damaging gardens, moles burrowing in yards, or mice living in their homes (Figure 14.6). In the United Kingdom, nuisance problems include mice and rats in buildings and pigeons and gulls defecating in yards and on roofs (Baker et al. 2020). These are mostly nuisance problems that reduce the quality of life of metropolitan residents. More serious wildlife problems

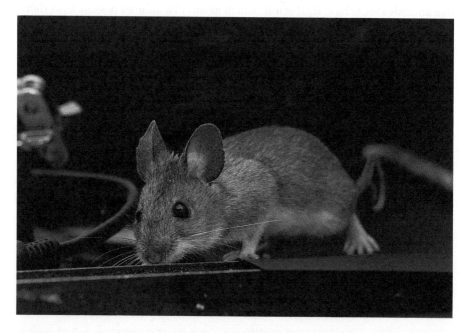

FIGURE 14.6   One of the more common, but unpleasant, ways in which metropolitan residents interact with wildlife occurs when they find mice in their kitchen.

Source: Horvath82, Shuttlerstock 1574343130.

that worry metropolitan residents include deer–automobile collisions and wildlife spreading zoonotic diseases.

Most metropolitans prefer nonlethal techniques when dealing with wildlife problems, due to ethical considerations. Some believe a deer's life is more valuable than the risk it poses to human health and safety; others believe the opposite. Attitudes of metropolitan residents toward the depredating species become more negative when wildlife damage is perceived to be severe or chronic or when densities of depredating species are increasing (Siemer et al. 2013; Baker et al. 2020). When this happens, more people support lethal measures to limit wildlife populations. Wildlife management agencies often find themselves caught in the middle between metropolitan residents who want nuisance animal killed and their neighbors who have emotional ties to the animals and oppose the killing of animals.

14.2.7 RURAL RESIDENTS

Sixty million people in the United States live in rural areas. They include farmers and ranchers along with people in farm-related professions, residents of small cities and towns, urban commuters, retired people, and urban refugees. An increasing exchange of people and ideas between rural and urban areas is occurring, homogenizing the views and attitudes of the rural and urban residents; yet, differences remain between rural and metropolitan residents. Rural residents are more knowledgeable than urban residents about wildlife because they have more first-hand experience with wildlife and are more likely to have farmers or ranchers as friends. A higher proportion of rural residents fish, hunt, or engage in wildlife-related recreational activities than urban residents. Rural residents have a more utilitarian attitude toward animals than metropolitan residents and are more interested in the practical or material value of animals (Kellert 1980a, 1980b). Rural residents are more worried than others about the expansion of large predator populations and less supportive of protecting large predators (Smith et al. 2014). Due to these differences, conflicts can occur between rural and urban residents. As one example, Ontario, Canada, is home to ten million people and 100,000 black bears. Most of the people are located in southern Ontario, while most of the bears and bear problems occur in the northern part where few people live. Clashes occurred over the passage of a moratorium on spring hunting of black bears. This moratorium was popular in the southern part of the province where there were few bears, but hated in the north. This heightened frustration in the north was fed by a feeling of being ignored. These feelings developed into a northern resistance movement that endorsed the concept of "northern sovereignty" (Lemelin 2008).

14.3 WHY ARE PEOPLE'S PERCEPTIONS OF RISK IMPORTANT?

Many factors create an individual's perception of risk, including risks caused by wildlife. Many people have deep-seated phobias and psychological dread, which drive their perceptions of wildlife. Phobias of spiders, insects, snakes, reptiles, birds, and mammals diminish a person's willingness to spend time outdoors and his or her

FIGURE 14.7   The 1975 horror movie *Jaws* terrified people across the world. This statue of an unnaturally large shark named "jaws" delights tourists at Universal Studios in Florida.

Source: Kamira, Shutterstock 218290723.

enjoyment of wildlife. These phobias are less common in people who live alongside wildlife. People with phobias and dreads can dramatically overestimate the risk and damage caused by wild animals. Rare, devastating losses have a much greater impact on people than one would expect. Examples abound. A bear killed seven people in Japan in 1915, but the event is still remembered today, and this memory causes some Japanese to fear bears (Dickman 2010). Half of Norwegians stated that were very afraid of wolves despite the fact that the last wolf attack on a person occurred over two centuries ago (Linnell et al. 2003). The movie *Jaws*, about a fictional great white shark that went on a killing rampage, caused thousands of viewers, after the movie was released, to stop swimming in the ocean (Figure 14.7).

Perceptions of risk are modified by societal expectations, social norms, gender, education, and beliefs (Thornton and Quinn 2010). For example, people's perceptions of bats are based, in part, on vampire mythology. In Africa, some people believe that their enemies use magical powers to punish them by inciting predators to kill their livestock (Dickman 2010). Perceptions of risk increase when people perceive themselves as being vulnerable or unable to cope with the consequences of an event. Individuals who have multiple sources of income or have the financial means to withstand crop losses are less worried about wildlife damage to their crops than someone who faces starvation if crops fail. People are less tolerant of wolves when they fear for their own safety or that of their family (Olson et al. 2015). The step that someone takes to reduce the potential dangers is based on that person's answer to the age-old question: how much risk is too much?

14.4 WHAT IMPACT DO HUMAN–WILDLIFE CONFLICTS HAVE ON A PERSON'S ATTITUDES TOWARD WILDLIFE?

Wildlife damage can alter a person's perceptions about wildlife, especially when damage exceeds his/her tolerance. People who have had a dangerous encounter with a bear or cougar have a higher sense of risk or fear toward large predators than people who have not experienced that horror (Thornton and Quinn 2010; Sakurai and Jacobson 2011). For example, 80% of people in Wisconsin who have lost a pet or livestock to a predator favor reducing wolf populations, compared to 38% of people who have not had a personal experience with a predator (Naughton-Treves et al. 2003). The risk of zoonotic diseases, especially if the disease is new or not well understood, increases the willingness of people to support the use of lethal control of wildlife (Peterson et al. 2006). Alternatively, farmers and ranchers are tolerant of predators if they are not losing livestock to them. In South Africa, farmers became more tolerant of cheetahs after they started using Anatolina guard dogs to protect their livestock from predators. In fact, cheetahs were spotted more frequently on farms that employ guard dogs, presumably because the farmers no longer felt the need to kill them (Rust et al. 2013).

In a national survey of agricultural producers, 53% of respondents reported that the amount of wildlife damage they experienced exceeded their level of tolerance (Conover 1998). The same survey found that 40% of all agricultural producers reported that wildlife damage on their farm or ranch was so severe that they would oppose the creation of a wildlife sanctuary near them; 26% reported that wildlife damage reduced their willingness to provide wildlife habitat on their property. Even among metropolitan residents, individuals who have previously experienced a wildlife problem are more likely to be concerned about local wildlife populations and more supportive of their government taking steps to control wildlife populations (Baker et al. 2020). Residents who had experienced problems with beavers or who lived in areas with high densities of beaver had a lower acceptance level toward beaver and a greater willingness to resort to lethal methods to resolve beaver problems compared to other folks (Jonker et al. 2009; Siemer et al. 2013).

In many parts of the world, people who live or farm near a park suffer a myriad of problems caused by the park's wildlife (Hegel et al. 2009). These wildlife problems, in turn, impact villagers' perceptions of both wildlife and the park. Elephants and baboons venturing out of Uganda's Kibale National Park caused considerable damage to local villagers, most of whom were subsistence farmers. Nineteen percent of local farmers had at least one period of food insecurity during the prior year (MacKenzie and Ahabyona 2012). Farmers facing food insecurity experienced higher levels of wildlife damage, particularly losses to corn, yams, and cassava than other farmers. These losses occurred despite the efforts of farmers to protect their crops from wildlife. During the months when crop raiding was high, the average number of days per week spent guarding crops from wildlife was 5.2 for men, 3.9 for women, and 1.5 for children. Most school children (88%) around Kilombero Game Controlled Area, Tanzania, reported that they guarded crops; 60% reported that they missed classes to guard (Haule et al. 2002). Not surprisingly, student who miss school did poorer on standardized tests than other students. People in rural areas of Sri Lanka where elephants occur refrain from walking outside at night because they are terrified of being attacked (Gamage and Wijesundara 2014). Although most of these rural residents will never be threatened by an elephant, they have suffered a loss in the quality of life because their fear is restricting them from activities they would otherwise enjoy.

Perceived losses by small-scale farmers impact wildlife conservation; without a positive opinion of wildlife, local villagers will not support local conservation efforts (Gillingham and Lee (2003). For example, farmers surrounding the Selous Game Reserve in Tanzania blamed the game reserve for wildlife losses to their crops and livestock and were opposed to the reserve and its wildlife (Sidebar 14.2). Villagers complained that government receives the income from safari hunting, while the villagers were prevented from taking direct action to protect their livestock or crops from wildlife, even on land owned by the village.

In Kenya, villagers hunted wildlife for food and clothing and viewed this as a trade-off for wildlife damage to their crops, livestock, and property. But this traditional relationship between people and wildlife changed in 1997 when the government banned hunting and the consumption of wild animals. The ban resulted from the government's realization that poaching threatened the Kenya's tourism industry, which produced $2 billion during 2019 (Kenya Government 2020). But little of the tourist revenue reached the poor villagers who suffered the brunt of wildlife problems. Villagers started to resent wildlife with the result that many villagers were willing to use illegal, lethal means to protect their farms and livestock from wildlife.

These illegal methods include the use of toxins, traps, guns, arrows, and leaving nails sticking up on paths used by wildlife. Sifuna (2011) argued that Kenya government needed to develop a fair system of sharing tourism revenues with rural villagers and to give local residents some say in how wildlife will be managed in their area.

SIDEBAR 14.2 WHY DO MAASAI WARRIORS ILLEGALLY KILL LIONS?

Areas in Tanzania and Kenya that are controlled by the Maasai people have some of the largest concentrations of wildlife. Maasai warriors (ilmurran in the Maasai language) hunt lions, but this is illegal unless a sports hunting permit is obtained from the Director of Wildlife, which most ilmurran fail to obtain. Some conservation groups want to persuade Maasai to stop killing lions, but until the reasons why ilmurran kill lions are understood, such a goal cannot be achieved. To obtain this information, Goldman et al. (2013) interviewed 246 ilmurran and learned that they hunt lions for social, emotional, and political reasons. The duty of ilmurran is to protect the community and their cattle from neighboring groups, predators, and droughts. Specific benefits that ilmurran obtained by hunting lions included achieving prestige (identified as important by 29% of ilmurran), testing one's bravery (22%), keeping lions fearful of Maasai (18%), killing depredating lions (14%), maintaining Maasai culture (10%), and impressing women (7%). Part of this motivation is due to the Maasai's emotional attachment to their livestock. As one elder said, "We cannot stop the ilmurran because we already lost our cattle, and this loss hurts deep into our soul." Some lion hunting was motivated by revenge against the government; Maasai feel that they have little say about local wildlife management decisions, fail to benefit from wildlife tourism, and face restrictions on livestock grazing. Until wildlife biologists can address these complex motivations, Maasai will continue to kill lions (Lichtenfeld 2005; Goldman et al. 2013).

14.5 WHAT IS THE CONCEPT OF CULTURAL CARRYING CAPACITY?

The original goal of wildlife management was to increase wildlife populations to just below the biological carrying capacity to create abundant wildlife to hunt, trap, and view. Wildlife management was successful in achieving this for a remarkable number of wildlife species, but these large populations caused considerable damage. Public perception started to shift from loving wild animals to the belief that some species had become overabundant; this led to the development of the concept of the cultural carrying capacity (CCC). The CCC is the maximum wildlife population that is acceptable to the public. Said another way, it is the number of animals that can compatibly coexist with the local human population. For many wildlife species, the CCC is below the biological carrying capacity (Organ and Ellingwood 2000; Lischka et al. 2008).

The difficulty of determining what the CCC is for a particular wildlife species is the diversity of the many groups of stakeholders. One approach to determining the CCC is to ask each stakeholder group what is the highest density of a wildlife species that they could tolerate; this density is called the group's wildlife acceptance capacity. This density could be obtained by having meetings with each stakeholders group or sending the people in each group a questionnaire to determine their opinion (Organ and Ellingwood 2000; Lischka et al. 2008). The cultural carrying capacity would be set by the stakeholder group with the lowest wildlife acceptable capacity (Decker and Purdy 1988). This approach minimizes human–wildlife conflicts because the wildlife density does not exceed anyone's tolerance (Figure 14.8).

Attitudes of stakeholders about wildlife are influenced by rare events that represent the worse-case scenario rather than by more common situations. A rancher's memory will be seared by the year that coyotes killed 30 lambs, and this memory will carry more weight than the other years when no lambs were killed by predators. A goose hunter's perceptions about whether goose populations should be increased will be shaped by that one year when he did not see a goose. Hence, wildlife managers need to be mindful not only of what losses or conditions occur during a normal year but also in worse-case scenarios. Attitudes can be shaped by faulty memories of the "good old days." I have heard hunters speak nostalgically about hunting as a child when duck flocks were so large they blackened the sky.

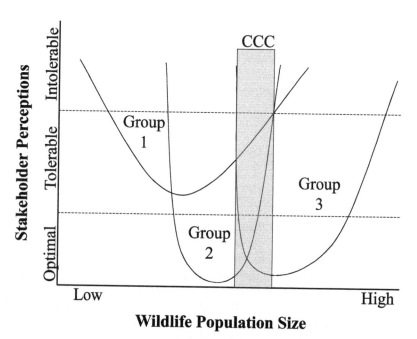

FIGURE 14.8 The optimal and tolerable range of deer densities for three different groups of stakeholders. The cultural carrying capacity or CCC (gray region in the figure) is the range of deer densities that all three groups consider to be tolerable.

Source: This is Figure 15.8 in the first edition of this book.

These exaggerated or false memories create a utopic view and produce dissatisfaction when current conditions do not match memories.

14.6 WHY IS THE MANAGEMENT OF HUMAN– WILDLIFE CONFLICTS SO CONTROVERSIAL?

Given the diversity of stakeholders, disagreements over wildlife population are not surprising. Sometimes, the ranges of tolerance for all stakeholder groups do not overlap (Figure 14.9). When this happens, there is a lack of consensus within society about how the wildlife population should be managed. That is, for any wildlife density, some people will complain that there are too many animals and, concomitantly, other people will complain that there are too few. Human–wildlife conflicts create a difficult situation for the government agency charged with managing the wildlife resource because any action it implements will displease some people. In these situations, one can argue that the ideal solution is one that displeases everyone equally.

To reduce these controversies requires a realignment of the benefits and liabilities of wildlife to fall more evenly upon all segments of society. Consider Zimbabwe, which has a community-based natural resource management program called CAMPFIRE (Communal Areas Management Programme for Indigenous Resources) aimed at realigning the benefits and costs of wildlife. This program is based on the

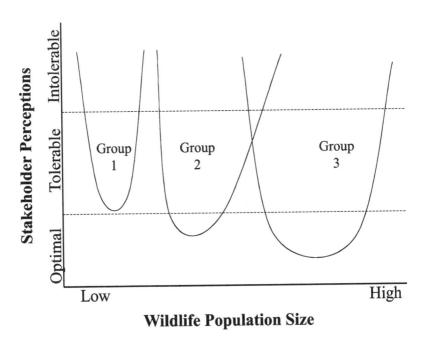

FIGURE 14.9 The optimal and tolerable range of deer densities for three different groups of stakeholders (in this case, there is no cultural carrying capacity [CCC] because there is no deer density that all three stakeholder groups consider tolerable).

Source: This is Figure 15.9 in the first edition of this book.

principle that rural communities should benefit directly from local wildlife. Under the program, rural district councils can market access and hunting rights to communal lands to safari operators, who them market hunting to foreign sports hunters (89% of revenue) and photographic safaris to ecotourists (11%). The rural district councils then disperse 50% of the funds to rural communities on the communal lands, 35% for wildlife management, and retain 15% for administrative costs. Millions of dollars have been generated since CAMPFIRE began during the 1980s, and the program has been copied in other African countries. But CAMPFIRE has not always lived up to its potential. The program is designed to provide enough revenue to rural households that they would manage for wildlife habitat, become more tolerant of wildlife, and limit their own taking of wildlife for the greater good of the community. Yet, payments to households are usually less than $150 annually. In exchange, rural households have to deal with more human–wildlife conflicts and a reduction in the wildlife protein in their diet from a loss of their own opportunities to hunt (Mutandwa and Gadzirayi 2007; Frost and Bond 2008).

14.7 HOW ARE POLICY DECISIONS REGARDING HUMAN–WILDLIFE CONFLICTS MADE?

Government officials need public input to make sound management decisions. This requires time and resources, but the extra work will result in more public ownership in the outcome and enhanced credibility for wildlife agencies. Input from stakeholders can be sought by holding public forums in which citizens are allowed to air their views. Governments may also create citizen boards to oversee wildlife policy (Sidebar 14.3).

SIDEBAR 14.3 DISENTANGLING SCIENCE FROM HUMAN VALUES IN POLICY DECISION-MAKING

Sometimes, the roles of science and human values can be difficult to separate when contentious decisions about wildlife policy must be made. Montana's Department of Fish, Wildlife, and Parks created a science team and a citizen working group to allocate harvest quota for cougars. The science team consisted of cougar biologists and population ecologists. The science team was tasked with estimating changes over a 5-year period in cougar populations under five different harvest quotas and four different estimates of cougar densities. The science team's analyses demonstrated that the alternate harvest quotas and current density estimates had little impact on cougar populations. Armed with this information, the citizen working group discussed the real problem: differences in values among stakeholder groups. By distinguishing between the roles of science and values, the citizen working group was able to work collaboratively and recommend a compromise solution. In doing so, the working group produced buy-in among stakeholders and minimized disagreements. The working group presented their recommendation to the Montana Fish and Wildlife Commission in 2004, and their recommended quota was accepted and incorporated in that year's hunting regulations (Mitchell et al. 2018).

Many wildlife agencies use a consensus-building approach to address disagreements over controversial wildlife policy. This approach is based on a series of face-to-face meetings in which leaders of different stakeholder groups seek to achieve resolution of their differences. Usually, these processes are led by a mediator, who serves as a neutral third party in a negotiation process and helps the group establish a framework for discussions. Elements of a successful consensus-building process include (1) identification of clear objectives; (2) agreement among participants on how group decisions will be made; (3) inclusion of team-building activities, such as dining together or participating in activities unrelated to the issues; and (4) achievement of success with smaller issues prior to addressing larger ones (Guynn 1997).

14.8 HOW CAN PARTNERSHIPS BE BUILT BETWEEN WILDLIFE AGENCIES AND THE VICTIMS OF HUMAN–WILDLIFE CONFLICTS?

One task of wildlife managers is to persuade landowners to adopt management practices that are beneficial to wildlife. Unfortunately, wildlife damage makes it more difficult to convince landowners that their best interests are served by to do so. As Tanner and Dimmick (1983) stated, "The incentives for a farmer to [manage for] wildlife are ethereal and few: aesthetic values, sporting opportunities, perhaps an important source of food. The disincentives, however, are glaring and many: damage to crops and/or livestock, nuisance animals, negative interactions with fellow citizens (e.g., hunters, animal-rights groups), and the myriad of social and legal entanglements that may arise from these problems." The formation of a working partnership between landowners and wildlife managers requires time, trust, and a shared sense of mission; none of which are easily accomplished. To achieve success, wildlife managers must have good interpersonal skills, tolerance for diverse views, and a willingness to listen. They also need to address the problem of wildlife damage in an open, proactive manner. Too often, wildlife managers are unconcerned about wildlife damage or gloss over the problem (Kirby et al. 1981). This attitude is counterproductive and conveys the impression to farmers that the wildlife manager is naive or uncaring (Tanner and Dimmick 1983).

Human–wildlife conflicts can escalate when local people feel their needs and desires are subverted to those of wildlife or when local people feel that government agencies dismiss their concerns out of hand, and people do not feel empowered to address local wildlife conflicts (Madden 2004; Hegel et al. 2009). Historically, local farmers and herders in Africa were given a free hand by the government and could make their own decisions about how to deal with depredating animals; but, when governments started regulating the harvest of wildlife, decision-making power shifted from the local community to a government agency located far away. Former methods to deal with depredating animals were now illegal, and when the local villagers continued to employ them out of necessity, the villagers became criminals. The situation was made worse when wildlife refuges or parks were created, turning local villagers, who were forced to move, into refugees. This was true even for people who remained in their village because they were prevented from using the land that now was inside the park; they were confronted with an influx of new people who arrived after the refuge or park opened. All of these consequences made local villagers feel disempowered in their own lives and lands (West et al. 2006).

One conservation organization attempted to reduce human–wildlife conflicts in villages near the Budongo Forest Reserve, Uganda, by constructing large live traps that could be used by the local farmers to catch baboons: the main agricultural threat. The traps were baited with local produce. The conservation organization held two meetings in each village to explain the trap, and groups of local farmers agreed to take responsibility for the traps and their maintenance. In return, the local farmers agreed to stop using snares and leg-hold traps. After two years, however, the traps were no longer in use. To understand why the project failed, Webber et al. (2007) queried the local farmers and learned that 84% believed the traps were ineffective because baboons avoided them. The traps also were hard to maintain and had to be checked and baited regularly. Another reason for the failure was that the traps were developed externally and then brought to the area. Those farmers with baboon problems were not involved in the project or given responsibility for the traps. The farmers concluded that the cost of maintaining the traps was higher than their value.

14.9   CAN HUMAN–WILDLIFE CONFLICTS BE MITIGATED THROUGH THE HUMAN DIMENSION?

Human–wildlife conflicts can be resolved by reducing wildlife populations (Chapters 12 and 13), translocating animals (Chapter 11), changing wildlife behavior (Chapters 6, 7, and 9), excluding wildlife from specific sites (Chapter 8), or modifying the habitat or the object being damaged (Chapter 10). Likewise, wildlife problems can be resolved by focusing on the people who are the victims. An extreme method of solving human–wildlife conflicts through the human dimension is removing the people experiencing the problems. This happened in India where entire communities were moved for the benefit of tigers (Karanth 2005; Shahabuddin et al. 2005). Uncontrolled grazing of livestock by Guijjar villages had degraded habitat within Sariska Tiger Reserve and created tiger–human conflicts, including crop raiding by herbivores from the reserve, depredation of livestock, and loss of human life. To resolve the conflict, the Indian government decided to relocate people who were living in villages inside or adjacent to the tiger reserve. Each family was given $19,000 and 2.5 ha of land in a new area to compensate them for the costs of relocating. Such methods reduced conflicts with the reserve's wildlife but were highly controversial. A less radical approach was recommended by Coltrane and Sinnott (2015). Grizzly bears and humans used the same trail system in Anchorage, Alaska, and human–bear encounters were common. The scientists recommended that human access to the trails be limited to certain times of the day so that the bears could adjust their activity patterns to avoid the trails when humans could be expected to use them.

14.10   CAN HUMAN–WILDLIFE CONFLICTS BE RESOLVED BY CHANGING HUMAN BEHAVIOR?

Human tolerance of predators is impacted by attitudes (Rabinowitz 2005; Ramañach et al. 2007), perceptions (Marker et al. 2003; Madden 2004), religion

(Hussain 2002), poverty (Ale and Karky 2002), social status (Hazzah et al. 2009), and the importance of livestock to the community (Bagchi and Mishra 2006). Bears can learn that humans inadvertently provide food to them and quickly habituate to humans after raiding garbage cans and food left out at camp sites. Once this happens, the bear starts spending time in campgrounds or human-dominated areas and, too often, will have to be euthanized because it poses a threat to human safety. Several education programs have been developed to educate people about why they should not leave food accessible to bears and what to do if they should see a bear. Many of these programs have successfully reduced the frequency of bear–human conflicts (Beckmann et al. 2004; Gore et al. 2006). Replacing 175 dumpsters that bears could easily open with bear-proof containers decreased the number of complaints about bears by 75% at the Massanutten Village in Virginia (Scott et al. 2018).

Many wildlife agencies discourage the public from feeding birds in urban areas because the fecal material from large flocks of gulls and pigeons can create water quality issues. The Massachusetts Division of Water Supply Protection tried to discourage people from feeding birds in urban parking lots by erecting signs asking people not to feed birds and informing people about the problems caused by this activity (Figure 14.10). When someone was observed feeding birds, Division employees would walked up and asked them to stop doing so. The education program was successful in reducing the number of people feeding birds, but gull numbers did not decrease (Clark et al. 2015). Another useful program involved a policy change in Yellowstone National Park (Sidebar 14.4).

SIDEBAR 14.4 MANAGING BEAR JAMS IN YELLOWSTONE NATIONAL PARK AND GRAND TETON NATIONAL PARK

Each year, over three million people visit Yellowstone National Park and Grand Teton National Park, which also have high densities of black bears and grizzly bears. Human-habituated bears often cause traffic jams (called bear jams) along the roads in the national park as hundreds of people stop to watch the bears. Usually, the bears that feed on natural food close to roads are females with cubs, perhaps because they are safer there from aggressive male bears. The close proximity of bears and humans can be a recipe for conflicts. Beginning in 1990, park managers adopted the proactive management strategy of managing people at bear jams and not the bears. The key components of the strategy were to prevent bears from becoming conditioned to human foods, making human behavior as predictable as possible, and setting boundaries for both people and bears. Under this strategy, park rangers were dispatched to bear jams to ensure that visitors parked their cars safely and did not walk in or set up camera tripods in traffic lanes. Rangers also ensured that people did not approach, encircle, or feed the bears. This strategy was successful. Despite thousands of bear jams from 2008 to 2017, bears have not injured people at bear jams, but at least six people at bear jams have been stuck and injured by a vehicle. Negative aspects of bear jams include traffic congestion that leads to angry motorists and accidents. The new strategy toward bear jams was labor intensive, requiring about 3,000 hours of park employees annually. Still benefits outweighed costs. Human-habituated bears benefited from being able to forage on high-quality food resources adjacent to roads, and park visitors enjoyed the opportunity to view and photograph bears (Gunther et al. 2018).

Persuasive communication is an intentional effort on behalf of a communicator to elicit a desired response by a person. It is often used by public health and public safety

FIGURE 14.10 A sign used by Massachusetts Division of Water Supply Protection erected in parking lots to discourage people from feeding birds.

Source: Daniel Clark and used with permission.

agencies to convince people to engage in healthy behavior (e.g., washing hands, getting flu shots, and wearing seat belts). A common aim of persuasive communication campaigns is to motivate people act in ways not directly beneficial to them, such as donating blood or registering as an organ donor. Persuasive communication may be useful in wildlife management. For example, it is a challenge to convince hunters to harvest enough deer in areas where a pathogen is endemic in the deer. Triezenberg et al. (2014) employed persuasive communication to alter hunters' intentions to harvest more antlerless deer where bovine tuberculosis (BT) exists in wild deer populations. The persuasive message covered the risks of BT, what other hunters were doing to reduce its risk, and what they could do. Respondents exposed to persuasive communication materials changed their perceptions of risks from BT and increased their intentions to hunt. The results demonstrated that persuasive communication can be effective when it focuses on the activity of interest (deer hunting), communicates goals of management (wildlife disease management), and communicates actions that individuals (deer hunters) can take to reduce risks.

By changing driver behavior, the frequency of ungulate–vehicle collisions can be reduced. In Sweden, moose–vehicle collisions are more common in the fall during the hunting season and the rut because moose are more active during these periods. Neumann and Ericsson (2018) recommended that the Swedish government take steps to inform vehicle drivers to slow down during this period when more moose are crossing roads.

Unfortunately, getting people to slow down can be difficult to achieve. Drivers in Michigan who had been in a DVC within the past five years were more likely than other drivers to know about deer, to believe that were a serious problem, and to prefer a decrease in deer populations. Despite this, they were only willing to make modest changes to their driving behavior because they believed that deer–vehicle collisions were inevitable (Marcoux and Riley 2010).

14.11 CAN HUMAN–WILDLIFE CONFLICTS BE ALLEVIATED BY INCREASING THE VICTIM'S APPRECIATION OF WILDLIFE?

When private property is damaged by wildlife, the loss falls mainly on the owner of the property. If a cat is killed by coyotes, it is the cat's owners who grieve. If bats roost in an attic, it is the homeowner who suffers. One way to solve wildlife damage problems is to change the perceptions of people experiencing the damage (i.e., the victims) so that they are more willing to tolerate it. This can be accomplished by enhancing their appreciation for both the tangible and nontangible benefits of wildlife. For instance, most suburban residents like having deer in their neighborhoods, although they recognize that the price they pay for the presence of deer includes damage to gardens and landscaping plants and some risk of Lyme disease or deer–automobile collisions.

Farmers who enjoy hunting are more tolerant of deer damage to their crops than those who do not because the deer also provide them enjoyment during the hunting season. Many farmers who complain about starling or blackbird damage to their grain crops are tolerant of turkey damage because they enjoy hunting turkeys or allowing their friends to do so (Craven 1989; Gabrey et al. 1993). Other landowners suffering from damage by game species tolerate the damage because they can generate money by leasing out the hunting rights to their land. In some rural areas, access fees paid by hunters can be quite high and can exceed the income landowners receive from timber production, farming, or grazing (Burger and Teer 1981). Other farmers and landowners who do not hunt may derive so much pleasure from seeing wildlife on their land that they do not mind the economic losses they suffer from wildlife damage.

Everyone likes to be recognized, and many people suffering from wildlife damage seek nothing more than empathy and understanding. Hence, another way to increase the value of wildlife for landowners is to ensure that these people feel appreciated for their willingness to tolerate damage. Letters of thanks, phone calls, personal visits, and offers of help all convey the notion that other people appreciate the efforts of farmers and landowners to help wildlife. As one innovative example, color calendars were sent to farmers who participated in a wildlife enhancement project as a token of thanks. Landowners who received these calendars developed a deeper appreciation of wildlife and were more willing to take steps to help wildlife (Messmer et al. 1996).

In India, the dominant religion is Hinduism, which takes a benevolent view of wild animals (Karanth et al. 2013). This tolerance toward animals allows India to have a large wildlife population despite its large human population. For example, the Terai Arc Landscape (TAL) of northern India includes five million ha that encompasses both the lowlands and foothills of the Himalaya Mountains (Figure 14.11). It has a dense human population of 550 people/km^2. Yet, it also has 350 tigers on the Indian side of TAL and many more leopards. Both tigers and leopards kill livestock and occasionally humans. Nonetheless, most villagers in the TAL are tolerant of these felids, and there are few attempts to poison them (Malviya and Ramesh 2015). Buddhism predominates in Nepal, and this religion also is tolerant of animals (Sidebar 14.5).

SIDEBAR 14.5. RELIGION AND SNOW LEOPARDS

Snow leopards live in the high mountains of northern Nepal and share this region with people, livestock, and wild herbivores (Figure 14.12). Snow leopards kill livestock and are both revered and feared by herders. The local people are Buddhist and have incorporated many indigenous beliefs into their religion. One local belief forbids herders from roasting meat or else the mountain god will send his snow leopard to depredate the livestock, and the herders have to accept this as a just punishment. There are stories of great lamas disguising themselves as snow leopards before making trips to Tibet to seek medicinal herbs. Other folk stories describe snow leopards as a barrier standing between the crops and wild herbivores that otherwise would eat their crops. Local inhabitants believe that spirits are reincarnated as cats, including snow leopards, so that they can atone for the sins of their former lives. It is believed that anyone killing a snow leopard will take on the leopard's sins. Given the danger of killing a great lama by mistake or taking on the sins of snow leopards, it is not surprising that people in Nepal prefer to coexist with snow leopards (Ale and Karky 2002).

FIGURE 14.11   Map of India showing the location of the Terai Arc Landscape in shading.

Source: Adapted from Malviya and Ramesh (2015) and drawn by Tara Larkin.

14.12   CAN TOLERANCE OF HUMAN–WILDLIFE CONFLICTS BE INCREASED THROUGH EDUCATION?

When perceptions of risk differ from reality, public education can be used to provide accurate information to stakeholders and reduce their unfounded fears. Doing so can increase public tolerance for wildlife and their damage. Education can also increase

FIGURE 14.12   Snow leopard.

Source: Jim Cummings Shutterstock 1808068270.

a person's appreciation of wildlife (Slagle et al. 2013; Mcgovern and Kretser 2015), while the lack of knowledge about wildlife can produce unfortunate results. For example, local residents in Iran are more likely to kill any wild felid they encounter (even endangered species) when residents cannot distinguish among species and do not know which species is actually depredating their livestock (Hunter et al. 2007).

Providing information to campers about the importance of not leaving food where bears can access it can alter human behavior (Beckmann et al. 2004; Dunn et al. 2008). Durango, Colorado, took a multiprong approach to solving its human–bear conflict, which involved developing an educational program to change the behavior of its residents, increasing enforcement of the city's bear ordinances, and distributing over 1,000 bear-proof containers. As a result, trash-related bear problems declined by 60% and compliance with local bears laws increased by 39% (Johnson et al. 2018). Modifying human behavior can be more effective when education is paired with warnings and enforcement action (Baruch-Mordo et al. 2011).

In Brazil, losses of livestock to jaguars on one's own farm or neighboring farms increased negative attitudes toward jaguars, and poor knowledge about jaguars exacerbated these attitudes. That is, many ranchers could not identify which carcasses were jaguar kills and blamed jaguars for a high proportion of their dead cattle (Marchini and Macdonald 2018).

Ignorance causes harm in many forms. The parasitic nematode *B. procyonis* lives in the intestines of raccoons, and its eggs are shed in the feces of raccoons. This parasite can cause larva migrans if the feces are consumed by humans. In serious cases, the parasite can cause blindness, head and body tilt, nervous behavior, and coma. For this reason, raccoons should be kept out of buildings and yards, and feces should not be touched. Surprisingly, Ogdee et al. (2016) found that people in Texas, where raccoons are common, had only superficial knowledge of raccoon behavior and virtually no knowledge of the parasite or its inherent dangers as a zoonotic disease. Few parents realized that children are especially at a risk of infection because raccoons like to defecate in sandboxes where children play. The incidence of the disease could be decreased if people understood these factors.

14.13   CAN TOLERANCE OF HUMAN–WILDLIFE CONFLICTS BE INCREASED USING COMPENSATION?

Some landowners resent the fact that wildlife, which are owned by society, are damaging their property. They note that if their livestock escaped and damaged another person's property, they would be liable for any damage. They question why the government is not responsible for wildlife damage if they own and manage the wildlife. Several landowners have sued the government over wildlife damage, and the courts have ruled that the government is not responsible for wildlife damage because individual animals are not under its direct control (Musgrave and Stein 1993). The World Parks Congress in 2003 recommended that local people affected by wildlife in parks be compensated for their losses. The Congress believed that this would help encourage local support of conservation objectives (Ogra and Badola 2008).

Despite immunity from lawsuits for wildlife damage, many U.S. states and Canadian provinces financially compensate landowners for certain types of wildlife damage or provide landowners with damage-abatement material, such as fencing material to build deer-proof fences (Wagner et al. 1997). However, none of these states or provinces compensate for all forms of wildlife damage, raising the interesting question of why some wildlife damage is compensated but not others. The answer seems to be that compensation is more likely to be provided when damage is caused by a game species or a large predator. For these species, governments restrict the ability of landowners to kill depredating animals because of their value. In many cases, government agencies also have taken management actions that have increased the populations of these species. Under these circumstances, some governments acknowledge that their actions may be responsible for an increase in wildlife damage and compensate landowners for it. In contrast, no state compensates for damage caused by voles because the government does not take actions to increase vole numbers, nor does it restrict the ability of landowners to kill voles (although there are restrictions on the use of toxicants due to environmental concerns).

Although compensation programs are often perceived to be an appealing alternative to lethal control, not everyone supports them (Hegel et al. 2009). Agricultural producers are often unhappy because compensation programs involve a lot of paperwork for not much money. Disagreements often arise between agricultural producers and government agencies in charge of compensation programs because agency employees accuse farmers of overestimating losses, while farmers complain that agencies deliberately underestimate them. Disagreements over damage estimates can affect the relationship between the agricultural community and the wildlife agency. One way to avoid this is to have neutral third parties, such as crop adjusters from insurance companies, estimate losses.

Many people worry that compensation programs discourage farmers and ranchers from taking actions to reduce the level of wildlife damage (Bulte and Rondeau 2005). To avoid this problem, Alberta, Canada, only compensates farmers for elk damage to stacked hay if the farmer has taken preventative steps, such as surrounding the hay with an elk-proof fence (Hegel et al. 2009). Some compensation funds in Africa reduce payments if livestock are allowed to stray or not kept at night in a predator-proof fence or structure (Maclennan et al. 2009).

Ranchers are particularly unhappy with compensation programs because funds are only paid if it can be confirmed that a large predator killed the livestock, and most kills are never found. Also, it takes time to find a carcass and for an official to come out and look at it; by then, it is often impossible to determine what killed the animal, let alone which predator may have been responsible. Wyoming recognizes this problem and pays ranchers seven times the value of any confirmed kill in recognition that only one in seven actual predator kills are ever confirmed. Few other states or countries do more than just pay the value of a confirmed kill. In fact, many countries cannot do more than pay a fraction of what the animal is actually worth.

In Sweden, wolverines kill many reindeer, and reindeer herders were compensated for their losses by the government. Then Sweden switched from compensating herders for their losses and, instead, paid herders for the number of wolverines that reproduced in their district. Authorities followed wolverine tracks in the snow to locate natal dens and females with cubs; payments averaging €2.7 million were made annually to local reindeer herders based on these numbers. This program greatly benefitted the wolverines. There were only 57 wolverines in Sweden when the program became fully operational in 2002; there were 125 a decade later (Zabel and Holm-Müller 2008; Persson et al. 2015).

Compensation programs have other problems. They can be expensive for the state or federal governments that fund them, often exceeding $1 million annually. Wildlife agencies are generally opposed to these programs because they do not want to become trapped in a payment system for an indefinite period of time. Others argue that wildlife agencies, however, should view compensation programs as a tool to encourage the provisioning of wildlife on private land (Wagner et al. 1997; Yoder 2002).

In Europe, livestock producers are often compensated for losses due to predators because Europeans like knowing that populations of large predators are stable in their countries. During 2001, Norway paid livestock producers for 10,000 lambs killed by lynx (Linnell and Brøseth 2003). Sweden compensates for 50,000–60,000 sheep and lambs killed by predators annually (Widman et al. 2019).

Third-world countries often do not have the money to adequately compensate agricultural producers for their losses. Botswana compensated ranchers $240,000 for livestock killed by predators, but the payments were so small that they did not increase ranchers' willingness to coexist with predators. Instead, some ranchers resorted to illegal killing predators because they were upset with the government's response to the predator problem (Tjibae 2001; Gusset et al. 2009).

Tigers in Chitwan National Park, Nepal, and its surrounding buffer zones kill both people and livestock (Figure 14.13). In response, the government created a compensation program to reduce public animosity toward tigers. The government could only afford to compensate for losses at a fraction of the actual losses. For example, a payment for a human life was set at $3,000. Other payments averaged less than $500 per person and covered 81% of medical costs for injured person and 47% of the value of killed livestock. The compensation program lacked broad support among local residents because payments were meager and often delayed for months (Dhungana et al. 2016). Still, Nepal is a poor country, making higher payment difficult.

Common leopards kill over 100 livestock annually in Binsar Wildlife Sanctuary, India. The sanctuary compensates villagers for their losses, but payments are less than the actual value of the livestock and vary by the type of livestock. Compensation for goats is 12% of their actual value, 18% for water buffalo, and 51% for cattle (Kala and Kothari 2013). In Uganda, village farmers around Kibale National Park are confronted by crop-raiding elephants and baboons that leave the park seeking food. The park shares revenues with local farms to compensate them for their losses, but the amount that each household received annually is only about $1 (Mackenzie and Ahabyona 2012).

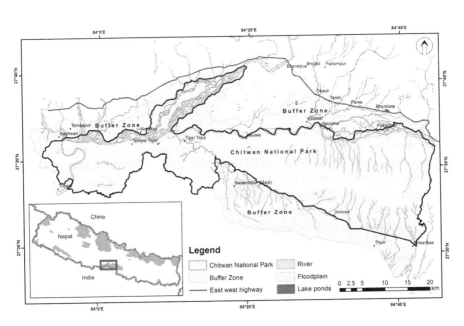

FIGURE 14.13 Map of Chitwan National Park, Nepal, and the buffer zones around it. Within both the park (green color) and the buffer zones (tan color), compensation is paid for tiger attacks on humans and livestock.

Source: From Dhungana et al. (2016) and used with permission.

14.14   SUMMARY

In the past few decades, the goal of wildlife management has shifted from trying to maximize wildlife populations to a more difficult goal of trying to maximize wildlife values for society. A major difficulty in trying to achieve this goal is that the benefits and liabilities of wildlife fall unevenly upon different segments of society. This causes disagreements over what the ideal wildlife population really is and how wildlife should be managed. For this reason, each stakeholder group has its own "wildlife acceptance capacity." When combined, these become the "cultural carrying capacity" or the wildlife population which everyone can tolerate.

Important stakeholders in wildlife damage management often include agricultural producers, hunters, fur trappers, animal welfare activists, animal rights activists, rural residents, and metropolitan residents. Experiencing wildlife problems can change one's perception of wildlife and one's tolerance of wildlife damage, especially if the problem is serious and chronic. People suffering from wildlife damage are reasonably accurate in estimating the extent of damage wildlife. One way to alleviate wildlife damage problems is to increase the injured person's tolerance for damage by increasing their appreciation of wildlife, expanding their knowledge about wildlife, allowing them to reap economic benefits from wildlife, and compensating them for their losses.

14.15   DISCUSSION QUESTIONS

1. How do the following terms differ from each other: wildlife acceptance capacity, cultural carrying capacity, and biological carrying capacity?
2. Nepal tries to realign the benefits and liability of wildlife to they fall evenly upon all segments of society. Half of the revenue generated by Chitwan National Park is returned to the communities around the park for development, conservation, and awareness programs in partial compensation for damage caused by the park's wildlife (Dhungana et al. 2016). In the United States, Yellowstone National Park has the same problem because wolves, bison, and elk venture out of the park during the winter and cause problems for local agricultural producers. Do you think that Yellowstone National Park should share some of its revenue with local ranchers and communities to compensate them for their losses?
3. If you were the newly appointed manager of a migratory bird refuge in North Dakota, what actions would you take during your first year to improve relationships with local farmers?
4. What stakeholder groups would be interested in the question of whether recreational trapping should be outlawed in Massachusetts? How would you assembly the stakeholders together to try to reach an agreement on the question? Would you invite groups from outside the state to participate?
5. The Idaho Department of Fish and Game maintains a Big-Game Depredation Trust to compensate ranchers and farmers for big-game damage. It receives about $1 million annually from the state government. During 2019, one farm filed a claim for $1 million in damage to his crops from elk. This one

claim entirely drained the Trust, leaving all of other agricultural producers in Idaho empty handed. In response, the Idaho legislature did not increase funding for the Depredation Trust; instead, it passed a bill to cap the payment amount for any claim to no more than 10% of the funds available in the Trust (Schaefer 2019). What do you think of this situation?

LITERATURE CITED

Ale, S. B., and B. S. Karky. 2002. Observations on conservation of snow leopards in Nepal. Pages 3–14 *in Contributed papers to the snow leopard survival strategy summit.* International Snow Leopard Trust, Seattle, WA.

American Society for the Prevention of Cruelty to Animals. 2019. *ASPCA about us.* www. aspca.org/about-us. Accessed 8 July 2019.

Andersone, Ž., and J. Ozoliņš. 2004. Public perception of large carnivores in Latvia. *Ursus* 15:181–188.

Animal Welfare Institute. 2019. *Annual report.* Animal Welfare Institute, Washington, DC.

Association of Fish and Wildlife Agencies. 2018. *Characteristics of U. S. trappers.* www.fish-wildlife.org/application/files/4915/2942/8278/Characteristics-of-Trappers-06-18-18_reduced.pdf. Accessed 5 July 2019.

Bagchi, S., and C. Mishra. 2006. Living with large carnivores: predation on livestock by the snow leopard (*Uncia uncia*). *Journal of Zoology* 268:217–224.

Baker, S. E., S. A. Maw, P. J. Johnson, and D. W. Macdonald. 2020. Not in my backyard: public perceptions of wildlife and "pest control" in and around UK homes, and local authority "pest control". *Animals* 10(2):222.

Baruch-Mordo, S., S. W. Breck, K. R. Wilson, and J. Broderick. 2011. The carrot or the stick? Evaluation of education and enforcement as management tools for human-wildlife conflicts. *PLoS One* 6(1):e15681.

Beckmann, J. P., C. W. Lackey, and J. Berger. 2004. Evaluation of deterrent techniques and dogs to alter behavior of "nuisance" black bears. *Wildlife Society Bulletin* 32:1141–1146.

Berg, N. A. 1986. USDA goals for strengthening private land management in the 1980s. *Transactions of the North American Wildlife and Natural Resources Conference* 46:137–145.

Bulte, E. H., and D. Rondeau. 2005. Why compensating wildlife damages may be bad for conservation. *Journal of Wildlife Management* 69:14–19.

Burger, G. V., and J. G. Teer. 1981. Economic and socioeconomic issues influencing wildlife management on private lands. Pages 252–278 *in* R. T. Dumke, G. V. Burger, and J. R. March, editors. *Wildlife management on private lands.* Wisconsin Chapter, The Wildlife Society, Madison, WI.

Clark, D. E., J. J. Whitney, K. G. MacKenzie, K. K. G. Koenen, and S. DeStefano. 2015. Assessing gull abundance and food availability in urban parking lots. *Human-Wildlife Interactions* 9:180–190.

Coltrane, J. A., and R. Sinnott. 2015. Brown bear and human recreational use of trails in Anchorage, Alaska. *Human-Wildlife Interactions* 9:132–147.

Conover, M. R. 1997. Wildlife management by metropolitan residents in the United States: practices, perceptions, costs, and values. *Wildlife Society Bulletin* 25:306–311.

Conover, M. R. 1998. Perceptions of American agricultural producers about wildlife on their farms and ranches. *Wildlife Society Bulletin* 26:597–604.

Craven, S. R. 1989. Farmer attitudes toward wild turkeys in Southwestern Wisconsin. *Proceedings of the Eastern Wildlife Damage Control Conference* 4:113–119.

D'Angelo, G. J., and M. D. Grund. 2015. Evaluating competing preferences of hunters and landowners for management of deer populations. *Human-Wildlife Interactions* 9:236–247.

Decker, D. J., and T. L. Brown. 1987. How the animal rightists view the "wildlife manage-ment – hunting system". *Wildlife Society Bulletin* 15:599–602.

Decker, D. J., and K. G. Purdy. 1988. Toward a concept of wildlife acceptance capacity in wildlife management. *Wildlife Society Bulletin* 16:58–62.

Dhungana, R., T. Savini, J. B. Karki, and S. Bumrungsri. 2016. Mitigating human-tiger con-flict: an assessment of compensation payments and tiger removals in Chitwan National Park, Nepal. *Tropical Conservation Science* 9:776–787.

Dickman, A. J. 2010. Complexities of conflict: the importance of considering social factors for effectively resolving human – wildlife conflict. *Animal Conservation* 13:458–466.

Dunn, W. C., J. H. Elwell, and G. Tunberg. 2008. Safety education in bear country: are people getting the message. *Ursus* 19:43–53.

Frost, P. G. H., and I. Bond. 2008. The CAMPFIRE programme in Zimbabwe: payments for wildlife services. *Ecological Economics* 65:776–787.

Gabrey, S. W., P. A. Vohs, and D. H. Jackson. 1993. Perceived and real crop damage by wild turkeys in Northeastern Iowa. *Wildlife Society Bulletin* 21:39–45.

Gamage, A., and M. Wijesundara. 2014. A solution for the elephant-human conflict. *Texas Instruments India Educators' Conference* 169–176. doi:10.1109/TIIEC.2014.35.

Gillingham, S., and P. C. Lee. 2003. People and protected areas: a study of local percep-tions of wildlife crop-damage conflict in an area bordering the Selous Game Reserve, Tanzania. *Oryx* 37:316–325.

Goldman, M. J., J. R. De Pinho, and J. Perry. 2013. Beyond ritual and economics: Maasai lion hunting and conservation politics. *Oryx* 47:490–500.

Gore, M. L., B. A. Knuth, P. D. Curtis, and J. E. Shanahan. 2006. Education programs for reducing American black-bear conflict: indications of success? *Ursus* 17:75–80.

Gunther, K. A., K. R. Wilmot, S. L. Cain, T. Wyman, E. G. Reinertson, A. M. Bramblett. 2018. Managing human-habituated bears to enhance survival, habitat effectiveness, and public viewing. *Human-Wildlife Interactions* 12:373–386.

Gusset, M., M. J. Swarner, L. Mponwane, K. Keletile, and J. W. McNutt. 2009. Human-wildlife conflict in northern Botswana: livestock predation by endangered African wild dog *Lycaon pictus* and other carnivores. *Oryx* 43:67–72.

Guynn, D. E. 1997. Miracle in Montana – managing conflicts over private lands and public wildlife issues. *Transactions of the North American Wildlife and Natural Resources Conference* 62:146–154.

Haule, K. S., F. H. Johnsen, and S. L. S. Maganga. 2002. Striving for sustainable wildlife management: the case of Kilombero Game Controlled Area, Tanzania. *Journal of Environmental Management* 66:31–42.

Hazzah, L., M. B. Mulder, and L. Frank. 2009. Lions and warriors: social factors underlying declining African lion populations and the effect of incentive-based management in Kenya. *Biological Conservation* 142:2428–2437.

Hegel, T. M., C. C. Gates, and D. Eslinger. 2009. The geography of conflict between elk and agricultural values in the Cypress Hills, Canada. *Journal of Environmental Management* 90:222–235.

Hooper, J. K. 1992. Animal welfarists and rightists: insights into an expanding constituency for wildlife interpreters. *Legacy* 20–25, November–December.

Hunter, L., H. Jowkar, H. Ziaie, G. B. Schaller, G. Balme, C. Walzer, S. Ostrowski, P. Zahler, N. Robert-Charrue, K. Kashiri, and S. Christie. 2007. Conserving the Asiatic cheetah in Iran: launching the first radio-telemetry study. *Cat News* 46(8):e11.

Hussain, S. 2002. Nature and human nature: conservation, values, and snow leopard: observa-tions on conservation of snow leopards in Nepal. Pages 67–75 *in Contributed papers to the snow leopard survival strategy summit.* International Snow Leopard Trust, Seattle, WA.

Hygnstrom, S. E., R. M. Timm, and G. E. Larson. 1994. *Prevention and control of wildlife damage.* University of Nebraska Cooperative Extension, Lincoln, NE.

Johnson, H. E., D. L. Lewis, S. A. Lischka, and S. W. Breck. 2018. Assessing ecological and social outcomes of a bear-proofing experiment. *Journal of Wildlife Management* 82:1102–1114.

Jonker, S. A., J. F. Organ, R. M. Muth, R. R. Zwick, and W. F. Siemer. 2009. Stakeholder norms toward beaver management in Massachusetts. *Journal of Wildlife Management* 73:1158–1165.

Jonzén, N., H. Sand, P. Wabakken, J. E. Swenson, J. Kindberg, O. Liberg, and G. Chapron. 2013. Sharing the bounty – adjusting harvest to predator return in the Scandinavian human – wolf – bear – moose system. *Ecological Modelling* 265:140–148.

Kala, C. P., and K. K. Kothari. 2013. Livestock predation by common leopard in Binsar wildlife sanctuary, India: human-wildlife conflicts and conservation issues. *Human-Wildlife Interactions* 7:325–333.

Karanth, K. K. 2005. Addressing relocation and livelihood concerns. *Economics and Political Weekly* 440:4809–4811.

Karanth, K. K., L. Naughton-Treves, R. DeFries, and A. M. Gopalaswamy. 2013. Living with wildlife and mitigating conflicts around three Indian protected areas. *Environmental Management* 52:1320–1332.

Kellert, S. R. 1980*a*. Americans' attitudes and knowledge of animals. *Transactions of the North American Wildlife and Natural Resources Conference* 45:111–124.

Kellert, S. R. 1980*b*. American attitudes toward and knowledge of animals: an update. *International Journal of the Study of Animal Problems* 1:87–119.

Kenya Government. 2020. *Kenya tourism revenue.* www.ceicdata.com/en/indicator/kenya/tourism-revenue. Accessed 5 April 2020.

Kirby, S. B., K. M. Babcock, S. L. Sheriff, and D. J. Witter. 1981. Private land and wildlife in Missouri: a study of farm operator values. Pages 88–101 *in* R. T. Dumke, G. V. Burger, and J. R. March, editors. *Wildlife management on private lands.* Wisconsin Chapter, The Wildlife Society, Madison, WI.

Lemelin, R. H. 2008. Impacts of the cancellation of the spring bear hunt in Ontario, Canada. *Human-Wildlife Interactions* 2:148–150.

Leopold, A. 1933. *Game management.* Charles Scribner's Sons, New York.

Lichtenfeld, L. L. 2005. *Our shared kingdom at risk: human – lion relationships in the 21st century.* Ph.D. dissertation, Yale University, New Haven, CT.

Linnell, J. D. C., and H. Brøseth. 2003. Compensation for large carnivore depredation on domestic sheep 1994–2001. *Carnivore Damage Prevention News* 6:11–16.

Linnell, J. D. C., E. J. Solberg, S. Brainerd, O. Liberg, H. Sand, P. Wabakken, and I. Kojola. 2003. Is the fear of wolves justified? A Fennoscandian perspective. *Acta Zoologica Lituanica* 13:34–40.

Lischka, S. A., S. J. Riley, and B. A. Rudolph. 2008. Effects of impact perception on acceptance capacity for white-tailed deer. *Journal of Wildlife Management* 72:502–509.

Mackenzie, C. A., and P. Ahabyona. 2012. Elephants in the garden: financial and social costs of crop raiding. *Ecological Economics* 75:72–82.

Maclennan, S. D., R. J. Groom, D. W. Macdonald, and L. G. Frank. 2009. Evaluation of a compensation scheme to bring about pastoralist tolerance of lions. *Biological Conservation* 142:2419–2427.

Madden, F. 2004. Creating coexistence between humans and wildlife: global perspectives on local efforts to address human-wildlife conflicts. *Human Dimensions of Wildlife* 9:247–257.

Malviya, M., and K. Ramesh. 2015. Human-felid conflict in corridor habitats: implications for tiger and leopard conservation in Terai Arc landscape, India. *Human-Wildlife Interactions* 9:48–57.

Marchini, S., and D. W. Macdonald. 2018. Mind over matter: perceptions behind the impact of jaguars on human livelihoods. *Biological Conservation* 224:230–237.

Marcoux, A., and S. J. Riley. 2010. Driver knowledge, beliefs, and attitudes about deer-vehicle collisions in Southern Michigan. *Human-Wildlife Interactions* 4:47–55.

Marker, L. L., M. G. L. Mills, and D. W. Macdonald. 2003. Factors influencing perceptions of conflict and tolerance toward cheetahs on Namibian farmlands. *Conservation Biology* 17:1290–1298.

Mcgovern, E. B., and H. E. Kretser. 2015. Predicting support for recolonization of mountain lions (*Puma concolor*) in the Adirondack park. *Wildlife Society Bulletin* 39:503–511.

Messmer, T. A., C. A. Lively, D. MacDonald, and S. A. Schroeder. 1996. Motivating landowners to implement conservation practices using calendars. *Wildlife Society Bulletin* 24:757–763.

Mitchell, M. S., H. Cooley, J. A. Gude, J. Kolbe, J. J. Nowak, K. M. Proffitt, S. N. Sells, and M. Thompson. 2018. Distinguishing values from science in decision making: setting harvest quotas for mountain lions in Montana. *Wildlife Society Bulletin* 42:13–21.

Musgrave, R. S., and M. A. Stein. 1993. *State wildlife laws handbook.* Government Institutes, Rockville, MD.

Mutandwa, E., and C. T. Gadzirayi. 2007. Impact of community-based approaches to wildlife management: case study of the CAMPFIRE programme in Zimbabwe. *International Journal of Sustainable Development and World Ecology* 14:336–344.

Naughton-Treves, L., R. Grossberg, and A. Treves. 2003. Paying for tolerance: rural citizens' attitudes toward wolf depredation and compensation. *Conservation Biology* 17:1500–1511.

Neumann, W., and G. Ericsson. 2018. Influence of hunting on movements of moose near roads. *Journal of Wildlife Management* 82:918–928.

Nolen, J. L. 2019. Humane society of the United States, American organization. *Encyclopedia Britannica.* www.britannica.com/topic/Humane-Society-of-the-United-States. Accessed 8 July 2019.

Ogdee, J. L., S. E. Henke, and D. E. Wester. 2016. Lack of human awareness and the need for increased public education regarding the zoonotic parasite, *Baylisascaris procyonis*. *Human-Wildlife Interactions* 10:283–291.

Ogra, M., and R. Badola. 2008. Compensating human-wildlife conflict in protected area communities: ground-level perspectives from Uttarakhand, India. *Human Ecology* 36:717–729.

Olson, E. R., T. R. Van Deelen, A. P. Wydeven, S. J. Ventura, and D. M. Macfarland. 2015. Characterizing wolf – human conflicts in Wisconsin, USA. *Wildlife Society Bulletin* 39:676–688.

Organ, J. F., and M. R. Ellingwood. 2000. Wildlife stakeholder acceptance capacity for black bears, beavers, and other beasts in the East. *Human Dimensions of Wildlife* 5:63–75.

Persson, J., G. R. Rauset, and G. Chapron. 2015. Paying for an endangered predator leads to population recovery. *Conservation Letters* 8:345–350.

Peterson, M. N., A. G. Mertig, and J. Liu. 2006. Effects of zoonotic disease attributes towards wildlife management. *Journal of Wildlife Management* 70:1746–1753.

Rabinowitz, A. 2005. Jaguars and livestock: living with the world's third largest cat. Pages 278–285 *in* R. Woodroffe, S. Thirgood, and A. Rabinowitz, editors. *People and wildlife, conflict or coexistence?* Cambridge University Press, Cambridge.

Ramañach, S. S., P. A. Lindsey, and R. Woodroffe. 2007. Determinants of attitudes towards predators in central Kenya and suggestions for increasing tolerance in livestock dominated landscapes. *Oryx* 41:185–195.

Rust, N. A., K. M. Whitehouse-Tedd, and D. C. MacMillan. 2013. Perceived efficacy of livestock-guarding dogs in South Africa: implications for cheetah conservation. *Wildlife Society Bulletin* 37:690–697.

Sakurai, R., and S. K. Jacobson. 2011. Public perceptions of bears and management interventions in Japan. *Human-Wildlife Interactions* 5:123–134.

Schaefer, B. 2019. *Idaho farmer's elk damage claim exceeds $1 million*. Farm and Ranch, Boise, Idaho. www.postregister.com/farmandranch/crops/idaho-farmers-elk-damage-claim-exceeds-1-million/article_a6502657-167b-5ab9-837a-e20b72a7e523.html. Accessed 20 July 2020.

Schmidt, R. H. 1991*a*. Why do we debate animal rights? *Wildlife Society Bulletin* 18:459–461.

Schmidt, R. H. 1991*b*. Influence of the animal rights movement on range management activities – productive directions. *Rangelands* 13:276.

Scott, A. M., D. M. Kocka, and G. W. Mitchell, Jr. 2018. Human-bear conflicts in Massanutten Village: achieving success required partnerships. *Human-Wildlife Interactions* 12:405–410.

Shahabuddin, G., R. Kumar, and M. Shrivastava. 2005. Pushed over the edge: village relation from Sariska. *Economic and Political Weekly* 40:3563–3565.

Siemer, W. F., S. A. Jonker, D. J. Decker, and J. F. Organ. 2013. Towards an understanding of beaver management as human and beaver densities increase. *Human-Wildlife Interactions* 7:114–131.

Sifuna, N. 2011. Use of illegal methods in Kenya's rural communities to combat wildlife damage: a case study of Laikipia. *Human-Wildlife Interactions* 5:5–8.

Slagle, K., R. Zajac, J. Bruskotter, R. Wilson, and S. Prange. 2013. Building tolerance for bears: a communications experiment. *Journal of Wildlife Management* 77:863–869.

Smith, D. W., P. J. White, D. R. Stahler, A. Wydeven, and D. E. Hallac. 2016. Managing wolves in the Yellowstone area: balancing goals across jurisdictional boundaries. *Wildlife Society Bulletin* 40:436–445.

Smith, J. B., C. K. Nielsen, and E. C. Hellgren. 2014. Illinois resident attitudes toward recolonizing large carnivores. *Journal of Wildlife Management* 78:930–943.

Soulé, M. E. 1985. What is conservation biology? *BioScience* 35:727–734.

Tanner, G., and R. W. Dimmick. 1983. An assessment of farmers' attitudes toward deer and deer damage in West Tennessee. *Proceedings of the Eastern Wildlife Damage Control Conference* 1:195–199.

Thornton, C., and M. S. Quinn. 2010. Risk perceptions and attitudes toward cougars in the Southern foothills of Alberta. *Human Dimensions of Wildlife* 15:359–372.

Tjibae, M. 2001. Overview of problem animal control. Pages 25–34 *in National technical predator management and conservation workshop in Botswana*. Department of Wildlife and National Parks, Gaborone, Botswana.

Triezenberg, H. A., M. L. Gore, S. J. Riley, and M. K. Lapinski. 2014. Persuasive communication aimed at achieving wildlife-disease management goals. *Wildlife Society Bulletin* 38:734–740.

U. S. Census of Agriculture. 2012. *Farm demographics – U. S. farmers by gender, age, race ethnicity and more*. USDA National Agricultural Statistics Service. www.nass.usda.gov/Publications/Highlights/2014/Farm_Demographics/Highlights_Farm_Demographics.pdf. Accessed 5 July 2019.

U. S. Department of Interior. 2016. *National survey of fishing, hunting and wildlife-associated recreation*. U. S. Department of the Interior, U. S. Fish and Wildlife Service, and U. S. Department of Commerce, U. S. Census Bureau. https://wsfrprograms.fws.gov/subpages/nationalsurvey/nat_survey2016.pdf. Accessed 5 July 2019.

Wagner, K. K., R. H. Schmidt, and M. R. Conover. 1997. Compensation programs for wildlife damage in North America. *Wildlife Society Bulletin* 25:312–319.

Webber, A. D., C. M. Hill, and V. Reynolds. 2007. Assessing the failure of a community-based human wildlife conflict mitigation project in Budongo Forest Reserve, Uganda. *Oryx* 41:177–184.

West, P., J. Igoe, and D. Brockington. 2006. Parks and peoples: the social impact of protected areas. *Annual Review of Anthropology* 35:251–277.

Widman, M., M. Steen, and K. Elofsson. 2019. Indirect costs of sheep depredation by large carnivores in Sweden. *Wildlife Society Bulletin* 43:53–61.

Willcox, A. S., and W. M. Giuliano. 2011. Cattle rancher and conservation agency personnel perceptions of wildlife management and assistance programs in Alabama, Florida, Georgia, and Mississippi. *Wildlife Society Bulletin* 35:59–68.

Yoder, J. 2002. Deer-inflicted crop damage and crop choice in Wisconsin. *Human Dimensions of Wildlife* 7:179–196.

Zabel, A., and K. Holm-Müller. 2008. Conservation performance payments for carnivore conservation in Sweden. *Conservation Biology* 22:247–251.

Appendix

Latin Names for Species Mentioned in the Text

alder, green (*Alnus viridis*)
alligator, American (*Alligator mississippiensis*)
antelope, pronghorn (*Antilocapra americana*)
apple (*Malus domestica*)
armadillo, nine-banded (*Dasypus novemcinctus*)
ash, white (*Fraxinus americana*)
aspen (*Populus tremuloides*)
aspen, quaking (*Populus tremuloides*)
auklet, Cassin's (*Ptychoramphus aleuticus*)
baboon, chacma (*Papio ursinus*)
baboon, hamadryas (*Papio hamadryas*)
baboon, olive (*Papio anubis*)
badger, American (*Taxidea taxus*)
badger, European (*Meles meles*)
bamboo (*Phyllostachys* spp.)
barley (*Hordeum vulgare*)
bat, flying fox (*Pteropus* spp.)
bat, giant fruit (*Pteropus giganteus*)
bear, Andean (*Tremarctos ornatus*)
bear, Asiatic black (*Ursus thibetanus*)
bear, black (*Ursus americanus*)
bear, brown (*Ursus arctos*)
bear, grizzly (*Ursus arctos horribilis*)
bear, polar (*Ursus maritimus*)
bear, sloth (*Melursus ursinus*)
bear, sun (*Helarctos malayanus*)
beaver (*Castor canadensis*)
beaver, mountain (*Aplodontia rufa*)
beech (*Fagus sylvatica*)
beech, American (*Fagus grandifolia*)
bettong, burrowing (*Bettongia lesueur*)
bison (*Bison bison*)
bitterbrush (*Purshia tridentata*)
blackbird, common (*Turdus merula*)
blackbird, Eurasian (*Turdus merula*)
blackbird, red-winged (*Agelaius phoeniceus*)
blackbird, yellow-headed (*Xanthocephalus xanthocephalus*)
blackbush (*Coleogyne ramosissima*)
blueberry (*Vaccinium* spp.)
bluefish (*Pomatomus saltatrix*)

bluegrass, Kentucky (*Poa pratensis*)
boar, wild (*Sus scrofa*)
bobcat (*Lynx rufus*)
bobwhite (*Colinus virginianus*)
brant, black (*Branta bernicla nigricans*)
buffalo (*Bison bison*)
buffalo, African (*Syncerus caffer*)
buffalo, European (*Bison bonasus*)
buffalo, feral (*Bubalus bubalis*)
buffalo, water (*Bubalus bubalis*)
bullfinch (*Pyrrhula pyrrhula*)
burro (*Equus asinus*)
bush pig (*Potamochoeus procus*)
butterfly, monarch (*Danaus plexippus*)
caiman, black (*Melanosuchus niger*)
caiman, spectacled (*Caiman crocodilus*)
caiman, yacare (*Caiman yacare*)
camel (*Camelus dromedarius*)
camel, dromedary (*Camelus dromedarius*)
caracal (*Caracal caracal*)
cardinal, northern (*Cardinalis* cardinalis)
caribou (*Rangifer tarandus*)
caribou, Gaspé (*Rangifer tarandus caribou*)
carp (*Cyprinus carpio*)
cat, feral (*Felis catus*)
catbird (*Dumetella carolinensis*)
catfish (*Ictalurus* spp.)
cattail (*Typha* spp.)
cattle, feral (*Bos taurus*)
cedar, northern white (*Thuja occidentalis*)
cedar, western red (*Thuja plicata*)
chaffinch, common (*Fringilla coelebs*)
chamois (*Rupicapra rupicapra*)
cheetah (*Acinonyx jubatus*)
cherry (*Prunus* spp.)
cherry, black (*Prunus serotina*)
cherry, choke (*Prunus virginiana*)
chimpanzee (*Pan troglodytes*)
chipmunk (*Tamias* spp.)
civet (*Viverra zibetha* or *Viverricula indica*)
cockatoo, sulphur-crested (*Cacatua galerita*)
cocoa (*Theobroma cacao*)
cod, black (*Anoplopoma fimbria*)
condor, California (*Gymnogyps californianus*)
coot, American (*Fulica americana*)

copperhead (*Agkistrodon contortrix*)
cormorant, double-crested (*Phalacrocorax auratus*)
cormorant, great (*Phalacrocorax carbo*)
corn (*Zea mays*)
corn borer, European (*Ostrinia nubilalis*)
cottontail, desert (*Sylvilagus audubonii*)
cottontail, eastern (*Sylvilagus floridanus*)
cougar (*Felis concolor*)
cowbird, brown-headed (*Molothrus ater*)
coyote (*Canis latrans*)
crab, ghost (Ocypodinae)
crane, sandhill (*Grus canadensis*)
crake, Henderson (*Zapornia atra*)
crane, whooping (*Grus americana*)
crocodile, American (*Crocodylus acutus*)
crocodile, Australian freshwater (*Crocodylus johnstoni*)
crocodile, Morelet's (*Crocodylus moreletii*)
crocodile, mugger (*Crocodylus palustris*)
crocodile, saltwater (*Crocodylus porosus*)
crocodile, West African (*Crocodylus suchus*)
crow, American (*Corvus brachyrhynchos*)
crow, carrion (*Corvus corone*)
crow, fish (*Corvus ossifragus*)
damselfish (*Plectroglyphidodon lacrymatus*)
deer, barking (*Muntiacus muntjak*)
deer, black-tailed (*Odocoileus hemionus columbianus*)
deer, fallow (*Dama dama*)
deer, Florida key (*Odocoileus virginianus clavium*)
deer, hog (*Axis porcinus*)
deer, mule (*Odocoileus hemionus*)
deer, muntjac (*Muntiacus* spp.)
deer, red (*Cervus elaphus*)
deer, roe (*Capreolus capreolus*)
deer, sika (*Cervus nippon*)
deer, white-tailed (*Odocoileus virginianus*)
dhole (*Cuon alpinus*)
dingo (*Canis familiaris dingo*)
dog, feral (*Canis familiaris*)
donkey (*Equus asinus*)
dove, eared (*Zenaida auriculata*)
dove, Henderson fruit (*Ptilinopus insularis*)
dove, Inca (*Columbina inca*)
dove, mourning (*Zenaida macroura*)
dove, red-eyed turtle (*Streptopelia decaocto*)
duck, wood (*Aix sponsa*)

dunlin (*Calidris alpina*)
dunnock (*Prunella modularis*)
eagle, golden (*Aquila chrysaetos*)
egret, cattle (*Bubulcus ibis*)
eider, common (*Somateria mollissima*)
elephant, African (*Loxodonta africana*)
elephant, Asian (*Elephas maximus*)
elk (*Cervus elaphus*)
falcon, peregrine (*Falco peregrinus*)
ferret, black-footed (*Mustela nigripes*)
fescue, tall (*Festuca arundinacea*)
finch, African weaver (*Quelea quelea*)
finch, house (*Carpodacus mexicanus*)
fir, Douglas (*Pseudotsuga menziesii*)
fir, Fraser (*Abies fraseri*)
flycatcher, pied (*Ficedula hypoleuca*)
flycatcher, southwestern willow (*Empidonax traillii extrimus*)
flying squirrel, southern (*Glaucomys volans*)
fody, red (*Foudia madagascariensis*)
fox, arctic (*Alopex lagopus*)
fox, gray (*Urocyon cinereoargenteus*)
fox, kit (*Vulpes macrotis*)
fox, red (*Vulpes vulpes*)
fox, San Joaquin kit (*Vulpes macrotis mutica*)
fox, swift (*Vulpes velox*)
foxglove (*Digitalis purpurea*)
gadwall (*Anas strepera*)
galah (*Eolophus roseicapillus*)
gaur (*Bos gaurus*)
gerbil, Mongolian (*Meriones unguiculatus*)
gharial (*Gavialis gangeticus*)
gnatcatcher, coastal California (*Polioptila californica californica*)
goat, feral (*Capra hircus*)
goat, mountain (*Oreamnos americanus*)
goose, Aleutian Canada (*Branta canadensis leucopareia*)
goose, brant (*Branta bernicla*)
goose, Canada (*Branta canadensis*)
goose, Egyptian (*Alopochen aegyptiaca*)
goose, Hawaiian (*Nesochen sandvicensis*)
goose, pink-footed (*Anser brachyrhynchus*)
goose, Ross' (*Chen rossii*)
goose, snow (*Chen caerulescens*)
gopher, pocket (*Geomyidae*)
goshawk, northern (*Accipiter gentilis*)
grackle, boat-tailed (*Quiscalus major*)

grackle, common (*Quiscalus quiscula*)
ground squirrel (*Spermophilus* spp.)
ground squirrel, Belding's (*Spermophilus beldingi*)
ground squirrel, California (*Otospermophilus beecheyi*)
ground squirrel, golden-mantled (*Spermophilus lateralis*)
grouse, red (*Lagopus lagopus scoticus*)
grouse, ruffed (*Bonasa umbellus*)
grouse, sage (*Centrocercus* spp.)
grouse, sharp-tailed (*Tympanuchus phasianellus*)
gull, black-backed (*Larus marinus*)
gull, California (*Larus californicus*)
gull, glaucous-winged (*Larus glaucescens*)
gull, herring (*Larus argentatus*)
gull, laughing (*Larus atricilla*)
gull, ring-billed (*Larus delawarensis*)
gull, yellow-legged (*Larus michahellis*)
gum tree, manna (*Eucalyptus viminalis*)
gyrfalcon (*Falco rusticolus*)
hare, snowshoe (*Lepus americanus*)
harrier, hen (*Circus cyaneus*)
hawk, Harris's (*Parabuteo unicinctus*)
hawk, red-shouldered (*Buteo lineatus*)
hawk, red-tailed (*Buteo jamaicensis*)
heather (*Calluna vulgaris*)
hemlock, eastern (*Tsuga canadensis*)
heron, black-crowned night (*Nycticorax nycticorax*)
heron, gray (*Ardea cinerea*)
heron, great blue (*Ardea herodias*)
hippopotamus (*Hippopotamus amphibius*)
holly, American (*Ilex opaca*)
holly, China girl (*Ilex X meserveae*)
holly, Japanese (*Ilex crenata*)
horse, feral (*Equus caballus*)
horse, Przewalski's (*Equus caballus przewalskii*)
hummingbird, black-chinned (*Archilochus alexandri*)
hyacinth (*Muscari* spp.)
hyena (*Hyaena hyaena*)
hyena, brown (*Hyaena brunnea*)
hyena, spotted (*Crocuta crocuta*)
ibex, alpine (*Capra ibex*)
impala, black-faced (*Aepyceros melampus petersi*)
iris (*Iris* spp.)
jackal (*Canis aureus*)
jackal, black-backed (*Canis mesomelas*)
jackal, golden (*Canis aureus*)

jackdaw (*Corvus monedula*)
jackrabbit, black-tailed (*Lepus californicus*)
jaguar (*Panthera onca*)
jay, blue (*Cyanocitta cristata*)
jay, Steller's (*Cyanocitta stelleri*)
junglefowl, red (*Gallus gallus*)
kangaroo (*Macropus* spp.)
kangaroo, eastern gray (*Macropus giganteus*)
kangaroo rat, California (*Dipodomys californicus*)
kestrel, American (*Falco sparverius*)
kestrel, Eurasian (*Falco tinnunculus*)
killdeer (*Charadrius vociferus*)
kingfisher, belted (*Ceryle alcyon*)
koala (*Phascolarctos cinereus*)
langur, gray (*Semnopithecus* spp.)
lapwing (*Vanellus vanellus*)
leopard (*Panthera pardus*)
leopard, snow (*Panthera uncia*)
lion, African (*Panthera leo*)
lion, Asiatic (*Panthera leo persica*)
lion, mountain (*Felis concolor*)
lizard, alligator (*Elgaria*)
lizard, western fence (*Sceloporus occidentalis*)
llama (*Lama glama*)
lorikeet, Henderson (*Vini stepheni*)
lynx, Euarasian (*Lynx lynx*)
macaque, Japanese (*Macaca fuscata*)
macaque, pig-tailed (*Macaca nemestrina*)
macaque, rhesus (*Macaca mulatta*)
magpie, Australian (*Gymnorhina tibicen*)
mallard (*Anas platyrhynchos*)
mange, sarcoptic (*Sarcoptes scabiei*)
maple, sugar (*Acer saccharum*)
marmot, yellow-bellied (*Marmota flaviventris*)
mink (*Mustela vison*)
minnow, pike (*Ptychocheilus oregonensis*)
mockingbird (*Mimus polyglottos*)
moles (Talpidae)
mongoose, Indian (*Herpestes javanicus*)
monkey, red-tailed (*Cercopithecus ascanius*)
monkey, vervet (*Chlorocebus pygerythrus*)
moose (*Alces alces*)
mouse, cotton (*Peromyscus gossypinus*)
mouse, house (*Mus musculus*)
mouse, striped field (*Apodemus agrarius*)

mouse, white-footed (*Peromyscus leucopus*)
mouse, wood (*Apodemus sylvaticus*)
munias, chestnut (*Lonchura atricapilla*)
munias, scaly-breasted (*Lonchura punctulata*)
mouse, yellow-necked (*Apodemus flavicollis*)
muntjac (*Muntiacus muntjac*)
murrelet, marbled (*Brachyramphus marmoratus*)
murrelet, Scripps's (*Synthliboramphus scrippsi*)
murrelet, Xantus's (*Syithliboramphus hypoleucus*)
muskrat (*Ondatra zibethicus*)
night-heron, black-crowned (*Nycticorax nycticorax*)
nilgai (*Boselaphus tragocamelus*)
nutria (*Myocastor coypus*)
ocelot (*Leopardus pardalis*)
oldsquaw (*Clangula hyemalis*)
oleander (*Nerium* spp.)
opossum (*Didelphis virginiana*)
oriole, northern (*Icterus galbula*)
osprey (*Pandion haliaetus*)
otter, Eurasian (*Lutra lutra*)
owl, barn (*Tyto alba*)
owl, barred (*Strix varia*)
owl, burrowing (*Athene cunicularia*)
owl, great-horned (*Bubo virginianus*)
owl, northern spotted (*Strix occidentalis caurina*)
owl, spotted (*Strix occidentalis*)
oystercatcher (*Haematopus ostralegus*)
palm, oil (*Elaeis guineensis*)
parakeet, Mauritius (*Psittacula echo*)
parakeet, monk (*Myiopsitta monachus*)
parakeet, rose-ringed (*Psittacula krameri*)
peacock, Indian (*Pavo cristatus*)
peafowl, Indian (*Pavo cristatus*)
pear (*Pyrus communis*)
petrel, Bulwer's (*Bulweria bulwerii*)
pika, plateau (*Ochotona curzioniae*)
peccary (*Pecari tajacu*)
petrel, dark-rumped (*Pterodroma phaeopygia*)
pheasant, ring-necked (*Phasianus colchicus*)
pika (*Ochotona princeps*)
pika, plateau (*Ochotona curzioniae*)
pig, feral (*Sus scrofa*)
pigeon (*Columba livia*)
pigeon, passenger (*Ectopistes migratorius*)
pigeon, Picazuro (*Columba picazuro*)

pigeon, spot-winged (*Columba maculosa*)
pigeon, wood (*Columba palumbus*)
pine, Austrian (*Pinus nigra*)
pine, lodgepole (*Pinus contorta*)
pine, ponderosa (*Pinus ponderosa*)
pine, Scotch (*Pinus sylvestris*)
mountain plover (*Charadrius montanus*)
plover, piping (*Charadrius melodus*)
plover, western snowy (*Charadrius alexandrinus nivosus*)
pocket gopher (*Geomyidae*)
pocket gopher, Mazama (*Thomomys mazama*)
poplar (*Populus* spp.)
porcupine (*Erethizon dorsatum*)
porcupine, African crested (*Hystrix cristata*)
possum, brush-tailed (*Trichosurus vulpecula*)
prairie-chicken, lesser (*Tympanuchus pallidicinctus*)
prairie dog, black-tailed (*Cynomys ludovicianus*)
prairie dog, white-tailed (*Cynomys leucurus*)
pronghorn (*Antilocapra americana*)
puaiohi (*Myadestes palmeri*)
ptarmigan, willow (*Lagopus lagopus*)
python, Burmese (*Python bivittatus*)
quelea, red-billed (*Quelea quelea*)
rabbit, cottontail (*Sylvilagus floridanus*)
rabbit, European (*Oryctolagus cuniculus*)
rabbit, marsh (*Sylvilagus palustris*)
raccoon (*Procyon lotor*)
rat, Asian house (*Rattus tanezumi*)
rat, black (*Rattus rattus*)
rat, canefield (*Rattus sordidus*)
rat, cotton (*Sigmodon hispidus*)
rat, Gambian giant pouched (*Cricetomys gambianus*)
rat, kangaroo (*Dipodomys* spp.)
rat, Norway (*Rattus norvegicus*)
rat, Polynesian (*Rattus exulans*)
rat, rice (*Oryzomys palustris*)
rat, ricefield (*Rattus argentiventer*)
rat, roof (*Rattus rattus*)
rattlesnake (*Crotalus* spp.)
rattlesnake, eastern diamondback (*Crotalus adamanteus*)
rattlesnake, timber (*Crotalus horridus*)
rattlesnake, western (*Crotalus oreganus*)
reindeer (*Rangifer tarandus*)
rhinoceros (*Rhinoceros unicornis*)
rice, southern wild (*Zizania aquatica*)

robin, American (*Turdus migratorius*)
robin, North Island (*Petroica longipes*)
rock-wallaby, brush-tailed (*Petrogale penicillata*)
rock-wallaby, yellow-footed (*Petrogale xanthopus*)
rook (*Corvus frugilegus*)
rowan (*Sorbus aucuparia*)
salal (*Gaultheria shallon*)
salmon, Atlantic (*Salmo salar*)
sambar (*Rusa unicolor*)
sandpiper, pectoral (*Calidris melanotos*)
sea lion, California (*Zalophus californianus*)
seal, common (*Phoca vitulina*)
seal, harp (*Phoca groenlandica*)
seal, grey (*Halichoerus grypus*)
seal, earless (Phocidae)
seal, harbor (*Phoca vitulina*)
sheep, domestic (*Ovis aries*)
sheep, bighorn (*Ovis canadensis*)
shoveler, northern (*Anas clypeata*)
shrew, short-tailed (*Blarina brevicauda*)
silvereye (*Zosterops lateralis*)
skunk, striped (*Mephitis mephitis*)
skink, Whitaker's (*Cyclodina whitakeri*)
snake, brown tree (*Boiga irregularis*)
snake, garter (*Thamnophis sirtalis*)
snake, rat (*Elaphe obsoleta*)
sorghum, grain (*Sorghum vulgare*)
soybean (*Glycine max*)
sparrow, house (*Passer domesticus*)
sparrow, seaside (*Ammodramus maritimus*)
sparrow, Java (*Lonchura oryzivora*)
sparrow, Spanish (*Passer hispaniolensis*)
spruce, white (*Picea glauca*)
squirrel, Douglas (*Tamiasciurus douglasii*)
squirrel, fox (*Sciurus niger*)
squirrel, gray (*Sciurus carolinensis*)
squirrel, red (*Tamiasciurus hudsonicus*)
starling (*Sturnus vulgaris*)
starling, European (*Sturnus vulgaris*)
starling, glossy (*Lamprotornis chalybaeus*)
stoat (*Mustela erminea*)
storm-petrel, European (*Hydrobates pelagicus*)
sunflower (*Helianthus annuus*)
swallow, barn (*Hirundo rustica*)
swan, mute (*Cygnus olor*)

sycamore (*Acer pseudoplatanus*)
Tasmanian devil (*Sarcophilus harrisii*)
teal, blue-winged (*Anas discors*)
tern, California least (*Sternula antillarum browni*)
tern, common (*Sterna hirundo*)
tern, Forster's (*Sterna forsteri*)
tern, least (*Sterna antillarum*)
tern, little (*Sternula albifrons*)
tern, Sandwich (*Sterna sandvicensis*)
thick-knee (*Burhinus* spp.)
thorn bush, Mauritius (*Biancaea decapetala*)
thrush, song (*Turdus philomelos*)
tick, American dog (*Dermacentor variabilis*)
tick, blacklegged ticks (*Ixodes scapularis*)
tick, brown dog (*Rhipicephalus sanguineus*)
tick, cayenne (*Amblyomma cajennense*)
tick, Rocky Mountain wood (*Dermacentor andersoni*)
tick, western blacklegged tick (*Ixodes pacificus*)
tiger (*Panthera tigris*)
tiger, Siberian (*Panthera tigris altaica*)
tit, great (*Parus major*)
toad, cane (*Bufo marinus*)
tortoise, gopher (*Gopherus polyphemus*)
thylacine (*Thylacinus cynocephalus*)
tiger (*Panthera tigris*)
tiger, Amur (*Panthera tigris altaica*)
tiger, Siberian (*Panthera tigris altaica*)
tomistoma (*Tomistoma schlegelii*)
toad, cane (*Bufo marinus*)
tortoise, desert (*Gopherus agassizii*)
tortoise, gopher (*Gopherus polyyphemus*)
tulip (*Tulipa* spp.)
turkey (*Meleagris gallopavo*)
viper, pit (*Crotaline*)
vireo, black-capped (*Vireo atricapilla*)
vireo, least Bell's (*Vireo bellii pusillus*)
vole, bank (*Myodes glareolus*)
vole, meadow (*Microtus pennsylvanicus*)
vole, pine (*Microtus pinetorum*)
vole, southern red-backed (*Clethrionomys gapperi*)
vulture, black (*Coragyps atratus*)
vulture, griffon (*Gyps fulvus*)
wallaby, red-necked (*Macropus rufogriseus*)
wallaby, swamp (*Wallabia bicolor*)
wallaby, tammar (*Macropus eugenii*)

warbler, black-and-white (*Mniotilta varia*)
warbler, black-throated green (*Dendroica virens*)
warbler, golden-cheeked (*Setophaga chrysoparia*)
warbler, Kirtland's (*Dendroica kirtlandii*)
warbler, Henderson reed (*Acrocephalus taiti*)
warthog, common (*Phacochoerus africanus*)
water buffalo (*Bubalus bubalis*)
water monitor, Merten's (*Varanus mertensi*)
waxwing, cedar (*Bombycilla cedrorum*)
weasel, short-tailed (*Mustela erminea*)
weaver, black-headed (*Ploceus melanocephalus*)
weaver, village (*Ploceus cucullatus*)
weaver, yellow-backed (*Ploceus melanocephalus capitalis*)
wedelia (*Wedelia trilobata*)
whale, sperm (*Physeter macrocephalus*)
wheat (*Triticum aestivum*)
white-eye, Japanese (*Zosterops japonicus*)
wild dog, African (*Lycaon pictus*)
wildcat (*Felis* spp.)
wildebeest (*Connochaetes taurinus*)
willow (*Salix* spp.)
wolf (*Canis lupus*)
wolf, gray (*Canis lupus*)
wolfsbane (*Aconitum napellus*)
wombat, bare-nosed (*Vombatus ursinus*)
woodchuck (*Marmota monax*)
woodpecker, red-cockaded (*Picoides borealis*)
wood-pigeon (*Columba palumbus*)
woodrat, dusty-footed (*Neotoma fuscipes*)
woodrat, eastern (*Neotoma floridana*)
woodrat, Malayan (*Rattus tiomanicus*)
yellowhammer (*Emberiza citrinella*)
yew, Japanese (*Taxus cuspidata*)
zebra (*Equus spp.*)

Species Index

Note: Page numbers in *italics* indicate a figure and page numbers in **bold** indicate a table on the corresponding page.

Subject Index

Note: Page numbers in *italics* indicate a figure and page numbers in **bold** indicate a table on the corresponding page.